How Parliament Works

Sixth edition

Robert Rogers
Rhodri Walters

PEARSON

Longman

Harlow, England • London • New York • Boston • San Francisco • Toronto
Sydney • Tokyo • Singapore • Hong Kong • Seoul • Taipei • New Delhi
Cape Town • Madrid • Mexico City • Amsterdam • Munich • Paris • Milan

Pearson Education Limited
Edinburgh Gate
Harlow
Essex CM20 2JE
England

and Associated Companies throughout the world

Visit us on the World Wide Web at:
www.pearsoned.co.uk

First published 1987
Second edition 1989
Third edition 1995
Fourth edition 1998
Fifth edition 2004
Sixth edition published 2006

© Paul Silk 1987
© Paul Silk and Rhodri H. Walters 1989
© Pearson Education Limited 1995, 2006

ISBN-13: 978-1-4058-3255-7
ISBN-10: 1-4058-3255-X

British Library Cataloguing-in-Publication Data
A catalogue record for this book is available from the British Library

Library of Congress Cataloging-in-Publication Data
A catalog record for this book is available from the Library of Congress

10 9 8 7 6 5 4 3 2
10 09 08 07 06

Typeset in 10.25/13.25pt ITC Galliard by 35
Printed in Great Britain by Henry Ling Limited, at the Dorset Press, Dorchester, DT1 1HD.

The publisher's policy is to use paper manufactured from sustainable forests.

PEARSON
Education

We work with leading authors to develop the strongest educational materials in politics, bringing cutting-edge thinking and best learning practice to a global market.

Under a range of well-known imprints, including Longman, we craft high-quality print and electronic publications which help readers to understand and apply their content, whether studying or at work.

To find out more about the complete range of our publishing, please visit us on the World Wide Web at: **www.pearsoned.co.uk**

To those who believe that
Parliament matters

Contents

Foreword   xi
Acknowledgements   xiii

1 Parliament: its home and origins   1

2 Who is in Parliament?   21

The Commons   21
The Lords   34
The Queen   40

3 Running Parliament   44

The House of Commons   44
The Speaker   44
The Deputy Speakers   55
The Leader of the House   56
The Clerk of the House   57
The House of Commons Service   58
The House administration   59
The House departments   61
MPs' pay, allowances and staff   64
Finance for opposition parties   67
The House of Lords   69
The Lord Chancellor/The Lord Speaker   69
The Chairman of Committees, Deputy Speakers and
    deputy chairmen   72
The Leader of the House of Lords   73
The Clerk of the Parliaments and the staff of the House   74

House of Lords administration   75
Paying for Parliament   76
The House of Commons   76
The House of Lords   77
How much does Parliament cost?   77

**4 Parliamentary sovereignty, legislative supremacy
and devolution**   79

Sovereignty and supremacy   79
Human Rights Act 1998   82
The European Union   84
Devolution of government   85

5 Influences on Parliament   92

The House of Commons   92
The party   98
Members' interests and parliamentary standards   124
Members' interests: the current arrangements   126
Influences on the House of Lords   130

**6 The parliamentary day and the organisation
of business**   136

The parliamentary calendar   136
A parliament   136
A session   138
Adjournments   144
The sitting week in the Commons   146
The sitting day in the Commons   148
Time in the House   160
An MP's day   161
Sittings and use of time in the House of Lords   164
Parliamentary papers   168
Voting   171
The media   176
Broadcasting Parliament   179
Privilege   181
Procedure   185

7 Making the law — 189

Government bills — 192
Commons stages — 208
Lords stages — 234
Disagreement between the Houses: the balance of power — 242
Private legislation — 249
Delegated legislation — 252

8 Parliament and the taxpayer — 265

The Budget cycle — 270
The estimates cycle — 274
The reporting cycle — 280
Conclusion — 284

9 Debates — 287

Debates in the House of Lords — 306

10 Calling to account: questions — 311

Questions in the Commons — 311
Questions in the House of Lords — 338
Petitions — 340
Letters to ministers — 342

11 Calling to account: select committees — 344

Select committees in the House of Commons — 344
The committees — 347
How committees work — 357
A typical inquiry — 363
Select committees in the House of Lords — 378

12 Parliament and Europe — 386

13 The future of Parliament — 406

Modernisation, reform and effectiveness — 406
The House of Commons — 409

The House of Lords   431
The Lord Chancellor and the Lords of Appeal in Ordinary   437
Modernisation of practice and procedure in the Lords   440
Conclusion   443

Glossary of parliamentary terms   446
Sources of information about Parliament   470
Index   478

Foreword

IN THIS SIXTH EDITION OF *How Parliament Works* our aims remain the same: to explain a complex, and constantly evolving, national institution in straightforward language; to give an insider's feel for how and why things happen; to analyse strengths and weaknesses; and to examine ways in which Parliament might develop. Parliament's ancient functions of legislating, controlling expenditure, representing the citizen and calling government to account have never been more important; and the more effective Parliament is, the better it will serve its real owners – the people of the United Kingdom.

We hope that our readers will include those who have anything to do with Parliament in their daily lives: journalists, lawyers, civil servants, lobbyists, academics, researchers, students and teachers, and indeed Members of both Houses; and those who simply want to find how out their Parliament works, and what it can do for them.

The pace of political and parliamentary change continues to be rapid. Even though this edition is appearing only two years after its predecessor, we have both been surprised at the amount of updating that has been needed. At the same time we have included more explanation and analysis, and have extended the final chapter, which assesses how Parliament might change in the years ahead. In every way, this is a thoroughly new edition.

Our joint total of years in the service of Parliament is now more than 65 but, although we may think we know a thing or two about the institution, as always we are immensely grateful to many colleagues and friends inside and outside Parliament who have given so readily of their expertise and advice. To name any of them would be invidious; but our appreciation and thanks to one other person should be recorded here: Paul Silk, now Clerk of the National Assembly for Wales, who was co-author of the first edition in 1987, and of three subsequent editions.

Some criticisms of Parliament are well founded; some are not. Many of the latter make up in stridency what they lack in knowledge or realism. As we show in this book, Parliament in 2006 is a more active and vibrant institution than it has been for decades. But there is much that could be done to make it more effective, and many ways in which the institution as it is now could be used more effectively by its members. The other side of the equation is the value placed upon Parliament by those it represents. It is human nature to value something more if one really understands it; and we hope that *How Parliament Works* will continue to play its part.

Robert Rogers
Rhodri Walters
Westminster, April 2006

Acknowledgements

We are grateful to the following for permission to reproduce copyright material:

The Palace of Westminster on page 6, Parliamentary Copyright 2004; The Chamber of the House of Lords on page 8, Parliamentary Copyright House of Lords 2003, Terry Moore; The House of Lords in session on page 9, Parliamentary Copyright House of Lords 2005, Terry Moore; The Chamber of the House of Commons on page 11, Deryc R. Sands, Parliamentary Copyright House of Commons 2001; The House of Commons, 13 July 2005 on page 12, Parliamentary Copyright House of Commons 2005, Terry Moore; Part of the Order of Business for a typical day in the Chamber of the House of Commons on page 152, Parliamentary Copyright House of Commons 2006; Notices and Orders of the day: The House of Lords Order Paper on page 167, Parliamentary Copyright House of Lords 2005; The stages in the passing of a public bill on page 203, Parliamentary Copyright House of Lords 2005; The Terrorism Bill on pages 204–7, Parliamentary Copyright House of Commons 2005; House of Commons Oral Questions Rota on pages 318–19, Parliamentary Copyright House of Commons 2005; Oral Questions on the Commons Order of Business on page 323, Parliamentary Copyright House of Commons 2005; *Hansard* report of Question Time on 7th December 2005 on pages 324–7, Parliamentary Copyright House of Commons 2005; The Commons Health Committee taking evidence from Home Office and Health ministers about changing the law on smoking in public places, November 2005 page 365, Deryc R. Sands, Parliamentary Copyright House of Commons 2005; European Union Select Committee hears evidence from Rt Hon John Hutton MP, Chancellor of the Duchy of Lancaster, on effective regulation in the EU, May 2005 on page 379, Parliamentary Copyright House of Lords 2005, Terry Moore; parliamentary material is reproduced with the permission of the Controller of HMSO on behalf of Parliament.

Parliamentary Environs on page 20, Give Way Ltd; Table 8.1 The annual parliamentary cycles on pages 268–9, adapted from Evans, P. (2002) House of Commons Procedure, 3rd edition, page 108, Vacher Dod Publishing Ltd.

A typical selection list for the first day of a Commons standing committee's consideration of a bill under a programme order on page 218, Crown copyright 2005; A typical selection list for part of the report stage of a bill in the House of Commons under a programme order on page 219, Crown copyright 2005; Crown copyright material is reproduced with the permission of the Controller of HMSO and the Queen's Printer for Scotland.

1

Parliament: its home and origins

Mid-Victorian masterpiece: Parliament in its setting

The Palace of Westminster, that magnificent range of Gothic buildings along the banks of the Thames, is probably the United Kingdom's most famous landmark. The Clock Tower at the north end of the palace and the striking of Big Ben, the hour bell of the Great Clock, are known throughout the world. The palace is one of the greatest achievements of nineteenth-century architecture and art, and even those who work there every day remain awed by its power and confidence.

If the Palace of Westminster were empty, it would still be one of the great tourist attractions of Europe. But this Grade I listed building, part of the World Heritage site that includes Westminster Abbey as well as the palace, contains a parliament that is one of the biggest and busiest in the world. This is a source of many tensions. Whatever its working methods, and however effective it may be, it is very difficult for a parliament housed in a heritage icon to *look* modern and efficient. And the constraints of conserving and caring for such a building mean that any structural change for parliamentary purposes – from new door locks to constructing a visitor centre – must run the gauntlet of English Heritage, the planners of Westminster City Council, and countless others who love the building for its art and history. The building is expensive to maintain precisely because everything must be done to the highest standards for the benefit of future generations. Finally, the palace is a perfect example of how buildings shape the activity within them. As we shall see, the nature of the buildings of Parliament has a powerful influence on how business is conducted and the way that members of both Houses work.

The King's palace

It may seem odd that a parliament should meet in a palace; but the Palace of Westminster has been a royal palace for well over a thousand years. Before the Norman Conquest it was the residence of Edward the Confessor, and it continued to be used by the monarch until the reign of Henry VIII, who bought Whitehall from Cardinal Wolsey in 1529 and then built St James's Palace in 1532. Although Westminster was thereafter no longer a royal residence, it continued to be a royal palace. Property in what is now London SW1 was clearly as much in demand in the sixteenth century, and the buildings huddled around the great bulk of Westminster Hall were rapidly taken up for use by the two Houses, the law courts (which remained at Westminster until they moved to the Strand in 1882), courtiers, placemen and shopkeepers – and others plying less reputable trades.

The King's summons

Although parliaments have met at Westminster for some 750 years, there is no requirement to do so. Parliament has met, and could meet elsewhere, and still conduct its business with constitutional and legal propriety. Second World War bomb damage forced the two Houses from their own Chambers; and were the modern spectre of global terrorism to make it necessary, Parliament could meet elsewhere with the minimum of infrastructure – and indeed has plans to do so.

The word 'parliament', from the French *parler*, to speak or talk, was first used in England in the thirteenth century, when it meant an enlarged meeting of the King's council, attended by barons, bishops and courtiers, to advise the King on law making, administration and judicial decisions. The germ of the modern institution can be traced back to the parliament summoned on Henry III's behalf by Simon de Montfort in 1265, when representatives from the towns were present for the first time. Parliaments still meet in response to a royal summons; the parliament that met after the 2005 general election was summoned by a proclamation from the Queen, which in part said:

> *And We being desirous and resolved, as soon as may be, to meet Our people and have their advice in Parliament, do hereby make known unto all Our loving Subjects Our Royal Will and Pleasure to call a new Parliament.*

Those words may fall strangely upon a modern ear, and at a time when the role of the monarch in the governance of the nation is increasingly questioned; but the purport of Elizabeth II's proclamation was the same as those issued during the reigns of thirty-four of her predecessors.

The development of the two Houses

By the middle of the fourteenth century, the King's Parliaments were attended by knights of the shire and burgesses from the cities and boroughs (the Commons), the magnates (the Lords Temporal) and the bishops and abbots (the Lords Spiritual). At this time, the reign of Edward III, the Commons began to claim that their agreement was required for any taxation by the monarch, in particular the tax on wool. By now the Commons and Lords had emerged as two distinct houses. The Commons met in the Painted Chamber or in the refectory or the chapter house of Westminster Abbey, and they moved to St Stephen's Chapel in 1547. The Lords settled in the White Chamber of the old palace, moving to the larger White or Lesser Hall in 1801 when the Union with Ireland introduced extra members into the House. After the fire of 1834, they moved to the re-roofed Painted Chamber until they were able to move into their present accommodation in 1847.

The fire

The night of 16 October 1834 was fine, with some high cloud. By seven o'clock that evening the London sky was lit by flames. Two workmen had been told to dispose of large quantities of Exchequer tallies – notched hazel sticks used from early mediaeval times to show what each taxpayer owed; the stick could be split to provide both a record and a receipt. The workmen burned the tallies in the furnaces that heated the flues under the floor of the House of Lords, and their enthusiasm, or possibly their impatience, led to the destruction of the mediaeval palace and the meeting places of both Houses. Thousands watched.

> *An immense multitude of spectators assembled at Westminster to witness the ravages of the fire, the lurid glare of which was visible for many miles around the metropolis. Even the river Thames . . . was covered with boats and barges . . . and the reflections of the wavering flames upon the water, on the neighbouring shores and on the many thousands thus congregated, composed a spectacle most strikingly picturesque and impressive.*

wrote one contemporary observer.

The winning design

The destruction of a large part of the old palace and of much of its contents, including irreplaceable manuscripts, paintings and tapestries, was a great loss. Westminster Hall survived, as did other parts of the building that today would undoubtedly have been preserved or restored. But the authorities of the day saw the fire as an opportunity to start afresh. A competition was held for the design of a completely new parliamentary building, which resulted in an extraordinary architectural and artistic partnership. The scheme produced by the architect Sir Charles Barry and the interior designer Augustus Welby Pugin was chosen from among ninety-seven designs submitted, and the foundation stone was laid on 27 April 1840. The Palace that was built over the next twenty years is huge. It covers eight acres (3.24 hectares), and has 1,100 rooms, 100 staircases and three miles (4.8 km) of passages.

A Victorian Parliament

The Barry and Pugin palace had, apart from its visual merits, one great advantage: it was a purpose-built parliamentary building. As well as the two Chambers, it provided residences for the principal officers and officials, dining rooms, smoking rooms, writing rooms, committee rooms, libraries and all the paraphernalia of a grand country house and London club combined.

This was all a mid-Victorian Parliament needed. There were 658 members of the Commons, and some 500 members of the Lords, no more than 350 of whom turned up to speak in any session; but an MP or peer wrote his correspondence in longhand, and if he wanted to find something out, he went and looked it up, just as he would have done in his library or study at home. Members of the Commons were careful to keep on the right side of local political magnates, but modern constituency pressures were unknown. Indeed, illuminated addresses survive that were presented to the local MP 'on his visit (sometimes *annual* visit!) to the Constituency'.

The New Palace today

Sadly, the ever-present threat of terrorism has meant that public access to the Palace of Westminster has to be closely controlled. During term time, the parties of constituents and other visitors who tour the principal parts of the palace must be sponsored by an MP or peer (although visitors may pay to see the palace during the commercial summer opening (see page 475)).

Those who come to see the Palace of Westminster begin by following the Queen's route at the State Opening of Parliament, and in the part of the palace still devoted to the monarch. With the exception of the Commons Chamber, much of what they see has changed little and would have been familiar to Gladstone or Disraeli. A plan of the palace is shown on the next page.

The Robing Room and Royal Gallery

When the Queen opens Parliament, her state coach drives under the great archway of the Victoria Tower, the 323-foot (98.5 m) tower at the south end of the palace that houses the parliamentary archives. She then ascends the Royal Staircase and passes through the Norman Porch (so called because it was intended to place statues of the Norman kings there, but somehow Victorian prime ministers supplanted them) to the Robing Room, where she puts on the state robes and Imperial State Crown before walking in procession through the 110-foot (33.5 m) long Royal Gallery, into the Prince's Chamber and then into the Chamber of the House of Lords.

This southern end of the palace is magnificent and ornate – deliberately conceived as a backdrop to state ceremonial. The perfect proportions of Barry's rooms are complemented by the sumptuousness of Pugin's decoration. His themes of portcullis, rose, lily and lion, together with Queen Victoria's VR cipher, run throughout the palace's decoration, with its Gothic features and linenfold panelling, but his 'graceful fancy' is nowhere more evident than at the south end of the building – the Robing Room and the Royal Gallery.

The Robing Room has not been in use, except for the day of the State Opening, since the Lords sat there after the Commons Chamber was destroyed by enemy bombing during the Second World War. The Royal Gallery is occasionally used when a visiting head of state addresses both Houses of Parliament; the King of Spain and the presidents of France, Russia and the USA have done so in recent years. As there is no concept of joint sittings of the two Houses (unlike the practice of the US Congress, for example), the Royal Gallery is a convenient place for such events.

The Chamber of the House of Lords

The visitor then moves to the Chamber of the House of Lords, which is fitted out in the same rich style. At one end, the throne faces north under a gilded canopy and Cloth of Estate. In front of it is the Woolsack, on

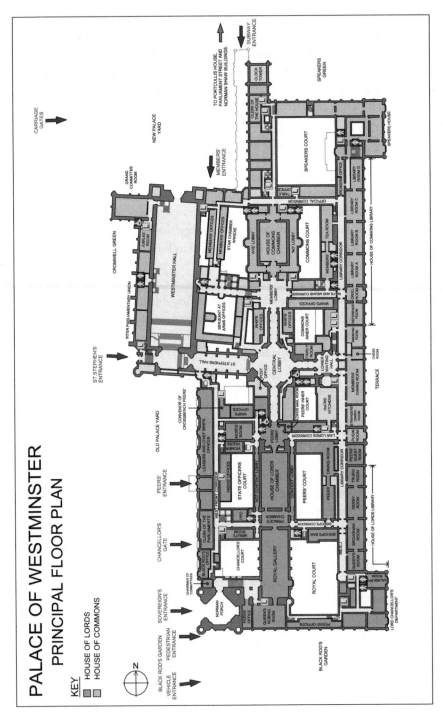

The Palace of Westminster

which sits the Lord Speaker as presiding officer of the House of Lords. The Woolsack is a seat stuffed with wool from the different countries of the Commonwealth. Edward III decided that a sack of wool would be a useful reminder to their lordships of the pastoral basis of the country's economy – and the chief source of his revenue – and the tradition has persisted. In front of the Woolsack are the two judges' woolsacks. These remind us that the Appeal and High Court judges still receive Writs of Assistance to attend the House. Nowadays they attend only in a representative capacity on the day of the State Opening. To the left and right of the Woolsack are four rows of red benches for peers, divided into three sections. In the centre of the floor is the Table of the House, and on the opposite side of the table to the Woolsack there are three further benches.

Looking from the throne, the right of the House is known as the spiritual side, because the bishops sit there, in the front rows of the section nearest the throne. The left is called the *temporal side*, while beyond the table are the *cross-benches*. As well as the bishops, government supporters sit on the *spiritual side*, with ministers who are peers in the front row of the central section. Other parties sit on the temporal side. Peers who do not belong to a party sit on the cross-benches. A labelled view of the Chamber and a photograph of the House in session taken in May 2005 are on pages 8 and 9.

Beyond the Lords Chamber, the visitor passes through Peers' Lobby to the Central Lobby, a large octagonal room at the very centre of the palace, beneath the third-largest of the palace's towers. Almost all visitors on business come to the Central Lobby; it is the place where constituents who wish to lobby an MP come to fill in a 'green card' requesting an interview. It lies directly between the two Chambers; and when on State Opening day all the doors are thrown open, the Queen sitting on the throne in the Lords can see the Speaker presiding over the House of Commons more than a hundred yards (91.4 m) away.

Members' Lobby and the Chamber of the House of Commons

Moving towards the Commons Chamber, the visitor passes into the Members' Lobby. This is a much larger space than Peers' Lobby. When the House is busy, especially before and after votes, it is thronged with MPs and is the haunt of 'lobby' journalists; and it is then a clearing-house of opinion, news and rumour. It contains a message board with a slot for each member's messages, pigeonholes for members' select committee papers, a counter where members can get a wide range of parliamentary and

The Chamber of the House of Lords

Source: The House of Lords 2003, Terry Moore

The House of Lords in session, May 2005

Source: The House of Lords 2005, Terry Moore

government papers, and a post office that deals with some 52,000 items every sitting day. The whips' offices of the major parties (see page 98) adjoin the Members' Lobby.

The Commons Chamber was destroyed in an air raid on the night of 10 May 1941. Even Barry's original Chamber was less ornate than that of the Lords; the rebuilt Commons Chamber, designed by Sir Giles Gilbert Scott, is austere by comparison with that of the Lords. A labelled view of the Chamber and one of the House in session are shown on pages 11 and 12. From the public gallery one now looks down through a massive 7-tonne glass screen, installed in September 2005 on security advice. Below, the Speaker's canopied Chair is the focal point. During Question Time and ministerial statements the Speaker's Secretary stands to the right of the Chair (as seen from the gallery) helping the Speaker to identify members and keeping a record of those he has called. To the left of the Chair, against the far wall, is the officials' box for civil servants advising ministers. In front of the Chair is the Table of the House, at which sit the bewigged Clerks at the Table, who advise the Speaker and his deputies, and any other member, on the conduct of proceedings, and who also compile the legal record of the House's decisions.

On each side of the Chamber are five rows of green benches, divided by a gangway into two sections. On the left as seen from the gallery are the benches occupied by the government party, and on the right those of the opposition parties. Ministers sit on the front bench by the Table, and the main opposition party's spokesmen and women (or 'shadow ministers') opposite them. Ministers and their shadows are thus known as 'front-benchers'; all other MPs are 'back-benchers'.

On each side of the Table are the despatch boxes at which ministers and their counterparts from the main opposition party speak; and at the near end of the Table is the Mace, which symbolises the authority of the House.

At our observer's eye level, above the Speaker's Chair, is the Press Gallery, with seats in the centre for the *Hansard* reporters who compile the verbatim record of proceedings. Other galleries are for members of the House of Lords, personal guests of the Speaker and distinguished visitors, as well as for the general public. Two galleries are reserved for MPs and are technically part of the floor of the House, although Speakers have indicated that they will not usually call members sitting there to speak. Down below, but not visible except from the front of the gallery, sits the Serjeant at Arms, responsible for order around the House and in the galleries. There too are the cross-benches; but as the 1997 and 2001 parliaments each contained only one member and the 2005 only two (apart from the occupants of the

The Chamber of the House of Commons, looking down from the public gallery

Source: Deryc R. Sands; The House of Commons 2001

The House of Commons, 13 July 2005, Prime Minister's Questions

Source: Terry Moore, House of Commons 2005

Chair), who owed no party allegiance, these are in practice extensions of the seating for government and opposition members (although MPs may not speak from them).

Westminster Hall

This brief description of the Palace of Westminster would be incomplete without reference to what must be one of the finest rooms in Europe – Westminster Hall, the great hall of the mediaeval palace and, along with the crypt Chapel of St Mary Undercroft, the only part of the original building to remain. The hall has been much restored over the years, but at its core it remains an eleventh-century building with a late fourteenth-century hammerbeam roof. It is used today for ceremonial occasions. The Lying in State of the Queen Mother took place in Westminster Hall in April 2002; and a few weeks later the Queen received the Humble Addresses of the two Houses of Parliament there on the occasion of her Golden Jubilee. The regular sittings of the House of Commons 'in Westminster Hall' (see page 296) take place not in the Hall itself, but in the Grand Committee Room at the north end.

The palace and parliamentary vocabulary

The layout of the Chambers, derived from earlier meeting rooms of the two Houses, is reflected in the vocabulary of Parliament, which in many cases has passed into general everyday use, as well as around the world with the Westminster model of parliamentary government.

The *opposition* parties sit physically opposite the government party (as well as opposing it). A meeting of the House is a *sitting*, at the end of which the House *rises*. Matters considered by either House are debated *on the floor*. If a member changes parties he or she is said to have *crossed the floor*. When MPs and peers hand in questions, amendments to bills or notices of motions, or when ministers place documents formally before either House, they are said to have *tabled* them, even if they do not place them on the massive Table of either House. If a bill has its committee stage in a Commons standing committee, it is said to be taken *upstairs* because the palace's committee rooms are on the first floor. When either House votes, it is said to *divide*, because those voting divide physically into two groups ('ayes' and 'noes' in the Commons, 'contents' and 'not contents' in the Lords) and walk through separate lobbies on either side of both Chambers to be counted. Securing something *on the nod* – that is, without debate or division – may derive from a member's brief bow of respect to the Chair when moving a motion formally.

Some supposed parliamentary derivations are bogus. *In the bag* stems not from the petition bag on the back of the Speaker's Chair but from the much older idea of a game bag. It is just as fanciful as the myth that the red lines on the floor of the Commons Chamber are two sword lengths apart. There is indeed a rule that a member speaking from the front row of benches (above or below the gangway) should not step over the lines; but there is no record of a time when members were permitted to bring swords into the Chamber. And *toe the line* has nothing at all to do with these lines; it comes from the Royal Navy of Nelson's time, when barefooted seamen lined up for inspection on the seams, or lines, in the deck planking. A more frequent error is the description of Westminster as 'the mother of parliaments'. When John Bright coined the phrase in 1865 he was referring to *England* as the mother of parliaments; but, given the immense influence Westminster has had on the development of parliaments around the world, perhaps the mistake is understandable.

'We shape our buildings, and afterwards our buildings shape us'

From the start the clublike rooms and common spaces of Barry's palace have encouraged members of both Houses to congregate and meet informally. In the Commons, the Smoking Room, the Tea Room and the Members' Lobby after a big vote (as well as the division lobbies themselves during it) are places where opinions are formed and exchanged, support is canvassed and tactics planned. This informality and personal contact also produces volatility: rumours travel quickly, even through so large a membership; views – and perhaps back-bench rebellions – can gather momentum with surprising speed.

A first-time visitor almost always finds the Commons Chamber smaller than expected; and, for an assembly of 646 members, it is surprisingly intimate – its floor area is almost exactly that of a tennis court. Its seating capacity (together with the galleries reserved for members) is usually said to be 427; but as there are no individual seats and members inevitably take up varying amounts of the green leather, this is an approximation.

There are no individual places, so also no desks, telephones or computer terminals; and members speak from their places, not from a podium. When the House is full, perhaps towards the end of a major debate or during Prime Minister's Questions, the atmosphere is made tense by the crush of MPs, and one can appreciate the way in which the House can become great political theatre. The small size of the Chamber also means that, even when only a few MPs are present for some abstruse debate, the feeling of speaking to empty space, which is a problem in many foreign parliaments, is minimised.

It is likely that the rows of benches facing each other derive from the use by the Commons of St Stephen's Chapel in the old palace. The clergy faced each other in choir stalls on each side of the altar, and the arrangement was unchanged when the Tudor House of Commons took over the chapel. Some feel that this encourages adversarial politics (and even, perhaps fancifully, a two-party system). The Commons, unlike the Lords, has no cross-benches spanning the width of the Chamber. It may be significant that standing committee rooms, where legislation is debated in the same way as in the House, are laid out like the Chamber; but for select committees, where there is a more consensual approach, members sit around horseshoe tables, and MPs and peers do not necessarily sit on party lines.

Certainly the idea of replacing the Chamber with a hemicycle, of the sort found in many continental parliaments and also in the European Parliament, has its supporters, especially among those who shun confrontational politics. A hemicycle would almost certainly bring with it individual desks and seats, but accommodating a Chamber of that size in Barry's palace would be next to impossible – although the House of Commons had an opportunity to break this particular mould after the old Chamber was destroyed in 1941. However, neither a hemicycle nor a larger traditional Chamber found favour. Churchill represented the majority view in the House when he said in the debate on the rebuilding:

> *if the House is big enough to contain all its Members, nine-tenths of the debates will be conducted in the depressing atmosphere of an almost empty or half-empty chamber . . . We wish to see our Parliament as a strong, easy, flexible instrument of free debate. For this purpose a small chamber and a sense of intimacy are indispensable . . . The conversational style requires a fairly small space, and there should be on great occasions a sense of crowd and urgency . . . We shape our buildings, and afterwards our buildings shape us.*

Time and space

In an echo of metaphysics, the way any parliament operates is dictated by time and space. *Time*: to allow full scrutiny of government, examination of draft legislation, airing of concerns affecting constituencies and constituents, and the political causes pursued by political parties and individual members. *Space* is almost as important: space to provide meeting rooms for committees, political parties and lobby groups; space for library and research facilities; adequate office accommodation for MPs and their staff to provide the service that their constituents expect, and for members of both Houses to support their parliamentary duties.

Add to that the space that is needed for the infrastructure of Parliament: support for the work of the two Chambers and of legislative and investigative committees; provision of IT, security, catering, housekeeping, maintenance, and administration of pay, allowances and personnel. Then there are those who are in Parliament but not of it: TV, radio and print journalists, civil servants supporting ministers, and lawyers appearing before the House of Lords Appellate Committee. Last, but emphatically not least, are the owners of Parliament: constituents and taxpayers and their families, who may want to bring problems to their local MP, or have a cause taken up by a member of either House, or who may simply want to see how Parliament works.

Nor are these demands constant. Parliament must react to expectations of it as well as to events. The creation of a new government department will need a new select committee to shadow it in the Commons; some major issue of the day may lead to the establishment of a new select committee in the Lords. More draft bills will need more select committee consideration, and in turn space for the staff to support the process. We consider below the ways in which the two modern Houses have tried to cope with the constant pressure on their accommodation.

The shoe pinches

The new Palace of Westminster was largely completed by 1852, although it was not finally finished until 1860. The Lords occupied their Chamber on 15 April 1847; the Commons first sat in theirs on 30 May 1850 but did not move in permanently until 3 February 1852. In 1854, Sir Charles Barry produced plans to build additional offices surrounding New Palace Yard, but these were never pursued. By 1867 a select committee was examining how the size of the Commons Chamber could be increased, and in 1894 another Commons select committee was looking at the adequacy of accommodation more generally.

The pressures

The shortage of accommodation was a recurring theme over the next hundred years. In the Commons, it became particularly acute during the last twenty or thirty years of the last century with the increasing burdens of constituency work, the need to house larger numbers of MPs' own staff, and the growth in select committee work and in research facilities. The administration and support of the House became more professional and better resourced, needing more staff and office accommodation. Every new facility, however desirable in itself, has imposed new strains, from the introduction of broadcasting (with its need for control rooms and archive space) to the establishment of information offices for the public.

A visitor following the route from the Victoria Tower to the Commons Chamber has an impression of lofty ceilings and spacious rooms, but on the floors above and below (except along the Committee Corridor on the river front) the story is rather different and includes subdivided rooms, mezzanine floors and even temporary huts on flat roofs.

For many years in the Commons, members were prepared, however reluctantly, to share offices – even with nine or ten of their colleagues – or to do much of their constituency work around the House, writing letters in the library or dictating to their secretaries in the Committee Corridor while waiting to vote. That this did not lead to changes may have been partly because of the 'never did me any harm' principle, but also because the scope for change was limited.

New building

The only realistic possibilities lay to the north of the palace, across Bridge Street towards Whitehall. Various schemes blossomed, were rejected and withered. Between 1984 and 1991, however, the buildings in Parliament Street, at the end of Whitehall, were converted to provide some ninety offices for MPs, together with library, catering and meeting facilities. Nearby, the old Scotland Yard police headquarters (the Norman Shaw buildings) have been taken over and refurbished and the next-door Canon Row buildings modernised for office accommodation. And at the other end of the palace, Westminster House at 7 Millbank contains most of the staff of Commons select committees, together with the Department of Finance and Administration of that House.

Portcullis House

However, if MPs and their staff were to have proper modern office accommodation that would allow them to give a proper service to their constituents, the key site was that overlooking the river. Here between 1998 and 2000 Portcullis House was constructed to provide offices for 210 MPs and 400 of their staff, together with a variety of meeting rooms. Designed by Michael Hopkins and Partners, from the outside the building appears austere, even forbidding, but inside, from the airy atrium to state-of-the art committee rooms and offices, it shows a confident and innovative style that has won a string of awards.

The £234 million price tag was controversial even for a building designed to complement a world-famous site and to outlast any conventional office accommodation – though the project came in under budget and almost exactly on schedule. The House of Commons Commission, responsible for the House's administration and for the construction of the building, said of it:

> *The building is often described as one purely for Members of Parliament and their staff. This is indeed an important function, and good working conditions play their part in the service which Members give their constituents. But more important are the outstanding facilities for public hearings of select committees, and for meetings of groups of all kinds. This access of the people to the political process is an essential part of the working of a modern Parliament.*

It is safe to say that those who commissioned the new palace after the fire of 1834 would not have recognised any part of this description of the uses of a parliamentary building.

Lords accommodation

Like the Commons, the House of Lords has outgrown the 40 per cent of the original palace that it occupies and, rather late in the day compared with the House of Commons, has started to acquire office space for staff and members in nearby streets. In 1994, 7 Old Palace Yard – an elegant Georgian house opposite the west front of the palace – was returned by the Commons to Lords use; in 2001, Millbank House was leased from the Church Commissioners for mixed office and member use; and in 2002 Fielden House, an office building in Little College Street, was bought for £13 million and occupied in 2005. Most recently, in March 2005, the House purchased from the Church Commissioners the whole of the Millbank island site comprising Millbank House (already leased to the Lords), 1 Millbank, and 5 Great College Street. The cost was £76 million; the building is expected to be ready for occupation in 2009 and should provide a long-term solution to the accommodation needs of members and staff of the House of Lords.

This expansion reflects both the increased activity of the Lords as a chamber of Parliament and the increased expectations of its membership in regard to desk space, IT facilities and so on. Unsurprisingly, as in the Commons, this scattering of staff and members' offices has made the Lords seem less of a homogeneous organisation.

The parliamentary estate

Today's parliamentary estate is like a small town. It covers 185,400 square metres in eleven buildings housing over 4,000 people – and this population is doubled by those from outside Westminster who have business in Parliament each day. A plan of the parliamentary estate appears on page 20.

We now move on to consider the institution housed in those buildings.

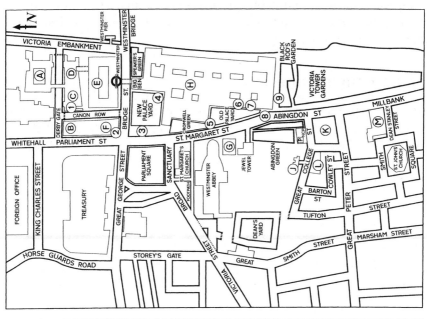

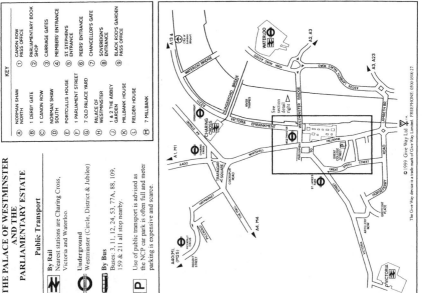

THE PALACE OF WESTMINSTER AND THE PARLIAMENTARY ESTATE

Public Transport

By Rail
Nearest stations are Charing Cross, Victoria and Waterloo.

Underground
Westminster (Circle, District & Jubilee)

By Bus
Buses: 3, 11, 12, 24, 53, 77A, 88, 109, 159 & 211 all stop nearby.

P Use of public transport is advised as the NCP car park is often full and meter parking is expensive and scarce.

KEY

Ⓐ NORMAN SHAW NORTH
Ⓑ 1 DERBY GATE
Ⓒ 1 CANON ROW
Ⓓ NORMAN SHAW SOUTH
Ⓔ PORTCULLIS HOUSE
Ⓕ 1 PARLIAMENT STREET
Ⓖ 7 OLD PALACE YARD
Ⓗ PALACE OF WESTMINSTER
Ⓙ 1 & 2 THE ABBEY GARDEN
Ⓚ MILLBANK HOUSE
Ⓛ FELDEN HOUSE
Ⓜ 7 MILLBANK

① CANON ROW PASS OFFICE
② PARLIAMENTARY BOOK SHOP
③ CARRIAGE GATES
④ MEMBERS' ENTRANCE
⑤ ST STEPHEN'S ENTRANCE
⑥ PEERS' ENTRANCE
⑦ CHANCELLOR'S GATE
⑧ SOVEREIGN'S ENTRANCE
⑨ BLACK ROD'S GARDEN PASS OFFICE

© 1999 Give Way Ltd

The Give Way device is a trade mark of Give Way Limited. FREEPHONE: 0500 0500 27.

Parliamentary Estate and Environs

Source: Give Way Ltd (for left-hand map)

Who is in Parliament?

The Commons

The size of the Commons

Even in the early fifteenth century there were more than 250 members of the Commons – two knights from each of thirty-seven counties, two citizens or burgesses from each of the eighty or so cities and boroughs, and fourteen members from the Cinque Ports. More were steadily added by statute and royal charter, and by 1673 the membership of the House – at that time only from England and Wales – stood at 513. Union with Scotland in 1707 added forty-five members, and a further hundred came from Ireland with the Union of 1801, making 658.

The House grew to 670 members in 1885, and to 707 – the most at any stage – in 1918. Irish independence reduced the numbers to 615 by 1922. The upward trend during the rest of the twentieth century produced a House of 659 members by 1997; but the post-devolution reduction in Scottish seats at Westminster from 72 to 59 means that there are now 646 members of the Commons. The number sitting for constituencies in England is 529, 59 in Scotland, 40 in Wales and 18 in Northern Ireland. There is thus one MP for every 90,995 people (or for every 68,390 people entitled to vote).

Too big?

Even for a population of some 61 million, this is a very large House. By comparison, the Italian Camera dei Deputati has 630 members, or one for every 94,430 people, the French Assemblée nationale has 577 members (one for every 104,700 people) and the Spanish Congreso de los Diputados has 350 members (one for every 115,100 people). A comparison with the US House of Representatives is even more striking (435 members, one for every 673,600 people) but of course in the USA representation at state level also has to be taken into account.

A big House of Parliament has some disadvantages – at least from the point of view of the individual member. Parliamentary time is at a premium. The back-bencher must compete with colleagues to ask questions or to be called in debate (it is sometimes said that more speeches are prepared for the House of Commons than are ever delivered). The individual's share of both influence and parliamentary resources is less than in a smaller House.

On the other side of the equation, the historically large numbers of MPs have led to a large number of ministers; in 2006, 93 (the maximum allowed by law is 95) sat in the Commons out of a total of 115 in both Houses. This means that many individual members get ministerial experience (although the proportion – 14 per cent – might well be the same in a smaller House). A large House provides more back-benchers to undertake the scrutiny of government through select committee work; in session 2004–05, some 300 MPs were members of investigative or scrutiny select committees.

However, from the point of view of the electorate, a large House means that an individual MP represents a relatively small number of people. An MP's focus on the constituency is very sharp, not only because it is a power base, and he or she must woo the electors to be re-elected, but also because most constituencies are small enough to be fairly homogeneous in terms of character, population and economic activity. Your chances of engaging an MP's attention on an issue are very much greater if it is something that directly affects his or her constituency. And the close and valued relationship between a single MP and a single constituency has undoubtedly been a factor in opposition to some forms of proportional representation.

The constituencies

Four Boundary Commissions, one for each part of the UK, keep under review the size, boundaries and numbers of parliamentary constituencies, especially to take account of population changes. The commissions are guided by the 'electoral quota': the total number of electors divided by the number of constituencies. The current quotas are: England, 69,934; Northern Ireland, 60,969; Wales, 55,640. The Boundary Commission for

Scotland used the quota for England in arriving at its recommendation for 59 Scottish seats at Westminster.

Drawing constituency boundaries is not mechanistic. The process must take account of geography, and of existing county and London borough boundaries, so constituencies vary considerably in size. The largest is the Isle of Wight at 108,253 electors (where there would be little to be gained in dividing the island into two constituencies), and the smallest is Na h-Eilanan an Iar (the Western Isles of Scotland) at 21,346 (where the identity of the islands is so distinct that combination with a mainland constituency is not an option).

The time-lag between population change and constituency change has benefited the Labour Party. The average size of the electorate in Labour-held seats is 65,000, compared with 73,000 in Conservative-held seats. Following a Boundary Commission report, it seems likely that six seats in Labour-dominated urban areas will be abolished, and eleven new constituencies created in rural areas where the Conservatives have the advantage.

The candidates

Anyone may stand for election to the Commons if he or she is a British subject or citizen of the Republic of Ireland, is aged 21 or over, and is not disqualified. Those disqualified include undischarged bankrupts, people sentenced to more than one year's imprisonment, members of the House of Lords (but hereditary peers not sitting in the Lords are eligible; one, Viscount Thurso, was elected to the Commons in 2001, and another, Douglas Hogg, succeeded his father as Viscount Hailsham in 2001 but still sits in the Commons) and holders of offices listed in the House of Commons Disqualification Act 1975. These last, often described as those 'holding an office of profit under the Crown', include civil servants, judges, members of the regular armed forces and police, some local government officers and some members of public bodies. They amount to about one in twenty-five of the electorate.

Independent candidates are occasionally elected. The first for many years was Martin Bell as the 'anti-sleaze' candidate in Tatton in 1997, followed by Richard Taylor in Wyre Forest in 2001 on a platform of saving Kidderminster Hospital (beating a sitting member, who was also a minister, by the large majority of 17,630). Remarkably, Taylor held the seat in 2005, although with a reduced majority of 5,250. Two other candidates caused upsets in the 2005 general election. Peter Law stood as an independent in Blaenau Gwent after the imposition of a women-only short-list prevented him standing as a Labour candidate, and won with a majority of 9,121; and in Bethnal Green and Bow, the maverick former Labour MP George Galloway, who had founded his own 'Respect' party but was in effect an independent, beat the sitting Labour MP Oona King by 823 votes.

But these results are very much the exception. You need to be the adopted candidate of a major political party to have a realistic chance of election to the House of Commons. In the 2005 general election there were 3,552 candidates altogether; 1,883 of these were from the three major UK-wide parties.

Candidates are chosen by the party organisations in the constituency concerned, although there has been increasing involvement of the central party organisation in the process, especially at high-profile by-elections. In the Labour and Conservative parties, a committee of the local party will draw up a short-list of five or six candidates from as many as a hundred names, who will usually also be on the party's 'approved' list, although it is possible for the central organisation to impose its own short-list. The Labour Party has reintroduced all-women short-lists for some seats in an attempt to increase the number of women in the Commons (which backfired in Blaenau Gwent). Candidates are interviewed at a meeting of local party members and then elected by eliminating ballot to be the 'prospective parliamentary candidate' (PPC).

The Liberal Democrats draw up panels of suitable candidates in England, Wales and Scotland, and the local party must advertise a vacancy to the people on the relevant list. The local party then prepares a short-list (which must include men and women and pay due regard to the representation of ethnic minorities), and all party members in the relevant constituency may vote to select their PPC.

The selection of candidates is thus subject to local control, although no procedure as elaborate as the primary system in the United States of America has evolved. However, unlike the USA, it is not necessary for a would-be MP to have considerable personal means. The deposit required is £500 and is forfeited only if the candidate receives less than 5 per cent of the votes cast. In any case, it is found by the party, as are most of the candidate's expenses (see below). In June 2003 the Electoral Commission suggested that the system of deposits might be abolished.

Once elected to the Commons, an MP can usually expect to remain the party's candidate at the next election. The Labour Party has a system of mandatory reselection; that is, the sitting member must undergo the selection process before being adopted by the constituency party. For the 2005 general election, one sitting Labour MP was 'deselected': Jane Griffiths in

Reading East. In the other parties an initiative has to be taken to force a reselection process (as happened with Nick Hawkins, the former Conservative MP for Surrey Heath in 2004, and Howard Flight, the former Conservative MP for Arundel and South Downs in 2005).

Elections: when?

General elections are held after Parliament has been dissolved, either by royal proclamation on the advice of the Prime Minister or because the maximum life of a parliament – five years – has expired. Since 1945, no parliament has run its full term, although the 1992–97 parliament came within a fortnight of doing so. The average length of parliaments since 1945 has been a little over three years and seven months. This contrasts with the fixed terms of the US Congress or the practice in countries such as Belgium or Germany, where parliaments are dissolved early only in exceptional circumstances. The ending of a parliament by royal proclamation – in effect, by decision of the Prime Minister, gives him or her a tactical advantage in the timing of the election, although this did not profit the party in government in June 1970 or February 1974.

Although elections are held only for the Commons (elections for any part of the Lords are some way off), a dissolution covers both Houses: the Queen's proclamation says that she dissolves 'the said Parliament accordingly; And the Lords Spiritual and Temporal, and the Members of the House of Commons, are discharged from further attendance thereat'.

A by-election takes place when a seat becomes vacant because the MP dies or is otherwise no longer eligible to sit (see *The candidates* above). A by-election is not required if an MP changes party. An MP cannot in terms resign from the House but in effect does so by accepting one of the 'offices of profit' of steward or bailiff of Her Majesty's three Chiltern Hundreds of Stoke, Desborough and Burnham, or of the manor of Northstead. These are not real jobs but purely symbolic offices used to allow an MP to stand down. By convention, a by-election takes place within three months of the vacancy occurring. Until a new MP is elected, constituency matters are normally handled by a neighbouring MP of the same party.

Elections: who can vote?

The United Kingdom is more generous than many countries in those whom it allows to vote in parliamentary elections. There is no property qualification, since 1928 no sex discrimination, and there are voting rights for Britons who live abroad and choose to register. Commonwealth and Irish citizens resident in Britain are entitled to vote, and the only main categories excluded are those under 18, convicted offenders still in prison, people detained under mental health legislation for criminal activity, and anyone with a seat in the House of Lords. You do not have to have an address in order to vote; homeless people may make a 'declaration of local connection'. However, you must be on the register of parliamentary electors in a constituency. The register is updated every year on the basis of who was resident in the constituency on 15 October, but under the rolling register introduced in 2000 you can have your name added at any time during the year.

Elections: the timetable

This is set out in the Representation of the People Act 1983, as amended in 1985. The whole process, from the last sitting of the old parliament to the State Opening of the new, can take as little as six weeks, although in 1992 it took just over seven. The basic rule is that a general election takes place on the seventeenth day (excluding Sundays and holidays) after the royal proclamation summoning the new parliament (which nowadays accompanies the dissolution of the old). On 5 April 2005 the Prime Minister made the long-expected announcement of a general election, and thereafter the timetable ran as follows:

Thursday 7 April: Parliament met for the last time.
Monday 11 April: Parliament was dissolved by royal proclamation.
Thursday 5 May: Polling day.
Wednesday 11 May: Parliament met to swear in members and, in the
                       Commons, to elect a Speaker.
Tuesday 17 May: State Opening of Parliament and Queen's Speech.

A dissolution on a Monday ensures that the general election itself will be held on a Thursday; not since 1931 (when it took place on a Tuesday) has a general election been held on a different day of the week. Strictly speaking, the last day on which the general election following that in 2005 can be held is Friday 4 June 2010; but if a Thursday polling day is retained, the last day would be Thursday, 3 June 2010.

South Staffordshire: what if?

The constituency of South Staffordshire exposed a loophole in electoral law. A week before polling day, the Liberal Democrat candidate died. As the law stood, there had to be a delay of seven weeks before the election could take place in the constituency. And as Sir Patrick Cormack, the sitting member, pointed out, if one person were to stand in the constituencies being fought by the Prime Minister and every member of the Cabinet, intending to commit suicide before polling day – perhaps in support of terrorist aims, or as part of a campaign for legalising euthanasia – the result would be constitutional chaos. Following a ten-minute rule bill (see page 229) presented by Sir Patrick when he was eventually returned to the House, and his amendment to the Electoral Administration Bill, this loophole has been closed.

Election expenses

We have seen that personal wealth is not a prerequisite for standing for Parliament. Indeed, however well-off a candidate or party may be, the law limits what may be spent in each constituency during an election. The general election limits were raised in 2005 to £7,150 plus 7p per elector in a county constituency (that is, one which is partly rural) and £7,150 plus 5p per elector in a borough constituency. For a by-election, the overall limit is £100,000. The total of a party's campaign expenditure over the 365 days before a general election is £30,000 times the number of constituencies that party is contesting: a maximum of £19.38 million if all 646 constituencies are contested. A general election also involves public expenditure; the cost of administering the 2005 election for the 569 constituencies in England and Wales was £71 million.

Is the Commons politically representative?

Electoral law on the timing of campaigns is clear, the franchise is wide and elections are frequent. But whether an election result is representative and properly reflects the views of the voters depends on the voting system. The British system is based on the relative majority method, sometimes called 'first past the post'. The voter marks a ballot paper with one X against the name of his or her favoured candidate – hedging bets with two Xs will mean that the ballot paper is spoiled and will not be counted – and the candidate with the most votes wins. In this system there are no prizes for coming second; and it also means that the proportions of MPs of each party are not the same as the parties' shares of the votes cast across the nation as a whole.

In the 2005 general election 25,580,549 votes were cast for parties that won seats in the House of Commons (leaving out votes cast for the Speaker

Table 2.1 Voting patterns in the 2005 general election

Party	Votes received	Percentage of all votes	Seats won (and percentage of all seats)	Seats in proportion to votes received
Labour	9,552,372	35.2	355 (55.0)	227
Conservative	8,785,942	32.4	198 (30.7)	209
Liberal Democrat	5,985,704	22.1	62 (9.6)	143
UK Independence Party (UKIP)	605,173	2.2	none	14
Scottish National Party	412,267	1.5	6 (0.9)	6
Green	258,154	1.0	none	10
Democratic Unionist Party	241,856	0.9	9 (1.3)	6
British National Party (BNP)	192,746	0.7	none	5
Plaid Cymru	174,838	0.6	3 (0.5)	4
Sinn Féin	174,530	0.6	5 (0.8)	4
Ulster Unionist	127,414	0.5	1 (0.2)	3
SDLP	125,626	0.5	3 (0.5)	3

Note: Figures are rounded to one decimal point; seats do not sum to 646 because of votes cast for independent candidates, and for parties not in the table.

and the three other independent and Respect MPs); 24,324,018 of these, or 95 per cent, were for one of the three main UK-wide parties. Shares of that total, and the number of seats that each party won in the House of Commons, are shown in Table 2.1.

But Table 2.1 also shows the seats that each party would have won if the numbers of MPs corresponded exactly to the votes cast. Labour would be the largest party – but only just – and Tony Blair's 2005 overall majority of sixty-six would be only a dream. UKIP, Greens and BNP, who won no seats in 2005, would have a parliamentary presence for the first time, with four-teen, ten and five seats respectively.

The other side of the story is what is sometimes known as the 'wasted vote'. For example, in 2005 as in 2001 all three major parties must have seen the constituency of Bristol West as winnable. The result was:

Liberal Democrat	21,987
Labour	16,859
Conservative	15,429
Green	2,163
UK Independence Party	439
Socialist Labour Party	329
Save the Bristol North Baths	190

Stephen Williams won the seat for the Liberal Democrats with only 38.3 per cent of the votes cast; 35,409 people voted for other parties, but their votes were not reflected in the result. However, the *potential* power of each voter in Bristol West (by switching parties as a 'floating voter') was much greater than that of a voter in Bootle who did not wish to vote for the Labour candidate. There Joe Benton won the safest Labour seat in the country with 75.5 per cent of the vote, 19,345 votes compared with his closest rival, the Liberal Democrat, with 2,988 votes. In the country as a whole, the different effect of votes cast for the three main parties was striking. It took 96,500 votes to elect a Liberal Democrat MP, and 44,400 to elect a Conservative MP, but only 26,900 to elect a Labour MP.

The 2005 general election showed some of the effects of the first-past-the-post system in an extreme form. The Labour Party remained in power with a reduced, but still very comfortable, majority (commentators who talked up Tony Blair's 'slashed' majority seemed to forget how many Prime Ministers would have delighted in such luxury; the margin of sixty-six was higher than in nine of the eighteen Parliaments since 1945). More important, Labour's 35.2 per cent of the poll was the lowest ever share of the vote for a winning party. The low turnout magnified the effect: the government was elected on the votes of less than a quarter of the electorate – 21.6 per cent – again a record for a winning party.

Proponents of the first-past-the-post system usually make three main points in its favour. It is a simple system – no preferences, or second and third choices – and it is easily understood by voters. It usually produces clear results, with one party having a strong mandate to govern. And it avoids 'smoke-filled rooms', shorthand for the situation where political choices are made by negotiation between parties after an election, where deals are made and policies agreed that have not been put before the electorate.

Critics of the system reply that voters are more sophisticated and canny than many pundits might think; that strong governments may be overbearing and insensitive, and actually the last thing the voters want; that, once in office, governments produce policies that have never been put before the electorate anyway; and that most voters would prefer consensus to adversarial politics.

Despite the Labour Party's traditional opposition to electoral reform, its 1997 manifesto pledged an inquiry into voting systems, to be followed by a referendum. The incoming Labour government set up the Independent Commission on the Voting System, chaired by Lord Jenkins of Hillhead, which reported in October 1998. Its main recommendation was for a two-vote 'mixed system'. The majority of MPs (80 to 85 per cent) would continue to be elected on an individual constituency basis by the alternative vote (AV) method, in which voters indicate their preferences for all the candidates. If a candidate wins more than half the votes cast on the first count of first preference votes, he or she is elected. If not, the candidate with the fewest first preference votes is eliminated and his or her second preferences allocated to the other candidates. This process continues until one candidate has achieved an overall majority. The AV method might have produced a different result in Bristol West in 2005, but it would not have produced a different result in Bootle.

However, in an attempt to correct disproportionality, Lord Jenkins recommended that to elect the remainder of MPs ('top-up members') voters should have a second vote, which could be cast for a party or for an individual candidate on a party list.

Ironically, forms of proportional representation are already in widespread use in the UK. The Scottish Parliament has 73 constituency members (elected using the first-past-the-post system) and 56 additional regional members drawn from party lists. Similar systems are used for the National Assembly for Wales (40 and 20) and for the Greater London Assembly (14 and 11). The 108 members of the Northern Ireland Assembly are elected using the single transferable vote (STV) system, and the 78 UK MEPs are elected using a 'closed-list' system in large multi-member regional constituencies.

The Labour government's policy, as stated in June 2005, is to assess the experience of the other voting systems in the UK before making any proposals for change in the Westminster system (which would be put to a national referendum). Immediately after the 2005 general election, the Liberal Democrats, the party in the vanguard of campaigning for electoral reform, claimed that Labour had won 130 more seats than their votes entitled them to, and pointed out that $1^{1}/_{2}$ million votes had been cast for parties that won no seats. The then LibDem leader, Charles Kennedy, called on Tony Blair 'to pick up the phone' for talks on electoral reform; but, despite the vote/seat mismatch in 2005, any early change seems very unlikely. The results of the 2005 German general election, where proportional representation produced a stalemate, provided ammunition for opponents of PR at Westminster – even though in 2006 there was a similar result in Italy, where 75 per cent of seats are first-past-the-post.

Are the members of the Commons representative?

Despite a local democratic element in the choice of candidates, the MPs who sit in the Commons are not a microcosm of the electorate as a whole.

Age

The House of Commons is overwhelmingly middle-aged. The average age of MPs in the last four parliaments has been almost exactly 50, with a slight drop in 2005. In the House elected in 2005, 416 MPs were aged between 40 and 60 (64 per cent of the total compared with 27 per cent of the population of the UK as a whole); and only three were younger than 30 when they were elected, compared with four in 2001 and eleven in 1997. The average age of the House is perhaps not surprising. Few young aspiring politicians are lucky enough to be selected for a winnable seat; constituency parties often prefer candidates with some experience outside politics. Nevertheless, although the average age of the population as a whole is rising, the age profile of the Commons may be a factor in distancing younger voters from the political process.

Occupation and education

In the 2005 parliament, 38 per cent of MPs in the three main parties had a professional background: 13 per cent had been school or university teachers, and 11 per cent were lawyers; 18 per cent had a business background, and 13 per cent had been in full-time politics (compared with 5 per cent in 1987). About a third of the adult population has been to university, but nearly three-quarters of MPs have had a university education (27 per cent at Oxford or Cambridge).

There are many reasons why certain occupations produce a disproportionate number of MPs while others, for example manual work (6 per cent in the House compared with 32 per cent in the country as a whole), nursing and engineering, are less well represented. MPs do not have secure jobs in Parliament and often want to retain part-time work in their old professions – something criticised by those who believe that election as an MP with a salary of just over £59,000 demands full-time attention. Some jobs are communicative and more likely to appeal to those who want to enter politics. In some jobs it is impossible to devote large amounts of time to politics – normally essential if one intends to stand for Parliament. And despite the fact that an MP's pay is more than two-and-a-half times the national median wage (the level below which 50 per cent of employees fall) of £22,941 (April 2005), some who might consider standing would have to take a substantial pay cut.

Women in Parliament

After decades of campaigning, culminating in the suffragette movement, the bill to allow women to stand for Parliament was passed on the day that

Parliament was dissolved for the 1918 general election. Paradoxically, it allowed women to be candidates at the age of 21, although women did not then have the right to vote until the age of 30 (reduced to the same age as men, then 21, in 1928).

The first woman elected to the Commons, Countess Markievicz, was elected in 1918 for the St Patrick's division of Dublin as a Sinn Féin member but, in protest against British policy on Ireland, never took her seat. It was ironic that the first woman to do so, Viscountess Astor, who was elected at a by-election on 15 November 1919, had never campaigned for women's rights. Since 1918, a total of 4,653 MPs have served in the House of Commons. Of these, 291, or 6.3 per cent, have been women.

The numbers of women MPs remained very low for seventy years, only passing 5 per cent at the 1987 general election, rising to 9.2 per cent in 1992 and sharply to 18.2 per cent in 1997. The 128 women MPs elected in 2005 (19.8 per cent) was the most ever, but still a very low proportion as women make up more than 51 per cent of the population. The devolved parliaments do much better them Westminster: 39.5 per cent of members of the Scottish Parliament are women, while in the National Assembly for Wales the figure is 50 per cent.

The average representation of women in national parliaments worldwide is 15 per cent. Rwanda comes closest to representing the population with 49 per cent women members, followed by Sweden with 45 per cent. In the league table published by the Inter-Parliamentary Union the UK comes 51st, some way ahead of the USA (67th), France (81st), Italy (85th) and Russia (98th), but behind Germany (16th), Australia (24th) and Pakistan (32nd).

Ethnic minorities

There have been non-white members of the House of Commons in the past (a Liberal, a Conservative and a Communist, who each sat for brief periods between 1892 and 1929) but, despite the substantial immigration into the United Kingdom from its former colonies in the West Indies and from the former Indian Empire in the 1950s and later, no representative of these communities was elected to Parliament until 1987 (although several had been created life peers). There is still no representative of the substantial ethnic Chinese community of more than half a million. Efforts have been made in all parties to nominate ethnic minority candidates, but not with great success. In the 1992 parliament there were six MPs who described themselves as being from an ethnic minority. This increased to nine in the 1997 parliament, to twelve, or 1.8 per cent, in the 2001 parliament and to fifteen, or 2.3 per cent of MPs, in 2005. That figure compares with some 7.9 per cent of the population in the country as a whole, which, in proportion, would mean fifty-one MPs from ethnic minorities.

Does it matter?

In one sense, it matters very little that the make-up of the membership of the House of Commons does not reflect the population as a whole. Every MP is there to represent all the people in a constituency, whether they voted for the MP, or one of the other candidates, or did not vote at all. A man, or a woman, or someone from an ethnic minority, or a single parent, may perhaps be thought to have a better understanding of the outlook of men, of women, of ethnic minorities, or of single parents. Nevertheless, the MP's job is to represent the diversity of the people in the constituency in a conscientious and professional way. Understanding your constituents is part of doing the job well, whether or not you have a particular affinity with one group or another.

The reputation of Parliament

Another factor is how the House of Commons is seen by the people it represents. There are many factors that affect the standing of Parliament. A powerful executive and a large parliamentary majority for one party condition the perception of Parliament's powers and what it can do for the citizen. Cynicism about spin and soundbites does not help. The behaviour, and thus the standing, of individual MPs is another factor.

Despite increasing direct access to Parliament and its work, through the BBC Parliament channel, webcasting on www.parliamentlive.tv and the Parliament website www.parliament.uk, most people hear about Parliament through the media. *Political* reporting in the UK is of a generally high standard, but *parliamentary* reporting, requiring a knowledge of the institution and the way it works, is less so. Trivial and ignorant coverage, especially in some of the print media, may sell newspapers, but it does not do justice to the institution.

It is an open question whether, if the House of Commons were seen by all sectors of the population as containing 'people like us', the institution would be held in higher esteem; and, if it were, whether that would increase public interest and participation. In this respect, the 2001 and 2005 general elections gave considerable cause for concern.

Turnout: reconnecting Parliament with the people

In the general election of 1992, nearly 78 per cent of those registered to vote did so. The turnout fell to 71.5 per cent in 1997, perhaps because so many people assumed that Labour would win. Even though the result of the 2001 election might also have been easily predicted, the fall in the turnout – to just over 59 per cent – was dramatic. It was lower than at any election since the introduction of the universal franchise, and it was of concern for two reasons. First, a government with an overwhelming Commons majority, and apparent carte blanche to do as it wished, had been elected with the support of only one in four people entitled to vote. Perhaps more seriously, the low turnout seemed to signal a loss of interest in the country's central democratic institution. The 2005 general election did not provide reassurance. The turnout went up slightly, to 61.5 per cent, but the government elected with a comfortable majority was now supported by only one in five of the electorate.

Many factors have been blamed. Was an adversarial style of politics putting the voters off? Or, equally, did people see the less polarised relationship of the two major parties as offering less choice than before? Did the result seem a foregone conclusion to many? Or did the electorate see Parliament as less able to control an over-mighty executive – the 'it won't make any difference' syndrome?

If there was no agreement on the cause, there is certainly no agreement on the cure. A change in the electoral system? More access to the political process, through online consultations, draft bills and the work of select committees? Fostering a wider understanding of what Parliament does and how it works? We will have a closer look at the possibilities in Chapter 13.

The Lords

Unlike the House of Commons, the House of Lords has never been representative. From its earliest times it was a chamber of individuals. Originally, members of the House were mainly the rich and powerful landed magnates on whom the King relied for his support and whose retainers would turn out to assist him (or when things went wrong, oppose him!) on the battlefield. From the late seventeenth century, the House came to include members whose influence lay elsewhere, in money, commerce and political patronage. During the twentieth century this changed as new members were increasingly drawn from the ranks of former MPs and others without landed or moneyed connection – such as trade unionists, academics, former public servants, local politicians and so forth. But members continued to have one thing in common throughout the ages: they represented no one but themselves.

Current membership

Membership of the House on 1 July 2005 was 731, eight of whom were on leave of absence – that is to say, they had been granted leave of the House not to attend in response to their writs of summons to Parliament. The categories of membership are as follows:

Archbishops and bishops	25
Life peers under the Appellate Jurisdiction Act 1876	28
Life peers under the Life Peerages Act 1958	586
Hereditary peers under the House of Lords Act 1999	92
Total	**731**

Let us now take a closer look at these different categories. Who are they and how are they selected?

Archbishops and bishops

The Anglican Archbishops of Canterbury and York, the Bishops of Durham, London and Winchester and the twenty-one senior diocesan bishops from other dioceses of the Church of England sit in the House as 'Lords Spiritual'. All the other Lords are known as 'Lords Temporal'. In the mediaeval Parliament the Lords Spiritual (bishops and mitred abbots) made up about half the membership. Currently they represent about one in twenty-eight. Only the Church of England is represented. The other established church, the Church of Scotland, has no nominees; nor do other religious denominations, non-Christian religions or the Anglican churches outside England. When the then Chief Rabbi, Lord Jakobovits, was made a peer in January 1988, it was personal to him. When a bishop retires, he loses his seat in the Lords.

Life peers under the Appellate Jurisdiction Act 1876

Besides exercising its purely parliamentary functions, the House of Lords also acts as the supreme court of appeal for the whole of the United

Kingdom in civil cases and for England, Wales and Northern Ireland in criminal cases. About seventy cases a year are heard, and the business is done in the Appellate Committee, although judgments are delivered in the Chamber at specially convened sittings. When Parliament is not in session – usually in early October – the appeals themselves are also heard in the Chamber. Lords who hold or have held high judicial office may sit on the Appellate Committee, provided that they are under 75 years of age, but the backbone is provided by up to twelve Lords of Appeal in Ordinary, salaried life peers appointed under the Appellate Jurisdiction Act 1876 specifically to hear appeals. Currently twenty-eight serving and former law lords sit in the House, having become members by this route. When the provisions relating to the establishment of a Supreme Court set out in the Constitutional Reform Act 2005 are commenced (in 2009) the twelve serving Lords of Appeal in Ordinary will become Supreme Court justices and cease to sit in the House (see page 437).

Life peers under the Life Peerages Act 1958

Until the passage of the House of Lords Act in 1999, the Life Peerages Act 1958 was the most significant influence in determining the House as we know it today. Under this legislation, men and women can be created peers for life. The title ceases on death. In July 2005 there were 586 life peers, eight of whom were on leave of absence. Many of them are politicians, often those who have worked for their party outside Parliament, who have retired from the Commons, or who have been defeated in elections. Other life peers have been drawn from different aspects of national life and have brought considerable and very valuable expertise to the House of Lords – former senior officers in the armed forces, civil servants, heads of large private sector industries, trade union leaders, doctors and academics and even the occasional actor or teacher.

The power to create peerages belongs formally to the Crown but in effect new peerages are a gift of the Prime Minister of the day – and a considerable source of patronage. By convention, other party leaders are also asked to make nominations for new peerages. This is often the only way open to opposition parties to strengthen their teams of front-bench spokesmen. The creation of most new peerages (other than Lords Spiritual and Lords of Appeal in Ordinary) is announced in the regular Honours Lists – the New Year and Queen's Birthday lists, which appear annually, and the Dissolution and Resignation lists, which occur when Parliament is dissolved or a Prime Minister resigns, respectively. But from time to time lists of so-called working peers – exclusively political appointees of the major parties – are presented. And occasionally individual peerages will be announced ad hoc.

Since May 2000 a non-statutory Appointments Commission has sat to make recommendations for non-political peers and to vet for propriety all nominations for peerages, including those from the political parties. Following a public nomination scheme conducted by the Commission, fifteen 'people's peers' were nominated in April 2001 and a second list of seven names was announced in May 2004. The right of invitation to make such nominations remains with the Prime Minister.

There are times when the House is required to absorb very large num-bers of new members, particularly following a change of administration. Thus following the 1997 general election the House witnessed a large influx of new members – twenty-one from the Dissolution list (19 April), three from the Birthday list (14 June), ten from the Resignation list (2 August) and forty-eight from a working peers list (2 August). Adding a further four peerage creations made outside these lists to enable people without seats in either Chamber to be offered ministerial posts, the House was required to absorb eighty-six new members within a very short period.

Sometimes there are periods when, other than ad hoc nominations of peerages to Law Lords, or Bishops, or for other specific purposes, no party lists appear. Thus from 2001 until May 2004 few new members joined the House, then in that month a list of forty-six new peerages was announced. Of these thirty-seven were party nominations, two were former holders of high office, and seven were put forward by the Appointments Commission. Then in the first half of 2005, thirty-five new peerages were created, twenty-seven in the Dissolution Honours list in May of that year. Towards the end of 2005, the existence of a further list of twenty-eight 'working' peers was reported in the press, but publication was delayed until 11 April 2006 after the Appointments Commission questioned the propriety of awarding peer-ages to four nominees who had lent money to the Labour Party.

Hereditary peers

Until the passing of the Life Peerages Act, all members of the House of Lords, except for the bishops and Lords of Appeal in Ordinary, were hereditary. The principle of a hereditary peerage is that, at some historical point, an individual is created a peer or lord (in one of the different ranks of dukes, marquesses, earls, viscounts or barons), and the legal document con-ferring that peerage (the 'letters patent') stipulates that his heirs (normally only the males) may inherit his title and with it the right to sit in the House of Lords. Some peerages descend through the female as well as the male line, and after 1963 women holders of hereditary peerages were also able to take their seats in the Lords.

Current membership of the House of Lords includes ninety-two hereditary peers who have seats as a result of the House of Lords Act 1999. This Act reformed the House's membership by excluding hereditary peers from sitting, but following an agreement between the government and the then Leader of the Opposition in the Lords, Lord Cranborne, the bill was amended so that seventy-five hereditary members were excepted from the general provisions of the Act by election from among their own party or group, a further fifteen by election by the whole House to serve as Deputy Speakers and committee chairs, and two (the Earl Marshal and Lord Great Chamberlain) ex officio.

These arrangements were expected to be transitional pending further reform of membership (see Chapter 13), but their effect meanwhile is to make the hereditary principle a continuing feature of British political life. From the passing of the House of Lords Act until the end of the 2001–02 session, vacancies arising out of the death of one of the ninety elected members were filled by the runners-up in the relevant category with the most votes. Two cross-bench vacancies were filled in this way. Thereafter a system of by-elections came into force. Anyone in receipt of a writ before the passage of the Act, or anyone who has subsequently established a right to be included, may ask to be on the register of eligible candidates. The electors are the whole House in the case of the fifteen excepted as Deputy Speakers or chairs but only the hereditary peers in a party or group in respect of the seventy-five elected by party or group. The first such election was held in March 2003, using a preferential voting system, and elections have since become commonplace.

Before the 1999 Act, the House of Lords was on paper at least a predominantly hereditary body, although in terms of regular attendance the hereditary element was just under 50 per cent. Now the ninety-two hereditary members represent just 12.6 per cent of membership. The government intends to remove the remaining hereditary element as part of its further reform proposals (see page 436).

Attendance

We have already noted that members of the House are not representative. They are also part time and do not always attend. In the long post-general

Table 2.2 Composition of the House of Lords, 1 July 2005

	Life	Hereditary	Bishops	Total
Conservative	159	49	–	208
Labour	211	4	–	215
Liberal Democrat	69	5	–	74
Cross-bench	155	32	–	187
Bishops	–	–	25	25
Other	12	2	–	14
Total	606	92	25	723

Note: Excludes eight members on leave of absence.

election session 2001–02, average daily attendance was 370; in the shorter pre-general election session 2004–05, it was 388. It is worth noting that the proportion of members attending is much higher since the exclusion of all but ninety-two of the hereditary peerage in 1999. In the 1996–97 session, average daily attendance was 381 out of a total potential membership of no fewer than 1,272! But the fact remains that, although many members of the House attend regularly, some life peers attend relatively infrequently.

Of the total current membership of 731, 133 are women, four of whom hold hereditary peerages. The percentage of women members is 18.2 per cent, close to that in the Commons.

Politics

Although members of the House are not representative and are unelected, they are nearly all political animals. Most members of the House take a party whip, and of course many of the life peers owe their membership of the House to political patronage. The non-aligned cross-bench members have political opinions on issues, although none of them supports a political party. Party political allegiance on 1 July 2005 is shown in Table 2.2.

The passage of the House of Lords Act 1999 and the creation of more Labour life peers since 1997 has done much to promote greater parity between the two main parties. The Labour Party is now the biggest single group in the House, but lacks an overall majority. In consequence, the government often relies on Liberal Democrat and cross-bench support to get its way in the face of Conservative opposition. On those occasions when such support might not be forthcoming, the government is more prone to compromise. We look more closely at this in Chapter 7.

The Queen

It is easy to think of Parliament as consisting simply of the two Houses; but the sovereign is also part of the institution. Indeed, the words that precede every Act of Parliament remind us that, to become law, a bill must be approved by the Queen as well as by both Houses:

> *Be it enacted by the Queen's most Excellent Majesty, by and with the advice and consent of the Lords Spiritual and Temporal, and Commons, in this present Parliament assembled, and by the authority of the same, as follows: –*

The Queen's name appears again and again in the proceedings of Parliament. Bills go for Royal Assent; if a bill affects the Royal Prerogative or the Queen's personal interests, then the Queen's consent must be signified before it is passed; the spending of taxpayers' money in connection with a bill must have the Queen's recommendation; the government's legislative programme is set out at the beginning of a session in the Queen's Speech; many papers presented formally to the two Houses are presented 'by Command of Her Majesty'; Orders in Council – a category of delegated legislation – are made in her name; the government is 'Her Majesty's Government'; and ministers are 'Ministers of the Crown'.

This terminology may seem more appropriate to the mediaeval relationship between the monarch and his fledgling parliament, and in the early twenty-first century the language is entirely symbolic. The Queen does indeed give her consent to bills – by signing a list of bills passed rather than each one – but she has no practical power of refusal. The last sovereign to refuse Royal Assent (to a bill for settling the militia in Scotland) was Queen Anne in 1707–08, and in subsequent centuries sovereigns have progressively distanced themselves from the business of politics.

Above politics: political neutrality

The conventional phrase is that the Queen is 'above politics' or, as Walter Bagehot said of royalty and Queen Victoria, 'Its mystery is its life. We must not let in daylight upon magic. We must not bring the Queen into the combat of politics, or she will cease to be reverenced by all combatants; she will become one combatant among many'. Most would agree that events of the last fifteen years, aided and abetted by the tabloid press, have dispelled much of Bagehot's 'magic'; but the Queen's political neutrality is still of constitutional importance. On the one hand, most people would regard it as unacceptable for the monarch to be identified with a particular political party (even a political party that they themselves supported); on the other hand, the Queen may have to perform a crucial constitutional task: deciding who should form a government after a general election.

Choosing a Prime Minister

Normally this is straightforward. The day after polling day the leader of the party with the most seats in the House of Commons – and so able to command the House and get the business of government through – is summoned to Buckingham Palace and asked as Prime Minister to form a government, which in practice means appointing the members of the Cabinet and other ministers and taking responsibility for the administration of the country.

Similarly, when a sitting Prime Minister resigns, as Harold Wilson did in 1976, or Margaret Thatcher did in 1990 having lost the confidence of her party, the sovereign's task is an easy one. The government party will choose a new leader under the procedure required by its party rules, and – assuming that that party still has a majority in the House – the Queen will invite the winner to form a government.

A hung parliament

However, in a hung parliament after a general election, where no one party has a majority, the Queen's task may be more difficult. When the final tally of seats is clear, there will probably be intense negotiation between the parties to see how much common ground there might be for the formation of a coalition (where ministers would be drawn from two or more parties) or for one party to govern with the formal support of another. When the Conservative Party lost its majority in the general election of February 1974, Edward Heath negotiated with the Liberal Party in an attempt to continue in government with Liberal support. When it was clear that he would be unsuccessful, the Queen asked Harold Wilson to form a minority government, which struggled on until a general election in October that year, at which Wilson won a narrow overall majority of three seats.

More difficult for the sovereign would be a situation where a general election produced a three-way split in seats in the Commons but very little common ground between any of the three parties. If it was quickly clear that the party leader first asked to form a government could not sustain it – for example by losing the vote on the proposed legislative programme in the

Queen's Speech – she would probably invite another party leader to attempt to form a government.

It would be a matter of judgement as to how long this process could be allowed to go on. On the one hand, the argument goes, the people have spoken (as former President Clinton famously said of the 2000 US presidential election, 'but we're not sure yet what they've said') and it is for politicians to agree a constructive way forward. To force another poll so soon after the first would inflict another general election on a weary electorate, with no guarantee that it would produce any different result. On the other hand, the business of government needs to be carried on, and a second general election might be preferable to months of inter-party squabbling and horse trading.

In these circumstances, the sovereign's political neutrality is crucial. While others may be concerned about party advantage, she must consider only the national interest. The process is not risk-free: when in Australia in 1975 the Governor-General dismissed the Prime Minister on the grounds that the two Houses of Parliament could not reach agreement on the budget and the business of government could not be carried on, that undoubtedly fuelled the flames of republicanism. By contrast, in Belgium, where coalition governments are the norm, there was little criticism of the King in 1985 when he refused the Prime Minister a dissolution because the coalition government had broken down.

Another method?

It is sometimes suggested that the Queen's powers to dissolve Parliament and invite a party leader to form a government should be delegated to the Speaker of the House of Commons (as has been the case in unicameral Sweden since 1974, where the King's functions are purely ceremonial). But even if it were acceptable to give the presiding officer of one House powers over the other – for a dissolution affects the Lords as well – the same problems would remain to be solved.

The sovereign as statesman

To quote Bagehot again: 'the sovereign has, under a constitutional monarchy such as ours, three rights – the right to be consulted, the right to encourage, the right to warn'. He was speaking of Queen Victoria, who perhaps exercised more influence than does her great-great-grand-daughter, but those principles still hold good today. It is worth remembering that the present Queen has more experience of the nation's affairs than anyone in politics. She sees a wide range of state papers and is briefed frankly by the government on the issues of the day. British ambassadors ('Her Majesty's Ambassadors') and high commissioners call upon her when they leave to take up their posts and when they return, and she sees their most important despatches.

She has known ten Prime Ministers, from Churchill to Blair, and at weekly audiences has discussed with them the crises and dilemmas that they have faced. Almost all have had an excellent relationship with her, and some have described the weekly audiences in terms almost of therapy: being able to talk about major problems in total confidence with someone of immense political experience who is neither a political opponent nor a rival. The role of the present Queen demonstrates that Bagehot's rights of the sovereign are still of great value.

The Crown prerogative

We saw how frequently the Queen's name is used in the business of Parliament, mostly in relation to matters that require the approval of Parliament or are subject to the authority of Parliament. However, the ability of a mediaeval monarch to wage wars, appoint ambassadors and conclude treaties without the approval of Parliament survives in a modern form through the government's use of the Crown prerogative. Ministers make between three and four thousand public appointments every year, many to posts of power and importance. The Prime Minister can reorganise government departments and their responsibilities overnight, and negotiate and sign treaties with few constraints. The government can even take the country to war without parliamentary approval; putting the matter to the House of Commons, as was done on 18 March 2003 before the invasion of Iraq, was a remarkable precedent.

All these things are done in the Queen's name through the use of the Crown prerogative, usually bypassing the two Houses of Parliament. We examine the implications of this in Chapter 4.

3

Running Parliament

The House of Commons

The Speaker

The Speaker of the House of Commons is the most visible player on the parliamentary stage. His 'Order, order' opens every parliamentary day in the Chamber; he is usually in the Chair for the stormiest parliamentary events, and he is the representative of the House on occasions of state ceremony, sorrow and rejoicing.

Not only does the Speaker have the task of chairing the House; he is also an enormously influential figure in almost every aspect of the way that the House and its administration are run. As the presiding officer of the Commons he may seem the exact counterpart of the Lord Speaker as the presiding officer of the Lords; but, as we shall see, their functions are very different.

The office of Speaker

The first member known as Speaker was Sir Thomas Hungerford in 1376, although it seems clear that individual members presided over the early mediaeval House before then, perhaps as early as Peter de Montfort in Henry III's 'Mad Parliament' at Oxford in 1258. The title of Speaker (Mr Speaker or Madam Speaker, as he or she is always referred to in the House) comes from the ancient position of official spokesman of the Commons to the monarch. In the days when sovereign and Commons were frequently at odds, this aspect of the job was rather more arduous than today, and more hazardous: between 1471 and 1535, six Speakers were executed.

Some of the ancient functions of the Speaker survive in more symbolic form. Once elected by the Commons, he makes claim to the Crown of the House's

> *ancient and undoubted Rights and Privileges, particularly to freedom of speech in debate, freedom from arrest, freedom of access to Her Majesty whenever occasion may require, and that the most favourable construction should be placed on all its proceedings.*

although this may perhaps appear a little at odds with the modern relationship between the monarch and a House elected by universal suffrage.

The Speaker still occasionally acts as the House's spokesman and representative. After the terrorist atrocities on 11 September 2001 he expressed the House's condolences to the US Congress; and on the occasion of the Golden Jubilee in 2002 he presented an Address of the House to the Queen in Westminster Hall. When parliaments around the world responded to the London bombings of 7 July 2005 it was to the Speaker that they sent their messages of sympathy.

The independence of the Speaker

In many foreign parliaments the presiding officer is a party politician. In the US House of Representatives, for example, the Speaker is a leading party politician and frequently takes part in controversial debate. In Germany, the president of the Bundestag is normally a senior member of the government party who continues to play an active part in his party's affairs, and the same is true of the president of the French Assemblée nationale.

However, in the House of Commons there is a long tradition of impartiality, which began with Arthur Onslow (Speaker for thirty-three years from 1728) and which is so strong that all Speakers are seen as genuinely independent of party. There was a welter of press comment when the current Speaker, in the Chair, thanked a government minister for the *content* of a statement the minister had just made to the House. Speaker Martin's words were not unduly controversial, and he made it clear that he was voicing a constituency concern that he felt was shared by all members, but the incident demonstrated how the real independence of the Speaker is valued not only in the House but also more widely. The Speaker could not do his job, or exercise the considerable powers that the House has given him, were he not seen as in every way above the party battle.

In practice, this means that the Speaker resigns from his party – perhaps after having been a party member for thirty years or more – and has nothing more to do with its internal affairs. When he stands at a general election, it is not under a party banner but as 'the Speaker seeking re-election'; and he is usually unopposed by the major parties. He draws the salary of a cabinet minister and can look forward on retirement to a generous pension and a peerage. He wears formal dress, a court coat and barrister's bands, and when in the Chair a gown – but as Speaker Boothroyd abandoned the full-bottomed wig and Speaker Martin has followed suit, that particular tradition has probably ended for good. When the Speaker goes to and from the Chamber he is preceded by a trainbearer. Warned by cries of 'Speaker!' from the doorkeepers, even the most senior MPs stop what they are doing and bow as he goes by.

In the Palace of Westminster the Speaker has a personal staff to support him and splendid state apartments, which are his official residence, with a comfortable and less formal flat above. He no longer eats with other MPs in the dining rooms or takes part in the political gossip of the Tea Room. Members now come to him. Every Speaker must keep a finger on the pulse of the House and the concerns of its members, and much of his time is taken up with meetings not only with, for example, the Leader of the House or the Chief Whips, but also with a wide variety of MPs with concerns, problems – or bright ideas.

The Speaker is also the embodiment of the House as far as the outside world is concerned. He receives ambassadors, Speakers and ministers from other parliaments, delegations of all sorts, and he presides over a number of parliamentary associations and other bodies.

The Speaker still carries out constituency work and duties like any other MP. It is sometimes suggested that the Speaker should sit for a notional constituency – perhaps called St Stephen's – but this idea has never found much favour. Speakers want to understand and share at first hand the constituency pressures and problems faced by other MPs; and their own constituents are fortunate in having the Speaker for their Member of Parliament as ministers understandably give special attention to constituency cases raised by the Speaker.

The election of the Speaker

Since 1945, some Speakers have been former ministers (Morrison, Selwyn-Lloyd and Thomas had all been cabinet ministers, while Hylton-Foster had been Solicitor-General and Weatherill had been government Deputy Chief

Whip); the careers of others had been mainly on the back benches (King and Martin; Boothroyd had been a government assistant whip for two years). However, since 1965 five out of the six Speakers have been former Deputy Speakers (King, Thomas, Weatherill, Boothroyd and Martin); not only did they come to the Speakership with experience in the Chair, but also the House had been able to make some assessment of them in that role.

Perhaps surprisingly in view of the rigid political independence of the office, all post-war Speakers except Betty Boothroyd have come from the government side of the House, whichever party has been in power. Given that one of the roles of the Speaker is to protect the House's interests when they conflict with those of the executive, this may have required a rapid reorientation; but it is often said that, particularly at the outset, Speakers tend to be harder on their former party than on the other side of the House.

Since 1945, there has normally been only one candidate for the Speakership. In 1992 there was rather more of a contest: the former cabinet minister, Peter Brooke, was defeated by 372 votes to 238, and Betty Boothroyd was elected. She was re-elected unopposed at the start of the 1997 parliament.

On her retirement in 2000 there was an unprecedented election for the Speakership, with no fewer than twelve candidates standing. Propositions are normally put to the House in the form of a motion to which amendments may be moved, and this had always been the procedure for the election of the Speaker, where the motion 'That X do take the Chair of this House as Speaker' could be amended by leaving out 'X' and inserting 'Y'. Thus in 2000 the motion named Michael Martin, and the other candidates were put to the House one by one in a series of amendments. Speeches proposing and seconding the candidates, and by the candidates themselves, together with the votes on each amendment and the final decision, took nine hours. As of course there was no Speaker, the member with the longest continuous service (the 'Father of the House'), Sir Edward Heath, presided.

In one sense, a day's sitting to fill a post of such importance to every single MP and to the House as a whole was not excessive; but there was understandable pressure to see whether matters could be handled differently. Following a report from the Procedure Committee, in 2001 the House agreed new arrangements. These favour a Speaker who returns to the House after a general election; only if a motion that he or she should take the Chair is defeated does the new procedure for a contested election come into play.

In a contested election, nominations (supported by twelve to fifteen MPs, at least three of whom cannot be from the candidate's own party) are submitted to the Clerk of the House on the morning of the election. When the House meets later that day, the candidates address the House in turn, in an order chosen by lot, and MPs then vote by secret ballot. If one candidate gets more than half the votes, his or her name is put to the House straight away; but if not, the lowest-scoring candidate and any candidate with less than 5 per cent of the votes are eliminated, a second ballot is held, and so on until one candidate gets more than half the votes. The system is designed to be as fair as possible and not to give an advantage to the candidate who is proposed first (as did the previous system). It is unlike any voting system used in any of the House's other decisions; but it has not yet been used; Speaker Martin was elected unopposed in 2001 and 2005.

The roles of the Speaker

Maintaining order

Perhaps the most obvious function of the Speaker and his deputies is to maintain order when the House is sitting. All speeches made in the Chamber are addressed to the Chair, and the Speaker 'calls to order' any MP who offends against the rules of the House. Some of these are conventions, and others are laid down in standing orders or in past resolutions of the House. The definitive guide to them is *Erskine May's Treatise on the Law, Privileges, Proceedings and Usage of Parliament*, usually known as *Erskine May*. Sir Thomas Erskine May, Clerk of the House from 1871 to 1886, edited the first nine editions, and fourteen more have been edited by his successors.

The House's rules range from the relatively trivial, such as requiring members to refer to each other by constituency rather than name, to the more serious, such as the *sub judice* rule (see page 303), which is designed to prevent criminal trials or civil actions in the courts being prejudiced by comment in the House. Other rules require speeches to be relevant to the matter before the House (and supplementary questions to be relevant to the subject of the question on the Order Paper), forbid the use of insulting words or 'unparliamentary expressions' (see page 303), specify when an MP may speak a second time in a debate, regulate the proper conduct of votes, and so on. The Speaker has both to make sure that these rules are observed and to give his rulings when MPs raise points of order about the application or interpretation of these rules.

In a democratic assembly passions can run high and tempers flare. It is then that the Speaker and his deputies need to be most sensitive in gauging the mood of the House. Will a humorous intervention from the Chair defuse the situation, or is there serious trouble that must be dealt with firmly from the outset? At need, they have powers to discipline individual MPs, either by ordering them to resume their seats, to leave the Chamber for the day or, for more serious offences (usually involving a disregard for the authority of the Chair), *naming* them. After a member has been named, a motion is moved by the senior minister present, which the House invariably agrees to, and which has the effect of suspending the MP, so barring him or her from the building for five sitting days on the first occasion, twenty sitting days on the second and indefinitely on the third (and stopping payment of the member's salary for those periods). If there is general disorder in the Chamber, the Speaker can suspend the sitting.

These are powers used with great reluctance by the Speaker. He does not want to create martyrs or give an individual MP's political protest added force by expulsion from the Chamber; but he has also to protect the reputation of the House and the business before it. In February 2003, the way in which Speaker Martin dealt with the protest by the Father of the House, Tam Dalyell, that Parliament was not being properly consulted on impending war with Iraq, was a good example of the merits of restraint. A whole column of *Hansard* was taken up with an exchange between the Speaker and the Father of the House, which was courteous rather than angry, and the incident ended with Mr Dalyell leaving the Chamber of his own accord. Precipitate disciplinary action can rebound upon the Chair, as with the Victorian Speaker who was foolish enough to have the police called to deal with disorder in the Chamber. Thereafter, whenever the House was rowdy, his authority was routinely undermined by shouts of 'send for the police'.

Holding the ring

The Speaker and his deputies have absolute discretion over which members they call to speak. There may be some fixed points in a major debate: perhaps a cabinet minister will open the debate, responded to by his or her opposition shadow, with a Liberal Democrat representative speaking shortly afterwards, and the winding-up speeches at the end might be made by another member of the shadow cabinet and by another cabinet minister.

In between, the character of the debate is shaped by which MPs the Chair calls to speak. Balancing their claims is no easy task. Let us suppose that there is a full day's debate on policy towards asylum seekers: in practice, five or six hours' debating time. The five front-bench speeches might leave no more than three or four hours for everyone else who wishes to take part. Let us also suppose that pressure on existing reception centres for asylum seekers has led the government to propose a number of additional sites. Unrest in two or three centres has been followed by violence and extensive damage. There will be MPs with asylum centres in their constituencies; those who represent people who are up in arms that a new centre might be located near them; those who represent Channel ports; those who are close to the unions representing asylum centre staff; perhaps the chairman and members of the Home Affairs Select Committee, who have just produced a critical report on asylum policy. And, as well as juggling these urgent claims to speak, the Speaker and his deputies have to ensure that the party balance is maintained.

During Question Time (see Chapter 10), the Speaker's ability to shape events is even more marked. He can cut short over-long supplementary questions (and ministerial answers), but he can also decide how long to go on calling MPs to ask supplementaries on a particular question. If the subject is one on which the government is vulnerable, eight supplementary questions – perhaps including some hostile ones from the minister's own side – instead of two or three may give a minister a torrid time at the despatch box. And it is the occupant of the Chair alone who decides how long questioning on a ministerial statement or an urgent question (see page 332) should continue. Again, if political and media pressure has forced a ministerial statement on some high-profile problem, the government's exposure will be much greater if questions run for an hour instead of half an hour.

The Speaker's powers in the Chamber

In sharp contrast to the House of Lords, the Commons has given its presiding officer extensive powers. The House of Lords may largely regulate itself, but in the much more contentious and politically polarised Commons the Chair has a considerable armoury.

First, as we have seen, there is *the power to call MPs to speak in a debate or to ask a question*, described by Speaker Thomas as his most potent weapon. Although Speakers strive to be fair to every MP, the member who is disruptive or abusive, or disregards the authority of the Chair, may find it difficult to catch the Speaker's eye at Prime Minister's Questions for some little while thereafter. Allied with this is the power to decide *how long questioning on a particular topic may continue.*

In most debates, the Speaker also has the *power to limit the length of backbench speeches*, down to a minimum of three minutes. He can also intervene to *prevent deliberate time wasting* by MPs either speaking repetitiously or calling for unnecessary votes. The decision on whether to accept the closure

– in other words, to *allow the House to decide whether a debate should end and a vote be taken on the subject under discussion* – is entirely in the hands of the Chair.

The Speaker also has absolute discretion on *whether amendments to bills or to motions before the House should be debated and voted upon*. This can be of great significance. For example, when in February 2003 options on the future composition of the House of Lords were put before the Commons by the government, the choices were in the form of seven free-standing motions, on each of which the House would take a decision (in fact, every one was defeated). There was no option that would have allowed a decision on whether there should be a House of Lords at all. However, a Labour back-bencher put down identical amendments to each of the options, declining approval as 'it does not accord with the principle of a unicameral parliament'. The Speaker selected the amendment (in other words, allowed it to be debated and voted upon) and it was defeated by 390 votes to 172. But it was only because of the Speaker's decision that a substantial minority in favour of abolition were able to record their view.

The debates on Iraq in February and March 2003 provide even more vivid examples. When on 26 February 2003 the Commons debated a government motion calling upon Iraq to recognise this as its final opportunity to comply with its 'disarmament obligations', the Speaker selected a Labour back-bench amendment to the effect that the case for military action against Iraq was 'as yet unproven'. The amendment was defeated by 393 votes to 199, but the 199 included 122 Labour MPs voting against the government's policy – a rebellion of huge political significance.

Less than a month later, the government put before the House of Commons a motion authorising the use of all means necessary to ensure the disarmament of Iraq's weapons of mass destruction – in effect authorising war. Again, the Speaker selected a Labour back-bench amendment asserting that 'the case for war against Iraq has not yet been established, especially given the absence of specific United Nations authorisation'. This time the amendment was defeated by 396 votes to 217; the 217 included 139 Labour MPs (twenty-nine of whom had not rebelled on the previous occasion), again a seismic political event.

The Speaker can also set part of the political agenda, and allow the House to call the government to account, through *urgent questions* (formerly called 'private notice questions' because they are applied for to the Speaker privately rather than being printed on the Order Paper). If the Speaker thinks a matter is sufficiently urgent or important, and there is unlikely to be another way of raising it in the House in the next day or so, he allows a question to be put to a minister (often by the Opposition spokesman on the subject) at the end of Question Time. Although ministerial statements are made voluntarily by the government, urgent questions are granted when in the Speaker's view the House needs to be informed but no ministerial statement is forthcoming. Urgent questions are described in more detail in Chapter 10 (page 332).

The Speaker also has the power to decide whether *a complaint of privilege* – in other words, an allegation that an MP, or a servant of the House, or perhaps a select committee, has been obstructed or threatened – should be put to the House. Such an allegation must be made privately to the Speaker – a procedure designed to prevent frivolous complaints. If the Speaker believes that there may be grounds for action, he allows the matter to take precedence over other business and a motion to be moved referring the complaint to the Committee on Standards and Privileges for investigation. Such complaints are rare. Privilege is described in more detail in Chapter 6 (page 181).

The casting vote

Once put to the vote in the House, a matter must be decided; it cannot be left as a draw. If the numbers of 'ayes' and 'noes' are equal, then the occupant of the Chair must decide the question by casting a vote; and it is only on these occasions that the Speaker or his deputies do vote. However, the Chair is protected from controversy by clearly established historical principles. These are, broadly, that a decision should be taken by a majority of the House, not just on the basis of a casting vote; and that there should be opportunity for further discussion. Thus the Chair will vote 'aye' on a casting vote on the second reading of a bill, because the bill can continue its progress and be amended if the House wishes. But the Chair will vote 'no' if the vote on the third reading is tied, because that is the moment at which the Commons approves the bill, and the law should not be changed except by a majority of the House. If the vote is on a motion for the adjournment, the Chair votes 'no' in order to allow the House to proceed with other business.

In the Thatcher and the Blair years, big government majorities made the need for casting votes much less (although on issues of conscience, or unwhipped votes on private members' bills the possibility was always there; and it is worth remembering that the 80 per cent elected/20 per cent appointed House of Lords option was defeated only by 284 votes to 281 on 4 February 2003). However, when the government has a small majority the more likely is the need for a casting vote; it was used seven times between 1974 and 1979. It was almost needed when the Callaghan government fell as a result of losing a vote of confidence on the night of 28 March 1979; 311 MPs voted against the government, and 310 for.

Had the casting vote been needed then, it would have been 'no' on the principle that the decision had to be taken by a majority and not on a casting vote. But so clear is the principle that, even in the greatest political controversy, there is no question of political bias. The most recent casting vote is a good example. On 22 July 1993 the House was voting on the Leader of the Opposition's amendment to a motion on the Social Protocol of the Maastricht Treaty. The votes were 317 ayes and 317 noes. Speaker Boothroyd voted 'no' on the basis that the decision should be taken only by a majority. The government lost the vote on the motion itself and put a motion of confidence before the House the next day, which it won comfortably, without the need for a casting vote. The closest to a casting vote since then was in November 2005. With Conservative and Liberal Democrat Support, a Labour back-bench amendment to the Terrorism Bill, limiting the definition of 'glorifying terrorism', was defeated by only one vote, and in January 2006 a Lords amendment to the Racial and Religious Hatred Bill was defeated by one vote.

Recalling the House
It occasionally happens that because of some grave event the House is recalled during a recess (as it was on three occasions in 2001 following the 11 September attacks in the USA, on 3 April 2002 following the death of the Queen Mother, and again on 24 September 2002 to debate possible action against Iraq), and the media normally report that it is the Prime Minister who has recalled Parliament. In fact, the standing orders provide that ministers may represent to the Speaker that the public interest requires an earlier meeting of the House; and, if the Speaker agrees, he appoints a time for the House to sit. This may be a distinction that is not much of a difference because, following precedent, the Speaker always agrees to the government's request. However, the Iraq crisis has given rise to concern in some quarters about the role of Parliament at a time of international tension, and to pressure for the Speaker to have the power to recall the House regardless of the views of the government. The Procedure Committee has now recommended that the decision should be one for the Speaker alone.

Statutory and other functions
The Speaker is ex officio chairman of each of the Boundary Commissions mentioned in Chapter 2, although the work falls to the other members, led

by a High Court judge (or Scottish equivalent). This function will end when the responsibilities of the Boundary Commissions are transferred to the Electoral Commission set up under the Political Parties, Elections and Referendums Act 2000. The Speaker also chairs the Speaker's Committee, which oversees the operation of the Electoral Commission.

The most important and time-consuming of the Speaker's statutory responsibilities is as chairman of the House of Commons Commission, which is the financial and employing authority for the House administration, and whose work we describe on page 60.

The voice of the House

The Speaker's role as official spokesman of the Commons to the monarch may survive only in ceremonial form, but the core of his job is still protecting and expressing the interests of the House. He protects the interests of the House through securing orderly proceedings, the courtesies of debate, and consistent and fair rulings on points of order and matters of contention. Expressing the interests of the House is more complex and potentially more politically exposed, as it centres upon the House's relationship with the government of the day. The Speaker can grant urgent questions, select unwelcome amendments, allow questions to run on, and ensure that a wide spectrum of opinion is called in debate if this helps Parliament better to air issues and hold the government to account.

One key area on which both Speaker Boothroyd and Speaker Martin have expressed strong views is what Speaker Martin has described as 'the fundamental importance for the proper functioning of Parliament that this House is the first to hear of important developments in government policy'. This is a sensitive area; governments of both political parties have wanted to set the media agenda outside the House, to brief selected journalists, perhaps to prepare public opinion for unwelcome news. But if Parliament is to be the focus of national attention, then, whether the news is momentous or not, the principle that the nation's representatives in Parliament are told first is an important one; and the Speaker must be its main advocate.

Precedent and change

Precedent provides the framework within which any Speaker operates. It is a powerful ally in making rulings robust against challenge and – as with casting votes – emphasising the impartiality of the Chair. But no Speaker can simply rest on precedent. Parliament is constantly changing, not only internally in terms of its membership and political complexion but also in terms of the influences and pressures upon it. There are always new problems and situations with which a Speaker must grapple, and set new precedents in the process. These may be as far-reaching as the procedures adopted by Speaker Brand in the 1870s and 1880s to deal with the Irish Home Rule MPs who were obstructing the House's business; before his unilateral action to limit MPs' rights to speak by the introduction of the closure, members could speak for as long as they liked on any question before the House. More often, changes come about almost imperceptibly as a result of a series of Speaker's rulings.

The Speaker works closely with the Clerk of the House and the Clerk's senior colleagues; he draws on their professional knowledge and long experience and has the political and professional advice of often highly experienced deputies. But the decisions are for him alone. Members may criticise the Speaker only by putting down a substantive motion for debate; if such a motion is not withdrawn, the government quickly finds time for a debate in order to resolve the matter. The fact that only three such motions have actually been debated since the Second World War suggests that, despite the fact that they exercise a great deal of power in a politically highly contentious House, Speakers do a pretty good job.

The Deputy Speakers

The Speaker is assisted by three deputies – the Chairman of Ways and Means and two Deputy Chairmen. They are senior back-benchers who are appointed by the House for the duration of the parliament, normally all at the same time on the first business day of a new parliament, and in a far less elaborate way than the Speaker is chosen; after informal soundings have been taken, a motion to appoint them appears in the name of the Prime Minister or the Leader of the House. This rather informal procedure has answered well enough for many years, although in April 2002 the Procedure Committee recommended a more formal approach with wider consultation.

The Chairman of Ways and Means is so called because from the late seventeenth century he presided over the Committee of Ways and Means (dealing with taxation) as well as the Committee of Supply (dealing with government expenditure), at that time the only two permanent committees of the House. It was not until 1853 that the Chairman began formally to deputise for the Speaker.

Today the Chairman of Ways and Means exercises most of the powers of the Speaker in the Chamber (and has the power to select amendments in Committee of the whole House, when the Speaker never presides). The

Chairman also has three other distinct roles. He oversees the consideration of private bills (as distinct from private members' bills) (see page 249); he supervises arrangements for sittings in Westminster Hall (see page 296); and through his chairmanship of the Chairmen's Panel (see page 212) he has general responsibility for the work of legislative standing committees. From 1902, a Deputy Chairman of Ways and Means was appointed, and a Second Deputy Chairman from 1971. They exercise the same powers in the Chamber as the Chairman of Ways and Means. No decision of any of the three may be appealed to the Speaker.

The three Deputy Speakers come from both sides of the House and, together with the Speaker, cancel out the loss of numbers from government and opposition sides of the House. Thus Speaker Martin came from the government (Labour) side; Sir Alan Haselhurst, the Chairman of Ways and Means, from the opposition (Conservative) side; Sylvia Heal, the First Deputy Chairman, from the government side; and Sir Michael Lord, the Second Deputy Chairman, from the opposition side. The deputies are rigidly impartial in the Chair and other House duties, and they do not vote (except to resolve a tied vote). However, unlike the Speaker they remain members of their parties, and they fight general elections on a party basis.

The Speaker and the deputies have a rota of duty in the Chair; normally the Speaker takes the first two hours, disposing of Question Time, one or more ministerial statements thereafter, and any points of order before the main business of the day begins. The deputies do stints of two hours or so, although the Speaker may return to preside over the end of the main business and any votes that take place.

In 2002, the Procedure Committee attempted a job description for the deputies:

> an ability swiftly to command the respect of the whole House . . . a
> demonstrable knowledge of procedure and its application, as well as wider
> experience of the House and the way it works, together with an ability to
> chair the most challenging debates with demonstrable fairness and authority
> . . . a good team player. An appetite for hard work, unremitting punctuality
> and a sense of humour and proportion are also highly desirable.

The Leader of the House

The Leader of the House of Commons – from April 2006 Jack Straw – is a key figure in both government and Parliament. He or she is a cabinet minister as well as an MP; but although the Leader has collective Cabinet responsibility for defending the government's policies in the House, he or she also has the wider task of upholding the rights and interests of the House. With the Chief Whip, the Leader is responsible for the arrangement of government business in the Commons, and for planning and supervising the government's legislative programme as a whole by chairing the Cabinet Committee on the Legislative Programme (known as LP).

He or she has an extensive power base in government through membership of some of the most important Cabinet committees and sub-committees, including those on domestic affairs, economic affairs, environment, local government, public services, international terrorism and European issues.

Following the Labour victory in the 1997 general election, a Select Committee on the Modernisation of the House of Commons was appointed (see page 353) and has been chaired by successive Leaders of the House – although not without criticism that a Cabinet minister chairing so influential a select committee was yet another aspect of the government's control of Parliament.

The Leader reports weekly to Cabinet on forthcoming parliamentary business. He announces that business – firm for the following week, provisional for the week after – to the House every Thursday, an event that emphasises the control that the government of the day has over the time of the House of Commons. He also answers oral questions once a month on his wider responsibilities as Leader.

The Leader usually moves (and defends) motions to determine how Commons business is to be dealt with, or to introduce procedural change, and often winds up at the end of major debates on behalf of the government. He also plays a role in House administration as an ex officio member of the House of Commons Commission and as the minister responsible for the Members Estimate (see page 77).

The Clerk of the House

The Clerk of the House of Commons is the House's senior official and combines a variety of roles. He is the House's adviser on all aspects of parliamentary procedure, practice and privilege, the editor of *Erskine May* and a frequent witness before Procedure Committees. He is the Speaker's right hand on a wide range of issues but is also available to advise any Member of the House. He is Chief Executive of the House Service, chairs the Board of Management, which is responsible for providing the services that support the work of the House, its committees and its members, and is the principal adviser to the House of Commons Commission (see page 60). He is Accounting Officer for the House of Commons Administration Estimate and the Members Estimate and so is personally responsible for the propriety and economy of expenditure. He is the House's corporate officer and so formally holds property and enters into contracts on the House's behalf, and is legally responsible for the actions of the House Administration. He is also the professional head of the Clerk's Department, which is the part of the House Service most closely concerned with the work of the House and its committees.

It may seem strange that the Clerk combines the somewhat academic precision of procedural matters with overall responsibility for the management of the House's services. In fact it would be strange if he were not to do so. He is the authority on all aspects of the House's core business – not just the drier matters of procedure – and no one is in a better position to understand from long experience how the main functions of the House need to be supported and how they can be made more effective.

The first known Clerk of the House – formally styled 'Under-Clerk of the Parliaments, to wait upon the Commons' – was appointed in 1363, and there has been an unbroken line since. The title 'Clerk' probably derives from the fact that in early mediaeval times literacy was by no means universal and was most widely found among priests, or clerks in holy orders. The Clerk of the House is appointed by the Queen by letters patent (as is the Clerk Assistant), which underpins his independence.

The House of Commons Service

The permanent staff of the House (some 1,700 people) are not civil servants but employees of the House of Commons Commission. This distinction may not be of great importance for those staff who are responsible for the upkeep of the buildings or for catering services, but for many it is of constitutional importance. The Clerk of a departmental select committee who manages a committee's inquiry into something that has gone wrong within government and then has to draft a report strongly critical of ministers and civil servants would face an intolerable conflict of loyalties if he or she owed allegiance to the Civil Service. To take another example, analysis prepared by the subject experts in the Library's research services is expected to be rigorous regardless of the possibility that their findings may not be palatable to the government of the day.

The House of Commons Service must also be politically impartial. Again, this is more important in some areas of work than in others. Staff in the Clerk's Department may find themselves in quick succession advising both government and opposition on procedural tactics for highly contentious business in the House, or within the space of a few minutes advising both the member in charge of a private member's bill and those MPs who want to scupper its chances of proceeding any further. If they are to retain the confidence of MPs, it is essential for their credibility that Clerks giving that advice are seen to be absolutely impartial as to both parties and issues.

The House administration

The administration of the House of Commons is fairly complex. This is not surprising; on the one hand, it has to deliver a wide range of disparate services, from regilding Pugin decoration in a Grade I listed building to supporting select committee work that covers every aspect of public life, to producing overnight a record of all the proceedings in the House and in Westminster Hall. On the other hand, professional management and planning must take into account the changing, and not always consistent, wishes of MPs as well as the unpredictable pressures on Parliament itself.

A 1999 review of the way the House services were run summed up the problem.

> *The effective operation of the House is of enormous constitutional and public importance. The elector (and taxpayer) expects Governments to be held to account; constituents to be represented and their grievances pursued; and historic Parliamentary functions to be extended and adapted to changes in the wider world.*
>
> *These things do not come cheap, and no-one should expect them to. Seeking to hold to account a complex, sophisticated and powerful Executive; dealing with an unremitting burden of legislation; and meeting ever-increasing expectations on the part of constituents; all this requires substantial, high-quality support. . . .*
>
> *There is no shortage of complicating factors. Each Member of Parliament is an expert on what he or she wants from the system, and what the system should provide. With their staffs, Members are in effect 659 [now 646] small businesses operating independently within one institutional framework. Managers in both the public and private sectors have to meet the needs of demanding customers; but they do not have customers every one of whom can*

take a complaint to the Floor of the House of Commons – perhaps televised nation-wide.

At the same time the House and its Members are funded by the taxpayer. This spending is inevitably high-profile, exposed to media interest which is not always friendly and which may not pause to assess the wider value of Parliamentary expenditure. The House must be able to demonstrate proper stewardship of public money, and to show that expenditure is efficient, effective and economical.

That is the task facing the House administration.

The House of Commons Commission

The Commission is the supervisory body of the administration, responsible for the House's finances and the employer of almost all its staff. Set up under the House of Commons (Administration) Act 1978, it is chaired by the Speaker; its other members are the Leader of the House, a member nominated by the Leader of the Opposition (in practice, always the Shadow Leader of the House), and three senior back-benchers, one from each of the main parties. The Commission operates in a wholly non-party way; in any event, it has never had a majority of government members.

The Commission meets monthly. Its meetings are private, usually with senior staff who are responsible for the subject under discussion; but it posts its minutes on the Internet and also publishes an annual report that is a mine of information about the activities of the House administration, its plans and performance. One member of the Commission acts as its spokesman and answers written parliamentary questions on its behalf, as well as oral questions in the Chamber once a month. The Commission is advised by two select committees of MPs: the Finance and Services Committee considers major items of expenditure, the three-year financial plan and the six-year business plan; the Administration Committee advises on services more generally.

Strategic planning

The House of Commons may not have a mission statement, but the House administration is subject to normal public sector disciplines. Each year the Commission approves a corporate business plan for the administration. The 2006–2011 plan has three core tasks: supporting the House and its committees; supporting individual MPs and their staff; and promoting public knowledge and understanding of Parliament. These core tasks are supplemented by objectives covering governance, value for money, flexibility, good working environments, the use of information and communications technologies (ICT), and so on. The tasks and objectives are the framework for a wide range of projects and plans, with specific objectives and milestones, in the more detailed corporate business plan.

The Board of Management

Responsibility for running the House services, and for employing staff, is delegated by the Commission to the Board of Management. This consists of the heads of all the House departments, plus the Clerk of Committees as a representative of the Clerk's Department so that the Clerk of the House himself can take an overall view as Chairman of the Board and Chief Executive. The Board is supported by the Office of the Clerk, which acts as a corporate office as well as the Board's secretariat. Four groups of senior officials work under the Board's direction on business planning, human resources, information technology and information for the public.

The Audit Committee

This consists of two members of the Commission (one as chairman) and two external members. Its has general oversight of internal audit and review, with emphasis on achieving value for money; it advises the Clerk of the House in the exercise of his responsibilities as accounting officer, and on the programme of internal audit; and it has the task of encouraging best financial practice, use of resources and governance in the House administration. It reports annually to the Commission, and its report is published with the Commission's own annual report. The National Audit Office are the House's external auditors.

The House departments

For reasons of good governance and economy, the House administration must seek to operate as a corporate whole. There are also issues such as financial planning, the use of accommodation, ICT, health and safety, data protection, human resources and so on that can be dealt with effectively only across the board. However, both their historical origins and the specialised nature of the services they provide mean that the individual House departments have distinct characters and roles.

The Clerk's Department

The Clerk of the House and some senior members of his department are perhaps the most visible of all the House staff; in television coverage of the Chamber they are seen sitting at the Table of the House in front of the Speaker, dressed as a QC would be in court: court coat, wing collar (but with a white tie rather than barrister's bands), wig and gown. Their task there is to advise the Chair, ministers, whips and any other MP on the business the House is transacting; to record the decisions the House has taken (but not what has been said, which is taken down by the *Hansard* reporters in the gallery above them) and to help to conduct votes. The Clerks at the Table have other roles as well, usually as head of one of the offices of the department.

The *Committee Office* provides the secretariat of each investigative select committee and contains half the 360 staff in the department. The *Legislation Service* deals with primary and secondary legislation on its passage through the House and provides the secretariat for legislative scrutiny committees. The *Overseas Office* represents the House overseas and provides secretariats for delegations to international assemblies. The *Journal Office* advises on parliamentary privilege and procedure generally and compiles the daily permanent legal record of proceedings. The *Table Office* prepares the Order Paper and processes parliamentary questions; and the *Vote Office* is responsible for the provision of official papers to MPs. The department also contains the *Legal Services Office*, the *Broadcasting Unit*, concerned with televising and archiving proceedings, and the *Parliamentary Office of Science and Technology*, which provides advice on scientific and technological issues to members of both Houses.

The Serjeant at Arms's Department

The first recorded Serjeant at Arms was given office by King Henry V in 1415, the year of the Battle of Agincourt. In previous centuries he was responsible for carrying out orders of the House, including making arrests; the splendid silver gilt Mace that the present Serjeant carries in the Speaker's Procession every day, and which then lies upon the Table while the House is sitting, was in times past a necessary symbol of the House's authority outside the precincts.

Today the Serjeant at Arms heads the largest Commons Department, of some 400 staff, together with a substantial security force. He is responsible for order inside the precincts, in the galleries of the Chamber and committee rooms, and for the security of the Commons part of the parliamentary estate. His *Operations Directorate* is also concerned with housekeeping, mail, car parking, visitor tours and other services. The *Parliamentary Estates Directorate* serves both Houses and is responsible for the preservation and strategic management of the parliamentary estate. The *Parliamentary Works Services Directorate* also serves both Houses and provides maintenance, engineering, furnishing and horticultural services.

The Library

Although the grand rooms running along the river front of the palace may seem reminiscent of the sort of Victorian library we mentioned in Chapter 1, the modern House of Commons Library, with some 230 staff, is a very different institution. As well as offering the reference facilities one might expect, it also provides MPs with high-quality, impartial research and information services.

The researchers are highly qualified, and their work is respected both inside and outside the House. When a member says in the Chamber 'the Library have told me', what they have said is unlikely to be challenged. Library staff undertake research in response to specific requests from MPs, as well as producing research papers on bills and other current issues. This research back-up is highly valued by MPs, and especially by opposition spokespeople in shadowing ministers, when the latter can call upon the extensive resources of government departments.

The Library is also a source of information for the public through the House of Commons Information Office, which answers queries by telephone and e-mail, and the Parliamentary Education Unit, which provides educational material and school tours on behalf of both Houses (see page 475).

Other departments

More commonly known as *Hansard*, the *Department of the Official Report* (110 staff) records what is said in the Chamber, in Westminster Hall and in standing committees, together with the answers to written parliamentary questions (some 25,000 pages a year) (see page 333). *Hansard* is substantially a verbatim report; repetitions and obvious mistakes are corrected, but the Editor strongly resists any attempt by an MP, no matter how senior, to make any change of substance. The *Department of Finance and Administration* (170 staff) is responsible for the pay and allowances of MPs and provides financial, payroll, personnel, health and safety, and internal review services for the House administration as a whole. The *Refreshment Department* (290 staff) supplies more than 1,450,000 meals each year across the Commons part of the Parliamentary Estate.

Services shared between the Lords and the Commons

The House administrations of the Commons and Lords are constitutionally separate, but they work jointly, or share services, when it makes sense to do so, for example on estates and works, communications, records, ceremonial, security, visitors and educational work. Costs are apportioned between the Houses, usually on a 60:40 Commons:Lords basis. In areas where each House has distinct needs, there is nevertheless informal consultation and cooperation. In 2005, the first joint department of the two Houses, the *Parliamentary Information and Communications Technology Service* (PICT) (90 staff) came into being and took over from the Serjeant at Arms's Department responsibility for the parliamentary data and video network, with 6,000 users at Westminster and across the UK, and a variety of online services. We look at ICT and Parliament in Chapter 13.

MPs' pay, allowances and staff

MPs' pay

Members of Parliament were first paid in 1911, when the rate was £400 a year. Ever since, their pay levels have been controversial, not least because MPs are one of the few groups of people who can in effect set their own salaries. However, in order to provide an objective assessment, pay and allowances have, since 1970, been referred to an outside organisation, now the Senior Salaries Review Body. The SSRB bases its recommendations on general principles: that pay should not be so low as to deter or so high as to make it the main attraction; that, although some MPs take on work outside Parliament, pay should be at a level reflecting the full-time job that it is for most MPs; that there should be no compensation for job insecurity or reflection of length of service; and that there should be a clear distinction between pay and expenses.

Starting in 2000, the SSRB now reviews MPs' pay every three years. Upratings between these reviews are linked to changes in the pay of senior civil servants. In recommending pay levels, the SSRB takes into account the pay of people with a similar 'job weight'; it equates the job of an MP with, for example, a director in a district general hospital, the head teacher of a large secondary school, a chief superintendent of police, or a lieutenant-colonel commanding a battalion. An MP's salary now (2006) stands at £60,277 with a generous pension scheme (there were reports in December 2005 that a rise of 22 per cent to £72,000 was being sought). Ministers are paid on top of their parliamentary salaries: the Prime Minister gets an additional £124,837, a cabinet minister £74,902, a minister of state £38,854 and a junior minister £29,491.

MPs' allowances

These are also based on SSRB reviews, but again it is the House that effectively decides their levels: a *staffing allowance* of £84,081 a year, allowing MPs to employ up to three full-time staff; an *incidental expenses provision* of £20,000 a year, mainly to cover the costs of constituency offices; and an *additional costs allowance* of £21,634 a year to cover the costs of staying away from home while at Westminster. In addition, MPs have free travel throughout the UK while on parliamentary business, a motor mileage allowance (40p per mile for the first 10,000 miles a year and 25p per mile thereafter). Three visits a year to EU institutions or the national parliaments of EU and EFTA member states or candidate countries are also paid for. IT equipment (three PCs, a laptop and two printers/scanners) is provided by the House for parliamentary business.

These allowances (the staff and office elements total some £104,000 a year) are in real terms more than twenty times the level of the first allowance of £500 a year introduced in 1969. They are nevertheless lower than those for the European Parliament or the German parliament but significantly higher than those for the devolved assemblies.

The driver for these allowances is to allow MPs to provide a better service to their constituents, but it is no surprise that the level of allowances and salary comes in for routine criticism in the media.

A particular frenzy occurs in October each year, when the House publishes the amounts claimed by each MP out of each allowance (in 2004/05, the highest total claim was £176,026, and the lowest £75,487). Much of the coverage presents allowances as part of MPs' salaries. They are not, but have to be claimed against expenditure – although it comes as something of a surprise to those used to claiming business expenses that documentary evidence is generally not required for items of less than £250. Nevertheless, headlines such as 'Is this Britain's most expensive MP?' ignore the fact that one of the main purposes of the allowances is to help MPs give a better service to their constituents. That said, there have been occasional abuses, and there was particular criticism in October 2005 when it appeared that MPs in marginal seats spent most on postage (four MPs each spent more than £35,000). There has also been criticism of the use by MPs of the additional cost allowance to pay a mortgage on a property, which may provide a substantial capital asset when they leave the House.

MPs' staff

MPs are the employers of their staff, although staff are paid centrally by the House administration and are hired on standard contracts. Increases in the staffing allowance have produced a substantial increase in MPs' paid staff, from 1,850 in 2001 to 2,580 in 2005 (in addition to unpaid staff).

There is no one pattern of the way an MP uses staff, and there are many permutations. Some MPs, particularly those with a heavy constituency caseload, base all their staff in the constituency. This makes practical sense: staff in constituency offices can network more easily with local agencies and make arrangements for surgeries, visits and so on more conveniently, and staff costs are lower outside London. Others, especially London members, whose constituencies are not far away have all their staff at Westminster (where they also have the advantage of free accommodation and other services). In the country as a whole, staff are split about one-third at Westminster and two-thirds in constituencies.

The types of people that MPs employ, and what they expect from them, vary from member to member, reflecting the fact that there is no standard way of doing the job of an MP. Some need caseworkers; some need a PA to organise a diary and act as their right hand; others need researchers to support work on their specialist subjects; yet others need a 'deputy MP' in the constituency, someone they can trust to handle their local profile and press relations, combined with a sure touch on constituency cases.

Opposition front-benchers have a particular need for specialist support because they are taking on ministers who can draw on the non-party-political but nevertheless substantial resources of government departments. Sometimes MPs pool their staff; for example, in opposition the Conservative Party established its own parliamentary research unit of a dozen or so graduates who researched topics in depth on request from subscribing MPs. Opposition front-benchers are also heavy users of the independent researchers in the House of Commons Library.

A number of MPs have worked at Westminster before winning a seat of their own, and a post as a researcher is a recognised apprenticeship in a political career. But it is also not unusual to find staff who do not identify fully with their MP's political views and see themselves as servants of the constituency as much as of a party politician.

Some, especially the traditional secretary or PA, spend much of their working lives in the job. For others, such as the 'interns' on the US model, working for an MP may be more for the experience than the pay, as a prelude to a career in a different field. A few universities now have a sandwich year as a formal part of a politics degree.

Just as the use made of staff varies, so too does its effectiveness. Having personal staff is a new experience for many newly elected MPs. Some take to it readily and use staff to add real value to their work. However, too many MPs allow researchers to operate with a good deal of independence, which leads to criticisms that these are surrogate members pursuing their own agendas and encouraging MPs to commission Library research or table parliamentary questions that are more for the benefit of researcher than member. The website **theyworkforyou.com**, which ranks MPs on crude activity measures (number of speeches made, questions asked, and so on) has probably encouraged this inappropriate use of researchers.

Finance for opposition parties

'Short money': parties in the House of Commons

Since 1975, there has been financial support for opposition parties in the Commons (often called 'Short money', after Edward Short, Leader of the House at the time) to go some way towards redressing the imbalance between the support available to opposition parties and that available to the government through the Civil Service. In order to qualify, a party must have at least two MPs – or one MP provided that the party also polled 150,000 votes nationwide. In either case, the MPs must have been elected for their party at the previous general election, which disqualifies new party groupings formed in the current parliament from claiming financial support.

There are three categories of support: the basic funding established in 1975; travel and associated expenses, introduced in 1993; and support for the Leader of the Opposition's Office, which began in 1999. All are uprated annually in line with the retail price index.

The current amounts for basic funding are £12,518 per MP and £25 for every 200 votes cast for the party in the last general election. The

2005/06 allocations were: Conservatives, £3,576,789; Liberal Democrats, £1,524,291; DUP, £142,887; SNP, £126,633; Plaid Cymru, £59,404; and SDLP, £53,254. These were full-year allocations; the amounts actually claimable were some 90 per cent of these figures, as the allocations were effective from 6 May 2005, the day after the general election.

For travel expenses, the opposition parties shared a total of £137,506 in the same proportions as their basic funding. Support for the Leader of the Opposition's Office was £583,169.

The basic funding may be used only for parliamentary business, which includes research to support shadow ministers and their work, and developing and communicating alternative policies. The money may not be used for political campaigning, fund raising or membership drives. Each party has to produce an auditor's certificate every year to verify that the money has been spent only on parliamentary business. In February 2006, the government's proposal to give the Sinn Féin MPs financial support along the same lines as Short money, although they had not taken their seats, was approved despite fierce opposition in some quarters.

Opposition salaries

Six opposition members in the two Houses receive a salary by virtue of the posts they hold. In the Commons, the Leader of the Opposition gets £68,662 a year, the Opposition Chief Whip gets £38,854 and his deputy and one other Whip get £25,005 – in each case in addition to their salaries of £60,277. In the Lords, the Leader of the Opposition receives £69,138 and the Opposition Chief Whip £63,933 a year.

Why subsidise the opposition?

It may seem reasonable for a taxpayer to say: 'I'm prepared to fund hospitals, or the education system; but why should I pay for party politicians?' Fair enough; but there is a powerful counter-argument. Ministers are not allowed to use their civil servants for overtly party political purposes, although they can still use the huge resources of their departments to research, develop and present new policies. But no government has a monopoly of truth and right. It must surely be to the advantage of the country as a whole when opposition parties have the resources to test and challenge those policies in a reasoned, well-researched way, and to put forward credible alternative proposals.

This was recognised in the Political Parties, Elections and Referendums Act 2000, which made provision for 'policy development grants'. The sum of £2 million a year is now available for work on policies for inclusion in a party's manifesto. Under the supervision of the Electoral Commission, the money is divided between parties with at least two MPs at Westminster (who have taken their seats, so Sinn Féin are not eligible). The money is allocated rather like Short money (see page 67): £1 million is split in proportion to numbers of MPs; £1 million in proportion to votes cast at the last election.

State funding for political parties?

More generally, the extent to which the non-parliamentary activities of political parties should be publicly funded remains contentious. The present combined membership of the Labour and Conservative parties is about 500,000, or about 2.7 per cent of those who actually voted for those parties in the low turnout of the 2005 election (and down from a total of about 800,000 at the time of the 1997 election). So the ability of major parties to fund themselves from their membership is declining. This inevitably makes them readier to look to major donations by wealthy individuals; but these in turn give rise to suspicions of peddling influence and politicians in hock to vested interests. By law, donations of over £5,000 to a party's central organisation and of over £1,000 to a constituency party must be reported to the Electoral Commission each quarter, and are published on the Commission's website www.electoralcommission.org.uk. However, as the 'loans for peerages' row in 2006 showed, this can be circumvented if the money is not given but lent.

There is considerable opposition in some quarters to the state funding of *all* the activities of political parties (in contrast to the parliamentary functions of challenge referred to above). And there are also the arguments that state funding tends to make recipient parties complacent and – because the obvious way of setting levels is to base them on the previous election results – that it over-rewards those who do well. But, for the time being at least, change in the present system seems unlikely.

The House of Lords

The Lord Chancellor/The Lord Speaker

The Speaker of the House of Lords was formerly the Lord Chancellor (from early July 2006 he was succeeded by a Lord Speaker, elected by the House). Important figure though he was, his role as presiding officer of the House of Lords was much more circumscribed than that of the Speaker of the House of Commons. Most of his duties lay elsewhere, for in him were combined functions relating not only to the legislature but also to the judiciary and executive – functions normally kept separate in other jurisdictions and in classical political theory.

The Lord Chancellor was first and foremost an appointee of the Prime Minister and a member of the Cabinet, heading a department responsible among other matters for the administration of the courts and tribunals, judicial appointments, constitutional and electoral matters, and justice. Only distinguished lawyers used to be appointed to the Lord Chancellorship because of the Lord Chancellor's second role as head of the judiciary and his function of presiding over the House of Lords when it sits in its special judicial capacity (a function he was able to perform only occasionally and which Lord Falconer of Thoroton never performed). His tasks as Speaker of the House of Lords, on the whole, were subsidiary to his work as a member of the government.

The Lord Chancellor's powers as Speaker were very limited indeed. The Lord Chancellor did not arbitrate on rules of order. The preservation of order in the House is the responsibility of all the Lords who are present, and any Lord may call the attention of the House to any breaches of order or laxity in observing its customs. If the House is in need of advice on matters of procedure and order, it is to the Leader of the House (also a government minister) that they look. And the Leader – or in his absence, the government Chief Whip – will often intervene to interpret and give voice to what he or she considers to be the wish of the House when procedural difficulties occur.

The Lord Speaker and Deputy Speakers do not call lords to speak. As we shall see on page 308, the order of speaking in debates is prearranged. Each item of the day's business set out on the Order Paper is called on by the Clerk at the Table. The Lord Speaker or his deputies will call members to speak to their amendments when the House is considering legislation, but no one calls the subsequent speakers in a debate on an amendment. The Lord Speaker cannot curtail debate, and when debate is concluded, his function is limited to putting the question – announcing what it is on which the Lords are about to vote – and then declaring the result of the vote. He votes just like any other Lord, and, if the vote is tied, he has no function – the standing orders of the House then govern the result.

The Lord Speaker is empowered to recall the House of Lords whenever it stands adjourned if public interest requires it – for example, for the debate on the outbreak of the Falklands War in 1982 and following the terrorist attack on the World Trade Center in September 2001. With the agreement of the House, from time to time he or his nominee represents it at conferences overseas. He also represents it on ceremonial occasions at home – for example when visiting heads of state address members of both Houses, on the opening of inter-parliamentary conferences meeting in the United Kingdom, or the presentation of Humble Addresses to the Queen.

In June 2003, following the resignation of Lord Irvine of Lairg, who had been Lord Chancellor since the 1997 general election, the government announced its intention to reform the office so that the Lord Chancellor's roles of Speaker of the Lords, as a judge and head of the judiciary, and as a minister of the Crown, would become separate. The House of Lords would be asked to decide on a means of appointing its own Speaker; the Lord Chancellor would no longer sit judicially in the Lords; a Judicial Appointments Commission would undertake the function of making judicial appointments; and the Lord Chancellor's Department was renamed the Department for Constitutional Affairs, also acquiring overall responsibility for the Scotland and Wales Offices. The office of Lord Chancellor, it was envisaged, would eventually be abolished. (At the same time, the government announced its intention to establish a supreme court to replace the appellate function exercised by the law lords sitting in the House of Lords.)

The Constitutional Reform Act 2005 gave effect to most of these changes (see page 438). Under its provisions, while the office of Lord Chancellor will continue (in deference to a Lords amendment made in Committee of the Whole House), the office-holder will no longer of necessity be a lawyer or sit in the Lords; the Lord Chief Justice became Head of the Judiciary from April 2006; and provision is made for the establishment of a Judicial Appointments Commission and a supreme court. While the Act does not in itself make provision for Speakership of the House (the Lord Chancellor presided as Speaker by virtue of Standing Order 18), by freeing the office-holder from the legal profession, from the House of Lords and from judicial appointments, it would be perfectly possible for a future Lord Chancellor to sit in the Commons. With this in mind the House of Lords resolved (without a division) on 12 July 2005 'that this House should elect its own presiding officer'. The House also set up a Select Committee chaired by Lord Lloyd of Berwick (a former Law Lord) 'to consider further how to implement this resolution with full regard to the House's tradition of self-regulation' and to report by 20 December 2005. It recommended that the Speaker should be elected using the alternative vote system. It reaffirmed the principle that the House should keep its own order, though it suggested that on occasion the Speaker might offer procedural advice during proceedings, and adjudicate on matters such as the *sub judice* rule and admissibility of Private Notice Questions. The Speaker would chair the House Committee and would usually preside in the Chamber (including Committee of the Whole House) for three hours each day. He or she would play a representative role on behalf of the House of Lords at home and abroad. The Procedure Committee and the House as a whole endorsed these recommendations early in 2006; the new Lord Speaker was elected on 28 June 2006 and assumed office the following week, following the Queen's approval. The Leader will still arbitrate at Question Time; the Chief Whip will determine speaking times in time-limited debates; and the front benchers and other members will intervene when rules are breached.

Nevertheless, the change will be momentous: while the House will retain much of the apparatus of self regulation, the presence of a well informed Lord Speaker on the Woolsack every day is bound to assist the smooth running of business and observance of the procedural brief.

The Chairman of Committees, Deputy Speakers and deputy chairmen

Even after the election of a Lord Speaker in 2006 the need for a panel of deputies (albeit reduced in number to twelve) continued – to preside when the Lord Speaker cannot.

The principal Deputy Speaker is the Chairman of Committees, a member of the House who is appointed by the House at the beginning of every session to take the chair in all Committees of the Whole House. The Chairman of Committees is a very influential figure in the Lords and is paid the salary of a minister of state in consequence. He organises the panel of Deputy Speakers and deputy chairmen and assigns them their duties week by week. He has considerable powers in the field of private legislation (see page 249) by selecting opposed private bill committees and himself presiding over unopposed bill committees. During the nineteenth century – the heyday of private legislation – this gave the holder of the post immense power and influence over many of the greatest public works projects of the day. This aspect of his work takes up far less of the Chairman of Committees' time today.

Indeed, most of his work is now concerned with the administration of the House. His role as chair of the House Committee – broadly the Lords equivalent of the House of Commons Commission – is now to be undertaken by the Lord Speaker. But the Chairman of Committees will still be the House Committee's spokesman in the House and he will continue to chair the Select Committee on Administration and Works, which is described below. The Chairman of Committees also chairs the Liaison Committee, which meets from time to time to review and allocate resources to the policy select committees of the House, and also the Procedure Committee. Such is his prominence in the life of the House that he often acted as its representative at international conferences in place of the Lord Chancellor in the days when the Lord Chancellor was Speaker. His former Chairmanship of the House Committee has passed to the elected Lord Speaker, who will also take a more prominent role than his predecessors in overseas matters.

The Leader of the House of Lords

Like the Leader of the Commons, the Leader of the House of Lords is a Cabinet minister, usually holding a non-departmental office such as Lord Privy Seal. Her allegiance is to the government and its policies, but she too has a wider task of upholding the rights and interests of the House as a whole. It is the Leader of the House, for example, who assists the House in keeping its own order during proceedings and who makes representations on behalf of the House on such matters as members' allowances.

She works closely with the Leader of the House of Commons in planning and supervising the government's legislative programme; she is a member of the Legislative Programme Committee of the Cabinet; and she reports to the Cabinet itself on business in the Lords. She is responsible for delivering the government's business in the House, although most of the planning of this is done on her behalf by the Government Chief Whip and in particular by the Chief Whip's private secretaries. These private secretaries, who are Clerks on secondment to the Cabinet Office, also assist the Leader of the House in her parliamentary work.

Much of the Leader's influence is exerted behind the scenes, for example through meetings of the business managers (as the Leaders and government Chief Whips of the two Houses are known). Within the Lords, she secures agreement on matters relating to the business of the House and other matters by discussions with other party leaders. Similar negotiations are held by the Chief Whip with other party whips. As in the Commons, these contacts are known as the usual channels. They are entirely informal and by their very nature devoid of any ground rules save perhaps one – that a deal struck through 'the usual channels' will normally stick. The Leader of the House, together with other party leaders, sits on all key decision-making bodies within the House – such as the House Committee, the Liaison Committee and the Procedure Committee.

The former Leader of the House, Lord Williams of Mostyn, also took an interest in the modernisation of working methods. In the 2001–02 session, he chaired a working group on the working of the House, many of whose recommendations on sitting hours, question time, legislative procedure, committee work and other matters have already been implemented.

The Clerk of the Parliaments and the staff of the House

The most senior official of the House of Lords is the Clerk of the Parliaments. Like the Clerk of the House of Commons he combines a variety of roles. He is the principal adviser to the House on all aspects of parliamentary practice and procedure, and the daily business of the House proceeds on the basis of briefs prepared by the clerks in the procedural offices. But he also has wide administrative responsibilities as Chief Executive of the service of the House and Chair of the Management Board (see page 75) – a pre-eminence derived from his position as accounting officer for money spent under the two Lords Requests for Resources (formerly Votes), and as the employer of all House of Lords staff under the Clerk of the Parliaments Act 1824 and the Parliamentary Corporate Bodies Act 1992. The 1992 Act makes the Clerk of the Parliaments corporate officer of the House of Lords, and in this capacity he gives the House legal personality and enters into contracts on its behalf. He is also Registrar of the Court when the House sits judicially, and signs its Orders. The Clerk of the Parliaments is appointed by the Crown under letters patent, usually from among the longer-serving Clerks of the House, following advertisement and interview by the party leaders. His immediate deputies, the Clerk Assistant and the Reading Clerk, are appointed by the Lord Chancellor in a similar way.

Different offices of the House's administration deal with finance, committees, legislation, human resources, the Journal of the House, overseas business, the official report or *Hansard*, catering services, and information services including the Library and Parliamentary Archive. The Department of the Gentleman Usher of the Black Rod, to give him his full title, deals with accommodation, services and security, reflecting Black Rod's appointment as agent of the Administration and Works Committee. (Although principally a servant of the House like any other, Black Rod also has ceremonial duties within the palace – it fell to him to make the arrangements for the Lying in State of Queen Elizabeth the Queen Mother in April 2002 – and in connection with the Order of the Garter. In the past the post used to be offered to a retired senior member of the armed forces, but the present holder was appointed following public advertisement and interview.)

The total number of staff employed in these offices is about 480. This figure excludes staff in services shared with the Commons – in the Parliamentary Works Services Directorate, the Parliamentary Estates Directorate and the Parliamentary Information and Communications Technology Service and the security staff contracted to both Houses from the Metropolitan Police.

House of Lords administration

The chief decision-making body in the administration of the Lords is the House Committee, a select committee of twelve members, including the Leader of the House and other party leaders and the Convenor of the Cross Bench Peers. The Clerk of the Parliaments and Black Rod also attend. Other senior officers attend as required. The committee's role is to determine strategy, to take major policy decisions, especially financial decisions not previously authorised, and to agree the House's business and financial plans and annual estimates of expenditure. Its work is assisted by a management board of senior officers of the House chaired by the Clerk of the Parliaments. Both the House Committee and the management board meet monthly when the House is sitting, and their decisions are published on the Internet.

Four further domestic select committees – on administration and works, refreshments, information, and works of art – have responsibility for determining policy in those areas. But any decision requiring major expenditure requires the agreement of the House Committee. To the extent that the House of Lords has an equivalent to the House of Commons Commission, it is the House Committee.

These arrangements were introduced at the beginning of the 2002–03 session following a review by a working group chaired by the Chairman of Committees. They supplanted the former Select Committee on House of Lords Offices and its sub-committees. The House has also established an

Audit Committee with two external members, as part of the modernisation of its administrative arrangements.

Expenses

Members of the House of Lords are unpaid, in the sense that with the exception of certain office holders they do not receive a salary. But they do receive expenses and allowances of various kinds, the most significant of which are free travel to and from Westminster, an overnight and day subsistence allowance and a modest secretarial and office expenses allowance. The levels of these allowances are kept under review by the SSRB. The allowances are free of tax; if all are claimed they amount to £290 for every day of attendance, excluding the value of any travel expenses. This is not meant to amount to a full-time salary, so many members, particularly those below normal retirement age, have other jobs elsewhere. Having said that, if a member were to claim all his or her expenses having attended every sitting day of, say, a financial year like 2004/05, he or she would now be eligible to receive £44,080.

Finance for political parties in the Lords: Cranborne money

For many years the chief opposition parties in the Lords received funding from money made available from public funds to opposition parties in the Commons (see page 67). Since October 1996, the Official Opposition (currently the Conservative Party) and the second-largest party (the Liberal Democrat Party) have been provided with a separate allocation, funded by the House. Since 1999, the Convenor of the Cross Bench Peers has received similar funding to provide secretarial support. These sums are determined by resolution of the House and are uprated annually in line with inflation. With effect from 1 April 2005, the amounts available were £426,351 to the Official Opposition, £212,873 to the Liberal Democrats and £38,208 to the Convenor.

Paying for Parliament

The House of Commons

The House of Commons is funded from two separate Estimates, or budgets of public expenditure (also called Accounts). The *House of Commons*

Administration Estimate pays for the staff of the House, the services supplied by all the House departments, and buildings, works, rates and energy costs. Unlike the rest of public spending, the government does not determine what the House's expenditure should be; the House of Commons Commission proposes an Estimate – after a lengthy planning process – and puts it directly to the House for approval, without intervention by the government.

However, the *Members Estimate*, which covers MPs' pay and allowances, is a government Estimate for which the Leader of the House is the responsible minister. Levels of pay and allowances are recommended by the SSRB, are put to the House by the government, and are then set following a free vote. MPs voting for increases above the SSRB recommendations (which has happened on occasion) inevitably comes in for criticism. The *Members Estimate Committee*, a select committee with the same membership as the House of Commons Commission, oversees the rules for MPs' allowances and may make minor changes – but without altering the rates. The *Members Estimate Audit Committee* has the same membership and functions as the Administration Estimate Audit Committee (see page 61).

The House of Lords

The House of Lords is funded directly from the Treasury on the same lines as a government department, but for constitutional reasons – and unlike a department – the House is not cash-limited. That does not mean that it can spend what it wants. Great self-restraint is, in fact, exercised on the demands made upon the public purse. The House has two Estimates, one for administration (including members' expenses) and one for works. Overall financial control rests with the House Committee, and as we have seen the Clerk of the Parliaments, who is head of the Lords administration, is the Accounting Officer and is responsible for all its expenditure, including its propriety and effectiveness. The House of Lords accounts are examined and certified each year by the National Audit Office.

How much does Parliament cost?

Parliament operates on the same 'resource accounting' basis as central government, so the costs of Parliament include not only what is paid in cash, such as salaries, rates and electricity, but also notional costs for the use of buildings and other assets.

On this basis, in 2004/05 the House of Commons cost some £328 million, £140 million of which went on MPs' pay and allowances. In the same year House of Lords administration cost £46 million, and works £73 million (much above the normal figure of some £20 million because of the fitting out of Fielden House and the purchase of the Millbank island site) – a total of £119 million.

To put these figures in context, in 2004/05 total government spending was £477 *billion*. Parliament thus costs some 0.09 per cent of what the government spends.

4

Parliamentary sovereignty, legislative supremacy and devolution

Sovereignty and supremacy

In this chapter we consider the nature of Parliament's powers: what many writers on the constitution would have described in the past as the 'sovereignty of Parliament' but for which a better modern term might be 'legislative supremacy'.

Let us look briefly at the ways in which Parliament is not sovereign. *First*, Parliament is clearly not sovereign in the sense that it embodies any concept of national sovereignty, although it may contribute to the sentiment. *Second*, it is not sovereign in the sense that it vies with the Queen to be head of state. *Third*, it is not the centre of the day-to-day decision making of government. It is the government that conducts the business of the state, often acting within the powers and resources that have been granted by Parliament, and claiming its authority to govern by virtue of its majority in the House of Commons. Although Parliament may try to influence the government's actions by a variety of means, it does not and cannot micromanage the affairs of state. Parliament does not govern.

Fourth, Parliament is not the sole source of the government's powers, many of which are derived from the government's exercise of the prerogative powers of the Crown with little or no recourse to Parliament at all. Prerogative powers and the concept of prerogative range widely. International treaties are entered into without any reference to Parliament. Although they are laid before Parliament, usually as Command Papers,

Parliament plays no formal role. Treaties involving the European Union are the exception, because they require amendment of the European Communities Act 1972. Parliament does not have to be consulted before the armed forces are used – whether as peacekeepers or in military conflict. Although the House of Commons was given the opportunity to vote on a substantive motion before the commitment of troops in Iraq in 2003, no such opportunity preceded the involvement of British troops in Kosovo in 1999 or previous deployments or conflicts. Parliament has no say in matters relating to honours or patronage. The Civil Service answers to the Crown, that is to say the government, and not to Parliament; and there is no concept of parliamentary oversight of appointments to public office (even though select committees are now seeking to remedy this – see page 373), or of control of the actual machinery of government. Finally, it is the government that, by royal proclamation, summons, prorogues and dissolves Parliament. There is increasing support for the view that Parliament should have a greater role in the exercise of these prerogative powers, most recently in 2006 from David Cameron, the new Leader of the Opposition.

Legislative supremacy

So when people use the phrase 'the sovereignty of Parliament', what they really mean is the legislative supremacy of Parliament, that is to say its unique ability, in the words of the nineteenth-century constitutional writer A. V. Dicey, to 'make or unmake any law whatever'.

The principle was set out elegantly in 1844, when Thomas Erskine May published the first edition of his *Treatise on the Law, Privileges, Proceedings and Usage of Parliament* – a work that was to become the authoritative text on the procedures of Parliament. He began his second chapter with this paragraph:

> *The legislative authority of Parliament extends over the United Kingdom, and all its colonies and foreign possessions; and there are no other limits to its power of making laws for the whole empire than those which are incident to all sovereign authority – the willingness of the people to obey, or their power to resist. Unlike the legislatures of many other countries, it is bound by no fundamental charter or constitution; but has itself the sole constitutional right of establishing and altering the laws and government of the empire.*

Parliament no longer legislates for an overseas empire, but Erskine May's words are in all other respects still applicable. Clearly this legislative supremacy is the source of enormous power.

Characteristics of legislative supremacy

Legislative supremacy is essentially a legal concept, and it manifests itself in a number of different ways. For example, the courts of law are under a duty to apply legislation, even if that legislation might appear to be morally or politically wrong. This is a powerful reason why legislation must always be got right so as to avoid the possibility of unexpected consequences. Moreover, unlike other countries with written constitutions – the United States for example – it would not be possible to challenge an Act of the United Kingdom Parliament in the courts on the grounds that it was 'unconstitutional'. The 2005 challenge to the Hunting Act (which was appealed all the way to the House of Lords) was based on the alleged effects of the Parliament Acts (see pages 81 and 244–6), not on a conflict with the constitution. And in any event, even the constitution can be subject to statute. New constitutional principles can be established, such as reform of the membership or powers of the House of Lords or devolved government in Scotland, Wales and Northern Ireland. Moreover, existing principles can be modified or changed, such as the succession to the throne or the parliamentary privileges set out in the Bill of Rights of 1688–89.

One of the consequences of Parliament's legislative supremacy is that one parliament cannot bind its successor parliaments, which, after all, have an equal claim to legislative sovereignty. In some cases, things that Parliament does by legislation are in practical terms so difficult to reverse that successor parliaments are, in effect, bound by those Acts – such as the Acts that gave self-government or confederation to the former dominions, or independence to the former colonies, or votes to women, or even devolution to Scotland and Wales. (Devolution in Northern Ireland has been revoked, restored and then revoked again by Parliament, as is considered more fully below.)

But in other areas the principle of legislative supremacy remains strong – even in the field of human rights. It was for many years held that a bill of rights – in modern language, a bill to incorporate the European Convention on Human Rights into UK law – could never be entrenched into law so as to protect such fundamental rights from the possibility of subsequent infringement by a future parliament. Indeed, when the government brought forward its Human Rights Bill in 1997–98, it made no attempt to do so.

Limitations upon legislative supremacy

Parliament's legislative supremacy is a powerful concept, but it has its limitations. Erskine May put his finger on the chief limitation – 'the willingness of the people to obey, or their power to resist'. Most of the time, in these days of universal suffrage, this manifests itself through the ballot box rather than in mass civil disobedience, but the repeal of the disliked community charge or poll tax legislation in 1992 was undoubtedly hastened by the mass demonstrations of 1990.

Other limitations derive from the radical changes in society since Erskine May first wrote. On the one hand, the law has covered more and more areas that formerly went unregulated or were considered private matters not deserving the intervention of the state – such as education, working conditions, social security, health, and so on. But on the other hand, modern technology, and in recent years especially information technology, has placed some activities almost beyond the reach of UK law making – electronic international transfer of funds, for example, or intellectual property rights in material placed on the Internet.

Apart from the ultimate limitations of public consent and of practical constraint, the legislative supremacy of Parliament has been limited in practical ways in recent years, by:

♦ the passing of the Human Rights Act;

♦ accession to the European Union (at that time the European Economic Community); and

♦ devolution to Scotland and Wales, and, with some qualifications, to Northern Ireland.

Each of these represents a major constitutional development worthy of separate consideration.

Human Rights Act 1998

Background

The incorporation of the European Convention on Human Rights (ECHR) into UK law in 1998 potentially had a major impact on the legislative supremacy of Parliament. This is the background. The ECHR was originally drawn up by the Council of Europe both as an affirmation of principles in a post-war Europe and as a test that potential new members of that body would be required to pass. The United Kingdom took a leading role in drafting it and duly ratified it in 1951. However, the British government – unlike other signatories – did not subsequently incorporate it into domestic law; nor, until 1966, did the United Kingdom accept the optional provisions allowing individuals to petition the European Court of Human

Rights (set up under the ECHR to adjudicate on infringements) and the compulsory jurisdiction of the European Court of Human Rights.

The rights covered by the ECHR are for the most part unremarkable and would be taken for granted by most British people. They include the right to life, liberty and security of person; the prohibition of torture; the freedom of expression; and the right to a fair trial. One might well wonder why successive administrations, both Conservative and Labour, declined to incorporate the ECHR into British law. After all, they had modified the law in a number of areas where the European Court had found the United Kingdom to be in breach of the ECHR – for example on homosexuality in Northern Ireland, the right of appeal against life sentences and corporal punishment in schools.

One of the chief reasons revolved around legislative supremacy. Previous schemes for incorporation had raised the possibility that, by invoking a bill of rights or the European Convention, UK courts would have been able to strike down provisions in Acts of Parliament and thus undermine Parliament's supremacy in legislative matters. This was the line taken by the Conservative government during debates in the House of Lords on Lord Lester of Herne Hill's Human Rights Bill (a private member's bill that sought to incorporate the ECHR into UK law) during the 1996–97 session. Another reason was the impossibility of entrenchment of the provisions of any such Act into UK law in a manner that would render its provisions unamendable at some future date.

The Human Rights Act 1998

Following the 1997 general election, the new Labour government carried through a commitment to incorporate the ECHR, and the Human Rights Act was passed in 1998. It enables the rights of an individual under the ECHR to be tested in UK courts without recourse to the European Court of Human Rights. Central and local government must act in a way that is compatible with the convention. If in any case the courts decide that an Act of Parliament is itself incompatible with the convention, a declaration of incompatibility may be made. Although that will not in itself change the law, it will certainly prompt the government and Parliament to take action, by means of primary legislation or a remedial Order – a statutory instrument subject to affirmative resolution of both Houses of Parliament. Since the passage of the Act, three such Orders have been made.*

---

* The Mental Health Act 1983 (Remedial) Order 2001, the Naval Discipline Act 1957 (Remedial) Order 2004, and the Marriage Act 1949 (Remedial) Order 2006.

So far as the Westminster Parliament is concerned, the concept of legislative supremacy has been preserved more or less intact. But the powers of
the courts are different in respect of legislation by the Scottish Parliament
and of Orders issued by the Welsh Assembly. The courts are able to hold
Scottish legislation to be unlawful if it is incompatible with the ECHR; and
Welsh Assembly Orders may be quashed. Secondary legislation passed at
Westminster may also be quashed by the courts.

So the legislative supremacy of Parliament is preserved – or is it? The
government has said that there may be circumstances in which it may be
unwilling to act upon a declaration of incompatibility. But in most cases it
will almost certainly feel morally bound to take steps. In any event, without
remedial action the legislation in question would be fatally weakened and
liable to further challenge. Parliament often legislates, or amends existing
legislation, because the courts have found the statutes wanting, or have
exposed loopholes. But the Human Rights Act is novel in that it forges a
direct link between a declaration in a court of law and an expectation of
remedial action by Parliament.

The European Union

In 1973, following the passage of the European Communities Act 1972, the
United Kingdom joined what is now called the European Union. Parliament's
relationship with the European Union is fully set out in Chapter 12, but
some discussion of this in the context of legislative supremacy is inevitable.
Parliament's legislative supremacy is compromised by EU membership in a
number of different ways.

First, Parliament plays no part in the European legislative process. As we
see in Chapter 12, it may try to influence the stand taken by the government at meetings of the EU Council of Ministers where EU legislation is
agreed, but national parliaments play no formal part in European decision
making. Once agreed, regulations become directly applicable throughout
all member states without the involvement of Parliament, while directives
have to be incorporated into United Kingdom law, usually by means of
secondary legislation in the form of statutory instruments. As we will see in
Chapter 7, secondary legislation is not amendable and is poorly scrutinised
at Westminster. And of course this legislation comes before Westminster
parliamentarians very late in the day, after the contents have effectively been
agreed in Brussels.

Second, the 1972 Act provides that any existing or future legislation passed at Westminster shall be subject to any directly applicable obligations under EU law. Where Acts of Parliament are inconsistent with EU law, it is expected that the latter will prevail. This is the line adopted by the UK courts, which will not apply national legislation, whether enacted before or after 1972, if to do so would conflict with EU law. Thus, in areas of EU competence, any conflict of laws will always be resolved in the EU's favour.

The fact remains that Parliament acquiesced in these arrangements in passing the 1972 Act (and the subsequent amending Acts to take account of successive treaties). In theory these Acts could be repealed. But meanwhile Parliament has chosen that in certain areas of EU competence, EU legislation will prevail – legislation, what is more, that it had little or no part in formulating.

Devolution of government

The new Labour government of 1997 was committed to establishing devolved government in Scotland and Wales and to attempting to resurrect devolved arrangements in Northern Ireland. The Referendums (Scotland and Wales) Bill was passed by the summer recess of 1997, and referendums were held in Scotland and Wales in September 1997. These endorsed (ringingly in Scotland, more equivocally in Wales) the government's proposals for a Scottish Parliament with tax-varying powers, and for a Welsh Assembly. The referendums were held before the details of the bills to implement the proposals were published. In 1998, three Acts were passed – the Scotland Act, the Government of Wales Act and the Northern Ireland Act – to give effect to these devolution proposals. Each Act is very different from the others, both in the detailed arrangements relating to the assemblies they established and – more particularly – in the extent to which legislative powers were transferred.

The Scotland and Northern Ireland Acts – but not the Government of Wales Act – transferred primary legislative powers to a Scottish Parliament and Northern Ireland Assembly. Under both Acts, the Westminster Parliament reserved the power to legislate for both Scotland and Northern Ireland. And of course both Acts could in theory be repealed – and the Northern Ireland Assembly was in fact suspended and then restored. But in effect the Westminster Parliament has chosen to forgo its powers to legislate in the wide areas of policy that are specified as devolved matters in both Acts. We shall now look at each region in turn.

Scotland

Since 1999, Scotland has had its own unicameral Parliament consisting of 129 members (MSPs), seventy-three of whom are elected directly on the basis of the current Westminster constituencies (although Orkney and Shetland have been split into two constituencies), with fifty-six additional MSPs (seven from each of the eight European Parliament constituencies) elected under a form of the additional member system of proportional representation. MSPs are elected for four-year terms; the second election was held on 1 May 2003. Early dissolution of the Parliament may occur if more than two-thirds of the members vote for it or if the Parliament fails to agree on the appointment of a First Minister. The First Minister is appointed by the Queen on the advice of the Parliament's Presiding Officer and is normally the leader of the party able to command the support of a majority in the Parliament. The First Minister appoints the other Scottish ministers, and this executive has, in all essentials, the same relationship to the Scottish Parliament as UK ministers have to the Westminster Parliament.

The Scottish Parliament has powers to legislate for Scotland in certain areas, but other areas are reserved to Westminster – such as foreign affairs, defence, the armed forces, finance and the economy. A schedule to the Scotland Act also lists more specific reserved matters within policy areas that are otherwise devolved. These tend to be areas where it would make no sense for different parts of the UK to have different laws – for example, import and export control, misuse of drugs, immigration and nationality, and broadcasting. The Act also provides that matters may, by Order in Council (a particular type of secondary legislation), be transferred from and to the list of reserved matters.

The Westminster Parliament retains power to legislate for Scotland on any matters, and it could override decisions taken by the Scottish Parliament on devolved matters. But a convention has arisen that Westminster will not legislate on a devolved matter without the prior agreement of the Scottish Parliament, demonstrated by its passing of a so-called 'Sewel motion' (Lord Sewel was a minister in the then Scottish Office when the Scotland Act was passed).

In addition to these legislative powers, the Scottish Parliament has powers of scrutiny over the activities of the executive, power to determine spending priorities within devolved areas, and a power, not yet exercised, to vary basic rate income tax by up to 3 per cent.

The effect of these developments at Westminster has been considerable. There is no longer specific Scottish legislation, and ministers may not be asked questions about matters that are now the responsibility of the Scottish Executive. The Scottish Affairs Select Committee in the Commons has continued in existence, but with narrower formal terms of reference (although they now include 'relations with the Scottish Parliament').

As we saw in Chapter 2, the government recognised that the present seventy-three Scottish MPs would need to be reduced in number to reflect the changes. Early in 2005 the passing of the Parliamentary Constituencies (Scotland) Order 2005 reduced the number of seats to fifty-nine with effect from the next general election. Thus since May 2005, Scotland has fifty-nine rather than seventy-two MPs. A continuing issue is the West Lothian question, named after Tam Dalyell, then MP for West Lothian (later MP for Linlithgow and Father of the House), who frequently raised the issue during the devolution debates of the late 1970s – why should Scottish MPs at Westminster be able to speak, question and vote on matters affecting the rest of the United Kingdom when in Scotland the same matters are devolved?

Wales

Unlike the Scottish Parliament, the National Assembly for Wales does not have the power to pass primary legislation, which remains with the Westminster Parliament, but it does have the power to make secondary legislation. The Assembly consists of forty constituency members and twenty proportionately elected additional members (five from each European Parliament constituency). The Assembly has a fixed four-year term with no possibility of early dissolution, and the second elections were held on 1 May 2003. It is fully bilingual, conducting its business in both Welsh and English.

The Assembly has been established on an executive model with a cabinet-style system. The Scottish Parliament has a staff independent of the executive, but the Welsh Assembly is staffed by civil servants. In theory they are like the staff of a county council, who provide services to the council in its deliberative role but more importantly execute and administer the decisions it takes. In practice, the staff who provide the chamber and support services to the Assembly itself have developed some sense of separate identity. The Assembly took over the Welsh Office's function for the distribution of almost all the block grant allocated by the Treasury to Wales, and it acquired the Welsh Office's functions in relation to local authorities in Wales and other public bodies such as the Welsh Development Agency.

At the apex of the Assembly structure is the equivalent of the Cabinet – the Executive Committee, chaired by the Assembly First Minister, who is elected by the Assembly as a whole. The other members of the 'Cabinet' (Executive Committee), the Assembly Ministers, are appointed by the First Minister, and one serves on each of the subject committees of the Assembly. The Executive Committee is able to meet in private, and it consists of members of one party only (except when there is a coalition administration). The number and size of the subject committees, currently seven, is determined by the Assembly First Minister, and their political balance will reflect the membership of the Assembly as a whole. Each committee has a chairperson, and the chairs are allocated proportionately between parties. The standing orders of the Assembly designate the functions that can be discharged by the hierarchy ranging from the Assembly as a whole to the Cabinet, subject committees, leaders of subject committees and unelected officials.

The Assembly's legislative role is currently restricted to making secondary legislation that formerly would have been made by the Secretary of State for Wales or for which, since 1998, powers have been delegated to the Assembly by subsequent Acts of Parliament. Pre-1998 secondary legislation within the Assembly's area of competence can be replaced, revoked or amended. Assembly Orders are prepared by subject committees and the Executive Committee; and, before being laid before the Assembly as a whole, Orders go before a committee known as the Legislation Committee in order to ensure that the Assembly has the powers to make the Order proposed. Any dispute about the Assembly's use of its powers can be referred by the Attorney General to the Judicial Committee of the Privy Council for decision.

In addition to these executive and limited legislative functions, the Welsh Assembly also has some parliamentary functions. The Assembly First Secretary is subject to questioning by the Assembly as a whole; Assembly Orders are approved by the Assembly before they can pass; and the Assembly acts, in accordance with the government's July 1997 White Paper, as the forum for the nation, able to debate all matters of concern in Wales, not only those that it directly controls. The Assembly has committees representing the regions of Wales, but without executive functions, and an Audit Committee. However, the Public Accounts Committee of the House of Commons can still investigate Assembly spending. Moreover, the Parliamentary Commissioner for Administration continues to be able to investigate Welsh matters not within the competence of the Welsh Assembly, although in such cases she reports to the Assembly. A new (2005) Public Services Ombudsman for Wales (uniting the offices of Welsh Administration Ombudsman, Health Service Commissioner for Wales and Commission for Local Administration in Wales) investigates complaints about the exercise of functions that have been transferred to the National Assembly.

The Secretary of State for Wales retains all his functions so far as primary legislation affecting Wales is concerned, and he negotiates the block grant with the Treasury. His role is thus much stronger than that of the Secretary of State for Scotland.

As all primary legislation for Wales remains the prerogative of the Westminster Parliament, there has been no proposal to reduce the number of Welsh MPs – at present forty. If Wales were represented pro rata with England, it would have thirty-three MPs. However, the creation of the National Assembly for Wales has considerably reduced the number of matters on which the Secretary of State for Wales is answerable and on which secondary legislation comes before the Westminster Parliament. There has thus been some diminution in Westminster MPs' role in Welsh affairs. But the Welsh Affairs Select Committee in the Commons continues (as does the Scottish Affairs Select Committee) with a narrower formal remit, but one that now includes 'relations with the National Assembly for Wales'. Matters are by no means static, however. The House of Commons and the National Assembly for Wales have developed a procedure of 'reciprocal enlargement' of their respective committees to allow joint scrutiny of items of common interest relating to Wales, either by the Welsh Affairs Committee in Westminster, or in Cardiff. Enlarged 'Westminster' proceedings would be conducted according to Westminster procedure and attract parliamentary privilege. Enlarged 'Cardiff' proceedings would follow National Assembly procedure and attract the more limited statutory protection against suit for defamation that applies there. The precedent for enlarging a committee with participating (but non-voting) members is the Joint Committee on Indian Constitutional Reform 1933–34, which included representatives of the Indian States and of British India.

Meanwhile the National Assembly is likely to evolve further in coming years on more parliamentary lines. A Commission set up by the Assembly under the Chairmanship of Lord Richard to review the working of the Assembly reported in March 2004. It recommended, amongst other things, that the Assembly be given primary legislative powers in devolved matters; that meanwhile more scope should be given to the Assembly to devise its own policies through existing secondary legislation powers; and that its current corporate structure be replaced with a separated executive and legislature. The government responded cautiously, though positively, to many of the Commission's ideas in its White Paper of June 2005. It agreed to bring forward legislation to effect a formal separation between the Assembly and the Welsh Assembly government. And it undertook to draft bills in a way that would allow the Assembly more power to determine the application of provisions in Wales under existing powers to make delegated legislation. More significantly perhaps, and as a first step towards primary powers, the government has agreed to use Orders in Council (a form of affirmative instrument) in the Westminster Parliament to give the Assembly greater legislative latitude in devolved areas. These Orders in Council will authorise the Assembly to legislate in a particular area. While the Orders themselves – to be known as *Enhanced Legislative Competence Orders* – are likely to require the affirmative resolution of both Houses of the Westminster Parliament, the legislation passed by the Assembly (to be known as *Assembly Measures*) will not.

A bill to give effect to these changes was introduced in 2005–06, although full powers to initiate primary legislation are unlikely to be granted soon, and not without a further referendum. This provision is also included in the bill. Meanwhile other recommendations of the Richard Commission – on the granting of revenue-raising powers and on increasing the size of the Assembly – have received a more mixed reception.

The legislative supremacy of the Westminster Parliament has been compromised far less by the establishment of the National Assembly for Wales than by the setting up of the Scottish Parliament. It remains the case that if at some future date a Welsh Assembly Cabinet promoted secondary legislation not in tune with the policies of the United Kingdom government, the government could introduce primary legislation at Westminster to override anything the Assembly did. But within that overall constraint it is clear that in coming years the Assembly will be given opportunities to exercise more and more discretion in legislative matters.

Northern Ireland

Unlike Scotland and Wales, Northern Ireland government was first devolved long ago – under the Government of Ireland Act 1920, which gave Northern Ireland its own executive (Prime Minister and Cabinet) and two-chamber legislature. A reduced number of MPs continued to sit at Westminster. Foreign affairs and defence, customs and excise and certain other matters were reserved, and the ultimate legislative supremacy of Westminster was preserved. These arrangements continued until 1972, when, due to civil unrest, direct rule was resumed and in 1973 the former arrangements were brought to an end. This is an example of how, ultimately, the legislative supremacy of the Westminster Parliament can be reasserted under devolved arrangements, albeit in extreme circumstances.

Despite attempts in 1973 and 1982 to revive some kind of devolved arrangements, not until 1998, in the wake of the Belfast (Good Friday) Agreement between the Northern Ireland political parties, were new devolved arrangements attempted and the Northern Ireland Act 1998 passed. The new Northern Ireland Assembly consisted of 108 members, six for each of the eighteen Westminster constituencies, under the single transferable vote system. A complicated system of power sharing between the major parties governs all major decision making, so that power is effectively shared between the Unionist and Nationalist communities. The First Minister, Deputy First Minister and other ministers are appointed under power-sharing arrangements and constitute the Executive Committee of the Assembly.

Devolved arrangements do not apply to defence, immigration, elections and political parties, and other issues such as aviation, criminal law and emergency powers are reserved. Westminster still reserves the right to make laws for Northern Ireland on transferred matters. The Assembly has no power to vary rates of tax.

At Westminster, the Northern Ireland Affairs Select Committee considers matters within the responsibilities of the Northern Ireland Office, but, by contrast with the Scottish and Welsh select committees, it does not have relations with the Northern Ireland Assembly in its terms of reference. The Northern Ireland Grand Committee meets for occasional debates (ten times in the first three full sessions after devolution). Both the select committee and the grand committee operate against the background of some political uncertainty in Northern Ireland.

Continuing political difficulties caused the Assembly to be suspended from February to May 2000 and again in October 2002, and it was dissolved in April 2003. The elections due to take place in May 2003 were deferred until 26 November 2003, but the results showed an increased polarisation of the Unionist and Nationalist communities, making a return to devolved government more difficult. The announcement in July 2005 that the Provisional IRA (Irish Republican Army) was to disband led to hopes that the Assembly might be restored; but this depended on the willingness of the parties to work together. In April 2006 the British and Irish Prime Ministers announced that, following the passage of an expedited Bill, members of the Assembly would be recalled on 15 May with a view to re-establishing the executive and devolved arrangements by 24 November at the latest. During these periods of suspension and direct rule Northern Ireland legislation is passed by the Westminster Parliament in the form of Orders in Council – in other words, as secondary legislation requiring only an affirmative resolution in each of the two Houses.

5

Influences on Parliament

The House of Commons

The job is what you make it

Almost everyone in employment in the United Kingdom has a job description. And those who are self-employed – perhaps running a shop or other small business – have pretty clear indications of what constitutes success or failure. Members of Parliament have neither, unless it is to be re-elected at the next election. As we shall see, there is no shortage of people who will tell the newly elected MP what he or she should be doing; but there is no formal statement of what the job involves.

In 1996, consultants working for the Senior Salaries Review Body (SSRB) had a go at writing an MP's job description. It had three main elements:

◆ Contributing, whether in the Chamber, Committees, or to the party, to developing policy on general or specific issues, and communicating this outside Westminster, especially within the constituency. This encompasses the fundamental responsibility to scrutinise and monitor the Executive.

◆ Representing the interests of the constituency as a whole, for example on planning and development matters; and staying closely in touch with local business and significant public services within the constituency (e.g. education and the health service) to understand and feed back experience.

◆ Representing, especially to public authorities, individual constituents who may need what they perceive to be high level support to understand their rights, obtain what they need, or explain why their wishes cannnot be satisfied.

This was a very good description of 'what MPs do', but it was strictly a *description*, drawn from observing the many, and not a *definition*. And the truth is that no definition exists. As a newly elected MP, it is entirely up to you to decide how you do the job. Will you devote yourself entirely to your constituents and their problems? (Unless you are both selective and realistic, you will rapidly discover that you could easily spend twenty-four hours in every day on this.) Will you become a standard bearer for some product of your constituency – apples, computer software, shellfish, sports cars? Will you pursue an abiding political interest which you had before you came into the House: perhaps Third World debt, or renewable sources of energy? Possibly you are attracted by select committee work, the business of calling the government to account, and making yourself an expert on a particular area of policy. Perhaps you might set yourself to contribute to better understanding between the United Kingdom and the Arab world, or to ensuring that the UK makes the most of commercial opportunities on the Pacific Rim. If you are in the party of government, might your ambitions be focused on ministerial office and getting a foot on the first rung of the ladder as a parliamentary private secretary (PPS; see page 94)?

In practice, most MPs will do some or all of these various aspects of the job. But few will do exactly what they expected when first they came into the House. And the main reason for that is the complex web of influences on the House and its members.

The government's control of the House of Commons

We saw in Chapter 2 how, in order to be invited to form a government, a prospective Prime Minister must have control of the House of Commons – that is, for his or her party to have enough of a parliamentary majority to be certain of getting approval for the legislative programme (announced in the Queen's Speech) and for government taxation and spending (through the Finance Bill and the Estimates). But the government's day-to-day control of the Commons is much more extensive.

Control of time

Perhaps the most evident symptom of that control is the fact that, every Thursday, the Leader of the House announces what the business will be – that is, what items will be taken on each day – for the next fortnight. In many parliaments, particularly those on the continental model, there is a business committee or *bureau*, involving not only the business managers and other party representatives but also the president of the assembly and his deputies, who decide what business to propose. And even then, that draft agenda is subject to approval by the assembly as a whole.

However, in the House of Commons, it is primarily for the government of the day to propose and to dispose. Ever since the Balfour reforms at the turn of the nineteenth/twentieth centuries, all House of Commons time that is not ring-fenced is at the disposal of the government of the day. In 150 or 160 sitting days in a parliamentary session, only twenty 'opposition days', thirteen days for private members' bills, some time for private bills, three 'Estimates days' for debates on select committee reports, the daily half-hour adjournment debate, urgent questions and the daily Question Time are not in the gift of the government. Even then, it is for the government to decide *when* the opposition days, private members' bill days and Estimates days shall be taken. In terms of time in the Chamber, nearly three-fifths of business is initiated by the government, about a tenth by the opposition and about a quarter by back-benchers. Even though business initiated by the government provides debating opportunities for the opposition and for back-benchers generally, the extent of that power of initiative is considerable. In addition, the standing orders provide that only ministers may move certain key motions for the arrangement and organisation of business. The vast majority of legislation passed by Parliament is government legislation, and even private members' bills stand little chance of enactment unless they have government support.

The 'elective dictatorship'?

The former Conservative Lord Chancellor, Lord Hailsham, described the Westminster system of parliamentary government as an 'elective dictatorship': that is, one in which a government, once elected, is free to do very much what it wants. To an extent, Lord Hailsham was and is right. The Westminster system is not government by Parliament but government through Parliament, and (perhaps especially obvious when the government has a large parliamentary majority) one of the roles of Parliament is to legitimise what the government does.

Government patronage and collective responsibility

The government's position is further entrenched by the Prime Minister's ability to choose the members of the government. In 2006 there were 115 paid ministerial posts in both Houses: ninety-three in the Commons and twenty-two in the Lords. In addition, in the Commons there were fifty-two parliamentary private secretaries, who are not ministers but who act as unpaid aides to secretaries of state or ministers of state.

Not only is the power of ministerial appointment a key prime ministerial weapon, but it is also allied to the constitutional doctrine of 'collective responsibility', under which all the members of a government support any public statement of the government's policies. Ministers may (and often do) disagree privately and seek to change or modify their colleagues' minds and policies, but if they disagree publicly they are expected to resign (as did the Leader of the House, Robin Cook, in March 2003 over the government's proposed military action against Iraq) or face the sack from the PM of the day. This doctrine also applies to PPSs and means that in any vote the government can always rely on the support of all ministers and PPSs (often called collectively 'the payroll vote').

Theory and practice

It might appear that little stands in the way of the government doing precisely what it wants (or, perhaps more precisely, what the Prime Minister with the backing of the Cabinet wants). But the picture is more subtle than that. There is indeed an expectation that a government having won a mandate at a general election, with a majority in the House of Commons, will be able to 'get its business through'. However, in practice this depends on a number of factors. A government must retain the support of its back-benchers; and, as we shall see, it is not enough to issue orders; persuasion is often needed. Public and media opinion also needs to be benign – or, at least, not so critical as to give government back-benchers cold feet.

In addition, all governments are aware of the fact that, perhaps not too long distant, they may be on the opposition benches. In the heady days after a big election victory, or with the insulation of a large parliamentary majority, this recollection may be sometimes less vivid, but it underpins any government's need to maintain a working relationship with the opposition, and especially with the largest opposition party ('the official Opposition'). New MPs who have known only the government benches may want to press on regardless, but their enthusiasm tends to be tempered by longer-serving MPs who can remember all too many occasions when in opposition they won the arguments but lost the votes.

This working relationship with the opposition means, in House terms, general agreement on the arrangement and timing of business and accord on less contentious matters such as the dates of parliamentary recesses, normally through 'the usual channels' (see page 100). An effective working relationship may also colour the relationships between the parties on much more significant matters, such as a measure of agreement on how to approach a firefighters' strike, or the possible imposition of sanctions against a foreign country.

The opposition, too, has a considerable interest in maintaining this working relationship. The traditional statement that the opposition's power is one of delay is now out of date given the routine programming of government bills (see page 198). However, cooperation with the government in the arrangement of business will give the opposition the chance to express (and sometimes secure) priorities for debate, and to trade time and tactics, perhaps along the lines of 'no division on second reading of bill X and only half a day on its report stage', but in return 'an extra day on the report stage of bill Y'. The opposition gets the extra day on bill Y, which it sees as more important; the government saves some time on bill X and also knows that it can slacken the voting requirements for its MPs on the second reading of that bill.

Accountability and responsibility

A distinction is sometimes made between ministerial accountability (being answerable to Parliament for the government's actions) and ministerial responsibility ('taking personal responsibility for what has been done in the minister's name – even without the minister's knowledge – and, if necessary resigning') but in practice the second is really an extension of the first.

A. J. Balfour (Prime Minister 1902–05) described democracy as 'government by explanation'. Even if it is inevitable that the government will in the end get its way, Parliament is the forum in which it must explain itself and be held to account. Explanation may take various forms: responding to criticisms of proposed legislation at the second reading of a bill, or on detailed amendments put forward at report stage; explaining and defending a broader policy, perhaps on education reform or NHS funding, as part of a full day's debate initiated by the opposition; or giving a detailed account of its actions to a major select committee inquiry. The requirement on governments to explain and justify can in itself be a brake on executive power; but it is up to members of Parliament in both Houses to make this process effective.

Ministerial accountability is a concept that it is easier to recognise than to define. There is extensive case law over a number of years, beginning with the Crichel Down affair in 1954, when the Minister of Agriculture, Sir Thomas Dugdale, resigned apparently because he was taking responsibility for errors made by his civil servants (but more likely because he was left high and dry by a change in government policy), to the Westland affair in 1986 and the special adviser Jo Moore 'burying bad news' in 2001, which led eventually to the resignation of Stephen Byers as Secretary of State for Transport, Local Government and the Regions. On Westland, Leon Brittan resigned as Secretary of State for Trade and Industry, taking responsibility for errors by officials but refusing to explain exactly what had happened. The Defence Select Committee, which investigated the saga, remarked drily: 'A Minister does not discharge his accountability to Parliament merely by acknowledging a general responsibility and, if the circumstances warrant it, by resigning. Accountability involves accounting in detail for actions as a Minister'.

The principle of accountability to Parliament is now underpinned by resolutions of both Houses in March 1997 (following the Scott inquiry into the supply of arms to Iraq) on how ministers should behave towards Parliament:

Ministers of the Crown are expected to behave according to the highest standards of constitutional and personal conduct in the performance of their duties. In particular, they must observe the following principles of Ministerial conduct:

i.   *Ministers must uphold the principles of collective responsibility;*

ii. *Ministers have a duty to Parliament to account, and be held to account, for the policies, decisions and actions of their Departments and Next Steps Agencies;*

iii. *It is of paramount importance that Ministers give accurate and truthful information to Parliament, correcting any inadvertent error at the earliest opportunity. Ministers who knowingly mislead Parliament will be expected to offer their resignation to the Prime Minister;*

iv. *Ministers should be as open as possible with Parliament and the public, refusing to provide information only when disclosure would not be in the public interest, which should be decided in accordance with relevant statute and the Government's Code of Practice on Access to Government Information;*

v.   *Similarly, Ministers should require civil servants who give evidence before Parliamentary Committees on their behalf and under their directions to be as helpful as possible in providing accurate, truthful and full information in accordance with the duties and responsibilities of civil servants as set out in the Civil Service Code.*

In Chapters 10 and 11 we will look more closely at the ways in which the government is called to account.

The party

However close an MP's relationship with the constituency, the party to which he or she belongs is the key element in an MP's parliamentary life. This is not surprising; as we saw in Chapter 2, the only realistic prospect an aspiring politician has of being elected to the House of Commons is to join a political party and then have the backing of that party to fight an election. But for most MPs, their relationship with their party has an element of compromise about it. No party is ever in the happy position that every one of its MPs would sign up to every last detail of every one of its policies. Some would like to see greater emphasis in this or that direction; others are uneasy about the party committing itself on something else. However, just as the collective responsibility of ministers has its strength in public unity, so MPs are content to exchange occasional disagreements or private doubts for the shelter and support of the party that best represents their political outlook.

Given the enormous importance of political parties in Westminster politics, it is perhaps surprising that they are not more explicitly recognised in the rules of the two Houses. In the Commons, the standing orders notice parties only so far as 'committee memberships reflect the composition of the House', that smaller opposition parties have a share of opposition day debates, and that one MP speaking for the Liberal Democrats is exempted from any limit that may be imposed on speaking time for back-benchers in a particular debate. In a formal sense, party structures and disciplines exist in parallel with the regulation of the House and its proceedings, although in practice they interlock at every level.

By contrast, in some parliaments – for example the Canadian House of Commons – the role of parties is explicitly recognised in the allocation of oral questions and speaking time, which means that the Speaker plays a smaller role in allocation than at Westminster.

The whips

The whips are key players in party organisation and discipline, and in the arrangement and timing of business, on both sides of the House. The title derives from 'whippers-in' or 'whips' in the hunting field – rather ironic in view of the political furore over the banning of hunting. Whips act as a two-way channel of communication between the party leadership and the back benches, on the one hand feeding back MPs' views and warning of areas of possible difficulty or dissent and, on the other, making clear to back-benchers what the leadership wants from them.

An effective whip needs to be a strong character and a shrewd operator but also has to balance personal authority with an understanding of the pressures on the MPs for whom she or he is responsible. Much is written and more speculated about the black arts of the whips – their techniques for bringing recalcitrant MPs into line – and of their intelligence gathering. There is no doubt that whips can on occasion be fearsomely effective, whether by use of stick or carrot, in persuading potential rebels to live with their doubts rather than express them; and there is no doubt, either, that a good whips' office knows more about the views and foibles of its back-benchers than it would ever wish to see made public.

However, whips also need to be good personnel managers. New (and some more experienced) MPs may find life at Westminster difficult and frustrating; and spending much of the working week perhaps hundreds of miles from home and family, combined perhaps with constituency casework that is especially tragic or emotionally draining, can impose real strains. In such circumstances, a good whip is a source of advice and support.

Whips are ever-present in proceedings in the House, Westminster Hall and standing committees. In the House there is always a government and an official opposition whip sitting on the front benches keeping an eye on proceedings, jotting down notes on speeches (and speakers) in the debate and alert for any procedural or political difficulty that may arise. Whips have a talent-spotting role, and their good opinion (and especially that of the Chief Whip) may lead to ministerial office, a shadow post, or perhaps a coveted place on a popular select committee.

The government Chief Whip is known formally as the Parliamentary Secretary to the Treasury (and sometimes as the Patronage Secretary – a reminder of the carrot rather than the stick of parliamentary discipline). It is her responsibility to get the government's business through the Commons with the greatest efficiency and the least dissent from government back-benchers. She normally attends Cabinet meetings and advises the Prime Minister and his senior colleagues on opinion within the parliamentary party, and how proposed policies are likely to play with back-benchers. On the government side, the next three senior whips carry formal titles of posts in the Royal Household: the Deputy Chief Whip is the Treasurer of HM Household, followed by the Comptroller and the Vice-Chamberlain. There are five other whips (known as Lords Commissioners of the Treasury) and usually seven assistant whips.

The Conservative official Opposition has a Chief Whip and a deputy (who receive additional salaries even though they are in opposition) and ten or eleven other whips (one of whom receives an additional salary). The Liberal Democrats have a Chief Whip, a deputy and four other whips. The smaller parties each have someone who acts as a Chief Whip, although with relatively few MPs their role is more as their parties' voice in the arrangement of business than as organisers and disciplinarians. In the major parties, the whips have regional and subject responsibilities: for example, the north-east and defence, and they attend the relevant party committees and groups.

The usual channels

This is deliberately vague shorthand for the informal discussions that take place between the business managers on both sides of the House. It embraces the Leader of the House and shadow Leader, and the government and opposition Chief Whips (and of other parties as circumstances require), but it also includes day-to-day and minute-to-minute conversations and arrangements between whips on both sides. A key player is the private secretary to the government Chief Whip, who although a civil servant plays a highly political role as a go-between.

The usual channels deal with a wide range of business, from issues such as the amount of time to be spent on a government bill in committee and which party should get which select committee chair, to extempore arrangements in which a whip will go round the Chamber asking his side's last two or three speakers to limit their speeches so that the 'winding-up' speeches from the front benches can start at the time agreed. Off-the-cuff arrangements are sometimes referred to as being done 'behind the Chair', which is indeed where they happen when whips from both sides have whispered conversations behind the Speaker's Chair.

Discussions through the usual channels are private – were they to be made public it is unlikely that they would take the same form or be so effective. But this secrecy, and the feeling on the part of some that deals cooked up behind the scenes may be more for the convenience of the participants than of back-benchers on one side or another, has led to criticism: the former Labour cabinet minister Tony Benn, for example, described the usual channels as 'the most polluted waterway in Europe'.

There is no doubt that, on occasion, the whips on both sides are closer to each other than to some elements of their own parties. It was widely thought, for example, that an alliance of the whips on both the government and opposition sides was responsible in October 2002 for defeating a proposal by Robin Cook as Leader of the House that would have greatly reduced the power of the whips over which MPs should serve on which select committees.

The Whip

A vital document for every MP is *The Whip*. This is circulated weekly by the whips of each party to their own members and lists the business for the following two weeks, together with the party's expectations as to when its MPs will vote. The importance of the business is reflected by the number of times it is underlined, hence the phrase 'a three-line whip' for something seen as an unbreakable commitment. An example is shown overleaf.

By arrangement with the whips, an MP may miss even an important vote if he or she is paired – that is, if an MP from the other side makes a formal arrangement not to vote, so that the effect is neutral. This is of less importance when the government of the day has a very large majority, but it may be of considerable importance when the numbers are close; for example, it allows the Foreign Secretary to be at the UN, or other ministers to take part in crucial negotiations in Brussels, rather than being called back to vote. When the government party can rely on a large majority, it will normally excuse some of its MPs from voting, on a rota basis, so that they can spend time in their constituencies.

Occasionally it happens that the usual channels break down, and the opposition withdraws pairing arrangements. This can be a considerable inconvenience to the government, which must keep many more of its MPs in the precincts or nearby in case of a snap vote.

Party discipline

The whips are responsible for delivering the votes to give effect to their parties' policies and intentions. On matters that are likely to be contentious within the party, the leadership normally takes care to trail proposals in advance to assess whether there is likely to be dissent. It follows that, for the whips, a back-bencher's cardinal sin is to abstain, or worse, vote against his or her party, without giving any warning. An MP who expresses doubts about being able to support the party will normally be asked to discuss those doubts with his or her own whip, and probably also with the Chief Whip (such meetings are sometimes known ironically as 'career development inter-views'). For crucial votes, the party leader may want to try to change minds. In the two key votes on policy towards Iraq in February and March 2003, and on the Education and Inspections Bill in 2006, for example, the Prime Minister sought to persuade waverers personally.

PRIVATE & CONFIDENTIAL

MONDAY 11ᵀᴴ JULY 2005.   The House will meet at 2.30pm.

1. Culture, Media and Sport, Church Commissioners, Public Accounts Commission and Speaker's Committee on the Electoral Commission Questions.   Last tabling date for Education and Skills, Solicitor General.

2. RACIAL AND RELIGIOUS HATRED BILL: REMAINING STAGES
(Rt Hon Charles Clarke and Paul Goggins)

   YOUR ATTENDANCE FROM 3.30PM IS ESSENTIAL.

3. At the end of the sitting: Adjournment – Hepatitis C.
(Bob Laxton)

   TUESDAY 12ᵀᴴ JULY 2005.   The House will meet at 2.30pm.

1. Health Questions.   Last tabling date for Work and Pensions, Wales

2. OPPOSITION DAY (5ᵀᴴ ALLOTTED DAY). THERE WILL BE A DEBATE ON "THE FAILURE OF THE TAX CREDITS SYSTEM" AN OPPOSITION MOTION.

   FOLLOWED BY

3. A DEBATE ON "THE GOVERNMENT'S FAILURE TO DEAL WITH LICENSING CHAOS" ON AN OPPOSITION MOTION

   YOUR ATTENDANCE AT 6.00PM FOR 7.00PM AND/OR 9.00PM FOR 10.00PM IS ESSENTIAL.

4. At the end of the sitting: Adjournment – Proposed closure of the meteorological office in Aberdeen. (Malcolm Bruce)

   WEDNESDAY 13ᵀᴴ JULY 2005.   The House will meet at 11.30am.

1. Northern Ireland and Prime Minister Questions.   Last tabling date for Foreign and Commonwealth Office.

2. MOTIONS TO APPROVE THE MEMBERSHIP OF SELECT COMMITTEES AND OTHER HOUSE MOTIONS.
(Rt Hon Geoff Hoon and Nigel Griffiths)

   FOLLOWED BY

3. MOTION TO TAKE NOTE OF THE FOURTH REPORT OF THE COMMITTEE ON STANDARDS AND PRIVILEGES, HC 472, SESSION 2004-05 AND TO APPROVE THE REVISED CODE OF CONDUCT.
(Rt Hon Geoff Hoon and Nigel Griffiths)

   YOUR ATTENDANCE IS REQUESTED.

3. At the end of the sitting: Adjournment – Availability of Co-proxamol.
(Anne Begg)

****

DEFERRED VOTING
YOUR ATTENDANCE TO HAND IN YOUR VOTE PAPER
BETWEEN 12.30PM AND 2.00PM IS ESSENTIAL.
****

A political party's 'Whip', which tells its MPs when they should be present for votes in the Commons

A former Cabinet minister once advised his new MP colleagues 'to tread that narrow path between rebellion and sycophancy'; but party discipline is normally not a problem for most MPs. They accept that membership of

---

THURSDAY 14TH JULY

The House will meet at 10.30 am.

1. Education and Skills, Solicitor General Questions.   Last tabling date for Prime Minister.

2. CONSUMER CREDIT BILL: REMAINING STAGES
    (Gerry Sutcliffe)

    YOUR ATTENDANCE FROM 11.30AM IS ESSENTIAL.
    ═══

3. At the end of the sitting: Adjournment – Eviction of travellers from the Crays Hill site, Billericay.
    (John Baron)

    FRIDAY 15TH JULY 2005.

    THE HOUSE WILL NOT BE SITTING

---

a party, with all the advantages that its structures and organisation bring, involves some degree of compromise; and they are usually content to vote as the party wishes, especially in subject areas of which they have no close knowledge. They are also well aware that a divided party is a parliamentary, and certainly an electoral, liability. It is ironic that, on the one hand, there is public pressure for MPs to be more independent, but at the same time, a feeling that a party which cannot keep its own members on side has somehow failed.

Dissent and rebellion

An MP will think very carefully before voting against the party, or even abstaining in an important vote. Unless it is unassailably on a matter of personal conscience, the action will be seen as disloyal and will often have an effect on the prospects for preferment; whips have long memories.

The reasons for rebellion are varied: the issue may be one of general principle, as on limiting the right to jury trial, or on the prospect of military action against Iraq. It may be on an issue that is seen by some of its members as contrary to a party's traditions and best interests, for example for the Conservatives on the Maastricht Treaty in the 1992 parliament, and for the Labour Party on university tuition fees in the 2001 parliament.

The size of a government's majority is obviously an important factor. In 1992, the Conservatives under John Major were returned with an overall majority of twenty-one. By the end of the parliament, by-election defeats and defections to other parties had reduced this to a minority of three. Rebellions amongst Conservative MPs resulted in a total of nine defeats for the government during that parliament. By contrast, in 1997 Tony Blair had an extraordinarily high majority of 179 over all other parties. Actual defeat on the floor of the House was therefore much less likely; but rebellions were still of no less concern to the leadership.

Dissent since 1997

In the 1997 parliament, the level of dissent on the government back benches was less than in previous parliaments, perhaps because of a feeling of being on trial after eighteen years in opposition, perhaps because of memories of damaging divisions in the party during the last Labour government in 1974–79. Nevertheless, there were 104 occasions on which Labour members voted against the government on the floor of the House – the fourth largest number of rebellions in parliaments since 1945. In the 2001 parliament, Labour back-benchers rebelled in 20.8 per cent of votes, the highest *rate* of rebellion since 1945.

The biggest rebellions since Labour came to power in 1997, and in fact the biggest for more than a quarter of a century, took place over the government's policy on military action against Iraq. On 26 February 2003, 122 Labour MPs voted against the government on an amendment asserting that the case for military action was 'as yet unproven'; and on 18 March, 139 Labour MPs voted for an amendment to the effect that the case for war had not been established.

Dissent in the 2001 parliament

Indeed, in the first two sessions of the 2001 parliament the government experienced the greatest level of back-bench dissent since 1945, with more than two-thirds of Labour back-benchers voting against the government on one or more occasion. This dissent continued throughout the parliament: in January 2004, seventy-two Labour MPs voted against the second reading of the Higher Education Bill on the issue of tuition fees, and the bill scraped through by only five votes. In November 2004, abstentions and votes against knocked ninety-five votes off the government's majority on second reading of the Gambling Bill, which would have authorised a number of 'super-casinos'; and in March 2005 sixty-two Labour MPs voted against the government's proposals for house arrest of terrorist suspects on the authority of a minister and not of a judge.

Dissent in the 2005 parliament

In June 2005 the government's majority of sixty-six was reduced to thirty-one on second reading of the Identity Cards Bill, which suggested that the smaller majority in the 2005 parliament would need careful management. And so it proved.

In October 2005, twenty-five Labour MPs voted against the proposal that personal details which could be used for an identity card should be provided when applying for a passport. In November 2005, thirty-three Labour MPs helped to cut the government's majority to a single vote on the definition of 'glorifying terrorism' in the Terrorism Bill. And on 9 November 2005 forty-nine Labour MPs helped defeat the government's proposal that suspected terrorists could be held without charge for up to ninety days and substitute for it a period of twenty-eight days. Worse was to follow. On 31 January 2006 the government lost two votes on Lords Amendments to the Racial and Religious Hatred Bill: one, by ten votes, to narrow the definition of an offence so that actions had to be 'intended' to stir up hatred rather than 'likely' to do so; and the second, by one vote, to make 'threatening' behaviour an offence, rather than 'threatening, abusive or insulting'. However, these defeats were not primarily the result of dissent: twenty-six Labour MPs voted against the government on the first vote, and twenty-one on the second. Rather it was a complete miscalculation on the part of the government Whips, who allowed too many of their MPs to be away (some campaigning in the Dunfermline and West Fife by-election) and even allowed the Prime Minister to leave the Commons before the division, which was lost by one vote.

Whatever the reasons, it was unprecedented for a government with a majority of over sixty to lose a total of four key votes in the first nine months of a new Parliament.

The dynamics of dissent

Voting against one's party, however good the reasons, is not a decision lightly taken. The aims vary. Quite apart from their views on matters of principle, MPs may want to make a point about being consulted by the party leadership. They may want to establish their credentials, both within the party as a whole and with their constituents, on a major issue (many Labour MPs came under a great deal of pressure in their constituencies on the impending war with Iraq).

Especially if the government's majority is small, a threatened revolt may secure substantial changes in policy. But small majorities work both ways; when the boat is low in the water, people are less inclined to rock it, and, however strongly they feel, government MPs will be reluctant to risk the 'nuclear option' of defeating their party on a major issue and perhaps triggering a vote of confidence (as happened when in July 1992 the

Conservative government was defeated by 324 votes to 316 over the Social Protocol to the Maastricht Treaty – even though it won the confidence motion the next day by the luxurious margin of 110 votes).

Dissent and rebellion can become a habit for some MPs. More than 80 per cent of the Labour rebels on the second Iraq vote had voted against their party at least once since 1997. Repeated rebellion sometimes indicates a growing disenchantment with the mainstream views of the party – for a few, this may be the first step towards defection to another party (see *Crossing the floor* below). It is also the case that rebellion becomes easier; an MP may think that, having damaged his prospects by voting against the government several times, full membership of the 'awkward squad' will not make things much worse. The presence of a major figure, perhaps a former Cabinet minister who is on the back benches because he or she resigned over a major policy difference, may also be a potential focus of dissent. The number of sacked ministers and of MPs who are unpromoted and resentful (the 'ex-would-be-ministers') are also contributory. In 2005 and 2006 the wish of a number of Labour MPs to see Tony Blair step down was an additional factor.

Because of their wish to present a united front to the electorate and the media, political parties tend to undervalue dissent – or at least, dissent in public. In most organisations and businesses, challenge is seen as a healthy process, leading to better decision making. Had Margaret Thatcher's government taken more account of its dissenters over the Local Government Finance Bill in 1988 (which introduced the community charge or 'poll tax'), and particularly the proposal of one back-bencher, Michael Mates, that there should be banding of the charge according to income, the political history of the next two or three years might have been rather different.

Punishment

Voting against the party is not normally a good career move; most parties are unwilling to reward rebels with promotion. There are more formal sanctions. The Parliamentary Labour Party (PLP) has a code of conduct that requires its MPs to behave in a way that is consistent with the policies of the party, to have a good voting record and not to bring the party into disrepute. However, it does contain a 'conscience clause', which recognises a right of dissent on 'matters of deeply held personal conviction'. The Chief Whip may reprimand an MP in writing (which may also be reported to the member's constituency party). The PLP as a whole may 'withdraw the whip' from one of its MPs – in effect expelling them from the party. In a case of alleged serious misconduct, an MP may be suspended from the party pending an investigation, as happened with the Labour MP George Galloway in May 2003. He later left the party.

The Conservative Party has similar rules, also with 'conscience' provisions. But in the 1992 parliament eight Eurosceptic Conservative MPs had the whip withdrawn from them for six months because of their repeated voting against the party on European issues, and crucially on the Maastricht Social Protocol, which became an issue of confidence for the government.

Whether to make an example of rebels is a matter of judgement. There is a balance between doing so *pour encourager les autres* and the risk of creating martyrs. And if dissent is on a large enough scale, the whips may have little practical power; the solution then is for the party to re-examine its policy.

Crossing the floor

In an extreme case, an MP who falls out with his or her party may leave altogether and join another party. This is relatively rare; there were eight in the period 1992–2005. An MP changing parties does not trigger a by-election, as he continues to represent constituents whether or not they voted for him; but there is usually some local pressure for the defector to resign so that a new candidate can be chosen.

Large-scale defections may rewrite part of the political map, as in 1981 when twenty-seven Labour MPs and one Conservative joined the newly formed Social Democratic Party founded by the 'Gang of Four' former Labour ministers Roy Jenkins, David Owen, Shirley Williams and William Rodgers. The importance of established party backing was demonstrated by the fact that only four of the twenty-eight survived the 1983 election (and one of those lost in 1987).

Party organisation in Parliament

The whips do not spring political surprises on MPs, for MPs are themselves part of the decision-making processes in their party, and their influence is felt in the committees and groups that each party organises. This organisation is obviously more complex in larger parties, but each party has a formal structure, supported by its own secretariat.

The Labour Party

The PLP

All Labour MPs, back-bench and front-bench, and Labour peers, are members of the Parliamentary Labour Party. The PLP meets at 6.00 p.m. every Monday for between 45 and 90 minutes. The main agenda item is normally forthcoming business in the House, and the Chief Whip tells MPs what the whipping will be. A Cabinet minister will normally be a guest speaker, reporting on plans and current issues (with a chance to shine in front of the party's rank and file). An important agenda item may be a top-ical subject raised under 'any other business'. Individual MPs may move motions to make a point or to test opinion; notice of these must be given to the Chief Whip at least a week before the meeting. Attendance at the weekly PLP meetings is usually between 100 and 150. The chair of the PLP (since 2005 Ann Clwyd) is elected by a ballot of all Labour MPs (not just back-benchers) and is a key party figure.

The Parliamentary Committee

When the Labour Party is in government, the Parliamentary Committee of the PLP, in effect its executive committee, consists of the Prime Minister and Deputy Prime Minister, four ministers including the Leader of the House and the Chief Whip in the Commons, the chairman of the PLP and four back-bench MPs elected by other back-benchers, and one peer elected by back-bench Labour peers. In opposition, the Parliamentary Committee is elected by the PLP as a whole and forms the shadow Cabinet.

Subject committees

Each of these monitors the work of a government department from a party point of view; there is also a Women's Group, which only women mem-bers may join. Labour MPs may belong to a maximum of three subject committees (not counting the Women's Group) but may attend any other committee in a non-voting capacity. The committees meet approximately fortnightly, often with the participation of ministers; attendance varies greatly according to the interest of the agenda, down to half a dozen or so. When the party is in government, the chairman and officers of a subject committee keep in close touch with the ministers of the relevant depart-ment. Committees are consulted about forthcoming policy initiatives and legislation, and ministers report to the relevant committee on the work and plans of their departments.

Regional groups

Every Labour MP belongs to the appropriate regional group: for example, Greater London, the North-East or Wales. These usually meet fortnightly and focus on issues of particular local concern or interest. They can play an important part in setting the broader agenda within the party, and they are also a target for local government, agencies and institutions that want to shape opinion amongst the MPs for their area.

The Conservative Party

The 1922 Committee

The Conservatives' equivalent of the PLP is the 1922 Committee, which was founded in 1923 by MPs who came into the House for the first time at the 1922 general election. Despite its former formal title of 'the Conservative Private Members' Committee', it has always been known as 'the 1922 Committee' or 'the 22'. In opposition, every Conservative MP is a member of this committee; when the party is in government, it is usual for ministers and whips not to attend unless invited. Conservative Members of the European Parliament (MEPs) and peers may attend but do not vote. The 1922 Committee meets on Wednesdays at 5.30 p.m.; the business taken is similar to that in the PLP. The chairman of the 1922 Committee (since June 2001 Sir Michael Spicer) plays an important role in the party as the representative of the interests of back-benchers, with direct access to the leader of the party, and he also sits as the representative of the parliamentary party on the Conservative Board, the governing body of the party.

The Executive Committee of the 1922 Committee

This consists of the chairman of the 1922 Committee, two vice-chairmen, a treasurer, two secretaries and twelve other back-benchers, elected each year. The Executive Committee meets for an hour on Wednesday afternoons at 4.30 p.m., immediately before the meeting of the 1922 Committee itself. The Executive Committee has always had a significant influence on party policy and direction.

Policy groups

In the 2001 parliament these played very much the same role as the Labour Party's subject committees, engaging in dialogue with shadow ministers and feeding back-bench views into the formation of policy. Following the 2005 election defeat their future structure was uncertain, awaiting the election of a new party leader instead, back-benchers interested in a particular policy area now attach themselves to the relevant front-bench team – perhaps a good way of getting noticed.

The Liberal Democrats

Liberal Democrat MPs meet on Wednesdays at 5.30 p.m. for an hour or more. The first item is usually a report by the leader of the party, followed by a discussion of forthcoming business in the House, and items submitted by individual MPs. Occasional longer meetings take place, including 'awaydays' outside Parliament during recesses. Partly attributable to the size of the party (62 MPs in the 2005 parliament), there is no formal committee structure.

Other parties

The six Scottish National Party and three Plaid Cymru MPs meet jointly on Wednesday evenings, with the chair alternating between the leaders of the parties. An important purpose of these weekly meetings is to arrange for the coverage of debates and to develop coherent tactics. This is a problem for small parties – business is arranged principally between the two major parties, and the Nationalists might find that they have to decide between support for the government and support for the opposition when they may not wholly support either. The option of abstention is not recorded officially and so is not distinguishable from absence.

The Democratic Unionists, with nine MPs, hold weekly meetings, usually on Wednesdays at 2 p.m. The five Sinn Féin MPs elected in 2005 have not taken their seats (nor did the four elected in 2001), and take no part in the business of the House.

Political groups

We said earlier that membership of a party involved a degree of compromise, that some MPs would like to see greater stress placed on some areas of policy or might be uneasy about other areas. For many years, in all political parties, these differences of emphasis have led to the formation of political groups within parties that more closely represent particular currents of opinion. The Labour Party in government probably has less formal activity of this sort than for many years. However, the reduced majority in 2005 seemed likely to give the left-wing Campaign Group, with some forty MPs, a new lease of life. The Conservative Party's dining clubs come and go, but the more enduring are the centre-left Nick's Diner and the No Turning Back and the 92, which are to the right of the party. The Cornerstone Group is described as 'the religious right' and interviewed each of the candidates for the party leadership in 2005.

Party leadership

No assessment of influences on MPs within their own parties (and the influence that they in turn can exercise) would be complete without a mention of the way in which party leaders are elected. Dissatisfaction with a party leader, or the perception that there is a leader-in-waiting, can produce blocs of opinion within a party – as witness the press's enthusiastic labelling of Labour ministers as 'Blairite' or 'Brownite'.

It can also give rise to an extreme form of dissent, as when in 1990 Margaret Thatcher was deposed as party leader (and so as Prime Minister) following a leadership challenge by Michael Heseltine, who had resigned from the Cabinet over the Westland affair almost five years before. Thatcher won the ballot by 204 votes to 152, but the scale of support for Heseltine led her to withdraw from the contest. In the early months of the 2005 parliament, dissent by some Labour MPs seemed aimed at Tory Blair's premiership almost more than the issues on which they voted against him.

In the Conservative Party, a challenge to the leadership may be triggered only if 15 per cent or more of Conservative MPs (in the present parliament, at least twenty-four) ask the chairman of the 1922 Committee for a vote of confidence in the leader. If the leader then receives a majority of the votes cast, there can be no further challenge for a year. If the leader loses, votes of all Conservative MPs then reduce the number of candidates for the leadership to two, and the contest is decided by a ballot of all party members in the country at large (despite an unsuccessful attempt by Michael Howard in 2005 to make the views of party members advisory, and that of Conservative MPs decisive). In 2003, Iain Duncan Smith lost the party leadership following a vote of confidence amongst Conservative MPs (90 votes to 75); Michael Howard was the only candidate to succeed him, and became leader with no further vote by MPs, nor a ballot of party members. But in 2005, after ballots of Conservative MPs had eliminated Kenneth Clarke and Liam Fox, it was on a vote of party members, by 134,446 to 64,398, that David Cameron beat David Davis for the leadership.

In the Labour Party, the leader and deputy leader are elected by three elements of the party: Labour MPs and MEPs, party members, and affiliated organisations (mainly trade unions), each element disposing of one-third of the vote. A candidate with more than half of the votes is elected (after elimination ballots if necessary). A nomination must be supported by 12.5 per cent of the PLP (in the present parliament, fifty-one MPs) if there is a vacancy, and by 20 per cent (eighty-two MPs) if there is a challenge. In government, a Labour leader is more secure than a Conservative leader: a challenge may take place only if requested by a majority of the party conference on a card vote – something virtually impossible to achieve.

The Liberal Democrat leader is elected by a ballot of the party in the country as a whole under the alternative vote system. Candidates must be

Liberal Democrat MPs, and they must have the support of ten per cent of MPs in the parliamentary party, and of 200 party members in at least twenty local parties. In March 2006 Sir Menzies Campbell beat Chris Huhne for the leadership, polling 29,697 votes of party members to 21,628, third-placed Simon Hughes having been eliminated.

The party – conclusion

Political parties consist of much more than Members of Parliament, but MPs are at the forefront of political activity, and they have an important role in the determination and presentation of their parties' policies. The multi-faceted organisation of parties in Parliament is a constant influence on the individual MP, in terms of voting expectations, exposure to the views of other MPs and changing currents of opinion, and, in the major parties, inter-action with ministers when the party is in government and with shadow ministers when it is not.

In turn, MPs have the opportunity to take part in the development of party policies through formal committee and group structures, and also through informal personal contacts and relationships – the newest MP may spark off an important new idea with the leadership in a three-minute con-versation in the Tea Room or the division lobby.

Personal influences

People are shaped by their experiences, and MPs are no exception. They bring with them into the House what they have acquired in previous careers, whether as teachers, lawyers, social workers, as craftspeople (in the case of Speaker Martin, as a sheet-metal worker) or in other fields, such as the Labour MP who was a microbiologist, the Liberal Democrat with a doctorate in logic or the Conservative who was a fireman. MPs are also influenced by more personal experiences. In the present parliament, members' contributions have reflected, for example, being on the receiving end of racial discrimination, being a single parent, acting as a carer for a terminally ill partner, and being gay. Many of these experiences will condi-tion how an MP reacts to some of the myriad issues of parliamentary life.

The constituency: the MP's relationship

The constituency is a vital part of the life of every MP. As we noted in Chapter 2, it is a power base, and its voters must be wooed to maximise the chances of being elected. An MP's identification with the interests and concerns of a constituency is also sharpened by the fact that UK constituencies are small enough to be fairly homogeneous in terms of character, population and economic activity.

An MP represents all the people in a constituency, whether or not they voted for him or her, or indeed whether they were old enough to vote; an average constituency in England may have 70,000 electors but a total population of 90,000 if you count those under 18. This non-party representation of a constituency is emphasised by the fact that in most cases (and especially in the low turnout in the 2001 and 2005 general elections) the majority of people entitled to vote will not have voted for the person elected as an MP. In the super-safe Labour seat of Bootle, for example, the elected MP won 75.5 per cent of the vote, but this represented only 36 per cent of those entitled to vote.

The closeness of an MP's relationship with the constituency, and the extent of its influence on the MP's actions in Parliament, has steadily increased. The classic statement of the relationship of member and constituency is that contained in Edmund Burke's speech to the electors of Bristol in 1774:

> *It ought to be the happiness and glory of a representative to live in the strictest union, the closest correspondence, and the most unreserved communication with his constituents. Their wishes ought to have great weight with him; their opinion, high respect; their business, unremitted attention. It is his duty to sacrifice his repose, his pleasures, his satisfactions to theirs – and above all, ever, and in all cases to prefer their interest to his own. But his unbiased opinion, his mature judgement, his enlightened conscience, he ought not to sacrifice to you, to any man, or to any set of men living. . . . Your representative owes you, not his industry only, but his judgement; and he betrays, instead of serving you, if he sacrifices it to your opinion.*

The first part of this antithesis – the close relationship with and unremitting attention to the constituency – may be seen as years before its time, even though Burke was speaking to electors a century and a half before universal suffrage. For the whole of the nineteenth century and in many cases into the twentieth, constituencies were simply platforms on which MPs stood to take part in public life and which they visited rarely. Such absenteeism would not wash today, and below we describe some of the constituency pressures on the modern MP.

The second part – the assertion that an MP is the representative of a constituency who votes according to his judgement and conscience, and not a delegate who votes according to constituents' instructions – has undergone a transformation. An MP may still exercise judgement and conscience, and in doing so may represent a minority of opinion in the constituency – for example for additional rights for gay couples, or for additional powers for the European Union – but, as we saw earlier in this chapter, the main constraint on the way an MP *votes* is now the party to which he or she belongs.

Listening to constituents

Almost every MP has a constituency office to deal more effectively with constituency matters and to have a presence close to local issues; and increasingly MPs base their support staff in constituencies rather than at Westminster.

In recent years, the core of an MP's work on behalf of constituents has been the 'surgery', when the MP's availability to discuss problems is advertised in the local press and elsewhere. In a small constituency, this may be at a central constituency office; in a larger one, it may be in a succession of town and village halls during the day, or even in a caravan that the MP tows around. Surgery work is on the increase; many MPs have moved to twice-weekly surgeries, and the changed sitting patterns of the Commons since 2002 have included many more non-sitting 'constituency' Fridays.

Constituents also raise issues and problems with their MP by letter – most MPs receive fifty or more letters a day, rising into the hundreds when there is a matter of great local or national contention. E-mail is increasingly used, but brings its own problems: the speed of communication leads many constituents to expect an equal speed of reply on what may be a hideously complicated problem, and some very conscientious members prefer not to use e-mail for this reason.

Constituents' problems

People will raise literally any subject with their MP. They do so for a variety of reasons: they think the MP will be able to get action; they have exhausted all other possibilities; they do not know whom to approach and so start with the MP; or they go to the MP as a personification of an establishment that they see as being the problem itself. This last category inevitably includes the desperate and the disturbed, and at surgeries security is often an issue; it is not long since an MP's researcher was killed and the MP himself badly injured, and other MPs have been attacked.

When a constituent seeks help, the MP must first establish exactly what the problem is. This is often much more difficult than it might seem. The constituent may be coming to the MP only after months or years of struggle with some organisation or agency, and his or her opening gambit may be to present a box file overflowing with documents of all sorts, some more legible than others. Unravelling the tangled skein to find out exactly what has happened, whose fault it was and what can be done about it can be enormously time-consuming. On the other hand, the problem – perhaps 'neighbours from Hell' – may be very straightforward, but what can be done without legal action, which the constituent cannot afford, may be much more difficult.

People often assume that an MP can do something about anything but, strictly speaking, an MP's role is limited to matters for which ministers are answerable to Parliament – in general, the responsibilities of government departments or executive agencies. This nevertheless covers a huge range of things that give rise to constituents' problems: immigration and asylum, pensions and social security, income tax, the Child Support Agency, the National Health Service, and animal health and farming subsidies being just a few.

The MP does not have a direct role in matters that are the responsibility of a local authority – the running of local schools, rubbish collection and recycling, council housing, council tax, and so on, as 'constituency cases' here are the responsibility of local councillors. But although an MP will be careful not to step on the toes of councillors (whether of the same party or not), he or she may on the basis of local difficulties pursue a broader issue of principle for which central government *is* responsible: for example, in the extent of central government funding for local authorities and what is taken into account in setting the level of that funding.

A constituent may bring to the MP a 'private sector' problem: perhaps the mis-selling of pensions, rogue builders, or rocketing insurance premiums in an area prone to flooding. A letter from an MP may or may not have any influence directly with the company concerned, but in cases such as these the MP's best bet is to engage the responsibilities of ministers for regulating these sectors of industry in the public interest, or perhaps to seek the assistance of an industry's own watchdog body, which has an interest in the reputation of the industry as a whole. If the problem is a failing company and job losses, the MP may be looking for government support for European Union grants, or money for retraining redundant workers.

Even if the MP really has no direct role, and the possibility of doing something constructive is very limited, there is always the risk that an honest answer to this effect may be misrepresented by the constituent, the press or a political opponent as 'Ms X doesn't care' or 'Mr Z isn't prepared to put himself out'. There is thus a good deal of pressure on the MP to make some sort of positive or helpful response, even if it is only to suggest some other person or agency to approach.

MPs are extremely careful to check that the person raising a problem is indeed their constituent and not that of a neighbouring member (you can find out who your MP is by putting your postcode into the *Locata* system on the parliamentary website: **www.locata.co.uk/commons/**). Occasionally an MP faced with a case in which he or she might be thought to have a personal interest may ask another MP to take it on. This also happens from time to time when an MP has taken a strong public stand on an issue, in order to avoid a constituent with a contrary view feeling that there might be a conflict of interest. However, if an MP dies or resigns, it is usual for constituents' problems to be dealt with by one or more neighbouring MPs.

A new MP is always warned by colleagues not to take up planning cases; planning has its own machinery at both local and national level, and the applicants and the objectors are usually all constituents; to favour one is to disadvantage another. Similarly, although the 'neighbours from Hell' referred to above may be a public nuisance for a whole local area, MPs are generally reluctant to take up neighbour or family disputes; all concerned are likely to be constituents.

What can the MP do?

An MP does not have executive power but is an analyst and advocate. In taking up a constituent's case, he or she must identify what the problem is and who is responsible (or direct a constituent elsewhere if someone else is more likely to be able to take effective action). Then it is a matter of exposure and persuasion. A letter on House of Commons writing paper may be enough to break a bureaucratic log jam or to persuade a company that it has indeed treated someone unfairly.

On most things for which central government is responsible, the most usual first step is the letter to the minister. This may ask for a case to be reviewed, for the minister's observations on the problem or simply for a clear statement of the department's policy on the point at issue. We return to MPs' letters to ministers in Chapter 10.

If the minister's response does not solve the matter, and the constituent has a good case that the MP is determined to take forward, the possibilities are limited only by energy and ingenuity. The MP may seek a meeting with the minister. If the problem is a wider one within the constituency, perhaps involving mass redundancies, or a manufacturing or farming sector in crisis, this may take the form of leading a deputation to a formal meeting in the department, with the minister and civil servants present. The MP may make an informal approach – the classic way is to corner a minister in the division lobby during a vote in the House. Perhaps there are other members who have had similar problems in their constituencies, who can make common cause. Maybe the issue can be given a higher profile through parliamentary questions or an early day motion (see page 300); or the MP may apply for one of the daily half-hour adjournment debates in the House or Westminster Hall, when there will be an opportunity to set out the case in detail and the responsible minister will have to reply. A case of maladministration may be referred to the Ombudsman (see page 351). At any of these stages, the support of the local or possibly the national media may be enlisted.

However good the constituent's case, success is not guaranteed. But, as with so many issues in parliamentary and political life, a good argument, persuasively and energetically deployed, the support of sympathisers, and above all, persistence and determination, offer the best chance of success.

Constituents' views

Constituents also write to MPs on the issues of the day. These naturally vary with the political agenda, but over the last two or three years Iraq, terrorism, embryo research, the European Union, hunting, the National Health Service, immigration, 'binge-drinking' and asylum seekers have been at or near the top of the list. In most cases, an MP's response will reflect party policy or personal views. However, the strength of popular opinion shown by the size of the postbag – provided that it consists of individually written letters and not duplicated campaign mailings – may influence both individual MPs and their parties.

Constituency profile

A new Labour MP for a Welsh valley constituency had previously been an energetic local councillor. Within weeks of being elected to Westminster, he was stopped in the street by a constituent he had known for a long time. 'We don't see much of you now', she said. He replied that he had been elected as an MP. 'Yes', she said. 'I voted for you. But we still don't see much of you'. He explained that he was very busy in the House for most of the week. 'So you're not going to be here as much as you were?' 'No', he said. 'I'm sorry, but I'm not'. 'Oh', she said. 'If I'd known that, I'd never have voted for you'.

This anecdote (not apocryphal) illustrates a tension in the life of the constituency MP. The centre of parliamentary life is Westminster, and to satisfy the requirements of the parliamentary party and the whips, to promote constituency interests and to take part in select committee work, as well as to pursue personal political priorities, that is where the MP needs to spend a good deal of time. But there is a strong gravitational pull from the constituency as well. The local MP is expected to be on the spot: to open bazaars and fairs; to speak to working men's clubs and the WI; to put in an appearance at school prize givings or road safety days; to comment knowledgeably on livestock at an agricultural show or present quality awards at the diesel engine works; to read the lesson at the civic service; to attend the Remembrance Day parade; or to draw the fund-raising raffle.

Those activities are public duty rather than party duty; but an MP must also spend time cultivating local party links and support (especially, perhaps, in the Labour Party with its mandatory reselection process; see page 24). This may involve party social events, from wine and cheese to beer and crisps, and a round of dinners and lunches (the so-called 'rubber chicken circuit') as well as reporting back on the MP's work at Westminster.

For many MPs, constituency activity fills up the rest of the week not occupied by work at Westminster. Some constituencies are within easy distance of Westminster and the distinction is less sharp, but, for most members, the Westminster week finishes on Thursdays; they travel to their constituencies that afternoon, and Friday, the weekend and Monday mornings are given over largely or even entirely to activity in the constituency; they then travel back to Westminster on Monday in time for votes in the evening.

Fighting the corner

In 2001 the Senior Salaries Review Body reported on the work of MPs in representing the constituency as a whole:

> Our interviewees [a sample of MPs] were nearly unanimous that expectations in this area had grown substantially from business, public institutions such as schools, and indeed the public generally. The Press have become much more insistent on the local MP contributing to local debate (for example through regular columns) and everyone expects them to 'fight the local corner' with Ministers and other influential players at national or European level.

Dealing effectively with constituents' problems is only half of being a 'good constituency MP'. The local member is also expected to be an advocate and ambassador for the constituency as a whole. This may involve seeing that his or her patch is not left out when EU grants or subsidies are bid for, or ensuring that ministers do not forget how the crisis in farming is hitting the constituency, or perhaps (for some Scottish MPs with distilleries) making the case against a Budget tax rise on spirits. As well as direct approaches to ministers and the media, subject debates and particularly Question Time are good opportunities for this; but there is a convention that members should not use select committee work to make the constituency case.

In the last analysis, constituents expect important constituency matters to be paramount for the MP, even if that means rebellion against the party line. For example, during the last Conservative administration the otherwise loyal Tory MPs in the south-west consistently expressed their willingness to vote against the government if they thought that their fishermen were getting a raw deal in EU Common Fisheries Policy negotiations.

The constituency comes to Westminster

The closer a constituency is to London, the more likely an MP is to see his or her electors at Westminster. This may be an individual visit to put a problem to the MP; it may be an organised party to see around the Palace of Westminster and perhaps listen to a debate; it may be a school visit as part of the Education Unit programme; or it may be tea on the Terrace for senior members of the party in the constituency and their spouses. MPs value these connections; they give constituents a chance of seeing the other side of an MP's life and understanding more about Parliament – and of course they may be a special day out that demonstrates the MP's regard for his or her constituents.

The changing role of MPs – from parliamentarians to caseworkers

Constituency work, and particularly casework on constituents' problems, has taken more and more of MPs' time over the last twenty to thirty years. But over the last five or six years it has become the determining influence upon the great majority of MPs. Although the 'golden age' of Parliament yearned after by some commentators probably never existed, it is certainly true that fewer MPs than ever before are now classic 'parliamentarians', speaking with authority on the great issues of the day or developing the expertise to challenge the government on some complex or technical subject. For most of their time, the majority are caseworkers, more interested in effective intervention in local issues, or establishing a reputation as a constituency champion. There is no right and wrong about this, of course; but the change has meant that the parliamentary opportunities afforded by the House of Commons are used less effectively than they might be. We return to this in Chapter 13.

All-party groups

Some 320 'all-party groups' bring together MPs and peers to discuss issues of common interest. These groups must consist of at least ten members of the government party and at least ten from other parties. About forty associate parliamentary groups also include people who are not members of one or other House; the most significant is the Parliamentary and Scientific Committee, which brings together MPs, peers, scientific organisations, science-based companies and universities.

In addition to these are 120 country groups, which are formed of MPs and peers who are interested in the affairs of particular countries. States such as Kazakhstan and Yemen, as well as many more familiar countries, have their own group. Most country groups receive briefing from the embassies of the countries in which they are interested, and their members are sometimes invited to visit or to receive overseas delegations to the UK. Country group members do not normally see themselves as defenders of the governments of the countries concerned but as people who know something of the politics, culture, economics and history and so are able to make some contribution to the UK's relationship with that country. Most country groups are under the auspices of the Inter-Parliamentary Union or the Commonwealth Parliamentary Association.

All three types of group meet as often as enthusiasm sustains them; they elect their own officers and (because they are often seen as potential lobbying targets and in some cases receive outside funding) they are officially – and publicly – registered. The principal groups are Westminster fixtures; others are established or disappear as the mood takes. Some have formal secretariats and planned programmes; others may simply have a social event from time to time, perhaps with a guest speaker.

The extent and variety of activity is well shown by the meetings advertised in the *All-Party Whip* (this is not about party voting requirements but is a sort of Westminster noticeboard) for the first week of December 2005. Among nearly forty group meetings during the week, the Civil Contingencies Group had a meeting to discuss the UK's plans to counter an outbreak of bird flu, and the Animal Welfare Group considered the implications of the same disease. The British-Norwegian Group held a meeting with the Speaker of the Norwegian Parliament; and the Overseas Development Group discussed agricultural policy with the Secretary of State for International Development. The Fisheries Group prepared for the annual fisheries debate in a meeting with leaders of fishermen's associations; the Beer Group looked at smoking in licensed premises in the context of the Health Bill that had just been given a second reading; while the Drug Misuse and Hepatology Groups held a joint meeting to hear a Professor of Hepatology talk about Hepatitis C. The Royal Air Force Group gave a reception for the Red Arrows aerobatic team, the Renewable and Sustainable Energy Group invited a minister to talk about biofuels for transport, and the Chile Group held a discussion with the Chilean Ambassador.

All-party and associate groups give MPs and peers the opportunity to discuss a wide range of issues, often with major players. Their work influences members, but it also provides an opportunity to focus opinion and in turn to influence ministers. The groups are also invaluable to lobby groups and lobbyists in assessing parliamentary and political opinion. In early 2006 the influence of lobbyists over all-party groups, and the funding of some groups, was highlighted in the media, with allegations that the nuclear, pharmaceutical and drinks industries among others were writing policy reports for some of them. Although all-party groups must disclose any funding they receive, the Chairman of the Committee on Standards in Public Life, Sir Alastair Graham (see page 125), called for a tightening of the rules on sponsorship.

Lobby groups and lobbyists

The word 'lobby' used in the sense of a House of Commons ante-room first appears in 1640. It later crossed the Atlantic to be applied to the geography of the US Congress. But 'to lobby', meaning to seek to exert influence on parliamentarians, and 'lobbyist', one who does so, are American coinages first appearing in 1850 and 1863 respectively. By the end of the nineteenth century, both had crossed the Atlantic the other way and became commonly used in the Westminster Parliament.

The term 'lobby group' is usually used of political pressure groups that might, for example, be campaigning for more resources to provide clean water in the Third World, or for healthier children's diets, or homeopathy – or for the ordering of new aircraft carriers or lower taxes on electric cars. 'Lobbyist' is usually used of the professional advocate whose skills in presentation, making contacts and persuasion are for hire.

Modern lobbying is mainly directed at governments, whose executive power and power of initiative make them obvious targets, and covers the whole field of government activity. Political pressure groups, charities or commercial interests may try to have particular provisions included in (or, just as often, excluded from) forthcoming legislation, or seek favourable tax treatment in a forthcoming Budget. The government is a huge contractor and purchaser (for example of defence equipment), and selling to government is a major area of lobby activity.

Single-issue politics, embracing campaigns such as those on, for example, animal rights and anti-globalisation, often with an international dimension, have become more prominent in recent years. They tend not to use traditional lobbying methods but use the Internet both to bring their supporters together and to target politicians who are seen as opponents, often running campaigns against those with slim majorities. Some organisations that have used more traditional techniques in the past are either switching to this approach or are running both methods in tandem.

Lobby groups and lobbyists are interested in MPs for two main reasons. First, if they espouse a cause they can give it a high profile through writing to ministers, parliamentary questions, early day motions or tabling of helpful amendments to legislation. Second, they can influence opinion, both outside the House through the media and, more important, with their colleagues, both back-bench and front-bench. This influence will usually be greater if their party is in government.

Effective lobbying means effective targeting, either through knowledge of an MP's interests and experience, or by exploiting the vital constituency link. Too many would-be lobbyists have an entirely unrealistic idea of how interested most MPs will be in what they have to say. In the view of the Conservative MP for North Wiltshire, who had been a director of one of the larger lobbying consultants:

Bombarding decision-makers with excess and useless information will often be counter-productive. Those people who believe that they are achieving something useful by sending their annual accounts out to MPs with a stereotyped covering letter with 'Dear James Gray' at the top (only worse is 'Dear James Gray, Esq., MP', which happens all too often) are mistaken . . . waste paper baskets round Westminster will be the only beneficiaries.

By contrast, a simple letter along the following lines will hit the mark every time: Dear Mr Gray [preferably handwritten], the widget-makers of North Wiltshire are very concerned about the effects of a forthcoming government Statutory Instrument about widget specifications, which may put 25 jobs in your constituency at risk. I know that Mr Blodgett, the managing director of Widgets to the Gentry, Bumpers Farm, Chippenham, would very much welcome the opportunity of meeting you to explain the matter and to introduce you to his workforce if you could spare an hour or so, perhaps one Friday, in the near future. *[Handwritten:]* Yours sincerely, Fred Plunket, National Association of Widget-Makers.

This description of an MP's reactions is reinforced by Paul Tyler, the former Liberal Democrat MP, who had run a public affairs consultancy:

Anything that looked like a real message from a real constituent – preferably a local postmark – got priority attention . . . Targeting from a constituency viewpoint, and timing to coincide with the parliamentary agenda, has always seemed to me to be much more likely to achieve impact than the most elaborate hospitality or printed material.

Although lobby groups and lobbyists influence MPs, they are also extremely useful to MPs – and to others – as well. James Gray again:

. . . those of us in Parliament, and no doubt in government, find truly professional lobbying very useful indeed. A shadow minister handling an obscure statutory instrument debate; a back-bencher searching for an original line in a select committee or during oral questions; a journalist looking for a new perspective on legislation; a civil servant seeking to summarise an industry or public response to a ministerial initiative – all of these and others will value a truly professional, concise and targeted exposition of a particular argument.

Good lobbying (objective, factual, well argued) provides some of the research resource that many MPs feel they lack, despite the support of their own staff and the work of the researchers in the House of Commons Library. And if it obeys the golden rules of being on an MP's particular political interest, or relating to the constituency, it is likely to be used.

Lobbyists, or parliamentary or public affairs consultancies, are used by many organisations and interests. Some simply want to have parliamentary and government activity monitored in order to have early warning of what is coming forward. Others feel they need help in making their case. A typical assignment might be to attempt to head off a policy proposal that the client believes might damage his business. The lobbyist will need to understand the proposal and its context and master the arguments against it.

Contacts between ministers, MPs, civil servants, journalists and others must then be used, or new ones developed, to get the message over. The EU dimension is increasingly important, both at the stage when a proposal is only a gleam in the eye of the European Commission and as it advances through the European Parliament. Above all, the earlier the problem is tackled, before political capital is invested and it quickly becomes much harder to get a proposal modified or dropped, the better.

One fundamental difference between lobbying in the USA and in the UK is that lobbyists in Washington are advocates for their clients; US politicians seem to prefer dealing with a 'hired gun' than directly with the client. In the UK, however, parliamentarians prefer to hear the message direct, and lobbyists prepare their clients for meetings rather than being the principal actors.

In the late 1980s and 1990s, some types of lobbying acquired a doubtful reputation, becoming associated with the parliamentary sleaze described below and appearing to be based more on lavish entertainment than strength of argument. In 1994, the Association of Professional Political Consultants was set up by a group of lobbyists who wanted to brighten the industry's rather tarnished image by promoting high ethical standards. The APPC operates a code of conduct that bans any financial relationship with politicians or advisers, and the association also publishes a register of members, including the names of consultants, and their client lists for the last six months. Other trade bodies have followed suit.

However, no survey of the influences on MPs would be complete without an examination of the ways in which possible financial influence is regulated and policed.

Members' interests and parliamentary standards

Although individual MPs may not have executive power, they do have influence through the ability to bring subjects to public notice; to raise the profile of particular issues through parliamentary questions (see Chapter 10) or early day motions (see page 300); or to press their cause in debate. All these processes can move matters up the political agenda or persuade the government of the day to take action.

It is clearly of the first importance for public confidence in Parliament that MPs act in the national and constituency interest rather than with the expectation of private gain. This has not always been so; the seventeenth- and eighteenth-century approach seems to have been rather more relaxed, although when Sir John Trevor as Speaker received the then colossal bribe of £1,100 from the Common Council of London for helping to get a bill passed, the House expelled him in short order. The fact that he remained Master of the Rolls for the next twenty-two years may say something about the judicial standards of the day.

The Victorian House of Commons recognised the importance of MPs' advocacy in the House being divorced from private gain and in 1858 resolved that: 'It is contrary to the usage and derogatory to the dignity of this House that any of its Members should bring forward, promote or advocate in this House any proceeding or measure in which he may have acted or been concerned for or in consideration of any pecuniary fee or reward'. This was aimed especially at MPs who were practising barristers, but it was reinforced in 1947 by a further resolution forbidding contractual arrangements under which, for any benefit, a member promoted any point of view on behalf of an outside interest. In 1974, the House agreed that MPs should be required to declare any financial interest that they might have in matters being debated or otherwise before the House or its committees, and that they should register their financial interests. A Select Committee on Members' Interests was established to supervise this process.

Parliamentary sleaze

In the late 1980s and early 1990s there was a steady growth in professional lobbying firms on the US model, many with multi-million- or multi-billion-pound businesses as clients. They saw parliamentary influence as a valuable commodity, and by 1995 more than a quarter of MPs had paid consultancies with lobbyists (26) or with other bodies outside the House (142).

Whether or not this was against the public interest, public unease was greatly increased by some high-profile incidents: the 'cash for questions' affair, in which *Sunday Times* journalists approached twenty MPs offering £1,000 for simply tabling parliamentary questions (which was accepted by two of them); and the allegations by the businessman and owner of Harrods, Mohamed al-Fayed, that he had rewarded MPs for lobbying on his behalf.

The Committee on Standards in Public Life

At the same time there was a growing public suspicion – both reflected in and to an extent fuelled by a high media profile – of the uses that certain individuals made of their position or wealth. Donations to political parties to buy influence, newly retired or resigned ministers and senior civil servants obtaining lucrative directorships, important public appointments being made on the basis of personal connections rather than merit – however widespread (or not) this might have been, the important thing was that it was widely believed. Finding his government dogged by such allegations, Prime Minister John Major set up the Committee on Standards in Public Life in October 1994.

The committee has ten members; it has no parliamentary character (although three peers are members) but is appointed by the Prime Minister and reports to him. It has taken on the title of each of its chairmen: first, 'the Nolan Committee' (Lord Nolan, a Lord of Appeal), then 'the Neill Committee' (Lord Neill of Bladen, a QC and academic), 'the Wicks Committee' (Sir Nigel Wicks, a retired civil servant) and, most recently, 'the Graham Committee' (Sir Alastair Graham, a former trade unionist and former chairman of the Police Complaints Authority and Northern Ireland Parades Commission).

Following the first report of the Nolan Committee in 1995, the House of Commons set up a Select Committee on Standards in Public Life to consider the Nolan findings and to recommend how they should be reflected in the rules of the House. The main changes made in 1995 were:

♦ *the appointment of a Parliamentary Commissioner for Standards;*
♦ *the setting up of a new Committee on Standards and Privileges to replace the separate Committees on Privileges and on Members' Interests; and*
♦ *the drawing up of a code of conduct for MPs.*

Members' interests: the current arrangements

Registration of interests

The purpose of the Register of Members' Interests is 'to provide information of any pecuniary interest which a Member receives *which might reasonably be thought by others* to influence his or her actions, speeches or votes in Parliament, or actions taken in his or her capacity as a Member of Parliament'. New MPs must submit a registration form to the Parliamentary Commissioner for Standards within three months of their election; thereafter, they are responsible for reporting any change in their circumstances within four weeks of it occurring.

The main categories of interests that have to be registered are paid directorships; paid employment, including practising in a profession or being a member of Lloyd's; clients and consultancies, including those arising out of being an MP (and any agreement to provide services must also be deposited with the Parliamentary Commissioner for Standards); sponsorships for fighting an election or supporting an MP's work once elected; gifts and hospitality; overseas visits as an MP that are not paid for wholly out of public funds; land and property; and shareholdings.

Various thresholds are used, mostly by reference to the level of the current parliamentary salary. Generally, an interest worth less than 1 per cent of the current salary (so, at present, less than £600) does not have to be registered. (This comes in for some criticism at county and parish council level, where the threshold is £25.) A shareholding must be registered if it is more than 15 per cent of issued share capital, or if it is worth more than the current parliamentary salary). For land and property, the threshold for registration of income is 10 per cent of salary, and for value, 100 per cent of salary. Sponsorships must be registered if they amount to £1,000 or more from a single source.

The Register of Members' Interests is published soon after the beginning of each parliament, and annually thereafter; in between, a version is kept up to date as changes occur. Both are available at www.parliament.uk.

There are also registers of the interests of MPs' staff (to make transparent a situation where an individual may be working part time for an MP and part time for a pressure group or commercial organisation); for parliamentary journalists; and for all-party groups. These too are available on the parliamentary website.

Declaration of interests

An MP must disclose a financial interest when speaking in a debate, in a way sufficiently informative to allow a listener to understand the nature of the interest, although it is up to the member whether he or she draws attention to a registered interest or explains it in more detail. Interests must also be declared when tabling parliamentary questions, when tabling early day motions or amendments to bills (or adding names to them), and when introducing private members' bills. When an interest is declared, the symbol [R] appears on the Order Paper beside the name of the member concerned.

An MP must also declare if he or she has a reasonable *expectation* of future financial advantage – for example, an MP whose family business made industrial cleaning equipment would be expected to declare an interest when speaking on a bill that would set up an inspectorate to monitor standards of cleanliness in schools and hospitals.

In select committees, all the members declare their registrable interests before electing a chairman, on the grounds that this aspect of an MP's independence is a factor in his or her suitability for the chair. Thereafter, members of a select committee must declare any relevant interest, or even withdraw from an inquiry completely if there is a conflict of interest.

Voting

The classic rule was stated from the Chair almost two centuries ago, when Speaker Abbott ruled that 'no Member who has a pecuniary interest in a question shall be allowed to vote upon it'. In modern times this is interpreted as a *direct* financial interest, and in the context that an MP's interests have been declared. To take two examples: in 1983 the Speaker ruled that MPs who were solicitors might vote on a bill that removed their exclusive rights on conveyancing, as the bill was a matter of public policy; however, in 1981 MPs who were also members of Lloyd's were advised not to vote on a bill to regulate the Lloyd's insurance market.

Lobbying for reward

This rule, based on the 1858 and 1947 resolutions referred to above and borrowing some of their language, takes the declaration of interests several steps further. It outlaws paid advocacy – that is, doing anything in the House (speaking, voting, tabling amendments or urging other MPs to do so, or approaching ministers or civil servants) directly for payment. In practice, this means that an MP who is a director of a company, or a paid adviser for an organisation, may not try to get any preferential treatment for that company or organisation (for example in tax relief, subsidies or some special treatment or opportunity) in any use of his or her functions as an MP.

The Ministerial Code

MPs (and peers) who are ministers are also covered by the Ministerial Code laid down by successive Prime Ministers with the aim of ensuring that there is no actual or apparent conflict between their private interests and their public duties as ministers. The Code became more contentious with a series of high profile cases (notably David Blunkett's second resignation from the Cabinet in November 2005 following allegations of a conflict of interest, and the financial dealings of Tessa Jowell's husband). It was increasingly argued that policing the Code should be a matter not for the Prime Minister but for an independent figure. In March 2006 the Prime Minister appointed Sir John Bourn, the Comptroller and Auditor General, as an independent *adviser* on the Code; but it remains for the Prime Minister to judge whether a minister has breached the Code.

The Parliamentary Commissioner for Standards

From 2002 the Commissioner has been Sir Philip Mawer, formerly Secretary-General of the General Synod of the Church of England. His main responsibilities are maintaining the Registers of Interests; advising MPs (especially new MPs) about the rules; monitoring the operation of the code of conduct; and investigating complaints against members.

When a complaint is made that an MP has broken the rules, the Commissioner decides whether there is enough evidence to justify a preliminary inquiry; if so, he investigates further and decides whether a full investigation is warranted. If he judges that it is, he interviews those involved and reports to the Committee on Standards and Privileges. The committee may make further inquiries and report to the House with its recommendations, which may include suspension from the House (with loss of pay) or loss of pay without suspension. It is for the House itself to decide what penalty should be imposed.

Concerns about parliamentary sleaze in the early 1990s should not be underestimated; but, as so often when urgent political solutions are sought in the glare of publicity, what resulted was a set of complex and rather legalistic rules (the Code of Conduct and the Guide occupy some 40 pages), some of which had unexpected results. For example, in its original form the advocacy rule meant that, if an MP had been invited to visit, say, Brazil at the expense of the Brazilian government (as the British government has for years invited foreign politicians on study visits so that they may better understand the UK and its concerns) he or she could not have initiated a debate on UK relations with Brazil for a year thereafter, despite the fact that the MP concerned might have been much better informed than other speakers in the debate. That rule has now been relaxed, but the rules on interests remain detailed and more complex – and more restrictive – than in many parliaments.

Standards now

There has been a sea-change since the assumptions of 'MPs for hire' of the early 1990s, when the offenders were in any event a very small minority. This is probably as much to do with changed attitudes three parliaments on as with tough rules properly enforced. In the 2001 Parliament, the Committee on Standards in Public Life concluded '. . . standards in the House of Commons are generally high, and the overwhelming majority of members seek to, and in practice do, uphold high standards of propriety'. The previously frequent tit-for-tat complaints, party against party, have virtually disappeared, and the emphasis is now on 'education and prevention'. In addition, the 'rectification procedure' has introduced a much simpler way of disposing of cases of admitted failure to register or declare interests where the interest involved is minor, or the failure to register or declare is inadvertent.

No system will satisfy everyone. There are those who believe that all MPs should be full time; others believe equally strongly that current outside experience makes an MP more knowledgeable and effective. But if outside interests are to be allowed, then public disclosure of those interests, allied to rigorous investigation of complaints and effective sanctions when the rules are broken, is the right way to build public confidence.

Influences on the House of Lords

Lords and Commons

Members of the House of Lords are subject to much the same influences as MPs, except that they do not have constituencies. Perhaps the chief influence – constraint even – on the House of Lords is its unequal position in Parliament vis-à-vis the House of Commons. The limitations on Lords' powers to reject or amend bills are fully described in Chapter 7, but it is important to grasp at this stage that the Lords, by not being elected and therefore being unrepresentative, are put at considerable disadvantage in terms of power compared with the Commons. If the Lords always attempted to insist on its will against that of the elected House, especially if the Commons were giving effect to policies endorsed by the electorate as part of the election manifesto of the governing party, there would be a constitutional showdown between the two Houses that would almost certainly result in further diminution of the Lords' powers. Because of this, the Lords tacitly recognises the right of the government to govern and of the House of Commons to see its will prevail most of the time. They willingly sacrifice their power in the same sort of compromise as that involved in the supremacy of the government in the House of Commons.

The introduction of an elected element into the House under any proposal for further reform of composition of the House (see page 433) would be bound to lead to a readjustment of these assumptions – assumptions that have held good since the House of Commons became a truly representative chamber following the extension of the franchise in the nineteenth and early twentieth centuries. That said, the House of Lords is also subject to government, party, personal and external pressures just like the House of Commons, although these influences are perhaps less obtrusive in the Lords.

Government

The position of the government in the Lords is not as well entrenched as in the Commons. Following a general election the party with the majority of seats in the House of Commons forms the government, and it is this party that occupies the government benches in the Lords too. The government front bench in the Lords currently consists of two Cabinet ministers and twenty other ministers, from junior whips to ministers of state. Thus the government presence is, relatively speaking, much smaller in the Lords than in the Commons, and promise of ministerial office is accordingly much less influential. The government's influence over its own back-benchers and over other members of the House is, in the absence of a large 'payroll' membership, that much weaker. And party discipline – including that of the government party – is weaker because peers do not have to submit themselves to the rigours of selection by the constituency parties.

However, there is an understanding that the government can expect to get its business through. As we will see on page 246, under the 'Salisbury convention' the Lords will not reject at second reading legislation relating to commitments contained in an election manifesto. But a more general understanding on business is indispensable for the proper functioning of the House, as there are no procedural devices for curtailing debate on legislation; nor do the Lords' standing orders give government business precedence over other business. In the House of Commons, we have seen that a high proportion of sitting time is reserved for government business. In the Lords, anything up to 60 per cent of sitting time can be occupied with government business, but none of it is formally reserved for government use. In the last resort, a government might try to suspend standing orders in order to give its own business precedence, but fortunately this is rarely necessary. Provided that the government business managers respect the conventions of the House, consult the opposition through the usual channels and do their best to accommodate the demands of the private member, the other parties and private members alike are content to leave the arrangement of business to the government Chief Whip. Governments are able to get their business through because they make sure that they are seen to deal fairly with the other parties and interests in the House.

The political parties

Although the members of the House are not elected, many of them – but by no means all – belong to political parties. A breakdown appears on page 39. Because lords are not elected, it is important to remember that the political composition does not change after a general election.

Officially, the House scarcely recognises the existence of the political parties. They are nowhere referred to in standing orders, and they are barely mentioned in the *Companion to Standing Orders*, the House's own procedural handbook. But the reality is very different. Each party has its leader and its whips and a small secretariat. We have already seen how opposition parties and the Convenor of the Cross Bench Peers receive public funding (the so-called 'Cranborne money') to assist them in their activities. The government party has the advantage of an office manned by civil servants to organise its affairs. Committees of the House tend to reflect the composition of the House, as in the House of Commons, and the government party negotiates through the whips' offices of the other parties (the usual channels) and, where appropriate, with the Convenor nominated by the cross-benches in the arrangement of business.

As in the Commons, the party whips send their members statements of forthcoming business in the House, with items underlined to indicate their importance to the party leadership. But discipline is not as strong as in the House of Commons, and there is no pairing system. There are weekly party meetings – every Wednesday afternoon – at which future business is discussed and there is, even in the Lords, a general predisposition to toe the party line. However, for many members of the House, their political careers are not their principal interest, and the allure of office carries less weight. So there is often some cross-voting. And the cross-benchers – who profess no party line – are all, theoretically, floating voters.

The leader of the government party in the Lords is the Leader of the House, who, together with the government Chief Whip, advises ministerial colleagues on any problems that might be encountered in getting their business through the House.

Personal interests

The composition of the House guarantees great diversity of interest. The non-political element provides a lay presence. Then there are the politicians – either those elected hereditary peers who have taken up political careers based in the Lords or those created peers who have formerly been MPs or prominent in local government. Finally there are those, mainly but not exclusively life peers, who are experts in their field. Very often they are retired or approaching retirement, but their expertise still places them at an advantage where detailed scrutiny of policy is required – in debates on funding of scientific research or in scrutiny in committee of some abstruse piece of EU agricultural legislation, for example. The diversity of the members of the House ensures that personal interest and influences are very strong in the Lords.

And, of course, many have business interests. A survey conducted in 1996 (before the passage of the House of Lords Act 1999) by Pensions Investment Research Consultants found that 134 peers were directors of eighty-eight companies. Some were directors of companies formed to manage family assets, but many were successful business people who had been ennobled in recognition of their achievements or had been appointed for the useful contacts they brought or the status they gave. Two sectors, banking and transport, had a particularly high proportion of 'lords on the board'.

Registration of interests

It is a long-standing custom of the House that lords speak always on their personal honour but, unlike the Commons, there was for many years no registration of members' interests in the Lords. In November 1995, however, following a study by a sub-committee of the Procedure Committee chaired by Lord Griffiths, a former Lord of Appeal in Ordinary, the House clarified its rules governing members' interests and resolved that lords should never accept any financial inducement as an incentive or reward for exercising parliamentary influence.

A simple but rigorous set of rules was put in place with voluntary registration of interests. Failure to register consultancies or interests in lobbying firms could be investigated by the Committtee for Privileges. Following a review of these arrangements by the Committee on Standards in Public Life, a system of compulsory registration of interests and a code of conduct came into force on 1 April 2002.

The code reminds members of their public duty under their oath or affirmation of allegiance and that they should observe the seven general principles identified by the Committee on Standards in Public Life (the 'Nolan Principles': selflessness, integrity, objectivity, accountability, openness, honesty and leadership). Members must comply with the code, must act on their personal honour, must never accept financial inducement for exercising parliamentary influence and must not vote or ask questions or promote any matter in return for money or other benefit (the 'no paid advocacy' rule). And they must register all relevant interests, that is to say interests which might reasonably be thought by the public to affect the way in which a member discharges his or her parliamentary duties. When they speak or otherwise act in a parliamentary capacity they must declare any interest relevant to the subject matter in hand. Those interests may be financial, such as paid consultancies, or involvement in the lobbying business, or regular employment, or shareholdings, or receipt of any payment or service: or they can be non-financial, such as membership of or the holding of office in organisations or institutions, trusteeships and so on.

Allegations of non-compliance may ultimately be determined by the Subcommittee on Lords' Interests of the Committee for Privileges. If an allegation is proved, the member complained against can appeal to the Privileges Committee itself. The reports of both committees are made to the House. Under these arrangements, the House of Lords, unlike the House of Commons, has no power to suspend its members. The whole process of investigation and the publicity that surrounds it are thought to be sufficient sanction.

In a House which is essentially unpaid and to that extent is sometimes described as 'amateur', the personal connections and outside activities of individual members provide the House with a valuable source of talent and expertise. On the whole, this was not diminished by the 1995 registration scheme and only slightly diminished by the more demanding 2002 code.

Territorial

Members of the House of Lords have no constituencies: they are not representatives. As Lord Birkenhead once remarked of a member of the House who had incurred his ire, 'The noble Lord represents no one but himself and I don't think much of his constituency'. It follows therefore that they do not have 'surgeries' or make representations to government or other authorities in respect of individuals' problems or grievances. Nor are they answerable to local party organisations or selection committees.

However, sometimes members of the House will be approached by interests in the locality in which they live or whose title they bear by reason of some long – and sometimes extinct – association, asking them to take up a particular stance on a public matter. Members are undoubtedly responsive to such approaches.

Lobby groups

As we examine in detail later on, all legislation has to be considered in the Lords as well as in the Commons, and some legislation begins its passage through Parliament in the House of Lords. Members of the House therefore find themselves courted in much the same way as members of the House of Commons by lobby groups either directly or through parliamentary consultants. The dramatic increase in lobbying since the end of the 1970s has been a conspicuous feature of the revival in the House of Lords' influence in recent years – part cause and part effect. Some lobbyists are skilful and selective in their targets. Others resort to an indiscriminate 'mail-drop'. These organisations will prepare evidence for committees, draft amendments to be moved to bills and provide briefing notes, offer to take peers on visits, or arrange lectures at which their policies are expounded. Thus over forty groups, for example, lobbied peers during the passage of the Criminal Justice and Public Order Bill in 1994, from the National Gypsy Council to the Prison Reform Trust and Save the Children. More recently, over thirty organisations lobbied members on the Communications Bill in 2003. Of these, one organisation was a consortium of twelve well-known charities, and another represented over a thousand businesses active in IT, telecommunications and electronics.

As a result of these contacts, some peers form potentially close associations with, for example, local authority organisations, industry groups, bankers, major exporters or libertarian groups. These contacts not only influence members of the House but also help to provide briefing and a wide range of assistance to what is essentially still a part-time – even amateur – Chamber of the legislature.

Like MPs, peers also belong to the all-party and registered special interest and country groups (see page 120).

The independence of the Lords

Despite party and other influences, members of the House of Lords are rather more unpredictable in their allegiances and voting than MPs. This manifested itself strongly under the successive Conservative administrations between 1979 and 1997 and continues to do so under the subsequent Labour administration, with marked consequences for legislation, as we shall see in Chapter 7.

The parliamentary day and the organisation of business

The parliamentary calendar

Before we look at the various items of business that make up a typical day in Parliament, and how members of both Houses are likely to spend their time, it is worth looking more broadly at the parliamentary calendar and the cycle of business in each House.

A parliament

In Chapter 2, we encountered the main division of parliamentary time: *a parliament*. This is the period between one general election and the next. Under the Septennial Act of 1715, the maximum life of a parliament was set at seven years. This was reduced to five years by the Parliament Act of 1911, although during the First and Second World Wars, to avoid a war-time general election, the life of the 1911 parliament was extended to eight years; that of the 1935 parliament was extended to ten years. Although the maximum life of a parliament – that is, the period between the day of first meeting and dissolution – is five years, few parliaments run their course, because the Prime Minister of the day seeks a dissolution at a time that he or she sees as giving the best electoral advantage. The average length of parliaments since 1945 has been a little over three years seven months, and four years or so is the modern norm. Parliaments are numbered; the 2005 parliament is the fifty-fourth parliament of the United Kingdom since the Union with Ireland in 1801.

The beginning of a parliament

Some events always happen at the start of a parliament. Both Houses assemble on the day specified in the Sovereign's proclamation dissolving the previous parliament. The Commons go to the House of Lords, where they are directed to elect a Speaker (see page 46). Having gone back to their own House and done so, the Commons return to the Lords the next day, where the Queen's approbation of the Speaker-Elect is signified. (These ancient usages reflect a mediaeval relationship with the Sovereign; but should it ever happen that the Commons were unwilling to go to the Lords on either occasion, it would be difficult to imagine that their choice of a Speaker could be challenged as being somehow illegal or ineffective.)

The Commons then return to their own Chamber, and the new Speaker takes the oath of allegiance, standing on the upper step of the Speaker's Chair and holding a New Testament: 'I swear by Almighty God that I will be faithful and bear true allegiance to Her Majesty Queen Elizabeth, her heirs and successors, according to law. So help me God'. Other MPs then take the oath, starting with the Prime Minister and the Cabinet, and the shadow Cabinet, then Privy Counsellors (usually former Cabinet and other senior ministers), then other back-benchers. The order of taking the oath is of significance only when the longest-serving MPs were elected in the same year; if their seniority is equal, the Father of the House (there has not yet been a Mother of the House) is the member who takes the oath first.

MPs queue up before the Table; the oath is administered by the Principal Clerk of the Table Office; under the supervision of the Clerk Assistant each MP then signs the 'test roll', a bound parchment book, and is then formally introduced to the Speaker by the Clerk of the House. The swearing in of members goes on for three or four hours that day and then continues on the next three or four days.

Jews may swear on the Old Testament, and Muslims on the Qur'ān; and an MP who does not wish to take the oath may instead make a solemn affirmation. The oath or affirmation must be taken in English, but the Speaker has allowed it to be said additionally in Welsh, Scots Gaelic or Cornish. An MP must take the oath or affirm before sitting, speaking or voting in the House (except for the election of a Speaker); and if by chance he or she does not, the penalty is severe: the seat is vacated and there must be a by-election.

Most MPs take the oath or affirm in these first days of a new parliament, but those remaining may do so in the days following the first Queen's Speech of the new parliament (and occasionally much later if prevented by illness). When the 'swearing days' are completed, the House adjourns to the day of the State Opening, which takes place at the start of a new parliament and also at the start of each of the sessions of that parliament.

Similarly, the Lords sit for oaths and affirmations and then adjourn until the State Opening.

A session

This is the period that begins with the State Opening of Parliament and the Queen's Speech outlining the government's plans for legislation during the remainder of the session. It ends with prorogation (see below), or with a dissolution (see page 25) if it is the last session of a parliament. The timing of general elections often means that the final session of a parliament is a short one.

A session normally lasts from a State Opening in the first or second week in November until prorogation a year or so later, and it is denoted by both years (thus the '2005–06 session'). When a general election takes place in the spring or summer (as has been the case since 1979), the first session of a parliament is usually a long session lasting until the November of the following year. This is convenient for a new government as it provides a long first legislative period.

The State Opening

A session begins with colourful ceremony as the Queen drives in procession to Westminster with an escort of Household Cavalry, normally arriving at about 11.30 a.m. The processional route is lined with troops and thronged with tourists; bands play; the police even wear white gloves. The Queen arrives under the Victoria Tower at the south end of the Palace of Westminster and proceeds to the Robing Room, where she puts on the Imperial State Crown and then moves in procession to the House of Lords, which is a bright theatre of peers' scarlet and ermine, judges' robes and wigs, and ambassadors and high commissioners in evening dress and decorations.

Black Rod ('the Gentleman Usher of the Black Rod') is directed to summon the Commons. In a symbolic reminder of the right of the Commons to exclude any royal messenger, the doors leading to the Chamber are closed in his face; he knocks, is admitted and delivers the summons. Led by the Speaker and Black Rod, and followed by the Clerk of the House, Prime Minister and Leader of the Opposition, and members of the Cabinet and shadow Cabinet, MPs walk the hundred metres or so to the House of Lords, where they crowd behind the Bar of the House (the formal boundary of the Chamber) to hear the Queen's Speech.

The Queen's Speech

The Queen's Speech is the parliamentary core of this state ceremony. The speech is drafted by the government and will have been approved by the Cabinet. It normally refers to any recent or forthcoming royal events or state visits, and it contains some very broad policy intentions; the 2005 speech began: 'My Government will continue to pursue economic policies which entrench stability and promote long-term growth and prosperity'. A sentence in the speech tells the Commons (because they, rather than the Lords, have financial authority) that estimates for financing the public services will be laid before them.

The meat of the speech is the legislative agenda for the coming session: the 2005 speech foreshadowed 29 bills and draft bills. Bills are usually described in very broad terms; in 2005, for example, Parliament was told that 'A Bill will be introduced to give police and local communities new powers to tackle knives, guns and alcohol-related violence'. Bills do not have to be in the Queen's Speech to be introduced, but the speech outlines the main legislative activity for the year ahead.

When the Commons return to their Chamber the sitting is suspended until 2.30 p.m., when the Speaker makes a statement welcoming new MPs and encouraging them to learn about the House, reminding all MPs about standards of conduct and behaviour, and in 2005 concluding with a reminder of the importance of security. The House then passes an Order directing the Commissioner of the Metropolitan Police to allow free access for MPs to the House and around the parliamentary estate. The House also gives a formal first reading to the Outlawries Bill 'for the more effectual preventing of clandestine outlawries', whose purpose belongs to the distant past but which is a symbol of the right of the House to proceed with its own business before considering what the Sovereign has just told Parliament. Thereafter Deputy Speakers are normally appointed.

The Lords sit at 3.30 p.m., when certain sessional orders, including that to prevent 'stoppages in the streets', are passed; some office-holders such as the Chairman of Committees are appointed; and a pro forma bill (in the Lords it is the Select Vestries Bill) is read a first time.

Debate on the Queen's Speech
This is the first debate of the session, normally lasting four or five days. The debate is formally on a motion to present 'an Humble Address' to the

Queen thanking her for the 'most Gracious Speech' addressed to both Houses, but it is in practice a review of the government's policies and intentions. The debate is opened by a mover and a seconder from the government back benches (the only occasion on which a motion in the House of Commons is seconded). It is something of an honour to be selected (by the whips) to make these first two speeches. The MPs concerned (usually one new and one long-serving) are expected not to be contentious but to be reminiscent and witty and to extol the virtues of their constituencies.

Then the business gets more seriously under way. The Leader of the Opposition speaks next, with the disadvantage that he gets no advance text of the Queen's Speech and has only a couple of hours to decide on much of what he will say. Then the Prime Minister makes what is in effect the keynote speech, outlining the government's plans and programme and going into much more detail than in the Queen's Speech itself. The leader of the Liberal Democrats follows, and then the debate is open to MPs generally. The first day is a general debate, when any aspect may be raised; the subsequent debates are themed as agreed through the usual channels, perhaps on home affairs, foreign affairs and defence, health, and the economy, and are opened and closed by the relevant ministers or shadow ministers. On the last two days amendments in the name of the Leader of the Opposition are moved and voted upon, usually regretting the fact that the Gracious Speech contains no plans to legislate to do this or that. When the government has a comfortable majority the outcome is not in doubt; but were there to be a minority government or a shaky coalition, these votes, and that on the substantive motion at the very end of proceedings, would be the first test of whether the Prime Minister of the day could command a majority in the House. On the last day, a further amendment may be voted upon; this is usually in the name of the Liberal Democrats, and it provides an opportunity to have a formal vote on the key policy priorities of that party.

In the Lords, the motion for 'an Humble Address' in reply to the Queen's Speech is moved and seconded from the government back benches, but the debate proper is then adjourned and takes place over the subsequent five days. As with the Commons debate, each day has a theme, but unlike the Commons no vote is taken at the end.

The pattern of the session

The reference points in any parliamentary session are a combination of the sacred and the secular: the State Opening, Christmas, Easter, Whitsun, the summer adjournment, the 'spillover' and prorogation.

Early business in a session usually includes a government motion to fix the thirteen Fridays on which private members' bills will be taken (seven for second readings and six for 'remaining stages'; see page 228) and the non-sitting or 'constituency' Fridays for the rest of that session. In the first few days of a new session the first two or three of the major government bills foreshadowed in the Queen's Speech will be introduced (at that stage they will be given a purely formal first reading, with second reading debates on the principle of each bill following ten or so days later).

Second readings of government bills starting in the Commons (others will be beginning their parliamentary journey at the other end of the building in the House of Lords) are a feature of business in the Chamber up to Christmas and again after the House returns in January, usually almost to Easter. Also before Christmas, the Commons will normally approve the *Vote on Account* for the current financial year and the *Winter Supplementary Estimates* on the first *Estimates day* (see page 277).

After their second reading in the Chamber, the *government bills will go into standing committees* (see page 211) and from Christmas onwards, standing committee activity builds up. At its peak, six or seven standing committees may be sitting for much of Tuesdays and Thursdays, occupying 100 to 150 MPs altogether, with big bills taking several weeks in committee, and each being the main focus of activity for the ministers responsible for each bill and for the shadow ministers opposing them. As the bills complete their committee stages they return to the House for *report stages*, and in the period up to Easter and beyond this starts to take up time on the floor of the House. Government legislation will usually be contentious between the parties and so will require the presence of MPs to vote even if they are not directly involved in the business.

Most *second readings of private members' bills* will normally be taken between Christmas and Easter, but many will fall by the wayside. Around Easter the successful (up to then!) private members' bills will be coming through their standing committee stages and queuing up for the *six remaining stages days* in the summer. An MP's presence on a private members' bill Friday is less likely to be required by the whips (with the exception of the payroll vote of ministers and PPSs), so unless the MP has agreed to support a colleague's bill (or wants to obstruct or kill a bill) these may be days when the MP can work in the constituency.

Before Easter, the House approves the remaining *Supplementary Estimates* for the current financial year and any *Excess Votes* for the previous financial year (see page 279). A key event before Easter (it took place in the autumn from 1993 to 1997) is the *Budget*, usually in March or early April, followed by four days' debate on the Chancellor of the Exchequer's proposals.

From early spring onwards, *bills that started in the Lords begin coming down to the Commons* and going through all the same stages as those bills that originated in the Commons. The Commons rises in late July, and then has an unbroken summer recess until the first or second week in October. In 2003 and 2004 the House sat for two weeks in September; but this innovation had a mixed reception and may not be repeated.

At a fairly late stage in the session, the two Houses consider the amendments each has made to bills that started in the other House: *Commons amendments* and *Lords amendments*. If amendments made by one House are not accepted by the other (most often this arises because the government wishes to reverse a defeat it has suffered in the Lords) a passage of 'ping-pong' between the two Houses may ensue, with alternative amendments being offered in an effort to get agreement before the bill is killed by the end of the session.

The *spillover* of two or three weeks in the second half of October and early November is usually a hectic and often unpredictable period of tidying up the to and fro of bills between the two Houses, often with other business being inserted as a makeweight while waiting for one House or the other to complete proceedings on this or that bill.

We have described the pattern of the session largely in terms of legislation and financial business, but a great deal else is going on. Time must be found for the twenty *opposition days*, each of which is a full day's debate on a subject on which the opposition feels the government may be vulnerable; the second and third *Estimates days*, on which select committee reports linked to particular Estimates are debated; time may need to be found for private bills; and there will also be a number of debates on general subjects, from the hardy perennial of the Welsh affairs debate on or near St David's Day to general debates, often 'on the adjournment' (in other words, not with a substantive motion before the House) on subjects in which there is general parliamentary interest: perhaps defence, the introduction of broadband technology, manufacturing industry or European Union affairs. And every day except Friday there is the framework of Question Time, ministerial statements, and the half-hour adjournment debate at the end of each day's proceedings, as well as debates in Westminster Hall on Tuesdays, Wednesdays and Thursdays (see page 296).

Business in the Lords follows a slightly different cycle. Although the business managers make every effort to introduce a certain number of bills in that House to occupy it in the early part of the session, most bills start in the Commons and arrive in the Lords after Easter. This makes for longer sitting hours and more sitting days in the latter part of the session. Thus the

Lords often sit later in July than the Commons and start their spillover one or two weeks earlier. Unlike the Commons, the Lords have no fixed points in the calendar for consideration of financial matters, except for their formal consideration of the Finance Bill in July.

Prorogation

This is the formal end of a session. It is a 'prerogative act' of the Crown, another survival of the early relationship between sovereign and Parliament (and used on occasion by monarchs to curb an inconvenient House of Commons). In modern times such royal powers are exercised by the government of the day, so it is the government that decides the length of the parliamentary session. There is no formal requirement for an annual October–November session (and the first session of a parliament in recent years has been one of eighteen months or so), but the constitutional convention of an annual session is a strong one.

The timing of prorogation is often settled in the last few days of the session; the government business managers want to be sure that they have left enough time to get the last bills through, which may involve a degree of brinkmanship in achieving agreement between the two Houses.

At prorogation, the House of Commons goes up to the House of Lords just as at the State Opening, although in rather fewer numbers; but on this occasion the Queen will not be there. The Queen's Speech – a retrospective of the session – and the proclamation proroguing Parliament and setting the date for the State Opening will be read out by one of the five peers who form the Royal Commission to do this on the Queen's behalf. Parliament may also be prorogued by proclamation when both Houses are adjourned. During the period of prorogation neither House, nor any committee, may meet.

Clearing the decks

A prorogation brings to an end almost all parliamentary business (which is why the business managers are so keen to secure the passage of government bills before the end of the session). There are a few exceptions: private bills (see page 249) and hybrid bills (see page 252) may be carried over from one session to the next; and in 1998 the House agreed to a procedure whereby public bills may also be carried over. Up to the 2005 dissolution, this had been used for only five bills in seven years. In some ways it is surprising that the procedure has not been used more often for government bills. Although in some ways it is convenient for the business managers, it can also allow longer scrutiny of legislation – the pressure of time is both a bone of contention between government and opposition and a source of criticism of the quality of legislation. It could also smooth the legislative programme by allowing major bills to be introduced later in the session.

This 'sudden death' at the end of the session is practised by relatively few parliaments and may have disadvantages in the case of legislation; but it also acts as a clear-out of the parliamentary agenda and imposes some discipline on the legislative process. Early day motions (of which there may be more than two thousand by the end of the session) lapse, and private members' bills die – both those that are clearly going to make no progress however much time might be available and those that their backers feel might have had a chance 'if only'.

Adjournments

The standing orders prescribe when the House of Commons sits, both in terms of time and days of the week, so when the House finishes its sitting ('adjourns') on any day, it will automatically meet on the next sitting day. Longer times of adjournment, commonly called recesses – although strictly speaking this word applies only to the time during prorogation – are discussed through the usual channels and decided by the House on the basis of a motion moved by the Leader of the House.

The normal pattern of recesses and sitting periods (sometimes called 'terms') is:

November   State Opening

December

              Christmas adjournment: about two weeks

January

February   A 'constituency week' coinciding with school half-term

March

              Easter adjournment: one or two weeks

April

May

              Whitsun adjournment: one or two weeks

June

July   House rises in the second half of July (summer adjournment)

August

September

October   House returns in the first or second week for the 'spillover'
                Prorogation in late October or early November

November

It should be clear from the earlier account of constituency pressures that recesses are not MPs' holidays. Constituents do not stop writing because the House of Commons is not sitting, and many MPs will do more surgery work, and certainly more constituency engagements, than during a sitting week. But every year when the House rises in July, the media remorselessly report that 'MPs are off on *x* weeks summer holiday'.

Sittings of the Lords follow the same pattern but with some small variations; for example, the Lords do not always have a February break. Although in 2005 they rose in July at the same time as the Commons, congestion of business has often resulted in their continuing to sit a week or two longer. And in October the Lords invariably start their spillover a week or two before the Commons.

The annual calendar

Although the pattern of sitting times has always been broadly predictable to within a week or two, exact dates used not to be announced until a short time before each recess. In October 2002, following a recommendation of the Modernisation Committee, a parliamentary calendar for the next twelve months (something that has long been routine in many parliaments) was introduced. This has proved extremely useful, allowing those who deal with Parliament as well as those in it to make long-term plans. There is a tension between announcing sitting times a long way ahead and the wish of business managers to retain flexibility; and any change (as for example when the Easter 2003 recess was changed to allow for the Budget debate) may lead to criticism.

The annual calendar is a prediction of *likely* sitting and recess dates. Some suggestions for reform have gone further, with proposals for a fixed parliamentary year (so that, for example, the summer adjournment would always begin on the third Thursday in July), and the other non-sitting periods would be fixed in the same way. This, it is argued, would mean that the government would have to make concessions to get its business through without running out of time and could not use the threat of sitting into late July or even August. However, if such a fixed calendar were to be introduced (and it is hard to see government business managers being enthusiastic about such a change), the result might be a greater proportion of parliamentary time given over to legislation, and stricter programming of bills to ensure that time did *not* run out.

As long as the pressure of government legislation remains at the levels of the last few years, the same might be the result of the more radical suggestion that the Commons should meet in alternate weeks, with the rest of the time being allotted to constituency or committee work. Given the size of the House, a net reduction in parliamentary time would limit the debate and question opportunities for back-bench MPs.

Recalls of Parliament

In Chapter 3 we noted the Speaker's role in recalling the House if, as Standing Order No. 13 says, 'it is represented . . . by Her Majesty's Ministers that the public interest requires' that the House should meet during an adjournment. The Speaker always grants such a request; and in the last 25 years there have been 14 days on which the House has been recalled to debate events, including the invasion of Kuwait (1990), the UK's withdrawal from the European exchange rate system (1992), the Omagh bombing and subsequent emergency legislation (1998), the terrorist attacks in New York and Washington (2001), possible military action against Iraq (2002), and to mark the death of the Queen Mother (2002). There might well have been a recall in 2003 or 2004 to debate events in Iraq, but in both those years the House had a planned September sitting. On 3 April 1982 the House met on a Saturday to debate the invasion of the Falklands; this was not strictly speaking a recall, as the House would have been adjourned only over the weekend, as the standing orders provide; on the Friday a motion to meet additionally on the Saturday was agreed to. The only Sunday sitting in the last century was on 3 September 1939, on the outbreak of the Second World War.

The sitting week in the Commons

From April 1946, the House sat at 2.30 p.m. each day, with the 'moment of interruption' (see page 158) normally ending the main business at

10.00 p.m., and on Fridays at 11.00 a.m., with the moment of interruption at 4.00 p.m. In each case, after the disposal of the business before the House (including business that was 'exempted' and so could proceed after the moment of interruption) there would be the daily adjournment debate (see page 295) for a further half-hour. In 1980, Friday sittings were moved to 9.30 a.m., with the moment of interruption at 2.30 p.m.

In 1994, following the recommendations of a select committee chaired by the former Conservative Chief Whip Michael Jopling, attempts were made to rein back the amount of business and the impact it had on the hours the House sat, particularly late at night. One of the changes was the introduction of Wednesday morning sittings starting at 9.30 a.m. As with the brief experiment under the 'Crossman reforms' in the 1960s (from the then Leader of the House, Richard Crossman), these were used primarily for non-contentious business and debates initiated by back-benchers. From 1999, Thursday sittings began at 11.30 a.m.; and at the end of 1999, with the additional back-bench opportunities afforded by the establishment of Westminster Hall as a second debating forum, the House went back to sitting on Wednesdays at 2.30 p.m.

A new timetable – and second thoughts

As a result of changes recommended by the Modernisation Committee chaired by Robin Cook as Leader of the House, 2003 saw a radical rearrangement of sitting hours. The original hours were kept for Monday (or for a Tuesday or Wednesday if this followed a recess), but with an 11.30 a.m. start Tuesday to Thursday, and an earlier finish on Thursday. The few remaining Friday sittings stayed at 9.30 a.m. The Modernisation Committee pointed out that over history the House's hours had changed in response to changes in social custom and business practice. Later hours were convenient when MPs were unpaid and could do much of a day's work in the City or the courts and still be at Westminster for the main business of the House. The committee felt that this was no longer appropriate when most members were full-time MPs.

It also observed that major events such as statements and PM's Questions came relatively late in the day; and the House responded to an agenda of public debate – in effect media coverage of events – which had already been set by then. Major votes usually came at 10.00 p.m., often too late for adequate coverage in the next day's papers.

In making its proposals, the Modernisation Committee warned that there was no consensus on sitting hours, and so it proved. Earlier sittings on Wednesdays were approved by 288 votes to 265, and those on Tuesdays by a narrower margin: 274 to 267. Opinion among MPs was sharply divided: on the one hand, some believed that more conventional working hours make Parliament seem less alien, and that a more family-friendly approach would encourage more people with family responsibilities to become MPs. Others disliked earlier starting times for committees and the House sitting during a morning that could be used for constituency and other parliamentary work.

Those with constituencies (and families) in or near London tended to prefer the new hours; those hundreds of miles from Westminster were less enthusiastic.

The new sitting hours remained contentious, and in January 2005 the traditionalists reclaimed the old sitting hours for Tuesdays, by a majority of 292 to 225. The start of the Thursday sitting was advanced to 10.30 a.m. to allow more substantial business to be taken on that day – but, in spite of this, Thursdays have remained the poor relation of the first three days of the week. The current sitting pattern is shown in Table 6.1.

A perverse result of the move to change sitting times is that on only two days of the week is the Commons timetable the same. Most parliaments have a consistent timetable to which members, parliamentary staff, the public and the media easily adapt. The House of Commons no longer does.

The sitting day in the Commons

This is often complicated and, although the business is taken in a pre-scribed order and subject to the House's rules, is never entirely predictable. Here we describe both the unchanging parts of the day and events that may happen only occasionally. Some of the more important proceedings are described in greater detail later in this book. The Order of Business for a typical day appears on pages 151 and 152.

Before the sitting, the *Speaker's Conference* will have taken place. Here the Speaker goes over the business for the day with the Deputy Speakers and the Clerk of the House and his senior colleagues, assessing possible problems or procedural complexities, deciding, for example, what will be a reasonable scope of debate on a particular item, or what response he will give to a likely point of order. The Speaker will also take a view on applications for urgent questions or urgent debates that may have been submitted. The Serjeant at Arms is also present and may know of a planned demonstration or mass lobby, which may affect access to the palace or may delay MPs getting to the House to vote.

Table 6.1 Programme for a normal sitting week in the House of Commons

	Monday	Tuesday	Wednesday	Thursday	Friday
House sits	2.30 p.m.	2.30 p.m.	11.30 a.m.	10.30 a.m.	9.30 a.m.
	Prayers (every day, for about three minutes)				
	private business after Prayers (not on Fridays)				
	Question Time (not on Fridays)				
urgent questions, statements by ministers	3.30 p.m.	3.30 p.m.	12.30 p.m.	11.30 a.m.	11.00 a.m.
(On Fridays, the main business will begin after Prayers and will be interrupted if there is a statement or urgent question at 11.00 a.m.)					
	main business (perhaps legislation, an opposition day or a debate on a topic in government time)				
main business interrupted	10.00 p.m.	10.00 p.m.	7.00 p.m.	6.00 p.m.	2.30 p.m.
	after the end of any votes (or of proceedings on 'exempted business'): daily adjournment debate (up to half an hour)				
Sittings in Westminster Hall:					
begin		9.30 a.m.	9.30 a.m.	2.30 p.m.	
suspended			11.30 a.m.		
resume			2.30 p.m.		
end		2.00 p.m.	5.00 p.m.	5.30 p.m.	
select committees					
(typically)			10.00 a.m.	9.30 a.m.	9.30 a.m.
	4.00 p.m.	4.00 p.m.	2.45 p.m.		
standing committees					
(typically)			10.30 a.m.	9.00 a.m.	9.00 a.m.
	4.30 p.m.	4.00 p.m.	2.30 p.m.	2.30 p.m.	
	(sittings in Westminster Hall, and in select and standing committees, are suspended for divisions in the House)				

The start of a sitting

Every sitting begins with the *Speaker's Procession* from Speaker's House. The Speaker, preceded by a doorkeeper and the Mace carried by the Serjeant at Arms, and followed by his trainbearer, secretary and chaplain, walks to the Chamber by way of the Central Lobby. Here the police inspector shouts 'Hats off, Strangers!', even though these days it is very unlikely that any male visitor will be wearing a hat. This is now a rare use of the term 'strangers' meaning visitors – see page 412. The Speaker and his chaplain (who is usually also Rector of St Margaret's, Westminster (the parliamentary church), and a canon of Westminster Abbey) and the Serjeant at Arms then enter the Chamber. The Serjeant places the Mace on the Table to show that the House is sitting, and the Speaker and chaplain kneel at the Table for *Prayers*. These Anglican *Prayers for the Parliament* take about three minutes and are in private. (A member who wants to reserve a seat in the House for the whole of a sitting may leave a prayer card on a place to show that he or she will be there for Prayers.)

As the Speaker rises, the doorkeepers shout 'Prayers are over'; the galleries are opened to guests and visitors; the Clerks' chairs are set at the Table; and, as the Speaker rises to begin proceedings with 'Order, order', television coverage starts.

Up to the end of Question Time

Although infrequent, any *report of the Queen's answer to an Address* (for example the 'Humble Address', which was formally before the House during the Queen's Speech debate) will come at the start of business. The sovereign's response is normally read out by one of the government whips who holds a post in the royal household (see page 99), and is generally very brief, as 'I have received with great satisfaction the dutiful and loyal expression of your thanks for the speech with which I opened the present session of Parliament'.

There may be a *formal communication by the Speaker*. When this happens, it is most often the announcement of the death of a member and is in brief, formal terms. There is normally no opportunity for a eulogy, although the House adjourns on the death of the Prime Minister or a former Prime Minister, or the Leader of the Opposition, after tributes have been given. The Speaker may also announce that he has sent or received messages of condolence or congratulation (for example to the Royal Family or to foreign parliaments or heads of state). He may announce the outcome of an 'election court' set up to resolve a dispute about the conduct of an election, which can declare a particular candidate to have been elected or can order a rerun of the election. He may even report the imprisonment of an MP (of which the courts must inform the House).

A *motion for a new writ* may be moved. This triggers a by-election in a seat made vacant by the death, resignation or disqualification of the sitting MP. It is normally moved by the Chief Whip of the party to which that member belonged but has occasionally been moved by a back-bencher wishing to make a point about a delay in holding a by-election, or to frustrate

| No. 83 | Order of Business: 9th January 2006 | 1729 |

At 3.30 p.m.   Urgent Questions (if any)

Ministerial Statements (if any)

Main Business

†   1   GOVERNMENT OF WALES BILL: Second Reading (*Queen's Consent to be signified*).   *[Until 10.00 p.m.]*

Mr David Cameron
Mrs Cheryl Gillan
Mr Dominic Grieve
Mr Oliver Heald
Mrs Theresa May
Mr Patrick McLoughlin

That this House declines to give a Second Reading to the Government of Wales Bill because there has been inadequate consultation about the electoral arrangements proposed in the Bill; and because the Bill fails to provide for a referendum on the introduction of the Orders in Council mechanisms for conferring enhanced legislative powers on the National Assembly for Wales.

The First Report from the Welsh Affairs Committee, Session 2005–06, on the Government White Paper: Better Governance for Wales, HC 551, is relevant.

Debate may continue until 10.00 p.m.

†   2   GOVERNMENT OF WALES BILL (PROGRAMME)   *[No debate]*

Mr Secretary Hain
Mr Geoffrey Hoon

That the following provisions shall apply to the Government of Wales Bill:

Committal

1. The Bill shall be committed to a Committee of the whole House.

Proceedings in Committee

2. Proceedings in Committee of the whole House shall be completed in three days.

3. The proceedings shall be taken in the following order: Clauses 92 and 93, Schedule 5, Clauses 94 to 102, Schedule 6, Clauses 103 to 107, Schedule 7, Clauses 108 to 115, Clauses 1 and 2, Schedule 1, Clauses 3 to 27, Schedule 2, Clauses 28 to 58, Schedule 3, Clauses 59 to 87, Schedule 4, Clauses 88 to 91, Clauses 116 to 144, Schedule 8, Clauses 145 to 148, Schedule 9, Clauses 149 to 159, Schedule 10, Clauses 160 and 161, Schedule 11, Clause 162, Schedule 12, Clauses 163 to 165, new Clauses, new Schedules, remaining proceedings on the Bill.

4. The proceedings shall (so far as not previously concluded) be brought to a conclusion at the moment of interruption on the third day.

5. Standing Order No. 83B (Programming committees) shall not apply to the proceedings on the Bill in Committee of the whole House.

Consideration and Third Reading

6. Proceedings on consideration and Third Reading shall be completed in two days.

† *indicates Government Business*

7. Proceedings on consideration shall (so far as not previously concluded) be brought to a conclusion one hour before the moment of interruption on the second day.

8. Proceedings on Third Reading shall (so far as not previously concluded) be brought to a conclusion at the moment of interruption on that day.

9. Standing Order No. 83B (Programming committees) shall not apply to proceedings on consideration and Third Reading.

Other proceedings

10. Any other proceedings on the Bill (including any proceedings on consideration of Lords Amendments or on any further messages from the Lords) may be programmed.

To be decided without debate (Standing Order No. 83A(6)).

† **3** GOVERNMENT OF WALES BILL [MONEY]: *Queen's recommendation signified.* *[No debate]*

John Healey

That, for the purposes of any Act resulting from the Government of Wales Bill, it is expedient to authorise—

(1) the payment out of money provided by Parliament of—

(a) expenditure incurred by a Minister of the Crown or government department by virtue of the Act, and

(b) any increase attributable to the Act in the sums payable under any other Act out of money provided by Parliament,

(2) the payment out of the National Loans Fund of any sums required by the Secretary of State for making loans under the Act, and

(3) the payment of sums into the Consolidated Fund and the National Loans Fund.

To be decided without debate (Standing Order No. 52(1)(a)).

† **4** NORTHERN IRELAND *[No debate]*

Mr Secretary Hain

That the draft Industrial and Provident Societies (Northern Ireland) Order 2005, which was laid before this House on 14th November, be approved.

To be decided without debate (Standing Order No. 118(6)).

† **5** PROCEEDS OF CRIME *[No debate]*

Mr Secretary Clarke

That the draft Proceeds of Crime Act 2002 and Money Laundering Regulations 2003 (Amendment) Order 2005, which was laid before this House on 22nd November, be approved.

To be decided without debate (Standing Order No. 118(6)).

† **6** CONSTITUTIONAL LAW *[No debate]*

Secretary Alan Johnson

That the draft Scotland Act 1998 (Modifications of Schedule 5) Order 2006, which was laid before this House on 29th November, be approved.

To be decided without debate (Standing Order No. 118(6)).

At the end of the sitting:

7 ADJOURNMENT

Proposed subject: **Standards of education in Plymouth schools** (*Linda Gilroy*).

Debate may continue until 10.30 p.m. or for half an hour, whichever is later (Standing Order No. 9).

Part of the Order of Business for a typical day in the Chamber of the House of Commons (an example of a preceding page containing oral questions is on page 323)

Source: The House of Commons 2006

later business. By convention, new writs are moved within three months of the vacancy occurring, but there is no formal limit. If a motion for a new writ is opposed at this time, it is taken later in the sitting, after statements but before the main business.

After these uncommon proceedings comes *private business* – that is, private bills and related motions (including motions relating to the Committee of Selection (see page 354)). At this time in the sitting day, only private business to which a blocking motion has not been tabled, or that is not opposed by even a single MP shouting 'object' can pass. Much private business is uncontroversial, and it is not unusual for private bills to go through all their stages on different days at this time.

A *motion for an unopposed return* may be moved. It may be that an official inquiry has criticised individuals who might sue if the report were published in the conventional way (for example, Sir Richard Scott's 'Arms for Iraq' inquiry in 1996, Sir Thomas Legg's Sierra Leone inquiry in 1998 and in 2004 Lord Hutton's inquiry into the death of Dr David Kelly). This device gives the report the protection of parliamentary privilege.

Even if all the items of business listed above were to take place, they would probably delay the House for only four or five minutes. *Question Time* then follows and continues for an hour (although it may be extended by another twenty minutes or so if an *urgent question* has been granted, or if a minister has decided to answer a *question at the end of Question Time*). This is described in greater detail in Chapter 10.

After Question Time and up to 'the commencement of public business'

The main events at this time are *statements by ministers*. These may announce a new policy initiative, progress on a major industrial dispute, or perhaps the government's reaction to the outcome of a court case or an official inquiry. A statement may report on an international meeting, perhaps of the UN or European Council, or the outcome of significant EU negotiations. Statements are also used to inform the House about serious accidents or terrorist crimes and to set out the government's response. A series of statements over several weeks kept the House informed about the political, diplomatic, military and humanitarian aspects of action against Iraq in early 2003. In cases of great urgency, a statement may be made at another time; on 6 May 2003, after the decision had become known in Dublin earlier in the day, the Secretary of State for Northern Ireland reported the government's decision to postpone elections to the Northern Ireland Assembly at

10.45 p.m., after the main business and before the half-hour adjournment debate.

Significant statements are made by the responsible cabinet minister (or by the Prime Minister); less important statements are made by more junior ministers directly responsible for the subject. Ministers notify the Speaker in advance of their intention to make a statement, but (although they conventionally begin a statement with the words 'with permission, Mr Speaker') they do not need his permission, or that of the House, to do so. Notice that a statement is to be made appears on the television annunciators around the House between one and two hours beforehand, and a minister will as a courtesy give his or her opposition 'shadow' an advance copy of the text an hour or so before it is delivered. However, unless the subject is one that has been simmering on the political agenda, much of the initiative rests with the government (especially so if the statement announces a surprise policy development), and the opposition will have to be quick on its feet to react effectively.

As we saw in Chapter 3, it is up to the Chair to decide how long questioning goes on. This will depend on the significance of the statement, but the Speaker will also have in mind the need to protect any important business that follows, at the same time as exposing the minister fully to questioning.

On Thursdays, the Leader of the House's *weekly statement of forthcoming business* is formally a reply to a question from the shadow Leader (and so follows immediately after Question Time) rather than a conventional ministerial statement. However, if there is another statement on a Thursday, the Leader's announcement may follow it and be technically a statement in its own right.

After statements, *any new Member of the House elected at a by-election* is formally introduced to the House and *takes the oath or makes affirmation* (see page 137) – normally on the Tuesday following the by-election. He or she waits below the Bar of the House (in other words, within the Chamber but just outside what is formally the floor of the House; the Bar itself does exist, but as it consists of two heavy metal rods that slide back into the woodwork of the benches on each side it is seldom seen). If there is a statement – or, worse, two statements – this can be a long and nervous wait for the new member.

When the moment arrives, the new MP, flanked by two members who act as sponsors (perhaps old friends or constituency neighbours), comes forward, clutching the certificate from the Clerk of the Crown that is proof of election. He or she bows and then takes the oath (or affirms), signs the test roll and is announced to the Speaker and the House by the Clerk of the House. There will have been a lot of political interest in the by-election campaign and its outcome – particularly if the seat has been captured by a different party – and the introduction of the new MP is in some ways the culmination of the campaign, hailed with cheers from MPs of the victorious party and fairly good-natured heckling from other parts of the House.

Also after statements, MPs have the opportunity of *requesting an urgent debate*, sometimes known as 'an S.O. No. 24 application', on what the standing order calls 'a specific and important matter that should have urgent consideration'. The MP must seek the Speaker's permission beforehand and has three minutes in which to make the case for an urgent debate. The Speaker then gives his decision (and is forbidden by the standing order from giving any reasons). If he allows the application and the House agrees, a three-hour debate will take place the next day (or the same day if there is sufficient urgency).

Urgent debates are very rare; the most recent was in March 2002 following the deployment of British troops to Afghanistan, but the one before that was in 1993. Applications are less frequent than in previous years, no doubt because Speakers do not encourage hopeless applications; but they are used as a means of raising a constituency crisis as well as events on a bigger scale: in May 2003, an MP applied for a debate on the heavy financial deficit of her constituency's main hospital; in October 2004, an MP tried for a debate on a multinational company's decision to close a factory in his constituency; and in March 2006 an MP sought a debate on local NHS redundancies.

There is then a slot for (rare) *ceremonial speeches* – perhaps on the death of a former Speaker or some other distinguished figure, *motions to give the Speaker leave of absence* for some specific reason, and *personal statements*. These may be of apology, perhaps for failing to register an interest or for using 'unparliamentary language', or a minister may apologise for giving the House wrong information; or they may be of explanation after resignation. This second category can be dramatic. Sir Geoffrey Howe's statement after resigning as Deputy Prime Minister in 1990, delivered in an electric atmosphere in the House, was a defining moment just before the end of Margaret Thatcher's Prime Ministership. Equally memorable were Norman Lamont's statement in June 1993 after he had been sacked as Chancellor of the Exchequer; Robin Cook's in March 2003 after he resigned from the Cabinet on the eve of war against Iraq (his personal statement was unusually made at 9.45 p.m., but that was just after the equally unusual timing of a statement by the Foreign Secretary that talks in the UN had broken down); and Clare Short's attack on the Prime Minister's style of government following her resignation in May 2003.

Personal statements may be made only with the permission of the Speaker, and because the practice of the House is to hear statements in (near) silence, and not to allow interventions, the Speaker sees the text beforehand.

Matters relating to privilege (see page 183) may be taken at this time. Alleged breaches of privilege have to be raised privately with the Speaker, so matters of privilege are raised on the floor of the House only if he is prepared to give them precedence over other business. An opposed motion for the issue of a new writ in a by-election would also be taken at this stage of the day.

Usually at about this time, MPs will raise *points of order* with the Speaker (although points of order on the business actually before the House may be raised at any time). The test of a 'genuine' point of order is whether the Chair can actually rule upon it because it relates to the rules and practice of the House – for example, whether a phrase is acceptable parliamentary language, or perhaps in some complex business, the order in which the House will take decisions, or whether something was amiss in one of the House's working papers. The Speaker will either give his decision on the spot (particularly if the MP has given him notice of the point to be raised) or undertake to give a decision later. These rulings are part of the case law that is an important element in the practice and procedure of the House.

Even if a point of order is genuine, Speakers will normally not rule on something that is hypothetical, or on something that has happened in committee; that is the responsibility of the chairman concerned. Nor will the Chair give detailed procedural counsel, normally suggesting that the MP seeks the advice of the Clerks.

Genuine points of order sometimes relate to the administrative responsibilities of the Speaker, such as access to the precincts or the use of facilities. But the majority of points raised at this stage in the parliamentary day are to a greater or lesser degree bogus in that they make political or debating points. One of the most frequent from the opposition benches is an inquiry as to whether the Speaker has received a request from a minister to make a statement on some contentious subject (usually implying undue reticence on the part of the government). Assertions by ministers, or the content of their replies to parliamentary questions, are often raised. There is a catch-22 in that the Chair has to allow the MP to go some way towards making the point, as it is only then that it becomes clear that this is not a real point of order. However, because of the limited opportunities that MPs have to raise current issues other than in relevant Question Times or debates (many parliaments have a period each day in which the members may speak briefly on any subject of current concern) these points of order can act as something of a safety valve. (A point of order specifically on the business before the House at that moment may be raised with the Chair at any time during a sitting.)

'At the commencement of public business'

It may seem strange that this title occurs only at this stage of the sitting day; but for almost all the preceding business most of the very few decisions that arise have to be taken by unanimity, and for much of the time there is no *question* before the House – that is, a matter put forward for decision by the House. Confusingly, there is no 'question' in this technical sense before the House during Question Time.

Three main types of business are taken at this time. The first is the *presentation and first reading of public bills* – a formality, which is explained in Chapter 7. Then come government motions to regulate the business of the House for that day – perhaps to allow several items to be debated jointly, or to allot time to a particular item of business, or to allow an urgent bill to be taken through all its stages at one sitting. Such motions can be debated and may be voted upon. To avoid the (perhaps unpredictable) loss of time for the main business, these are often taken on a previous day.

The best-known category of business 'at the commencement' is the *ten-minute rule bill* (strictly a motion, because the member seeks permission to bring in the bill rather than a decision by the House on the bill itself). Every Tuesday and Wednesday, a back-bencher has the chance to propose new legislation in a speech lasting not more than ten minutes; if there is opposition, one MP may put the contrary case, again for no more than ten minutes, and if necessary there is a vote. These are very popular opportunities for back-bench MPs, not least because a back-bencher's opportunities to initiate business on the floor of the House are very limited, but also because they take place in 'prime time', which may be immediately before a major debate. Ten-minute rule bills are discussed further in Chapter 7.

The main business

It is unusual for the events described so far (apart from ministerial statements) to go on longer than 15 or 20 minutes after the end of Question

Time. The House then embarks on the main business of the day, which consists of *orders of the day* (typically, a stage of a bill) and *notices of motions* (typically, a debate either on a substantive motion, as on an opposition day, or a motion for the adjournment, which allows a subject to be discussed on the 'technical' motion 'that this House do now adjourn').

It often happens that the usual channels have agreed that the main business should be in two halves, or that the Liaison Committee has recommended two estimates for debate on an estimates day. In that case, the halfway point is at about 7.00 p.m. on a Monday or Tuesday, 4.00 p.m. on a Wednesday, or 3.00 p.m. on a Thursday ('half days' do not happen on Fridays).

The moment of interruption

At 10.00 p.m. on Mondays and Tuesdays, 7.00 p.m. on Wednesdays, 6.00 p.m. on Thursdays and 2.30 p.m. on Fridays comes the 'moment of interruption'. This is normally the end of the main business and is the time when most major votes are taken. Unless there has been a previous decision of the House to the contrary, business still under way when that moment comes will lapse. Thus an MP can 'talk something out' by continuing to speak as the Speaker says 'Order, order' to signify that the business is being interrupted. To prevent this the closure (see page 50) must be moved, which will be granted by the Chair after a full day's debate and is normally agreed without a vote, the House passing straight on to a vote on the main business itself.

'Talking out' is a traditional weapon used against private members' bills; 100 MPs must vote for the closure for it to be effective, and the sponsor of a private member's bill may find it difficult to round up enough supporters at the end of business on a Friday. In addition, if the bill is second or third on the order paper on a private members' Friday, the Chair may think that there has been insufficient debate to allow the closure to be put to the House. Strictly speaking, 'talking out' happens only when there is opposition to further proceedings. Theoretically, if the Chair detected no objection from any member, debate on 'non-exempted' business could survive the moment of interruption, and the House could then take a decision at the end of that debate; but such cases are extremely rare.

Non-exempted business, which is not expected to be debated, is sometimes described as 'nod or nothing after seven o'clock' (or ten o'clock); in other words, either it is agreed 'on the nod' without any objection, or there is objection and the matter cannot be put to the House.

Exempted business

Not all business has to end at the moment of interruption. A motion moved (only by a minister, and only if notice has been given on the order paper) may allow an item to be proceeded with 'until any hour' or for a specific time.

Some other business is automatically exempted: finance bills (unlimited time); Statutory Instruments and European Union documents (an hour and a half – although any that have already been considered in standing committee cannot be debated again); and some thirty other types of business, although not debatable, may nevertheless be decided.

On the first four days of the week, after decisions and votes taken immediately after the moment of interruption have been disposed of, *public petitions* may be presented (on Fridays, this happens at the start of business). Petitions are described in more detail in Chapter 10. There is then the *half-hour adjournment debate*, which is covered in Chapter 9.

The last words spoken in the Chamber are the same as the first: 'Order, order'. The occupant of the Chair (by this time, usually one of the Deputy Speakers) leaves the Chair, and the Serjeant at Arms takes the Mace from the Table and joins the Deputy Speaker behind the Chair. The Deputy Speaker says '11.30 [or whatever the next day's sitting time is] tomorrow' or '2.30 on Monday', which is repeated by the Serjeant. The doorkeepers shout 'Who goes home?' – usually abbreviated to a long drawn-out 'ho-o-o-me', a relic of days when MPs homeward bound in the same direction would band together as a defence against footpads and highwaymen – the division bells ring for the last time, and the parliamentary day is over.

Late sittings

Late sittings were a regular feature of the House of Commons in the 1970s and 1980s. The average time the House rose in the decade to 1990–91 was well after midnight (so – taking Fridays into account – an average sitting of some nine hours), with some sittings lasting much longer. More than a fifth of sitting time was after the moment of interruption. Sometimes proceedings were greatly prolonged by back-benchers or by opposition parties to emphasise criticism of the government or its proposals. This occasionally went as far as sitting beyond the House's scheduled time of meeting the next day, thus 'breaking the sitting' and losing the government's planned business for the following day.

By contrast, in the 18 months up to the 2005 general election, the average sitting day was seven hours and 52 minutes, and the sitting time after the moment of interruption was only 11 per cent of total sitting time. There have been various reasons for this change – although all have their critics. They include the *routine programming of bills* (see page 198), whereby time limits are imposed on bills at an early stage in their passage through the House; *the move of a substantial amount of debating time to Westminster Hall* (and indeed a net increase in debating time thereby; in the 18 months up to the 2005 general election, the House sat for 1,747 hours in total, and sittings in Westminster Hall totalled 566 hours, or nearly three hours for each day that the House sat); the taking of *more business in standing committee rather than on the floor of the House*; and *money and ways and means motions* (authorising expenditure or taxation in relation to bills) normally *being taken without debate*.

Time in the House

The Modernisation Committee pointed out that the House of Commons (and, by extension, the House of Lords, which has similar sitting patterns)

> *spends far less time in recess than most other democratic parliaments. The House of Commons meets for more days than any of the parliaments of the larger Commonwealth countries and indeed for twice as many days as all of them except Canada. The typical pattern among European parliaments is for the legislature to sit around 100 days in the year, compared with 150 days for the UK Parliament.*

Comparisons with continental legislatures, where the work of the plenary is fuelled to a much greater degree by committees, are not exact; but there is no doubt that the Westminster Parliament is one of the longest-sitting parliaments in the world. There are a number of reasons for this: principally the unremitting legislative programme of successive governments; but also the number of members and so the pressure for parliamentary time to raise a wide range of issues; even, perhaps, a degree of habit.

Use of time

Taking the 2003–04 and 2004–05 sessions together to give a more representative picture, the sitting time of the House of Commons broke down as shown in Table 6.2.

Table 6.2 Breakdown of sitting time in the House of Commons, sessions 2003–04 and 2004–05

Business	Percentage of time
Daily prayers	1.1
Questions	11.1
Statements	5.4
Business statements	2.3
Ten-minute rule motions	0.9
Points of order	1.0
Government bills	33.6
Private members' bills	4.7
Private bills	nil
Estimates	1.1
Affirmative instruments	1.4
Negative instruments	nil
Government motions	12.5
Opposition motions	10.0
Petitions	0.2
Back-bench adjournment motions	7.8
Miscellaneous	6.9

This fairly typical breakdown shows that nearly three-fifths of the House's business is initiated by the government and that nearly two-fifths of time on the floor of the House is spent on legislation – not counting the hundreds of hours that are spent on legislation in standing committees.

Although questions, debates and statements provide opportunities for back-benchers, proceedings initiated by them took up only one-tenth of the time, whereas debates on select committee reports represented only 1 per cent. This picture was redressed to some extent by 566 hours of debates in Westminster Hall, where, as percentages of total *House* sitting time, debates initiated by back-benchers would have represented 24 per cent and those on select committee reports would have represented 5 per cent.

An MP's day

There are as many ways of doing an MP's job as there are MPs. The influences upon them, which we surveyed in Chapter 5, and the variety of priorities that they have, mean that there is no standard working week or day, although there are some common ingredients. An MP will normally come to Westminster from midday onwards on a Monday, depending on how far away the constituency is, and go back to the constituency on a Thursday or Friday, subject to the business in the House.

Some of the parliamentary agenda is set by the media, and devouring a variety of newspapers, together with breakfast news or the *Today* programme (or sometimes appearing on it), is a usual start to the day. Some time in the office at the House, talking over the in-tray with researcher and assistant, may be followed by attendance at a standing or select committee, and then to the House for Question Time (especially on a Wednesday, when Prime Minister's Questions are at noon). Or the morning may be given over to constituency work, perhaps also seeing a delegation representing an important local industry and then taking them to meet a minister in Whitehall. Lunch – these days for many MPs more likely to be a sandwich and a yogurt than anything more elaborate – may be in the office, hearing the case a pressure group wants to put, or chatting with other members in the Tea Room. In July 2005, a new Muslim MP remarked ruefully: 'Nothing is done without eating or drinking with colleagues, so I've drunk more water and Diet Coke than I thought possible'. The afternoon might include writing the MP's weekly column for the local newspaper, signing letters, an interview with local or national media, telephone calls following up constituency cases, or back to standing committee or select committee business – perhaps interrupted by votes in the House. If the MP retains business or professional interests outside the House, he or she may find time for these. Later in the day there may be a meeting of a party committee and an all-party group on a subject in which the MP is heavily involved.

Perhaps the MP wants to speak in the Chamber; in that case, most of the afternoon may be taken up waiting on the green benches, leaping up to catch the eye of the Chair at the conclusion of each speech, and then being in the Chamber again for the wind-up speeches by the front benches at the end. Or possibly he or she has been able to secure the half-hour adjournment debate; in that case, much of the time that day will have been spent looking over notes for the speech, and perhaps discussing the issues with the constituent whose case has been raised, or a group interested in the subject to be debated; and, as the parliamentary day nears its end, narrowly watching the progress of business so as to be in the Chamber in time. Thereafter, a telephone call home to a distant family to exchange news about the day.

Ministers

If the MP is one of the ninety or so ministers in the Commons, the day will be very different. Whitehall, not Westminster, is their focus; their departments' concerns rule their day, and their officials feel that they own a minister's time. As well as work at the desk, there will be a range of meetings – with civil servants, ministerial colleagues (for the more senior, in Cabinet and Cabinet committees), official visitors and delegations (perhaps led by one of their back-bench colleagues). There will be opening ceremonies, keynote speeches at conferences, ministerial visits, EU negotiations in Brussels, press conferences. Their relationship with the House will change; now they are concerned only with one subject area, and their time in the House will centre on when their department is top for Questions (see page 320), when they open or reply to a debate, take 'their' bill through its stages or appear as a witness before a select committee. Their weekends are dominated by red despatch boxes with papers they need to read or approve by Monday morning – in effect, the homework set by their department. And they still have to keep up with their constituency work.

Most ministers' workloads are very heavy; just how heavy often comes as a surprise to newly appointed ministers. A senior member of the former Conservative Cabinet said (sympathetically rather than critically) after the first few months of the Blair government: 'Labour ministers have one thing in common; they're all knackered'.

To a lesser extent, the same is true of opposition shadow ministers, who have fewer resources to support them. Although they do not have the burden of departmental work, much of their day is spent in keeping up with developments in their subject brief, or perhaps leading for the opposition on a bill in committee or a debate on the floor of the House.

Attendance in the Chamber

Most visitors to the galleries, or viewers of coverage of the House of Commons, comment on the relatively small attendance of members in the Chamber. Objective measures are hard to come by, but average attendance in the Chamber has been falling over the last fifteen years or so. Even though the Chamber is packed weekly for Prime Minister's Questions and at other times for major debates or statements, the routine level of attendance for some debates can be embarrassingly low, and is often a source of criticism from those who see on television an important subject being debated by only 1 or 2 per cent of the House's membership.

The level of attendance is influenced by various factors: there is continuous television coverage over the annunciator system, and there have been improvements in members' office accommodation, both of which have limited the tendency to 'drop in' to the Chamber rather than planning to be there for a particular item of business. When debate is predictable and the outcome certain – especially if it is by a large majority – this too will have an effect.

However, it will be clear from the description of an MP's day that members are also drawn away from the Chamber simply because there is so much else to do. For most of the day, there is a great deal of formal parliamentary activity going on elsewhere – in Westminster Hall, and in standing or select committees – in addition to the huge variety of party and group activity, as well as constituency work. Much is sometimes made of 'activity statistics': how many times an MP has voted, or how many times he or she has spoken in debate. These give a rather two-dimensional picture and can be misleading. Whips will score highly on divisions, because they are on the premises most of the time the House is sitting and votes are their business. But they will not feature in debates, because by convention they do not speak. Members with distant constituencies may not score as highly as London members; other MPs may decide that they can do more through select committee work than by interventions in the Chamber. And the shift towards constituency casework may be an additional reason why attendance in the Commons Chamber is often much lower than in the Chamber of the House of Lords.

Sittings and use of time in the House of Lords

The House of Lords usually sits from Monday to Thursday, and on Fridays in the latter part of the session. In the 1999–2000 session – a very busy one – it sat for 177 days, an average of 7 hours 29 minutes each day (the Commons sat for 170 days, averaging 8 hours 29 minutes per day). In 2003–04, by contrast, it sat for 157 days, averaging 6 hours 58 minutes each day. On Mondays and Tuesdays the Lords meets at 2.30 p.m., on Wednesdays at 3.00 p.m. and on Thursdays at 11 a.m., adjourning at 1.30 p.m. for one hour if legislative business is being taken (Thursday morning sittings began in the 2002–03 session, at first on a trial basis.) On Fridays, sittings begin at 11 a.m. and continue without interruption until the business before the House has been completed. As in the Commons, Saturday and Sunday sittings have taken place only at times of national crisis. The length of Lords' sittings has grown gradually – in the 1974–75 session, the average sitting lasted under six hours.

As in the Commons, the day begins with *prayers*. In the Lords, prayers are read by a bishop, and members kneel on the benches. Immediately after prayers, new members go through their ceremony of introduction and take the oath, as does any member who has not yet taken the oath in this parliament. The business starts with a short *question time*. Four questions – known as 'starred questions' because they are marked with a star on the order paper – are taken. Private notice questions are very rarely allowed in the Lords but, when they are, they come immediately after starred questions. *Business statements* – indicating the limitations on speaking time to be observed in time-limited debates, or the hour of adjournment for dinner during a particularly long piece of legislative business, for example – follow. *Ministerial statements* in theory come next, but only if the minister making the statement is a lord. Most statements are made in the Commons and repeated in the Lords. Occasionally statements to be made in the Commons are deemed by the usual channels not to be sufficiently important to the Lords to be repeated. When they are important, they are usually delivered in the Commons at 12.30 p.m. and in the Lords as soon after as is convenient. In the Lords, brief comments and questions for clarification from the opposition front benches and from back-benchers of all parties are allowed for a total period not exceeding forty minutes following the end of the statement. Members clearly value this opportunity to comment and probe the government further on statements, and an attempt by the Lords Procedure Committee to restrict comment to front-bench spokesmen of the main political parties received very short shrift from the House.

The substantive business then begins. Discussion of *private legislation* comes first, followed by *Business of the House motions*, usually moved by the Leader of the House and signifying a change in the order of business. Then, when necessary, comes *Chairman of Committees' business*. This usually relates to the discussion of any reports by committees for which the Chairman of Committees has responsibility – such as reports of the House Committee on some matter of internal management, or the Procedure Committee. Discussion of *public bills, delegated legislation and reports from select committees* come next, followed by other motions. At the end of business, any *questions for debate that have been tabled for oral answer* by the government may be taken. These are called 'unstarred questions' (to distinguish them from the questions put at the commencement of business, which do not give rise to debate, they are not prefixed by a star on the order paper). Proceedings on unstarred questions are time-limited to one and a half hours. They are somewhat akin to adjournment debates in the Commons. Indeed, so popular have they become that, if time permits, they are now sometimes taken during the adjournment for dinner of proceedings on a major bill.

The order of business is slightly different on Thursdays, when by standing order motions have precedence over bills and other business. The practical effect of this is to make Thursday a day of debates. Any other business has to come last.

It would be very unusual to find all the different kinds of business set down for any one day. A typical day might begin with prayers, followed by starred questions and business statements; proceedings on a private bill might come next but would usually be very brief (discussion of a controversial nature will, at the Chairman of Committees' discretion, usually be deferred until later in the day); there may then come a business motion; then would follow the legislative stages of one or more bills. If the principal business consists of a lengthy stage of a major bill requiring constant attendance, then at 7.30 p.m. that stage may be adjourned for an hour, in which time short items of business – say an uncontentious piece of delegated legislation or a private member's bill or, as has recently become the practice, an unstarred question – might be taken. The adjourned proceedings on the major bill will then be resumed and the House might adjourn at any time between about 9 p.m. and 10 p.m. If it is likely that business will finish earlier in the evening, an unstarred question may have been set down as last business.

A day's business in the Lords is illustrated by the Order Paper reproduced on the next page. After questions a Business of the House motion was moved to allow a motion for debate to precede a second reading of a private member's bill on Friday 18 November (only on Thursdays do motions have precedence); this was followed by a government motion of 'instruction' to provide on a later day for a government bill to be considered at its Committee Stage (on this occasion in Grand Committee) in a particular order; then came a motion to approve an item of delegated legislation requiring the approval of the House (since the suspension of representative government in Northern Ireland all Northern Irish legislation has taken this form); and then followed the Third Reading and Second Reading of two government bills. Meanwhile, in the Moses Room, another government bill continued its Committee Stage in Grand Committee. The House rose at four minutes past nine, comfortably within the target rising time.

In July 2002, the Procedure Committee endorsed the recommendation of a working group chaired by the then Leader of the House, Lord Williams of Mostyn, that it should be a firm convention that the House should rise by about 10 p.m. on Mondays to Wednesdays and that on Thursdays any

NOTICES AND ORDERS OF THE DAY

Items marked † are new or have been altered.
Items marked ‡ are expected to be taken during the dinner adjournment.

WEDNESDAY 9TH NOVEMBER

At half-past two o'clock

*The Baroness Knight of Collingtree—To ask Her Majesty's Government what proposals they will make following the end of the consultation period on local government takeover of privately owned homes.

*The Lord Judd—To ask Her Majesty's Government what arrangements they have made for cooperation with the Russian Federal Security Service (FSB) on anti-terrorism activities; and what is their assessment in this context of the recent troubles in the North Caucasus Region.

*The Lord Hylton—To ask Her Majesty's Government what representations they have made to the government of Israel about the 23 square miles of land in the West Bank alleged to have been expropriated from Palestinian owners since July.

*The Baroness Scott of Needham Market—To ask Her Majesty's Government what is their response to the Local Government Association's assessment of the financial outlook for the coming year.

†Business of the House—The Lord President (Baroness Amos) to move, That Standing Order 41 (Arrangement of the Order Paper) be dispensed with on Friday 18th November to allow the motion standing in the name of the Lord Goodhart to be taken before the second reading of the Estate Agents (Independent Redress Scheme) Bill [HL].

†Transport (Wales) Bill [HL]—The Lord Evans of Temple Guiting to move, That it be an instruction to the Grand Committee to which the Transport (Wales) Bill [HL] has been committed that they consider the bill in the following order:

          Clauses 1 to 3   Clauses 4 to 17.
          Schedule

Northern Ireland (Sentences) Act 1998 (Specified Organisations) Order 2005—The Lord Rooker to move, That the Order laid before the House on 14th September be approved. [*4th Report from the Joint Committee and 9th Report from the Merits Committee*]

Equality Bill [HL]—Third Reading [The Lord Falconer of Thoroton]

Commissioner for Older People (Wales) Bill [HL]—Report [The Lord Evans of Temple Guiting]

In the Moses Room
At 3.30 pm

Commons Bill [HL]—Further consideration in Grand Committee [The Lord Bach]   [*3rd Report from the Delegated Powers Committee*]

Notices and Orders of the day: the House of Lords Order Paper

Source: The House of Lords 2005

business should be completed by 7.00 p.m. This 10 p.m. convention is by now well on its way to becoming established though on occasion due to pressure of business it is simply not observed.

The sitting time of the House of Lords in the 1995–96 and 2003–04 sessions broke down approximately as shown in Table 6.3.

Table 6.3 Comparisons of sitting time breakdowns in the House of Lords, Sessions 1995–96 and 2003–04

| | Percentage of time spent | |
	1995–96	2003–04
Prayers	1.2	1.3
Introductions	0.5	0.5
Starred questions	6.7	7.4
Private bills	0.1	0.4
Statements	3.1	3.6
Public bills (government)	47.8	52.7
Public bills (private members)	4.3	1.9
Statutory instruments	5.7	5.6
Debates	25.1	20.1
Unstarred questions	3.0	4.8

We conclude this chapter with four topics that are ever-present in a parliamentarian's day: parliamentary papers, voting, the media and the broadcasting of Parliament; and two that form a preface to the more detailed examination of some of the functions of Parliament that follows: privilege and procedure.

Parliamentary papers

The parliamentary process generates a great deal of paper. Much of it is private and relates only to a particular group – for example the working papers of a select committee – but there is also a central core of printed material that provides MPs with their bread-and-butter information and that is also available to people outside Parliament.

The Vote bundle

Every MP receives a daily bundle of papers known as 'the Vote'. This will be no more than a few pages in the first few days of the session, but for many sitting days it may be as much as 200 pages. The front page is the *Summary Agenda*, which lists the titles of business to be taken in the House and Westminster Hall. Then follows the *Order of Business* or Order Paper, a detailed agenda that gives all the items for which notice is required; so, for example, the texts of oral questions and of any motions to be debated (or to be put for decision without debate), in the order in which they will be taken. The Order Paper 'freezes' at the moment when the House adjourns on the previous sitting day; nothing can be slipped in thereafter (although of course some things are permitted to be done without notice). Statements and urgent questions are not included; they are notified by way of the television annunciators before the start of the sitting. The Order Paper tries to be informative without being misleading (for example, by implying that a practice normally followed will necessarily be followed). After all, it is often the opposition's aim not to achieve the agenda; and the government does not have to proceed with every item of business simply because it is on the Order Paper.

There is then a list of *standing and select committee sittings that day*, giving the time and place of each, and the witnesses for public sittings of select committees, followed by notice of *written ministerial statements* to be made that day (for less important announcements, an alternative to making an oral statement to the House). The next section is *future business*, section A of which covers *the provisional business announced by the Leader of the House* for the next week or more; B is *business for Westminster Hall*; C is *remaining orders and notices*, which covers future business (although each item is set down formally for that day, it is not expected to be taken); D, *other future business*, gives items scheduled for particular future days (normally ten-minute rule motions and private members' bills) and E gives notice of written ministerial statements for future days. Then follows the *Order Paper for Westminster Hall*.

Other items in the Vote bundle are *lists of amendments* put down to bills to be debated that day, both on the floor of the House and in standing committee; and the *Votes and Proceedings*. This is the formal legal record of what the House *did* the previous day rather than what was said: decisions on motions, amendments made to bills, papers laid before the House, the record of reports from select committees, and so on. Almost all of the papers listed above are available on the parliamentary website (**www.parliament.uk**).

Also in the Vote bundle are the parliamentary questions and amendments to bills that were tabled the previous day, and new early day motions (or those up to a fortnight old to which new signatures were added the previous day). These are all printed on blue paper to show that they are new notices rather than papers for the current working day. All parliamentary questions already tabled for that day or for a future day are contained in the separate *Question Book*.

Hansard

T. C. Hansard was the nineteenth-century printer and publisher whose daily record of the Commons was published privately. From 1909, staff of the House took on the recording of debates, but the name 'Hansard' stuck and was officially adopted in 1943. Properly called *the Official Report*, *Hansard* is the record of what is said in the House. It is substantially verbatim; *Official Report* staff tidy up obvious mistakes and repetitions, but they do not allow any change of substance.

Hansard contains not only everything that is said in debates in the House and Westminster Hall the previous day but also lists of MPs voting in divisions and a large section devoted to the answers given by ministers to written questions, as well as written statements by ministers. There are two columns on each page of *Hansard* (a column accounts for about three minutes of debate), and references are always to column or 'col.' rather than to page. Unlike many parliaments, Westminster does not allow speeches prepared but not delivered to be put into the record. The full text of every day's *Hansard* is published at 7.30 a.m. the following morning and put on the parliamentary website at 8.00 a.m. and at the end of 2005 a 'rolling' *Hansard* of the Chamber was introduced, with chunks of text being posted on the Internet about three hours after the words were spoken in the Chamber. *Hansard* staff also record all the debates in standing committees; these appear a little more slowly than the Chamber *Hansard*. Evidence given by witnesses before select committees is recorded not by *Hansard* but by the private firm of W. G. Gurney (the founder of the firm invented his own form of shorthand), which has done so for more than 150 years. Select committee evidence appears either with the committee's eventual report or in 'daily parts'; transcripts of the more important hearings are put on the website in uncorrected form.

Other parliamentary papers

A wide range of papers are presented to Parliament, which MPs may obtain in hard copy from the House's Vote Office, and members of the public may buy from the Stationery Office. Most papers generated by Parliament itself are also available at www.parliament.uk; those produced by government departments are usually on their own websites.

Bills are published when they are first introduced and again at subsequent stages if they are amended. More than 300 *Command Papers* (so called because they are formally presented by the government 'by command of Her Majesty') are presented each year. These may be treaties and other agreements with foreign governments, reports of non-parliamentary committees of investigation or Royal Commissions, 'White Papers' (statements of government policy) or 'Green Papers' (documents for consultation on possible policy options). *Act Papers* are laid before Parliament because an Act of Parliament requires it; the majority are Statutory Instruments (see page 252) – about 1,500 a year – but this category also includes reports and accounts of a wide range of public bodies, government statistics, and reports by the Comptroller and Auditor General (see page 283).

House of Lords working papers

The most important of these is the *Minute*. The Minute is, broadly speaking, the Lords equivalent of the Commons Order of Business, Votes and Proceedings and other notices rolled into one. It is compiled each day and sent out to peers overnight. It begins with a formal record of the business conducted in the Chamber that day, including the judicial decisions of the House; next come the motions and orders of the day for the coming month in so far as business will have been set down (the next day's business is also printed separately as the *Order Paper* (see page 167) each day); and finally there are listed motions awaiting debate, questions for written answer, bills and orders of various kinds in progress, and forthcoming meetings of committees. The format of the *Minute* is being reviewed and a number of changes may be made in late 2006. One suggestion is that it should be reordered so that notices of forthcoming business come first. The document might be re-named *House of Lords Business*. A *Weekly Bulletin* of meetings of select committees for up to one month ahead is published by the Committee Office. There is also a sessional journal, the formal record of proceedings.

The House of Lords also has its own *Hansard*, and nearly all the papers presented to the Commons are also laid before the House of Lords.

Voting

Votes are called 'divisions' because MPs 'divide' physically, going through different lobbies depending on which way they are voting. Although during a sitting day many things are decided without a division, disagreement between government and opposition (or dissent by a smaller group of MPs on either side of the House) will produce a vote. And forcing votes as a means of taking time and disrupting or delaying the business is a tactic used in every parliament.

Voting in both Houses of Parliament is on the basis of approval or disapproval; there is no provision for formally recording abstentions and no means of ranking competing choices in a single decision (which might have led to a rather different outcome on the future composition of the House of Lords); the only exception is in the new procedure for the election of a Speaker.

When a proposition has been put before the House for debate (for example, when a member has moved that a bill 'be now read a second time', or that an amendment be made), when the mover sits down, the Speaker *proposes the Question* – in other words, says formally to the House 'The Question is, that the Bill be now read a second time' or whatever, making clear exactly what it is that the House then has to decide or debate. This may seem a pointless duplication, but it is important as a formality – and vital if the House is proceeding rapidly through a flock of amendments (or, for example, the eight different options for the future composition of the House of Lords). At the end of a debate the Speaker *puts the Question*, saying 'The Question is, that the Bill be now read a second time. As many as are of that opinion say "Aye". Of the contrary, "No"'. If the matter is uncontroversial, the only response he hears is a muffled 'Aye' from the government whips, and the matter is decided without a vote.

But if there is disagreement and the opposition as a whole, or a group of back-benchers, wants to press the matter to a vote, the two sides will shout out 'Aye' or 'No' in response to the Chair. The Speaker, in what is known as *collecting the voices*, says, judging what he thinks is the louder cry, 'I think the Ayes/Noes have it'. If his decision is challenged by the other side still shouting 'Aye' or 'No' then he says 'Division. Clear the Lobby' (in the singular, this refers not to the division lobbies but to Members' Lobby beyond the Chamber, which the doorkeepers now clear of all but members and officers of the House to allow MPs easier access to vote). The division bells ring throughout the parliamentary precincts (and in nearby flats, pubs and restaurants whose owners pay to be connected to the system), and a division is under way.

After two minutes, the Speaker *puts the Question again* to check that there is still disagreement between the two sides. He then *names the tellers*. These are usually two whips on each side, although any MP may act as a teller. 'The Ayes to the right, the Noes to the left [referring to the two division lobbies]. Tellers for the Ayes, Geoffrey Clifton-Brown and Henry

Bellingham. Tellers for the Noes, Joan Ryan and Gillion Merron [or whoever it may be]'. If no teller (or only one) has come forward on one side, the
Speaker declares the result in favour of the other side.

The tellers, one from each side so that they agree on the numbers, then
go to the exit door of each division lobby and count MPs as they emerge
(whips will be at the other end of the lobby to encourage their own MPs
to vote the right way). Inside the lobby their names will have been taken by
the division clerks, and the lists that result will be published in *Hansard* the
following day. After eight minutes from first calling the division the Speaker
says '*Lock the doors*'; the doorkeepers lock the doors leading into the lobbies
and no more MPs can get in to vote. When every member has passed the
division clerks and then the tellers, the results are reported to one of the
Clerks at the Table, who writes them on a 'division slip', which is handed to
one of the tellers on the winning side. The tellers then form up at the Table,
by the Mace and facing the Speaker, with the Clerk at the despatch box to
one side, and the teller with the division slip reads out the result to the
House – a soundbite often used on the television news when a major vote
has taken place. The Clerk takes the slip to the Speaker, who repeats the
result: 'The Ayes to the Right, 307. The Noes to the left, 271. So the Ayes
have it, the Ayes have it. Unlock'. The doorkeepers unlock the doors to the
division lobbies, and the House moves on to the next part of the business
of the day. From start to finish, the division has taken anything from twelve
to fifteen minutes.

This may seem unnecessarily complicated, but there is a lot of common
sense about it. Collecting the voices allows an expression of disagreement
but does not commit the House to a division unless the disagreement
is persevered with. Putting the question again after two minutes allows
for second thoughts; and if no disagreement is expressed then (or if it is
not enough to provide two tellers for one side or the other) the matter is
decided. This avoids unnecessary votes (and in complicated proceedings
allows for the occasional mistake, for example when a group of MPs actually wanted a vote on the next amendment rather than this one). Requiring
tellers on each side to agree on the number of votes they have counted also
means that the numbers are unlikely to be challenged.

If the result of a division shows that fewer than forty MPs were present
(that is, fewer than thirty-five actually voting, plus the two tellers from each
side and the occupant of the Chair) then the division is not valid and the
House proceeds to the next business. In fact, many MPs may be present but
not voting; staging an inquorate vote in this way is, for example, a very
good way of killing a private member's bill.

Electronic voting?

But for many people the idea of taking a quarter of an hour of valuable parliamentary time on a vote is inexplicable. Why not vote electronically? There is a good case for it, but also some powerful arguments against. From a practical point of view, the fact that MPs do not have individual seats in the Chamber means that there would have to be voting stations outside the Chamber. Then, because MPs would have to come to the Chamber to vote, perhaps from offices some distance away, and queue up at the voting stations, not a lot of time might be saved after all. Remote electronic voting is canvassed by some – after all, if you can pay your London congestion charge by text on your mobile phone, why couldn't you vote? However, for many proponents of electronic voting, this goes too far. The public perception of MPs not even having to come to the Chamber to vote on some vital issue, at a time when Parliament is struggling to 'reconnect' with the public, might not be favourable. The same might go for a more modest solution, such as voting stations in more distant parts of the precincts.

There is also the question of security; how do you ensure that in every case a vote is registered only by an MP entitled to do so? Swipe cards may not be enough and may need validation by biometric systems such as palmprints or iris recognition. After all, what is at stake is not whether or not you can get £100 out of a cash machine. A vote 'to take note' of a particular EU document may not be of huge significance, but the House of Commons also votes on the biggest national issues – whether a government survives a vote of confidence, or, in March 2003, whether there should be a war. Any system of electronic voting has to deliver the same confidence in the result as the present system; and it is interesting to note that, in the later days of the Major government, with close results on important votes and even the government's survival in the balance, the accuracy of those votes was never challenged.

However, for many MPs, a powerful argument for the present system is that it collects large numbers of members together for a few minutes, often at a predictable time. This brings back-bench and front-bench MPs together (and many back-benchers may not actually see very much of those in government) and is a valuable opportunity to buttonhole ministers, or to gather support for some initiative or signatures for an early day motion. For most MPs, this adds a great deal of value to the otherwise often mundane business of voting.

Deferred divisions

In June 2000, the Modernisation Committee recommended a new procedure to 'reduce the number of occasions on which [the House's] judgements have to be delivered in the small hours of the morning' and to allow debate without requiring other members to be on hand for a vote that might in the event not take place. Following an experimental period, this procedure has been made permanent.

The procedure does not apply to bills or to motions that authorise expenditure or charging in relation to bills; nor does it apply to consideration of Estimates and to some types of motion to regulate the business of the House. But where it does apply, if after the moment of interruption (see page 158) an attempt is made to force a vote, that vote is held between 12.30 p.m. and 2.00 p.m. on the next sitting Wednesday. In one of the division lobbies members mark 'Aye' or 'No' on a form that lists all the votes to be taken, the numbers are totalled by the Clerks, and the Speaker announces the result to the House later during that sitting.

The procedure is a departure from the general practice of the House of taking a decision immediately following a debate (although this could already happen on Estimates and on some amendments to bills (see page 200), and it has some strong critics. To an extent it reduces the power of the opposition (or dissenters anywhere in the House) to force votes on the spot to demonstrate disagreement and to have that disagreement reflected in inconvenience for the government. Others see it as preserving the opportunity to vote, but at a more sensible time (although the fact that the change in sitting hours means that on three days of the week votes that are now able to be deferred would have taken place in the early evening has somewhat weakened this argument).

Some would like to go further, and have all votes delayed to a single 'decision time'. Although some parliaments have this system, it also has strong critics, on the grounds that it would be seen by the public simply as a means of making MPs' lives easier, and would reinforce the image of MPs as 'lobby fodder'. In some types of proceedings, it might actually distort the process of decision making. For example, on the Terrorism Bill in November 2005 there was an amendment to reduce the government's proposed ninety-day detention without charge to twenty-eight days, and another to 'sunset' any such period (that is, to make it law only for a limited time). If the decisions had been postponed to a later time, the debate on 'sunsetting' would have taken place with no idea of what period of detention without charge was being discussed.

Voting in the Lords

Voting is very similar in the Lords, the principal difference being one of terminology. Three minutes elapse before the question is put a second time, and eight minutes pass before the doors are locked. Generally speaking, the numbers of members voting in divisions in the Lords are fewer than in the Commons, but a vote can still take ten minutes or more from beginning to end. Because party discipline is weaker in the Lords, there is no tradition of pairing. But the whips nevertheless try to keep their members in the House as long as they can when important divisions are likely. In a busy session this can be fatiguing: there were 250 divisions in 1985–86, compared with 165 in 1992–93, 110 in 1995–96 and 176 in the session of 2003–04. There are no deferred votes in the Lords, and the same considerations apply to electronic voting as in the Commons.

The media

The gallery and the lobby

The relationship between politicians and journalists has always been, and will always be, an equivocal one. Politics is about publicity; opinions will gather force and support if they are positively presented to a mass audience. But good political reporting has to be critical; it must show up weaknesses as well as strengths, which politicians find less attractive. And political disasters make the best copy of all. There is a partnership – or perhaps a fatal attraction; journalists need the stories that politicians provide, and politicians need the oxygen of publicity to further their own aims.

For many years, the House of Commons treated reporting of its proceedings with the gravest suspicion. In 1694, the writer of a newsletter that carried an account of debates was summoned to the Bar of the House and there – on his knees – was rebuked by the Speaker. In 1738 the House resolved that:

> It is a high indignity to, and a notorious breach of privilege of, this House for any news writer, in letters or other papers . . . or for any printer or publisher . . . to give . . . any account of debates or other proceedings of this House . . . ; and that this House will proceed with the utmost severity against such offenders.

However, by the end of the eighteenth century, although the resolution still stood, reporters were starting to appear in the gallery of the House (where they had to compete for space with members of the public). The 'press gallery' was established 200 years ago, when in 1803 Speaker Abbott directed that seats should be reserved for the press. In the eighteenth and nineteenth centuries, literary luminaries appear as parliamentary reporters: Johnson, Hazlitt, Coleridge, Cobbett and Dickens, as well as (before note taking was permitted) 'Memory' Woodfall, a prodigy who could remember hours of debate verbatim and would later return to his office to dictate from memory.

Today there are about 170 print, radio and television journalists in the gallery and some 200 in the lobby. Many of these represent national papers or channels, but others report for a regional audience; given their constituency focus, MPs are particularly keen to establish good relations with these. All journalists must be accredited by the Serjeant at Arms before they get a pass – and they too must make a declaration of their interests. Members of the gallery used to report proceedings in the House and in committees, and members of the lobby were more concerned with interpreting parliamentary and political events to the outside world; but in practice the distinction has disappeared. Most national newspapers also have sketch writers, who contribute satirical – and more or less witty – pieces about one or two events the previous day. When they are at Westminster, journalists inhabit cramped and somewhat Dickensian quarters behind the actual press gallery in the House.

The lobby have access to a number of places around the palace frequented by MPs but denied to the general public: principally the Members' Lobby and some of the bars. They will also receive advance copies of documents, such as government White Papers or select committee reports 'under embargo', which allows them a vital twenty-four or forty-eight hours to write their stories on what may be a complex subject in time for publication. More importantly, lobby correspondents have access to MPs and ministers in both Houses on 'lobby terms'; the journalists are given information on the basis that it may be disclosed but not attributed. Politicians will use this channel in a number of ways: a secretary of state whose policy has proved damagingly unpopular may be able to hint at a U-turn; public opinion may be prepared for some new initiative; or disenchantment with the party leadership may be aired, and a warning shot fired, without actually putting a head over the parapet.

There are more formal ways in which the lobby is briefed and ministers and others may be questioned. On sitting days, the Prime Minister's press secretary holds twice-daily briefings usually at 11.00 a.m. and 3.45 p.m. (since May 2002, the morning briefing has been open to other journalists as well). On Thursday afternoons, the Leader of the House holds a briefing, mainly covering the parliamentary business for the following week. The Leader of the Opposition gives a briefing on Thursdays, and press conferences are held by ministers and others as occasion demands.

The lobby system has its critics; it is alleged to be too cosy and open to manipulation by those – especially governments – eager to spin the best story. Partly in response, after the 2001 general election the No. 10 briefings became attributable (although not by name, but as the Prime Minister's official spokesman (PMOS)), and summaries of these briefings are now put on the No. 10 website. The Prime Minister also holds regular televised press conferences.

The days when every reputable newspaper devoted many column-inches and even pages to detailed reporting of Parliament are long gone; but serious parliamentary reporting hit a low point in the late 1980s and early 1990s, illustrated by the decision to abandon the parliamentary page in *The Times* (and to save a dozen staff). MPs criticise what they see as the press's lack of interest in the institution of Parliament; journalists (and newspaper proprietors) respond that they report what is newsworthy and relevant, and that they cannot be expected to report Parliament only because it is Parliament. Interestingly, in the build-up to war against Iraq the amount of straight reporting greatly increased. In its coverage of the decisive debate on 18 March, *The Times* report ran to 7,500 words, including a 2,500-word account of the Prime Minister's speech, and there was lengthy coverage in most other papers. However, later in 2003, the new editor of *The Daily Telegraph* decided to dispense with that paper's parliamentary page.

Most reporting is political rather than parliamentary; Westminster is more often part of the backdrop than the main focus. And although much political reporting is sharp and insightful, it sometimes displays an ignorance of the workings of Parliament even on occasions when knowledge is crucial to a real understanding of what is happening.

Politicians and journalists each have something the other wants – information on one side, and a national or local platform on the other – but journalists can also exercise a great deal of influence on politics. MPs and, more important, senior ministers take notice of Nick Robinson's dissection of an issue, of Peter Riddell's magisterial analysis, or of the results of a mugging in an interview by John Humphrys or Jeremy Paxman. Sometimes the media are partisan; the *Sun*, the UK's biggest selling daily at over four million copies, headlined the Conservative victory in the 1992 election with 'IT WAS THE SUN WOT WON IT'. Yet following the Labour victory in 1997, many observers saw Trevor Kavanagh, the political editor of the *Sun*, as especially influential with No. 10. But whether the relationship is by turns supportive or critical, suspicious or friendly, the media are an integral part of British politics and so of the Westminster Parliament.

Broadcasting Parliament

Although it was as long ago as 1923 that the BBC sought unsuccessfully to broadcast the King's Speech at the State Opening of Parliament, it was not until 3 April 1978 that regular sound broadcasting of both Houses and their committees began. The Lords has been televised since 23 January 1985 and the Commons since 21 November 1989. Both Houses began with an experiment, which was then made permanent. The initial reluctance to be televised – the Commons rejected it in 1966, 1971, 1975 and 1985 – is slightly reminiscent of the House's view of journalists in previous centuries. Even when the Commons approved televising, the majority was not overwhelming: 320 in favour and 266 against; but now it is very hard to imagine Parliament not being televised.

Committees of the two Houses have drawn up rules of coverage concentrating on what is actually being said rather than distractions elsewhere in the Chamber: 'a full, balanced and accurate account of proceedings, with the aim of informing viewers about the work of the House'. This means that the use of cutaway shots is limited, which can be frustrating to broadcasters who want more atmospheric coverage; but the pictures ('the clean feed' – in other words, with no captions or other material added) are also used by broadcasters who want brief inserts for a news bulletin and so need pictures of MPs speaking rather than reacting. The rules for the use of material prohibit it being used for comedy or satire, or for advertising.

Proceedings in both the Commons and the Lords are covered gavel to gavel by remote-control cameras in each Chamber operated from a control room across the road at 7 Millbank – eight cameras in the Commons and five in the Lords. All sittings in Westminster Hall are televised, but coverage of committees, either live or recorded (or in sound only) is decided (and charged) on the basis of how many of the broadcasting organisations want to take the feed. These arrangements, and the rules of coverage and use, are supervised by the Director of Parliamentary Broadcasting, who is an officer of both Houses.

The opening of Portcullis House, with six camera-equipped rooms (four of which are primarily for select committees) and two permanent control rooms, brought in digital broadcasting for the first time. All parliamentary broadcasting is now digital and is available in widescreen format. BBC Parliament, the digital channel, carries the House of Commons Chamber live, time-shifted coverage of the House of Lords and unedited coverage of about ten committees each week. BBC 2, BBC News 24 and Sky News take Prime Minister's Questions live together with some ministerial statements and committee evidence. The main domestic channels, regional companies and some international organisations use recorded extracts.

All material is archived by the Parliamentary Recording Unit, which keeps tapes for about two years before they are deposited at the National Film Archive. This is developing into a fascinating historical record; many will regret that televising or filming was not permitted many years before, and that the archive does not show us debates at the time of Munich, during the Second World War or during the Suez crisis; and that we have only the written word and contemporary recollections to tell us how Chamberlain, Churchill, Bevan, Macmillan, Wilson and many others performed in the House of Commons.

In January 2002, the two Houses launched experimental webcasting, transmitting audio and audio-visual coverage of proceedings over the Internet (www.parliamentlive.tv). This was made permanent in May 2003, also covering select committees, and is likely to develop extensively in the years ahead.

The microphones used in the Chambers are highly selective and directional to reduce extraneous noise, especially in the often noisier Commons. Perversely, this makes the coverage slightly less realistic. A minister may be under a great deal of pressure, being barracked as he or she winds up a debate; but if the minister keeps going, talking directly at the microphone, it sounds as though the ride is fairly smooth. The one-liners that spice proceedings are often lost: in one statement during the Iraq war, the Prime Minister was asked about arranging a surrender. He was replying that one of the difficulties was finding someone with authority to surrender, when a wag behind him shouted out 'George Galloway?' The House collapsed with laughter; but the intervention was almost inaudible on the television.

It is understandable that broadcasters should make the most use of moments of confrontation on the floor of the House, but a good contrast is provided by coverage of select committee hearings, which can be compelling television (it is interesting to speculate what additional political impact the Defence Select Committee's hearings on Westland, some of the most high-profile in recent years, might have had if they had been televised). The televising of proceedings is now a fact of parliamentary life, and its effect on proceedings and behaviour, feared by its original opponents, is to that extent an academic question. What is certain is that it has made Parliament and its proceedings much better known and more accessible to the country at large.

Privilege

The privilege of Parliament allows the Houses, and their members, to perform their duties without outside threat or interference: rights absolutely necessary for 'the due execution of [Parliament's] powers' as the eighteenth-century Clerk of the House of Commons John Hatsell described them. 'Privilege' is an unfortunate term, as it implies a special advantage rather than a special protection. 'Public interest immunity' would be a better description.

The privileges of Parliament, and especially of the House of Commons in its struggle for power with the sovereign, have been established over many years in a series of cases that are charted in *Erskine May*. In later years, assertion of privilege became less important, and in the nineteenth and twentieth centuries these cases became more a matter of defining the limits of privilege – actions to which it did or did not apply.

From 1997 to 1999, the whole question of privilege was examined by a joint committee of both Houses, chaired by a law lord. The committee made a number of detailed recommendations, which have not yet been implemented, including setting out the extent of privilege clearly in an Act of Parliament; its overall approach was that privilege was needed for the proper functioning of Parliament in the public interest, but that it should be limited to what was essential in practice. It is worth noting that Westminster MPs are in any event less protected than those of many other parliaments, where a parliamentary immunity from arrest or civil suit exists.

There are two key elements in modern parliamentary privilege: the first is *freedom of speech*. The classic statement of this is in Article 9 of the Bill of Rights 1688–89: 'That the freedom of speech, and debates or proceedings in Parliament, should not be impeached or questioned in any court or place out of Parliament'. This means that no MP can be sued or prosecuted for anything he or she says as part of the proceedings of the House or any of its committees. This ensures that a Member of Parliament can speak up on behalf of constituents, or can express any opinion on a public issue, without fear of legal action. Rich and powerful individuals or companies cannot use the threat of writs to silence criticism. Anyone giving evidence to a committee of the House also has the absolute protection of privilege; no civil or criminal action can be brought against them on the basis of what they have said. In a recent case in which a constituent sought to bring an action against her MP for identifying her family in the House as socially disruptive, the European Court of Human Rights acknowledged the public interest of free speech in a national parliament, and the attempt to bring the action failed.

The protection of privilege is balanced by a need for it to be used responsibly, as has been emphasised by successive Speakers (and the Chair, both in the House and in committees, does have some control over MPs' opportunities to speak). Nevertheless, it does happen that individuals are unfairly criticised, or even unjustly accused of a crime, but as Robert Blackburn and Andrew Kennon (see page 470) comment:

> *As in the courts themselves, the House of Commons could not work effectively unless its Members were able to speak and criticise without having to account to any outside body. Freedom includes the freedom to make mistakes. There would be no freedom of speech if everything had to be proved to be true before it was uttered.*

However, this freedom of speech is limited to *proceedings*. This includes anything said in debates on the floor or in standing or select committees; it also includes anything put in writing that forms part of a proceeding, such as the text of any question (or a minister's written answer), amendment or early day motion, and, by virtue of the Parliamentary Papers Act 1840, any document published by order of the House (select committee reports, *Hansard* and potentially sensitive reports by outside bodies that are the subject of a motion 'for an unopposed return' (see page 153)).

The privilege of freedom of speech does not include press conferences, letters to constituents or to ministers, or words said at ordinary public meetings (even if they are held within the parliamentary precincts). Strictly speaking, it does not even include distributing a speech from *Hansard*, as the protection applies to the whole of the document rather than excerpts; but, unless the excerpts were selected and edited in a distorting and malicious way, it would be very unlikely that any action would succeed.

Exclusive cognisance

The second key element in modern parliamentary privilege is *the freedom of each House to regulate its own affairs* – to use the language of the Bill of Rights, not to have its proceedings questioned. This freedom is sometimes known as 'exclusive cognisance', and in practice it means that the validity of what one House or the other has done, whether in making amendments to a bill, deciding not to proceed with some matter or in regulating the conduct of its own members, cannot be adjudicated upon by any other body.

Parliament and the courts

The scope of exclusive cognisance has contracted in recent years, as Parliament has made certain legislation – for example on employment protection, anti-discrimination, health and safety, and latterly the Freedom of Information Act 2000 – applicable to itself. It is also the case that the courts may find legislation incompatible either with the Human Rights Act 1998 or with EU law; but both these possibilities arise as a result of decisions by Parliament itself, and in both cases what is at issue is the final content of the legislation rather than the way in which Parliament has passed it. In addition, following the *Pepper* v. *Hart* case in 1993 (where the Inland Revenue interpreted a piece of tax law in a way at odds with what a Treasury minister had said about it when the bill was before Parliament), the courts may try to resolve ambiguities in law by looking at ministerial statements and speeches setting out the intention of a piece of legislation.

With the exception of these closely defined categories, the courts are careful to follow the principle set out by the jurist Blackstone in 1830, that 'the whole of the law and custom of Parliament has its origin in this one maxim, that whatever matter arises concerning either House of Parliament, ought to be examined, discussed and adjudged in that House and not elsewhere'. The rules of both Houses seek to return the compliment, through the rules on matters *sub judice* (see page 303) and on criticism of judges.

If the extent of parliamentary privilege were to be set out in an Act of Parliament, as recommended by the Joint Committee on Parliamentary Privilege, the courts would have a bigger interpretative role (as they do in Australia, for example), which might not make the relationship easier.

Even in the legal challenge to the Hunting Act (passed in 2004 using the Parliament Acts (see page 244)), which was appealed all the way to the House of Lords, the case turned on the *nature of the law* that had been passed, and not *what the Commons had done* in passing it; perhaps a fine distinction, but an important one.

Complaints of privilege

Until 1978, complaints that parliamentary privilege had been infringed could be made by any MP in the Chamber, and this became a regular slot (rather like the 'bogus point of order') for raising political matters that had nothing to do with privilege. Now MPs have to write privately to the Speaker; in the exceptional cases where he agrees that there has been a serious breach, he makes a statement to the House and allows the MP the opportunity to move a motion relating to the matter, normally the following day, and usually referring the matter to the Committee on Standards and Privileges for detailed examination. The most recent reference was in October 2005, of differences between what Stephen Byers had said on oath in a court case about Railtrack, and what he had said to a select committee when he was Secretary of State for Transport.

Contempts

The privileges of free speech and exclusive cognisance protect the proceedings of Parliament in the public interest. Attempts to interfere with proceedings in Parliament, or to obstruct or threaten MPs in the performance of their parliamentary duties, are known as 'contempts'. Examples of contempts might include disrupting a sitting, giving false evidence to a select committee or threatening an MP on account of something he or she had said, or intended to say, in the House, or for voting in a particular way – or for threatening or taking action against a witness because of what he or she had said to a select committee. A contempt may also be committed by an MP: examples in the last twenty years are the leaking of a draft select committee report to a government department and agreeing to ask parliamentary questions in return for payment. In 2004, for example, the Lord Chancellor and others were found to have committed a contempt by dismissing Judy Weleminsky from the board of the Children and Family Court Advisory and Support Service (CAFCASS) on account of evidence she had given to a select committee.

There is no automatic definition of whether something is a contempt or not. Only if the Committee on Standards and Privileges finds that a contempt has been committed, and its view is endorsed by the House, is the matter decided.

Punishment

From early times, both Houses have had the power to imprison, fine or reprimand anyone (including an MP), and to suspend or expel MPs from the House. The last time the Commons imprisoned someone was in 1880, and it is difficult to see the House attempting to do so in modern times.

The last time the House fined someone was in 1666; but the power has never been formally discontinued, and indeed select committees in 1967 and 1977 recommended that a power to fine should be put on a statutory basis, although nothing was done.

The sixteenth to eighteenth centuries are dotted with expulsions of members from the House, from the rather grand crime of 'being in open rebellion' through forgery, fraud and perjury to the social discrimination of 'having behaved in a manner unbecoming an officer and a gentleman'. Expulsion became less frequent in the nineteenth and twentieth centuries; the last occasion was in 1954, for a criminal conviction. Suspension, on the other hand, is used more frequently; when an MP is named by the Speaker in the House (usually for disorderly conduct challenging the authority of the Chair), the House suspends the member for five sitting days on the first occasion, twenty sitting days on the second occasion and indefinitely on the third.

Suspensions are also used as punishments for other offences: twenty days for damaging the Mace (1988); ten and twenty days for 'cash for questions' (1995); three, five and ten days for leaking a draft select committee report (1999); three weeks for not disclosing a financial interest (2002); one month for non-disclosure and for obstructing an inquiry (2002); three weeks for claiming an allowance without entitlement (2003) and two weeks for conflict of interest, followed by indefinite suspension if an apology was not made (2005). An MP who is suspended is not paid during the period of the suspension.

Procedure

Procedure regulates the proceedings of the House and its committees. It has four sources. *Practice*, sometimes called 'ancient usage', refers to matters so clearly established over centuries that there is no need to set them down formally – for example the process of moving a motion, 'proposing the question' on it to the House, debating that question, and then deciding it by 'putting the question'.

Standing orders are general rules for the conduct of business and are amended or added to as the House alters its procedures. They govern matters as diverse as the election of the Speaker, the appointment and powers of most select committees, and the length of debate on different types of business. As *Erskine May* remarks, in a phrase which has survived many editions of that work, 'their chief characteristic is that they are intended to expedite the progress of business by reducing the opportunities for debate and checking its luxuriance'; and it is probably not a coincidence that standing orders became significant in the early nineteenth century when the government began to exert more control over the time of the House. Today 165 standing orders occupy 157 pages of the blue booklet which these days is republished annually – sometimes more often – to keep up with changes.

Rulings from the Chair are an important part of the case law of procedure. These usually arise because the view of the Speaker is sought on a point of interpretation, or some new matter not otherwise covered. The rules on admissibility of parliamentary questions, motions and amendments to bills have grown up in this way. Rulings have a close relationship with precedent – that which has been done before, and judged to have been in order by the Speaker of the day. Rulings and precedents are distilled in successive editions of *Erskine May*.

Finally, some parliamentary proceedings are regulated by *Acts of Parliament*, covering such things as the way Royal Assent to bills is signified to Parliament, how secondary legislation (see page 252) is dealt with, and making an affirmation or taking an oath.

Like the Commons, the House of Lords derives its procedure from practice, from standing orders, and to some limited extent from Acts of Parliament. But as the House has no Speaker with powers of order, there are no Speaker's rulings in the Lords. Instead, procedure is developed and refined by the House itself by agreeing recommendations from its Procedure Committee. Sometimes these may result in amendments to standing orders, but more usually they are set out in the House's own procedural handbook, the *Companion to Standing Orders*.

Why procedure? And why is it complicated?

Every deliberative body, from a parish council to the General Assembly of the United Nations, needs rules to a greater or lesser extent. Rules regulate how business is initiated; they provide a framework for consideration; and they define how a valid decision is reached.

Many organisations can manage with simple rules, and perhaps no great damage is done if even those rules are not followed very closely. The procedure of Parliament is not simple, for three main reasons.

◆ **Contention.** If a group of people are in complete agreement about something, rules are barely necessary. The Supreme Soviet in the old USSR had little need of procedure. The Westminster Parliament is a forum where often profound disagreements on politics and principles are argued out and decided. Procedure thus has to provide a means of focusing points for decision, allowing challenge to take place, and balancing the will of the majority against the arguments of the minority.

In addition, procedure has to protect the rights not only of the opposition parties but also of groups of MPs, or individual members, wherever they may sit in the House. In a House the size of the Commons, this is especially important; one MP out of 646 may be in a very small minority, but he or she may have constituents whose interests might be threatened by a decision of the majority.

Where the balance should be struck between the will of the majority (in effect, the government of the day) and the arguments of those who disagree is controversial. There has always been an understanding that a government that has a majority will get its way in the end; but governments are always impatient. Both the Conservative official Opposition and the Liberal Democrats have been highly critical of the effect of programming of bills (see page 198) upon scrutiny of legislation. The legislation to ban hunting perfectly encapsulates the tension between the wishes of a majority and the interests of a minority.

◆ *Control.* The standing orders are about setting limits – defining what powers select committees may have, how long various types of business may be debated, when certain things happen, and so on. The more tightly those limits are drawn, and the more circumstances that have to be controlled, the more complex the rules. For example, the standing orders on the programming of bills run to twelve pages.

◆ *Complexity of business.* Parliament has to deal with a huge range of material: every issue for which the government is responsible, and legislation on any subject, often extremely detailed. It approves taxation and grants the government the money required to run the country. At the same time, it must try to fulfil its role of calling government to account. Small wonder that procedures to regulate this business are often complicated.

Consistent, certain and clear

We have seen why there have to be rules, and why they are complicated. But rules are not an end in themselves. As the United Kingdom has no written constitution, and as the way Parliament operates cannot be reviewed by any other body, its rules must be robust. Good procedural rules have three qualities:

♦ They must be *consistent*; things of the same type must be dealt with in the same way; when something is not, that must be on the basis of a formal decision to handle it in a different way.

♦ They must be *certain*, with notice given of matters for substantive decision and rules enforced firmly but fairly. Punctuality is an important part of this; if the moment of interruption is 7.00 p.m., the Speaker will say 'Order, order' precisely on the stroke of seven o'clock, not a moment earlier or later.

♦ Rules may be complex, but they must be *clear*. Vagueness will mean that the rules themselves, not what they regulate, will become a source of disagreement; and it will also tend to cast doubt on the validity of what has been done.

7

Making the law

IF ASKED 'Who makes the law in the UK?' most people would instinctively reply 'Parliament'. It seems to be an obvious feature of our democracy that the law under which it operates has been decided by elected representatives in Parliament. And if we were asked 'Where can one find the law?' we might point to the long series of volumes entitled 'Statutes' or 'Acts of Parliament'. As we saw in Chapter 2, each of these Acts of Parliament begins with the formula:

> *Be it enacted by the Queen's Most Excellent Majesty, by and with the consent of the Lords Spiritual and Temporal, and Commons, in this present Parliament assembled, and by the authority of the same, as follows . . .*

However, if we look at any particular instance of the law in operation, the picture is less simple. The way the law works in practice may differ from the intentions of Parliament when the law was passed, or the application of the law may vary in different parts of the country.

For example, the driver of an antique lorry used in a funfair is stopped by the police as he drives the wrong way down a one-way street. The police find that he has no tachograph in his cab, and they take the view that this is required by law to record his hours of work and the miles he has travelled. The driver is charged with driving the wrong way down the street and with not having the tachograph and is convicted by the magistrates on both counts. He accepts the first but goes all the way to the Court of Appeal on the second, on the grounds that his lorry is an exhibit and is not used for commercial haulage purposes, so it is not required to have a tachograph. The appeal court judges agree and quash the conviction.

What has Parliament to do with this process? The enforcement of the law was the duty of the police. The interpretation of the law was a matter for the courts. The street was not designated as one-way by Parliament but by the district council. The law about tachographs was set out in regulations made by the Secretary of State for Transport, not by Parliament. And all the Secretary of State for Transport had done was to give effect in the UK to European Union legislation brought forward by the European Commission and agreed by the Council of Ministers and the European Parliament.

However, all the actors in this drama have been operating within a framework that derives from statute law as made by the Westminster Parliament. The district council was able to make the street one-way because an Act of Parliament gave it the power to do so; the European Union was able to legislate because an Act of Parliament – in this case the European Communities Act 1972 – provides that such legislation shall apply to the UK; and the Secretary of State for Transport was able to make regulations because the same Act of Parliament allows the translation of general EU legislation into detailed domestic law. The Westminster Parliament retains the power to repeal the European Communities Act 1972 and end the power of the EU to make any law applying to the UK; and although such a thing might be politically highly unlikely, it remains possible.

This chapter will look in detail at these Acts of Parliament and how they are made. It will also examine delegated legislation: that is, legislation made directly by the government and other bodies that have been authorised by Parliament to do so.

Types of legislation

First, some definitions. The *Acts of Parliament* we have been talking about are a level of legislation known as *primary legislation*. A piece of draft primary legislation is a *bill*. When a bill is passed, it becomes an *Act* and part of *statute law*. An Act is referred to by its title and the year it was passed.

There are two types of bill and Act: *public* and *private*. The majority, and by far the more important, are public. They affect the public general law, which applies to everyone in the UK – although some Acts may apply specifically to England, Wales, Scotland or Northern Ireland, and the Scottish Parliament has power to make primary legislation for Scotland on a range of subjects defined by the Westminster Parliament in the Scotland Act 1998.

Private Acts confer private and particular rights or are local and personal in their effect. A private Act might allow a local authority to close a cemetery, or to confer powers to manage and control access to areas of common land. A private Act may also allow an exception to the general law: for example, the Birmingham City Council Act 1985 allows motor racing – when authorised by the City Council! – on public roads in Birmingham. In recent years, the rare cases of personal legislation (once used for divorces) have been to allow people to marry who otherwise would be prevented from doing so (for example stepfather and stepdaughter).

Sometimes a public bill contains provisions that do not apply generally but affect particular individuals or bodies differently from others who would otherwise be in the same situation. If these were the only provisions in the bill, it would be a private bill; but combining them with changes to the general law turns the bill into a *hybrid bill*. Different procedures apply to public bills, private bills and hybrid bills.

Private members' bills are sometimes confused with private bills, but they are public bills to change the general law; their title comes from the fact that they are brought forward by a private member (that is, a back-bencher) rather than by the government.

Bills of all types may start their parliamentary passage in either House, although those whose purpose is mainly or entirely financial will generally start in the Commons. At the beginning of a parliamentary session, the government business managers will try to maximise the use of parliamentary time available by deciding which bills will start in the Lords and which in the Commons. A bill that begins in the Lords has [*Lords*] suffixed to its title when in the Commons and [HL] when in the Lords.

Delegated legislation is made by a minister (or occasionally a public body) under powers conferred by an Act of Parliament. Individual pieces of legislation may be called *orders*, *rules*, *regulations*, *schemes* or *codes*, depending on what the original Act (called the 'parent Act') says; but they are generally known as *delegated legislation, secondary legislation* or *Statutory Instruments* (SIs). A special type of order, an *Order in Council*, requires the approval of the Queen in the Privy Council.

Delegated legislation is normally used for detailed arrangements that flesh out broader provisions in the parent Act, or to specify things – such as, for example, the arrangements for licensing some activity – the details of which may need to be changed and for which an amending bill would be a poor use of time. But the balance between what is contained in primary legislation, which can be examined in detail during the passage of a bill, and what is left for ministers to determine in much less scrutinised secondary legislation, is an important issue. We deal with delegated legislation in greater detail on pages 252 to 264, which also covers *regulatory reform orders*, *remedial orders* and *Church of England measures*.

Government bills

Origins

After a general election, the legislative programme is dominated by *bills reflecting commitments that the winning party has made in its manifesto*. Reversing the policy of the previous government on a key issue may be a priority, as for example when the Labour government introduced a bill soon after it was elected in 1997 to repeal legislation passed seventeen years before under a Conservative government that provided for some pupils at independent schools to have their fees paid by local authorities. In the same way, the incoming Conservative government in 1979 repealed the previous Labour government's Education Act 1976, which had compelled local education authorities to introduce comprehensive schools.

Examples of 'manifesto' bills for the incoming Labour government in 1997 were the Human Rights Bill, legislation to devolve power to the Scottish Parliament and the National Assembly for Wales and to create the Greater London Authority and Assembly, and the Firearms (Amendment) Bill, fulfilling a manifesto pledge to allow a free vote on the banning of handguns. Following the 2005 general election, 'manifesto' bills included the Violent Crime Reduction Bill (aimed at reducing public disorder and violent crime, controlling replica guns and giving powers to schools and to the police to search for knives), the Identity Cards Bill (to provide for a new type of passport or driving licence with biometric data), and the Immigration and Asylum Bill (to control immigration where it was in the national interest, and to prevent it otherwise).

During a government's term of office, its legislative programme will *reflect new and developing policies* as a result of changing circumstances, subjects moving up the general political agenda or sometimes the personal priorities of a senior member of the Cabinet in his or her area of policy – although he or she will also need Cabinet support. In the 2005–06 session, such bills included the Education and Inspections Bill (to give more autonomy to schools through three-year budgets and incentives for success) and the Health Bill (among other things, to restrict smoking in public places and to help control hospital-acquired infections such as MRSA).

Financial bills are required both to raise revenue and to authorise how it is spent. The Finance Bill, introduced following the Budget, authorises taxation as well as embodying the Chancellor of the Exchequer's proposals for tax changes; and Consolidated Fund and Appropriation Bills authorise government spending.

Bills may be needed to *give effect to international commitments*, such as the European Union (Accessions) Bill to incorporate into UK domestic law the Treaty of Accession for Romania and Bulgaria as new member countries of the EU. Treaties are not required to be approved by legislation, but in the case of EU treaties bills are necessary to incorporate their provisions into domestic law.

Government bills may *respond to events*. Fear about the potential for fraud in postal voting gave rise to the Electoral Administration Bill, and London's success in the competition to host the 2012 Olympic Games was followed by the Olympic Games and Paralympic Games Bill to set up the Olympic Delivery Authority. Past examples include legislation on the safety of sports grounds following the Hillsborough disaster, on firearms after the Hungerford and Dunblane massacres, and on dangerous dogs after incidents in which children were attacked. Legislation may also be needed *to respond to court decisions*, which may perhaps demonstrate that ministers do not have a power they thought they had, or which otherwise show that the law needs clarification.

In addition, most government departments will want what might be called *housekeeping bills*. These may or may not be substantial, are often not controversial in party political terms and are about keeping the business of government and public affairs up to date. Thus the Regulation of Financial Services (Land Transactions) Bill of session 2005–06 extended the powers of the Financial Services Authority with the aim of improving consumer choice and protection.

Also in the housekeeping category are *consolidation bills*, which set out the law on a particular subject in a clearer and more up-to-date form without changing its substance, and *tax law rewrite bills*, which with some greater latitude do the same for tax law.

From proposal to bill

Political pressures and day-to-day departmental pressures – to say nothing of the proposals from special interest groups for changes in the law – ensure that no government department is ever short of ideas for legislation. When those ideas have been formulated, a process of consultation begins, the length and detail of which depends on what sort of legislation is being considered and how quickly it is needed. Inside government, the Treasury will be consulted as well as other departments with an interest, together with the devolved administrations in Scotland, Wales and Northern Ireland. Outside government, the views of the pressure groups, public bodies, industries or trade unions affected will be sought.

The process of consulting outside government is covered by a Cabinet Office Code of Practice, which requires a consultation period of twelve weeks. Consultation documents are widely circulated and available on the Internet. Nevertheless, the process is sometimes open to criticism. Political pressures may mean that there is in fact little time for *effective* consultation. The process may sometimes focus too much on 'the usual suspects' – those organisations with a national profile – rather than opinion more widely. Consultation often has to be on the broad intentions of a proposal, but 'the devil is in the detail', and some important elements of a proposal may be decided only when the business of drafting begins. Finally – and crucially – there is no point in consulting if the opinions expressed are ignored and the government of the day steams ahead regardless.

These criticisms are met to a certain extent if legislation follows a Green Paper, where the government has sought views on various legislative options, or a White Paper, where is has made its intentions clear. Increasingly, though, the use of draft bills (see page 201), where a complete legislative proposal can be considered in detail before it begins its formal parliamentary stages, is seen as a way of allowing the widest consultation as well as resulting in better legislation.

In due course the sponsoring government department will have proposals to put before a policy committee of the Cabinet. This will often be done by correspondence, and only if disagreements arise or if major issues are at stake will the subject need to be discussed at a meeting of the committee itself. In 2005 there were 28 ministerial committees of the Cabinet, covering broad areas such as Domestic Affairs, Economic Affairs, Productivity and Competitiveness, and Defence and Overseas Policy, but also specific areas of current concern, such as Anti-Social Behaviour, Animal Rights Activists, and Serious Organised Crime and Drugs.

But even if the relevant ministerial committee endorses a proposal, this does not mean immediate legislation. A minor change may have to wait until a more extensive bill in that subject area comes along. A major policy development, or a series of related proposals, may need a whole bill and so a place of its own in the government's legislative programme.

Parliamentary time is scarce, so further decisions need to be taken centrally about priorities and about balancing the programme of bills for each session of a parliament. This is the task of the Ministerial Committee on the Legislative Programme – known as 'LP' – which includes the Leaders and government Chief Whips in both Houses. That committee recommends to the Cabinet what proposals will actually find a place in the next Queen's Speech. As the new session approaches, LP will decide which bills will start in the Commons and which in the Lords, and which should be published in draft; it makes an assessment of how much parliamentary time will be needed for each and any difficulties on the way – perhaps dissenting government back-benchers in the Commons, or a critical reaction in the Lords; and it decides on the phasing of bills, in order to make the best use of the time available.

Meanwhile, those proposals that have been approved for the next session's programme have been moving from concept to detail. The sponsoring department prepares drafting instructions for parliamentary counsel. These instructions will set out what the bill needs to do but not the detail of how it will do it. This is the job of parliamentary counsel, an elite group of lawyers specialising in legislative drafting. Despite the name, they are servants of the government rather than of Parliament, and they draft all government primary legislation (secondary legislation is normally drafted by lawyers in the government department concerned).

In converting a department's instructions into a bill, parliamentary counsel have a number of tasks. They must achieve clarity and precision, not only so that the bill's provisions will be tightly defined but also so that, once it is passed, the possibility of legal challenge is minimised. They must ensure that the bill fits with legislation already in existence – both the statute book of primary legislation and any relevant EU or delegated legislation. This may mean that the bill must amend or repeal provisions of UK legislation that may be scattered through a number of Acts of Parliament. Finally, they must ensure that the provisions of the bill work – in terms of logic rather than political policy. To take a simple example, if you make something illegal you need to ensure that there is a penalty for doing it, and you also need to define what will constitute evidence that the offence has been committed. Small wonder that it is said to take seven years to acquire the skills needed to draft a medium-sized bill.

This process of turning instructions into drafting often throws up new questions of policy, and for most bills there will be a continuing dialogue between the sponsoring department and parliamentary counsel while the bill is being drafted. Even then the bill may go through several further drafts before it is finally approved by its sponsoring department and minister, agreed by LP, and is ready to begin its parliamentary journey.

Just before it does so, the text must be submitted to the authorities of the House in which it is to start. In the Commons, the Clerk of Legislation ensures that the bill complies with the rules of the House; that everything in it is covered by the long title – the passage at the start of a bill which says that it is 'A Bill to . . .' and then lists its purposes; that any provisions which would require expenditure or would levy charges or taxes are identified (and are printed in italics); whether the Royal Prerogative is affected (in which case the Queen's or Prince of Wales's Consent will be required); whether any uncertainties exist as to what sort of amendments might be relevant to the bill; and whether it conflicts with or duplicates a bill or part of a bill that has already been introduced. In the Lords, the Public Bill Office offers advice on the same range of issues, except on financial matters. Once these consultations are complete, the bill is ready for introduction.

Is a government bill really draft legislation?

Every textbook of parliament and politics says that a bill is a draft Act of Parliament, but governments tend not to see it like that. For each bill, there has been a lengthy process of development and debate between departments and ministers; the government has consulted those it feels have an interest; the contents of the bill have been minutely considered by officials and by parliamentary counsel; and the bill has been through a series of drafts.

Small wonder, then, that by the time the bill reaches Parliament it is not so much draft legislation for discussion and amendment as word for word what the government of the day wants to see on the statute book. Moreover, ministers identify personally with major bills; 'their' bills are part of their political achievements as ministers, and significant amendment of a government bill, such as the November 2005 defeat of the proposal in the Terrorism Bill for a 90-day period of detention without charge – which was closely identified with the Prime Minister – is seen as a loss of face.

The pressure of legislation

This might matter less if there were more time to consider legislation and the lead times were longer. However, governments of both parties are always in a hurry: to demonstrate their dynamism; to seek to deliver on commitments; and to put their stamp on key areas of policy. This means in turn that the machinery for preparing legislation is frequently overloaded. The result is that the consultation process is rushed or curtailed; too many large and complex bills are attempted in a session; policy is sometimes not settled well in advance of drafting (and sometimes it changes after introduction of a bill); and instructions from departments to parliamentary counsel are sometimes late.

This often leads to 'drafting on the hoof', when significant amendments to a bill are made not because of effective criticism inside or outside Parliament but in order to reflect the government's changing views. Some government amendments are brought forward to meet such criticism (and one of the strengths of a bicameral system is that it allows an undertaking to amend to be given in one House and the time to bring forward the amendment in the other House).

However, although it is difficult, if not impossible, to be sure of the genesis of every amendment that a government puts down to one of its own bills, a large proportion are the result of second thoughts rather than a response to a measured critical process. To give examples of the general and the particular: in the 1999–2000 session, 3,892 government amendments were made in the Lords to government bills coming from the Commons; and in the 2002–03 session, the government tabled at the report stage of the Criminal Justice Bill 13 new clauses introducing additional provisions, some of them major matters of policy. That bill was being considered under a programme order (see below), which meant that there could be little or no substantive consideration in the Commons. Drafting on the hoof has an additional perverse effect in that it occupies the time of parliamentary counsel, who could be working with a longer lead time on the next session's bills.

Looking at the 1997–98 session, Blackburn and Kennon (see page 470) observe that fifteen of the twenty main government bills ended up with more sections than they had clauses when introduced, with the Finance (No. 2) Bill more than tripling in size. The 131 clauses of the Crime and Disorder Bill attracted 558 government amendments and the 90-clause Competition Bill 343 government amendments. In the 1999–2000 session, the total page count of government bills increased from 2,760 to 3,600, an increase of 30 per cent. Blackburn and Kennon comment: 'This shows that in many cases the legislative process is really a mechanism for the government of the day to tidy up under-prepared bills'.

The Ministerial Committee on the Legislative Programme has exerted increasing pressure to reduce the need for government amendments (especially late amendments), but the results have been patchy. One example was the return of the Criminal Justice Bill from the Lords to the Commons in November 2003, with 496 amendments occupying 134 pages of text. The Lords Amendments were printed overnight and taken in the Commons *the next day*. And when the Constitutional Reform Bill [*Lords*] reached the Commons in February 2005, the government tabled ninety-two pages of amendments to its own bill.

Programming and guillotines

In the Lords, the intervals between the different stages of the passage of a Bill are prescribed by a recommendation of the Procedure Committee in 1977: two weekends between introduction of a bill and second reading, fourteen days between second reading and committee, fourteen days between committee and report for large and complex bills, and three sitting days between report and third reading. Intervals in the Commons are governed by practice and a degree of negotiation between the two sides but are usually much shorter than in the Lords. The 1985 Commons Procedure Committee recommendation for two weekends between introduction and second reading, and ten days between both second reading and committee, and committee and report, was never adopted.

Bills may need little – or sometimes no – debating time if they are narrow and technical or if they command support on all sides (although all-party agreement may not make for good legislation, as was shown by the Dangerous Dogs Act 1991 and especially the Child Support Act 1991). However, for most bills there is pressure, both from the opposition and from government back-benchers, for more debating time than the government is prepared to concede. The purposes and motives of such debate are varied: to set out a contrary political position; to seek explanation and clarification from the government; to explore and criticise the details of the legislation and its likely effects, and to make alternative proposals; and, in the case of the more contentious bills, to make opposition clear, and to inconvenience the government, by delaying the bill.

There are various ways in which debate may be limited. We have already looked at the closure (see pages 50 and 158), where, after what in the view of the Chair is a reasonable period of discussion, the use of the government's majority can bring debate to an end and have the particular question before the House at the time put; but this is of little practical use to the government where legislation is concerned. A more draconian power was introduced into the Commons in the nineteenth century following the disruption of proceedings over several sessions by Irish MPs campaigning for Home Rule. It was generally recognised that the rights of the majority needed to be preserved and, despite considerable reservations at the time, the *guillotine* or *allocation of time order* was introduced. This has been modified over the years, but in essence it allows the House to agree, at any stage in proceedings on a bill, strict time limits for the remainder of its progress. A timetable is set out in a motion that is put to the House. If it is agreed, then delaying tactics are of no use; committee and report stages come to an end after a fixed period whether all amendments selected by the Chair have been discussed or not, and sometimes with many clauses of a bill not having been debated at all.

At one time the guillotines were considered wholly exceptional and could arouse outrage both inside and outside the House. The procedure was thus used just over seventy times in the ninety years 1881–1970. However, from the late 1970s its use increased under governments of both parties, and it was routine for three or four, or more, bills to be guillotined in each session. The highest numbers were in 1988–89 (ten guillotines out of thirty-seven government bills passed), 1998–99 (eleven out of twenty-seven) and 1999–2000 (thirteen out of thirty-nine).

One of the problems with a guillotine is its undiscriminating nature; the knife falls to conclude a stage of a bill, such as its consideration in standing committee, without taking account of how much of that bill has been considered. From the government business manager's point of view, the solution to this is in the hands of MPs on the committee; a degree of self-control would allow the time to be used more effectively. But with a contentious and complex bill this simply does not work – not least because in some cases in the past there has been political mileage for the opposition in spinning out proceedings in standing committee in the knowledge that the government will respond with a guillotine and can be criticised for that response.

In 1985, the Procedure Committee argued that the weapon of delay probably does nothing to change a government's mind, and that the guillotine response usually meant patchy scrutiny. It recommended that for controversial bills (those likely to need more than twenty-five hours in standing committee) there should be a timetable agreed by a Legislative Business Committee on which all parties were represented, which would allocate time in committee and on report to reflect the importance of different parts of the bill. This proposal had a good deal of support on the back benches but not on the front benches, and in February 1986 it was defeated in the House by 231 to 166. The Jopling Committee (see page 147) returned to this in 1992 and endorsed the earlier approach. In the event this was introduced in an informal way, with some timetabling agreed through the usual channels and guillotines avoided whenever possible (and indeed from 1994 to 1997 there were only six guillotines).

In 1997, the newly established Modernisation Committee returned to the issue. It recommended a halfway house between informal agreement and guillotine, to be known as 'programming'. When a bill was selected for programming, there should be discussions that would take account of representations from all sides of the House, including back-benchers. In the light of those discussions, the government would move an amendable motion immediately after second reading specifying the type of committee to which the bill should be sent and the day by which it should be reported. The committee would then decide how to use that time.

A *programme order* differs from a guillotine in that it is imposed on proceedings on a bill immediately after second reading rather than later, when the speed of progress (or extent of delay) is known, and, if taken immediately after second reading, is not debatable (guillotines are debatable for three hours). And, as noted above, unlike a guillotine it specifies the type of committee to which the bill should be sent. The programme order may be amended later, for example if the opposition persuades the government to provide more time.

When under a programme order the time allotted for part of a bill expires, only certain specified questions may be put to the standing committee or the House: in particular, on the amendment already under discussion, on any amendment selected by the Chair for a separate vote (in practice, amendments on which the opposition parties particularly want to register their position); thereafter, government amendments and new clauses may be taken en bloc.

When a programme order applies to proceedings in standing committee, the allocation is proposed by a sub-committee comprising the chairman of the committee and seven of its members and may be debated by the committee for half an hour (and may be amended). A standing committee can also make proposals to the House for changes in the date for reporting a bill, or in the programming of the report stage and third reading.

Following its introduction early in the 1997 parliament, programming operated on a fairly consensual basis, even when applied to controversial bills such as the devolution measures, but from 2000 onwards it has increasingly become a matter of contention, indeed bitter contention, between the two sides. In a debate in 2001, Eric Forth, the then shadow Leader of the House, said 'The Government seem determined to minimise or dispose of all opportunities for proper scrutiny of legislation', and in October 2004 his successor Oliver Heald said of programming 'no Opposition could tolerate the way in which this government want to operate'.

There are various reasons why programming of bills is now a source of such strong disagreement. *First*, the original proposals were seen as something of a compact, in which constraints on time would be balanced by more effective means of scrutiny, with a greater use of special standing committees (see page 222), as the Modernisation Committee had recommended.

However, in the four sessions 1998–2002 there were forty-eight programme motions; but only one bill was sent to a special standing committee.

Second, when the 'knives' of a programme order fall, large parts of a bill, and many proposed amendments, may be undebated (just as with a guillotine). In the 2002–03 session, when twenty-nine bills were subject to programming, 276 groups of amendments and 523 clauses or schedules went undebated in this way.

Third, although programming offers the prospect of more effective use of time, it can do nothing to increase the total time available; nor in itself can it reduce the pressure of the government's legislative programme. In a letter to the Modernisation Committee in June 2000 Speaker Boothroyd observed that 'Government legislation introduced in this House or brought from the House of Lords in the session to date comprises a total of 2,537 pages (excluding consolidation bills). The equivalent figure for the long 1997–98 session was 1,901, and for session 1998–99 was 1,590'. And as long as the pressure of the legislative programme leads to the 'drafting on the hoof' described in the previous section, any means of allocating time to the consideration of legislation will come under strain. One way of improving scrutiny – and perhaps of saving time in the long run – might be the use of draft bills.

Draft bills and 'pre-legislative scrutiny'

It has been the case for many years that a bill may be sent to a select committee for detailed examination after second reading. The select committee format has several advantages. The committee is not just a debating forum but can take oral and written evidence, involving many more people in a formal process of consultation and making the legislative process more accessible to those outside Parliament. A select committee has to return to the House the text of a bill just as a standing committee (see page 211) does, but unlike a standing committee it can also report its views and the reasons for its decisions. Even on highly contentious issues, select committees have a long history of operating in a consensual rather than an adversarial way, which is likely to make for more effective scrutiny of legislation. They are also much more flexible than special standing committees (see page 222) – even though the latter are often canvassed as a means of improving the legislative process.

Scrutiny of bills *in draft* by select committees (or joint committees of both Houses) goes several steps further. A draft bill has not begun its formal parliamentary progress, and it really is draft legislation in a way that a bill, once introduced, is not. Ministers have invested less political capital in it, and changes will not necessarily be seen as defeats. The Liaison Committee, consisting of the chairmen of all select committees, described the scrutiny of bills in draft as 'a development of great significance. It offers the prospect of properly examined, better thought out and so higher quality legislation'.

Between 1992 and 1997 the Conservative government published eighteen bills in draft for consultation, but they were not subject to systematic parliamentary scrutiny. In 1997 the incoming Labour government made a commitment to bring forward more bills in draft, and in the four sessions of that parliament there were three, eight, three and two respectively. The four sessions of the 2001 parliament saw five, nine, eight and twelve draft bills being examined by select or joint committees. The 2005 Queen's Speech foreshadowed seven draft bills for the 2005–06 session. So the numbers are going up, but they need to be seen against a background of between thirty and forty government bills in most sessions.

However, draft bills are not a panacea – at least, not for governments. They add to the time before a proposal passes into law (and circumstances may change during that time); they tie up more resources in the preparation and drafting of bills, as substantial changes may be needed in the bills eventually introduced; and, as there is the opportunity for criticism well supported by argument and evidence, they may make it harder for the government of the day to get its way. However, unless a way is found of slackening the *overall* pressure on a government's legislative programme, the contribution that draft bills can make may be limited.

The scrutiny of the draft Communications Bill in session 2001–02 is a case in point. This was a major and complex bill that proposed significant changes to the regulation and ownership of the media in the UK. The joint committee had two months to examine the draft bill. In that time it took oral evidence from more than fifty organisations, received 200 written submissions, set up an online forum for consultation, held three seminars and had thirteen deliberative sittings on the contents of the bill itself. Only extraordinary efforts by the members and staff of the committee produced an effective piece of scrutiny.

For pre-legislative scrutiny to work, it must be allowed enough time, and the tendency to 'bunch' draft bills in May, June and July needs to be tackled. We return to these issues in Chapter 13. We now follow the passage of a government bill (formally introduced into the Commons and not a draft bill) through Parliament. (A chart showing the stages of legislation in the two Houses is overleaf.)

STAGES *of* LEGISLATION

HOUSE *of* COMMONS

		TIMING
First Reading	• Formal reading out of title of the Bill by the Clerk at the Table. • Ordered to be printed.	
Second Reading	• Main opportunity to debate the principle of the Bill. A 'reasoned amendment' may be tabled. A division at this stage represents a direct challenge to the principle of the Bill. • After Second Reading, Government Bills are usually timetabled by Programme Motions.	Usually two weekends after First Reading.
Committee Stage R	• Chance to conside and vote on the detail, clause by clause. • Amendments **selected** by Chairman (advised by Clerk). • All Bills go to one of four Committee types: (i) *Committee of the whole House*:- for 'constitutional' Bills and parts of the Finance Bill; (ii) *Standing Committee* - most usual procedure. 16-50 Members, in proportion to overall party strengths. (iii) *Select Committee* [Infrequently used]. (iv) *Special Standing Committee* [Rarely used] - has powers to send for persons, papers and records; holds 4 sittings and hears oral evidence in private and public.	Usually starts shortly after Second Reading and can take anything from one meeting to several months.
Report Stage	• A further chance to consider amendments, new clauses and, for MPs not on the Committee, to propose changes.	Usually shortly after Committee Stage
Third Reading	• Final chance to debate the Bill. • A vote gives chance to show dissatisfaction with amended Bill. • The Bill now goes to the Lords.	Usually immediately after Report Stage on the same day.

HOUSE *of* LORDS

		No significant delay in the transfer of a Bill between the two Houses.
First Reading R	• Formal. • The Bill is reprinted in the form finally agreed by the Commons (*see note below*).	
Second Reading	• Debate on general principles of the Bill. • **Government Bills included in the election manifesto are, by convention, not opposed at the Second Reading**, but "reasoned" amendments may be tabled as a means of indicating dissent and can be voted on.	Two weekends must elapse after First Reading.
Committee Stage R	• Bills usually go to a Committee of the Whole House or Grand Committee away from the Chamber and rarely to other types of committee. • Detailed line by line examination. • **Unlike the Commons, there is no selection of amendments - all can be considered.** • **No programme, unlike the Commons, and debate on amendments is unrestricted.**	Usually starts at least fourteen days after Second Reading. Often spread over several days.
Report Stage R	• Further chance to amend Bill. • May be spread over several days.	Usually starts at least fourteen days after the end of Committee Stage.
Third Reading and Passing	• **Unlike in the Commons, amendments can be made** provided the issue has not been voted on at an earlier stage. • Passing: The final opportunity for peers to comment and vote on Bill.	Usually at least three sitting days after the end of Report Stage.
Consideration of Amendments	• Depending on which House the Bill started in, each House now considers the other's amendments. • Bills with contentious amendments pass back and forth between the Houses until agreement is reached. If each House insists on its amendments, a Bill is lost. • Bills with agreed amendments await Royal Assent.	
Royal Assent	• Queen's assent formally notified to both Houses. • Bill becomes an Act.	

Notes
(1) For the purpose of this chart, the Bill is assumed to have started in the Commons. Bills may equally be introduced first into the Lords. There are no differences in the stages followed by a Bill starting in the Lords.
(2) **R** = Bill is reprinted at these points if amended at previous stage.
(3) To follow the progress of a Bill, **Contact**: Information Office: (Lords) 020 7219 3107 (Commons) 020 7219 4272
            Consult: Weekly Information Bulletin (*see Progress on Bills*)
            Visit: Parliament website at www.parliament.uk

The stages in the passing of a public bill

Source: The House of Lords 2005

Anatomy of a bill

Part of the controversial Terrorism Bill of the 2005–06 session is reproduced below and on pages 205 to 207 and shows some of the main features
of any bill. Every bill has a *short title*, which is the title by which it is known
during its passage and which will normally be the same as the title of the Act
that will result. Also on the cover page of the bill will be a statement by the
relevant minister as to whether the provisions of the bill are compatible
with the European Convention on Human Rights. After the cover page will
be a list of contents, if the bill is long enough to need one. At the start of
the bill is the *long title*, which sets out the contents of the bill; all the provisions of the bill must fall within the long title. This is followed by the words
of enactment: 'Be it enacted by the Queen's Most Excellent Majesty . . .'.

    Clauses are the basic units of a bill; they are divided into *subsections*,
paragraphs and sub-paragraphs. This particular bill contained thirty-eight
clauses, but a long bill may contain 100 to 500 clauses or more and be
divided up into several *parts* or *chapters*. When a bill becomes an Act, the
clauses become known as *sections*. To reduce complexity, the *schedules* to a
bill fill in some of the fine detail (for example, one of the schedules will usually list amendments and repeals affecting existing legislation). A schedule
is always dependent on the clause that introduces it and has no effect unless

---

Terrorism Bill

EXPLANATORY NOTES

Explanatory notes to the Bill, prepared by the Home Office, are published separately
as Bill 55–EN.

EUROPEAN CONVENTION ON HUMAN RIGHTS

Mr. Secretary Clarke has made the following statement under section 19(1)(a) of the
Human Rights Act 1998:

In my view the provisions of the Terrorism Bill are compatible with the Convention
rights.

A

BILL

TO

Make provision for and about offences relating to conduct carried out, or capable of being carried out, for purposes connected with terrorism; to amend enactments relating to terrorism; to amend the Intelligence Services Act 1994 and the Regulation of Investigatory Powers Act 2000; and for connected purposes.

B E IT ENACTED by the Queen's most Excellent Majesty, by and with the advice and consent of the Lords Spiritual and Temporal, and Commons, in this present Parliament assembled, and by the authority of the same, as follows:—

PART 1

OFFENCES

Encouragement etc. of terrorism

1   Encouragement of terrorism

(1)   A person commits an offence if—   5
   (a)   he publishes a statement or causes another to publish a statement on his behalf; and
   (b)   at the time he does so—
      (i)   he knows or believes, or
      (ii)   he has reasonable grounds for believing,   10
      that members of the public to whom the statement is or is to be published are likely to understand it as a direct or indirect encouragement or other inducement to the commission, preparation or instigation of acts of terrorism or Convention offences.

(2)   For the purposes of this section the statements that are likely to be understood   15
by members of the public as indirectly encouraging the commission or preparation of acts of terrorism or Convention offences include every statement which—

    (a)   glorifies the commission or preparation (whether in the past, in the future or generally) of such acts or offences; and

    (b)   is a statement from which those members of the public could reasonably be expected to infer that what is being glorified is being glorified as conduct that should be emulated in existing circumstances.   5

(3) For the purposes of this section the questions what it would be reasonable to believe about how members of the public will understand a statement and what they could reasonably be expected to infer from a statement must be determined having regard both —

    (a)   to the contents of the statement as a whole; and   10

    (b)   to the circumstances and manner in which it is or is to be published.

(4) It is irrelevant for the purposes of subsections (1) and (2) —

    (a)   whether the statement relates to the commission, preparation or instigation of one or more particular acts of terrorism or Convention offences, of acts of terrorism or Convention offences of a particular   15 description or of acts of terrorism or Convention offences generally; and

    (b)   whether any person is in fact encouraged or induced by the statement to commit, prepare or instigate any such act or offence.

(5) In proceedings against a person for an offence under this section it is a defence   20 for him to show —

    (a)   that he published the statement in respect of which he is charged, or caused it to be published, only in the course of the provision or use by him of a service provided electronically;

    (b)   that the statement neither expressed his views nor had his endorsement   25 (whether by virtue of section 3 or otherwise); and

    (c)   that it was clear, in all the circumstances, that it did not express his views and (apart from the possibility of his having been given and failed to comply with a notice under subsection (3) of that section) did not have his endorsement.   30

(6) A person guilty of an offence under this section shall be liable —

    (a)   on conviction on indictment, to imprisonment for a term not exceeding 7 years or to a fine, or to both;

    (b)   on summary conviction in England and Wales, to imprisonment for a term not exceeding 12 months or to a fine not exceeding the statutory   35 maximum, or to both;

    (c)   on summary conviction in Scotland or Northern Ireland, to imprisonment for a term not exceeding 6 months or to a fine not exceeding the statutory maximum, or to both.

(7) In relation to an offence committed before the commencement of section 154(1)   40 of the Criminal Justice Act 2003 (c. 44), the reference in subsection (6)(b) to 12 months is to be read as a reference to 6 months.

2   **Dissemination of terrorist publications**

(1) A person commits an offence if he —

    (a)   distributes or circulates a terrorist publication;   45

    (b)   gives, sells or lends such a publication;

    (c)   offers such a publication for sale or loan;

Terrorism Bill

A

BILL

To make provision for and about offences relating to conduct carried out, or capable of being carried out, for purposes connected with terrorism; to amend enactments relating to terrorism; to amend the Intelligence Services Act 1994 and the Regulation of Investigatory Powers Act 2000; and for connected purposes.

Presented by Mr Secretary Clarke
supported by
The Prime Minister, Mr Secretary Prescott,
Mr Chancellor of the Exchequer,
Mr Secretary Straw, Mr Secretary Darling,
Mr Secretary Hain and Hazel Blears.

Ordered, by The House of Commons,
to be printed, 12th October 2005.

Bill 55   (317905)   54/1

ISBN 0-215-70623-4

The Terrorism Bill, passed by Parliament in 2006

Source: The House of Commons 2005

the clause is agreed to. Any provisions that would cost public money (other than routine administration by the government department concerned), or that would impose taxes or levy a charge, are printed in italics in bills introduced in the Commons.

The last page of the bill is the *backsheet*, which repeats the long and short titles, gives the bill number and the session it was introduced, and lists the MP introducing the bill (the 'Member in charge') and his or her 'supporters'. For a government bill, the member in charge will be the secretary of state heading the relevant department, and the supporters will be senior ministers with an interest in the subject matter.

Explanatory Notes are a separate document that accompanies a government bill. They set out the bill's intention and background, explain the clauses in lay person's language and give an assessment of the bill's effects on public service manpower and costs and on business in the private sector (for example, if a bill were to introduce a new system of regulation or licensing).

Commons stages

Introduction and first reading

The most usual method of introducing a bill is by the member in charge giving notice of the bill's long and short titles and of the intention to introduce it on a particular day. This notice appears on the Order Paper for that day, the MP is called by the Speaker at the commencement of public business (see page 157), and brings the so-called 'dummy bill' (merely a sheet of paper with the short and long titles and the names of up to twelve supporters) to the Clerk of the House at the Table. (In the case of a government bill, a 'dummy bill' is not brought to the Table.)

The Clerk reads out the short title and the Speaker says 'Second reading what day?' For all government bills the response is 'tomorrow' (or the next sitting day if there is a break for a weekend or recess) as the government can bring any of its bills forward on any sitting day. For a private member's bill, however, naming a day can be a matter for careful tactics (see page 227).

The bill is now said to have been read the first time; it is recorded in the Votes and Proceedings as having been ordered to be printed and to be read a second time on whichever day has been named. A bill introduced in this way is known as a *presentation bill*; bills may also come before the House by being *brought from the Lords*, by being *brought in upon a resolution* (the

Finance Bill is founded upon the resolutions agreed by the House to give effect to the Chancellor's Budget proposals) or when an MP gets *leave to bring in a ten-minute rule bill*.

Second reading

This is the first time the bill itself is debated, and it is a discussion of the principle of the bill rather than the details of individual clauses. It is considered good practice for second reading to be delayed until at least two weekends have passed since the bill's introduction (although, if the bill has not been seen before in draft, even this does not give much time to assess it). The government does not always comply with the 'two weekends' convention; nor, less importantly, do back-benchers with private members' bills.

A second reading debate on a major government bill will normally take a day (in practice about six hours; on a Wednesday, for example, from about 1.00 p.m. to 7.00 p.m.). Less important bills will get less time, and wholly uncontroversial measures (including some private members' bills) can receive their second reading 'on the nod' – that is, without any debate at all. It is also possible – but unusual – for uncontroversial bills to be referred either to a *second reading committee* 'upstairs' or, in the case of a bill relating to Wales, second reading may be taken in the Welsh Grand Committee. The Scottish and Northern Ireland Grand Committees may in theory consider bills in relation to their principle, but following devolution this is now less likely, certainly for Scotland. Second reading committees are also used for bills prepared by the Law Commissions; but these are usually technical reworkings of the law and will normally have started in the Lords and have been considered by a select committee there.

Some major bills have in the past had lengthy second reading debates on the floor of the House. In 1972, the bill to enable the United Kingdom to join the then EEC was debated over three days on second reading, and the 1976 bill on Scottish and Welsh devolution (which eventually failed) was debated for thirty-two hours over four sitting days.

A second reading debate on a government bill takes place on a motion moved by a minister 'That the bill be now read a second time'. At the end of this debate, on bills which are opposed, a vote is taken. This can be a straight vote against second reading, or a vote on what is known as 'a reasoned amendment' (if it has been selected by the Speaker). This spells out the reasons why the bill's opponents do not wish it to have a second reading. If the reasoned amendment is carried, or the House votes against second reading, the bill can go no further – nor can exactly the same bill be reintroduced in the same session. It is extremely rare for a government bill to be defeated on second reading; the last example was in 1986, when the Shops Bill, which had been intended to relax the law on Sunday trading, was passed by the Lords but defeated in the Commons by a majority of fourteen. However, as we saw in Chapter 5, voting against the second reading of a controversial bill may be a powerful way for government back-benchers to register dissent.

These days, the second reading of a bill will normally be followed immediately by a *programme motion*, which is decided without debate (although almost always with a vote), followed if necessary by a motion to authorise government expenditure in relation to the bill (*a money resolution*) or the raising of a tax or charge (*a ways and means resolution*). These also give the committee on the bill authority to consider provisions that would require expenditure or impose a tax.

'Fast-track' bills

Certain types of bill are dealt with on a 'fast-track' procedure. *Consolidation bills* are prepared by the Law Commissions as a sort of housekeeping of the statute book. These bills draw together the law on a particular subject, which may be in a series of Acts of Parliament, and present it in a more logical and user-friendly way. *Statute law repeal bills* remove parts of the law that have become redundant. Bills of both sorts are checked by a joint committee of both Houses to ensure that no change of substance has been made in the process of restating the law, and that no 'live' legislation is to be repealed. If no amendments are put down, such bills are passed without debate. There is also a fast-track procedure for *tax law rewrite bills*, which are considered by a separate joint committee. *Consolidated Fund and Appropriation bills*, which authorise government spending, have no committee or report stage; the questions on second and third reading are put successively without debate.

Committee

As soon as a bill has had its second reading, it is sent to a committee for a detailed examination of the text. The choices are *standing committee*, *Committee of the whole House*, *select committee* and *special standing committee*. The Finance Bill is routinely divided between Committee of the whole House for its most important provisions and a standing committee for the rest, and other bills are occasionally treated in the same way. As standing committees are the default setting – if no other decision is taken, a bill goes automatically to a standing committee – we start with this method of consideration.

Standing committees

To begin with, the very name is misleading. Standing committees are not permanent; new members are appointed to a committee specifically for each bill; and, when the committee has reported the bill back to the House, it is effectively dissolved. When standing committees were first introduced at the end of the nineteenth century as a means of saving time spent in Committee of the whole House, the intention was actually one that modern advocates of reform would applaud; there were to be four permanent committees, each specialising in broad areas of public policy, which could develop expertise and deliver better scrutiny. However, it took only a few years for this to fall victim to expediency.

Standing committees are set up as bills receive their second readings. Each is designated by a letter; in the short session 2004–05 before the general election Standing Committees A, B, C, D, E, F and G sat, but there is no limit on the number (apart from the practical one of MPs available to sit on them). Standing Committee C is reserved for the committee stages of private members' bills; but once a standing committee is set up it remains available for other bills, and, as we shall see, this can be tactically important for private members' bills.

To take a standing committee dealing with government bills in a typical session: in 2003–04 Standing Committee B dealt with

◆ the Asylum and Immigration (Treatment of Claimants, etc) Bill (which occupied twelve sittings between 17 December and 27 January);

◆ the Armed Forces (Pensions and Compensation) Bill (six sittings between 22 January and 26 February);

◆ the Pensions Bill (twenty-two sittings between 2 March and 27 April);

◆ the Energy Bill [*Lords*] (fourteen sittings between 10 May and 22 June);

◆ the Children Bill [*Lords*] (eight sittings between 13 September and 21 October); and

◆ the Gambling Bill (six sittings between 1 and 16 November).

Standing Committee B was sitting for a good proportion of the session, but for each bill its membership was different and it had a different chairman or chairmen for each bill.

Membership

A standing committee on a bill must have between sixteen and fifty members, but in practice the membership is usually between sixteen and thirty. Its members are chosen by the Committee of Selection, which includes whips of the three main parties. Membership of a standing committee reflects the party proportions in the House as closely as possible. Where there was a free vote on second reading (as on the Hunting Bill in the 2002–03 session), the membership reflects the numbers of supporters and opponents in the House on the second reading vote. The Committee of Selection appoints members directly to a standing committee; the names do not have to be approved by the House, unlike the membership of select committees.

At least one government minister will always be a member of a standing committee (including standing committees on private members' bills), together with a government whip, and front-benchers from the other parties are also appointed. The remaining back-benchers are a combination of those who are interested in the subject (and who spoke in the second reading debate) and those who are drafted in by the whips but are ready loyally to support their party's line on the subject. Obviously the strength of the second group becomes more important when very contentious legislation is being considered, but the Committee of Selection has generally appointed a spread of MPs, so that dissent within a party is represented as well.

The Law Officers (Attorney General, Advocate General and Solicitor-General) may, if they are members of the Commons, attend a standing committee and speak (but not vote), although this is in practice very rare. Any minister may do the same in the committee on the Finance Bill, but in practice this is handled by Treasury ministers. Other MPs not appointed to a committee on a bill may not take part in its proceedings.

Chairmanship

Each standing committee is chaired by a member of the Speaker's Panel of Chairmen. (We should perhaps note that both Houses use the word 'chairman' in their standing orders. 'Chair', chairwoman' and 'chairperson' are not formally used by either House, so in this book 'chairman' is used whether the occupant of the Chair is male or female.) The Panel is a group of thirty to thirty-five senior MPs chosen by the Speaker to chair standing committees. It also includes the Deputy Speakers (and is itself chaired by the Chairman of Ways and Means), thus connecting the business of chairmanship in the House with that of standing committees. The Panel meets from time to time as a committee to consider matters affecting standing committees generally (for example, whether MPs should be allowed to use laptops and palmtops in committee). Since November 2005 standing committee chairmen have been paid a salary depending on their experience on the Panel: from £2,165 a year for under one year's service to £13,368 a year for chairmen with more than five years' service.

If a standing committee is taking a big bill, there may be two or three chairmen sharing the duties. The chairman has most of the powers to control proceedings that the Speaker has in the House, including power to select amendments (see below), but not including the disciplinary powers listed on page 49. As in the House, he or she does not vote unless there is a tie, and then strictly according to precedent (see page 52).

Meetings
Standing committees meet in the suite of committee rooms on the riverside first floor of the Palace of Westminster (hence a bill in standing committee is sometimes referred to as having been 'sent upstairs'). The room is laid out very much like the Chamber, with the two sides facing each other across the floor. The chairman sits on the dais at one end, with the clerk on his or her left (see the plan overleaf).

Meetings of standing committees are open to the public and, as in the House, debates are recorded verbatim by the *Official Report* (*Hansard*) and published and placed on the parliamentary website. Standing committees may meet on any day on which the House sits, but committees on government bills normally meet on Tuesdays from 10.30 a.m. to 1.00 p.m., resuming at 4.00 p.m., and on Thursdays from 9.00 a.m. to 11.25 a.m., breaking then to allow members to attend Question Time in the House and resuming at 2.30 p.m. Depending on how keen the government is to make progress with the bill, and how contentious it is, the committee may then go on until late in the evening.

The normal first business of a standing committee is to consider the resolution of the *programming sub-committee* (the chairman of the committee and seven members), which makes proposals about the time to be allotted to the various parts of the bill and sometimes the order in which parts of the bill are to be taken.

Amendments, selection and grouping
The committee deals with the clauses of the bill one by one. Any MP may put down an amendment to a bill in standing committee (or an entire new clause or schedule), but only a member of the committee may actually move it.

Amendments can serve a variety of purposes. If the bill is highly contentious in party political terms, many amendments will be pegs for debate

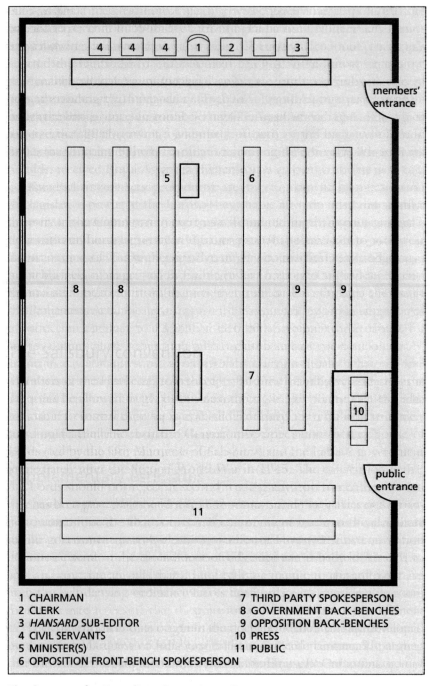

1 CHAIRMAN   7 THIRD PARTY SPOKESPERSON
2 CLERK   8 GOVERNMENT BACK-BENCHES
3 *HANSARD* SUB-EDITOR   9 OPPOSITION BACK-BENCHES
4 CIVIL SERVANTS   10 PRESS
5 MINISTER(S)   11 PUBLIC
6 OPPOSITION FRONT-BENCH SPOKESPERSON

The layout of a Standing Committee Room

to give publicity to government and opposition viewpoints – although this is more the case in Committee of the whole House (see below) as standing committees get very little media coverage. So-called 'probing amendments' are used to get the minister to clarify provisions of the bill and outline the thinking behind them. However, for the reasons we have seen, it is extremely unlikely that the opposition will table an amendment, convince the government of its merits and have it agreed to.

The chairman of a standing committee, like the Speaker in the House or the Chairman of Ways and Means in Committee of the whole House, has the power of *selection and grouping* (which does not exist in the House of Lords). This is crucial in allowing an orderly and logical debate on amendments, and it also prevents the proceedings of the committee being clogged up by hosts of amendments being tabled for their own sake.

Amendments are tabled on the days before the committee first meets (usually, at this stage by the opposition parties and possibly government back-benchers, but as we have seen, the government may even at this stage want to modify its own bill, and amendments may go down in the name of the minister in charge of the bill). The day after they are tabled, amendments will appear on blue paper in the Vote bundle (see page 168); but on the day the committee first meets, it will have before it a *marshalled list*, printed on white paper, of all the amendments that have been put down up to and including the previous day. This list of amendments is the committee's order paper.

The marshalled list sets amendments down by reference to where they apply to the bill. As each amendment is tabled, it is given its own unique reference number, so the numbering will jump about: for example, if the very first amendment tabled was to the last schedule, it will still be 1; and if, after 500 amendments have been tabled, an amendment is put down to the first line of the bill, it will be 501.

The process of selection and grouping, in which the chairman is advised by the clerk of the committee, begins with weeding out amendments that are *out of order*. Disorderly amendments include those that are irrelevant or outside the scope of the bill (or of the clause to which they are tabled); inconsistent with a decision that the committee has already taken (or that the House has taken in approving second reading – so-called 'wrecking' amendments); ineffective or incomplete; tabled to the wrong place in the bill, or to a part of the bill that the committee has already considered; 'vague, trifling or tendered in a spirit of mockery'; or that would impose charges outside the scope of any money or ways and means resolutions agreed to by the House. These rules are sometimes quite complex in their application, but they are a common-sense way of clearing out amendments that are irrelevant or ineffective (although an MP whose pet amendment is ruled out of order may not always see it like that).

Then begins the process of *selecting* from among the remaining amendments those that will be debated. Selection in standing committee is fairly generous (at report stage it is not), and unless an amendment is fairly trivial, or one of a multiplicity on the same point, it is likely to be selected. Amendments proposed by the member in charge of a bill, whether a minister or a private member, are normally selected automatically provided they are in order. An amendment that has been tabled only the previous day (and is marked by a star against it on the marshalled list), rather than the minimum two days in advance, will usually not be selected, although the chairman has power even to select a 'manuscript' amendment put forward within the previous few minutes if the circumstances warrant it.

At the same time, the chairman and clerk will be looking for themes that will help to *group* amendments. There are three main ways of doing this: the first is to group amendments that offer *alternative proposals on the same point*. An example might be where the bill proposes that a search can be authorised by any police officer. The opposition think that this is not stringent enough and so have put down an amendment that would require the authorising officer to be of the rank of inspector. Back-benchers on the committee (on both sides) would like to go further, and amendments are down variously specifying a superintendent, a magistrate and a High Court judge. If the 'inspector' amendment were selected on its own, the debate would take place only on the issue of whether the minimum authority should be constable or inspector. Separate debates would have to take place on the other proposals – and if the 'inspector' amendment were to be agreed to, then that would rule out debate on any alternative as being inconsistent with the decision the committee had reached. So all the amendments about the level of authorisation are grouped.

The second method is to group *interdependent amendments*. An example here might be where the opposition has an amendment early in the bill to appoint a statutory investigator of complaints. It has a raft of other amendments throughout the bill that specify how different types of case will come to this investigator. If the principle of appointing an investigator is defeated early on, all the later amendments will fall, so it is sensible to debate them together.

The third method is to *group amendments on a theme*. For example, there might be a number of amendments designed to require the secretary of state to make a regulatory impact assessment before using any of a number of powers that the bill would confer. Grouping these together allows a debate on the principle of requiring such an assessment. If the amendments were not so grouped, the result would be a series of very similar debates as the committee got to each of the clauses that would give the secretary of state each of those powers.

The result of this is a *selection list*, a new edition of which appears for each sitting day. The chairman gives no reasons for his or her decisions on selection, and there is no appeal to the Speaker. Two examples of selection lists appear on pages 218 and 219: one for the first day of a standing committee's consideration of a bill; and one for part of the report stage of a bill in the House. Both of these bills were programmed.

How the committee goes through the bill

Once the recommendations of the programming sub-committee have been considered, the committee begins with the first clause of the bill. Let us suppose that the first amendment in the first group – *the lead amendment* in that group – is to Clause 1. That amendment is moved, and the debate on the question 'That the amendment be made' then includes debate on any other amendment (or new clause) that is grouped with it. At the end of the debate the question is decided, on a vote if necessary: after a short interval the doors of the committee room are locked, the clerk rises and reads out the names of members of the committee. MPs say 'Aye' or 'No' or 'No vote'; the clerk totals the votes and hands the list to the chairman. She or he declares the result, says 'unlock' and moves on to the next question to be decided.

If a second group has its lead amendment to Clause 1, that group will be dealt with in the same way. But if not, the chairman proposes the question 'That Clause 1 stand part of the bill'. This gives the opportunity of a 'stand part debate' on the clause as a whole. If debate on a number of amendments to a clause has covered the ground, the chairman can decide to put the question on clause stand part without further debate.

An important feature of this way of going through a bill – and one that often causes confusion – is that the *amendments are decided not in the order in which they are grouped for debate but in the order in which they apply to the bill*. This can mean that an amendment to a clause near the end of the bill may be debated with the first group at the first sitting; but it will be put to the vote only when the committee gets to that clause, which may be after many hours of consideration. If amendments have already been debated (unless they are in the name of the member in charge of the bill), they are

---

Standing Committee A

NATIONAL LOTTERY BILL

Tuesday 25th October 2005 at 10.30 a.m. and 4.00 p.m.

Chairmen's provisional selection and grouping of Amendments

[Programme Motion – ½ hour]

Clause 7
24 + 25 + Govt 4 + 55 to 58 + Govt 7 to Govt 9
26 + Clause 19 stand part
27 + 28 + 94 + 95 + 38 + 42 + 61 to 63
29
30 + 77 + 79 + 82 + 84 + 85 + 37 + 60

Clause 19
Clause 13

Schedule 2
76 + 78 + 75 + 80 + 81 + 83 + 86 + 87
91 + 88 + 89 + 92 + 90 + 93
96

Clause 14
15 + 35 + 36 + 99
41 + 39 + 40
43 + 44 + 45
46 + 47 to 50 + 52 + 73
53 + 59 + 54 + 64 + 65

Clause 8
98 + Govt 5 + Govt 6
32

Clause 9

Clause 10
12

Clause 11
14 + 13

Clause 12

Clause 15
Govt 10 + 66 to 70

Clause 16

Clause 17
71 + 72

Clause 18
Govt 11

Clause 20
Schedule 3
Clauses 21 to 23

Clause 1
18 + 19 + 20

Clause 2
Govt 2 + Govt 3

Clause 3

Clause 4
21 + 22 + 74

Clause 5
23

Clause 6
Schedule 1

New Clauses
NC 1
NC 2

Proceedings to be concluded by 5.00 p.m. on Thursday 3rd November

Frank Cook
Mr Roger Gale
CHAIRMEN
[1]

A typical selection list for a Commons standing committee considering a bill under a programme order

Source: The House of Commons 2005

CONSIDERATION OF BILL

IDENTITY CARDS BILL

Provisional selection of amendments

Purpose of the register and of identity cards
8 + 9 + 6 + 10 + 24 + 15 + Govt 2 + 16 + 20

Content of the Register
Govt 1 + 33 + 12 + 34 + 17

[5.45 pm]

Compulsion and attendance
5 + 39 + 36 + 37 + 38 + 13 + 14

[7.15 pm]

Costs
7 + 19

Use of data
40 + 41 to 45 + 29

Miscellaneous and drafting
Govt 3 + Govt 4

[9 pm]

By Order of the Speaker
18 October 2005

A typical selection list for the report stage of a bill in the House of Commons under a programme order

Source: The House of Commons 2005

often passed over in silence when they are reached. But if the opposition or a back-bencher wants a vote – a separate division – and the chairman agrees, a vote on a specific amendment may take place, but without further debate. Government amendments that are reached in this way are called formally whether or not a vote is expected; the minister says 'I beg to move' and the question on the amendment is put to the committee.

If no lead amendment is down to any clause, the committee must never-theless agree whether or not the clause should stand part of the bill. When the committee has got to the end of the bill, any new clauses and new schedules (and any amendments to them) are decided upon (and debated if they have not been grouped with earlier amendments).

When the committee has completed its consideration of a bill, the mem-bers of the committee are discharged, the formal report of the bill appears in the Votes and Proceedings for that day, and the bill – if it has been amended – is reprinted for the *report stage* (see page 223). The process of going through the bill may have taken only a few minutes at a single sitting, or it may have taken a hundred hours of often fierce debate over thirty or forty sittings in the space of several weeks.

Scrutiny by debate and amendment: how useful is it?
Richard Crossman, Labour Leader of the House in the 1960s, wrote 'The whole procedure of standing committees is insane . . . under the present system there is no genuine committee work, just formal speech-making, mostly from written briefs'. Consideration in standing committee occupies a great deal of time: in the sessions 1998–99 to 2004–05 standing com-mittees on bills held a total 1,596 of sittings, and it is reasonable to ask how good a use of the time of the MPs involved this was, and how effectively the legislation was scrutinised.

Unlike select committees, standing committees have no research or staff resources of their own (the concern of the clerk of a standing committee is the conduct of the proceedings, not the merits of the bill). MPs have to rely on briefings from outside pressure groups (which are naturally often advocacy for a particular point of view). However, the minister taking a bill through standing committee has the support of the 'bill team' of civil servants, and behind them the substantial resources of his or her own department.

It is rare for the government to accept opposition (or individual back-bench) amendments in standing committee; when the other side feels that it has won the argument this is dispiriting and fuels pressure for a more consensual, evidence-based scrutiny, perhaps by select committee. How-ever attractive measured, non-partisan scrutiny of that sort may be, one should not lose sight of the role of the Commons as a place where political ideologies clash and where deep divisions between parties (often reflect-ing different views in the country at large) are played out in an adversarial way. However, there is no reason why select committee-type scrutiny (and especially the use of draft bills) should not be complemented by the full-dress political occasion, either in Committee of the whole House or at report stage.

Committees of the whole House

At one time, almost all bills were considered in Committee of the whole House. As its name suggests, it consists of all MPs (although only a relatively small proportion of those will be present during its proceedings) and takes place in the Chamber during part of a normal sitting of the House. The only evident differences are that it is presided over by the Chairman of Ways and Means and his deputies and not by the Speaker, that the Chairman sits at the Table beside the Clerk and not in the Chair, and that the Mace is placed on brackets below the Table rather than on it. Votes are taken in the same way as in the House.

The manner of going through a bill is similar to that in standing committee; and, as in standing committee, an MP may speak more than once in any debate. Selection and grouping of amendments is the responsibility of the Chairman of Ways and Means.

In recent years, Committees of the whole House have been confined to three types of bill. For convenience, *uncontroversial bills* (for which there would be no point in setting up a separate sitting of a standing committee) are considered in this way to save time. Also taken in Committee of the whole House are *bills of great urgency* that need to become law quickly, such as, in April 2006, the Northern Ireland Bill to pave the way for the restoration of the Northern Ireland Assembly.

The third category is of major *bills of first-class constitutional importance*. Since 1945, governments have been committed to having such bills dealt with in this way, but there is no formal definition, and whether a bill does or does not fall into this category can be a matter of political argument. Legislation to incorporate EU treaties into domestic law, to devolve powers to Scotland and Wales, or to reform the House of Lords clearly qualifies. In 2004 the Hunting Bill and the Scottish Parliament (Constituencies) Bill, and in 2005 the Constitutional Reform Bill [*Lords*] (for three days), the Electoral Registration (Northern Ireland) Bill [*Lords*] and the Terrorism Bill (for two days) were taken in Committee of the whole House.

It may thus be a matter of argument (or negotiation) as to what measures are treated in this way. The opposition will want time on the floor of the House and the higher profile of Committee of the whole House, but the government business managers will generally be reluctant, not only to take floor time on a bill they feel could be dealt with in standing committee, but also to have the burden of votes taking place in a forum of 646 MPs when they could take place in a committee of twenty or thirty members upstairs. And, historically, Committees of the whole House have presented problems for government business managers: the Parliament (No. 2) Bill to reform the House of Lords was considered for twelve days before it was dropped; and devolution to Scotland and Wales took up thirty-four days in Committee of the whole House in the 1976–77 and 1977–78 sessions. Nowadays, the prospect of being able to programme proceedings and so make them much more predictable and controllable may make government business managers slightly less reluctant to take committee stages on the floor of the House.

Select committees

We considered earlier the advantages of scrutinising *draft* legislation in a select committee. A bill that is on its *formal* passage through the House may be committed to a select committee after second reading, although this is rare. The main example is the bill every five years to renew disciplinary law for the armed forces (most recently in 2005–06), although in 2000–01 the Adoption and Children Bill was considered by a specially appointed select committee.

More frequently it happens that a select committee seizes the moment and conducts a swift inquiry into a bill and reports in time to influence later proceedings upon it, as when in 2005 the Constitutional Affairs Committee reported on the Constitutional Reform Bill [*Lords*] in time for its three-day examination in Committee of the whole House. However, if the bill has not been formally referred to a select committee by the House, the committee cannot make amendments to it.

Special standing committees

This provides a hybrid procedure; a special standing committee may have four sittings in select committee mode (one private deliberative session and three to take evidence, often with the chairman of the relevant departmental select committee in the chair) and then turns into a standing committee debating the bill. The advantage of this is that the committee is able to hear outside expert opinion on the bill, which will inform debate, and the committee will probably work more cooperatively as a result.

However, a special standing committee is more constrained than a select committee; the procedure is less flexible; and, although its members are likely to work more cooperatively, the majority of its proceedings will be in the usually adversarial debating format of a standing committee. It is perfectly possible for a bill to be examined by a select committee (perhaps by an existing committee specialising in the subject area that is used to working on a cross-party basis) and then given the standing committee treatment.

From the government's point of view, the disadvantage is that the process will take more time and that the party with the majority has less control. This may be why the special standing committee procedure has been used fairly infrequently, and mainly for non-controversial and fairly technical bills. The procedure was established in 1980 but used for only seven bills in the four years to 1984 and then not again for eleven years until two Scottish bills in 1995 and 1996. Although the Modernisation Committee recommended greater use of special standing committees, only the Asylum and Immigration Bill was so referred in the 1997 parliament, and only the Adoption and Children Bill (an earlier version of which had already been considered by a select committee) in the 2001 parliament.

Report stage

Except for bills that are considered in Committee of the whole House *and* are not amended there, all bills come back to the floor of the Commons for their *report stage*, properly called *consideration*. The bill returns in the form in which it left committee, and report stage is a further opportunity for amendments to be made. The important difference is that all MPs have an opportunity to speak to amendments on report.

Even for major bills the programme order is unlikely to give them more than two days on report (in May 2003, the Criminal Justice Bill had three days, but this was a major and complex measure, some of whose provisions – especially on the limitation of the right to trial by jury – were contentious with government back-benchers as well as with the Conservative and Liberal Democrat parties). Many government bills complete their report stage and third reading in a single sitting. Report stages of government bills in the two sessions 2003–04 and 2004–05 occupied about 10 per cent of the total time on the floor of the House.

New clauses and amendments for debate on report are selected by the Speaker on the same principles as in standing committee. However, selection is much tougher than in standing committee; the Speaker is unlikely to select amendments on a topic that has been fully aired in committee, unless the government indicated in committee that it was prepared to think again. However, major matters of public policy that were debated in committee may reappear, on the grounds that the House as a whole rather than a small group of MPs in committee should have the opportunity of expressing a view.

Procedure on report is somewhat different from Committee of the whole House. The Speaker (or one of the deputies) is in the Chair, and the Mace is on the Table. New clauses and schedules are normally taken first (although as in committee the minister may propose a particular order in which proceedings should be taken). The House is now revising the bill as a whole rather than going through it clause by clause, so there is no 'clause stand part', and the amendments are set out in a slightly different way.

Third reading

When all the selected amendments have been disposed of (or when the time allotted to report stage under the programme has expired), the House moves on to the third reading (usually at the same sitting). If there are no amendments on report, that stage is omitted and the third reading is taken immediately.

Third reading is the final review of the contents of the bill (debate is limited now to what is actually in the bill rather than, as at second reading, what might have been included). Except on highly controversial bills, where the opposition has the opportunity to fire some last shots, third reading debates tend to be quietly valedictory affairs in which those most closely involved (front-benchers and other MPs who were on the standing committee) look back rather sentimentally on the bill's progress through the House. Since the introduction of programming, however, the opposition front bench has often taken the opportunity to express hopes that the House of Lords will deal in more detail with this or that provision which they feel has had inadequate scrutiny in the Commons.

The procedure is akin to second reading: a minister will move 'That the bill be now read the third time', and a debate takes place on that question. As at second reading, it is possible to move a reasoned amendment (if selected by the Speaker), but this is very rare. Third readings occupy relatively little time on the floor of the House: about 2 per cent of the total in the 2001 parliament.

Once the third reading has been agreed to, the bill has been passed by the Commons. One of the Clerks at the Table, in wig and gown, then 'walks' the bill to the Lords. The doorkeepers shout 'Message to the Lords', the doors are thrown open, and the Clerk proceeds in stately fashion through the Members' Lobby, the Central Lobby and eventually to the Bar of the House of Lords. There the bill, tied up in Commons green ribbon (known as 'ferret', from *fioretti*, a sixteenth-century Italian name for a kind of silk), is handed over to one of the Lords Clerks.

This may seem a somewhat archaic way of taking a bill from one House to the other, but bill text is compiled and amended using highly sophisticated software, and at the same time an electronic version of the bill text has gone from the Public Bill Office in the Commons to its counterpart in the Lords. It can happen, though, near the end of a session, with the 'ping-pong' of amendments between the Houses, that the exact moment of a bill's formal arrival is of some importance. Handing it over in the Chamber makes this publicly evident in a way that its electronic appearance in a distant office does not.

Private members' bills

Before we move to the other end of the building to see how the House of Lords considers legislation, let us look at a category of legislation that often attracts publicity even though many more bills in this category fail than ever find their way on to the statute book: private members' bills.

These are not private bills but public bills that aim to change the general law of the land. They are introduced in one of four ways: the first private members' bills in each session appear following the *private members' bill ballot*; then there are *presentation bills*, (described on page 208), sometimes called 'back of the Chair bills'; when leave is given under the *ten-minute rule*; and private peers' bills that have been passed by the House of Lords may be *brought from the Lords* and *taken up* by a private member in the Commons.

Ballot bills

Ballot bills are introduced in the same way as presentation bills, but an MP gets the right to introduce such a bill through success in the ballot, a sort of legislative prize draw. On the Tuesday and Wednesday in the second week of each session MPs sign a book kept in the No Lobby, being allotted a number in the process. On the Thursday at 12 noon in Committee Room 10, normally televised live, the Clerk Assistant draws twenty numbers from a despatch box. The Chairman of Ways and Means matches the numbers to the MPs who have signed in and calls out the names. The twenty MPs get priority in introducing their own bills – but absolutely no guarantee that any of those bills will become law.

Some MPs are enormously keen to win the ballot; others strenuously hope not to be successful, as they have a good idea of how much sponsoring a private member's bill may interfere with their daily work. However, the reluctant are 'encouraged' by their whips to sign in, as the whips would prefer to see their own people successful rather than the other side. In most sessions 400 MPs will enter the ballot. Those whose names are drawn – especially those in the first seven places – are immediately mobbed in person, by post, telephone and e-mail by pressure groups who hope to persuade an MP to take on their special cause (and who may just happen to have a bill ready for the MP to adopt).

The ballot bills are presented on the fifth Wednesday of the session; and each of the twenty MPs has up to the rising of the House the previous day to decide what sort of bill to introduce. For some this will be a simple matter; this may at last be the opportunity to introduce legislation for which they have spent much of their parliamentary careers campaigning. For others, there are choices to be made. Should they accept that any bill is unlikely to become law and so produce a sort of manifesto on a subject they think important, hoping that as a bonus they might get a chance to debate it? Or should they temper their ambitions and go for a narrow bill that is likely to be uncontroversial but could make a modest but worthwhile change to the law?

One of the factors that will help an MP to come to a decision is the extent of outside support likely to be available. A pressure group may be a large and influential body, with resources including lawyers who can help with drafting the bill and people who can write speeches and briefings on hostile amendments. In these circumstances, an MP will feel a little less like David pitted against Goliath.

In a sense, the ultimate pressure group is the government itself. We saw earlier that it can be difficult for a government department to get its bills included in the legislative programme for any session. Persuading a friendly MP (not always from the government party) to take on one of its smaller hoped-for bills can be another route to the statute book. If an MP decides to take on one of these so-called *hand-out bills*, he or she will act rather like a minister, supported by departmental civil servants; and the bill itself will have been drafted by parliamentary counsel. However, the bill itself will proceed just like any other private member's bill and will get no special treatment (unless it is one of the very small number of private members' bills to which the government of the day is prepared to give some of its own time).

By the evening before the fifth Wednesday of the session, the MPs successful in the ballot must have given in the short and long titles of their bills (the latter will limit the scope of the bill when drafted), and they will have collected the names of their supporters for the back of the bill. At the commencement of public business (see page 157) the next day, the twenty MPs form a queue at the back of the Speaker's Chair, and as their names are called they come forward and hand their bills to the Clerk, who reads the title. The Speaker says 'Second reading what day?' and the MP names a day.

Tactics and procedure

It is at this point that the tactics essential for success in private members' legislation begin. There are normally seven days for private members' second readings. Obviously it is best to be the first bill on any day, because that means a full day's debate and the prospect (if 100 MPs can be found to vote for the closure) of getting a second reading and going into committee; and the earlier one can do that, the better. So if the twenty MPs name the days strictly according to those criteria, the bills will come on like this (the dates of the Fridays below are illustrative):

9 January	16 January	23 January	6 February	20 February	12 March	19 March
1	2	3	4	5	6	7
8	9	10	11	12	13	14
15	16	17	18	19	20	

However, it may be that the sponsor of bill 5 is not too concerned about her bill and cannot be in the House on 20 February anyway. So she names 9 January, which leaves a first-place slot open on 20 February. A quick-witted MP with a much lower-placed bill may then be able to get the first slot on 20 February, and a full day's debate. And unless the sponsor of bill 8 has those quick wits, and when it comes to his turn he names 9 January as he had planned, he will find that he is now the third bill on that day and not the second as he had hoped. And once a day is named, there is nothing to be done; a bill can be deferred but not advanced. The picture may be further complicated by MPs guessing that a particular bill will be fairly uncontroversial and may get through quickly and so putting their bill on for that day rather than the earlier day they could have taken (but when they would have been behind a fiercely contested bill and would have had no chance of getting debating time).

The next step for all the MPs successful in the ballot is to get their bills drafted. They may have the help of an outside body, of parliamentary counsel for a hand-out bill, or a kindly Public Bill Office (although this is not a formal part of the office's role). The drafting does not have to be perfect at this stage. If a bill gets into committee and looks to have a chance of getting further, the government will normally put down amendments so that if the bill is eventually successful it will be in properly drafted and workable form.

For those in the top slots on the second reading days, it will not be enough simply to have a majority of those in the House on the Friday in question. Even a few opponents can 'talk the bill out' by continuing to debate it up to the moment when the Deputy Speaker says 'Order, order' at 2.30 p.m. It will be important to muster at least 100 supporters, so that when the sponsor of the bill claims the closure just before 2.30 p.m. by saying 'I beg to move that the Question be now put', the closure is agreed with at least 100 MPs voting in the majority. With most MPs wanting Fridays for constituency work, this may take some silver-tongued persuasion – private members do not have the armoury of the whips at their disposal.

The rule that financial initiative rests with the Crown means that only a minister may bring in a bill whose main purpose is to create a charge. However, if a private member's bill that gets a second reading would incidentally involve an increase in public spending, the government will normally put down a money resolution to authorise such expenditure and to allow the bill to be considered in committee.

As with government bills, the next stage after second reading is standing committee, where opponents may seek to delay the bill by putting down a great many amendments, or – more subtly – may hurry the bill through to report because they can put amendments down at that stage, not to kill this bill but to deny time to the bill that is behind it on report.

The astute MP can get an advantage when going into committee. Standing Committee C is the one reserved for private members' bills, and as they get their second readings they join the queue for this standing committee. However, if a government bill comes out of one of the other standing committees and there is no government bill waiting to go in, the MP can ask to have his or her bill assigned to that standing committee. If the Committee of Selection can be encouraged to nominate the members of the standing committee before another government bill has appeared, the MP has overtaken the Standing Committee C queue on the inside lane.

The next hurdle will be the six 'remaining stages' days. On these Fridays the bills are ranked with the most advanced stage first: so, Lords amendments, third readings, report stages, Committee of the whole House (which is an option, although a high-risk one, for the private member) and second readings, in that order. Much the same tactics (and the need for closures) will apply, but at this stage it is much easier for opponents to take up time with amendments rather than on the single question of second reading, and so easier to kill the bill. The MP who is successful at this stage and secures third reading will rely on a colleague in the Lords to sponsor the bill there, and he will hope that that House does not amend the bill as this will produce another chance of 'sudden death' when the Commons considers those Lords amendments.

When a stage of a private member's bill is on the Order Paper on any of the first twelve private members' days but is not completed (because it is talked out or objected to after 2.30 p.m.), the member in charge may name one of the later private members' days for continuing with the bill. As the session proceeds, unsuccessful bills are put off from Friday to Friday, until on the thirteenth and last day (widely known as 'the massacre of the innocents') there may be fifty or sixty to be 'called over' at 2.30 p.m. Even if an MP is lucky enough to get third reading at this stage, eventual success will depend on the Lords agreeing to the bill without amendment in the relatively short time that then remains in the session.

Presentation, ten-minute rule and Lords bills

Much of what we have said about the procedure and tactics of ballot bills also applies to ordinary presentation bills, to ten-minute rule bills and to bills brought from the Lords. However, all of these have more of a hill to climb, as none may be proceeded with until the ballot bills have been presented (and those will have taken up two or three slots on each of the days devoted to second readings).

Both presentation bills and ten-minute rule bills are thus used more often to make a point than seriously to seek to change the law. Ten-minute rule bills have the additional advantage that an MP has the opportunity to gauge opinion in the House. Beginning in the seventh week of the session, on every Tuesday and Wednesday before the main business of the day, one MP is called to make a speech of not more than ten minutes setting out the case for a bill and seeking the leave of the House to introduce it. Other MPs are alerted to the subject matter by a brief description on the Order Paper. If there is objection to the proposal, one opponent may speak against, again for a maximum of ten minutes; and, if necessary, there is a vote. If the proposer is successful, the bill is introduced in a little ceremony that involves the MP walking from the bar of the House to the Table, bowing three times en route. (In a strange historical survival, the second of those bows, halfway up the Chamber, is just at the point where the great chandelier hung in the Chamber destroyed by fire in 1834, where MPs presenting a bill would stop and bow two centuries and more ago.)

Ten-minute rule bills are very popular with MPs. They could of course introduce exactly the same bill by the ordinary presentation method, without seeking the leave of the House. However, ten-minute rule bills come on at prime time immediately after questions and statements, and they are often a high-profile way of floating an idea and getting media attention – and perhaps laying the foundations of a later successful attempt. The right to introduce them is on a first come, first served basis. In the past an MP would spend the night in a room next to the Public Bill Office in order to be the first to give notice fifteen sitting days before the slot came up; but informal arrangements between the parties have ended this 'January sales' tactic.

Success and failure

Even with government backing, the success of a private member's bill is not assured. Against government opposition, failure is virtually certain; and even half a dozen determined back-bench opponents can make it exceedingly difficult to get a private member's bill on the statute book. An additional obstacle may be encountered every four years or so: a spring or early summer general election will probably kill all the private members' bills that are not on the point of being passed, even if they are entirely uncontroversial – as happened in 2005.

Over the last 25 years, about nine private members' bills a session have become law; but these figures are skewed by 'handout bills' (see page 226) where an MP is in effect taking through legislation on behalf of a government department. The numbers of bills passed in the last four complete sessions are shown in Table 7.1.

It is difficult to categorise successful back-bench legislation. Many are minor pieces of tidying up of the statute book to remove generally recognised anomalies, and a number of these will have been suggested to sympathetic

Table 7.1 Bills dealt with by Parliament, 2001–05

Session	2001–02 long session	2002–03	2003–04	2004–05 short session (general election)
Passed	8 (39)	13 (33)	5 (33)	0 (21)
Not passed	115 (0)	(89) 3*	(90) 3*	(56) 11

Figures for government bills are in brackets.
*Including bills not passed in that session because they were carried over to the next.

private members by government departments. Other Acts have dealt with small social reforms, particularly in areas affecting the rights of the disabled; marriage, children and the family; gaming and alcohol; care and control of animals; and the environment.

Overall, though, the scope has been very wide. Examples include the British Nationality (Falkland Islands) Act 1983, which gave British nationality to the inhabitants of the islands; the Pet Animals Act 1951 (Amendment) Act 1983, which made the sale of pets from market barrows illegal; the Race Relations (Remedies) Act 1994, giving industrial tribunals new powers in cases of racial discrimination; the Dogs (Fouling of Land) Act 1996, which gave local authorities new means of dealing with this problem; the Law Reform (Year and a Day Rule) Act 1996, which abolished the old rule of law that a person could not be found guilty of murder if the victim died more than a year and a day after being attacked; the Building Societies (Distributions) Act 1997, which removed some of the anomalies in the distribution of shares when building societies were 'demutualised'; the Protection of Animals (Amendment) Act 1999, which dealt with the welfare of animals when a prosecution for cruelty had been brought; the Private Hire Vehicles (Carriage of Guide Dogs etc.) Act 2002, which made it illegal to refuse to take a person in a taxi or similar vehicle on the grounds that he or she had a guide dog; and the Christmas Day (Trading) Act 2004, which prevented supermarkets and other large stores from opening on Christmas Day. Although the scope of these private members' bills may have been relatively small compared with major government bills, they have had important consequences in particular areas.

Some private members' bills have had a much wider application; they have brought about the abolition of the death penalty, the legalisation of abortion and homosexuality and the end of theatre censorship. More recently, the Knives Act 1997 prohibited the carrying of knives as offensive weapons; the Video Recordings Act 1984 regulated the sale of 'video nasties'; the National Audit Act 1983 established the National Audit Office and introduced important reforms to make government more accountable to Parliament; the Housing (Homeless Persons) Act 1977 placed requirements on local authorities to house the homeless; and the Unsolicited Goods and Services (Amendment) Act 1975 regulated the sending of unsolicited material to private citizens.

Success can be measured in other terms. Sometimes the government will take over the intention of a private member's bill, and it will appear in a subsequent session as a government bill. In 1994, the then government's embarrassment following its blocking of a private member's bill on disability discrimination led to a government bill being introduced, which became the Disability Discrimination Act 1995. The Wild Mammals (Hunting with Dogs) Bill failed in the 1997–98 session but appeared in the 2000–01 session as the Hunting Bill; was passed by the Commons but overtaken by the dissolution of Parliament in 2001; a similar bill was introduced by the government in 2002–03 but was not passed by the Lords; and in 2005 the Hunting Act, still not passed by the Lords, became law using the provisions of the Parliament Acts.

It is possible for the government to give a private member's bill government time in the same session that it began as a private member's bill. This was done in the 1950s and 1960s on such subjects as the abolition of the death penalty and the legalisation of abortion, but it is now very unusual – no doubt because of the 'me too' principle; the government would find it hard to pick and choose among worthy bills. In 1976 the Sexual Offences Bill, which provided for anonymity in rape cases, was given government time; so too was the Census (Amendment) Bill [*Lords*] in 2002. A slightly different case occurred in 2002, when the Tobacco Advertising and Promotion Bill [*Lords*], a private peer's bill, was taken over as a government bill when it arrived in the Commons. (An identical bill had originally been introduced in the 2000–01 session as a government measure but had been lost at the general election for want of time.)

Success may have nothing to do with eventual legislation. The former Labour Cabinet minister Tony Benn used substantial presentation bills to put forward his ideas on a Commonwealth of Europe to replace the European Union, on giving Parliament control over Crown prerogative, and on the reform of Parliament. None of these had a chance of succeeding, but setting out these detailed political proposals was an end in itself (and an MP whose bill is printed can receive up to 150 free copies of it).

The MP who seeks leave to bring in a ten-minute rule bill rarely expects that his or her bill will get on to the statute book (although ten did so in the period 1992 to 2005); and many bills for which leave is given are never actually printed. The ten-minute rule slot is a way of attracting attention to a subject, gauging opinion and putting it on the future political agenda. In the twelve-month 2003–04 session, thirty-one bills were brought in under the ten-minute rule. None became law (although one got as far as report stage); but the others gave an opportunity to air subjects for possible legislation such as rogue car-clampers, loan sharks, safety of mobile phone masts, and permanent summer time.

Should it be easier?

Private members' bills are fragile vessels. The sponsor of a bill from scratch (rather than a government hand-out) will have to compromise on what is desirable to achieve what is realistic; he or she has to be an astute tactician; must try to ensure that the government is at the least neutral on the proposal; will have to persuade doubters and potential saboteurs; and needs a bit of luck. And even then success is by no means guaranteed.

This process can be frustrating – perhaps never more so than when a bill gets a second reading by a large majority but is then defeated by guerrilla warfare in standing committee and on report. The Wild Mammals (Hunting with Dogs) Bill (the precursor of the bill which became the Hunting Act 2005) is an example; it received a second reading by 411 votes to 151, a majority of 260 on a vote of 86 per cent of MPs, but it did not become law. It may be said that the principle is one thing but the details another, and that scrutinising those is what the committee and report stages are for. And even if the degree of scrutiny – as opposed to obstruction – that a bill gets in those circumstances is open to question, many would argue that protecting the rights of the minority to disagree is especially important in the case of private members' legislation – in contrast to the assumption that a government with a majority will get its bills in the end.

Most proposals for making it easier for private members' bills to pass into law centre on providing more time, although, to make real difference, a substantial amount of time would have to be provided (and in a House that already sits for longer than many other parliamentary chambers). Recently there has been pressure to use Wednesday evenings (when the House would normally rise between 7.00 p.m. and 8.00 p.m.) for private members' bills. Apart from adding yet another three hours or so of sitting time, a mid-week slot, when most MPs are at Westminster, would undoubtedly be officially whipped on both sides, and the character of private members' business would be lost.

Another suggestion has been to make a few bills, perhaps the first five in the ballot, subject to a form of programming that would allow them to be voted upon at all their stages and would prevent their simply being 'talked out'.

But opinion is divided, even amongst MPs themselves. Some believe that taking initiatives to change the law should be a key part of an MP's role, and one in which MPs generally could act more independently of government; others are reluctant to see the amount of legislation already made every year increased, and they take Churchill's view that 'not every happy thought which occurs to a Member of Parliament should necessarily find its way on to the statute book'.

Lords stages

Bills can begin the parliamentary process in either House, and they have to pass through both Houses before they can be presented for Royal Assent, unless the Parliament Acts (see page 244) are used. A bill introduced in the Commons, and passed by that House after it has completed the various stages just described, is sent to the Lords. A bill introduced in the Lords will, after going through its stages in that House, be sent to the Commons for similar treatment. Consideration by the two Houses is – unlike the practice in the United States – never simultaneous, although on very rare occasions, to save time, identical bills are introduced in both Houses. One is later dropped, but the other can then proceed more quickly because its main points have been discussed already by both Houses.

The Lords spend a great deal of their sitting time discussing bills. All stages are normally taken on the floor of the House, although the House has in recent years developed the grand committee procedure with a view to considering more bills in committee off the floor. Indeed, a greater proportion of time is spent on bills in the Chamber in the Lords than in the Commons – between 50 and 60 per cent of the total sitting hours as opposed to one-third.

Bills in the Lords go through the same stages as in the Commons – a formal first reading, a substantial debate on second reading, detailed amendments at committee stage and report, and further debate (and, in the Lords only, consideration of amendments) at third reading. But outward appearances hide substantial differences in procedure, many of which reflect the more flexible and less constrained procedures that have survived in the Lords long after their demise in the late nineteenth-century House of Commons.

Differences in Lords procedure

The principal difference between Lords and Commons procedure is that bills are mostly considered at committee stage by a Committee of the Whole House. For many years, the only means of considering a bill in a committee off the floor was to commit it to a Public Bill Committee, roughly the equivalent of a Commons standing committee. But these committees have seldom been considered a success except for considering wholly uncontentious bills. Thus their scope for saving time on the floor of the House is limited. Their chief problem is that, as currently composed, it is virtually impossible to recreate the House in microcosm to form a committee in which only those named on the committee can vote in divisions. Only nine bills have been subjected to this procedure since 1968.

Since 1995, it has been possible to consider bills in a grand committee. The committee considers the bill, and amendments are tabled in the usual way; all Lords can attend and participate, but no divisions may take place. In 2003–04, eighteen bills were subjected to this procedure. Although used at first for relatively uncontroversial measures, it has proved a potentially useful way of saving time on the floor and has recently been used for longer and more substantial bills. Indeed, this was the intention of the 1994 Group on Sittings of the House (the Rippon Committee), which had originally recommended the procedure, and endorsed by the Group on the Working Practices of the House in 2002.

In 2003 it was agreed that Northern Ireland Orders might be debated in grand committee so as to improve scrutiny of what is, effectively, primary legislation during the suspension of the Northern Ireland Assembly. The orders then return to the floor of the House for decision. Since 2004 other statutory instruments, unstarred questions and select committee reports may also be debated off the floor in what has now become a parallel chamber (used for a wider range of business than the Commons parallel chamber in Westminster Hall (see page 296)).

In 1994 the Lords adopted a procedure akin to special standing committees in the Commons: a special public bill committee may take written and oral evidence on a bill within twenty-eight days of its appointment. Thereafter, these committees proceed as public bill committees. Originally devised to expedite Law Commission bills, the procedure was used only in 1994–95 and may now be considered defunct.

It has always been possible for a bill to be committed to a select committee at any stage between second and third reading, usually after second reading, for consideration of its merits (see also page 378). The committee undertakes detailed investigation of the subject matter and reports on the main provisions, recommending whether the bill should proceed or not, and if so in what form. If a bill is to proceed it is recommitted to a Committee of the whole House. The procedure is often used as a way of considering controversial issues raised in private members' bills, such as the Assisted Dying for the Terminally Ill Bill in 2004. Exceptionally, after the government lost a crucial vote in the House, the Constitutional Reform Bill (a government bill) was committed to a select committee in March 2004.

The committee, which included the Lord Chancellor as a member, sat until the end of June, hearing evidence, reporting on the policy of the bill and making amendments. Nevertheless, despite vigorous efforts in the 1990s to move legislative work off the floor, the norm is for the committee stage of bills containing any controversial material to be taken in Committee of the whole House.

A second difference between the Lords and Commons legislative procedures is that there is no selection by a chairman of amendments to be discussed. All the amendments that have been tabled may be considered. Third, there is no guillotine or programme procedure, so in theory proceedings could be very protracted indeed. Fortunately, filibustering is rare. Most members – and especially the party whips – realise that the excellent opportunities that arise in the Lords to consider all clauses and to take all amendments could not long survive persistent abuse by any one member or any one party.

Another substantial difference is that in the Lords it is possible to move amendments at third reading. The principal purposes of amendments at this stage are to clarify remaining uncertainties, to improve drafting and to enable the government to fulfil undertakings given at earlier stages of the bill. It is not permissible to raise an issue that has been fully debated and decided upon at a previous stage. A general debate may also take place on the motion 'that the bill do now pass', after any amendments have been considered, although this practice is now discouraged.

Since 1992, all government and some private members' bills are considered by a Lords Select Committee on Delegated Powers and Regulatory Reform, which reports to the House whether the provisions of any bill inappropriately delegate legislative powers to ministers using Statutory Instruments; or whether they subject the use of any delegated powers to insufficient parliamentary scrutiny. All bills are considered – usually on the basis of memoranda supplied by the government – after Lords first reading; and the committee reports quickly so that its findings can if necessary be acted upon by the House at committee stage. There is no equivalent committee in the House of Commons. All bills, whether introduced in the Lords or Commons, are also scrutinised by the Joint Committee on Human Rights in respect of any human rights issue; and by the Lords Constitution Committee for any constitutional issue. Reports are published by these committees on the issues raised, but the bills themselves are not committed to them and they cannot amend them.

It is worth noting that the government has no formal priority over other peers in introducing or debating legislation. In practice, government business is recognised to take priority, but at the same time – possibly as a quid pro quo – generous provision is made for private members' bills in the Lords. Because there is no limitation on the number of days on which they can be considered, the government has little control on the number of these bills that will actually be considered on the floor of the House. Ultimately this does not cause any trouble for the government, because a private member's bill to which the government is opposed and that survives in the Lords can always be blocked in the Commons.

Lords impact on legislation

House of Lords practice and procedure give a persistent back-bench (or opposition front-bench) peer a far better chance of getting a point of view across than the equivalent MP in the House of Commons. And these advantages, when combined with the comparative political independence of members of the House of Lords, can result in opposition to the elected government of the day, to the extent of sometimes radical amendment of bills. Until the passage of the House of Lords Act in 1998 the House of Lords was a predominantly Conservative body. All the more remarkable, then, that between 1979 and 1997 the Lords were often highly critical of aspects of government policy. During the Conservative administration of 1970–74, the government was defeated twenty-six times on a vote in the House of Lords, but between 1979 and 1997 these occasions became more frequent (see Table 7.2).

Most of these amendments were accepted by the government either as they stood or with modification when the bills returned to the Commons. But if reversed, the Lords only rarely insisted upon their disagreement. In the 1984–85 session, for example, the government suffered seventeen defeats in the Lords. Of these, sixteen related to amendments to bills; only two were reversed by the government in the Commons (we describe later what happens when the two Houses disagree). Some of these amendments made substantial dents in government policy.

Table 7.2 Government defeats in the House of Lords, 1979–97

Parliament	Number of defeats
1979–83	45
1983–87	62
1987–92	72
1992–97	56

Some writers have contended – usually in the context of discussions of Lords reform – that the Lords should have done more to modify or even curb the more radical Conservative policies of the 1979–97 era; and the fact that they did not showed that the House was on the whole content to acquiesce in those policies. While it is true that on certain major issues the government was, with strong whipping, able to carry the day, it is perhaps unfair to censure the Lords for not doing more. Political composition aside, the House of Lords, however composed, will always need to be mindful of its secondary position in relation to the Commons and use its remaining – and in theory still very considerable – powers sparingly. Under our current constitutional arrangements, Parliament, as a bicameral legislature, would rapidly become inoperable unless the upper House continued to be sensitive to the delicacy of its position.

Ironically, since the election of a Labour government in 1997, the Lords have continued to inflict defeats over unwelcome provisions in bills – notwithstanding the exclusion of many opposition hereditary peers in late 1998 (see Table 7.3).

One such bill was the Criminal Justice (Mode of Trial) Bill in 1999–2000, a Lords bill that sought to abolish trial by jury in so-called 'either way' cases. The provisions on jury trial were removed by the Lords and the bill abandoned. Reintroduced in the Commons as a No. 2 bill later that session, it was rejected by the Lords at second reading. It was not reintroduced, although somewhat different provisions limiting the right to jury trial reappeared in the strongly contested Criminal Justice Bill in 2003. The Sexual Offences (Amendment) Bill, which lowered the homosexual age of consent for males from 18 to 16, was rejected at second reading by the Lords in the 1998–99 session, reintroduced in the following session and received Royal Assent under the Parliament Acts at the end of the session. The Hunting Bill, opposed and radically amended in the Lords in two successive sessions, had to be given Royal Assent under the Parliament Acts at the end of the 2003–04 session.

Other bills have been heavily amended. A provision in the Local Government Bill in the 1999–2000 session that sought to repeal the now infamous 'section 28' of the Local Government Act 1986 (preventing local author-

Table 7.3 Government defeats in the House of Lords, 1997–2005

Parliament	Number of defeats
1997–2001	128
2001–05	245

ities from 'promoting' homosexuality) was removed by the Lords and not insisted upon by the government. (The Lords finally assented to the repeal of this section in 2003!) An amendment to the Transport Bill in the same session had the effect of delaying the proposed privatisation of the National Air Traffic Service until after the expected general election in 2001; and safeguards on privacy relating to e-mail interceptions were written into the Regulation of Investigatory Powers Bill. There were many other such examples as the pressure of time at the end of that very crowded session made the government receptive – perforce – to Lords amendments.

In the 2001–05 Parliament the Lords successfully modified aspects of anti-terrorism legislation that they considered excessive, particularly the Anti-Terrorism, Crime and Security Bill – a 126-clause bill containing measures in response to the terrorist attacks in New York and Washington on 11 September 2001. Although proceedings were accelerated, the Lords spent fifty-three hours seeking to amend this bill. As a result, changes were made in key areas, in some cases after the Lords had insisted on their amendments. Thus, among other things, an appeal mechanism against deportation was provided for; the additional police powers conferred by the bill were confined to anti-terrorism and national security matters; the offence of inciting religious hatred was struck out; and a 'sunset clause' was inserted to time-limit many of the bill's provisions.

Similarly, the Lords were to insist on a number of amendments to the Prevention of Terrorism Bill in March 2005, chiefly aimed at making the proposed control orders subject to judicial rather than political decision, under rules of court, consistent with the ECHR and subject to clearer statutory definition. The passage of the bill was in the end secured by agreement to Commons amendments in lieu of Lords amendments and an undertaking on the part of the government (not on the face of the bill) to review the bill's provisions with a view to renewal one year later. These final exchanges obliged the House to hold its longest sitting in modern times – beginning at 11 a.m. on Thursday 10 March 2005 and ending at 7.31 p.m. on Friday 11 March. This included four long adjournments for Commons consideration and the necessary negotiations.

But Lords interests extended beyond prevention of terrorism. In the 2002–03 session vigorous opposition led by Lord Puttnam and the prospect of certain defeat in the lobbies led the government to amend its Communications Bill at third reading so as to protect UK television channels from undesirable foreign or multi-media ownership. In the 2003–04 session the Civil Contingencies Bill was amended in response to Lords pressure so that regulations could only be made in respect of a particular emergency and be subject to a maximum life of 30 days. In the same session the Constitutional

Reform Bill was amended in Committee of the whole House so as to preserve the slimmed down office of Lord Chancellor. The government accepted the amendment but resisted successfully later attempts to insist on amendments to ensure that the Lord Chancellor would be a member of the House of Lords and a lawyer. The Higher Education Bill was amended to allow students who had deferred university entrance from 2005 to 2006 (the start of top-up fees) to be treated as though they had entered in 2005, and to ensure that the new Director of the Office of Fair Access would be appointed under the terms of the Civil Service Recruitment Code.

The 2005–06 session did not start well for the government in the Lords. The Racial and Religious Hatred Bill, which sought to create a new offence of inciting religious hatred, was amended radically in the Lords so as to separate the two offences, to provide that only intentional behaviour would be caught by its provisions and, as part of a 'freedom of speech' provision, confine the offence only to 'threatening speech and behaviour' rather than the looser 'abusive and insulting behaviour' in the original bill. In the Commons the government, while accepting the separation of the offences and the amendment on intention, sought to introduce the new concept of 'reckless behaviour' and to reinstate the 'insulting and abusive' provision. The government lost two critical votes, failed to modify the Lords Amendments, and so the bill received Royal Assent in the form that it left the Lords. The Lords amended the Terrorism Bill so as to remove the provisions creating a new office of glorification of terrorism which many thought unworkable. They insisted on their amendments but finally gave way to the Commons. The Lords persisted in their opposition to the provision in the Identity Cards Bill which would have compelled all applicants for a new passport from 2008 to accept an identity card too. The Commons was eventually obliged to accept an amendment in lieu offered by the Lords which, while allowing applicants' details to be entered in a new national identity register, would not require them to accept a card until 2010 – after the next general election – thus making the acceptance of a card an election issue. Finally, the prospect of almost certain defeat in the Lords on the Legislative and Regulatory Reform Bill (allowing the Government to amend existing legislation and give effect to Law Commission Recommendations by secondary legislation) caused the Government to announce a u-turn in April 2006 before the bill began its Lords stages. To counter arguments that the bill gave too much power to the Executive, the government announced that the respective regulatory reform committees in each House would be given a statutory power to veto any inappropriate use. It remained to be seen whether this would satisfy the bill's many opponents inside and outside parliament.

Lords independence

Why has the House of Lords been ready on occasion to impose its will on both Conservative and Labour administrations? The chief reason is that over the last twenty years or so neither party has been able consistently to control the House at critical moments. Table 7.4 shows how neither of the two major parties has, in terms of actual attendance of its members, held an absolute majority in the House in recent years.

The Conservative administrations, despite the relative strength of the Conservative Party in the pre-1998 House, were vulnerable to defeat on a vote if Labour, Liberal and cross-bench members united in opposition. Similarly, in spite of the strengthening of the Labour group in the House by the new peerage creations following the 1997 general election and the expulsion of the hereditary peers in 1998, the Labour Party has proved vulnerable in the same way.

But in addition to simple arithmetic, a number of other factors are at play. Party discipline is weaker in the Lords than in the Commons and back-bench rebellion more frequent. There are a number of reasons for this. As the House is not elected, its members are not directly accountable – as are members of the House of Commons – to an electorate and a party manifesto. Moreover, professional politicians or former politicians are in a minority, and even they may on occasions be out of sympathy with certain aspects of their party's policy. Furthermore, the payroll vote (of office holders) is very small in the Lords (see page 131), so members of the House, many of whom are in the twilight years of their political careers, are on occasion less cautious in voting than are aspiring MPs.

Why, then, does the government not reverse in the Commons every Lords amendment with which it disagrees? Some of the defeats are on matters of principle that command some support from the ranks of back-benchers in the Commons and from the country at large. So the government accepts amendments of this kind graciously rather than risk unnecessary unpopularity for itself among its own supporters both inside and outside Parliament.

Table 7.4 Average daily attendance in the House of Lords by party (%)

Session	Conservative	Labour	Liberal	Cross-bench	Other
1988–89	46.6	22.1	11.7	18.0	1.7
1998–99	37.0	34.4	10.6	15.9	2.0
1999–2000	35.3	36.0	11.4	15.4	1.9
2004–05	28.7	36.2	12.7	18.5	2.9

As in the Commons, compromise amendments will be accepted by a government to expedite a bill's progress, and any government may even admit defeat on part of its bill in order to get the other provisions through on time – well-illustrated by the government's partial climbdown on the Identity Cards Bill in March 2006.

But amendments to bills following the defeat of the government on a vote are a very small element in the total number of amendments made in a session, for the fact remains that most of the Lords' work is of a revising character – revising bills received from the Commons. Whichever party is in power, this aspect of the Lords' legislative work continues unchanged. In recent heavy legislative sessions, between 2,000 and 3,000 amendments have been made to bills in any one session. Thus in the 2003–04 session, 9,604 amendments to bills were tabled and 3,344 were made. The majority of them are drafting amendments of no real significance, amendments introduced by the government to meet points made in either the Commons or the Lords, or to introduce new provisions of its own into bills. One study (Shell and Beamish 1993) analysed proceedings in the Lords on eight bills in the 1988–89 session. It traced the origins of the amendments made and showed that the vast majority were made by the government itself, with, relatively speaking, a few more being made with government approval but on the initiative of others. Thus, of the 1,164 amendments moved by the government, 1,161 (99.7 per cent) were accepted: of the 1,047 moved by non-government members, only sixty-five (6.2 per cent) were accepted. A further look showed that, of these sixty-five, only four followed defeats in the lobbies (in fact two of these were later reversed in the Commons). Of the remaining sixty-one, thirty-nine were consequential or drafting amendments and only twenty-two involved matters of substance that the government accepted without a vote. Of the amendments moved by the government, about thirty-five were identified as arising out of ministerial undertakings to look again at aspects of the bills following criticisms in the Lords in the early stages. This analysis, though now somewhat dated, still serves as a good illustration of the nature of Lords amendments to bills.

Disagreement between the Houses: the balance of power

Ping-pong . . . or poker?

In the previous section, we saw that on occasion there is disagreement between the two Houses on a bill. We now explore this more fully. We also consider constraints on the Lords' powers to amend bills. A bill that passes without amendment through the second House then needs only the Royal Assent – or formal approval by the Queen – before it becomes law. It does not go back to the House where its progress began. However, if the second House makes amendments to a bill, those amendments (but no other part of the bill) must be considered by the first House. If they are agreed, the bill is ready to become law. If they are not, the second House looks at the matter again and can either insist upon its amendments or attempt compromise proposals. Theoretically, alternative compromises can be shuttled between the two Houses indefinitely. Each time, messages are exchanged between the two Houses. These can become fiendishly complicated.

The final stages of the Prevention of Terrorism Bill in 2005 are a good example. The Commons sat from 11.30 a.m. on Thursday 25 March until nearly eight o'clock in the evening of Friday 26 March, and during that time the Bill (which had the previous week gone from the Lords to the Commons and back again without agreement on the most contentious provisions) went back and forth between the Houses seven times with proposals and counter-proposals being considered each time (and new working papers being printed on each occasion – even at three in the morning). The Lords finally gave in, and their message to the Commons read:

> *The Lords do not insist on their Amendment to the Prevention of Terrorism Bill to which this House has disagreed and do agree with this House in its Amendments in lieu thereof; they do not insist on an Amendment in lieu of certain other Lords Amendments to which this House has disagreed, and do agree to the Amendments proposed by this House in lieu thereof; and they agree to the Amendments proposed by this House to words so restored to the Bill.*

Shortly after the arrival of this message, Royal Assent to the Prevention of Terrorism Act 2005 was announced to both Houses. Although dressed in archaic language, the exchanges were a classic political struggle between two Chambers of a bicameral Parliament, in one of which the government had a majority, and where the second had the power to destroy the government's bill, but was mindful of the possible political consequences of doing so. The process was perhaps more poker than ping-pong.

If a compromise were not reached, the bill would be lost, as happened to the House of Commons Distribution of Seats Bill in 1969 (which was not reintroduced); to the Trade Union and Labour Relations Bill and Aircraft and Shipbuilding Industries Bill in 1976 (reintroduced in 1977 and enacted in the conventional manner following compromise); and to the Hunting Bill in 2002–03 (enacted under the Parliament Acts at the end of the 2003–04 session). The point of *final disagreement* is normally thought to have been reached when each House has taken up its position and insisted upon it (*double insistence*).

In the past, final disagreement has usually been defined with respect to individual amendments even where they may have been grouped for purposes of debate. In the Commons, since 1997 the practice had arisen of grouping amendments together for the purpose of both debate and decision. This Commons practice of 'packaging' created difficulties in the Lords in May 2004 in respect of the Planning and Compulsory Purchase Bill. The Lords authorities took the view that double insistence had been reached on an amendment and that the bill was lost, whereas the Commons intention was that the bill could be further considered because that amendment had been decided as part of a 'package' with another amendment to which an amendment in lieu had been offered. Exceptionally, the bill was further considered by the Lords.

It was however subsequently agreed by the House that it would consider packages of amendments during ping-pong only if they were confined to single or closely related issues, not disparate issues joined together simply for convenience. In the case of the former, the House would be willing to consider such amendments in packages, in which case the double insistence rule would apply to the whole package. This development will have the benefit that consideration of Commons amendments may often become procedurally easier as the amendments can be printed together, whether consecutive or not. On the other hand, on complex issues it may be that the moment of double insistence will be longer deferred unless opposition parties remain vigilant.

Limitations on Lords powers: ancient practice and the Parliament Acts

The Lords do not have free rein in amending certain types of Commons bill. By ancient practice set out in Commons resolutions dating from the late seventeenth century, the Lords may not amend bills 'of aids and supplies' – a type of bill that includes the annual Finance Bill, which implements the tax proposals made by the Chancellor of the Exchequer in his Budget, and Consolidated Fund and Appropriation Bills, which sanction government expenditure.

If the Lords insist on their amendments to any other public bill in a manner that renders the bill wholly unacceptable to the majority in the Commons and to the point that the bill is lost by the close of the session, or if they reject altogether a bill passed by the Commons, the procedures of the Parliament Acts 1911 and 1949 may be invoked. These Acts were passed to ensure that important reforming legislation introduced by the Liberal and Labour governments of the time was not frustrated by the then overwhelming Conservative majority in the Lords.

The severest restrictions in the Parliament Acts apply to 'money bills'. These are bills that deal only with certain specified central government finance matters. The most important of them are pure taxation bills or the Consolidated Fund and Appropriation Bills that formally vote money to the government. These will be described in more detail in Chapter 8. (The annual Finance Bill, which implements the budget proposals, is often not a money bill because it contains wider provisions than those defined in the Parliament Acts. This is somewhat paradoxical, since the 1911 Parliament Act was passed as a reaction to the Lords' rejection of the 1909 Finance Bill.) Under the Parliament Acts, money bills passed by the Commons are allowed one month to pass through the Lords. If the Lords do not pass them within a month, they can be sent for Royal Assent without the Lords' approval. The provisions relating to money bills have never had to be invoked for the purpose of giving Royal Assent.

All other public bills passed by the Commons may be delayed for a minimum effective period of thirteen months by the Lords. The rule is strictly as follows: any bill (except one to extend the life of a parliament – that is, to postpone a general election) that passes the Commons in two successive sessions (whether or not a general election intervenes) can be presented for Royal Assent without the agreement of the Lords, provided that (1) there has been a minimum period of one year between the Commons giving it a second reading for the first time and a third reading for the second time, and (2) the Lords have received the bill at least one month before the end of each of the two sessions.

The rigours of these provisions of the Parliament Acts have on only four occasions been taken to their final stage since the 1949 Act (which reduced by one year the delaying time of the 1911 Act) was itself passed without the agreement of the Lords. In 1991, the War Crimes Act received Royal Assent under these provisions after the bill had been passed by the Commons and rejected by the Lords at second reading in two successive sessions. This bill sought, retrospectively, to create a new criminal offence so as to enable charges to be brought against alleged perpetrators of atrocities, chiefly against Jews, in continental Europe during the Second World War. Many lords felt that such prosecutions would be difficult to secure and that too many legal principles were offended by the proposed legislation. As the bill was not a manifesto commitment by the government, the Lords felt entitled to reject it. In 1998, the European Parliamentary Elections Bill was lost following disagreement over the electoral system proposed. The Lords rejected the reintroduced bill at second reading in the following session, thus enabling Royal Assent to take place in time for the elections to proceed notwithstanding the initial delay. In 2000, Royal Assent was also given under the Parliament Acts to the Sexual Offences (Amendment) Bill, which lowered the age of consent for homosexual activity and buggery to 16. In 2004, the Hunting Bill which outlawed hunting deer, foxes and hares with hounds, received Royal Assent in the same way.

The Parliament Acts procedures are the fundamental limitation on the legislative power of the Lords. They enable any administration with a majority in the Commons to exert its will and ultimately to pass its legislation without Lords agreement. But its procedures are akin to a nuclear deterrent, and of course they involve delay. For practical reasons, government business managers often find it easier to accept Lords amendments than to attempt to overturn them every time, let alone threaten the use of the Parliament Acts.

The Salisbury convention

Members of the House of Lords accept that the elected government of the day must be allowed to get its business through. The nearest that this idea has come to formal expression is in the Salisbury convention – an understanding reached between the Conservative opposition in the House of Lords (led by the fifth Marquess of Salisbury) and the Labour government immediately after the Second World War in 1945. The convention is that the Lords should not reject at second reading any government legislation that has been passed by the House of Commons and that carries out a manifesto commitment – that is to say, a commitment made to the electorate in the government party's election manifesto. However, this convention does not extend to the amendment of bills; nor can it be held, strictly, to apply to government bills that do not reflect a manifesto commitment. So even this self-denying ordinance leaves the Lords with considerable room for manoeuvre.

The convention had its origin in the doctrine of the mandate developed by the third Marquess of Salisbury in the nineteenth century. He argued that the will of the people and the views of the House of Commons did not necessarily coincide and that the Lords had a duty to reject – and hence refer back to the electorate at a general election – contentious bills, particularly those with constitutional implications. Like the doctrine of the mandate before it, the Salisbury convention is perhaps more a code of behaviour for the Conservative Party when in opposition in the Lords than a convention of the House. Indeed, it is a moot point whether, following the passage of the House of Lords Act 1999, the expulsion of the hereditary members and the ending of the overwhelming numerical advantage of the Conservative Party, the Salisbury convention as originally devised can have any continuing validity. But the notion that government bills (whether in fulfilment of a manifesto commitment or not) should not be denied a second reading – whatever the party of government – has certainly persisted for a very long time. There is now some evidence (articulated mainly by the Liberal Democrats who no longer accept it) that the convention is losing some of its force.

In spite of the Parliament Acts, and historical conventions on matters of supply, and more recent conventions on manifesto commitments, in practice – and under certain conditions – the Lords powers to amend bills other than money bills are real and influential. What is more, these powers have recently been reconfirmed by the Joint Committee on House of Lords Reform in December 2002; and by the Royal Commission on Reform of the House of Lords in 2000.

Royal Assent and implementation

A bill passed by both Houses needs the Royal Assent – from the Sovereign as the third element of Parliament in addition to the Lords and the Commons – before it can become law. The Queen's agreement is automatic (Queen Anne in 1707–08 was the last monarch to refuse to accept a bill passed by both Houses). Although in theory the Royal Assent can be given by the Sovereign in person, this was last done in 1854, and in 1967 it was decided to stop the procedure by which Black Rod would interrupt the proceedings of the Commons, summoning them to the Lords Chamber to hear the Lords Commissioners announcing Royal Assent. This now occurs only at prorogation. At other times, the Speaker in the Commons and the Lord Speaker in the Lords announce the Royal Assent at a convenient break in each House's proceedings.

Although Royal Assent to a bill turns it into an Act and makes it law, the law does not necessarily come into force immediately. The Act will normally contain *a commencement provision*. Typically, this allows the secretary of state concerned to make an order at some future date to bring part or all of the Act into force, although a date may be specified, for example three or six months after Royal Assent. Sometimes the appropriate date never comes: the Employment of Children Act 1973 has never been brought fully into effect. Nearly 100 Acts passed over the last thirty years have still to be brought fully into force.

The question of whether it was legal for a minister simply not to bring into force something that had been decided by Parliament was considered by the Court of Appeal in 1994. That court decided that as Parliament had not set a time for commencement the minister had not acted illegally; but the then Master of the Rolls, in a dissenting judgment, suggested that the power given to the minister was to decide *when* rather than *whether* an Act should come into force. However, it is not clear when delay becomes long enough to regard the Act passed by Parliament as ineffective.

If there is no commencement provision (whether a date, or a power given to a minister), the Act comes into force from midnight at the beginning of the day on which Royal Assent was given.

What is the law?

Acts of Parliament are available in bound copies of the statutes for any particular year, and Acts from 1988 are available on the parliamentary website. However, these sources will not show whether an Act is wholly or partially in force, or whether it has been amended (or even repealed), or what delegated legislation has been made under its authority. The picture is complicated when an Act legislates 'by reference' – not setting out the law anew but changing it by inserting new material in a series of other Acts. UK legislation is not codified; in other words, there is not a single Act covering, say, immigration law, that is republished every time there is an amending bill. To some extent, the work of the Law Commissions addresses this problem by compiling *consolidation bills* that bring together the existing law in a more logical and convenient form. For want of resources, the programme of consolidation has produced very little in recent sessions of Parliament. So the reader who wishes to know what a particular Act says needs to be careful to consult a fully revised and updated version, or to go to a publication such as Halsbury's *Laws of England* for a statement of how the law stands, and then look up the individual statutes or delegated legislation. The Internet is now an invaluable source too. Law publishers such as Halsbury and Butterworth offer an online subscription version of the statute book; and the government expects its own statute law database, with the fully revised and updated text of all legislation from 1275, to be available online to the general public in 2006.

Private legislation

The reader of the House of Commons Order of Business will often see at the beginning of the day's agenda on Mondays to Thursday references to private business. Occasionally the words 'At four o'clock [or three o'clock or seven o'clock] private business set down under Standing Order No. 20' can be seen. The private business is not private in the sense of being confidential or related to the internal affairs of the House; it is business related to private legislation.

As we saw earlier in this chapter (pages 190 and 191), private bills are nothing to do with private members' bills. Private members' bills seek to change the general law, but private bills affect individuals, groups of individuals or corporate bodies in a way different from other individuals, groups or bodies. Their effect is private and particular as opposed to public and general. For example, the Dartmoor Commons Act 1985 was promoted by Dartmoor farmers to give powers to stop the overgrazing of the moors; the Southampton International Boat Show Act 1997 allowed a park in Southampton to open for one extra day a year; and the City of London (Ward Elections) Act 2002 made changes to the franchise for local elections in the City. The Hereford Markets Act 2003 allowed a livestock market that by royal charter had to be held within the city limits to be moved outside and so release a prime site for other uses.

The first step in private legislation is for the person or group seeking the legislation to petition for the bill. Private bills are not presented by MPs or peers but by the promoters of the legislation, who are represented by special lawyers known as parliamentary agents. Throughout the bill's passage – but especially before it is even introduced – the promoters will be working to ensure that the bill attracts as little opposition as possible. Promoters need to comply with an elaborate set of standing orders, which try to ensure that interested parties (who may know nothing of the promoters' intentions) are given notice of the bill. When this has been done, the bill is allocated to one House or the other for first consideration, and, after second reading, is sent to a special committee. Private bill procedure is particularly complex and is set out in detail in *Erskine May*, but the main elements are described here.

Anyone who is aggrieved by the bill's provisions has the right to petition against it, but only those directly affected by the bill (who have what is known as *locus standi*) have the right to be heard. If the bill is not opposed by petitions, or if all the petitions are withdrawn because the promoters have been able to meet the petitioners' wishes, the bill is considered by a committee on unopposed bills, through which it usually passes swiftly after an explanation of its purposes by the promoters. Opposed private bills are considered much more elaborately over many days by a committee of four MPs (or five peers), who must have no personal interest in the matter.

The committee acts in a semi-judicial capacity, examining witnesses and hearing barristers who appear for and against the bill. In effect, it displays the character of Parliament both as a court, inquiring into and adjudicating on the interests of private individuals, and as a legislature safeguarding the public interest. The committee has to decide whether the promoters have demonstrated that the bill is necessary, whether those affected by it have been treated fairly, and whether there is any objection to it on public policy grounds. The committee has the power to make amendments, or even to recommend that the bill should not proceed (as happened with the first Crossrail Bill in 1994, which failed).

After their committee stage, private bills are considered on report (in the Commons, but not the Lords), read a third time and passed to the other House for similar stages to be taken. It is quite usual for a private bill not to complete all its stages in one session; an order is made that allows it to be taken up in the following session at the stage it had reached. By contrast, the carry-over procedure for public bills has been used only three times. Private bills are not covered by the Parliament Acts, so there is no restriction on the power of the Lords to delay them.

Most private bills do not encounter sustained opposition from MPs or peers, but the opportunities for delay are considerable. Each stage of a bill's progress is advertised on the Order of Business 'at the time of unopposed private business' and can be stopped from proceeding further by an MP shouting 'Object!' or by the tabling of a 'blocking motion'. If this objection is sustained on each appearance of the bill on the Order of Business, the bill cannot proceed without time being found for a debate. This is in the hands of the Chairman of Ways and Means, who has a general responsibility for the way that private bills are handled (but not for the success or failure of any bill). He can set a bill down for a three-hour period (on a Monday or Tuesday, from 7.00 p.m. to 10.00 p.m.; on a Wednesday, from 4.00 p.m. to 7.00 p.m.; or on a Thursday, from 3.00 p.m. to 6.00 p.m.).

The government business managers are naturally anxious not to have much scarce parliamentary time taken up with opposed private business, so an MP who objects to an aspect of a private bill has a strong bargaining counter with the promoters. Unless they go some way towards meeting the MP's wishes, he or she can delay the bill by insisting on a debate at each stage, and this may eventually mean that the bill is lost.

Table 7.5 Private bills presented and petitioned against, 1988–92 and 2001–05

Session	Number of bills	Number petitioned against (new bills in each session: so not including those 'revived' in a subsequent session)
1988–89	39	12
1989–90	32	12
1990–91	28	11
1991–92	24	10
2001–02	5	1
2002–03	3	2
2003–04	4	0
2004–05	6	0

In the Lords, private bills that have been reported from a select committee are not usually opposed further on the floor. The Chairman of Committees oversees private legislation proceedings in the Lords in the same way as the Chairman of Ways and Means in the Commons.

The amount of private legislation has fallen dramatically in recent years, especially following the Transport and Works Act 1992. This removed from the parliamentary process private bills dealing with matters such as railway, tramway and harbour building, and other types of development. These were often the most controversial private bills. Nowadays, parliamentary involvement in such projects will occur only when a project is seen by the government as being nationally significant, when a single debate on its desirability will take place on the floor of the House. An example is the debate on the proposal to build a new railway from Leicester to the Channel Tunnel via Rugby, which was rejected by the Commons in 1996.

Table 7.5 shows the numbers of new private bills in the four sessions before the passing of the Transport and Works Act 1992 and in the last four complete sessions, together with the numbers that attracted opposition and so were petitioned against.

There will no doubt be private bills in the future that do not deal with transport and works but that will still prove controversial, as for example did the City of London (Ward Elections) Bill, which encountered opposition on the grounds that it provided for a weighted franchise, and which took nearly four years to get through Parliament. And any private bill may be of great importance both for its promoters and for those who will be affected. But, compared with their nineteenth-century heyday, private bills have become something of a parliamentary backwater.

Hybrid bills

These bills – which are fairly unusual – combine characteristics of a public bill and a private bill. Bills that are introduced by the government but that would otherwise be private bills are also treated as hybrid. Examples of hybrid bills include the Channel Tunnel Bill in 1987, the Cardiff Bay Barrage Bill (which was enacted in 1993 after starting out as a private bill and then being taken over by the government), and the Channel Tunnel Rail Link Bill in 1994, which became law in 1996. One of the classic examples of a hybrid bill was the Aircraft and Shipbuilding Industries Bill of 1976, which was intended to nationalise these two industries. It was discovered that this bill did not apply to one shipbuilding company which otherwise fulfilled the bill's criteria for nationalisation. Because this company was thus being treated differently from all other companies in the same class, the bill was ruled by the Speaker to be hybrid. Although this ruling was set aside by the Commons, the bill was committed to a select committee in the Lords.

Hybrid bills are treated as public bills, except that the promoters do not need to prove the need for the bill. Bills are examined to see whether they comply with the standing orders that relate to private bills, and there is an additional stage – they are referred to a select committee in each House, which can hear petitions from those affected. This may be a major exercise; the committee on the Channel Tunnel Bill received several thousand petitions. In 2005–06 the Crossrail Bill, which was carried over from the previous Parliament, continued its hotly contested passage. The bill would authorise the construction of a new east–west rail link across London. Those whose homes or businesses would be adversely affected were able to lodge objections: 358 petitions against the bill were received in the three-month petitioning period.

Delegated legislation

Definitions

Delegated legislation is law made by ministers or certain public bodies under powers given to them by Act of Parliament, but it is just as much part of the law of the land as are those Acts. The volume of delegated legislation is huge, and this presents particular challenges for parliamentary scrutiny.

Individual pieces of delegated legislation, often called *secondary legislation* to distinguish them from primary legislation contained in Acts of

Parliament, or *subordinate legislation*, are found under many different names. They can be *orders, regulations, Orders in Council, schemes, rules, codes of practice* and *statutes* (of certain colleges rather than in the sense of Acts). Even the Highway Code is a form of secondary legislation.

Delegated legislation may be made by any person or body empowered to do so by an Act of Parliament ('the parent Act'); and although some institutions and professional bodies have this power in particular cases, the bulk of such legislation is made by ministers.

Before the Second World War there was very much less delegated legislation, and parent Acts prescribed a variety of different parliamentary procedures, often designed for the particular case. Most of these were unified by the Statutory Instruments Act 1946, which describes what a statutory instrument is and prescribes the principal procedures for parliamentary approval. Not all pieces of delegated legislation are *Statutory Instruments*, but this general term (abbreviated to SI, with individual instruments numbered in an annual series, for example 'SI 2006/875') will serve. About half of the 3,000 or so Statutory Instruments made each year have only a local effect and may be for only a temporary purpose. Our concern is with the general instruments that form part of the law of the land.

Purpose

The original idea of an SI was to supplement what was set down in an Act of Parliament, for two particular purposes. The first was to prescribe things that were too detailed for inclusion in an Act of Parliament. The second was – again, for fairly minor matters – to provide the flexibility to change the law to meet changing circumstances without the sledgehammer (and the delay) of new primary legislation.

As long as this remained the guiding principle, one would expect there to be little difficulty. However, over the years the boundaries of delegated legislation have been tested.

The increase over the last thirty years has been of the order of 50 per cent, although it appears that the upward trend may have levelled out. However, the *volume* of delegated legislation is huge: the 1,297 SIs laid before Parliament in 2004 took up 9,552 A4 pages.

The second area of strain has been in the *use* of SIs. Ministers naturally find it more convenient to be able to legislate in a way that is subject to more limited parliamentary scrutiny than primary legislation, and there is thus a temptation to leave to delegated legislation matters that arguably should be set out in a bill and so in an Act. The most extreme examples of

Table 7.6 Statutory instruments laid before Parliament, 1955–2004

Year	Number of statutory instruments
1955	657
1960	733
1965	899
1970	1,040
1975	1,362
1980	1,197
1985	1,204
1990	1,408
1995	1,666
2000	1,373
2001	1,502
2004	1,297

this have been in so-called 'skeleton' or 'framework' bills, where the use of delegated powers is so extensive that the real operation of the bill would be entirely by the regulations made under it. The Education (Student Loans) Bill in 1990, the Child Support Bill in 1991 and the Jobseekers Bill in 1995 all attracted criticism on these grounds, as have 'Henry VIII powers', which allow ministers to amend primary legislation by the use of secondary legislation (see also page 260).

The speed of the legislative process encourages an overuse of delegated powers. A minister may want to put a new provision into a bill during its passage, but the limited time available to settle the details may lead to the provision being drafted in very general terms, with even quite significant matters being left to delegated legislation. There is also the question of where the threshold should be set between the more important *affirmative instruments*, which Parliament must approve explicitly, and *negative instruments*, which have effect unless Parliament says otherwise.

Since 1992, the House of Lords has sought to address the balance between delegation and control through the work of the Delegated Powers and Regulatory Reform Committee (formerly the Delegated Powers and Deregulation Committee). For each bill introduced into the Lords (and for substantial government amendments), this committee examines the powers to make delegated legislation that are proposed to be given to ministers. It reports on both whether those powers are justified and whether the level of parliamentary control is appropriate (in other words, which powers should be exercised through negative instruments, which through affirmative instruments, and which should be matters for an Act of Parliament rather than delegated legislation). The vast majority of the committee's recommendations have been accepted, and it plays an important role in striking a balance between executive freedom and parliamentary control.

Two other features of the system should also be mentioned. The first is that the vast majority of SIs are not amendable. This is inevitable in that both Houses must take the same view on an SI, and amendable instruments would be like another class of bills going back and forth for both Houses to agree on any amendments. But it also means an element of 'take it or leave it', especially when an SI is substantial or complex.

The second is that the way the threshold is set between affirmative and negative instruments can become out of date with changes in society. For example, in an Act passed in 1950 it might have been thought essential to require a minister to come back to Parliament for permission to exercise a power that by 2003 would be thought to be a matter of routine. But the requirement remains in the 1950 Act, and only further primary legislation will remove it. The phenomenon may also work the other way – something routine in 1950 may have taken on a different significance fifty years later.

Parliamentary control

There are four levels:

1. Delegated legislation that may be made and come into effect *without any reference to Parliament*. This category includes a large number of SIs with only local effect, and many of these will be printed only if the responsible minister wishes them to be.

2. Delegated legislation that may be made and come into effect, and that *must be laid before Parliament, but on which there are no parliamentary proceedings*. These are really for information; commencement orders bringing an Act of Parliament into effect are typical.

3. *Negative instruments*: these are *laid before Parliament* and may *come into effect* immediately or on some future date *unless either House resolves that the instrument be annulled*.

4. *Affirmative instruments*: these do not normally (except in cases of urgency) come into effect until they have been *approved by resolution of each House*.

The third and fourth categories are the most significant; in the last four complete sessions, they averaged 217 affirmatives and 1,093 negatives a year (see Table 7.7 overleaf).

Table 7.7 Statutory instruments considered by Parliament, 2001–05

	Affirmative	Negative
2001–02, long session	262	1,468
2002–03	231	1,216
2003–04	247	1,038
2004–05, short session	126	650

Procedure

When an instrument has been laid before Parliament it is examined by the Joint Committee on Statutory Instruments (with members from both Houses), which is supported by specialist lawyers and reports on various technical aspects: whether in making the instrument the minister has exceeded the powers given by Parliament (this is also something that can be challenged in the courts); whether the drafting is defective or unclear; whether the instrument has retrospective effect, and so on. The committee reports its conclusions but, even if it finds fault, the progress of the instrument is not automatically halted. Some instruments, on finance and taxation, are laid before the Commons only and are examined by the Select Committee on Statutory Instruments, which consists of the Commons members of the Joint Committee.

Negative instruments

In the case of a negative SI, nothing will happen unless an opposition party, or a group of back-benchers, tables what is known as a *prayer*. This has nothing to do with religious devotion but is so called because of the form of the motion; because the instrument has been made by one of Her Majesty's ministers, it is the Sovereign who has to be asked to undo what has been done. To take a real example from the 2005–06 session (the SI that fixed the day on which all-day (and night) pub and bar opening would become legal), the motion would read:

> *That an Humble Address be presented to Her Majesty, praying that the Licensing Act 2003 (second appointed day) Order 2005 (S.I., 2005, No. 2091), dated 27 July 2005, a copy of which was laid before this House on 29th July, be annulled.*

Any annulment of an instrument must take place during a period of forty days (excluding time when both Houses are adjourned for more than four days) from the laying of the SI; this time is unsurprisingly known as *praying time*.

In the Commons, debate on a prayer on the floor of the House is unusual; most are taken upstairs in a *standing committee on delegated legislation*, which is very like a standing committee on a bill but which debates the prayer on a motion 'That the committee has considered' the instrument, for a period of one and a half hours (two and a half hours in the case of Northern Ireland instruments). Only a minister can move a motion in the House to refer a prayer to a standing committee, so even debates of this sort are in the gift of the government and are normally only granted to the principal opposition parties, and almost never to back-benchers. Moreover, the standing committee cannot reject the instrument, so any vote that is not on the floor of the House is purely symbolic; and on the floor of the House no prayer has been carried since 1979.

In an average session, thirty or forty prayers are taken in standing committee; but only two or three on the floor of the House.

Affirmative procedure

Because any instrument in this category must be explicitly approved, a decision of each House is required. In the Commons, affirmative instruments are automatically referred to a standing committee on delegated legislation. These operate in exactly the same way for affirmative instruments as for prayers against negative instruments, and they offer an opportunity for debate rather than substantive decision. When an affirmative has been debated in standing committee it returns to the floor of the House for decision, and a vote if necessary, but without further debate.

It is also possible for an affirmative to be 'de-referred': that is, so that it is both debated and decided on the floor of the House. The automatic referral to standing committee has existed since 1995; it was introduced as part of an effort to reduce sitting time on the floor of the House, but there was an understanding that the government would accede to a reasonable request to take particular affirmatives on the floor of the House.

Although, to begin with, substantial numbers of affirmatives were taken on the floor (seventy-three in 1994–95, forty-seven in 1995–96 and forty-two in 1996–97), there was a sharp decline thereafter, and now about a dozen affirmatives are considered in the House in an average session. Recent subjects taken on the floor have included: local government finance and the financing of police authorities, up-rating of social security benefits, the arms decommissioning amnesty in Northern Ireland, and the arrangements for a referendum on setting up an assembly in the north-east of England.

Every sitting week, the Journal Office in the House of Commons produces a *Statutory Instrument List* showing the state of play on all affirmative and negative instruments and, in the latter case, the number of 'praying days' remaining on each. It is available on the parliamentary website.

Lords proceedings on Statutory Instruments

Although delegated legislation is not subject to the Parliament Acts, the House of Lords rarely opposes negative or affirmative instruments. As we have seen, they are not amendable, so if the House pressed its opposition to a vote the result could be the wholesale rejection of the instrument. As the Lords usually consider instruments after they have been taken in the House of Commons, this has constrained opposition parties from pressing their disagreement. Between 1955 and the end of the 2004–05 session eighty-four statutory instruments were divided on, but such was the unease of the two major parties while in opposition about using the House's powers to the full that thirty-eight of those divisions were on motions that would not, if carried, have proved fatal to the instrument in question.

Only three times has the government of the day ever been defeated on a vote directly on an order. The Conservative Opposition divided the House against the Southern Rhodesia (United Nations Sanctions) Order 1968 and defeated the government, so provoking a constitutional furore. A virtually identical version of the order was approved a few weeks later. The two other instances occurred in February 2002 on a prayer to annul the Greater London Authority Election Rules 2000 and a motion to approve the Greater London Authority (Election Expenses) Order 2000. In addition, since 1955 one order has been withdrawn following debate with no vote taken and another – the Town and Country Planning General Development Order 1977 – was not proceeded with after the government lost a vote on a motion inviting it to withdraw the order.

The Royal Commission on Reform of the House of Lords recommended that the Statutory Instruments Act 1946 be amended to enable the Commons to override a Lords rejection of an affirmative or negative instrument. By diminishing the theoretical powers over delegated legislation slightly, it was argued, the House might make more use of the powers that remained to it. But this recommendation has not yet been taken up.

Improving parliamentary control

Parliament's control of secondary legislation has been criticised on a number of grounds. The remit of the Joint Committee is limited to technical issues of *vires* and drafting; opportunities for debate, particularly in the Commons, are limited; and SIs are unamendable in either House.

Lords Select Committees on Delegated Powers

The House of Lords, while cautious in the use it makes of its powers to reject affirmative or negative instruments in the Chamber of the House, has in recent years taken considerable steps in other directions so as to ensure that delegated powers are appropriately used. We have already noted the major contribution made by the Lords Select Committee on Delegated Powers and Regulatory Reform. Since 1992, this committee (originally the Delegated Powers Scrutiny Committee) has scrutinised all government and some private members' bills so as to establish whether any legislative power is inappropriately delegated to ministers, or whether any delegation is subject to sufficient parliamentary scrutiny. This 'up-stream' policing of the use of delegated powers has been very successful (see pages 254–5).

More recently the House has established a committee on the Merits of Statutory Instruments, to sift those of political significance from the rest. The establishment of such a committee had originally been recommended by the Royal Commission on Reform of the House of Lords in 2000 and endorsed by the Group on the Working of the House in 2002 and the Liaison Committee in 2003. The committee finally began its work in April 2004. The committee's remit is to consider every instrument laid before each House and subject to parliamentary proceedings (the so-called 'super-affirmative' procedure where draft proposals are first laid for a sixty-day period of consideration and possible amendments), and every draft statutory instrument. The committee does not consider Northern Ireland orders, human rights remedial orders, regulatory reform orders or Church Measures. The committee draws to the attention of the House any instrument that is important politically, legally or in policy terms; or is inappropriate in view of developments since the passage of the parent Act; or imperfectly achieves its objectives; or inappropriately implements EU legislation. (This latter provision arose out of fears that such regulations were over elaborate and 'gold plated' the original EU requirements). Recently (July 2005) the committee has been empowered to conduct inquiries into general matters relating to the scrutiny of merits of instruments and its first such inquiry – into the government's management of the secondary legislation process – has been held.

The workload is very considerable and the committee is supported by two lawyers in addition to the usual Clerk and clerical support. During approximately one calendar year of scrutiny (April 2004 to early April 2005) the committee considered 1,277 instruments of which 176 were affirmative and 1,099 negative. It reported on twenty affirmative instruments and fifty negative instruments, chiefly on grounds of public policy interest. All affirmative instruments are debated. But debate was sought on only twelve of the fifty negative instruments; and the Procedure Committee in July 2005 stated that it is 'debatable whether the House makes sufficient use of its output'.

The Commons Procedure Committee has twice recommended a sifting committee on merits of instruments like that now in place in the Lords (in 1996 and 2000), saying that 'the existing system of scrutinising delegated legislation is urgently in need of reform'. The committee also recommended that praying time for negative instruments should be increased from forty days to sixty; that no decision on an SI should be taken by the House until the Joint Committee on Statutory Instruments had completed its consideration; and that the most substantial and complex SIs should be given a super-affirmative treatment, being subject to pre-legislative scrutiny in the same way as a draft bill. The government has not so far taken action on these recommendations. We return to this in Chapter 13.

Regulatory reform orders

There are some Acts of Parliament that allow a minister to amend primary legislation by secondary legislation – to amend an Act by an SI. Such a provision in a bill is known as a 'Henry VIII clause' – reflecting that monarch's somewhat broad-brush approach to his powers. It is generally undesirable for a minister to be able to change what normally only Parliament may decide; however, in 1994 the Deregulation and Contracting Out Act gave ministers just those powers, but subject to a stringent system of parliamentary control.

As part of the then Conservative government's wish to lighten the weight of regulation, the 1994 Act allowed ministers to amend or repeal primary legislation that imposed a burden affecting any person carrying on a trade, business or profession. It introduced an entirely new parliamentary procedure whereby a minister had to consult on a proposal, which would then be laid before Parliament and examined by Deregulation Committees of both Houses, which could suggest amendments before the deregulation order was laid as a formal draft for approval. Nearly ninety deregulation orders were made under the 1994 Act, ranging from greyhound racing to the registration of marriages to the selling of salmon roe; but it is in the nature of deregulation that after the early quick hits it becomes harder to find areas to deregulate.

The scope of the procedure was then widened by the Labour government's Regulatory Reform Act 2001 to cover 'burdens affecting persons in the carrying on of any activity'; and some other limitations in the 1994 Act were relaxed. A power to make 'subordinate provisions' (a sort of further delegated legislation, but also to be considered by the committees) was introduced. The committees were renamed: that in the Commons became the Regulatory Reform Committee, and the Lords committee became the Delegated Powers and Regulatory Reform Committee.

Before a minister may make a regulatory reform order, he or she must *consult widely with those who would be affected*. This is part of the procedure on which the committees have been particularly insistent. After the consultation, the minister may lay before Parliament *a proposal for an order, together with an explanatory statement*. There is then a period of sixty days for consideration by the committees (as with praying time, not including recesses). They test the proposal against fourteen criteria, including whether this is the right method of changing the law; the adequacy of the consultation; whether the right balance of burdens and benefits has been struck, and whether the proposal would continue any necessary protection for those affected; whether it would limit any reasonable rights or freedoms; and whether the minister is acting within the powers given by the Act.

In assessing the proposal, the committees often take written or oral evidence, both from the government and from those who might be affected, and they then report separately on whether the proposal should go forward, with or without amendments.

At the end of the sixty days, the minister is able to lay before Parliament *a draft order*, taking into account the views of the committees and of anyone else who has commented during the sixty-day period, and setting out what changes have been made, and why. The committees look at the draft order within fifteen sitting days and report to each House upon it. In the Commons, there is then a graduated procedure. If the committee has unanimously recommended that the draft order be made, it is put to the House without debate; if the committee had a vote on the matter, there is an hour and a half's debate in the House; but if the committee recommends that the draft order not be approved there must be a debate of up to three hours on a motion to disagree with the committee. If that motion is successful, the question on approval of the draft order is put without further debate.

Once the draft order has been approved by both Houses, the minister may *make it* and so bring it into law. A list of regulatory reform business, and the stages each proposal or draft order has reached, is published weekly. At the beginning of the 2001 parliament, the government identified fifty changes to the law that it planned to address through the regulatory reform procedure; ten to fifteen proposals come forward in an average year.

This procedure, under both the 1994 and the 2001 Acts, has been innovative and effective. It has all the advantages of pre-legislative scrutiny: detailed, evidence-based scrutiny and analysis; wide consultation and public access to the legislative process; and the testing and amendment of proposed legislation to produce a better quality of outcome. Moreover, it is systematic; it is not up to the government of the day to decide, as with bills, whether they should be examined in draft before being formally introduced. If the regulatory reform route is taken, then the procedure outlined above applies automatically.

It has been rigorous; indeed, so much so that several government departments decided early on that they would not take this route but wait for an opportunity for the easier ride of primary legislation. It has been effective and has allowed back-benchers to have a real influence on the content of legislation; governments of both parties have almost always accepted the committees' recommendations. And it has been consensual; the committees have worked in a remarkably non-partisan way. The procedure is seen by many as offering lessons that could be applied more widely.

The government had signalled its wish to extend this procedure, but when the Legislative and Regulatory Reform Bill was published in early 2006 it caused consternation. The Bill would allow almost all amendments to or repeals of primary legislation to be made by Ministerial Orders; and the Commons Regulatory Reform Committee described it as having 'the potential to be the most constitutionally significant Bill that has been brought before Parliament for some years'. Without additional parliamentary safeguards – later promised by the government – it seemed likely to shift the weight of legislative advantage still further in favour of the government of the day. We return to this in Chapter 13.

Remedial orders

The Human Rights Act 1998, which came into effect in October 2000, allows ministers to make a new form of delegated legislation known as 'remedial orders'. These come about when a UK court finds that some provision of an Act of Parliament is incompatible with the Human Rights Act. A remedial order may amend primary legislation; the procedure for considering it is similar to that for a regulatory reform order, except that it is the task of the Joint Committee on Human Rights, rather than the two Committees described above, to consider and report on proposals and draft orders. Once it has been considered by the Joint Committee on Human Rights, and the statutory periods have passed, a draft order is treated in the same way as any other affirmative instrument.

If swift action is required, a minister may make an order, laying it before both Houses. It has immediate statutory effect, but it must be confirmed by both Houses approving it within 120 days of its being laid (as for praying time, excluding times when both Houses are in recess). During the first sixty of those days, representations may be made to the minister; and if as a result the minister decides to make a new order, it must be approved by both Houses within the remaining sixty days.

A list of proposals, draft remedial orders and any urgent procedure orders, together with time remaining on each, is published with the Vote bundle every sitting Wednesday. There have so far been only three remedial orders: in 2001, to amend the Mental Health Act 1983 in respect of the burden of proof for detaining someone under that Act; one urgent proce-dure order, on naval discipline legislation, in 2004; and the Marriage Act 1949 (Remedial) Order 2006.

Devolution: Northern Ireland

The principal post-devolution source of delegated legislation considered at Westminster is Northern Ireland. Under the Northern Ireland Act 1974, which introduced direct rule from Westminster, legislation is in the form of Orders in Council; these have normally been a version of legislation enacted for England and Wales. The Northern Ireland Act 1998 requires that pro-posals for Orders in Council dealing with matters reserved to Westminster (such as public order, criminal law, firearms, police, the Civil Service and emergency powers) should be referred to the Northern Ireland Assembly for its views during a sixty-day consultation period. At the end of that time, the government may lay before Parliament a draft order for approval, together with a report on representations made and any changes as a result – a form of super-affirmative instrument that has similarities with the regulatory reform procedure. If the Northern Ireland Assembly is suspended, then Orders in Council are dealt with as straightforward affirmative instruments.

Since the 2003 suspension, the House of Lords has debated such Orders in grand committee off the floor so as to increase the time available for consideration. The motions for approval continued to be taken in the House, but with shorter debate.

Church of England Measures

As the established church of the state, the Church of England has to have its legislation approved by Parliament, including the Royal Assent of the Sovereign. These *Measures* are a form of delegated legislation, although they eventually form part of the statute book. They are first agreed by the Church's parliament, the General Synod, which has procedures for debate and amendment very similar to the Commons and Lords. A draft of the Measure is then sent to the Ecclesiastical Committee, which consists of fifteen members of the House of Lords nominated by the Lord Speaker and fifteen MPs nominated by the Speaker. This is not a conventional joint committee appointed by the two Houses but a statutory body set up under the Church of England (Assembly) General Powers Act 1919.

The purpose of the Committee is 'to determine whether or not the Measure is expedient'. The committee cannot amend the Measure. To assist the Committee in coming to a view, comments and explanations are submitted by the General Synod, and members of its Legislative Committee assist the Ecclesiastical Committee in its deliberations. On difficult issues a conference with the full membership of the Legislative Committee may be held, but this is rare. The committee presents a short report on each Measure, together with its decision on whether the Measure in question is 'expedient'. The Measure is at the same time laid before each House of Parliament for approval.

The role of Parliament in the governance of the Church is sometimes a cause of controversy. After all, the General Synod as the Church's own representative body has already approved a Measure by the time it reaches Parliament. It is arguable that in its consideration of a Measure Parliament should not seek to second guess the Synod. Very occasionally, the Ecclesiastical Committee has, on some point of principle, suggested that a Measure be laid in a slightly different form. Once the Ecclesiastical Committee has found a Measure expedient, the proceedings in the two Houses are uncontroversial, although in 1989 a Measure dealing with the ordination of divorced men was actually rejected by the Commons.

Parliament and the taxpayer

TOTAL GOVERNMENT expenditure in 2005–06 was expected to be £477 billion, or about £7,950 for every man, woman and child in the United Kingdom. Taxation and public spending touch everyone's daily lives, from the amount of income tax we pay to the levels of social security and old age pensions we receive, and from standards in our local hospitals and schools to the quality of the environment and the number of police on the beat. It is not surprising, then, that the nation's finances are always at the heart of political controversy. Are the economic prospects hopeful? Is the taxpayer getting good value for money? Should a project be financed through a public/private partnership? How much will it cost to issue everyone with an ID Card? Should we be spending more on schools? On the NHS? On the police? If we do, what will that do to taxation?

These questions are central to much of the work of Parliament but, as we shall see in this chapter, although the big issues are always in debate, Parliament exercises little detailed control over public spending.

The constitutional principles

The modern role of Parliament (and especially the House of Commons) in financial matters reflects the ancient relationship with the Crown. The Sovereign needed the authority and agreement of the Commons for taxes and for spending; but from early times the House required the redress of grievances before granting through taxation (*ways and means*) the money (*supply*) that the Crown sought, and this was the basis of its growing influence.

It is still a basic constitutional principle that it is for the Crown (in fact, the government of the day) and not for Parliament to propose expenditure and taxation. This *financial initiative of the Crown* means in practice that only ministers may make proposals for spending and taxes. If Parliament agrees to those proposals, then they are given authority through legislation.

The House of Commons has a special role in financial matters, based on a resolution of 1671, which stated 'That in all aids given to the King by the Commons, the rate or tax ought not to be altered by the Lords', reinforced seven years later by a resolution that said in splendidly comprehensive language:

> *all aids and supplies, and aids to his Majesty in Parliament, are the sole gift*
> *of the Commons; and all bills for the granting of any such aids and supplies*
> *ought to begin with the Commons; and that it is the undoubted and sole*
> *right of the Commons to direct, limit and appoint in such bills the ends,*
> *purposes, considerations, limitations, and qualifications of such grants,*
> *which ought not to be changed or altered by the House of Lords.*

Despite the language, this did not put things permanently beyond doubt and it was arguable that the Lords retained a power to reject a supply bill outright. Thus in 1860 the Lords rejected the Paper Duty Repeal Bill and, more seriously in 1909, the Finance Bill, which gave effect to Lloyd George's controversial Budget. In the latter case, the result was the passing of the Parliament Act 1911 and the permanent restriction of the powers of the House of Lords to thwart the legislative will of the Commons.

Today the practical results of the *financial privilege* of the House of Commons are that *bills of aids and supplies*, principally the Finance Bill, which authorises the government's taxation proposals, and the Consolidated Fund and Appropriation Bills, which authorise government spending, originate in the Commons and are not amended by the Lords. Finance Bills are debated on second reading in the Lords, but other proceedings are only formal.

However, if the Commons passes what the Parliament Act 1911 defines as a *money bill* – that is, a bill whose *only* purpose is to authorise expenditure or taxation – it is certified by the Speaker as a money bill. If such a bill is sent to the Lords at least one month before the end of the session and has not been agreed by the Lords within a month, it may be sent directly for Royal Assent. Although it remains in theory possible for the Lords to amend money bills – and such amendments have in the past been made – the Commons are not obliged to consider them, and it is now inconceivable that any amendment would be attempted. The stages of money bills are taken formally in the Lords and no money bill has ever had to be presented for Royal Assent under the terms of the 1911 Act.

A bill whose provisions involve an increase in public expenditure or taxation may begin in the House of Lords, but it may proceed in the Commons only if a minister takes charge of it. In such a case the constitutional niceties are preserved by a *'privilege amendment'*: a subsection at the end of the bill that says 'Nothing in this Act shall impose any charge on the people or on public funds' or vary any such charge. This is a fiction, of course; and the privilege amendment is routinely removed when the bill is in committee in the Commons.

Another practical effect of Commons financial privilege is that any Lords amendments to a Commons bill that involve a charge upon the public revenue not sanctioned by the Commons money resolution in respect of that bill are deemed disagreed to upon the Speaker's declaration, 'by reason of privilege'. A privilege reason for disagreeing to such amendments is now not questioned by the Lords.

The financial pre-eminence of the Commons in matters of legislation does not mean that the Lords are inhibited in discussing or investigating financial subjects. Both in debate and through the work of select committees such as the Economic Affairs Committee and the European Union Committee, such matters are frequently pursued. Indeed, since 2003 a subcommittee of the Economic Affairs Committee has been established specially each year to consider certain policy aspects of the Finance Bill. It is interesting to speculate whether the climate of Lords reform may encourage that House to seek a more formal role in financial matters – something which would probably be resisted by the Commons.

The annual cycles

Financial procedure is hideously complex; this is partly because of the complexity of the subject matter but is also because the process takes place in three largely separate cycles. The *Budget cycle* deals with broad financial issues, the management of the economy and the authorisation of taxation. The *estimates cycle* covers the authorisation of public spending; and the *reporting cycle* provides information on what money has been spent and how effectively it has been used. We will examine these one by one (and hope to make them slightly less confusing); but Table 8.1 below shows how events in all three relate. The fact that the parliamentary year (the session, normally from November to the following October) does not coincide with either the calendar year or the financial year is a further complication.

Table 8.1 The annual parliamentary cycles

	Budget cycle	Estimates cycle	Reporting cycle
			(throughout year, continuous programme of value-for-money inquiries and reports by the Comptroller and Auditor General and the Public Accounts Committee
Start of parliamentary session			
October/ November	Pre-Budget report published	Winter supplementary estimates (for year 2) presented (must be approved by 6 February)	Resource accounts (for year 1) presented
	Treasury Committee and other select committees report	Votes on Account (for year 3) presented	Departmental performance reports (for year 1) published
December		Consolidated Fund Bill (Consolidated Fund Act) (for year 2) passed	Select committees review and report
January		First estimates day (debates on select committee reports)	
February		Spring supplementary estimates (for year 2) presented (for approval by 6 February)	
		Excess Votes (for year 1) presented (for approval by 18 March)	
		Ministry of Defence Votes A presented (for approval by 18 March)	
		Second estimates day (debates on select committee reports)	
March	Budget statement and debate	Main estimates (for year 3) presented (for approval by 5 August)	
		Consolidated Fund (Appropriation) Bill (Appropriation Act) passed (must be by 31 March)	

Table 8.1 (*Cont'd*)

	Budget cycle	Estimates cycle	Reporting cycle
Start of financial year 3			
April	Finance Bill published Second reading (Treasury Committee reports in time for second reading)		Departmental reports and spending plans (for years 3, 4 and 5) published. Select committees review and report
May	Finance Bill in Committee of the whole House and standing committee	Summer supplementary estimates (for year 3) presented (for approval by 5 August)	
June	Finance Bill report stage and third reading	Third estimates day (debates on select committee reports)	
July	Formal consideration by Lords (Finance Act)	Consolidated Fund (Appropriation) (No. 2) Bill (the Appropriation (No. 2) Act) passed (must be by 2 August) Spending plans (for years 4, 5 and 6) published (if a biennial spending review is taking place that year)	

Source: Adapted from Paul Evans (2002) *House of Commons Procedure*, 3rd edition, p. 108, Vacher Dod Publishing Ltd, London

Table 8.1 shows the main events in each of the Budget, estimates and reporting cycles. Dates are indicative rather than exact (except for the approval deadlines). The financial year beginning in April is designated year 3; during the session the House will consider business relating to year 1 (the financial year that ended seven months before the start of the new parliamentary session) and year 2 (the financial year that is about halfway through when the session begins).

It should also be remembered that some important economic factors are reported to Parliament but are not under parliamentary control: interest rates are set by the Bank of England rather than by the government; and the level of the public sector borrowing requirement – in which the House of Commons might reasonably have a say – is, at least in theory, under government control.

The Budget cycle

The word 'budget' comes from the archaic French *bougette*, a little bag, which in English had its literal meaning from the fifteenth century; later, 'to open one's budget' meant 'to speak one's mind'. In 1733, Sir Robert Walpole, then Chancellor of the Exchequer as well as Prime Minister, was depicted in a satirical pamphlet as a quack doctor opening a bag of pills. The term rapidly became applied to the Chancellor's review of the national finances, given annually from Walpole's time onwards.

The Chancellor of the Exchequer normally delivers his Budget in March. There will also usually be a Budget not long after a general election if there has been a change of government. In recent decades, the Budget statement has been on a Tuesday, but from 2001 to 2005 the statement was on a Wednesday. Budget day is always something of a media event, with the Chancellor being photographed outside his residence at No. 11 Downing Street before leaving for the Commons holding up the despatch box containing his Budget speech. For nearly 140 years Chancellors used a battered red box first used by Gladstone in the 1860s; in 1997, for his first Budget, Gordon Brown used a new box made by young trainees in his constituency.

The Budget speech comes immediately after Question Time; in order not to upstage the Chancellor, the ten-minute rule bill slot (which is normally on Tuesdays and Wednesdays) for Budget day is deferred to the following Monday. Before the Chancellor begins his statement, the Speaker's place in the Chair is generally taken by the Chairman of Ways and Means, a tradition reflecting the fact that between 1641 and 1967, when it was abolished, taxation proposals were made in the Committee of Ways and Means.

The Chancellor begins with the review of the nation's finances and the economic situation, which might be recognised in form – although not always in content! – by his predecessors over three centuries. In the later part of his speech – in which he does not usually take interventions – he moves on to his taxation proposals. Modern Budget statements have lasted an hour or so: a far cry from Gladstone's four-and-three-quarter-hour marathon in 1853. When the Chancellor has completed his statement, the motions to give effect to the proposals he has announced – fifty to sixty of them (fifty-eight in 2005) – are made available to the House. Strict secrecy is maintained on the Budget proposals until the Chancellor announces them – not least because of their market sensitivity – so, exceptionally, no notice is given of these motions.

The Chancellor then usually moves a motion to give immediate legal effect to certain of his proposals (five in 2005) to forestall the speculation that might take place if it were known that the duty on cigarettes or whisky, for example, would be raised, but not for days or weeks. Under the Provisional Collection of Taxes Act 1968, when this motion is agreed to the proposals it covers have the force of law, but the House must agree to the motions on the individual proposals within ten sitting days. This procedure may apply to any proposal continuing a tax or altering its rate, but not to new taxes.

The Chancellor then moves what is known as the 'amendment of the law' motion. This is a general statement that 'it is expedient to amend the law with respect to the National Debt and to make further provision in respect of finance', and it is the vehicle for the very broad Budget debate that follows. The Chancellor is followed not by the shadow Chancellor but by the Leader of the Opposition, who must make some shrewd guesses in advance so that he can react swiftly to what the Chancellor has said, in addition to setting out his own party's economic policies.

The Budget debate normally lasts for four or five days, and at its conclusion all fifty or sixty motions are put to the House, providing the opposition parties with an opportunity to vote against – usually three or four – individual proposals with which they particularly disagree. The Finance Bill is then formally introduced on the basis of what have now become the *founding resolutions*. Budget secrecy has meant that consultation on many specific provisions has not been possible, so the bill is not finally printed and published for a little while after the Budget statement.

The Finance Bill

The Finance Bill is a substantial document, often running to 250 or more clauses. Its provisions combine changes to levels and types of taxation with much detailed administration of the tax system, which makes for greater complexity. It also provides for the renewal for that year of taxes already in force. In 1992–93, the Commons Procedure Committee suggested that the process be simplified, with one bill making tax changes and a taxes management bill doing the rest. In the event, no change has been made.

The Finance Bill's second reading debate will be a single day, providing a further opportunity for a general debate on the government's fiscal policy. The bill is then divided; clauses dealing with the major, or most controversial, proposals are taken in Committee of the whole House. The rest of the bill is committed to a standing committee. The report stage and third reading usually occupy a further two days on the floor of the House.

Standing committees on the Finance Bill have a character rather different from those on other bills. They are larger, often with thirty to forty members rather than twenty or so; because of the regularity of Finance Bills, and of debates on economic affairs, the participants will know each other well and be old sparring partners; and the level of expertise is high. Both the opposition parties and government back-benchers will be extensively briefed by groups that will be affected by the Chancellor's proposals and assisted by them in drafting amendments to the often highly complex provisions of the bill. In addition to the usual rules about the admissibility of amendments (see page 215), MPs' ability to propose changes is restricted by the scope of the resolutions to which the House has agreed and, where the resolutions simply said 'that provision may be made about the level of' such and such a tax or charge, the levels actually proposed in the bill. For example, if the House agreed to a resolution that said that the rate of corporation tax for small companies should be 19 per cent, amendments seeking to raise that rate would not be in order, although it would be possible to move to reduce it.

Governments are usually even less willing to accept substantial amendments to the Finance Bill than they are in the case of other legislation, although disquiet among back-benchers can cause changes, whether following defeat on a vote, as with the scrapping of the second tranche of VAT on domestic fuel in December 1994, or by the government altering its proposals to head off possible defeat, as in the halving of the increase in petrol duty that was proposed in the 1981 Budget. However, to a great extent the Budget is a package and, for MPs of the government party in particular, voting to defeat one proposal implies voting to increase revenue elsewhere – or to reduce public expenditure. However, less dramatic changes are not unusual as a result of the committee stage of the Finance Bill. One example in 1998 was the proposal to tax agricultural earnings applied to the upkeep of historic houses. The Historic Houses Association briefed MPs on the standing committee, they took up the case, and the taxation was phased in rather than being introduced immediately, with considerable benefits for the national heritage. In 2004 the Bill was amended to allow those who did not want to share their pension arrangements with others – in this case, the Exclusive Brethren – to remain separate.

The Finance Bill then goes to the Lords. As we have seen, Lords stages of supply bills, such as the Finance Bill and any money bill, are taken formally.

However, a general economic debate is held on second reading of the Finance Bill. Remaining stages are then taken formally, without debate.

Budget information

On Budget day the Treasury publishes the *Financial Statement and Budget Report* (FSBR), now a glossy-covered production but often known as the Red Book, from its former plain red cover. The FSBR is now combined with an *Economic and Fiscal Strategy Report*. The document is a substantial one, in 2005 running to nearly 300 pages. It sets out the features of the national economy in a global context, reports on a wide range of economic and financial measures, and seeks to integrate financial and taxation proposals into a broader context of policy across government. It is accompanied by a raft of press releases, and fifty to sixty notes by HM Revenue and Customs on specific proposals, setting them out in less technical language.

An important part of the 'Budget bundle' is the report by the Comptroller and Auditor General, provided for in the Finance Act 1998, on those conventions and assumptions underlying the Treasury's fiscal projections that the Chancellor has asked him to validate. In 2005, the C&AG examined how levels of unemployment were forecast.

The papers published on Budget day make up a bundle between five and ten centimetres thick, on a wide range of measures and policies, often of great technicality and complexity. Their audience is of course much wider than Parliament, and the proposals and analysis are closely examined in the financial, commercial and industrial sectors. Nevertheless, the Budget proposals and information set the House of Commons a substantial task of scrutiny, which the lengthy Finance Bill committee stage struggles to perform.

However, the Treasury Committee reports rapidly upon the Budget in order to inform consideration of the Finance Bill. It takes oral evidence not only from the Chancellor himself but also from the Permanent Secretary and senior officials at the Treasury, as well as from outside financial and economic experts. Despite a government majority, it often provides a critical counter-weight to the government's proposals.

The unified Budget

One of the features of financial procedure in the House of Commons has been that taxation – the Budget cycle – is dealt with separately from public spending plans and the related estimates cycle. From 1993 to 1996 under the Conservative government the Budget statement was made in November of each year, and it covered not only taxation proposals for the forthcoming financial year but also public spending for the next three years.

The pre-Budget report

In the first Labour Budget statement in July 1997, the new government announced a return to the separate approach, but with the introduction of a 'pre-Budget report', sometimes called the 'Green Budget' (as in 'Green Paper', because of its consultative character). The first of these was published in November 1997; the Chancellor described its purpose as to report the government's assessment of the economy, to outline the government's Budget aims and to encourage an informed debate on the issues.

This too is a substantial document; the December 2004 edition ran to 258 pages, with thirty tables. As with the Budget report itself, it places economic assessments in the context of policy priorities such as economic stability, productivity, employment opportunities, high-quality public services, and protecting the environment, so there is some element of read-across to detailed spending plans. The pre-Budget report provides an opportunity for select committees other than the Treasury Committee to examine implications for their areas of interest; for example, the Environmental Audit Committee may report on the environmental implications of particular policies.

The estimates cycle

The process of voting 'supply' has its origins in a time when monarchs needed to spend money that the Crown did not have, usually on wars. Parliament then had to be asked to supply the funds. Even though state expenditure is now on a very different scale and for a multitude of different purposes, the Sovereign's government must still ask the Commons for the money it needs. This request is conveyed through the *estimates*. Expenditure for which supply is voted is not the whole story. There are large areas of public expenditure that the supply estimates do not cover – for example, national insurance, expenditure by local authorities and net payments to the European Union.

Resource accounting

From 2001–02, as a result of the Government Resources and Accounts Act 2000, the estimates have been presented to Parliament on a resource accounting basis (although they still also contain some cash figures).

Resource accounting records the economic costs of the provision of services and the consumption of assets (including depreciation, the cost of using capital assets, and future liabilities such as those for compensation for early retirement). It is designed to give a more accurate picture of how resources are being used and makes government accounts much more like company accounts. It also allows a better assessment of how resources have been applied to the achievement of policy objectives. Cash accounting, the method used until 2001, just tracked the movement of cash.

Public spending plans

Over the last seven years, government spending reviews have taken place every two years. They are run by the Treasury, and government departments put in proposals for extra resources (or for not cutting existing budgets), which Treasury ministers then evaluate. The result of this process – in which Parliament has no role – is the *three-year spending plans* published in July. These give for each government department a brief summary of key objectives (including *public service agreements* – see page 280) and a short report on progress so far. Then follows total planned expenditure for that department for the next three financial years, expressed as a *departmental expenditure limit* (DEL) (split into a resource budget and a capital budget). DELs are totals of expenditure that departments can control, even though some elements may be demand-led.

The spending plans also bring together broader and cross-cutting policies and show how resources are to be applied to their achievement. A statistical annex sets out the figures across government and gives figures for new allocations and net investment. It also shows planned *total managed expenditure* for each of the next three years: that is, the totals of all the DELs plus expectations of *annually managed expenditure* (AME). AME covers expenditure that is less predictable or controllable than DELs: for example, social security and Common Agricultural Policy payments.

This government-wide forward look, which provides an opportunity for debate on the floor of the House as well as material for examination by the departmental select committees, is followed each spring by a *departmental report*, which reports annual progress against the three-year spending plan, with any adjustments.

Votes on account

These come before the House in November. They cover about 45 per cent of the estimated expenditure of each government department in the coming financial year and are in effect to tide the government over until the main estimates are approved in the following July. Votes on Account must be agreed by the House by 6 February.

Ministry of Defence Votes A

These are published in February. The Bill of Rights 1688–89 prevented the Crown from maintaining a standing army in time of peace without the approval of Parliament, so these 'Votes A' laid before the House by the Secretary of State for Defence invite the annual authorisation by the House of Commons of the maximum numbers of personnel in the armed services.

Main estimates

These estimates, one for each government department (and for other bodies such as the Office of Rail Regulation and the NHS Pension Scheme), are published at roughly the same time as the departmental reports. The Treasury aims to issue main estimates within three weeks of the Budget, which means that they are usually published in April or early May. They form the principal request from the government to the House of Commons for the resources required to run the state in the following financial year. They vary from small departments such as the Cabinet Office, which in 2005–06 sought £224 million to run its operations, to major areas of government expenditure: in 2005–06, the National Health Service was set to cost £89 *billion*.

The key elements of each estimate are, in Part I, the *net amounts sought*. It is the headline *request for resources* figures and the accompanying cash totals in Part I of the estimates that are presented for parliamentary approval. Even though government accounting is on a resource basis, the amounts sought are expressed in cash terms as well as in resource terms. This is because resources are an accounting concept in which amounts may not be finally determined until the books are audited after the end of the financial year, and there is in the meantime a need to control the cash flowing out of the Consolidated Fund (the government's account at the Bank of England).

Each estimate also contains a formal description of the services to be financed from the estimate (known as the *ambit* of the estimate). When the estimate has been approved by the House, this part will be reproduced in an Appropriation Act. The ambit is an important part of the authorisation; it provides the statutory description of the purpose for which the money is sought, and expenditure must fall within that description.

Part I also says who will account for the estimate; for each estimate there must be an *Accounting Officer*, usually the Permanent Secretary of the government department concerned or the chief executive of an executive agency. Accounting Officers have a personal responsibility for the regularity and propriety of expenditure – including ensuring that money is spent only on purposes authorised by Parliament – as well as for the quality of internal financial controls in the department concerned. Finally, Part I of the estimate notes any amounts already allocated in the *Vote on Account*.

Part II of the estimate shows the resource requirement from Part I, broken down into more detail of what is going to be provided with the money. This breakdown forms the basis for in-year control of expenditure by the Treasury. If there is an underspend in one area and a requirement in another, funds may be moved between these subheads with Treasury approval but without further parliamentary authority (a process known as *virement*). The rationale for this is that Parliament approves the headline figures but not the detailed breakdown. The flexibility that *virement* gives also means that there is less need to build in a contingency into each subhead, which would encourage an over-provision in the estimate as a whole.

Also in Part II is a detailed reconciliation between a department's net resource requirement and the cash it needs (its *net cash requirement*). Part III sets out any additional income that the department expects to receive in the course of the year, but which it will surrender to the Consolidated Fund and not use to finance its own expenditure.

Each estimate is accompanied by a *forecast operating cost statement*, which shows net administration costs and net programme costs. It also notes any *contingent liabilities*: commitments that, if they were to be called upon, would require further expenditure. Although ministers may give guarantees or indemnities, Parliament is not bound in advance to honour any liabilities arising unless by law the liability is charged on the Consolidated Fund. Any other type of liability of more than £100,000 must be reported to Parliament.

Estimates days

In each session, three days are allotted for the House to consider the estimates. Given the huge sums involved, and the myriad purposes for which they are used, this may not seem much, and the process is indeed highly selective. The Liaison Committee, consisting of all the chairmen of select committees, proposes an estimate (or part of an estimate) for debate on each of these days or half-days. However, rather than inviting the House's detailed examination of the particular part of the estimate concerned, there is normally a reversal of the process. The estimate is used as a peg for a debate upon a select committee report that is usually much more about policy than about the money the government is seeking from the House of Commons.

The three estimates days are usually taken close to the other supply deadlines of 6 February, 18 March and 5 August (see Table 8.1 on page 268), but they must all happen before 5 August. The arbitrary date of 5 August was fixed in 1896, reportedly when A. J. Balfour suggested that the House of Commons was 'not in its best parliamentary form' after the August Bank holiday.

Because of the financial initiative reserved to the Crown – in effect to ministers – any amendment proposed to an estimate may only reduce the total of a request for resources, not increase it. In order to allow debate on the maximum number of select committee reports, estimates days are almost always divided into two halves, each with a different subject.

At the end of an estimates day, those estimates selected by the Liaison Committee for debate, and any amendments selected by the Speaker (usually such amendments indicate disapproval by means of a formulaic proposal to reduce an estimate by £1,000 or £10,000), are put to the House for approval. Immediately thereafter (although this can also be done on a non-estimates day) the question is put on outstanding estimates (that is, those that have to be approved before the next deadline); but these are put not in a detailed department by department form but as totals of resources and cash sought. For the winter and spring deadlines, this specifies only the resources to be used and the total sums to be paid out of the Consolidated Fund.

Supplementary estimates

The *winter supplementary estimates* allow departments to make adjustments four months into the financial year. The *spring supplementary estimates* allow similar adjustments nine months into the financial year. The *summer supplementary estimates* are published in the early summer, usually in May. They seek authority for any additional funds that government departments have found to be necessary since the main estimates were prepared. The government tries hard to ensure that these are for an identifiable new requirement rather than as a result of poor estimating; but, either way, a supplementary estimate focuses attention on a particular area of a department's spending and can trigger an inquiry by a select committee. *Revised estimates* may be presented in the early summer; the purpose of these is not to seek additional funds but to change the ambit of an estimate if it seems that funds authorised via the main estimate may have to be spent on something that would otherwise be outside its scope. Revised estimates, unlike supplementary estimates, can also be used to reduce expenditure.

If emergencies arise, the government can have recourse to the contingencies fund. This is limited by law to 2 per cent of the previous year's total authorised supply expenditure, and any money drawn out of the fund must be repaid. Alternatively, the House may be asked to agree an emergency supplementary estimate at any time; although, as for any supplementary estimate, fourteen clear days must elapse between presentation and approval.

Consolidated Fund and Appropriation Bills

When the House approves the estimates at the winter deadline, a *Consolidated Fund Bill* is brought in to provide legislative authority. Again, the bill does no more than specify the overall totals. On the basis that debate on the estimates has taken place on the items chosen for debate by the Liaison Committee, on a subsequent day the questions on second and third reading are put without debate; and there is no committee stage. Consideration in the Lords is purely formal, and the bill receives Royal Assent as the Consolidated Fund Act.

However, the Consolidated Fund (Appropriation) Bill brought in after the spring supplementary estimates have been approved gives much more detailed authority for the winter and spring supplementary estimates. It sets out the ambit of each request for resources and the amount to be *appropriated* – that is, paid – in respect of each. It also sets limits on the amount of their income from other sources that government departments can keep, and authorises numbers of personnel for the regular and reserve forces (the *Votes A* referred to on page 276). This bill, too, is passed without debate and is dealt with only formally by the Lords. Upon Royal Assent it becomes the Appropriation Act. Except for any *excess Votes*, the cycle of estimates and supply for the current financial year is almost over.

A second Consolidated Fund (Appropriation) Bill will be introduced in July to cover the main estimates and the summer supplementary estimates. This, too, is taken without debate, and purely formally in the Lords, and upon Royal Assent becomes the Appropriation (No. 2) Act.

Excess Votes

These seek retrospective authorisation when a department's spending in a financial year has exceeded what Parliament authorised (or has been incurred for a purpose that was not authorised), and there was not enough time to have a supplementary estimate approved in the course of the year (or if the overspend came to light only after the end of the financial year). Excess Votes are examined by the National Audit Office, which advises the Public Accounts Committee; no excess Vote may be put to the House for approval unless that committee has no objection.

The reporting cycle

We have seen so far how the government seeks authorisation for the taxes it wishes to levy and the different stages by which its proposed spending is approved. What about the other side of the process: how does the government account for how it has spent the money?

Departmental annual reports

These are normally published between March and May. They have been produced since 1991 and have developed substantially since then through initiatives by departments themselves, recommendations by select committees and, most recently, the additional transparency provided by the introduction of resource accounting. The Treasury exercises general supervision and lays down guidance. Departmental annual reports vary widely in format and presentation, but all contain core elements. They set out the names and responsibilities of the department's ministers and senior officials and the department's structure and purpose, and they survey the principal activities of the previous year. Departments also take the opportunity to explain to Parliament and the public how they go about their tasks and the main problems and challenges they face.

Departmental reports also give figures for each department's planned spending over the next three years (which are much more detailed than those in the government-wide spending plans published the previous July), together with the estimated spending for the current year and the actual spending for the four previous years. Other elements include changes to previously published plans, value-for-money initiatives, and departmental running costs and staffing.

A crucial part of every departmental report is its assessment of how it has delivered on its objectives and how it has used the resources provided by Parliament. This may be in terms of reporting on objectives and the extent to which they were achieved, often through formal *public service agreements* (PSAs). These are undertakings to deliver in the form of measurable targets over the period covered by the spending plans.

They are often very detailed – and measurable. In 2005, for example, the Department of Health's Target 1 within its overall Objective 1 'to reduce the incidence of avoidable illness, disease and injury in the population' was: 'reduction in the death rate from cancer amongst people aged under 75 years by at least 20 per cent by 2010 from a baseline of 141.2 deaths per 100,000 population for the three years 1995 to 1997'. Similar targets followed for heart disease, strokes and accidents. However, the progress reported was less clear. The Department said:

As a result of information from the 2001 Census, and subsequent Office of National Statistics Local Authority Population Studies, the population denominator has changed and rates for all years up to 2000 have been recalculated. Baseline data have been reset in accordance with these changes.

Which tells us very little, beyond the obvious fact that reporting of progress has to be consistent if it is to mean anything, and that changes in a statistical base have a way of obscuring what is actually happening.

Sometimes targets are unrealistic. The Department of Trade and Industry's Target 5 was 'to secure agreement by 2005 to a significant reduction in trade barriers leading to improved trading opportunities for the UK and developing countries'. Under 'progress' the DTI's 2005 departmental report recorded laconically 'slippage', together with the unsurprising news that 'the UK cannot deliver this target alone'.

An obsession with measurement can become an end in itself and get in the way of the activity concerned. Again, some activities – improving the state of diplomatic relations with a particular country, or the Cabinet Office's Objective 1 ('to support the Prime Minister in leading the government') – are difficult to measure in any exact way. The process of measurement becomes more one of totting up positive and negative factors. And there is a tendency for departments to report inputs (what they are doing) rather than outcomes and outputs (what they have got for it). Nevertheless, much of what the government does is capable of fairly rigorous measurement, and departmental reports – which have been greatly improved since they were first introduced – represent an important opportunity to do this. They are also a good way for taxpayers to see how a government department is spending their money. The glossy hard copies are very expensive (in 2005 anything between £24 and £32.50, depending on department) but they are also available on each department's website.

In October 2002, the House of Commons approved a set of core tasks for departmental select committees (see page 372). One of those core tasks was to monitor performance against targets in the PSAs. Select committees have increased their efforts in this area. They have focused especially on the need for targets to be both consistent year by year – measuring achievement is impossible if the goalposts move – and more consistent across government. A key player in this is the Committee Office's *Scrutiny Unit*, which, in addition to providing analysis for individual committees, also publishes its own review of the quality of departmental reports.

Select committees' examination of these reports, and assessments of the way that PSAs are formulated, measured and reported, seems likely to be an increasingly significant way of judging what the money voted by Parliament has actually bought.

Resource accounts

Resource accounts must be laid before Parliament by 31 January following the financial year to which they relate, although this is being speeded up; the more up to date the information, the more use it is. The target is now for all departments to lay their 2005–06 accounts by the end of July 2006, which would be a six-month improvement. Resource accounts are prepared according to GAAP (Generally Accepted Accounting Practice) and in some respects are similar to annual accounts of private sector businesses. They have the following elements: a foreword sets out the aims, objectives and main activities of the department. This is followed by statements of the accounting officer's responsibilities and on the system of internal financial controls that is in place.

All government departments (and many other public bodies, with some controversial exceptions, such as the BBC) are audited by the National Audit Office, headed by the Comptroller and Auditor General. The C&AG's certificate and report then sets out how the NAO has audited the accounts, and whether they represent a true and fair statement of the position. The *summary of resource outturn* compares actual expenditure with the estimate; there have been some substantial differences in the early stages of resource accounting, as departments have little historical experience on which to build, and some items (for example valuation of capital assets) have been difficult to forecast. The *operating cost statement* shows the resources consumed during the year; the *balance sheet* shows the assets and liabilities at year end; and the *cash flow statement* gives the cash flows during the year, including operating activities, capital expenditure and financing. Finally, there is an analysis of the department's expenditure to show what resources have been used in supporting each of its principal objectives.

The Comptroller and Auditor General and the National Audit Office

Resource accounts provide departmental select committees with more material in their monitoring of government departments; however, across government and other public bodies as a whole, audit and control is the task of the Comptroller and Auditor General backed by the Committee of Public Accounts.

The full title of the officer usually known simply as 'the C&AG' is 'Comptroller General of the Receipt and Issue of Her Majesty's Exchequer and Auditor-General of Public Accounts'. He heads a staff of about 800 (about two-thirds of whom are either professionally qualified or training for professional qualifications) in the National Audit Office, whose main buildings are about a mile from the Houses of Parliament. The C&AG has a direct responsibility to Parliament and works closely with the Committee of Public Accounts (usually known as 'the PAC'). This relationship is recognised by the C&AG's personal status as an officer of the House of Commons.

The C&AG's work has three elements. In relation to his Comptroller function, the Bank of England releases money to the government from the Consolidated Fund only on the authority of one of the C&AG's officials, who certifies that the release does not exceed the amount voted by the House. The C&AG also carries out an audit of the propriety and regularity of accounts – a total of some 600 accounts examined every year, including government departments, executive agencies and associated public bodies. Finally, the National Audit Act 1983, which established the NAO (previously the Exchequer and Audit Department), also gave the C&AG the task of examining the economy, efficiency and effectiveness of public spending. This side of his work is represented by about fifty value-for-money studies each year. Examples from 2005 are the quality of care for patients with strokes, consular services to British nationals abroad, The South Eastern Passenger Rail Franchise, and the financial management of the EU. The C&AG's reports are laid before Parliament and published.

The C&AG is not subject to operational direction from the PAC, or even from the House of Commons itself. He alone decides what to investigate and what conclusions he will reach. The great majority of his reports are taken up by the PAC, which enhances his status, while the committee's work is made more credible by the very substantial back-up of the C&AG and his staff.

The Committee of Public Accounts

The PAC was first established at Gladstone's instigation in 1861. The committee has sixteen members and is always chaired by an opposition MP. It meets twice a week while the House is sitting, and its principal witnesses are accounting officers. The standing orders give it the narrow task of 'the examination of the accounts showing the appropriation of the sums granted by Parliament to meet the public expenditure, and of such other accounts laid before Parliament as the Committee may think fit'; but for some years the committee has ranged more widely, principally following up the value-for-money reports of the C&AG but also moving into areas of policy, which leads to unnecessary duplication and overlap with departmental select committees. The PAC publishes some fifty reports a year. In combination, the C&AG and the PAC are an important means of checking the propriety of government expenditure – that money has been properly expended on authorised purposes – and, in selected areas, the extent to which value for money has been achieved.

Conclusion

We said at the start of this chapter that Parliament (in practice, the House of Commons) exercises very little control over the details of public spending. The examination of tax proposals is far less criticised – although the time available for debate on the Finance Bill is always a source of tension. Parliamentary examination of expenditure after the event, through the work of the C&AG, the PAC and other select committees, is seen as fairly effective. However, such examination always risks being somewhat academic; mistakes may have been made, or value for money may have been achieved, but either way, even though lessons have been learned, the money has been spent. Control over proposed spending is intrinsically more important.

The House of Commons has the ultimate deterrent of voting down the estimates – refusing supply – but that would be tantamount to a vote of no confidence in the government of the day and would almost certainly precipitate a general election. Nor would such an action really be one of *control*, which most people would see as analysis of each request for expenditure, followed by a decision on whether requests should be approved, or sums increased or reduced.

Because money is voted only on the initiative of the Crown, on the ancient principle that the Commons did not volunteer the money – the monarch had to ask for it – increasing estimates is not permitted. There is no fundamental reason why this should be so; increases are allowed in Germany, for example; and in France individual estimates may be varied up or down provided that the total remains the same (thus preserving the government's overall 'package' of income and expenditure). Suggestions that the practice in the Commons should be altered have been resisted by successive governments but, as a select committee examining the problem in the early 1980s pointed out, increases would have to be met by additional taxation. However, this would not apply to the 'tax-neutral' approach of keeping *total* expenditure the same.

In theory, estimates can be reduced, but here too effective power is limited. This is because the majority of money is voted, not line by line but on three occasions during the year, as a total of resources and cash for all the estimates before the House. True, there are the three estimates days, when specific estimates selected by the Liaison Committee are debated. But this does not provide effective control: first, the selected estimates represent a small proportion of the total; and, second, they are usually selected because they relate to a policy matter that merits debate, not a request for funds that needs to be analysed and challenged. And it is interesting to note that when in 1981 the Procedure Committee sought to address 'the myth of effective control' it recommended that there should be *eight* estimates days rather than the three that were conceded by the government of the day.

Select committees have traditionally been less interested in the spending that supports policies than in the policies themselves, although when the departmental select committee system was established in 1979 examination of expenditure was the first duty laid upon them, before examination of departments' administration and policies. The fact that the 'core tasks' now required by the House of all departmental select committees include examination of annual expenditure plans and outturns, as well as monitoring delivery against public service targets, may mean an increase in detailed examination. The increases in staff support for such committees has also been partly with the aim of better equipping them to carry out those core tasks.

However, even if committees major on the estimates, they have – especially for the often significant supplementary estimates – little time to carry out their work. Moreover, the opportunities for connecting the analysis and judgements of a select committee with the decisions taken in the House are very limited.

In 1998–99 the Procedure Committee, speaking as had its predecessor twenty years earlier of the House's power over expenditure as 'if not a constitutional myth, very close to one', asserted that:

*the House and the government would both gain from a system in which
the House could engage directly in identifying priorities and examining the
effectiveness of spending. The House would have an opportunity to influence
the Government's plans; the Government would have the opportunity to
explain those plans to Members and ensure that the House understood the
constraints in which they worked.*

The Procedure Committee put forward a package of reforms. It wanted to
circumvent the restriction imposed by the financial initiative of the Crown
through debates on motions that 'in the opinion of this House' increases in
expenditure or transfers between budgets should be made. It also wished to
see automatic referral of the estimates to the relevant departmental select
committee, with no vote taking place on the estimate concerned until the
committee had reported (within a limit of sixty days), and the ability of
select committees to put forward motions relating to estimates or departmental plans or reports, rather than the often artificial link between a select
committee report and an estimate.

No action has yet been taken on the Procedure Committee's proposals.
We return to the subject in Chapter 13.

9

Debates

THE *Oxford English Dictionary* defines the principal meaning of 'debate' as 'to dispute about, argue, discuss, especially to discuss a question of public interest in a legislative or other assembly'. Most proceedings in Parliament, whether on legislation or any other matter, take the form of debates. The main exceptions are questions and the examination of witnesses by select committees. In this chapter, we look at how debates take place on the floor of the House and elsewhere, how motions are moved and amended, and at some of the conventions of parliamentary debate.

Substantive motions

A substantive motion is one that expresses an opinion about something. The subject matter may range from 'That this House takes note of the Four-teenth to Thirty-Seventh Reports from the Committee of Public Accounts, Session 2005–06', for which there may be a dozen MPs in the Chamber (and probably no journalists in the Press Gallery) to 'That this House has no confidence in Her Majesty's Government', which will be a full-dress occasion, with intense media interest and the Chamber packed, perhaps to see the Prime Minister of the day fighting for his or her political life and the survival of the government.

A motion is *moved*, or proposed, by an MP who sponsors it. No sec-onder is required in the House of Commons; the seconding of the motion for the reply to the Queen's Speech is a tradition rather than a requirement.

If the motion requires notice, then the names of that member and any others who are putting the motion forward will appear on the Order of Business. The MP moving the motion argues for its approval by the House.

When he or she sits down, the Speaker will *propose the Question*, stating to the House what must be decided. Rather than read out a long text, he will normally say 'The Question is, as on the Order Paper'. A debate then takes place, with the Chair normally calling MPs alternately from one side of the House and then the other.

If an *amendment* is down to the motion and is *selected* by the Speaker (see page 51) then at some point in the debate the Chair will ask one of the MPs whose names are to the amendment on the Order of Business to move it. It is possible for the Speaker to select a *manuscript amendment* – that is, one that was not tabled before the rising of the House at the previous sitting and so does not appear on the Order of Business, but this is very unusual.

Once the amendment has been moved, the Speaker proposes the Question upon it, saying 'The original Question was [as on the Order Paper]. Since when an amendment has been moved [as on the Order Paper]. The Question is, that the amendment be made'. Strictly speaking, the debate then takes place on the amendment rather than on the motion that was first moved, but in most cases the scope of debate covers both.

When the time for the debate has elapsed, because the Question must be put at the moment of interruption (see page 158) or at any particular time, or because the closure (see page 51) has been moved and agreed to – or simply because there are no more MPs wishing to speak – the Speaker *puts the Question* on the amendment first ('The Question is, that the amendment be made') and the House decides that question, if necessary, by dividing (see page 171). Once the House has made its decision on the amendment, the original motion – whether or not amended – is decided, again by dividing if necessary. If an amendment was moved, the original motion is also known as *the main Question*.

If the motion is agreed to, it becomes a *resolution* or an *order* of the House. The distinction is that a resolution expresses an opinion (for example, 'that this House has no confidence in Her Majesty's Government'); an order is something on which the House can exercise power directly ('that a select committee be appointed to examine . . .').

The Iraq debate

As an example of the House dealing with a substantive motion – in this case a very high-profile one – let us take the debate on war with Iraq on 18 March 2003. A 390-word motion stood on the Order of Business in the names of the Prime Minister and other senior ministers. Carefully crafted to attract the maximum support from wavering government back-benchers, it began 'That this House notes its decisions of 25th November 2002 and 26th February 2003 to endorse UN Security Council Resolution 1441 . . .', and, after a rehearsal of the circumstances, it contained the crucial words 'and therefore supports the decision of Her Majesty's Government that the United Kingdom should use all means necessary to ensure the disarmament of Iraq's weapons of mass destruction . . .'.

Other amendments stood on the Order of Business, including one in the name of the former Labour Cabinet minister Chris Smith and a number of other government back-benchers, asserting that the case for military action had not been established. At 12.35 p.m., the Deputy Speaker, Sir Alan Haselhurst, announced the main business of the day and informed the House that the Speaker had selected Chris Smith's amendment. The Prime Minister then rose to move the government's motion. He spoke for forty-eight minutes and gave way twelve times to interventions, eight of those from his own back benches. At 1.23 p.m., the Leader of the Opposition then spoke, for twenty-one minutes, giving way four times.

At 1.44 p.m., Peter Kilfoyle, a former Labour defence minister and one of the signatories to Chris Smith's amendment, was called to move it. He had only eight minutes in which to do so; after the Leader of the Opposition's speech, the Speaker had announced that he had imposed an eight-minute limit on back-bench speeches in the debate. Then the leader of the Liberal Democrats (to whom the time limit did not apply) spoke for twenty-one minutes. In the debate fifty-one MPs spoke (a remarkable number because the debate was extended by three hours and because the eight-minute time limit had been imposed): twenty-six Labour, seventeen Conservative, five Liberal Democrats, and the leaders of the Scottish National, Ulster Unionist and Democratic Unionist parties. Back-bench MPs who spoke included William Hague, the former leader of the Conservative Party, John Denham, the Home Office minister who that morning had resigned from the government on the issue, and the chairmen of both the Defence and Foreign Affairs Select Committees. The Chair called MPs alternately from each side of the House, but on this question being much less able than usual to predict whether they would support the government's line or not. In the winding-up speeches at the end of the debate the shadow Foreign Secretary spoke for seventeen minutes and the Foreign Secretary for twenty-eight minutes.

At 10.00 p.m., the amendment was put to the vote and defeated by 396 votes to 217. The government motion was then approved by 412 votes to 149, and the House had agreed to a resolution that, among other things, authorised the use of military force. The votes had taken twenty-nine minutes;

and, as soon as the numbers in the second vote had been announced by the Speaker, the House moved on to the daily half-hour adjournment debate (see page 295), a very different parliamentary occasion for which only four MPs and the Deputy Speaker were present.

This was for many reasons an unusual debate, but it contained all the key elements of debate on a substantive motion. As we saw in Chapter 7, debate on legislation is structured in much the same way: a member moves 'that the such and such Bill be now read a second time'; it is possible to move a 'reasoned amendment'; and at the end of the debate the amendment and the main question are disposed of. Similarly, when an amendment to the text of a bill (or a new clause or schedule), is proposed in Committee of the whole House or standing committee, or in the House on report, the amendment is moved, and the question is proposed and debated. Amendments to amendments or to new clauses or schedules are treated in the same way as amendments to motions.

The moving of an amendment, whether in the House or in committee, is subject to the Chair having selected it. As we saw in Chapter 3, this is a power through which the Chair exercises great influence on the shape of proceedings. However, the power of selection does not exist in select committees (when, for example, they consider draft reports).

Disposing of a motion

Once a motion has been moved and the question proposed, it may be disposed of by being decided one way or the other, as outlined above. It may also lapse because the moment of interruption arrives and there is no provision for it to be debated beyond that hour. It will then have been 'talked out' (see page 158). A motion may also be *withdrawn* or *superseded*.

Withdrawal

Once a motion of any sort has been moved, and before it has been put to the House or a committee for decision, it is possible to seek to withdraw it. But because the motion has been moved, it is in the possession of the House or committee and may be withdrawn only 'by leave' – that is, by unanimous consent. The MP who moved it says 'I beg leave to withdraw the motion [or amendment]'; and the Chair says to all and sundry 'Is it your pleasure that the motion [amendment] be withdrawn? . . . Motion [amendment], by leave, withdrawn'. But even one objection is enough to prevent this happening, and in that case the motion or amendment must eventually be put to a decision.

Superseding

It is possible to supersede debate on a question before the House or committee by what is known as a *dilatory motion*. This may be a motion for the adjournment of the debate, or of the committee, or of the House. In consideration of legislation, it may also be a motion that further consideration of the bill be adjourned, or 'that the Chairman do report progress'. The moving of such a motion is subject to the permission of the Chair, who must be satisfied that it is not an abuse. If it proceeds, however, debate upon it supersedes the original debate, which is not resumed until the dilatory motion has been decided (or, indeed, which will not be resumed at that sitting if the dilatory motion is successful).

A rare and old-fashioned form of dilatory motion is *the previous Question*: a motion 'that the Question be not now put'. If it is agreed to, the House immediately moves on to the next business; but if it is not agreed to, whatever matter was interrupted must be decided immediately (as when a closure is agreed to).

Debate may also be interrupted by a motion 'that the House sit in private'. This might be in earnest if extraordinary circumstances arose during some national emergency; the House sat in secret several times during the First and Second World Wars. Modern use of the motion (formerly in the words 'that Strangers do now withdraw') has been to attempt to disrupt business or express strong objection to some proceeding. The Chair must put the motion immediately to the House for decision; but it may not be moved more than once during a sitting. It is rarely successful; the most recent occasion was in December 2001, during proceedings on the Anti-Terrorism, Crime and Security Bill (as an expression of objection rather than to allow some confidential matter to be discussed). The government was unprepared for such a motion to be moved, the motion was agreed to, and the House sat in private for nearly an hour. As the *Hansard* reporters withdraw when the House sits in private, there is no record of what was said during that time.

Quorum

A motion to sit in private may also be used to test whether a quorum is present, which in the House or Committee of the whole House can be demonstrated only when a vote takes place. If the result of the vote shows that fewer than forty MPs are present (thirty-five voting, two tellers on each side and the occupant of the Chair), then the business that was under discussion beforehand stands over until the next sitting of the House. If the business is not government business, this may well be fatal, and this tactic is used from time to time to attempt to kill private members' bills.

In standing committees and select committees no such procedure exists; the specified quorum must be present throughout or the chairman must suspend the committee. In select committees, the quorum is three or a quarter of the membership, whichever is the greater; in standing committees, it is one-third of the membership. In both cases fractions are rounded up. Somewhat illogically in standing committees, the chairman is not counted in calculating what the quorum is but does count towards whether a quorum is present. In Westminster Hall (see page 296) the quorum is three.

If the number of members present on the government side of a committee alone does not provide a quorum, the opposition sometimes uses the tactic of removing its own MPs from the room and thus stopping the business. The rule of the business standing over does not apply 'upstairs', however, and as soon as a quorum is again present (provided it is within twenty minutes), debate proceeds.

We now look at several different types of motion.

Motions on opposition days

Each session twenty days are set aside for debates initiated by the opposition parties. Seventeen of these are allocated to the official opposition and three to the Liberal Democrats as the second-largest opposition party, and one of these latter days is often shared between two of the smaller parties; Opposition day debates account for about 9 per cent of the total time of the House.

These days are ring-fenced opposition time; but, although their scheduling is normally agreed through the usual channels (see page 100), exactly when opposition days are taken is formally in the gift of the government. Each is the main business of a parliamentary day, so usually about six hours' debate – although ministerial statements can cut into this (often producing objections from the opposition). Days are often informally divided into two halves so that two subjects can be debated.

These days are a key opportunity for the opposition parties, and especially for the official Opposition, to try to expose the government over an issue on which it may be vulnerable, or to provide a shop window for one of its own policies. Among the subjects selected by the Conservatives in 2005 were the EU Constitution, special needs education, the risks of postal voting, council tax, the licensing laws, and preparedness for an outbreak of bird flu. Among subjects selected by the Liberal Democrats were access to NHS dentistry and primary care, and tackling climate change.

The motion moved in the House is usually a strongly worded criticism of government policies; the government tables an amendment that normally seeks to remove all the words of the motion after 'That this House' and substitute a warm endorsement of what the government is doing. The front-bench speakers will be the relevant shadow secretary of state and shadow minister, and their counterparts in government. The debate is often combative. Some can be testing for ministers as well as a proving ground for opposition front-benchers; and opposition days can give newer MPs an opportunity to shine and perhaps catch the selectors' eye as possible ministerial material.

At the end of an opposition day debate, the Question is put in an old-fashioned form that survives only in this case. Normally, the government amendment would be decided first and would no doubt be approved. The next Question would be the main Question, as amended; so both votes would take place on the government's words, not those of the opposition. The device that is used to avoid this is that the first Question put is 'That the original words stand part of the Question' – in other words, a vote on keeping the opposition motion as it is. When this proposition has been defeated, the second Question put is 'That the proposed words be there added' – a vote to approve the government's amendment. When this is agreed to, the Chair declares the main Question, as amended, to be agreed to, without a further vote (which would be pointless, as it would be a second vote on the government's text).

This may seem a rather complex minuet, but it is important to opposition parties to be able to put their own proposition to the House rather than to be forced simply to vote upon the government's counter-proposition.

Government substantive motions

Most of the occasions on which the government needs to seek the approval of the House of Commons are on legislation or spending. Exceptionally, as in the debates on Iraq, it may wish to have the backing of an explicit resolution of the House of Commons. On most substantive motions in a session, the government is in the position of defending or explaining in the face of opposition challenge. However, there are some occasions when the government puts a substantive motion before the House for debate. These are often when procedural changes are being proposed; when the Standards and Privileges Committee reports on the conduct of an MP; the annual 'take note' debate on the reports of the Public Accounts Committee; domestic business such as approving arrangements for the summer opening for visitors; or money and ways and means motions that are taken other than immediately after second reading. The four or five days of debates on the Queen's Speech and on the Budget – although each is very much a special case – may also be counted as government substantive motions.

Back-benchers' motions

Until 1995, four half-days and ten Fridays were set aside for motions moved by back-benchers chosen by ballot. As part of the Jopling reforms (see page 147), these were abolished and replaced by extra opportunities for back-benchers to raise subjects on the adjournment on Wednesday mornings (later moved, with increased time, to Westminster Hall). Private members' motion days gave individual MPs an opportunity to put a proposition to the House – which could be as controversial as they wished. Their passing is still regretted by many MPs, and it is extraordinary that the House of Commons (unlike the House of Lords and most parliaments throughout the world) now has no way for an ordinary MP to put a proposition to the House and have it voted on. The only similar (but very much more limited) opportunity that now exists is the chance under the ten-minute rule (see page 229) to put a proposal for legislation to the House for decision.

Adjournment motions

It may seem rather strange that the House of Commons apparently spends so much time deciding whether to adjourn or not (15 per cent of the total time in the 2003–04 and 2004–05 sessions). In fact, adjournment motions are not really about whether to end the sitting (which would be brought to an end anyway under the standing orders); they are vehicles for debate.

Government adjournment motions

From the government's point of view, these have the advantage of avoiding substantive decisions; there is no need to put any form of words before the House other than 'That this House do now adjourn' and indicating the subject for debate. On matters where the government may feel vulnerable to back-bench dissent, this allows debate but avoids a motion whose terms might encourage disagreement. It also prevents hostile amendments being tabled, either by the opposition parties or by its own back-benchers, because a motion for the adjournment is not amendable. An example in December 2005 was on the controversial proposal to restructure police forces in England and Wales, where the Opposition wanted to register their protest by voting on a substantive motion, but the government was prepared to give time only for a debate on the adjournment.

On contentious subjects, the minister replying to the debate will normally try to speak right up to the moment of interruption (see page 158), so that the motion lapses, having been 'talked out'. However, the opposition – or any individual back-bencher – can force a vote by moving the closure, usually in the last few seconds before the motion would lapse. This does provide an opportunity for the expression of views, but as it is only on the question of adjourning – what the media normally call 'a technical motion' – even a significant vote against loses much of its sting.

Some debates on adjournment motions are great parliamentary occasions. One such in 1940 led directly to the replacement of Neville Chamberlain by Winston Churchill as Prime Minister. In recent years, the debates at emergency sittings of the House (for example, on the invasion of the Falkland Islands and on the 11 September 2001 terrorist attacks in the USA) have been on motions for the adjournment.

Less controversially, government adjournment motions are used to provide opportunities for general debates, often more to ventilate a subject and to allow the expression of individual MPs' opinions than to provide a set-to between government and opposition. Some examples in 2005 were debates on defence in the UK, EU affairs, and fisheries. Government adjournment debates are also used to test the view of the House before more formal proposals are brought forward (for example, in the early stages of Lords reform). About 10 per cent of the time of the House is taken up by government adjournment motions in an average session.

The daily half-hour adjournment motion

Every day, after other business has been disposed of, back-benchers have an opportunity to raise a subject in the half-hour adjournment debate. The government whip on duty formally moves 'That this House do now adjourn', and the back-bencher then has fifteen minutes or so to speak, followed by a minister replying for the remainder of the time. Brief interventions from other MPs are allowed with the permission of the initiator of the debate and the minister.

MPs apply to the Speaker for an adjournment slot (by the end of a Wednesday for the following week), and their applications are put into a ballot. The Speaker himself chooses the subject for the Thursday slot, often picking an MP who has an urgent constituency matter to raise or who has been consistently unlucky in the ballot.

Any subject can be raised, provided that it falls within the responsibilities of the government so that a minister can reply to the debate. MPs are not allowed to use the half-hour adjournment primarily to call for legislation, but in practice this rule is not especially restrictive. As an illustration of the topics raised, five successive sitting days in December 2005 produced debates on improvements to the A27, a local community partnership, the Kent rail franchise, Internet rogue dialling and traffic jams in Taunton.

The half-hour adjournment is a sought-after opportunity for back-benchers, providing about 150 to 160 mini-debates a year and occupying about 6 per cent of the total time of the House. Unlike the Westminster Hall debates (see below) the timing of the half-hour adjournment is not always predictable because it depends on the main business that precedes it; but many MPs see such debates in the Chamber as having a higher status.

The half-hour adjournment often shows the extraordinary flexibility of the House of Commons. Some great matter may have been decided at the end of the day's main business, eagerly reported by the media; but as MPs stream out of the Chamber after a dramatic vote, the House – albeit much depleted – may turn to a very specific local problem: perhaps the difficulties faced by a single constituent.

Recess debates

Before each recess, there is a debate on 'matters to be considered before the forthcoming adjournment'. This gives an opportunity for back-benchers to raise topics similar to the half-hour adjournment debates, although in this case they are replied to not individually by the departmental ministers responsible for the subject but in an omnibus reply given by the Leader or Deputy Leader of the House. This is nevertheless parliamentary time valued by back-benchers, as evidenced by the number of takers, which often means that a time limit on speeches is imposed.

Emergency adjournment debates

In Chapter 6 (page 155), we described how an MP can make a case for an emergency debate; if granted by the Speaker, a three-hour debate takes place on a motion for the adjournment. However, such debates are very rare; there have been only two in the last ten years. Debates during a recall of the House (see above and page 146) also have the character of emergency adjournment debates, although these happen on the initiative of the government.

Westminster Hall

Much of the business in Westminster Hall takes place on the adjournment, so this may be a convenient place to describe this important procedural innovation.

Following the House's approval of a recommendation from the Modern-isation Committee, from the beginning of session 1999–2000 a 'parallel chamber' was established, known as Westminster Hall but in fact in the Grand Committee Room, a large committee room off the northern end of Westminster Hall. The idea had its origin in the 'Main Committee', a parallel but subordinate chamber used by the Australian House of Repres-entatives in Canberra.

The Westminster parallel chamber was intended to allow debates, open to all MPs, on less contentious business for which it would be difficult to find time on the floor of the House. Such business was to be referred by agreement through the usual channels, and decisions in Westminster Hall would be taken only by unanimity. The more consensual approach of Westminster Hall was emphasised by a seating layout closer to the hemicycle found in many other parliaments, with two rows of seats on each side as in the Chamber but with two more rows in a semicircle at the end, facing the Chair.

The Modernisation Committee was keen to avoid two possible dis-advantages of a parallel chamber; that the additional time available should not simply provide an outlet for more government business – and especially not more legislation – and that the Chamber of the House itself should remain clearly pre-eminent.

Westminster Hall sittings take place from 9.30 a.m. to 2.00 p.m. on Tuesdays and on Wednesdays from 9.30 a.m. to 11.30 a.m., when they are suspended to allow MPs to attend the main Chamber, resuming at 2.30 p.m. until 5.00 p.m. On Thursdays the sitting time is 2.30 p.m. to 5.30 p.m. Sittings in Westminster Hall are suspended for any votes in the House but have 'injury time' to compensate.

On Tuesdays and Wednesdays, Westminster Hall is given over to back-bench adjournment debates, two of one and a half hours each – which are intended for broader subjects on which a number of MPs will want to speak – and three of half an hour each. Two ballots are held on the Wednesday of the previous week for each category of debate; MPs may enter for both but cannot be successful in both. To minimise the disruption to ministers' work, each government department is on call to respond to debates every other week rather than (as in the House) whenever a relevant debate comes up. The business for Thursdays may include debates on government adjourn-ment motions and *cross-cutting oral questions* (see page 320). Westminster Hall Thursdays also provide an important opportunity for debates on reports from select committees, giving the work of those committees a higher profile. In an average session more than sixty hours of debate is devoted to select committee reports. Forthcoming business in Westminster Hall is set out in Part B of *future business* (see page 169).

In a typical week in December 2005, broader ninety-minute subjects included the future of the Probation Service, the funding of children's hospices, and agriculture in Northern Ireland. Half-hour subjects included the safety of artificial sweeteners, school closures in Weaver Vale, Cheshire, and transport links with the Isle of Wight.

In Westminster Hall, the chair is taken by the Chairman of Ways and Means (who has overall responsibility for proceedings in the same way as the Speaker in the House), his two deputies (see page 55) and by members of the Chairmen's Panel. The proceedings are recorded in *Hansard* and published in hard copy and on the parliamentary website in the same way as proceedings in the Chamber. Westminster Hall sittings are also televised in their entirety.

Decisions in Westminster Hall may be taken only by unanimity; if a decision is challenged it is referred to the House. In addition, if six MPs object to further proceedings a debate stands adjourned. This has not yet happened, as no substantive business has been taken in Westminster Hall; all debates have been on the adjournment.

In each of the three sessions shown in Table 9.1, Westminster Hall has thus provided an additional 32, 32 and 28 per cent of the total time available in the House, largely to the benefit of back-bench debates on the adjournment. In an average year it is likely that there will be 320 such debates, about 130 of the longer ninety-minute slots and 190 of the half-hour debates.

Table 9.1 Recent sitting time in Westminster Hall compared with sitting time in the House, in hours and minutes

Session	2002–03	2003–04	2004–05 short session
On subjects selected by:			
The government	31.31	19.22	13.28
Back-benchers	317.07	307.25	111.28
The Liaison Committee (debates on select committee reports)	59.33	64.19	21.24
Cross-cutting questions	6.06	2.06	
Total	414.17	393.12	146.20
Time the House itself sat	1,287.15	1,215.19	531.16

Debates in the Grand Committees and the Standing Committee on Regional Affairs – and a European experiment

The Scottish, Welsh and Northern Ireland Grand Committees (not to be confused with the select committees on each of those parts of the UK) consist of all the MPs sitting for constituencies in each country. Additional MPs from elsewhere are added to the Welsh and Northern Ireland committees. In the years immediately before devolution, the roles of all three committees were widened, allowing them to hear statements from ministers (including ministers in the Lords), to hold sessions of oral questions, to consider bills and delegated legislation, and to hold adjournment debates. Post-devolution, the committees have met less frequently (although the suspension of devolved government in Northern Ireland has revived the role of the Northern Ireland Grand Committee). All three committees may, with the leave of the House, meet away from Westminster in their respective parts of the UK.

In the last four complete sessions, these committees have met on the numbers of days shown in Table 9.2.

The majority of sittings in the Scottish and Welsh committees have been for general debates on subjects such as the Scottish fishing industry, the Scottish economy, the government's legislative programme as it relates to Wales, the Welsh economy, and draft bills on public audit and on transport in Wales. The Northern Ireland Grand Committee has held similar types of debate (for example on public investment in Northern Ireland) but has considered more legislation.

The Regional Affairs Committee consists of thirteen MPs sitting for constituencies in England, although any MP with a seat in England may attend and speak. The committee considers matters referred to it by the House and with the leave of the House may sit away from Westminster. A sitting of the committee may begin with a ministerial statement, followed by questions, for one hour; then a debate for three hours. The committee

Table 9.2 Meetings of grand committees, 2001–05

Session	2001–02	2002–03	2003–04	2004–05 short session
Scottish	4	3	0	0
Welsh	4	4	4	1
Northern Ireland	3	5	6	3

meets once or twice a session, debating such matters as regional assemblies and government regional offices.

In the 2001 parliament, a new type of standing committee was set up to consider the drafting of an EU constitutional treaty, and the reports of the UK members of the Convention preparing the text. The committee, snappily entitled *The Standing Committee on the Inter-Governmental Conference on the Future of Europe*, consisted of the members of the Foreign Affairs and European Scrutiny Committees (see page 396) but any MP was able to attend and take part (but not vote). A unique feature was that members of the House of Lords were able to take part in this Commons proceeding, on the same basis as MPs. It has been suggested that this model might be used for the consideration of European matters in the future (see page 404).

Early day motions

Every sitting day fifteen to twenty motions are tabled 'for an early day' – that is, for debate on an unspecified day. Almost all these 'early day motions' (EDMs) are tabled by back-benchers (although 'prayers' – see page 256 – first make their appearance as EDMs), so the chances of their being debated are negligible. Very occasionally, as in the case of the 1989 EDM on war crimes, a really significant EDM will be given debating time by the government or may figure in an opposition day debate.

An EDM is simply an expression of a view that could be debated by the House (they all begin 'That this House . . .'). They may be tabled by any MP, must not be longer than 250 words and must conform to other rules of order (for example, no unparliamentary language, and no reference to matters *sub judice*). An EDM appears in the Vote bundle, printed on blue pages, the day after it is tabled, and is reprinted for the rest of that week and the following week if any other MPs add their names to it or if an amendment is tabled. It is reprinted on any Thursday thereafter if names have been added during the preceding week; but it falls at the end of the session.

EDMs are used for a wide variety of purposes; an MP may want to put on record the success of his local football team (perhaps attracting only the signatures of his constituency neighbours – and perhaps a hostile amendment from supporters of a rival team), or criticise somebody's opinion or action – almost like writing a letter to a national newspaper. EDMs are also used by MPs to defuse pressure from constituents and others by being seen to be doing something about an issue, or to put material on the parliamentary record under the protection of parliamentary privilege. EDMs are also used to test and gather support on major issues (recently, on the restructuring of police forces, the availability of treatment for strokes, and the abolition of post office card accounts), and they are a useful source of political intelligence for the whips.

A random selection of EDMs tabled in December 2005 wanted to see the St George's Cross flag flown at Westminster on St George's Day; welcomed the new Commission for Equality and Human Rights; congratulated the Commonwealth Parliamentary Association for holding a seminar on Africa; urged support for small shops at Christmas; criticised the subsidy to English National Opera; and regretted the withdrawal of Routemaster buses in London.

Getting on for 2,000 EDMs are tabled each session and may attract a total of six or seven hundred signatures from MPs on a single sitting day. The number of EDMs, and the fact that many are on relatively trivial matters, have led to criticism of them as 'parliamentary graffiti', especially as printing them costs more than £600,000 a year. On the other hand, it can be argued that they act as a safety valve, and that MPs (and people outside the House) value them as a means of expressing and testing views – although their increasing numbers are devaluing the currency. Apart from the 'prayers' referred to above, none will ever get debated, although it is sometimes suggested that time should be found for those with substantial numbers of signatures (see page 423).

The rules and conventions of debate

An MP is called to speak by the Speaker (or by the chairman in a committee). MPs who want to take part in debates in the House (but not when a bill is in Committee of the whole House or at report stage), write to the Speaker beforehand. This is not to say that those who do not write cannot be called, but those who do write have preference.

When there is great pressure to speak in a particular debate, the Speaker may impose a time limit on speeches, as in the Iraq debate described earlier. This does not apply to the two front benches (nor to one MP speaking on behalf of the Liberal Democrats). The minimum time limit is eight minutes. In order to preserve the exchanges of debate, MPs get 'injury time' for the first two interventions they take from other members; the clock stops while the other Member is intervening, and then the MP speaking gets an extra minute so that he or she can reply to the intervention. This injury time can be profitable if the reply to the intervention is very short! When there is particular pressure on speaking time, the Speaker may further reduce speaking time to three minutes, without injury time; but this power has been little used.

Unlike the practice in the House of Lords and in many other parliaments, no list is made available of those who are to speak (although there is some pressure for the introduction of such a list). When the previous MP sits down, all those in the Chamber wanting to speak will bob up, hoping to 'catch the Speaker's eye'. The Speaker then says 'Mr Smith' and Mr Smith begins his speech. It is said that the practice of calling out a Member's name originated with the corrupt Speaker Trevor at the end of the seventeenth century (see page 124). Up to then, the Speaker merely looked meaningfully at the Member he wished to call; but Speaker Trevor had a truly grotesque squint, which is supposed to have led to widespread misunderstanding as to which Member he had intended to call. This may be apocryphal; but Trevor's portrait confirms the squint, at least.

MPs must address the House through the Chair, referring to other Members in the third person, and by their constituency or the office they hold rather than by name. So an MP cannot say to another 'what do you mean by that?' but must say 'what does the honourable member for Loamshire East mean by that'; and an MP cannot talk about 'David Cameron' or 'you in charge of the Tories' but must instead refer to 'the right honourable member for Witney' or 'the Leader of the Opposition'. All MPs are referred to as 'honourable members' or 'the honourable lady' or 'the honourable gentleman'; those who are Privy Counsellors (usually present or former senior ministers) are styled 'right honourable'. This may sound rather antique, but it avoids the direct confrontation of two MPs addressing each other as 'you' and often helps to lower the temperature.

The practice of referring to QCs as 'honourable and learned' and officers retired from the armed forces (or still in the reserves) as 'honourable and gallant' is no longer a convention of debate, but the terms are still used by traditionalists.

When they enter or leave the Chamber, MPs are expected to bow to the Chair as a gesture of respect to the House itself. They should not cross the line of sight between the Speaker and the member who has the floor; and – very important – should sit down as soon as the Speaker or a deputy rises. Dress conventions – jackets and ties for men – are generally upheld. Eating, drinking, the use of mobile phones and smoking are forbidden: the House of Commons has been a no-smoking area since the resolution of 1696 'That no Member do presume to take tobacco in the gallery of the House or at a committee table'.

MPs must speak from the place where they are called, which must be within the formal limits of the Chamber (so not from the cross-benches below the Bar of the House or from the parts of the galleries reserved for members). MPs may refer to notes, but they should not read questions or speeches at length – although notes are used to a greater degree than was the case a few years ago. An MP should be present for the opening and winding-up speeches of the debate in which he or she takes part, and after speaking should stay in the Chamber for at least the next two speeches. The Speaker will not call an MP to ask a question following a ministerial statement (or an urgent question) unless he or she has been there for the whole of the opening statement.

The House of Commons has a long tradition of MPs seeking to intervene in each other's speeches, to ask a question or to make a point. This – different from the practice in many other parliaments – makes debate much more lively than would otherwise be the case and is easier in the relatively intimate style of the Chamber than it would be in a large hemicycle (see page 15). Interventions must be brief; and they may be made only if the MP who has the floor 'gives way', although the expectation is that the MP speaking will indeed give way. The Chair will stop an MP whose speech is irrelevant or tediously repetitive, although with a certain amount of ingenuity most things can be made relevant and unrepetitive.

In most debates MPs may speak only once, but this does not apply, for example, in a committee on a bill. The *sub judice* rule prevents any MP referring to a current or impending court case (more precisely, when someone has been charged in a criminal case or, in a civil action, when a case has been set down for trial). This is to avoid debate in the House – under the protection of privilege – possibly influencing the outcome of a case; but it also reflects the relationship between Parliament and the courts (see page 183). However, the rule may be relaxed at the Speaker's discretion, and it does not prevent the House considering legislation.

'Good temper and moderation'

The language of debate must be restrained. An MP may not accuse another of lying, or of deliberately misleading the House; the Chair will intervene immediately to require the withdrawal of the charge. And in December 2005 Dennis Skinner, the veteran Labour MP, was ordered to leave the Chamber for suggesting that the shadow Chancellor of the Exchequer had in the past used cocaine.

Erskine May no longer lists the words ruled to be 'unparliamentary', although the lists in earlier editions are entertaining. 'Villains' got a red card in 1875, as did 'Pecksniffian cant' in 1928. Rather surprisingly, so did 'rude remarks' in 1887. Animal words of all sorts ('jackasses', 'swine', 'rats' and even 'stool pigeons') have always been required to be withdrawn. However, the important thing (and the reason why *Erskine May* no longer lists examples) is the context in which language is used. After the general election in May 2005, in a letter to all MPs reminding them of the conventions and courtesies of the House, Speaker Martin echoed the words of several of his predecessors when he said 'Members should bear in mind Erskine May's dictum that good temper and moderation are the characteristics of parliamentary language. It is important that exercise of the privilege of free speech is tempered with responsibility'.

MPs are expected to inform their colleagues when they intend to refer to them in the Chamber; when they table parliamentary questions that specifically affect the constituency of another MP; and when they intend to visit another constituency (except in a purely private capacity).

All these conventions and constraints may sound a little like school rules, and some occasionally come in for criticism from new MPs and others. But where political views clash and passions can run high a little formality can make the House more dignified and tolerant. It is a pity that many people judge the House of Commons from what they see on television of the gladiatorial Prime Minister's Questions; the House is actually a much more courteous place than many might think, while still allowing challenge and lively disagreement. At a time when Parliament is seeking to reconnect with the people, this is no bad thing.

The purpose of debate

As the previous pages show, the House of Commons itself, Westminster Hall and a variety of committees provide a great many different occasions and circumstances where debate takes place. What is the purpose of the millions of words spoken as a result?

Much of debate is, in one way or another, about deploying political argument: seeking to make the case for a particular philosophy or interpretation and applying it to the issue of the moment. Although many in the country at large see a clash of ideologies as rather sterile and negative, it is part of political reality.

But debate is also about challenge, testing and explanation. Parliament is a place where the government should be forced to justify its policies and actions. That process is part of checking an executive that will always tend to be over-mighty. It is also a process that crosses political divides, and it involves both the shadow minister who aspires to be in government and the government back-bencher who is uneasy about a course that the government is taking. In these circumstances, debate provides the opportunity to point out the weakness in a case, to offer alternative solutions and to ask 'why?'

Debate is also about exposure. One purpose of this is to force – or provide an opportunity for – the government to set out its view and its policy. This may be on some major issue – the reconstruction of Iraq, the achievement of peace in the Middle East or whether the UK should adopt the euro. It may be on something with a lower profile but of great importance to those affected; for example a school closure, an accident black spot or a local industry. This will produce a statement of government policy, or a response to criticism, but it will also act as a mind concentrator, not only for the minister but also for the civil servants in his or her department, who should be asking 'Is this a reasonable line to take? How vulnerable are we on this? Should we do more?'

The uses of debate

Exposure through debate is a way of attacking and defending – but above all testing – policies and ideas. It is also a way of putting subjects on the political (and media) agenda. It may be some abuse – perhaps a holiday timeshare scam – or perhaps an ethical or moral issue, such as stem cell research, battery hens or cluster bombs. It may also be a way of swinging the spotlight on to some injustice – sometimes affecting only one person or one family – perhaps children kidnapped by an estranged father, a disability pension denied or the perverse application of some planning law.

Debate is also about representation: industries, regions, constituencies, pressure groups and individuals have a parliamentary voice through MPs taking up causes, setting out the case and gathering support.

Does debate change minds? On the spot, rarely. On most matters that come to the House of Commons, the parties will already have their view; individual MPs will have their opinions. On a non-partisan issue, a compelling speech may be influential; on a highly charged issue, the trend of debate may change minds (a significant number of MPs said that they finally made up their minds which way to vote on war with Iraq only during the debate in March 2003). In the case of most debates, effective advocacy will indeed change minds, but more slowly. It may modify the government's view, influence public opinion and put new subjects on the agenda. How effectively it does this is very much down to MPs themselves.

Debates in the House of Lords

Unstarred questions

About a quarter of the House of Lords' time is taken up with debates. Some of these, as we have seen already, arise on 'unstarred questions' and take the form of short debates time-limited to an hour and a half at the end of the day's business, rather like adjournment debates in the Commons. A minister answers the question at the end of the debate, and there is no right of reply. These debatable questions can also be held during dinner adjournments in the course of legislative business, when they are limited to one hour. Unstarred questions are hugely popular and occupy about 5 per cent of the House's sitting time. The availability of time for these debates varies widely from session to session.

Debatable motions

Most debates take place, as in the Commons, on a motion moved by the initiator. The form of the motion used will vary according to the purpose of the debate. Most debates in the Lords will take place on a neutral motion 'for papers', a procedural device that allows the mover to raise a subject with a right of reply for himself or herself. The motion is invariably withdrawn at the end of the debate. Debates initiated for the purpose of considering reports of committees, or documents, and debates initiated by the government itself will normally be on motions 'to take note', or if an opinion on the content is to be expressed, 'to approve'. Finally, when it is desired that the House express a view on the subject matter under debate, a motion 'for resolution' is moved – usually resulting in a vote at the end. Let us look now at the context in which these different debating tools are used.

Debates on reports of select committees

Select committees on public policy (see page 378) – such as the Economic Affairs Committee, Science and Technology Committee or European Union Committee – make their reports to the House in the expectation that at some stage they will be debated. In recent sessions, 2 to 3 per cent of sitting time was spent debating these reports, almost invariably on a motion to take note. Sometimes motions to take note of reports on similar subjects are debated together. The debates on the Economic Affairs Committee's reports on the Finance Bill are usually debated as part of the second reading of the bill.

Chairmen and members of select committees are often critical that insufficient time is offered by the government Whips Office for debates on select committee reports or that time, when it is offered, tends to be at short notice or subject to last-minute change. On the other hand, there are those who point out that such debates rarely attract interest from the wider House and, save for a few members with knowledge of the subject matter, most of the participants tend to be members of the committee that made the report. In some ways this does not matter. The dialogue with the government over a committee's recommendations takes place not only on the floor of the House but also in the direct exchanges between the committees and ministers.

Opposition and back-bench debates

Most debates on motions moved by opposition parties and back-benchers take place on Thursdays (formerly Wednesdays), when motions have precedence over bills and other business. Most of these Thursdays are given over to the political parties to initiate debates, usually on the neutral motion 'for papers' or occasionally a 'take note' motion. The days for these debates are allocated to the various parties by agreement between party whips, with by far the most going to the official Opposition. They are not time-limited. However, the mover of the motion can ask the Leader of the House to move a Business of the House motion limiting the time. This is often done by the political parties to create the opportunity for two debates to be held. The limit on a single debate is usually five hours: the limits where two debates are held can vary but must not exceed a total of six hours.

In the earlier part of the session, up until the spring recess, one Thursday a month is set aside for two balloted debates limited to two and a half hours each and initiated by back-benchers or cross-benchers. The subjects are chosen by a ballot conducted some weeks beforehand by the Clerk of the Parliaments in the presence of chief whips and the Convenor of the Cross Benches.

In the 2003–04 session Thursday opposition and back-bench motions included such themes as foreign affairs (Iraq, Zimbabwe, the European

Constitution, Development Aid, Afghanistan), public policy (Science and Politics, Maritime Policy, Defence, Climate Change, Pensions, Local Government, Energy Supply), and moral and ethical issues (Marriage, Alcohol Abuse, Religious Offences, Dementia).

Government motions

Sometimes the government will itself wish to initiate a debate on a matter of public concern or potential concern to the House. Thus debates on reform of the House in recent sessions have usually been held on government motions to take note. Debates on pressing issues of foreign policy fall into the same category. On 18 March 2003 the Lords, like the Commons, debated the situation in Iraq, but on a take note motion, in the full knowledge that war was probably imminent. Unlike the Commons, however, no vote followed the end of the debate.

But there have been occasions in recent sessions where the government has sought to test the opinion of the two Houses of Parliament on issues of policy, placing a series of options before each House. Thus in March 2002 the government itself tabled motions for resolution on a series of options relating to hunting with dogs; in February 2003, although the debate had already taken place, a series of votes were held on seven motions to approve one or other of the options relating to the reform of the composition of the House that had been proposed by the Joint Committee on Reform of the House; and on 12 July 2005 the House resolved, after a short debate, that it should elect its own presiding officer (an issue that had been debated at greater length in early 2004).

Conventions of debate

Certain conventions apply to all debate in the House, whether on legislative business or on the general motions that are the subject of this chapter. We have noted in Chapter 2 that the Chair does not call members to speak in the Lords. Peers usually give advance notice to the government Whips Office of their intention to speak in debates, and lists of speakers are prepared by the Leader of the House (in fact by the Private Secretary in the Whips Office) in consultation with the usual channels and published before the debate begins. Any lord not on the list may speak, but only after those already on the list and before the winding-up speeches, and then only briefly. So there is no problem in the Lords of 'catching the Speaker's eye'. And of course the House keeps its own order.

As in the Commons, there are conventions governing the way in which other members are addressed. Thus remarks are addressed to the House as a whole. Other participants are addressed in the third person, never as 'you'. And the style of address is always 'The Noble Lord, Lord . . .' or 'The Right Reverend Prelate, the Bishop of . . .'.

Generally speaking, a lord can speak only once in debate, except when the House is in committee on a bill, and must not read (although many do). Unless speaking from the front bench, where lords speak from a despatch box, members speak in their places. Speeches must be relevant and, indeed, in 1965 the House even resolved that they should be shorter. Today a rather generous fifteen-minute rule applies in debates that are not time-limited, with a twenty-minute limit for members opening or winding up. Members must avoid 'asperity of speech'. And relevant interests must be declared (see page 134).

In addition to these rules of debate various rules of conduct apply – such as speaking 'uncovered' (without a hat!) or the custom of making obeisance to the Cloth of Estate behind the throne on entering the Chamber. Such customs help to lend the House a veneer of good, even courtly, manners that are sometimes sorely tested in the debates themselves.

Value of debate: the chamber of experts

It is no easier to set a value on Lords debates than it is for the Commons. We take it for granted that debate is free and open. It is of course protected by parliamentary privilege. That in itself is something to be cherished. But what purpose is served? Minds are certainly not swayed, especially where arguments follow party lines. Given that most speeches are pre-prepared, that is hardly surprising.

The value of debates is that they offer different opportunities and attractions to different participants. For a back-bencher initiating a debate, they offer the chance to air a policy matter of personal interest with the guarantee of a government response that is likely to represent the latest government thinking on the issue. For opposition parties, they offer the chance to set out their wares: to expose some aspect of government policy of which they do not approve, perhaps to say how things might be done better or differently, and to try to put the government on the spot. And for government itself they offer the opportunity to set out some new policy development or change in world events, and to test opinion across the parties.

Are the debates of good quality? Many are. And in most debates a few speakers can be deemed to have expertise that is relevant to the subject matter. This expertise stems in part from the fact that the House of Lords has never been a chamber of salaried members. Many, whether life peers or hereditary, have or have had full-time careers elsewhere. And life peerages have been bestowed on a wide range of men and women distinguished in their field – some irrespective of party, others because they have espoused a party cause. Thus among the sixty-seven speakers in the debate on Iraq and weapons of mass destruction on 24 September 2002 there were three former Chiefs of the Defence Staff, three former Foreign Secretaries, two former Home Secretaries, six bishops, two former ambassadors and two former Secretaries of State for Defence. The twenty-two speakers in a government debate to take note of developments concerning the draft European Union Constitutional Treaty in May 2004 included four former Cabinet Ministers, one of whom had also served as an EU Commissioner, the two Lords members of the 'Convention' on the draft Treaty, a former Secretary-General to the EU Commission, a former MEP, the Chairman of the EU Committee, two eminent retired diplomats and a professor of international relations.

Some commentators now view the House of Lords as a chamber of experts. This is perhaps to exaggerate the expert element in the House. Most of the peerages bestowed in the last fifty years or so have gone to politicians, active at either the national or local level. And many of the 'experts' have retired or are about to retire when they become members of the House. Their expertise might be thought a little dated. But the fact remains that the House of Lords as currently composed is a knowledgeable place in a way that distinguishes it from most other parliamentary assemblies in the world.

Calling to account: questions

IN THIS CHAPTER we will look at one of the best-known inquisitorial functions of Parliament: parliamentary questions, often known as PQs. This will also be a convenient place to look at public petitions and MPs' letters, which are other ways in which the actions of government can be influenced or exposed.

Questions in the Commons

By comparison with the processes of debate, legislation and examination by select committees, questions evolved relatively late in parliamentary history. Although the first recorded question to a minister was in the House of Lords in 1721, questions in the Commons did not develop until the nineteenth century, when all questions were asked orally; questions for written answer (now a major part of parliamentary activity) were not introduced until 1902.

What are questions?

Erskine May states that the purpose of a question is 'to obtain information or to press for action'. The people who have the information – and the ability to act upon it – are government ministers, and it is they who have to answer questions. Some questions are asked (or, in parliamentary language, 'tabled' or 'put down') of MPs who are not ministers but who speak on behalf of bodies such as the House of Commons Commission (see page 60) or the Church Commissioners. However, well over 99 per cent of all PQs are asked of ministers by back-benchers, and this process is part of the way in which government can be held to account.

Questions are one of the best-known, but often misunderstood, features of the House of Commons, and it is on that House that we will concentrate. Questions are also asked in the House of Lords, but in much smaller numbers and less restricted by rules than in the Commons.

The rules for questions

First and foremost, questions must be about something for which a minister is responsible. In many cases this is clear-cut: the Secretary of State for Defence is responsible for ordering a new aircraft carrier, and the Secretary of State for International Development is responsible for how the UK's aid budget is spent. But, although the government has an overall responsibility for local government finance, it is not responsible for the detail of how local authorities spend their money. Nor, for example, is it responsible for what the courts do, for the operational details of policing or the actions of EU institutions (although it is responsible for its own policy towards them).

Ministers are responsible to Parliament for their own policies and actions, not for those of the opposition parties; so a government back-bencher could not table a question that asked 'What would be the effect on public services of the spending plans announced by the Conservative Party?' even if the minister was eager to answer. But if the MP were to ask the Chancellor of the Exchequer an oral question such as 'What factors he takes into account in allocating resources to public services' then that is a matter for which he is responsible, and the reply may well take a side-swipe at the policy of the Conservative Party.

There are a variety of other rules. Matters that are *sub judice* (see page 303) cannot be raised. Questions must not offer information ('Is she aware that . . . ?') or be argumentative ('Does he agree that it is unacceptable that . . . ?'). They must have some reasonable basis in fact, rather than being purely speculative – they cannot, for example, ask whether a press report is correct. The government is treated as a single entity, so it is not in order to ask one minister to intervene with or influence another (although the same result may be achieved by asking the Prime Minister a question about improving coordination between two government departments).

A question that has already been answered in the current session may not be asked again unless there is reason to think that the situation may have changed (although in practice this is often interpreted as allowing a question to be repeated after three months). This is a common-sense rule that prevents cluttering up both the question book (see page 169) and *Hansard* with identical exchanges. The tabling of numerous but very similar questions is not allowed for the same reason. A related rule prevents an MP asking for information that is readily available – for example, in official publications or on government websites.

Since devolution to Scotland, Wales and Northern Ireland, ministers at Westminster may not be asked about things for which responsibility has passed to the devolved administrations. However, they may be asked about matters on which they have the power to require information from the administrations, or about concordats or liaison arrangements. This also applies to the government of London, which is the responsibility of the Mayor and the Greater London Authority – frustrating for MPs who want to ask questions about public transport in London.

The rules about questions have developed over the years; for the most part, they either reflect other rules of the House (such as the *sub judice* rule) or try to ensure that questions keep to their principal purposes of obtaining information or pressing for action. MPs can find the rules frustrating; but it is remarkable how often a slightly different question – or the same question in a different form – avoids running foul of the rules and may even get closer to what the MP really wants to ask.

The answers

There is a rather hackneyed story of a minister and a senior civil servant being driven to some remote government establishment. The fog closed in, the car went slower and slower, and finally the driver, dimly seeing a passer-by, rolled down the window and said 'Where are we?' Back came the answer: 'You're in a car, in the fog'. 'Do you realise, Minister', said the civil servant, 'that's a perfect answer to a parliamentary question. It's short, it's absolutely true, and it tells you nothing you didn't know already'.

In Chapter 5 we quoted the 1997 resolution of the House of Commons on ministerial accountability, which states the duty of ministers to account for policies, decisions and actions. So far as questions are concerned, the key passages are those that require ministers 'to give accurate and truthful information to Parliament and to be as open as possible with Parliament, refusing to provide information only when disclosure would not be in the public interest'. Answers to PQs provide a huge amount of information on the whole range of government responsibilities, but attention inevitably focuses on occasions when answers are not given. Although few would expect ministers to answer on the operations of the intelligence services, or where a major criminal investigation of VAT fraud was under way, some refusals to answer PQs are more contentious.

In the 2003–04 session, for example, ministers refused to answer on the outcomes of leak inquiries 'so as to safeguard security and investigative arrangements'; to publish a Cabinet Office audit of public services because it was held to be 'advice to ministers' and so confidential; to reveal the amount spent by the Ministry of Defence on water and sewerage because it 'could prejudice the competitive position of the Department'; to say when the outspoken British Ambassador to Uzbekistan would return to that country because it would be 'inappropriate to comment'.

And although the awarding of contracts for the reconstruction of Iraq was of great political interest, ministers blocked PQs on the subject on the grounds of commercial confidentiality – the reason also given for not publishing the investment case for closing small prisons and building larger ones, the operational availability of windfarms, and the number of containers carried each year by freight trains.

From a government perspective, it is easy to understand a reluctance to answer particular types of question – not least because answering one question may produce a flood of questions on a sensitive topic. Nevertheless, MPs find a minister's refusal to answer extremely frustrating when it prevents them pursuing a subject that they see as of political or constituency importance, where an answer is in the public interest. If a minister refuses to provide information on a particular subject for a stated reason it usually also prevents the same question being asked for the remainder of the session, which adds to the frustration.

The Freedom of Information Act

Ministers' judgement of what was 'not in the public interest' used to be based on the *Code of Practice on Access to Government Information*, which was introduced in 1994. This listed fifteen categories of exempt information, for example where disclosure would harm international relations, or the proper and efficient conduct of the business of a government department.

The Code was in effect replaced when on 1 January 2005 the *Freedom of Information Act 2000* came into force. The Act applies to all public authorities, including government departments and agencies. It gives a general right of access to information, but lists exemptions that echo some of those in the Code; for example: security matters, prejudice to international relations or the UK's economic interests, law enforcement, prejudice to the effective conduct of public affairs, and so on.

However, the Freedom of Information (FoI) Act does not apply to PQs (nor to inquiries by select committees). This may seem strange, but it is logical: PQs and select committee inquiries are 'proceedings in Parliament' and so are covered by parliamentary privilege (see page 181). FoI requests, on the other hand, are requests under a statute. And if a public authority does not provide the information requested, its decision can be challenged by an appeal to the Information Commissioner and then to the Information Tribunal. If a refusal to answer a PQ were pursued by this route, then an outside tribunal would be judging whether Parliament had the right to a particular piece of information. It is easy to imagine the constitutional outcry if the Commissioner or the Tribunal were to conclude that Parliament did *not* have a right to know.

This means that ministerial refusals have to be pursued by parliamentary means. Of course, it is perfectly possible for an MP (or his or her researcher, spouse or next-door neighbour, for that matter) to put in an identical request under the FoI Act, and pursue it through the Commissioner and Tribunal if necessary.

Even though it does not apply directly to PQs, the FoI Act has concentrated the government's mind. Ministers and civil servants are well aware of the political risks of refusing information in answer to a PQ, only to give it out to a member of the public under FoI. A key player in ensuring that the government responds properly to Parliament in these new circumstances will be the *Public Administration Committee*, a Commons Select Committee, often known as PASC.

The Public Administration Committee

PASC reports each year on ministerial accountability through PQs, following up ministers' refusals to answer; its 2004–05 report contained a forty-page list of such cases. PASC has pressed for the relevant part of the Code to be quoted in each case of refusal, and it is likely that it will seek to have the FoI equivalent quoted now that the Code has been replaced.

We should keep the scale of refusals in proportion: in the 2003–04 session 49,814 written PQs were asked, and an answer was refused to 819 of them, or 1.64 per cent. But of course many of those refusals were on subjects high on the political agenda.

And the content of answers remains a matter for ministers; successive Speakers have refused to comment on the ways in which ministers answer – or avoid answering – and many back-benchers feel that it is unfair that ministers can decide without any independent check to refuse to answer particular questions that everyone accepts come within their responsibilities. There are also occasions when an answer is given that is rather less than helpful, as when a question seeks the timing of some publication or event, and the answer is 'shortly' or 'in due course'; or when a reply simply refers the questioner to a previous answer to a slightly different question.

It is important to set such concerns against the reality that, if questions really are a means of holding the government to account, one cannot expect the answers always to be a friendly volunteering of information. And, of course, questions – and especially oral questions – are an important dimension of the party clash between opposition and government.

Cost

Ministers may refuse to provide an answer to a PQ if the cost of doing so would exceed a certain amount, known as the 'advisory cost limit', at present £600 (which is also the cost limit under the FoI Act). A minister's 'disproportionate cost' answer can be a source of annoyance to MPs: not only may they think that the expenditure of, say, £800, is not excessive if it puts important information in the public domain; they may also suspect that estimating the cost of answering is a fairly rough and ready business, and that if ministers wanted to answer the question, they would do so (and indeed a minister may decide that a question is to be answered irrespective of cost). However, the government's internal guidance emphasises that even if to give a full answer would cost more than the limit, any readily available information should be given.

In March 2005, the Treasury estimated the average cost of answering a written question at £134 and of answering an oral question at £369. These figures are averages, not the price tag of each question; it does not cost very much to reply 'No' to a question asking for a particular document to be published, for example. The higher cost of answering oral questions is because of the additional research and briefing needed for possible supplementaries (see below), so the extra cost is more that of defending the minister's position than of actually answering the question.

Oral questions

Civil Service guidance for answering oral PQs describes Question Time as:

> *usually the highest profile Parliamentary occasion of the month as Members can question Ministers on any topic for which they are responsible, to seek*

facts and to challenge and question Government policy. Supplementary
Questions in particular are used by opposition Members to raise matters with
the aim of putting Ministers on the defensive.

Many questions for oral answer receive a written reply, either because time
runs out before they are reached or because the MP concerned cannot in the
event be in the House that day and asks for a written rather than an oral reply.

But even though oral questions account for a relatively small part of the
total, Question Time, when they are answered, is one of the liveliest parts
of the parliamentary day, and Prime Minister's Questions (PMQs) each
Wednesday is normally the highlight of the week.

Question Time

Question Time takes place every day except Friday and begins immediately
after prayers are over and any private business (see page 153) has been
disposed of. This means that on Mondays and Tuesdays it runs from about
2.35 p.m. to 3.30 p.m., on Wednesdays from about 11.35 a.m. to 12.30 p.m.
and on Thursdays from about 10.35 a.m. to 11.30 a.m.

The ministers from each government department answer questions
every four weeks according to a rota that the government itself decides.
Thus, when in May 1997 Tony Blair decided that he would answer questions for half an hour on Wednesdays rather than for a quarter of an hour
on Tuesdays and Thursdays as his predecessors had done, it required no
decision of the House to make the change. Similarly, when the Department
of Constitutional Affairs was created in June 2003, the government simply
revised the rota to provide a slot for the new department.

The change in the arrangements for PMQs was strongly criticised by the
opposition, and indeed in June 2002 the Procedure Committee recommended that any future change should be open to debate and subject to the
formal decision of the House, which will thus be seen to have 'ownership
of its procedures'.

The rota for a typical fortnight appears on pages 318 and 319.

The day on which a department is top for questions can be a testing
time for ministers answering at the despatch box, but it can also be a shop
window for the department concerned, in which ministers have the opportunity of emphasising their successes and putting their interpretation of
events on the record. The balance between the two depends on how quick
ministers are on their feet, how well they prepare and how sharp opposition
MPs are with their supplementaries.

Note: The shuffles of oral questions for answer on Monday 9th, Tuesday 10th and Wednesday 11th January 2006 will take place on Tuesday 20th December 2005 at 12.30 p.m.

Mon. 9 Jan	Tues. 10 Jan	Wed. 11 Jan	Thurs. 12 Jan
Work and Pensions	**Foreign and Commonwealth Office**	**Northern Ireland Prime Minister[1]**	**Education and Skills Solicitor General[2]**
Last tabling at 12.30 for			
Education and Skills Solicitor General	*Home Office Wales*	*Transport Chancellor of the Duchy of Lancaster*	*Prime Minister*

Mon. 16 Jan	Tues. 17 Jan	Wed. 18 Jan	Thurs. 19 Jan
Home Office	**Transport Chancellor of the Duchy of Lancaster[3]**	**Wales Prime Minister[1]**	**Trade and Industry Minister for Women and Equality[2]**
Last tabling at 12.30 for			
Scotland Trade and Industry Minister for Women and Equality	*Defence*	*Constitutional Affairs Leader of the House and House of Commons Commission*	*International Development Prime Minister*

[1] At 12 noon
[2] At 11.20 a.m.
[3] At 3.20 p.m.

Mon. 23 Jan	Tues. 24 Jan	Wed. 25 Jan	Thurs. 26 Jan
Defence	**Scotland Constitutional Affairs**[4] **Leader of the House and House of Commons Commission**[5]	**International Development Prime Minister**[6]	**Treasury**
Last tabling at 12.30 for			
Treasury	*Culture, Media and Sport, Church Commissioners, Public Accounts Commission and Speaker's Committee on the Electoral Commission*	*Health*	*Deputy Prime Minister Prime Minister*

Mon. 30 Jan	Tues. 31 Jan	Wed. 1 Feb	Thurs. 2 Feb
Culture, Media and Sport Church Commissioners, Public Accounts Commission and Speaker's Committee on the Electoral Commission[7]	**Health**	**Deputy Prime Minister Prime Minister**[6]	**Environment, Food and Rural Affairs**
Last tabling at 12.30 for			
Environment, Food and Rural Affairs	*Work and Pensions Northern Ireland*	*Foreign and Commonwealth Office*	*Prime Minister*

4 At 3.00 p.m.
5 At 3.20 p.m.
6 At 12 noon
7 At 3.15 p.m.

The House of Commons oral questions rota for a typical fortnight

Source: The House of Commons 2005

Tabling oral questions

For many years, oral PQs had to be tabled ten sitting days (which usually meant a calendar fortnight) before the day for answer. However, in June 2002 the Procedure Committee concluded that this was 'a major barrier to the effective operation of questions' in that it often prevented Question Time dealing with the issues of the day; a question tabled a fortnight earlier might well be stale by the time it was answered. The committee thought that the only defence of the fortnight's notice was that it allowed civil servants longer to brief their ministers, and recommended that the period of notice should be reduced from ten to three sitting days. This was endorsed by the Modernisation Committee, approved by the House, and came into force in January 2003.

An MP can now table a PQ for oral answer any time after the previous Question Time for a particular department up to 12.30 p.m. three sitting days before that department's next Question Time; so, if the department is top for questions on a Tuesday, questions have to be tabled by 12.30 p.m. the previous Wednesday. For questions to the Secretaries of State for Northern Ireland, Scotland and Wales the notice period is five days because of the extra complication of there being devolved administrations in those parts of the UK. An MP may table only one oral question to a department on any one day, and no more than two in total on that day (which, for example, allows an MP to have a question to the Prime Minister as well as to the Secretary of State answering the same day).

Questions are tabled to the responsible Secretary of State or senior Commons minister in a department if the Secretary of State is in the Lords, rather than to an individual minister within a department, although there are other slots such as those for the Leader of the House and the Minister for Women and Equality.

As well as Question Time in the House, oral questions may be asked at some sittings of the Scottish, Welsh and Northern Ireland Grand Committees (see page 299), although these are not frequent occurrences. An interesting innovation has been the introduction of occasional cross-cutting oral Question Times in Westminster Hall, in which questions are about a subject that involves a number of departments rather than about the responsibilities of a single department: for example, a cross-cutting session on domestic violence has involved ministers from the Home Office, the Department of Health, the Department for Education and Skills, the Department for Constitutional Affairs and the Office of the Deputy Prime Minister. Westminster Hall Question Times have also covered youth, drugs and older people.

Whatever the forum, MPs must table questions in writing, either personally with the Clerks in the Table Office (a small room behind the Speaker's Chair), or by post. Since January 2003 they have also been able to send questions in electronically, using a system of authentication. By December 2005, 284 MPs had registered for this method of tabling questions, although only 183 had used the system. Electronic tabling now accounts for about 33 per cent of questions.

An MP's question is examined by one of the Clerks, who checks that it does not breach any of the rules for questions (see page 312), and who will where possible suggest to the MP how to avoid breaching the rules, or perhaps how to put the question in a more effective form. As well as conforming to the rules that operate for all questions, an oral question must be a single question (rather than having two or more sub-questions); and, except in the case of questions to the Prime Minister (see below), they must be precise enough to give an indication of the intended supplementary – open questions are not allowed.

Just after 12.30 p.m. on the last tabling day, there is a random computer shuffle of the questions that have been tabled to the department or departments concerned. The successful questions are printed next morning in the blue pages of the Vote bundle (see page 168) in the order in which they will be called on the day. Not all questions tabled are printed; if a single department is to answer for the whole of Question Time (in practice fifty-five minutes) then twenty-five questions to that department will be printed. If the slot is for forty-five or fifty minutes, twenty will be printed, and so on down to a ten-minute slot, for which eight questions will be printed. The remainder are treated as 'lost', are not printed and do not receive answers (unless the MP concerned wants a written answer).

If a question is put down to one government department but is more properly the responsibility of another, it will be transferred and answered by a minister from the second department. This does not matter for written questions, but an MP who has an oral question that is transferred after the shuffle has taken place will lose the opportunity to ask the question orally. When this happens it often produces a row; but it is a matter within the discretion of the government, and the Speaker will not intervene, although he has deprecated moving questions where there is some shared responsibility.

Both government and opposition parties are keen to get their MPs to table questions, because it shortens the odds of their party being successful in the shuffle and so beginning a question exchange with a friendly (or, for the opposition, a critical) supplementary. An opposition front-bench team will also identify themes it wants to raise in a forthcoming Question Time and encourage its back-benchers to table questions on these subjects.

Question Time: on the day

The Speaker announces 'Questions to the Secretary of State for the Home Department' (or whichever department is answering), 'Mr Philip Dunne' (or whoever). Mr Dunne simply says 'Number One, Mr Speaker' (there is no point in reading out the question as it is printed on the Order of Business), and the minister gets up to give his reply. Mr Dunne is then called to ask a supplementary question, to which the minister replies. Two or three (or more) back-benchers (called alternately from each side of the Chamber) then ask supplementaries. If the subject is an important one, the opposition shadow minister may ask the final supplementary, and the Speaker calls the name of the next MP with a question down for answer. As we saw in Chapter 3 (page 50), the number of supplementaries called is entirely a matter for the Speaker; on a subject on which the government is vulnerable, calling more MPs to put supplementaries may put the minister under greater pressure; conversely, if fewer supplementaries are called, more questions on the Order of Business will be reached.

All the ministers in a department – in a large department, the secretary of state, two ministers of state and two junior ministers (parliamentary under-secretaries) – will be present for their slot at Question Time. Which questions they answer will depend on their particular responsibilities within the department, but the secretary of state will usually take the biggest political subjects.

The list of questions on the Order of Business may not be followed exactly. With the Speaker's permission, a minister may group similar questions for answer if they are reasonably close together on the list, and the MPs who tabled those questions are called first to ask supplementaries. If an MP is unable to be present, he or she may withdraw a question, or convert it from an oral to a written question (known as 'unstarring' because oral questions are denoted by a star against them on the Order of Business).

The art of the supplementary

If Question Time is seen as a duel, the tabling of the question and the minister's often low-key reply are rather like two fencers squaring up to each other before the swords clash. The real conflict of Question Time is in the supplementaries. Thus an opposition MP may table a question that simply

House of Commons

Wednesday 7th December 2005

Order of Business

At 11.30 a.m.   Prayers

Afterwards

Oral Questions to the Secretary of State for International Development

★1   **Christine Russell** (City of Chester):   What steps his Department is taking to promote economic growth in Africa.   (34883)

★2   **Ian Lucas** (Wrexham):   If he will make a statement on the Government's plans to mark international AIDS Day.   (34884)

★3   **Daniel Kawczynski** (Shrewsbury & Atcham):   What percentage of his budget for overseas development will be given to Commonwealth countries in 2005-06.   (34885)

★4   **Anne Main** (St Albans):   What recent assessment he has made of the effects of protectionist trade policies on poor countries; and if he will make a statement.   (34886)

★5   **Mr Edward Vaizey** (Wantage):   What assessment his Department has made of the implications for developing countries of President Bush's recent comments on reducing global tariffs; and if he will make a statement.   (34887)

At 12 noon

Oral Questions to the Prime Minister

Unless otherwise indicated the Members listed below will ask a Question without notice.

★Q1   **Mr Stephen O'Brien** (Eddisbury):   If he will list his official engagements for Wednesday 7th December.   (34898)

★Q2   **Mr Philip Hammond** (Runnymede & Weybridge):   (34899)

★Q3   **Andrew Selous** (South West Bedfordshire):   (34900)

★Q4   **Mr Michael Fallon** (Sevenoaks):   (34901)

★Q5   **Mr Jeremy Browne** (Taunton):   (34902)

★Q6   **Mr Shailesh Vara** (North West Cambridgeshire):   (34903)

★Q7   **Mrs Theresa Villiers** (Chipping Barnet):   (34904)

★Q8   **Sir Michael Spicer** (West Worcestershire):   (34905)

★Q9   **Mr Brooks Newmark** (Braintree):   (34906)

★Q10   **Mr Ian Taylor** (Esher & Walton):   (34907)

★Q11   **Mr Bob Blizzard** (Waveney):   (34908)

★Q12   **David Mundell** (Dumfriesshire, Clydesdale and Tweeddale):   (34909)

★Q13   **Mr Sadiq Khan** (Tooting):   (34910)

★Q14   **Andrew Miller** (Ellesmere Port & Neston):   (34911)

★Q15   **Dr Nick Palmer** (Broxtowe):   (34912)

Oral Questions on the Commons Order of Business, Wednesday 7th December 2005 (questions to the Secretary of State for International Development after No. 5 have been omitted).

Source: House of Commons 2005

Trade Policies

4. **Anne Main** (St. Albans) (Con): What recent assessment he has made of the effects of protectionist trade policies on poor countries; and if he will make a statement.   [34886]

5. **Mr. Edward Vaizey** (Wantage) (Con): What assessment his Department has made of the implications for developing countries of President Bush's recent comments on reducing global tariffs; and if he will make a statement.   [34887]

The Secretary of State for International Development (Hilary Benn): We welcome moves to reduce tariffs, subsidies and other barriers to the free flow of goods and services. The UK has made assessments based on research by the World Bank, United Nations organisations and the Organisation for Economic Co-operation and Development that suggest that substantial gains for developing countries could result from the liberalisation of agricultural and industrial trade. The actual gains will depend, of course, on the level of reform and the policies that developing countries themselves put in place to take advantage of a more open trade system. Assistance to help the poorest countries to do this will be important, and the UK Government are committed to trebling trade with them and increasing support to £100 million a year by 2010.

Anne Main: The Secretary of State talks about a logjam in Europe. Instead of dealing with generalities, would he like to be specific: which countries are causing the logjam?

Hilary Benn: The hon. Lady is well aware that agriculture support is a big issue in France, is she not? I made the point earlier that there are 25 member states in Europe that have different views. In the end, there must be agreement in Europe so that progress can be made.

Mr. Vaizey: The Secretary of State said earlier that someone has to move in the world trade talks. Is it not the case that the United States has moved and that President Bush has said that he is ready to eliminate all tariffs? Is that not an offer that the European Union and Britain cannot refuse?

Hilary Benn: I welcome the offers that are on the table, but the question is how we unlock the logjam that we have got into. As far as Europe is concerned, some movement on the part of the G20 might allow progress to be made when we actually get to Hong Kong, but there is precious little time in which that can happen.

Mr. Lindsay Hoyle (Chorley) (Lab): My right hon. Friend is aware that moving trade barriers can have a real effect on the poorest countries, such as those in the Caribbean which have been dependent on protection for sugar cane. Will he ensure that there will be help and support for those Caribbean countries that have benefited from trade protection?

Hilary Benn: I share my hon. Friend's concern about the problems that sugar producers in the Caribbean face. What is currently on offer is €40 million of support

from Europe. The British Government's view is clear: that is insufficient. We will continue to press for more support to help those countries to adjust to changes that have to take place.

David Taylor (North-West Leicestershire) (Lab/Co-op): To take the example of one industry, in textiles and clothing the combination of low quotas and high tariffs means that north America and the EU cost 27 million jobs and $50 billion-worth of exports, which is not helping to alleviate poverty. Is not it true that we are helping to stitch up those poorer countries?

Hilary Benn: My hon. Friend makes a powerful case for why the current trade rules need to change so that developing countries can use their skills and expertise to bring a better life to their people.

PRIME MINISTER

The Prime Minister was asked—

Engagements

Q1. [34898] **Mr. Stephen O'Brien** (Eddisbury) (Con): If he will list his official engagements for Wednesday 7 December.

The Prime Minister (Mr. Tony Blair): This morning I had meetings with ministerial colleagues and others. In addition to my duties in the House, I will have further such meetings later today.

Mr. O'Brien: Does the outgoing Prime Minister— *[Interruption.]* Does he agree with the chairman of the Cheshire police authority, Labour Councillor Peter Nurse, when he says in his recent letter to the Home Secretary:

"Restructuring policing with such haste and without considering the long term implications is dangerous and not in the interests of the people of Cheshire"?

The Prime Minister: That is precisely why we must consult fully on it, which we will, and ensure that we get the right proposals for policing in the hon. Gentleman's area and others. However, I point out that he has record numbers of police in Cheshire, just as he has record numbers of people across the entirety of the public services. On every score—health, education and crime—things are better today than they were in 1997.

Jeff Ennis (Barnsley, East and Mexborough) (Lab): Can my right hon. Friend tell me how he will deal with a young, handsome, intelligent, charismatic politician, such as myself—*[Laughter.]*—and how Parliament can better engage ordinary people in the political process?

The Prime Minister: I have always thought that my hon. Friend was a model to follow, although I have never quite managed it myself.

The best way to make progress is to continue with the strong economic growth and the investment in our public services that we have seen across the whole of the public services. Every single indicator has improved since 1997.

Hansard report of Question Time on Wednesday 7th December 2005

Source: House of Commons 2005

Mr. David Cameron (Witney) (Con): The first issue that the Prime Minister and I are going to have to work together on is getting the good bits of his education reforms through the House of Commons and into law. *[Interruption.]* That is the problem with these exchanges—the Labour Chief Whip shouting like a child. *[Interruption.]* Is the right hon. Lady finished?

The Prime Minister and I both agree that schools with greater freedom produce the best results. Will he confirm that all of the freedoms for schools in the White Paper will survive into the Bill?

The Prime Minister: Yes. It is important that we give schools the freedoms that they need. I am delighted to hear that the hon. Gentleman supports these reforms. I assume, therefore, that the Conservative party will be voting for them.

Mr. Cameron: Absolutely. *[Interruption.]* With our support—*[Interruption.]* With our support, the Prime Minister knows that there is no danger of losing these education reforms in a parliamentary vote. So he can afford to be as bold as he wants to be. That is when he is at his best—or so I am told. Can we agree that that means trust schools owning their own buildings and land, employing their own staff, setting pay locally, developing their own culture and ethos and controlling their own admissions?

The Prime Minister: Of course it means all those powers that currently are available to foundation and voluntary aided schools being extended to other schools as well. That is the purpose of the proposals. Incidentally, before I answered any questions, I should have welcomed the hon. Gentleman to his new position and congratulated him on winning the Conservative leadership election. But can I tell him where I feel that we may—and I am sorry to say this—have a disagreement? As I understand it, his position is that all schools should be free to set their own admissions procedures. I am afraid that I believe that the present admissions code should remain in place. So perhaps we can clear that up, too.

Mr. Cameron: I want schools to control their own admissions. That is what is in the White Paper, and let us see that it turns into the Bill. *[Interruption.]* It is only our first exchange, and already the Prime Minister is asking me the questions. This approach is stuck in the past, and I want to talk about the future. He was the future once. Education is one of the public services in desperate need of reform, so does he agree with me that our aim should be to ensure that all schools have these freedoms? Will he ensure that this is one reform where he will not look back and wish that he had gone further?

The Prime Minister: I certainly can say, as I have said before, that it is important that all schools get these freedoms. However, it is obvious that we disagree on the issue of admissions. I think that if schools are free to bring back selection at the age of 11, that would be regressive for our country. So I am afraid that in this grand new consensus we have to disagree on that point.

The other point, which is very important, is this: we also have to keep the investment going into our schools. As the hon. Gentleman knows, the Conservative party

voted against that investment, but as a result of the investment and the change, through specialist schools, city academies and the literacy and numeracy strategy, we now have the best ever results at 11, at 16, at 18 in our schools. Therefore, I have to say to him that it is not merely in respect of education policy that we have to agree. We have also to agree that the investment that is so necessary to back up that reform continues. I am afraid that his economic policy, which is to cut back investment, because of his desire—*[Interruption.]* I am happy if this is another policy that he is about to change. He is saying that this year he would not have put all the investment in but rather have shared that investment half and half between tax cuts and investment. That would mean substantial cuts in public investment. I am very happy to have this new consensus with the hon. Gentleman, and I am delighted that he has said today that the Conservative party will vote for these education reforms, but it has to be on the basis of agreeing the investment also.

Hon. Members: More.

Mr. Speaker: Order.

Mr. Sadiq Khan (Tooting) (Lab): Would my right hon. Friend like to comment on the experience of Mr. Chuttun, a Tooting resident, who unfortunately was sick on Sunday and had to go to St. George's? He had an ECG, two types of blood tests, X-rays and various blood pressure tests, and was treated wonderfully by doctors and nurses. He said:

"This is the first time that I have used St. George's A and E. I was thoroughly impressed by the hospital and the conscientious staff."

Does my right hon. Friend not agree that if Opposition Members are serious—

Mr. Speaker: Order. I think that the Prime Minister will be able to answer the hon. Gentleman's question.

The Prime Minister: The type of improvement that my hon. Friend is describing is one that is happening right across the national health service at the present time. It is extremely important that it continues. It is the result of investment and reform, which means that over the past eight years waiting lists have come down by almost 400,000. We have the lowest waiting lists that this country has had since records began.

Mr. Charles Kennedy (Ross, Skye and Lochaber) (LD): The United States Secretary of State said yesterday that "extraordinary rendition" had been conducted in co-operation with European Governments. To what extent, therefore, have the Government co-operated in the transport of terrorist suspects to Afghanistan and elsewhere, apparently for torture purposes?

The Prime Minister: First, let me draw a very clear distinction indeed between the idea of suspects being taken from one country to another and any sense whatever that ourselves, the United States or anyone condones the use of torture. Torture cannot be justified in any set of circumstances at all. The practice of rendition as described by Secretary of State Condoleezza Rice has been American policy for many years. We have not had such a situation here, but that has been American policy for many, many years. However, it must be applied in accordance with international conventions, and I accept entirely Secretary of State Rice's assurance that it has been.

Mr. Kennedy: Given that assurance, can the Prime Minister therefore explain why the published evidence shows that almost 400 flights have passed through 18 British airports in the period of concern? When was he as Prime Minister first made aware of that policy, and when did he approve it?

The Prime Minister: In respect of airports, I do not know what the right hon. Gentleman is referring to. In respect of the policy of rendition, it has been the policy of the American Government for many years.

Bob Russell (Colchester) (LD): Why?

The Prime Minister: The hon. Gentleman says, "Why?" It is as well to remember that we need to detain some of the people we are talking about for reasons of action against international terrorism. Some of those people are highly dangerous, and some of them can provide information that is of fundamental importance in preventing terrorism. Of course, there should be proper treatment of anyone who is detained, and I have already made it clear that, as far as I am aware, it is not an issue here. However, the American policy has been clear for ages. That is not a matter of contention, and I fully endorse what Secretary of State Rice said yesterday.

Rosemary McKenna (Cumbernauld, Kilsyth and Kirkintilloch, East) (Lab): In the week of additional moneys for local government and the Scottish Parliament, will my right hon. Friend join me in condemning East Dunbartonshire Liberal-controlled council, which this week cut 64 jobs, reduced services and increased charges?

The Prime Minister: That is very typical of the Liberal Democrats. It will not surprise my hon. Friend that whenever the Liberal Democrats get their hands on any power in local government there is a clear difference between what they say they will do and what they actually do.

Q2. [34899] **Mr. Philip Hammond** (Runnymede and Weybridge) (Con): In 1998, the Chancellor of the Exchequer said that productivity was the

"fundamental yardstick of economic performance".

Does the Prime Minister agree that the collapse in Britain's productivity growth from 2.7 per cent. in 1997 to 0.5 per cent. today represents a fundamental failure by his Chancellor?

The Prime Minister: I do not accept the figure that the hon. Gentleman gave. Productivity in this country has been catching up with and even surpassing Japan and Germany. As the Chancellor of the Exchequer pointed out on Monday, the only year in which productivity fell was in a period of Conservative government.

Hugh Bayley (City of York) (Lab): What plans do the Government have to increase the supply of affordable

housing, especially family housing with gardens, in house-price hotspots in the north of England such as the City of York?

The Prime Minister: Both in my hon. Friend's constituency and elsewhere, the proposals introduced by my right hon. Friends the Chancellor and the Deputy Prime Minister for shared equity in homes are a major step forward that will allow many couples who want to get their feet on the first rung of the housing ladder, but who may not be able to afford the full 100 per cent. equity, to build up their equity stake over time. Together with the very considerable investment in social housing, that will make a difference in my hon. Friend's constituency and elsewhere.

Mr. David Cameron (Witney) (Con): The Montreal climate change conference is taking place this week. We support the goal of a new Kyoto-style treaty that will tackle carbon emissions. Earlier this year the Prime Minister said that he had been changing his thinking on the issue. Can he set out his new thinking? In particular, is he still committed to a proper successor to Kyoto based on clear targets and including all the major carbon-producing countries of the world?

The Prime Minister: Yes, I most certainly am committed to that. The reason it is important that we change our thinking on the matter is that I do not believe that the successor to Kyoto can work unless it has not just the United States involved in such targets and such a framework, but India and China, because they are the major emerging economies of the world. In China, for example, one power station is being built every week or every two weeks. Therefore, unless we manage to get a comprehensive framework that also involves India and China, it will not be of much use to us. I entirely agree that the issue is immensely important. That is one of the reasons, of course, why we passed the climate change levy. I hope the hon. Gentleman's question indicates that he will support us on that, too.

Mr. Cameron: I am grateful for the Prime Minister's answer. His Secretary of State for Environment, Food and Rural Affairs said in advance of Montreal:

"Without mechanisms in the form of compulsory action, such as targets to cut emissions, existing and new technologies will never be rolled out on the scale we need",

and I agree with that. The Prime Minister said last month that people get

"very nervous and very worried"

about this approach, and that we need a

"better, more sensitive set of mechanisms".

Will he confirm that he still genuinely agrees with what his Secretary of State for Environment, Food and Rural Affairs said?

The Prime Minister: I just said in answer to the previous question that it is important that we get binding targets. Emerging economies will want those to be sensitive to the needs of their economic growth, but one of the important issues that was not part of Kyoto but needs to be part of a new protocol is technology transfer. As we develop the research that allows us to have clean energy, we need to share that research and that technology with others. I am sorry—I was pointing my finger; I would not want that to break up the new consensus. It is important not merely that we say how much we care about climate change, but that we take the action necessary. Therefore, it will be no use the hon. Gentleman's saying that he supports the aim unless he also supports the climate change levy, the renewables obligation and the extra investment that we put into energy efficiency. If he is prepared to have a consensus on that basis, I welcome it.

asks the Home Secretary how many police officers there are in England. The Home Secretary gives the figure, and the MP then asks 'But is the right honourable member aware that in the police authority that covers my constituency police numbers have fallen by 9 per cent over the last three years, and violent crime has increased by 13 per cent? Doesn't that demonstrate that the government is soft on crime? Will the Home Secretary tell my constituents why he is not committed to improving their safety?' This not only makes the political point on behalf of the MP's party but will also play well in the MP's local press.

A government back-bencher may table exactly the same question, but the supplementary will be very different: 'Will the Home Secretary accept the thanks of my constituents for the government's commitment to beating crime, for extra officers on the beat, and for the reduction of [some category of crime that has gone down rather than up]?'

Short and sharp

By comparison with the *tabling* of oral and written questions, there are very few rules for oral supplementaries. If they are evidently wide of the original question, or if they refer to matters *sub judice* (see page 303), or if they clearly have nothing to do with the minister's responsibilities, the Speaker will call the MP to order. However, there is a catch-22 about this: it is not easy to tell that a supplementary is out of order until the MP is a fair way through asking it, although one type of disorderly supplementary from the government side is usually spotted very quickly: inviting the minister to comment on the policies of the opposition. Ministers are responsible for the government's policies, not those of their opponents. Even in the more knockabout atmosphere of Prime Minister's Questions, the Speaker has stopped the Prime Minister responding overtly to supplementaries that seek criticism of Conservative or Liberal Democrat policies.

Question Time is above all a political exchange; it is not about seeking information, which is what written questions are for. Oral questions are about exposing and criticising, or helping and supporting. This means that there is a tendency for both supplementary questions and ministers' replies to be too long. In its major survey of parliamentary questions in June 2002, the Procedure Committee said:

> We strongly support Mr Speaker in his attempts to restrain the prolixity of some Members. Long, rambling questions are counter-productive, whilst long, rambling answers are an abuse of the time of the House . . . We believe that the Chair should take a pro-active role in seeking to change the culture of Question Time and foster more incisive, tightly focused exchanges.

The committee also felt that it was too easy for ministers to brush off awkward questions with vague answers, and it recommended that the MP who tabled the question should be able to ask a second supplementary after other MPs had been called (not so far implemented).

Long supplementaries are tempting as a way of getting one's point on the record, but they also make things much easier for ministers. Not only is there plenty of time to turn to the relevant part of the briefing file for ammunition in reply, but long supplementaries are less focused and less likely to hit the target. Ministers are much less comfortable with the classic sharp supplementaries such as 'Why?' or 'How much?' or 'How many?'

Preparing for Question Time

For the government, Question Time is an opportunity to tell the story the way ministers see it. It can also be a high-risk occasion, and government departments prepare very carefully for their 'top day'. Ministers will have had briefing meetings with their civil servants, and each minister will take into the Chamber a ring-binder with the answer he or she is to give to each question, together with a survival pack of information and briefing, according to a fairly standard template used by the Civil Service:

◆ *The reason for the question*: why is the MP asking it? Is there a particular constituency focus? What has he or she raised with the department recently? [When a government MP puts down a question, he or she will often helpfully let the department know what is behind it, or what he or she plans as a supplementary question. Opposition MPs will also do this on occasion, especially if their intention is to flag up some issue of constituency concern rather than to attack the government.]

◆ *Elephant traps*: any information that the minister should know about potential gaps in the policy or problems with the figures on the main issues likely to be raised.

◆ *Positive/defensive*: three or four key best positive lines and three or four key defensive lines to take on the main issue covering government achievements and positive activity in the area of policy, and defending against the most likely lines of criticism.

◆ *Key background facts and figures* and, with a page for each issue, *other issues that may be raised* with bullet point lines to take.

◆ *Key quotes*: any useful third-party endorsements or supportive comments from members of the opposition.

The official Opposition team shadowing the government department will also lay its plans for Question Time, highlighting areas where it believes the government is open to criticism and seeking the help of back-benchers to reinforce the line being taken by the front-bench team.

When a government department answers oral questions, at least it knows what subjects are going to be raised, because specific questions have been put down. This is rarely the case in Prime Minister's Questions. Let us now look at one of the highest-profile parliamentary occasions.

Prime Minister's Questions

The Prime Minister answers for half an hour every Wednesday from 12 noon to 12.30 p.m. Only the top fifteen questions in the shuffle are printed, and the vast majority are in the form 'If he will list his official engagements for [Wednesday 9th July]'. Only the first such question is printed out in full on the Order of Business; if other MPs want to ask the same question, their names alone are printed alongside the question numbers.

Why the 'engagements question'?
It may seem strange that so many MPs want to ask the Prime Minister what he happens to be doing on a particular Wednesday. The reason is historical, but the habit persists even though in practice it is not really necessary. Thirty and more years ago, the Prime Minister of the day would transfer a specific question to the relevant secretary of state if the latter had ministerial responsibility for the subject, and the MP concerned would lose the chance of an oral question to the Prime Minister. Prime Ministers are in a sense responsible for everything, but there are relatively few things for which they have *specific* responsibility and a departmental minister does not; examples include coordination between government departments, sacking and appointing ministers, setting up Cabinet committees, and the intelligence services as a whole.

So the 'transfer-proof' question was devised: either to ask the Prime Minister his official engagements for the day, or a related open question – whether he would visit some particular place (usually the questioner's constituency) or country. When she became Prime Minister, Margaret Thatcher indicated that she would not transfer specific questions, as did John Major and Tony Blair when they came to office. However, the open question persisted for two reasons. It allowed MPs to raise the issue of the moment even though the question had been tabled a fortnight before; and it was easy – no thought had to be given to constructing some cunning question when it was odds-against that it would be successful in the shuffle. And even though the period of notice has shortened from ten sitting days to three with the express purpose of allowing more topical questions, the 'engagements question' still flourishes.

Prime Minister's Questions: on the day

As for departmental questions, the Speaker calls (say) 'Mr Graham Allen'; Mr Allen stands up and says 'Number One, Mr Speaker'. The Prime Minister gives the standard response: 'This morning I had meetings with ministerial colleagues and others. In addition to my duties in this House, I shall have further such meetings later today'. Mr Allen is then able to ask a supplementary on anything that is the responsibility of the government. After the Prime Minister has replied, the Speaker will call other MPs who were successful in the shuffle, interspersed with other back-benchers. Unlike departmental questions, MPs whose names are on the Order of Business simply ask their supplementary; they do not go through the process of calling out the number and having the Prime Minister repeat his original answer.

If the Leader of the Opposition rises, the Speaker will call him; he has a normal allocation of six questions in PMQs, which he may take in groups of three on two different themes. The leader of the Liberal Democrats gets two supplementaries.

Questions in PMQs are the usual mixture of the supportive and the critical, but the main event is the gladiatorial contest between the Prime Minister and the Leader of the Opposition. The House is full, noisy and partisan, which raises the stakes; and national newspapers carry 'post-match' comment the next day, sometimes rating the encounter in terms of goals scored or punches landed. The Prime Minister of the day has a built-in advantage; he is centre-stage for the whole play, while the Leader of the Opposition has only two scenes; and the Prime Minister can build on questions from his own back-benchers to project a positive presentation of government policy and achievements.

Even those who criticise PMQs often tend to be fascinated by the occasion; in a highly political House it distils the clash between government and opposition. However, PMQs are about putting the Prime Minister under political pressure rather than exploring policies and intentions; and, in this respect, the Prime Minister's appearances before the Liaison Committee (see page 349) are an important complement to the rough-and-tumble of PMQs.

On pages 323–327, we reproduce the oral questions on the Order of Business for Wednesday 7 December 2005, together with the *Hansard* report of the last oral questions to the Secretary of State for International Development, and the first few minutes of Prime Minister's Questions – which also happened to be the first PMQs in which the Prime Minister faced David Cameron, who had become Leader of the Opposition the day before.

On the Order of Business the questions are marked with a star to show that they are oral questions. Because questions 4 and 5 (both from Conservative back-benchers) were on the same subject, the Secretary of State (Hilary Benn) 'grouped' them and gave an answer covering both. Anne Main and Edward Vaizey then got their supplementary questions, following which the Speaker called two back-benchers from the government side to maintain the balance. The House was filling up rapidly, and the background noise made it hard to hear the questions and replies. The galleries for the public, for members of the House of Lords, and even for MPs who could not get a seat in the Chamber, were crammed.

The Conservative Stephen O'Brien (a shadow minister, but asking his supplementary as a back-bencher), combined a question on the hot topic of police restructuring with a swipe at the PM's plans for the future. (The prosaic '*[Interruption]*' in Hansard in fact indicates deafening roars from each side of the House.) The PM countered on police restructuring, and took the opportunity to make a broader point on his party's record in power.

The Speaker then called Jeff Ennis, a Labour back-bencher, to balance the Opposition supplementary, even though Mr Ennis did not have a question on the Order of Business: it happened that in the 'shuffle' for that day (see page 321) Opposition MPs had done unusually well.

David Cameron then had his first taste of PMQs as Leader of the Opposition, with three questions on the government's plans to reform education. The questions and responses were long, reflecting the style of oral questions – and especially PMQs – as mini-debates rather than interrogation. And indeed the Speaker decided that the next back-bencher to be called, Labour's Sadiq Khan, had taken rather too much time over his supplementary. Charles Kennedy as Leader of the Liberal Democrats then had his two questions on the contentious issue of 'extraordinary rendition' of suspected terrorists; questions went to government, opposition, and then government backbenchers, after which David Cameron had three more questions, during which the House was much quieter for the calmer exchanges on the climate change conference in Montreal.

It was an unusual PMQs in that it was a test of a new Leader of the Opposition, but the structure was typical: longish questions and answers making political points rather than seeking or providing information; the mixture of hot current issues and important but less contentious subjects; and the gladiatorial exchanges between the party leaders.

Urgent questions

On any sitting day, an MP can seek the Speaker's leave to ask an urgent question. These were formerly known as 'private notice questions' or PNQs because notice of them was given directly to the Speaker and not printed on the Order Paper as for other oral questions. The MP must make a request before noon on a Monday or Tuesday, before 10.00 a.m. on a Wednesday and before 9.00 a.m. on a Thursday, and the Speaker must be satisfied that the matter is of public importance and is genuinely urgent. If he grants the application, warning is displayed on the television annunciators around the parliamentary estate, and the MP concerned is called to ask the question at the end of Question Time (or, very rarely, on a Friday, at 11.00 a.m., interrupting the business then under way).

The Speaker's power to grant an urgent question is a significant one. It brings a minister to the House at very short notice to answer on something on which the government may be in some disarray and is still deciding how to respond to a problem that may have arisen only a few hours before. The Speaker does not usually allow questioning to run for as long as for ministerial statements, but he has absolute discretion, and on major issues the minister concerned has been exposed to questioning for up to an hour.

In the 2003–04 session, the Speaker granted twelve urgent questions, and four in the short 2004–05 session. In the early months of the 2005 parliament, subjects included the collapse of a court martial in which seven paratroopers were accused of murdering an Iraqi civilian; the adequacy of gas supplies for an expected cold winter; and the culling of badgers to curb TB in cattle. Even the Prime Minister can be brought to the despatch box in this way, as in November 2002 when the Leader of the Opposition was granted an urgent question on the firefighters' dispute.

The business question every Thursday at 11.30 a.m., in which the shadow Leader of the House asks the Leader of the House to announce forthcoming business in the House, is technically an urgent question, although of a specialised type. The Leader of the House lists the items of business, usually firm for the following week, more provisional for the week after, and then answers questions. Strictly speaking, these must relate to the forthcoming business, but they are often on more general political matters; and it does not take much ingenuity to ask for a debate on 'the government's failure to deliver on targets' or on 'the government's successes in carrying through public service reform'.

Questions answered at the end of Question Time

A minister may choose to answer an oral question not as it is reached during Question Time but at the end of oral questions (3.30 p.m. on Mondays and Tuesdays, 12.30 p.m. on Wednesdays, and 11.30 a.m. on Thursdays). This is relatively unusual, but it tends to happen when a question on the Order of Business is a convenient hook for an announcement a minister wants to make but at greater length than would be permissible in answer to a conventional oral question. As this is in effect a mini-statement, the Speaker allows more supplementaries than during Question Time. A minister may answer an oral question in this way even though it would not have been reached during Question Time (and may even answer a written question in this way if it is down for answer on that day).

Written questions

In the last twelve-month session before the 2005 general election, 2,060 questions received an oral answer in the House. By contrast, 54,875 written questions were tabled during that session, 9 per cent of which – over 6,000 – were to the Department of Health. The Home Office answered 5,500, and Environment, Food and Rural Affairs just over 4,000. Defence, Education and Skills, Trade and Industry all answered more than 3,000. At the other end of the scale, the Solicitor-General answered 208.

Written questions are of two types: *ordinary written questions*, which are put down for answer two sitting days after they are received, and which by convention the government answers within a week. There is no limit to the number of this type of question that an MP may table. *Named-day questions* are for answer on a stated day, with a minimum notice period of three sitting days (including non-sitting Fridays). The named-day system was originally intended for genuinely urgent questions, but it became greatly overused, and increasing numbers of questions received holding replies ('I will reply to the hon. member as soon as possible'). From January 2003, a limit of five named-day questions per member per day was imposed.

Written questions have a wide variety of purposes. They are used by MPs to raise the profile of particular subjects, to tease out details of the government's policy on some issue with a view to deploying the material in political debate inside or outside the House, or to press ministers in an area where the government appears vulnerable. They are tabled to gather information in order to be able to respond to constituency concerns, or to give a constituent's case wider publicity. Shadow ministers use them to monitor what the government is doing in their policy areas. Outside organisations will ask MPs to put down questions in order to assist a campaign, or to obtain an authoritative statement on a situation or of the government's policy towards it.

Written questions have one great advantage over oral questions: they can be pursued much more relentlessly. Whereas in Question Time an MP gets one supplementary and the moment is past, with the ministers concerned not answering again until a month later, written questions can follow up in detail, almost as a barrister would in cross-examination, the precise conduct of government policy in a particular area.

Although, as we noted above, there are rubbing points when MPs see no good reason for the government refusing to answer, replies to written questions (which occupy forty to fifty pages of *Hansard* on a typical day) put a staggering amount of official information into the public domain. But there is no doubt that the increasing use of written questions, and the type of question asked, is starting to devalue the currency, a point we return to below.

Written ministerial statements

It used to be the case that if the government wanted to put something formally on the record in the House that was not important enough for an oral statement (see page 153), a friendly back-bencher would be found to put down an 'arranged question' drafted in the department concerned, in answer to which the government could make the statement it wanted. These arranged questions or 'plants' were a rather opaque way for the government to make an announcement, and from October 2002 a system of written ministerial statements was introduced.

Statements to be made on any day are listed on the Order Paper at the end of the day's business, and statements on a future day appear in Section E of the *future business* part of the Vote bundle (see page 169). When made, the statements are printed before the written answers to questions in the next day's *Hansard* (and so are available online).

Are questions effective?

As part of its review of PQs in 2002, the Procedure Committee analysed the responses of 167 MPs to a questionnaire. One of the questions was 'How do you use the system of questions to assist in your work as a Member?' The responses confirmed the purposes of eliciting information (often about constituency matters), getting the government's position on the record, putting pressure on ministers, making a constituency point, researching an issue in depth and helping with a local campaign. One MP said 'It is one of the few areas where, as a back-bench MP, you can have a direct impact'; another said that it proved to constituents 'that you really are trying to get answers out of the government'.

MPs were also asked how effective they thought questions were in bringing information into the public domain, contributing to political debate and holding the executive to account. For oral questions, 43 per cent replied either 'quite' or 'very effective' and 31 per cent 'not very' or 'not at all effective'. Written questions scored better, with figures of 60 and 21 per cent, respectively, and this probably reflects the different character of oral and written questions.

Of the sample, 57 per cent received requests from outside organisations to table questions on their behalf, and about two-thirds 'occasionally' acceded to such requests. Over two-thirds of respondents said that their staff were involved in preparing questions for the MP to table, which may be seen by some to confirm their suspicions that staffers play too great a part in this area of parliamentary activity; certainly the trend has continued.

There is no doubt that, whereas thirty or forty years ago an MP would often first write to a government department for information or seek a meeting to put some point to a minister and would table a PQ only if he or she had to, putting down a question has for some time been the first step, not the last.

The survey on pages 313–16 of reasons for refusing to answer questions may seem daunting, and it is certainly the case that competent ministers and departments have the odds stacked in their favour. However, as in so many areas of parliamentary life, the determination and hard work of an individual MP can produce remarkable results. For example, it was the inexorable series of written questions tabled by the back-bench Labour MP Tam Dalyell which led to the admission from Margaret Thatcher's government that during the Falklands War the Argentinian cruiser *General Belgrano* had been torpedoed when steaming away from British forces rather than towards them, as the government had previously implied.

Devaluing the currency?

In recent years, the numbers of written PQs tabled in the Commons have soared: in financial year 2000–01 there were 32,821; but by 2004–05 this had risen to 54,428, an increase of 66 per cent. And the trend is now rising even faster: in November 2005 there were 62 per cent more written questions tabled per sitting day than in November 2004.

This would not be of concern if the increase were attributable to more MPs making greater use of the *inquisitorial* opportunity of PQs: requiring government to explain its actions; probing the details of a government policy; above all calling the executive to account. But much of the increase has been in what one might call the 'research' or 'general knowledge' type of question, which seeks statistical information, with extensive comparisons. Thus an MP might ask for progress on the clearance for use of one particular drug in which he was interested, perhaps with five or six other questions about how the drug was being evaluated, but at the same time might ask for all the same details for each of fifteen or twenty other drugs that were also being tested.

Similarly, an MP might ask for detailed statistics on housing and registered social landlords in her own constituency, but would then also ask for the same information for every constituency in her region, for every other region in England, and in respect of each of the last ten years.

There has also been a sharp growth in the 'round robin' PQs, which are put separately to each of the twenty-two government departments. Recent examples have sought to find out how many people have been dismissed for misconduct in each of the last five years; what new offences have been created in legislation sponsored by each department over the last ten years; and what each department's ten most valuable moveable assets and immoveable assets are. The last series of questions produced some interesting answers; but in no sense were they – or most of the statistical questions quoted above – remotely about *holding the government to account*.

Why has this happened? Probably for three main reasons. *First*, more MPs have got used to the PQ system as a free research facility (even though most such questions could probably be answered pretty easily by the excellent researchers in the House of Commons Library). *Second*, increased allowances have allowed MPs to employ more staff, and drafting PQs for their MP – often with little or no intervention from the MP – has become a growth industry. *Third*, outside pressures, from the media but especially from 'parliament-watchers' such as the **theyworkforyou.com** website, have increasingly valued activity over achievement. Thus **theyworkforyou.com** ranks MPs on how many PQs they have tabled, regardless of how good the questions were, whether they got good answers, or whether the MP followed up the questions and put the answers to effective use.

Does it matter? Yes. If the recent growth had been in incisive questions, systematically followed up, then the government would have been more effectively called to account in the public interest. But this has not been the case. In 2002 the Procedure Committee remarked in its survey of PQs that the scale of the increase 'risks a reduction in the quality of government replies'; and, although this can only be a subjective judgement, this does seem to be happening. More worrying is the fact that several government departments, overwhelmed by the volume of PQs, have set up 'answering divisions' to insulate the people actually dealing with the subjects from having to deal with PQs as well. This means that in those departments answers to MPs' questions are produced by a sort of research bureau rather than by the civil servants dealing with the issues first-hand.

Questions in the Commons – conclusion

The processes of oral and written questions are key functions of the House of Commons. Both can be means of exposing the government to criticism, and of requiring explanation and justification. Oral questions, although inquisitorial in theory, are more part of the political debate. Written questions, on the other hand, are a way of calling governments to account in detail, and they should be an important discipline on individual government departments and their ministers – the requirement to reply truthfully to a direct and precise question can mean that the spotlight swings on to something that the government would much preferred to have kept to itself.

Although, as we have seen, front-benchers use questions extensively, they are also one of the main opportunities for back-bench MPs on all sides of the House to pursue and expose issues, and to get the government of the day to put information on the public record. The very existence of parliamentary questions, and the opportunities that they provide for the representatives of the people to question the government of the day, are of constitutional importance. Their effectiveness has always been down to the tenacity and skill of individual MPs; but whether the system can survive the strains that are now being put upon it is also in the hands of MPs generally.

Questions in the House of Lords

The House of Lords also has a variety of ways of scrutinising the actions of, and eliciting information from, the executive by means of questions. These questions are always addressed to 'Her Majesty's Government'. (Questions on procedure or domestic House of Lords matters are usually addressed to the Leader of the House or Chairman of Committees respectively.) It follows that the government must have responsibility for the subject matter of the question. Fewer questions are tabled in the Lords than in the Commons, and the rules governing their content are less strict. It is ultimately for the House itself to determine what is in order and what is not. Nevertheless, there are some conventions. Questions casting reflections on the royal family or relating to the Church of England, or questions phrased offensively, are inadmissible. As in the commons, questions on matters 'reserved' to the Scottish Parliament, the National Assembly for Wales, and the Northern Ireland Assembly are also inadmissible. So too are questions that are *sub judice* (on matters awaiting decision by the criminal or civil courts) – subject only to the discretion of the Leader of the House, who may allow such a question if the case is of national importance and there is no danger of prejudice to the proceedings. It is considered undesirable to table questions on nationalised industries except for those asking for statistical information or on matters of urgent public importance, but following successive privatisations this rule is of less significance than it used to be. It is also undesirable to incorporate statements of fact or opinion in the text of a question.

Questions for oral answer

Every day except Fridays, at the beginning of a sitting, four questions for oral answer (*starred questions*) may be put to the government. They are marked on the Order Paper with an asterisk, and provided that they are not topical questions they may be tabled up to one month in advance. As in the Commons, questions in the Lords were losing their currency from being tabled too far in advance, and some members were, it was felt, hogging the Order Paper by tabling too many too far ahead. In recent years, the Procedure Committee has recommended that no member should have more than one on the Order Paper at any one time; and that on Tuesdays, Wednesdays and Thursdays one of the questions should be a 'topical question' selected by ballot by the Clerk Assistant two working days before they are to be asked. No starred question may be tabled less than twenty-four hours before it is to be asked.

Unlike the Commons, questions are not limited to any particular government department on any particular day, and there is no equivalent to Prime Minister's Questions. Every member asking a question is allowed one supplementary before other members' supplementaries are put. Supplementary questions must be in terms confined to the subject of the original question, but they frequently go wider. They must not give rise to debate. Question Time may not exceed thirty minutes. In the 1999–2000 session 630 starred questions were asked, which is typical for a session of normal duration. (In sessions 2002–03 and 2003–04 the House experimented by taking a fifth question on Tuesdays and Wednesdays but subsequently reverted to former practice.)

Questions for oral answer after debate

A question that may give rise to debate may be put down for any sitting day and is taken at the end of business. These debated questions are very popular with members. Such unstarred questions are time-limited to one and a half hours and are not marked by asterisks on the Order Paper. Any lord may make a speech upon the question, but after the minister has replied on behalf of the government there is no right of reply. Unstarred questions are normally taken when business appears to be relatively light and, although less frequent, they are in some ways akin to Commons adjournment debates (see also Chapter 9). Since March 1993, it has been possible to table unstarred questions for debate in the dinner break. An hour's time limit is imposed so that the resumption of legislative business is not delayed (see also page 165).

Questions for written answer

Members of the House may also obtain written answers by tabling questions on the Order Paper under the heading 'Questions for written answer'. The minister concerned will then write to the lord and the answer will also be published in *Hansard*. There is no limit to the number of questions a lord may ask in this way, although members are discouraged from tabling large numbers of questions or multiple requests for information masquerading as a single question, and no more than six a day may be tabled by a single member. Questions for written answer are answered within a fortnight. The government itself often used the medium of a written answer to a question to make an announcement or publish information, but written ministerial statements are now published in *Hansard* instead. In 1961–62, seventy-two questions for written answer were tabled; in 1998–99, 4,322; and in 2003–04, 4,524. Written answers on matters delegated to executive agencies are filtered through an appropriate member of the government and printed in the *Official Report* in letter form. They attract parliamentary privilege.

Private notice questions

A lord may seek to ask a question on a matter of urgency on any day, just as an MP may apply for an 'urgent question'. But it is the Lord Speaker who, in the first instance, decides whether the question is of sufficient urgency or importance to justify an immediate reply. Notice of such a question must be given by noon on the day it is proposed to ask it. Private notice questions are rare, and there are seldom more than one or two a session. They occur more frequently when a Cabinet minister with major departmental responsibilities sits in the Lords and during those periods when the House sits while the Commons remains in recess. But answers to many Commons urgent questions are repeated as statements in the House of Lords if the opposition requests it.

Petitions

The right to petition Parliament is an ancient one, summarised in a resolution of the House of Commons of 1699: 'That it is the inherent right of every commoner in England to prepare and present petitions to the House of Commons in case of grievance, and the House of Commons to receive the same'. The first recorded petitions date from the reign of Richard II (1377–99); and in 1571, a committee with the splendid name of the Committee for Motions of Griefs and Petitions was appointed to examine petitions.

Petitions were originally read at the start of a sitting, and debates could arise upon them. Huge numbers were presented during the nineteenth century; for example, 17,000 a year between 1837 and 1841; and 34,000 in 1893. The twentieth century saw a sharp fall in the numbers of public petitions, but they remain a way of giving local or more widespread concerns a higher profile.

Petitions must be presented by an MP. They may have hundreds of thousands of signatures, or only one, but the procedure is the same in each case. The basic rules are that they should state from whom they come, should be in 'respectful language' and should ask for something that it is in

Table 10.1 Petitions presented to the House of Commons in the
2001 Parliament

Session	Petitions	of which presented formally	Government observations
2001–02 (long session)	131	109	64
2002–03	220	194	178
2003–04	128	112	82
2004–05 (short session)	51	44	38

the power of the House of Commons to grant. The MP has the petition
checked by the Clerk of Public Petitions to make sure that it is in order, and
he or she can then, at any time during a sitting of the House, simply put
it in the green baize bag that hangs on the back of the Speaker's Chair.
The MP can also present a petition formally in the House. Just before the
daily half-hour adjournment debate (or, on Fridays, at the start of the day's
business) he or she is called by the Speaker and briefly introduces the
petition and reads the text. All petitions are printed and circulated with the
House's working papers. Government departments may (but do not have
to) make observations on them, and these observations are also printed.
Recent statistics are given in Table 10.1 (it should be remembered that a
campaign of petitions on a single subject can skew the figures).

Petitions cover a wide variety of subjects, both national and local. In
December 2005, for example, subjects included 'a fair and equitable replacement for council tax' (on which petitions were presented by a number of
MPs), the availability of the anti-cancer drug Herceptin, mental healthcare
in north-west Leicestershire, the expansion of Tees Port; and 'for a large and
conveniently placed post box' in the village of Westonzoyland in Somerset.

Petitions are sent to the relevant departmental select committee (see
page 347), but none has yet been taken up; and in that sense, they are not
a particularly effective way of making a case. But they can achieve a great
deal of publicity and on a local issue can have a snowball effect. On national
issues, either the sheer numbers of signatories to a petition or the fact that
similar petitions from scores of constituencies are presented week after
week can be a powerful statement of concern that for practical political
reasons the government must heed.

Petitions may also be addressed to the House of Lords by a member of
the House. No speech or debate takes place beyond the formal words of
presentation, and they are not printed. Although largely defunct, petitions
are very occasionally still presented there.

Letters to ministers

MPs' letters to ministers can be seen as part of the questioning process, although they are not 'proceedings in Parliament' (see page 182). The level of correspondence between MPs and ministers is approaching a quarter of a million letters a year (and has increased by more than 40,000 since 2002). Table 10.2 includes correspondence from peers, but the vast majority of letters are from MPs (who in this case also include ministers and the Speaker in their constituency roles).

It is not surprising that the departments that deal with the things which touch people's lives most closely – health, law and order, education, transport, immigration – have heavy postbags.

Typically, an MP receives a complaint from a constituent, perhaps that he was discharged from hospital too soon, or that he has a fiancée who is not being allowed to settle in the UK from Pakistan, or that his son is being kept in poor conditions in a remand prison. It would be impossible for the MP to investigate these complaints personally. He or she could table parliamentary questions or apply for an adjournment debate; but usually the

Table 10.2 Correspondence from MPs and peers received by government departments and executive agencies in calendar year 2004

Department for Constitutional Affairs	3,416
Department for Culture, Media and Sport	4,817
Ministry of Defence	5,989
Department for Education and Skills	15,313
Department for Environment, Food and Rural Affairs	14,305
Foreign and Commonwealth Office	26,942
UK Visas	12,849
Department of Health	20,140
Home Office (including Immigration and Nationality Directorate)	45,247
Inland Revenue	2,993
Department for International Development	4,686
Office of the Deputy Prime Minister	10,135
Department of Transport	8,593
Department of Trade and Industry	11,807
Treasury	4,316
Department for Work and Pensions	13,319
Child Support Agency	5,390
Others	16,589
Total	226,846

MP begins by forwarding the constituent's letter to the minister responsible for the subject and asking for comments. Not all letters are of complaint.
A small firm may want to know what government or EU grants it can apply
for or to seek the MP's help in negotiating some tangle of bureaucracy.

The constituent could have written directly to the department, whether
with a complaint or a query, but the fact that the letter is coming from an
MP means that the issue will be dealt with at a more senior level. The reply
– usually from a minister personally, but also from officials with operational
responsibility for the subject, or the chief executive of an executive agency –
will be in a form that the MP can forward to the constituent as a response,
but it may also give the MP useful background if similar cases arise.

Letters from members of the House of Lords to ministers are treated
in the same way inside government departments as letters from MPs. No
separate figures are published, but the numbers are much lower because
peers have no constituency work.

Letters have several advantages over parliamentary questions. They can
be sent at any time, whether or not Parliament is sitting. They can raise
confidential matters, or the personal details of a constituent's case, and can
go into great detail about the point at issue. And, unlike questions, there are
no rules restricting what an MP may say in a letter. The contents of letters
between MPs and ministers are private unless one side or the other releases
them; and although by convention the minister does not do this unless the
MP does, ministers are always aware that the MP may go public and their
letters are, whenever possible, written in a form that can be forwarded
directly to the constituent.

One disadvantage of letters is that they are more prone to delay than
the answers to PQs. All the departments in the table above have targets
for replying to MPs' letters, usually between fifteen and twenty working
days. In 2004, the Department for Education and Skills replied to 93 per
cent of letters within fifteen working days, and the Department for Work
and Pensions replied to 86 per cent within the same period. Some departments did less well: the Ministry of Defence replied to 62 per cent within
its fifteen-day target; and, although the Department for Constitutional
Affairs had a twenty-day target, it beat it in only 64 per cent of cases.

Most matters raised by constituents and taken up by MPs with ministers
are dealt with by correspondence. However, if the MP is unhappy with the
government's response, he or she can seek a meeting with the minister, or
put down parliamentary questions, or seek an adjournment debate, either
in the Chamber or in Westminster Hall, to which a minister will have to
reply. Proceedings in the House often start with a constituent's letter.

Calling to account: select committees

Select committees in the House of Commons

Introduction

People often associate select committees of the House of Commons with the system of departmental select committees set up in 1979; but in fact the House has used select committees for centuries to investigate, to advise, to consider complex matters – in fact for any task which is more effectively carried out by a small group of MPs than by the House as a whole. Indeed, the very name 'select committee' indicates that a task or function has been given, or *committed*, to that body, composed of MPs *selected* to sit upon it.

We have already encountered standing committees (see page 211) – strangely named because they are not permanent (with the exception of European standing committees (see page 397)): each one ceases to exist when it has finished considering the particular item of business committed to it. Some select committees are also appointed for a single purpose – to examine a draft bill, perhaps – and are dissolved when they have completed their work, but most are permanent institutions. They are appointed under standing orders and so do not die at the end of a session or the end of a parliament.

When the House meets after a general election, the permanent select committees are technically in existence but have no members. There is then a period of jockeying for membership of the most sought-after committees, and of negotiation between the parties for the chairmanships. Delays – sometimes of three months or more – in putting names to the House have been criticised as delaying the start of committee work and giving the new government a scrutiny-free run for the crucial early weeks after a general election. Largely due to the efforts of the new Leader of the House, Robin Cook, the delay at the start of the 2001 parliament was the shortest ever: the session began on 13 June 2001, and most select committees were nominated on 16 July. The timetable slipped in 2005: the session began on 18 May and most committees were nominated on 13 July.

The development of select committees

Select committees have long been a feature of the work of the House of Commons. If you look at the Journals of the House for the end of the sixteenth century, you will find select committees involved in, and advising the House on, some of the most sensitive political issues of the day. In 1571, there was a Committee for the Uniformity of Religion – a matter of life and death in Elizabethan England. The following year there was a Committee on the Queen of Scotts (*sic*) – in this case, a matter of death. In 1571 there was also a Committee for the Examination of Fees and Rewards taken for Voices (that is, votes) in this House – an early example of the House looking at appropriate standards of conduct. Just after the turn of the seventeenth century, select committees dealt with the Confirmation of the Book of Common Prayer and with the Union with Scotland (both in 1604).

Some committees were virtually permanent: committees on Grievances, on Privileges and on the Subsidy (the grant of money to the Crown) were regularly appointed. There were also select committees with wider responsibilities, such as the splendidly named Grand Committee for Evils (1623).

But most committees were ephemeral; something came up that the House wanted looked at, and it set up a committee. These would often operate very informally: the members nominated to the committee would go straight out of the House into another room, would deliberate, perhaps examine witnesses, and then come back to the House (possibly even later in the same sitting), when one of their members would report orally what view they had come to.

Until well into the twentieth century, most select committees were set up ad hoc to examine a particular issue of public policy, or often some disaster or scandal (and their appointment was often used as a political weapon). A classic case was the Sebastopol Committee, set up in 1855, which – with some resonances for the aftermath of the Iraq war in 2003 – investigated the conduct of affairs but also sought political scapegoats in the process. The committee sat almost every day for more than two months,

asked some 7,000 questions of witnesses and was bitterly critical of Lord
Aberdeen, the former Prime Minister (who gave evidence to the committee). Unlike a modern select committee, the Sebastopol Committee had
no staff (the role of committee clerks then was largely to ensure procedural
rectitude), and the final report was written by one of its members, Lord
Seymour (the draft report proposed by the fiery chairman, Mr Roebuck,
was rejected by the committee).

Unsystematic scrutiny

Committees such as the Sebastopol Committee played some part in calling governments to account (often after the event) but, with the possible
exception of the Public Accounts Committee (see page 284), set up in 1861
to see whether public money had been properly expended, there was until
the twentieth century little use by the House of Commons of select committees to monitor the detail of what the government of the day was
actually doing.

A move in this direction was made with the appointment in 1912 of
the Estimates Committee, which lasted until 1970, when it was succeeded
(until 1979) by the Expenditure Committee. Both committees worked
mainly through subject sub-committees, but their coverage of government
activity, although occasionally influential, was very patchy. In the late 1960s
and 1970s, a number of 'subject' select committees (for example, on agriculture, education and science, and overseas aid) were set up; but there was
no real system of select committees; and the Agriculture Committee, for
example, was wound up in February 1969 after a campaign of opposition
by government departments.

The real change came with the election of the Conservative government
in 1979. The new Leader of the House, Norman St John-Stevas, was quick
to put before the House the recommendation of the Procedure Committee
the previous year that there should be a select committee to shadow each
government department. The committee had also recommended that eight
days a year on the floor of the House should be devoted to debating the
committees' reports (and that their chairmen should be paid a small additional salary). These latter recommendations were not adopted by the
government, but the key principle of a system of select committees related
to government departments was approved in June 1979.

It was widely thought that, had St John-Stevas not moved so quickly,
the change would never have been made; by the autumn the Prime
Minister, Margaret Thatcher (who had other things on her mind in the

first few months of office), would have realised how inconvenient for the government these committees might be, and would have vetoed the proposal. But, for the first time, the House of Commons now had at its disposal a means of systematic scrutiny of the government of the day potentially much more rigorous than the traditional methods of debate and question.

Today these departmental select committees account for the majority of select committee activity; but they number less than half of the House's select committees. We now look at what select committees there are and what they do; then at their appointment and powers; and we will then use the example of a departmental committee to see how they work.

The committees

Departmental committees

There are eighteen of these (number of members on each in brackets):

◆ Constitutional Affairs (11)
◆ Culture, Media and Sport (11)
◆ Defence (14)
◆ Education and Skills (11)
◆ Environment, Food and Rural Affairs (14)
◆ Foreign Affairs (14)
◆ Health (11)
◆ Home Affairs (14)
◆ International Development (11)
◆ Northern Ireland Affairs (13)
◆ Office of the Deputy Prime Minister: Housing, Planning, Local Government and the Regions (11)
◆ Science and Technology (11)
◆ Scottish Affairs (11)
◆ Trade and Industry (14)
◆ Transport (11)
◆ Treasury (14)
◆ Welsh Affairs (11)
◆ Work and Pensions (11).

They have a very broad remit: 'to examine the expenditure, administration and policy of [the relevant government department] and associated public bodies'. They are thus concerned not only with the doings of 'their' department but also with any related executive agencies, and with regulators and inspectorates that operate in their field. All the committees have power to set up a sub-committee.

Because each committee shadows a government department, the system of committees has to change to match alterations in the structure of government. Thus, a Constitutional Affairs Committee was appointed in place of the Committee on the Lord Chancellor's Department, following the creation of the former department and the abolition of the latter. Similarly, when particular responsibilities move from one government department to another, the task of monitoring them moves from one committee to another.

'Cross-cutting' committees

The departmental committees look 'vertically' at all the responsibilities of a single department and its ministers (although the Scottish, Welsh and Northern Ireland Affairs Committees have a broader range of interests). The crosscutting committees, on the other hand, look 'horizontally' across Whitehall at themes or actions in which all or most departments are involved:

- ◆ Environmental Audit
- ◆ European Scrutiny
- ◆ Liaison
- ◆ Public Accounts
- ◆ Public Administration.

The Environmental Audit Committee

This was set up in November 1997. It has sixteen members, and its task is 'to consider to what extent the policies and programmes of government departments and non-departmental public bodies contribute to environmental protection and sustainable development', and 'to audit their performance against such targets as may be set for them'. The committee inquires into a range of 'green' issues, including the environmental implications of the government's spending plans and international policies on sustainable development (and the agendas and effects of successive world summits). Its recent inquiries have covered subjects such as corporate environmental crime, sustainable timber, and 'green' housing. Its priority for the 2005 Parliament is climate change. It has power to appoint a sub-committee.

The European Scrutiny Committee

This committee (formerly known as the European Legislation Committee) was established shortly after the United Kingdom joined the EEC in 1973. It examines a range of European Union business: not only European Union policies, spending and draft legislation, but also institutional issues – it reported in detail on the processes that led to the Maastricht, Amsterdam and Nice Treaties, and on the draft EU constitution. It has sixteen members and has power to set up as many sub-committees as it wishes. The work of this committee is covered in Chapter 12.

The Liaison Committee

This is an unusual committee whose work includes both detailed house-keeping (and so might be classed with the internal committees below) and some of the most high-profile hearings that any select committee holds. The committee consists of the chairmen of all the permanent select committees, plus two additional members, one of whom chairs the committee. The membership thus varies with the number of committees, but at present it stands at thirty-one. It has power to set up a sub-committee.

The Liaison Committee has the general task of considering 'general matters relating to the work of select committees'. This may be a change in the format of committee reports, for example, or the rules for putting uncorrected transcripts of evidence on the Internet, or adjudicating on overlap between the inquiries of two committees. The committee also decides how the budget for overseas travel by select committees is allocated, and it chooses reports for debate on the floor of the House on estimates days and in Westminster Hall (see pages 277 and 297).

In 2000, however, the committee changed its spots entirely and launched into a campaign to make select committees more effective. Its three reports, under the general theme of *Shifting the Balance* (between the executive and the legislature), put forward a reform programme that produced something of a confrontation with the government and with the then Leader of the House, Margaret Beckett. Her replacement by Robin Cook in 2001 led to the adoption of a number of the committee's proposals. The committee has followed up its work by publishing annual reports on the select committee system, assessing its effectiveness and examining innovations and problems.

One Liaison Committee recommendation produced an important result, although not immediately. In December 2000, the chairman of the committee wrote to the Prime Minister inviting him to give evidence to the committee on the government's annual report 'to spell out your policies in an atmosphere very different from that on the floor of the House'.

The request was turned down on the grounds of precedent and what was described as 'the important principle that it is for individual Secretaries of State to answer to the House and its individual Select Committees for their areas of responsibility, and not the Prime Minister' – even though the Prime Minister answers on those areas of responsibility every week during Prime Minister's Questions.

However, just over a year later the Prime Minister did indeed offer to appear before the committee twice a year to discuss domestic and international affairs, and the first session took place on 16 July 2002. The Prime Minister's appearances have become important parliamentary occasions, televised live and carefully analysed by the media. The size of the committee makes the normal style of examination more difficult, but questioning is focused on themes decided by the committee beforehand, each led by one MP. The Prime Minister is given notice of the themes but not of the detailed questions.

The calm questioning in depth at these sessions has been a valuable antidote to the knockabout of PMQs. They are opportunities for the Prime Minister as well as for MPs, but the fact that the PM now appears before a select committee in this way is symbolically important as well as making the head of the government more accountable. It is difficult to see a future Prime Minister being able to discontinue the practice.

The Committee of Public Accounts
The work of this committee, usually known as 'the PAC', and of the Comptroller and Auditor-General who supports it, is described in Chapter 8.

The Public Administration Committee
This committee was set up in 1997, taking on the functions of two previous committees, the Public Service Committee and the Committee on the Parliamentary Commissioner for Administration. In its public service role, the committee has conducted inquiries into matters that affect the government as a whole: for example at the start of the 2005 parliament, the role of government special advisers, the rules for political memoirs (among others, taking evidence from Sir Christopher Meyer, the ex-ambassador to Washington, whose gossipy memoirs had gone down badly with some); and into 'governing the future', studying the balance between strategic thinking and everyday administration in government. As we saw in Chapter 10, the committee also conducts regular reviews of ministers' refusals to answer particular types of parliamentary question. The committee has eleven members and the power to appoint a sub-committee.

In its other role, the committee considers the reports of the Parliamentary Commissioner for Administration (or Ombudsman, a Swedish name reflecting the fact that there were similar officials in Scandinavia in the nineteenth century; the concept was adopted by the UK in 1967, when the Parliamentary Commissioner Act was passed).

The Ombudsman is an entirely independent official who reports to Parliament. Assisted by a staff of 230, she investigates complaints about maladministration and the actions (or inactions) of government departments and other public bodies that seem to have caused injustice that has not been put right. Her main aim is to obtain a remedy for those who have suffered injustice, and her secondary aim is to ensure good standards of public administration. If she finds serious faults, she can recommend to the public body concerned what redress it should offer and the action it should take to avoid a repetition of the failure. The Ombudsman has no power to enforce her recommendations, but they are almost always accepted. She also holds the separate posts of Health Service Commissioner for England and for Wales, and Ombudsman for Administration in Wales. In the two latter roles she reports to the National Assembly for Wales. Her Scottish equivalent reports to the Scottish Parliament.

The relationship between the Ombudsman and the Public Administration Committee is not unlike that between the Comptroller and Auditor General and the Public Accounts Committee (see page 283). The Ombudsman has the additional clout of the committee's backing, and the committee is able to draw on the work of the Ombudsman's office with its substantial resources. The committee considers the Ombudsman's annual reports (and those of her Northern Ireland equivalent); but, rather than following up the details of individual investigations, it draws more general lessons for public administration as a whole.

'Legislative' committees

Although most legislation is considered by standing committees, several select committees are concerned with different types of legislation:

◆ Consolidation, &c., Bills
◆ Human Rights
◆ Regulatory Reform
◆ Statutory Instruments
◆ Tax Law Rewrite Bills.

The European Scrutiny Committee might also be included in this list, but as it deals with a wide range of EU policy matters as well as legislation, we have treated it as a cross-cutting committee.

The *Joint Committee on Consolidation, &c., Bills* is a joint committee of both Houses on which both MPs and peers sit (we look at joint committees more closely on page 384). Established in 1894, the committee has twenty-four members, half from each House, and is traditionally chaired by a law lord, who does much of the scrutiny work. Its task is to examine bills that 'consolidate' the law – that is, restate it in a more logical and convenient form without changing its substance, although errors and ambiguities may be corrected. Such bills are always introduced in the House of Lords rather than in the House of Commons. The committee considers the form rather than the merits of legislation. It meets only when a bill is referred to it: only four times in the seven sessions 1998–2005.

Following the enactment of the Human Rights Act 1998, the *Joint Committee on Human Rights* was appointed in 2001. It has a general remit to consider matters relating to human rights in the United Kingdom (but not individual cases), and in 2004–05 its inquiries included deaths in custody and UK compliance with the UN Convention against Torture. It also has an important role in legislation. It examines every government bill as soon as possible after introduction to see whether the bill, if enacted, might risk violating a human right, and it reports its views to both Houses. The committee also examines proposals for, and drafts of, remedial orders, which come about when a court finds that an Act of Parliament is incompatible with the Human Rights Act, and amendment of the legislation is necessary (see page 262).

This joint committee has twelve members, six from each House, and is chaired by a Labour MP (but the government does not have a majority on the committee). It is an active committee; in the 2001 parliament it met 106 times and issued eighty-six reports. Its staff includes an eminent human rights expert as legal adviser.

The *Regulatory Reform Committee* is a Commons select committee (the Lords equivalent is the Delegated Powers and Regulatory Reform Committee), consisting of eighteen MPs. The committee considers proposals and draft orders under the Regulatory Reform Act 2001; this process is described in Chapter 7 (page 261). Its staff include legal advisers.

The *Joint Committee on Statutory Instruments* is responsible for examining the technical aspects of delegated legislation rather than its merits – unlike the new sifting committee in the House of Lords (see page 259). It has seven members from each House with an opposition MP as chairman; it normally meets weekly when Parliament is sitting, but it reports only when it wishes to draw the attention of both Houses to some defect in a statutory instrument. The analysis of well over a thousand statutory instruments each year is carried out by a staff that includes three specialist lawyers. Delegated legislation on financial matters, which is laid only before the House of Commons, is examined by the *Select Committee on Statutory Instruments*, consisting of the seven Commons members of the joint committee. Delegated legislation is described in more detail in Chapter 7 (page 252).

The *Tax Law Rewrite Committee* is another joint committee, of fourteen members and chaired by an opposition MP (the former Conservative Chancellor of the Exchequer, Kenneth Clarke). It was set up in January 2001 to consider bills that simplify the law on taxation but, as with consolidation bills, do not make changes of substance.

Internal committees

These committees are concerned with the way the House and its members work, both procedurally and administratively:

◆ Modernisation of the House of Commons
◆ Procedure
◆ Selection
◆ Standards and Privileges
◆ Administration
◆ Finance and Services.

The Select Committee on the Modernisation of the House of Commons

The Modernisation Committee was set up in June 1997, a month after the general election at which the Labour government was returned. The Leader of the House, Ann Taylor, became chairman, and the committee of fifteen members also contained her Conservative and Liberal Democrat counterparts. The committee's task is 'to consider how the practices and procedures of the House should be modernised, and to make recommendations'. The committee was set up for the length of the 1997 parliament and was reappointed in 2001, again for the length of the parliament. On the grounds that there is already a wealth of opinion – perhaps too much! – expressed on the subject of reform of the House of Commons, the committee has proceeded largely through discussion and informal talks with MPs, Clerks and others rather than taking formal oral and written evidence.

The Modernisation Committee has produced reports on the legislative process and programming, the scrutiny of European business, the parliamentary calendar and sitting hours, sittings in Westminster Hall and connecting Parliament and the public. The fact that – very unusually for a select committee – it is chaired by a Cabinet minister has meant that its recommendations already carry some sort of government stamp of approval, although not all have been implemented (its proposal of a more open and independent way of choosing members of select committees, backed by Robin Cook, was defeated in the House).

We examine modernisation issues in greater detail in the final chapter of this book.

The Procedure Committee

Procedure Committees used to be appointed ad hoc to examine particular aspects of the House's business, or to address some problem. A Procedure Committee was appointed in each parliament from 1979, but the committee did not become permanent until 1997. The committee has thirteen members, and it has the job of considering the practice and procedure of the House in the conduct of public business (so not including private legislation – see page 249) and making recommendations.

The committee considers matters that are referred to it, usually informally by the Speaker or the government rather than formally by decision of the House. It also chooses its own subjects for investigation, although these are often picked because the committee is aware of a general feeling that some topic needs examination. There is inevitably an overlap with the work of the Modernisation Committee (although the chairman of the Procedure Committee is also a member of Modernisation). Over the last five years, the committee has reported on such things as delegated legislation, early day motions, parliamentary questions and the method of election of a Speaker (after the day-long process to elect a successor to Betty Boothroyd in 2000). Its recommendations on the last two subjects were substantially implemented, but it does not have the fast track to implementation that the Modernisation Committee usually enjoys through its connection with government.

The Committee of Selection

The main task of this committee, which meets weekly while the House is sitting, is to select MPs to serve on standing committees on bills and statutory instruments and private bill committees. At the beginning of a parliament it also puts forward names of MPs to serve on all the permanent select committees (except for Liaison and Standards and Privileges), and it nominates any replacements needed thereafter. It has nine members, six or seven of whom are whips. As we will see later (page 360), the involvement of government whips in the selection of MPs for committees that scrutinise government has been the cause of some criticism.

The Committee on Standards and Privileges
The committee was first appointed in 1996, combining the ancient institution of a Privileges Committee with the modern (from 1974) Committee on Members' Interests. The committee has ten members and is chaired by a senior opposition back-bencher. Most of its work has been concerned with MPs' conduct, although it also investigates and reports on any complaint of privilege referred to it by the House (see page 184). It works closely with the Parliamentary Commissioner for Standards (see page 129), considers his reports on complaints against MPs, taking evidence if necessary, and recommends to the House what action (such as suspending an MP for a specified period or withholding salary) should be taken. The committee also oversees the operation of the rules of conduct, and the compilation and publication of the registers of interests. It has the power to set up sub-committees, but has not done so.

Unusually, it has the power to order an MP to give evidence to it, or to produce documents; most committees have these powers only in respect of people who are not members of either House.

The Finance and Services Committee and the Administration Committee
As we saw in Chapter 3 (page 60), the *Finance and Services Committee* (usually known as 'F&S') advises the House of Commons Commission on the financial and business plans of the House administration. The Committee is chaired by a member of the Commission and has ten other members. The sixteen-member *Administration Committee* reflects the views of MPs generally in the planning and provision of services provided to and by the House. Their role is to advise the Speaker and the Commission.

Ad hoc committees

The House can set up new committees at any time, although the formal initiative to do so is invariably a motion moved by the government (in the nineteenth century and earlier, this was not the case; the Sebastopol Committee described earlier was appointed in the teeth of ministerial opposition, and the approval of the motion to set it up finished the government led by Lord Aberdeen).

In the more recent past, such ad hoc committees have considered domestic matters such as MPs' pay (1980–82) the televising of the House (1988–90), the sitting hours of the House (the 'Jopling Committee'), and matters of public policy such as the royal family's pay and expenses (1971–72), a possible 'wealth tax' (1974–75), abortion (1974–75) and violence in the family (1975–76). The existence of the Modernisation Committee and the Procedure Committee means that select committees are now less likely to be set up to consider individual in-House issues; and the existence of the departmental committees (two or more of which are able to conduct joint inquiries if they wish) means that select committees are also less likely to be appointed to consider specific issues of public policy. However, from time to time, special circumstances arise, usually when a particular subject affects both Houses (see page 384 for the joint committees on parliamentary privilege and Lords reform).

These days, most ad hoc committees are appointed to consider bills or draft bills. In 2004 and 2005, the Gambling Bill, the Charities Bill, the Mental Health Bill, the Disability Discrimination Bill and the draft Children (Contact) and Adoption Bill were examined in draft by ad hoc committees. Other draft bills were considered by departmental select committees (see page 372).

The Intelligence and Security Committee

One committee is often referred to by the media as a 'select committee' or a 'parliamentary committee' but in fact is neither. The Intelligence and Security Committee was set up under the Intelligence Services Act 1994. It consists of eight MPs and one peer, all back-benchers, and at present is chaired by Paul Murphy, the former Labour Secretary of State for Northern Ireland. Although its members are parliamentarians, they are chosen by the Prime Minister and not by Parliament, and it reports to the Prime Minister, not to Parliament (although its reports are presented to Parliament by the Prime Minister once sensitive material has been excised). The staff of the committee are civil servants and not servants of the legislature.

Although the committee has shown considerable independence of view (for example in its reports on the intelligence aspects of the Bali bombings and Iraqi weapons of mass destruction), there has been increasing pressure to have oversight of intelligence matters undertaken by a genuine select or joint committee directly responsible to Parliament. In its report on the decision to go to war in Iraq, the Foreign Affairs Select Committee recommended that the Intelligence and Security Committee be recast as a select committee of the House of Commons; this was endorsed in principle by the Foreign Secretary in his evidence to the committee, but there has been no sign of a change.

How committees work

Although in this section we have a departmental committee particularly in mind, most of it applies to most select committees.

Orders of reference and powers

A committee's task is set out in its *orders of reference*, which also define its powers and specify how many members it shall have. In the case of permanent committees, these orders of reference will be in the House's standing orders; but the House can set up a committee for as long or short a time as it sees fit and can give it other tasks or instructions (such as reporting by a certain date).

As the committee remits quoted in this chapter demonstrate, tasks are usually widely defined: 'to examine expenditure, administration and policy' or 'how the practices and procedures of the House should be modernised', although committees such as those on statutory instruments or regulatory reform are much more circumscribed. Most committees thus have a good deal of latitude; and it is also a basic principle that (subject to any instruction from the House) the interpretation of their orders of reference is a matter for them. Committees generally do not take kindly to being told by the government or by witnesses that they should not be looking at this or that subject; indeed, such comments are normally entirely counter-productive.

Committees are subordinate bodies of the House; they have only those powers that the House gives them and cannot exercise any power that the House itself does not have. The normal menu is 'to adjourn from place to place', which means that they do not have to sit only at Westminster ('within the United Kingdom' is added for those committees that may not travel abroad); to report 'from time to time', which means that they may continue reporting on their subject area rather than making one report at the end of their work; to appoint specialist advisers; (in most cases) to appoint one or more sub-committees; to exchange evidence with other committees (and with the Scottish Parliament, the National Assembly for Wales and the Northern Ireland Assembly); and to meet jointly with any other committee of either House. This last power provides a good deal of flexibility when a subject affects several committees: for example, the Defence, Foreign Affairs, International Development and Trade and Industry Committees have formed what is in effect a joint committee on arms exports (known as the 'Quadripartite Committee').

The power of compulsion

A key phrase in a committee's powers is 'to send for persons, papers and records' (known as 'PPR'). This means that they have the formal power to compel witnesses 'within the jurisdiction' (that is, within the UK) to attend, answer questions and deliver up any papers that the committee may wish to see.

Most witnesses before select committees are willing, even enthusiastic; they want the opportunity to make their case on a very public stage. But some are not, for a variety of reasons from a generalised reluctance to answer a committee's questions to having something discreditable or damaging to hide. In such cases, the committee may make an order to attend (or produce documents), which is served personally on the witness. If he or she does not comply, the committee may report the matter to the House as a breach of privilege. But there are disadvantages to this: the matter is put into a wider political forum, which means that the committee loses control of events; the procedure is cumbersome; and – especially if the matter becomes a party political football – there is no guarantee that the committee in the end will get what it wants.

A select committee's strongest weapon is publicity rather than the use of formal powers. A recalcitrant witness looks as though he or she has something to hide; the trick is for the committee to make *not* giving evidence more embarrassing or awkward than acceding to the committee's request.

Ministers and civil servants have a special status that occasionally leads to conflict with select committees. Civil servants are agents of their secretary of state and carry out his or her instructions; they cannot be forced to divulge information against the secretary of state's wishes. A committee can ask a minister for information but (although the 'embarrassment factor' can come into play here as well) cannot demand it. The House could do so (technically by an address to the Crown, because the information is in the hands of Her Majesty's ministers), but the House does not delegate this power to select committees.

There have been celebrated tussles between investigating select committees and reluctant governments. In its investigation of the Westland Affair in 1986, the Defence Committee sought to interview the civil servants most closely involved with the selective leaking of an opinion of the Solicitor-General. The government refused to allow them to attend, but the Cabinet Secretary appeared twice before the committee, which – because of the political pressure building on the government – also secured internal government documents that had previously been refused. Although the government's internal guidance states that, when there is disagreement between a minister and a committee about the attendance of a civil servant, the minister should appear personally (and in 1990 the then Cabinet Secretary said that a civil servant called by a select committee had a duty to attend), this issue is still an occasional source of friction. In 2003, for example, in its investigation of the decision to go to war in Iraq, the Foreign Affairs Committee was critical of the government for not allowing intelligence personnel to appear before it. More recently, the Transport and Public Administration Committees tried unsuccessfully to secure the attendance of the Prime Minister's 'blue skies' policy adviser Lord Birt.

The degree of disclosure of internal government documents to Lord Hutton's inquiry into the death of Dr David Kelly in 2003 compared unfavourably with the terms on which select committees get information; we look at the implications in Chapter 13 (page 426).

Membership

Almost all members of select committee are back-bench MPs; the most notable exception is the Leader of the House as chairman of the Modernisation Committee. Committees normally consist of between nine and eighteen MPs in as near as possible the party proportions in the House as a whole; thus, in the 2005 parliament, a committee of eleven usually had six Labour, four (or three) Conservative and one (or two) Liberal Democrat or other third party member. Once MPs are put on a committee, they remain on it for the whole of a parliament, unless they resign or become ministers or front-bench spokesmen.

The quorum of a committee – the number of members who must be present for business to be transacted – is three or a quarter of the number of members, whichever is the larger, with fractions counted as one.

MPs are appointed to committees by a motion put to the House (normally without debate). The names come either from the usual channels (see page 100) and the motion is in the name of the government Deputy Chief Whip; or (in the case of almost all permanent select committees) they are proposed by the Committee of Selection and the motion is in the name of a member of that committee. Either way, there has been suspicion that the whips exercise too much control over which MPs get on to committees; and criticism of the fact that government whips have a hand in selecting MPs whose job on the departmental committees is to scrutinise government – and would have an interest in picking MPs they thought would be less critical or independent-minded.

For many people, these suspicions were confirmed when, at the start of the 2001 parliament, the Committee of Selection did not put forward the names of two notably independent chairmen of committees in the previous parliament, the Labour MPs Gwyneth Dunwoody (Transport) and Donald Anderson (Foreign Affairs). This caused a row, and the names that were proposed for these committees were defeated in the House by substantial majorities. Dunwoody and Anderson were then reinstated.

However, a proposal from the Liaison Committee, later taken up by Robin Cook and the Modernisation Committee, that there should be an entirely open system in which the whips would not be involved, was narrowly defeated in the House in May 2002 – as some thought, as the result of an unholy alliance of the whips on *both* sides of the House. In fact, as we shall see, the way that committees work encourages MPs to be independent-minded, and it is remarkable how many conventional government supporters 'go native' when they are put on select committees.

Chairmen

Committees elect their own chairmen ('chairman' rather than 'chair' is the word used formally in both Houses). Although among the MPs put on a committee at the start of a parliament there is an obvious (or agreed) candidate for the chair, from time to time committees exercise their independence and elect someone else. Negotiation through 'the usual channels' results in a division of chairmanships between the parties that roughly corresponds to the party proportions in the House, although the governing party is always keen to have the chairmanships of committees that it sees as especially important: for example, Foreign Affairs, Home Affairs and Treasury. In the 2005 parliament, of the eighteen chairmanships of departmental committees, the Labour Party had ten, the Conservatives five and the Liberal Democrats three; and of the cross-cutting committees, the Labour Party had three chairmanships and the Conservatives two. Under a rule introduced in 2002, no MP may be elected chairman of a committee that she or he has chaired for the two previous parliaments, or for eight years, whichever is the longer.

The chairman is the key figure on any select committee. She or he takes a full part in the committee's work (unlike the chairman of a standing committee, who presides impartially over proceedings) and is usually the committee's spokesperson. The committee itself decides subjects for investigation and what witnesses to call, but the chairman's views will be highly influential; and, although chairmen have varying inputs into committees' reports, the draft considered by the committee is almost always in the chairman's name.

Styles of chairmanship vary: some are less interventionist 'chairmen of the board'; others are much more 'managing directors' driving the committee's work. Whichever style they adopt, the role of a good chairman is crucial in keeping the committee together: giving all its members a chance, promoting consensus, foreseeing political problems, establishing good – but not cosy – relationships with ministers in the relevant department, and providing leadership when the going gets tough.

The 1978 recommendation of the Procedure Committee that chairmen should be paid resurfaced in 2003 as a result of a Liaison Committee recommendation that the matter should be examined by the Senior Salaries Review Body. The latter's report recommended that, in recognition of their additional responsibilities, the chairmen of the main investigative and legislative committees should be paid in addition to their salaries as MPs. This was approved by the House; but some chairmen are strongly opposed to the principle, and do not draw the additional pay (at present £13,107 a year).

There is no formal post of 'deputy chairman'. If the chairman is absent, then the senior opposition MP (or government MP if the chairman is from an opposition party) often takes the chair; but the committee can decide to put any of its members in the chair on a temporary basis.

Staff

Select committees are supported by small teams of staff from the Department of the Clerk of the House; some thirty investigative committees are supported by about 160 staff in the Committee Office. A departmental select committee usually has five or six full-time staff. They are led by the *Clerk of the Committee*, usually a deputy principal clerk (equivalent to a Band

1 official in the senior Civil Service – what used to be called Assistant Secretary/Grade 5) with fifteen to twenty years of experience in the service of the House. In a nutshell, the Clerk's job is to help the committee to be as effective as possible in doing the job the House has given it. He or she is the committee's principal adviser, manages the staff team and the specialist advisers, works closely with the chairman on all aspects of the committee's work, and will be responsible for some of the committee's inquiries. *The Second Clerk* manages inquiries and will usually clerk any sub-committee. One or two *committee specialists*, subject experts on short-term contracts, provide in-depth research and briefing. The *committee assistant* is primarily an administrator, supervising arrangements for hearings and committee visits, and overseeing printing and publication of evidence. The *secretary* is a specialist desktop publisher; even substantial committee reports are published extraordinarily quickly; sometimes agreed one afternoon and published by The Stationery Office, and posted on the parliamentary website, the next morning.

The permanent staff are augmented by *specialist advisers*, who work to the Clerk of the Committee. They are people, often of great eminence, who assist the committee part time and are paid on a daily rate. This is a flexible and effective system; a committee can draw on a lifetime's experience in the precise area of what may be a very technical or complex inquiry. Some committees maintain panels of a dozen or fifteen advisers; others appoint one or two for specific inquiries. There are normally about 150 specialist advisers at any one time.

Committees also draw on the resources of the *Scrutiny Unit*, a group of sixteen staff who specialise in the analysis of estimates, departmental annual reports (see page 280) and other financial information; and also in the scrutiny of draft legislation (which allows a committee to deal at short notice with a draft bill without having its programme of work blown off course).

A committee's work

Select committees always meet in private except when they are taking oral evidence; as we shall see later, this has advantages. When a committee meets for the first time at the start of a parliament, its members first make a formal declaration of their registered interests. The chairman is then elected, and the next business is to agree a programme of work. The Clerk will put proposals before the committee: work outstanding from the last parliament; current and expected events in the subject area (including possible draft bills); previous recommendations on which the committee needs to maintain pressure; policies still in the process of formation, where the committee could have an influence; or perhaps some serious problem where the committee needs to keep up with developments. The chairman and committee members will have their own suggestions; and the committee will then agree and announce its programme of work.

In addition, the House has set *core tasks* for departmental select committees. These are listed on pages 372 to 374 together with examples of activity on each.

A typical inquiry

Just as a departmental select committee has wide discretion about *what* it investigates, so it also has great flexibility about *how* it does so. Inquiries may range from an in-depth examination of a complex subject lasting several months to a short sharp inquiry carried out in a week, perhaps with five or six oral evidence hearings crammed into that time. Inquiries may aim to analyse and influence a developing policy, to review a whole subject area, to carry out a 'what went wrong' investigation, or to look at a topical issue of the moment.

Most formal inquiries lead to reports to the House, but a committee may take evidence without reporting; and most committees hold regular one-off evidence sessions with public bodies, chief inspectors or regulators within their area, or with ministers or senior officials on current issues. However, let us take as an example a typical 'subject area' inquiry.

The start of an inquiry

The committee decides on a subject – let us say the government's policy towards domestic violence. The committee approves terms of reference for the inquiry, which are really to help potential witnesses who want to know what the main areas of interest will be – they do not bind the committee. Indeed, once an inquiry is under way, its focus often changes as the committee identifies particular aspects as more important. The committee publishes a press notice about the inquiry, and it may also circulate an 'issues and questions' paper to stimulate debate and the submission of evidence. Both will be put on the parliamentary website.

As well as issuing a general invitation to submit evidence, the committee will make more specific requests for written evidence (often called 'memoranda'). For our example of an inquiry into domestic violence, several government departments – the Home Office, the Department of Health, the Department for Education and Skills, the Department for Constitutional Affairs and the Office of the Deputy Prime Minister – are involved in different aspects of the subject. The committee may ask each department to prepare a paper on its own area of responsibility, or more likely (and to test coordination between the departments) will ask the government to provide a single paper addressing a series of written questions. At the same time, requests for evidence will go out to other key players: the NHS, the British Medical Association as representing GPs, the NSPCC, and national organisations representing social service providers, the police, and support groups for those who have suffered domestic violence.

The committee will at the same time draw up a list of likely witnesses. A programme of oral evidence often begins and ends with the responsible ministers; and there will be other obvious candidates to appear. However, committees try to make the process as open as possible, not limiting it to 'the usual suspects'; and on the basis of the written evidence that comes in – often not formal papers from prominent organisations but letters from local organisations or individuals who have heard about the inquiry – will select other people to give evidence. Several weeks after the call for written evidence first went out, the first oral evidence hearing takes place.

Taking evidence

The members of the committee sit around a horseshoe-shaped table with the chairman at the head and the clerk on his or her left (see page 367). Reflecting the more consensual approach in select committees, the members often do not sit by party affiliation (unlike standing committees). Witnesses sit at a table between the arms of the horseshoe. The shorthand writers who take a verbatim record of the evidence sit in the middle.

The MPs on the committee will have a detailed brief prepared by the committee staff. This will cover the background to the hearing, the key points from the witness's written evidence, including areas that could be explored further, anything that the committee especially needs to get on the record for its eventual report, and a list of suggested questions for the witness. The committee will often tell witnesses in advance the areas it wants to cover, but it does not normally give notice of particular questions unless some time for preparation would be needed to provide a full answer. The chairman opens the questioning, and other MPs follow. An oral evidence session usually lasts two to two and a half hours, but several witnesses,

The Commons Health Committee taking evidence from Home Office and Health ministers about changing the law on smoking in public places, November 2005

Source: Deryc R. Sands; House of Commons 2005

singly or in groups, may appear during that time. The hearing may be televised live, webcast, broadcast in sound only, or recorded. Seats are provided for the public and the press.

The vast majority of evidence is given in public, but committees can take evidence in private, usually if matters of personal or commercial confidentiality, or national security, are involved. Select committees, mainly the Defence Committee and the Foreign Affairs Committee, have dealt with national security or 'classified' material up to the highest levels of sensitivity.

Most hearings are fairly relaxed; the process is one of exploration and discussion of a subject about which the witnesses have special knowledge, on which the committee wants to draw. However, some hearings, usually if a committee is investigating something that has gone wrong, or where it believes that a government department or other witness is not being open, can be more adversarial. Committees can take evidence on oath if they wish, although this is extremely rare.

Those giving evidence before a select committee are taking part in a proceeding in Parliament (see page 180), so they are fully protected by parliamentary privilege – that is, neither their oral nor their written evidence may give rise to a criminal prosecution or civil action, nor, for example, to disciplinary action by an employer.

A few days after giving evidence, witnesses are sent a transcript to correct for accuracy; they can also add to answers in writing if they wish. Uncorrected transcripts are often published on the Internet as soon as they are available and are replaced with the final corrected version thereafter.

As the inquiry progresses, the committee will be following up oral evidence with requests for further papers, the staff will be researching other sources of information or possible evidence, and some thought will be given to possible visits.

Travel

Travel by select committees often gets a hard time in the media – but it contributes a great deal to a committee's effectiveness. In the inquiry example we have taken here, the committee will want to make visits within the UK, perhaps to see shelters for the victims of domestic violence in different parts of the country, to talk to social services, the police, GPs and support groups on their home ground, and possibly to take oral evidence as well. Visits make a select committee inquiry more accessible: not only do they bring the committee to a local community, but they also mean that people can talk informally to the MPs rather than giving evidence in the often daunting surroundings of Westminster.

Visits also mean that MPs see and hear for themselves; the often rather impersonal formal evidence is supplemented by the first-hand experience and opinions of the people actually involved, and a suggestion or criticism by a single individual often finds its way into the committee's final report.

Travel overseas plays a similar part. It may be that policy on domestic violence in Sweden, say, is better coordinated than in the UK; or that the Canadians have the most effective risk registers and techniques for early warning of violence. No amount of background reading and written evidence is a substitute for seeing for oneself, and finding out first-hand about the benefits and the problems.

The report

Towards the end of an inquiry, the Clerk of the Committee will usually prepare a 'heads of report' paper – identifying the possible main themes of the report and recommendations, and questions on which the committee itself

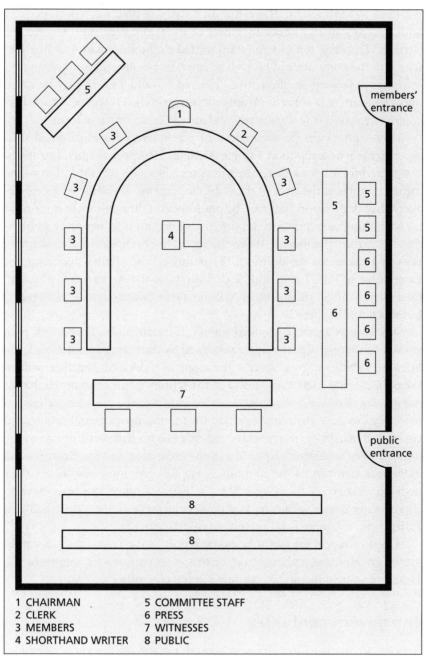

1 CHAIRMAN
2 CLERK
3 MEMBERS
4 SHORTHAND WRITER
5 COMMITTEE STAFF
6 PRESS
7 WITNESSES
8 PUBLIC

The layout of a select committee room

will need to form a view. Thereafter the Clerk will draft the report, perhaps
with the assistance of other members of the committee staff or specialist
advisers. The draft report will be submitted to the chairman and then presented to the committee in his or her name. In a contentious inquiry, other
members may want an alternative draft report (and a Clerk may be called
upon to draft two entirely incompatible reports!). However, most select
committee reports are unanimous and are the more effective for it.

Most committees go through draft reports very informally and then
agree to the whole report as a single decision. However, if amendments are
considered formally or there are any votes, these are set out in full in the
formal minutes at the back of the published report. The same is true of any
alternative draft report that may be put forward (although there is formally
no such thing as a 'minority report', the same aim is achieved by publication in the formal minutes). When the report has been agreed, the chairman
puts two questions for decision: 'That this be the [Fifth] Report of the
Committee to the House' and 'That I do make the Report to the House'.
One often hears in the media of MPs on a committee 'signing' the report;
but this never happens.

Shortly after a report is agreed – and it is usually in the next day or two,
as even substantial reports can be produced by the committee staff and The
Stationery Office at great speed – the report is published, together with all
the public oral evidence and many of the written papers submitted during
the inquiry. 'Embargoed' copies are often issued to the press beforehand so
that they can have their stories ready for the moment of publication; and
copies will usually go to witnesses and others who have contributed to the
inquiry. The committee may hold a press conference; and the chairman and
individual members of the committee will also give interviews to get their
own perspective on the record. (In a sensitive inquiry, they may have to
choose their words with care, as a press conference is not a proceeding in
Parliament, and there is no protection of privilege.)

A type of report known as 'a special report' is used as a vehicle for publishing government replies to committees, or sometimes for informing the
House of some difficulty encountered in the committee's work.

The government reply

Reports are made to the House, although the intended audience includes
everyone concerned with the subject, the media and – crucially – the government. Every select committee report should receive a formal government
reply within two months. This is a convention rather than a formal rule, but

committees have found that asking the minister concerned to appear to explain a delay often means the rapid appearance of the reply.

No one expects a government to put on sackcloth and ashes in this formal reply. If the committee has been highly critical, the government is more likely to be defensive and to restate its case than to say 'it's a fair cop'. If the committee has put forward challenging recommendations, the government is likely to be cautious rather than to accept them right away. But the 'delayed drop' effect of select committee reports should never be underestimated. Ambitious recommendations may change the whole public debate on a subject; they may be taken up by public bodies and pressure groups; and months (or sometimes two or three years) later they may contribute substantially to a major shift in government policy. Similarly, the effect of justified criticism may not be immediately apparent; but a department may be quietly changing its procedures to avoid making the same mistake again.

Whatever the contents of the government reply, committees are more influential if they follow up on their reports. Most departmental select committees have a 'continuous agenda' in which major policy issues recur, but returning to the detail of previous recommendations, and pursuing vague promises or non-committal responses through further inquiries, maintains the pressure and keeps the subject in the public eye.

Consensus

Select committees seem to be held in generally high regard – perhaps more than anything else that Parliament does. There may be several reasons for this: they provide access to the political process; they provide challenge and an alternative point of view; but probably most of all they show how politicians of different parties can work together.

There is no doubt that unanimous committees are more effective. They speak with a single voice, and it is much harder for governments to dismiss cross-party agreement. Some people see consensus as implying flabby compromise, but select committees show time and again that they can reach a tough agreed view on politically hot subjects. Given that select committees are made up of party politicians, how does this happen?

There are three main reasons. *First*, when they are not taking public oral evidence, *select committees meet in private*. Their discussions, working papers and draft reports are private. This means that it is much harder for party political pressure to be put on them – for example, by the whips – and it also means that the MPs can be remarkably frank with each other. For example, an individual back-bencher can put forward ideas totally at odds with party (or government) policy; and the readiness to see the other side of the argument is a key factor in getting cross-party agreement.

Second, the members of a select committee usually get to know each other well (even if, as can happen in a House of 646 members, they have never spoken to each other before the committee's first meeting). They will work together over many months, both formally and informally; there will be a good basis for trust; and they will then often see themselves as members of the committee more than as party representatives.

Third, select committees proceed on the basis of evidence (as shown by the wealth of footnotes in most select committee reports!). They do this because basing their conclusions firmly on evidence is part of the due process of investigation, but also because recommendations firmly grounded in fact, and explicitly supported by expert opinion, are much harder to challenge. This approach also helps to maintain consensus; a weight of evidence can lead MPs on a committee to agree on a conclusion even if it does not match their previous personal opinions.

Dealing with a select committee

As more and more people in all walks of life come into contact with the work of select committees, it may be helpful to say something about how to have an input into an inquiry (a fuller guide for witnesses is available on the parliamentary website together with a 'select committee calendar' showing current enquiries and planned meetings).

First, make sure that what you want to say is relevant to the committee's work. Look at the press notice and any issues and questions (on the website), and see what ground the inquiry will cover. If you are submitting written evidence – and this goes for government departments and some major national bodies as well as individuals – do not simply top and tail a paper prepared for some other purpose; make sure it is tailored to the requirements of the inquiry. If the inquiry is already under way, look on the committee's home page at transcripts that have already been published to see what the government and other bodies are saying to the committee. You may also be able to follow an inquiry via the BBC Parliament channel or, increasingly, through webcasts.

Keep written evidence concise and to the point; number the paragraphs and, for more than two pages or so, begin with a summary of what the paper says (and a table of contents if necessary). Say if you want any part of the paper to be kept confidential. An address for written evidence will be on the committee's home page. Committees prefer if possible to have written evidence electronically (in MS Word or rich text format) by e-mail attachment to the committee's mail-box address (on the press notice), with a hard-copy letter validating the e-mail, or on disk. Once you submit written evidence it becomes a committee document and, if you want to use it publicly before the committee publishes it, you should seek permission (which is almost always given).

You can ask to give oral evidence, but remember that the committee will have a full programme for the inquiry and will certainly not be able to accommodate all those who wish to do so. A witness who submits a constructive written paper, which suggests solutions rather than simply rehearsing criticism, may be more likely to be called to give oral evidence. If you are called, the committee staff will talk to you about the details and will usually be able to give you an indication of the committee's likely areas of interest. Let them know if you need disabled access.

When you appear, do not expect to be able to make an opening statement; this is better done in writing in advance, as most committees want to get straight on with questioning. The MPs on the committee will all have name-plates in front of them, but it is best to address your answers to the chair. Remember that giving oral evidence (or submitting a written paper) is not the one and only chance to contribute. You can provide additional information in writing (for example if you feel you did not answer a question fully) or comment on the evidence given by someone else. If you want to give any of your evidence in private, talk to the Clerk of the Committee well before your appearance. If you have a disability, you may want to let the committee staff know.

Whether you are contributing to an inquiry or not, you can attend the public hearings (subject to there being space; it is not possible to book seats in advance) either in the Palace of Westminster itself or in Portcullis House, or if a select committee takes evidence elsewhere in the UK.

Select committee activity

Activity is at a high level. Formal meetings of select committees (not including informal meetings, seminars and visits) are running at about 1,300 a year, of which some 500 are public evidence hearings. On average, about 375 MPs are members of select committees of one sort or another. With the advent of Westminster Hall (see page 296) there is more debate on select committee reports in addition to the three estimates days in the Chamber (see page 277); and there has been a noticeable increase in the use of committee reports in major debates in the House, as well as in Question Time, including Prime Minister's Questions.

Investigative select committees are also engaging in a wider range of activity. They hold seminars, often with outside experts, to focus and plan major inquiries; they undertake scrutiny of legislation; they have made a start on examining major public appointments and, although there is resistance in government to this sort of process, it is likely to spread. Committees have also widened political debate, taking evidence from opposition spokespeople on their alternative policies as well as from government ministers.

Particularly in the context of the core tasks and with the help of the Scrutiny Unit, committees now conduct more financial scrutiny of government departments, including estimates, annual reports and performance targets, than ever before. There is more 'joined-up scrutiny', for example on European issues between the European Scrutiny Committee and the departmental select committees. Committees themselves have become more accountable, publishing annual reports on their work, and how they have tackled the core tasks.

These core tasks are a good starting point for a look at the sorts of things select committees were doing in the months leading up to the 2005 general election. In each case, the examples give only a flavour of the range of activity.

What are select committees doing?

Task 1: scrutiny of policy proposals. Select committees carried out critical examination of the government's proposals for a Supreme Court; for changes in lottery licensing and regulation; on future defence capabilities; on identity cards; on company law; on health and safety; and on the reorganisation of fire and rescue services.

Task 2: identification and examination of areas of emerging or deficient policy. Here the Defence Committee carried out an inquiry into *the duty of care* in the wake of the deaths of army recruits at Deepcut; the Education and Skills Committee, in *Education outside the Classroom,* looked at the factors dissuading teachers from organising school trips; the Public Administration Committee published its proposals for *Reforming the Honours System;* and the Transport Committee's inquiry into *the Future of the Railway* was prompted by concerns about spiralling costs and poor performance.

Task 3: scrutinising draft bills. Departmental select committees scrutinised draft bills on animal welfare, the proposed Criminal Defence Service, identity cards, criminal justice in Northern Ireland, school transport, transport in

Wales and regional assemblies. Joint committees of both Houses examined draft bills on charities, disability discrimination and mental health. In almost every case the bills that were thereafter put before Parliament had been substantially changed to reflect committees' views, based on the evidence they took.

Task 4: examination of departmental decisions. Here the Quadripartite Committee (see page 358) continued its examination of licensing decisions on arms exports; and the Home Affairs Committee looked at draft sentencing guidelines, taking evidence from the Lord Chief Justice.

Task 5: scrutiny of expenditure plans and outturns. Committees focused on departmental Estimates (particularly Supplementary Estimates – see page 278) and picked out subjects for closer examination such as the Department of Work and Pensions' poor record of managing IT projects, the standard of care bought by health expenditure, the performance of the Office for National Statistics, poor financial management in the Department for Constitutional Affairs, and the costs of the UK military presence in Iraq.

Task 6: scrutinising Public Service Agreements and targets. Committees examined how government departments were performing on their PSA targets (see page 280) highlighting inadequate progress on such things as reduction of carbon emissions, child mortality rates in Africa, the protection of sites of special scientific interest, the handling of asylum applications, the rehabilitation of prisoners, and reducing the burden of regulation on business.

Task 7: monitoring the work of agencies and others. A variety of inquiries saw the Culture, Media and Sport Committee examining the BBC's Charter renewal, the ODPM Committee looking at the role and effectiveness of the Housing Corporation and of the local government ethical watchdog, the Standards Board for England. The Science and Technology Committee held separate evidence sessions with each of the seven Research Councils; and the Defence Committee picked out failings within the Defence Procurement Agency.

Task 8: scrutiny of major appointments. The Treasury Committee scrutinised appointments to the Bank of England's Monetary Policy Committee; other committees took evidence from new holders of major public appointments, quizzing them on how they were approaching their tasks. Although there is resistance in government to select committee scrutiny of public appointments, this is likely to be a growth area.

Task 9: examining the implementation of legislation. Legislation often has effects rather different from those intended, and among subjects to come under the spotlight were police anti-terrorism powers, universities charging of differential tuition fees to home and foreign students, landfill, electoral law (and fraud) in Northern Ireland, and pension credit.

Task 10: providing material for debate in Westminster Hall and the Chamber. As we have already seen (page 297) the work of select committees has been given a higher profile by an increased number of debates, which also give an opportunity to press the government on select committee recommendations and criticisms.

So far, so good. But what does all this activity achieve?

How effective are select committees?

In its March 2000 report *Shifting the Balance: Select Committees and the Executive*, the Liaison Committee said:

> *The 1979 select committee system has been a success. We have no doubt of that. At a bargain price, it has provided independent scrutiny of government. It has enabled the questioning of ministers and civil servants, and has forced them to explain policies. On occasion, it has exposed mistaken and short-sighted policies and, from time to time, wrong-doing in both high places and low. It has been a source of unbiased information, rational debate, and constructive ideas. It has made the political process less remote, and more accessible to the citizen who is affected by that process – and who pays the bill. Its very existence has been a constant reminder to Ministers and officials, and many others in positions of power and influence, of the spotlight that may swing their way when least welcome. It has also shown the House of Commons at its best: working on the basis of fact, not supposition or prejudice; and with constructive co-operation rather than routine disagreement.*

Objective measurement of the effectiveness or influence of select committees is impossible. Governments have accepted a great many select committee recommendations, even when they have not originally been disposed to do so, but it is always difficult to judge how far this has been down to the committee in each case and how far the committee has been the decisive advocate for a growing body of opinion. In 2002, for example, the government accepted the recommendation of the Home Affairs Select Committee to downgrade cannabis from a class B drug to a class C drug, but there was already some pressure for change. Had the committee come out against reclassification, on the other hand, the government would probably have used the committee's conclusion as the basis for *not* changing its policy.

Sometimes the mere fact of an inquiry leads to a change in government policy before the committee reports. To take another Home Affairs example, on the first day of hearings on the Criminal Records Bureau, the government caved in on the main issue, that of charging volunteers for criminal records checks. And public exposure can have wider influence. The mighty credit card companies found the Treasury Committee's hearings on the way they treated consumers extremely uncomfortable, and a wholesale review of their marketing practices followed.

There is no point in trying to measure effectiveness by totting up how many recommendations are accepted by the government. This process makes no distinction between 'soft' recommendations, on which the door is already ajar, and 'hard' recommendations, which have no chance of being accepted now, but which change the whole nature of public debate, and which may end up as government policy – perhaps the policy of an incoming government after a general election – months or years later (the 'delayed drop' effect referred to above).

However, having even tough recommendations accepted is not what effective scrutiny is about (although it may be one of the results). Scrutiny of government is the process of examining expenditure, administration and policy in detail, on the public record, requiring the government of the day to explain itself to parliamentarians as representatives of the citizen and the taxpayer, and to justify its actions.

This process of accountability is never comfortable for those being scrutinised; and it should not be. But the fact that the government's actions can be put under the spotlight of public examination at any time makes for better decision making; as Robin Cook when Leader of the House said, 'good scrutiny makes for good government'.

A sample of the work of just one departmental select committee over a period of eighteen months or so gives a flavour of this process. The Constitutional Affairs Committee's inquiry into the Children and Family Courts Advisory and Support Service resulted in the resignation of the entire Board; the Committee's criticism of the Asylum and Immigration (Treatment of Claimants) Bill led to the government dropping its proposal that there should be no oversight by the courts. The Committee's report on the treatment of one of its witnesses led to the Lord Chancellor having to apologise formally to the Committee on Standards and Privileges. The Committee's work on the Special Immigration Appeals Commission was influential in debate on the Prevention of Terrorism Bill (and its views were quoted by the House of Lords sitting judicially in *Roberts* v. *Parole Board*). The Committee's criticism of the government's Constitutional Reform Bill mortally wounded the government's proposal to abolish the office of Lord Chancellor, which was finished off by a Lords committee on the same subject; and major reform of criminal legal aid was rewritten as a result of the Committee's report on the draft Criminal Defence Service Bill.

In this chapter, we have described the role of Commons select committees largely in terms of scrutinising the government of the day. This accounts for much of their activity, but they also have a wider role. Their reports and recommendations may be aimed at particular public bodies, sectors of industry, or the professions. Select committees are often good at 'blue skies' thinking; they can examine some difficult topic of public policy and analyse possible courses of action – the relaxation of the law on drugs is a good example – that political parties would find more difficult. Where there is controversy about the factual basis of public debate, perhaps on a topic such as climate change or genetic engineering, a select committee is an excellent vehicle for analysing conflicting claims and setting out common ground. As with written questions (see page 333) but to an even greater degree, select committee written and oral evidence puts a mass of information, from both the government and other sources, into the public domain.

Effort equals success: the role of committee members

Whatever a select committee does, its effectiveness depends above all on its members. Their commitment and effort are crucial. As the Liaison Committee said in *Shifting the Balance*:

> *no pain, no gain: there is no easy route to success. A determined and hard-working committee, in which Members are prepared to devote substantial effort and put the interests of the citizen and taxpayer first, can be extraordinarily effective.*

MPs on select committees need an up-to-date understanding of the subject area. They do not have to be great technical experts – and indeed there is some reason for them not to be; it could be said that one of the strengths of select committees is that they are made up of well-informed lay people who can ask common-sense questions of the experts and make sure they get proper answers. Occasional attempts to browbeat witnesses for some easy headlines do nothing for the select committee system and are usually counter-productive. As a wise select committee chairman of another era used to say, 'more flies are caught with honey than with vinegar'.

On individual inquiries, members of a committee need to keep up with the written and oral evidence and to prepare for oral evidence sessions. The committee staff support the committee through briefing, and summarising and analysing evidence, but there is no substitute for individual MPs having command of the subject. Although, as we have seen in earlier chapters, there are many other calls on MPs' time, the most effective oral evidence sessions – especially with difficult and well-briefed witnesses – are those at which all the members of a committee are present throughout; are well prepared; divide up the areas of questioning between them; ask questions rather than make statements; and follow up each other's questions.

It is sometimes suggested that committees should have counsel to undertake part of the examination of witnesses. This misses the point on several counts; select committee work is a function of Parliament and should be undertaken by parliamentarians. It is also relatively rare that this sort of forensic examination is required: other types of inquiry are frequently more valuable and play to other select committee strengths.

But when forensic examination is required, a good many MPs are perfectly capable of extremely effective questioning. Anyone who saw or heard the clinical dissection of witness after witness by the Labour MP John Gilbert during the Defence Committee's inquiry into the Westland affair in 1986 will have a good idea of what is possible; but it cannot be done without hard work and a good deal of committee solidarity.

Being an effective member of a select committee is time-consuming. In its July 2003 report on pay for select committee chairmen, the Senior Salaries Review Body found that for most chairmen their select committee work occupied two days a week (or 50 per cent of the time that they spent in the House) and that for some chairmen this occupied up to 70 per cent of their time. The time commitment for members of a busy committee may not be much less. The average attendances each session for every committee are published in the Sessional Returns; it is noticeable that most of the committees generally seen as 'heavyweight' and effective have attendances around 80 per cent or higher.

A bargain price

The Liaison Committee described the achievements of the select committee system as having been 'at a bargain price'. This is still the case. Some forty-five select committees, including thirty or so investigative committees, are supported by about 160 staff (the Public Accounts Committee and the Public Administration Committee also draw upon the resources of the

Comptroller and Auditor General and the Ombudsman respectively). Staff costs are about £6.5 million a year, and all other costs, including printing, shorthand recording and transcription of evidence, specialist advisers, travel, and work commissioned, amount to a little over £4 million. 'Bargain' seems a fair description.

Select committees in the House of Lords

The committees

Since the early 1970s, the House of Lords has also developed an increasingly elaborate array of select committees reappointed every session to scrutinise various aspects of public policy. (For legislative committees, see page 235, and for domestic committees see page 75.) Some of these policy scrutiny committees enjoy a high reputation. Unlike the Commons, the Lords committee structure developed in a way that was thematic and cross-cutting rather than departmental, and there is now general acceptance that this enables Lords committee work to complement rather than compete with or duplicate that of the Commons.

The most elaborate of these committees is the European Union Committee, with its seven sub-committees, the work of which is described in the next chapter. A Science and Technology Committee, with two sub-committees, considers aspects of science policy and includes distinguished scientists amongst its members.

Since 2001, further committees have been established, not least because an expansion of select committee work has appealed to those interested in reform of the House. So, after the 2001 general election, an Economic Affairs Committee was established as a successor to what had originally been an ad hoc select committee on the Monetary Policy Committee of the Bank of England. In November 2002, this committee was empowered to set up a sub-committee in the expectation that it would consider policy aspects of the Finance Bill (other than the rates and incidence of tax). This was done for the 2003 Finance Bill and has continued since.

A Constitution Committee was also set up in February 2001, both to carry out policy inquiries and to examine and report on all public bills for any constitutional implications.

In addition, the House from time to time sets up committees to consider the merits of public bills. These are usually private members' bills that raise important policy issues such as the two charities bills in 1983, the

European Union Select Committee hears evidence from Rt Hon John Hutton MP, Chancellor of the Duchy of Lancaster, on effective regulation in the EU, May 2005
Source: The House of Lords 2005, Terry Moore

Infant Life Preservation Bill in 1987–88 or the Assisted Dying for the Terminally Ill Bill in 2004–05. Government bills are not committed to a select committee because of the delay that would be caused, so the setting up of a committee on the Constitutional Reform Bill in 2004 was most unusual. Select committees are also appointed to consider policy matters. In 1985, a committee considered overseas trade, particularly the trade deficit in manufactured goods, and in 1993–94 another considered medical ethics, specifically euthanasia; in 2001, one committee examined embryonic stem cell research, while another considered animal experimentation; in 2002–03 another looked at religious offences, and blasphemy in particular; and in 2005–06 another scrutinised the review of the BBC Charter. Such committees are not normally expected to continue in existence for longer than one session and usually try to fulfil their orders of reference in that time. Ad hoc select committees on matters of public interest are now regularly appointed annually.

One recent committee does not quite fit in with the general run of ad hoc committee activity and deserves brief mention by virtue of the oddity of both its subject matter and the manner of its being set up – the Select Committee on the Crash of Chinook Helicopter ZD576 on 2 June 1994. The pilots had been found grossly negligent by the RAF Board of Inquiry. On the motion of Lord Chalfont, a cross-bench member, the House agreed that the Liaison Committee (the work of this committee is discussed below) should consider appointing a select committee to consider the circumstances of the crash. Not surprisingly, the Liaison Committee took the view that select committees were not equipped to undertake quasi-judicial inquiries, and a precedent might be set. The Liaison Committee's advice was rejected by the House on a vote in March 2001, and a committee was then set up chaired by a Lord of Appeal. In January 2002, the committee found that the Board of Inquiry's finding could not be justified. The government rejected the committee's conclusion.

The process

How does the House decide when to establish a committee? Following a study of the House's committee work in 1991–92, a Liaison Committee chaired by the Chairman of Committees was set up to allocate resources between select committees and to make recommendations to the House on the appointment of committees. Discussions about committee work, which used to take place between the usual channels, now take place in the Liaison Committee, on which the party leaders, the Convenor of the Cross Bench Peers and a small number of back-bench members also sit.

The demand for establishing committees – usually temporary in the first instance – is strong. The initiative rests with the individual member promoting the idea, who now has to convince the Liaison Committee that the subject of inquiry is a suitable one for a Lords committee to consider. By no means all proposals meet with the approval of the Liaison Committee and, with the notable exception of the Chinook inquiry, the House follows its advice. As more committees are established, the demand for members to sit on them are sometimes not easy to meet, as the party whips can testify.

Once established, select committees in the Lords operate in a way that is almost identical to Commons committees, and they encounter many of the same logistical difficulties. Each committee or sub-committee is supported by its clerk, a secretary/administrator, a share of a committee researcher or specialist, and the assistance of an outside specialist adviser or advisers appointed for each particular inquiry in return for a daily fee. The permanent staff of the Committee Office is over fifty – even more modest than that in the Commons. The total spending of the Lords Committee Office in the financial year 2004–05 was about £3.5 million in support of up to sixteen active committees and sub-committees. These costs do not include any element for accommodation, IT, security or utilities. Nor do they have regard to the cost of members, whose expenses are paid by virtue of their attendance at the House. Indeed, a committee's members are its most important resource. But the fact is that, as with Commons select committees, the monetary costs are modest (especially by comparison with Royal Commissions and non-parliamentary committees).

Lords committees have an inherent power to send for witnesses; documents are produced voluntarily. An Order of the House would be required to compel witnesses (including members of the House) to attend or to produce papers, and none has in recent times been necessary. As with Commons committees, the prospect of embarrassment and potential adverse publicity in failing to comply has proved to be a powerful persuader. Lords committees have power to meet concurrently with Commons committees, although this rarely occurs.

As in the Commons, there are no minority reports in the Lords. Dissent – were there to be any – would have to be recorded by moving amendments and having these amendments printed in the minutes of proceedings. Lords committees usually succeed in achieving unanimity as members know that unless their conclusions can be supported by all they are unlikely to achieve the greatest impact. The chairman in the Lords has no casting vote.

The House usually finds time to debate the reports of its committees, although the timing may not always be to the liking of committee members (see page 307). Through these debates, the committee seeks to elicit a response from the government. In 2003–04, about 3 per cent of the House's sitting time was spent debating select committee reports. A written response is also provided. Following exchanges between committee chairs and the Leader of the House in 2005, the government agreed to provide responses within two months of publication, unless otherwise agreed with the committee in question. While this had always been done for reports of the European Union Committee, the period for other committees had been six months and this was felt to be too long.

Outcomes

It is difficult to say how far government policy adapts to the findings of Lords select committees, but where those committees produce reports that accord with government thinking, rather than being deeply critical, they seem to have effect. There are several examples of this happening in the case of the Science and Technology Committee, for example, in areas as diverse as hazardous waste disposal, regulation of biotechnology and research and development in the National Health Service. Its report on Systematic Biology Research in 1991–92 helped to preserve funding for that branch of science; and a follow-up inquiry in 2002 may have had the effect of an increase in the funding of at least one of the major institutions active in this field. In December 2004 a report on radioactive waste that was deeply critical of the lack of scientific expertise of the Committee on Radioactive Waste Management seems to have led to rapid remedial action on the part of the government; and a report on Air Travel and Health in 2000 led in 2003 to the government asking the Civil Aviation Authority to set up a unit to advise government on aviation health issues. The Science and Technology Committee was the first select committee of either House to propose, through one of its members, an amendment to a public bill – the Forestry Bill in 1981 – but this has not become common practice.

In some cases results can be more tangible. In 1985, government support (but no government time) facilitated the passage through Parliament (under the private members' procedure) of the Charities Bill, which had been drafted by the Select Committee on Charities in 1984.

The Select Committee on the Constitutional Reform Bill in 2004 was, not surprisingly, unable to agree on the chief points of principle concerning the abolition of the office of Lord Chancellor and the establishment of a Supreme Court, though it broadly confirmed the provisions on the appointments commissions and the terms of the 'concordat' whereby the Lord Chief Justice was to become head of the judiciary. Moreover it was able to ensure that significant changes were made to the bill in a number of areas, for example to give greater financial and administrative autonomy to the Supreme Court, to tighten the criterion of merit by which judicial appointments would be made and to include reference in the bill to the upholding of the rule of law. The presence of the Lord Chancellor as a member of the Committee facilitated these and other changes.

The report of the Economic Affairs Committee in July 2005 on the economics of climate change achieved rapid prominence in international forums and was seen, whether by design or no, as representing an alternative or supplementary approach to that of setting targets for reducing carbon emission. That debate can be expected to continue for some time.

The influence of other committees lies in helping to focus debate. Thus the Select Committee on the Infant Life Preservation Bill undoubtedly helped to focus the debate on the appropriate maximum period of gestation after which abortion would not be lawful; and it appears that the recent report on embryonic stem cell research, which recommended the continuation of such research under strict regulation, may have a similar effect in stabilising debate in this related area of public policy. The committee on religious offences accepted that it would be unable itself to agree on any recommendations on the future of the law of blasphemy and so focused instead on setting out the arguments and options for Parliament to consider in due course. The Select Committee on the Assisted Dying for the Terminally Ill Bill in 2004–05 set out very clearly the arguments for and against voluntary euthanasia for the terminally ill and the practice in some countries that allowed it. While the committee was unable to agree to the bill, it showed that a bill which facilitated assisted suicide might well receive more parliamentary support.

But whatever the response of the government may be to committee activity, and despite the procedural nicety that committee reports are made to the House, the reports of Lords committees also reach a wider audience and are usually meant to. Those of the European Union Committee are frequently used by members of the European Parliament and are widely read by those engaged in scrutiny in EU national parliaments. In 2002–03, its reports on the drafts of the Convention on the Future of Europe were used by the four British members of the convention. The report of the Select Committee on Overseas Trade, although its findings were on the whole rejected by the government at the time, achieved a certain notoriety: it received the rare accolade of an unfavourable mention in the Chancellor of the Exchequer's 1986 Budget speech, received wide media attention on publication in October 1985, ran through five editions and for some years served as a university teaching aid. More recently, the report of the Select Committee on Medical Ethics received wide media coverage because it proposed no change to the law governing euthanasia; and that on stem cell research because it supported continued research.

It follows that committee members are most anxious that their reports receive the widest possible publicity. The Committee Office retains its own press and publicity officer; the publication of every report is accompanied by a press notice; and for the more significant reports press conferences are held. But timeliness is all. A report of the European Union Committee on future financing of the EU was widely reported because it appeared in print just before the unproductive Luxembourg Summit of 2005; a report of the Economic Affairs Committee on the economics of climate change received extra coverage because it was published on the eve of the meeting of the G8 heads of government at Gleneagles, where climate change issues featured prominently on the agenda.

There can be no doubt that committee work has featured conspicuously in the renaissance of the House of Lords in recent times. It suits the non-partisan temper and character of the House, and it is certain to remain a permanent – and one suspects expanding – feature of its activities.

Joint committees

We have seen elsewhere that the two Houses are able to appoint joint select committees. There was a time when the best-known and most established, such as the Joint Committee on Statutory Instruments and the Joint Committees on Consolidation Bills and Tax Law Rewrite Bills were legislative in character (see pages 352 and 353). But nowadays the Joint Committee on Human Rights (see page 352) and the joint committees established ad hoc to scrutinise the policy in draft bills (pre-legislative scrutiny committees, see page 372) are probably better known because they consider policy matters. Joint committees are also occasionally set up for certain kinds of opposed private business – opposed Special Procedure Orders and opposed Scottish Provisional Order Confirmation Bills (though following devolution the latter will rarely be necessary).

Joint committees are also set up ad hoc to consider particular issues of concern to both houses. For example, in November 1997 a Joint Select Committee on Parliamentary Privilege was set up with a wide remit to review privilege and its application by the two Houses and to make recommendations. The committee reported in March 2000. Its report provided a definitive account of the state of parliamentary privilege at the end of the twentieth century. Its key recommendation was to restate the force of Article 9 of the Bill of Rights in respect of proceedings of Parliament (that they might not be impeached or questioned in any court of law), subject only to the possibility that either House might waive that privilege, provided that there was no risk of the member who spoke in the proceedings being exposed to legal liability as a result. Obscure, outdated and unnecessary privileges should be abandoned or redefined and the remaining privileges codified in an Act of Parliament (see also page 181). These recommendations have yet to be acted upon.

More recently, a joint select committee considered Lords reform. Set up in July 2002, its first task was to report on options for the composition and powers of the House once reform had been completed. After free votes in both Houses on the options, the committee would, it was envisaged, define in greater detail the proposed composition, role and powers of the second Chamber and recommend a transition strategy for transforming the Lords into its fully reformed state. The committee's first substantive report, published in December 2002, recommended no change in powers but set out seven options for composition ranging from fully nominated to fully elected. In February 2003, both Houses voted on these options. The Lords voted for continued nomination and rejected all other options. The Commons rejected all the options.

In a further report published in May 2003, the joint committee reported again, identifying areas of consensus and inviting the government to indicate what view it now took of Lords reform. In its response published in July, the government indicated that, in the absence of consensus, its interest now would be in making the existing House work more effectively. Its chief focus would be to review the role of the Appointments Commission and the continued presence of the remaining ninety-two hereditary members of the House. It was expected that a bill to implement these and other changes would be introduced in the Commons in March 2004 but the government decided not to proceed with further reform in that parliament. The joint select committee was not reappointed in the 2003–04 and 2004–05 sessions.

Following the 2005 general election and the references in the Labour Party manifesto to further Lords reform, a joint committee was set up in April 2006 to examine the conventions of the House (the Salisbury Convention and the practices on delegated legislation), the time taken on bills, and the practices governing the resolution of disputes over bills ('ping-pong'). We discuss the issue of Lords reform in Chapter 13.

12

Parliament and Europe

Background

The relationship between the United Kingdom and its parliament, and the European Union has been a key theme of British politics for more than thirty years. On 1 January 1973, the UK joined what were then three 'European Communities': the *European Economic Community* (EEC) or 'Common Market', together with the European Coal and Steel Community and the European Atomic Energy Community (Euratom). The 1992 Maastricht Treaty renamed the European Economic Community simply the 'European Community' and made it part of the new *European Union*.

Membership

There were six members of the EEC established by the 1957 Treaty of Rome: Belgium, France, Germany, Italy, Luxembourg and the Netherlands. In 1972, they were joined by Denmark, Ireland and the United Kingdom, in 1979 by Greece, and in 1985 by Spain and Portugal. In 1995, these countries – now the European Union – were joined by Austria, Sweden and Finland. The biggest ever enlargement of the EU took place on 1 May 2004, with the addition of Cyprus, the Czech Republic, Estonia, Hungary, Latvia, Lithuania, Malta, Poland, the Slovak Republic and Slovenia. Bulgaria and Romania are expected to join in 2007. Turkey, Croatia and Macedonia now have formal candidate status.

Closer union

The preamble to the Treaty of Rome set ambitious objectives of 'ever closer union of the peoples of Europe and elimination of the barriers which divide Europe'. However, it set the EEC the less politically sensitive task of 'establishing a common market and progressively approximating the economic policies of Member States . . . harmonious development of economic activities' and so on.

For nearly thirty years, the EEC was concerned mainly with commercial and economic affairs; and during that time the Community managed with only modest amendments to the original treaty (such as those required when new member states joined). Subsequent changes were more profound and fuelled political controversy about the balance between national sovereignty and an 'ever closer union'.

In 1987, the *Single European Act* allowed legislation for the completion of the Community's internal market to be made by qualified majority voting (QMV) in the Council of Ministers. The use of QMV, which has since been applied to many other areas of European legislation, means that the Council of Ministers makes decisions by a weighted system of voting in which larger countries have more votes. It also means that no single member state can exercise a veto. The Single European Act also increased the legislative role of the European Parliament and provided for political cooperation on foreign policy.

In some ways, it is surprising that the then Conservative government led by Margaret Thatcher accepted the concept of QMV, which in later years has eliminated member states' powers of veto in most areas. The completion of the internal market, which was due in 1992, was no doubt seen as a higher priority; and the introduction of QMV allowed some 280 internal market measures to be passed that would otherwise have been blocked by one state or another.

The *Treaty on European Union* of 1992 (*the Maastricht Treaty*) established three 'pillars' of the EU: the European Communities, and two intergovernmental pillars, a common foreign and security policy (CFSP) and cooperation on justice and home affairs (JHA); and it instituted the machinery to bring about monetary union.

The *Treaty of Amsterdam* (1997) formalised for the first time the concept of 'flexibility' in providing for some countries to cooperate on aims that were not necessarily shared by all member states. It moved the free movement of persons from the JHA pillar to the Communities pillar, making it a subject for legislation rather than simply cooperation, and it also incorporated the provisions of the social agreement.

The *Treaty of Nice* (2001) established a European Security and Defence Policy and extended the application of QMV. It also made provision for the institutional change that would be necessary on enlargement of the Union, including the size of the European Commission and a new weighting of votes for QMV.

In December 2001, the European Council set up the *Convention on the Future of Europe* to examine how the EU could be made more democratic and efficient, and to propose a constitution for the Union. The convention, which included representatives from national governments and parliaments, both of current member states and the applicant countries, as well as representatives of the European Commission and the European Parliament, reported in the summer of 2003. Its draft constitutional treaty, including additional powers for the European Parliament and a longer-term President of the European Council, led to opposition calls for it to be subject to a referendum in the UK. The future of the EU constitution is now uncertain. Although agreed by heads of state and government, and ratified by several member states, it was rejected in referendums in France and the Netherlands.

The European debate

The European Communities Act 1972, which took the UK into the Common Market, was passed by the narrow majority of seventeen (and the majority on second reading after three full days of debate was only eight). The UK's relations with the EC and EU have been a matter of political controversy ever since. In 1975, the Labour government led by Harold Wilson held a national referendum on renegotiation of the terms of the UK's membership; and the subject was so divisive that collective Cabinet responsibility was suspended so that senior ministers could campaign for opposite sides of the issue.

Disagreements about Europe, both between and within parties, were never absent in the succeeding years; but it was institutional change within the European Union that brought them to centre stage. In the 1992–97 parliament, John Major's government was dogged by dissent and open rebellion on European issues, made more hazardous by the Conservatives' small majority.

Major came into office with an overall majority of twenty-one, but after the loss of eight by-elections and the defection of four MPs to other parties, the Conservatives lost their overall majority and were in a minority of three before the end of the parliament. This meant that rebels on European issues – and especially on the Maastricht Treaty – had a real prospect of bringing about the government's defeat. In July 1992, the government did indeed lose a significant vote on the Maastricht Social Protocol, by 324 votes to 316, and had to put a motion of confidence – which it won comfortably – before the House the next day. Serious 'Eurosceptic' dissent nevertheless continued, leading to the withdrawal of the whip from eight persistent rebels from November 1994 to April 1995. And in June 1995, Major resigned the leadership of the Conservative Party, standing immediately for re-election in an attempt to bring matters to a head. Although he won by 218 votes to eighty-nine, the size of the minority indicated the level of (largely Europe-fuelled) dissent.

The broadly pro-European stance of the incoming Labour government in 1997 (and also its huge overall majority of 179) meant that European issues were less prominent in the 1997 parliament; but in the 2001 parliament the Convention on the Future of Europe and the draft EU constitution were issues between the parties, as well as within the Conservative Party.

Law making and sovereignty

It is easy to see why the EU has been a divisive issue. On the one hand, the argument runs, our interests are so similar to those of our neighbours that we should act in concert with them, giving up some freedom of action so that we can be more effective and influential as a union of states. On the other hand, this closer union is also seen as an unacceptable loss of sovereignty to a largely undemocratic and unaccountable EU in which distinct UK interests will be submerged.

It is certainly the case that the United Kingdom Parliament has lost its primacy in law making. EU directives set out what is to be the effect of the law in all the member states without specifying its detailed terms; it is up to each country to decide on the wording. However, under the European Communities Act 1972 implementation of EU directives in the UK takes place through delegated legislation (see page 252), which Parliament has no power to amend and is not particularly good at scrutinising. And EU regulations (see below) automatically become law in this country without the involvement of Parliament.

Moreover, as European law has precedence over the laws of member states, it is possible for the European Court of Justice to declare an Act passed by the Westminster Parliament to be incompatible with Community law and for a British court then to declare the law to be of no effect, as happened, for example, with the Merchant Shipping Act 1988 in the 1991 *Factortame* case.

It would be theoretically possible for Parliament to repeal the European Communities Act 1972 and the other legislation that has incorporated successive treaty changes into UK law. To that extent it remains a sovereign parliament; but how far repeal would be a practical possibility, with the withdrawal from treaty commitments and the unscrambling of the UK's relationship with the EU that would be involved, is another matter.

If a fundamental change in the relationship between the European Union and the UK and its Parliament is unlikely, then what role is there for Westminster (and for the national parliaments in each of the other member states, as well as the devolved assemblies)? Before we consider this in more detail, it may be helpful to review the institutions of the EU and how European laws are made.

The Council of Ministers

The Council is the principal legislative and decision-making body in the EU. It consists of ministerial representatives from each of the member states' governments, who vary according to the business under discussion. Thus for agricultural matters the Council will consist of agriculture ministers, finance ministers will deal with economic and financial matters, and so on. The great majority of Council meetings are held in private; most decisions are taken by agreement, but if votes are necessary they are usually by QMV (see page 387). Most Council of Ministers meetings take place in Brussels. The presidency of the Council is held by each member state in turn for a period of six months; this can be very demanding for small states and can also lead to problems of continuity.

The Council is supported by the Committee of Permanent Representatives (member states' ambassadors to the EU), known as COREPER, which prepares Council business and often negotiates agreement between member states so that the Council need take only a formal decision. The office of the United Kingdom's permanent representative – essentially the Brussels arm of government departments in Whitehall and elsewhere – is known as UKREP.

The European Council

This consists of the heads of state or government (prime ministers or presidents) of each of the member states and is the supervisory body of the EU, setting out strategic aims. It meets formally at least twice a year (there are also informal meetings) and is also attended by foreign affairs ministers and a representative of the European Commission. It is chaired by whichever country holds the presidency.

The European Commission

The Commission (based in Brussels) is the EU's executive – in some ways like a civil service, but with extensive powers of initiative, and of decision on a range of delegated matters. There are twenty-five Commissioners (one from each member state), each of whom is responsible for an area of policy. The work of the Commission is carried out by twenty-two Directorates-General.

The European Parliament

Since 1979, members of the European Parliament (MEPs) have been directly elected for fixed terms of five years; the next election will take place in 2009. The total membership is 732, seventy-eight of whom represent UK constituencies (sixty-four in England, seven in Scotland, four in Wales and three in Northern Ireland). The largest party in the parliament is the European People's Party (268 seats), to which the twenty-seven British Conservative MEPs are affiliated (although shortly after becoming Conservative leader in December 2005 David Cameron said that he wanted to break this link – and came in for criticism from his own MEPs). Then comes the Socialist Group (200 seats), to which the nineteen British Labour MEPs belong. The Alliance of Liberals and Democrats for Europe (eighty-eight seats) includes the twelve British Liberal Democrat MEPs. Other British MEPs are UK Independence (ten), SNP (two), Green (two), Plaid Cymru (one), Ulster Unionist (one), Democratic Unionist (one), Sinn Féin (one) and ex-members of UKIP (two).

The European Parliament operates on the 'continental' model, whereby most business in plenary sessions originates from the twenty permanent committees and their sub-committees, which carry out most of the legislative scrutiny. Extraordinarily, the European Parliament continues to sit both in Strasbourg, for a week of plenary sittings each month, and in Brussels, for a number of two-day plenaries and the majority of committee meetings.

The European Parliament employs some 4,500 people, 1,300 of whom are interpreters and translators for the twenty languages used by the Parliament. The budget for 2005 was £868 million, which does not include MEP's salaries. Exact comparisons are difficult, but in broad cash terms the European Parliament costs nearly three times as much as the Westminster Parliament.

Other institutions

The *Court of Auditors* (in Luxembourg) examines EU spending and makes both an annual report and reports on particular expenditure programmes. *The European Court of Justice* (also in Luxembourg) has a general duty of ensuring that in the operation of the treaties the law is observed. It decides on actions that challenge the legality of actions of the institutions of the EU, or that allege a breach of a treaty by a member state. It is assisted by the *Court of First Instance*. The 317 members of the consultative *Economic and Social Committee* (in Brussels) are drawn from trade union, employer, consumer and other interests; and the 317 members of the consultative *Committee of the Regions* represent the interests of regional and local government. The *European Central Bank* in Frankfurt has become the central bank for those countries that have joined the euro zone, while the *European Investment Bank* in Luxembourg is the EU's financing institution, providing long-term loans for capital investment.

European legislation: types

There are three forms of European legislation under the first, or Communities pillar: directives, regulations and decisions. (Strictly speaking, EU legislation is 'Community' legislation, as the European Community – within the structure of the EU – is the source of the European legal order, but for simplicity we will keep to 'European' or 'EU'.) *Directives* are binding on member states in terms of the result to be achieved by a specified date, but it is up to each country what form and method of implementation are to be used. *Regulations* have the force of law throughout the EU without member states having to take any action. Council *decisions* are binding on those to whom they are addressed; they are used for a range of matters, but especially to secure fair commercial competition throughout the EU. Regulations and directives must be published in the *Official Journal* of the EU.

European legislation: procedure

The legislative and decision-making processes of the EU are hideously complicated – much more complicated than legislative procedure at Westminster – and this book is not the place to set them out. Let us simply note the five main routes: (1) the Council of Ministers acts without the involvement of the European Parliament; (2) the Commission makes a proposal, but the Parliament has a right to be consulted; (3) the *cooperation procedure*, under which the Commission makes a proposal but the Parliament has the right to be consulted both on the proposal and on the 'common position' adopted by the Council on the proposal; (4) the *co-decision procedure*, in which both the Parliament and the Council must agree on a text for it to come into force; and (5) the *assent procedure*, used mainly for international agreements and applications by countries to join the EU. Where the member states take decisions inter-governmentally, rather than legislatively, they do so through *common positions*, *joint actions*, *declarations*, *common strategies* or *international agreements*.

A surprising feature of the process is that the Council legislates in private; comparisons are sometimes made with North Korea as the only other place where laws are made in secret. The European Parliament is part of this process, as meetings of *conciliation committees* (to agree texts with the Council) are also private. It is likely that the Council (but not conciliation committees) will soon meet in public (and the moribund draft EU constitution would have required it to do so when legislating). Nevertheless, it is hardly surprising that the EU has been criticised for a lack of openness and for being remote from its citizens.

How to influence European legislation?

We said earlier that a European regulation could become part of the law of the United Kingdom without the involvement of the British Parliament. Let us take a hypothetical example and then see whether British MPs might have been able to affect what happened.

A virus that causes severe food poisoning has been found in cockles and small clams harvested in the western Mediterranean. Several people have died. During questions to the Fisheries Commissioner at a sitting of the European Parliament he is urged to take action, and he undertakes to do so. The Commission then goes rather over the top and produces a whole new regulatory regime for shellfish, which amongst other things would require people catching shellfish of any kind to have their catch screened for the virus, and dealers to have similar checks carried out before selling shellfish to retailers.

The regulations go to the European Parliament and are considered in its fisheries committee. The Greens, who hold the balance of power on the committee, want the proposal strengthened to impose a ban on any catching or selling until procedures for the checks are in place EU-wide, and the Commission amends its proposed regulations. These are then discussed in the Council of Ministers. The Irish fisheries minister argues that the regulations are too sweeping, and she has the support of several others but not enough for a blocking minority; the British fisheries minister is doubtful but is unwilling to vote against for fear of unstitching an entirely separate agricultural negotiation on which the UK needs the support of countries that are in favour of the shellfish proposal.

The proposal comes into effect, and – because there is a three-month delay in manufacturing and supplying the equipment needed for the screening – effectively closes down the shellfish industry in northern Europe as well as in the Mediterranean. The proposal applies not only to the cockles and clams that were the cause of the problem but also to lobsters, crabs, prawns, scallops, mussels and oysters. Fishermen and fish merchants in Devon and Cornwall, and many other parts of the UK, face the loss of their livelihood and are outraged, as are their constituency MPs (and members of the Scottish Parliament, the National Assembly for Wales and the Northern Ireland Assembly). The only people who are delighted are the Norwegians, who are not in the EU; they are unaffected and can now sell their shellfish with very little competition.

How could the shellfish industry's case have been put more effectively? In this case, there have been three main actors: the Commission, the European Parliament and the Council of Ministers. As soon as the Fisheries Commissioner gave his undertaking to the European Parliament, industry representatives could have lobbied the Commission; and constituency MPs, alerted by fishermen's organisations, could have made the case to the Commissioner; but after giving the undertaking to the European Parliament he might well have been unwilling to change his proposal.

MPs could have contacted their European Parliament counterparts to emphasise the damage that could be done by the proposal. This might well have been effective with the MEPs (of whatever party) who had a constituency interest and were already concerned about the proposal – although with their much larger constituencies it might not have been quite such a priority as for some of our Westminster MPs. British MPs could also have approached British MEPs of their own party who did not have a direct constituency interest but who would appreciate the potential political damage. Once they had taken up the cause, the MEPs could have enlisted support from MEPs from other northern European countries that would be affected; and it might well have been that the proposal would have been toned down, or limited to the Mediterranean only, in the European Parliament's fisheries committee, rather than being toughened, as was actually the case.

But the decisive point at which to try to secure changes was in the Council of Ministers, through the stance taken by the British fisheries minister on behalf of the UK government. This is where the European scrutiny systems of both Houses would have come into play.

European scrutiny at Westminster

Two select committees – the European Scrutiny Committee in the Commons and the European Union Committee in the Lords – examine some 1,500 European documents a year on behalf of Parliament. For each one, they assess its importance (and seek any additional information or evidence they need in order to form an opinion), report upon it and, if necessary, recommend it for debate at Westminster. The Commons committee works quickly, reporting on a large number of documents it judges to be of importance (some 500 a year) and recommending some for debate; the Lords committee reports on many fewer (twenty-five or so a year) but in much greater depth, through inquiries by its sub-committees that are similar to the sort of inquiry carried out by departmental select committees in the Commons. Many other documents are scrutinised by the Lords committee by way of correspondence with the relevant minister. The two committees are doing rather different jobs, so they complement each other's work rather than duplicating it.

What is subject to scrutiny?

EU documents subject to the scrutiny process include draft regulations, directives and decisions; Commission green and white papers setting out future policy, including the Annual Work Programme; recommendations and resolutions of the Council of Ministers; and a range of other papers including proposed actions on justice, home affairs and foreign affairs, and the reports of the Court of Auditors. Any document that is subject to scrutiny must be deposited in Parliament and provided to the committees within two working days of its arrival in the Foreign and Commonwealth Office in London.

The explanatory memorandum

Then, within ten working days of deposit, the Whitehall department primarily responsible for the subject matter must submit an *explanatory memorandum* (EM) on the document. The EM sets out who is responsible for the subject matter (both in Whitehall and the devolved administrations); the legal authority under which the proposal is made, and what EU legislative and voting procedure applies; what the impact would be on UK law; whether the proposal meets the requirements of subsidiarity (in other words, whether action at a European level rather than at a national level is necessary); the government's view of the policy implications; a regulatory impact assessment if a proposal is likely to impose burdens on business; when required, a risk assessment and scientific justification; a note of what consultation has taken place; an estimate of the financial implications for the EU and the UK; and the likely timetable on which European decisions will be taken on the proposal. EMs are expected soon to include further information on the devolution and human rights implications of proposals.

EMs are an important element of accountability; one is submitted on every document and is signed by the responsible minister as formal evidence to Parliament. EMs are also public documents and so are useful sources of information for businesses and the public. Another advantage is that the process concentrates minds, both of the civil servants who draft the EM and the minister who signs it (especially when responsibility is shared between several departments and there is a risk of a subject not being gripped early enough). An EM can be a very comprehensive document; and in our shellfish example it would have set alarm bells ringing immediately, not least on the risk assessment, the scientific justification and possible burdens on business.

Once an EM has been submitted, the two Houses have different ways of dealing with documents, so this will be a convenient place to look at how the Commons and Lords committees operate.

The European Scrutiny Committee of the House of Commons

This is a select committee of sixteen MPs. It has a staff of fourteen (larger than any other Commons committee), which includes experts in European law and former senior civil servants with experience of negotiating in Brussels. As well as its main work of scrutinising European documents, it has produced a number of reports on EU constitutional issues, including improving democracy and accountability within the European Union. It also conducts pre- and post-Council scrutiny, in which ministers involved in particular meetings of the Council of Ministers explain, either in oral evidence or in writing, their approach to the agenda or the outcome of the meeting and the UK's role in it.

The committee is assisted by the National Parliament Office (NPO), which the House of Commons established in Brussels in 1998, and which now serves both Houses. This small office, headed by two Clerks, one from each House at Westminster on a two- or three-year posting, acts as the committee's 'eyes and ears' in Brussels, gathering intelligence on likely proposals from the Commission, views in European Parliament committees, and so on. The NPO also publicises the reports of the European committees in both Houses and assists other select committees investigating EU issues.

The European Scrutiny Committee meets every Wednesday, and considers forty or so documents at each meeting. On each document the committee has an analysis, brief and recommendation from the committee staff. In an average year, the committee considers about 1,000 documents. It reports on about 500 of them and recommends about forty for debate (see below).

The committee must first decide whether it has enough information to make a judgement. A comprehensive EM may be enough; but the committee may ask the government for further written evidence or occasionally call a minister to give oral evidence; this dialogue is a crucial part of the scrutiny process and of ministerial accountability. The committee decides whether the document is of political or legal importance. Our shellfish proposal would definitely be of political importance because of its likely impact on a UK industry. It might also be of legal importance if the proposal went beyond the EU's legal powers, for example. The committee may ask any departmental select committee (or the Public Administration, Public Accounts or Environmental Audit Committees) for a formal opinion on an EU proposal. There is increasing informal cooperation with other select committees, which often draw on the expertise of the Scrutiny Committee's staff.

If the committee decides that the document is indeed of political or legal importance, it will cover it in detail in its report on that week's crop of documents. The committee's weekly reports, which are published and put on the parliamentary website, are in effect a critical commentary on the EU agenda and a very useful source of analysis and information for anyone monitoring developments in the EU.

Debates

A further decision for the committee is whether the document should be debated. It can choose to recommend a debate in one of the three *European standing committees*. These have thirteen permanent members, but any MP can attend and speak (although not vote). European Standing Committee A deals with matters affecting the environment, food and rural affairs, transport, local government and the regions; B deals with finance, work and pensions, foreign affairs, home and legal affairs, and international development; and C with trade, industry, education, culture, media, sport and health. In 2005 the Modernisation Committee recommended that there should be five committees rather than three, to allow greater specialisation.

A European standing committee is a combination of questions and debate; a minister answers MPs' questions for up to an hour, and there is then an hour and a half's debate on a motion moved by the minister (to which amendments may be tabled and voted on), usually formally taking note of the documents with some words supportive of the line the government is taking. European standing committees can be a testing time for a minister; in addition to the normal debate format, he or she normally has to answer questions alone and without notice (unlike Question Time in the House, when four or five ministers will share the answering, and unlike appearing before a select committee, when the minister will have officials who can answer detailed questions). Attendances at European standing committees are not high, however, and it is surprising that MPs do not make more use of these opportunities to question ministers on what may be hot political issues. An increase to five committees, as recommended by the Modernisation Committee, may be hard to sustain.

After the standing committee proceedings the government puts down a motion in the House, which may be the same as the motion agreed to in the standing committee (even if that was defeated) or may be an entirely new motion. That motion is taken without further debate, but it may be voted on.

On the most important documents, the European Scrutiny Committee can recommend that a debate should take place on the floor of the House; but it is up to the government to agree to such a recommendation, and it has not always done so. However, if the Scrutiny Committee has recommended a debate, it must take place, in a European standing committee if not in the Chamber. The precise timing is up to the government, but ministers will usually want the debate to take place soon so that they can get 'scrutiny clearance'.

The European Union Committee of the House of Lords

The House of Lords established its Select Committee on the European Communities in 1974. Renamed the European Union Committee in 1999, it scrutinises all three 'pillars' of the EU, and receives the same documents and explanatory memoranda as the Commons committee. It draws the attention of the House to Commission proposals or other documents that raise issues of policy or principle with a recommendation as to whether or not a debate is desirable. The committee considers the merits of proposals for European legislation, and it uses Commission consultative documents or action programmes to undertake wide-ranging investigations of EU policy in a particular area. Like the Commons committee, it undertakes inquiries into broader EU issues. In the 2002–03 session, for example, the committee reported on various aspects of the work of the Convention on the Future of Europe.

The committee also monitors EU affairs in general. Thus, irrespective of the more specific policy work, regular meetings are held with Foreign and Commonwealth Office ministers, particularly following each European Council, and from the ambassadors of countries holding the EU presidency. The committee now makes a point of scrutinising the Commission's annual work programme.

The committee has nineteen members and seven sub-committees roughly covering the principal areas of competence of the European Community as well as justice and home affairs and common foreign and security policy matters. There is a total working membership (including co-opted members) of about seventy lords. The sub-committees consider whatever documents are 'sifted' to them by the chairman of the committee, as well as conducting free-standing inquiries. These sub-committees take evidence and make reports that draw on the knowledge and experience of a distinguished membership: for example, in 2003, the Common Foreign and Security Policy Sub-Committee (Sub-Committee C) included a former Chief of the Defence Staff, a former cabinet minister, a former senior foreign policy adviser to the government, a former Attorney General, a former Secretary-General of the EU Commission, and a former senior member of the intelligence community.

Every year, about a quarter of the 1,500 EU documents deposited by the government are referred by the chairman for more detailed consideration by sub-committees, but only a fraction of these will become the subject of a full-scale inquiry. Some reports of the committee are made for information only, and some for debate. Whether a report is debated or not, it is replied to in writing by the government within two months of publication. However, a substantial number of other documents are considered in detail by way of correspondence with the relevant minister. This is published, and much of it is available on the Internet.

The reports are useful as a source of both information and informed opinion. Although their target is, theoretically, the House and, through the

House, the government minister and government policies, the Lords reports, like those of the Commons committee, also have a wider market in the EU institutions, including the European Parliament itself and other national parliaments of the EU engaged in the scrutiny process.

Scrutiny clearance and the scrutiny reserve

The 1998 *scrutiny reserve resolution* of the House of Commons, and the Lords equivalent, constrain ministers from giving agreement in the Council of Ministers to an EU proposal that has not 'cleared scrutiny'. *Clearance* in the Commons means *either* that the European Scrutiny Committee has reported on it but has not recommended debate, *or* that the committee has recommended debate, the debate has taken place and the House has expressed a view on the proposal. A minister may give agreement to an uncleared proposal, but only with Committee agreement, or if the minister believes there are 'special reasons' for agreeing, such as urgency, or if UK interests might otherwise be damaged – in which case the minister must provide an explanation – or be called in to explain in person.

For the scrutiny system to work effectively, there must be time for examination and debate in national parliaments. Over-rapid legislating is just as much of a problem at the European level as it is at the national level. This is particularly so when a proposal has been through the Westminster scrutiny process but is then changed substantially in later negotiations.

The Commons committee had a remarkable success in getting included in the Amsterdam Treaty a protocol on the role of national parliaments that requires a six-week period of notice before the Council decides on a piece of legislation; but late changes to proposals often mean that this requirement is circumvented. In June 2003, the European Scrutiny Committee made recommendations designed to secure adequate time for scrutiny at all stages, remarking that 'the needs of national parliaments need to be built into the EU's legislative system rather than recognised only when wholly convenient'.

However, to return to our shellfish example: things might have proceeded like this. The European Scrutiny Committee recommends a debate, which takes place in European Standing Committee A. The minister is subject to some very hostile questioning from opposition MPs with fishing constituencies, and even some critical interventions from her own side. The government puts down a fairly bland motion about 'protecting public health and ensuring that all relevant factors are taken into account' but is unable to prevent the motion being amended to condemn 'an ill-thought-out proposal that will have a devastating effect on fishing communities throughout the United Kingdom'.

The same week, the Environment, Food and Rural Affairs Select Committee, which deals with fisheries, announces its intention of mounting a rapid inquiry into the possible effects of the proposal and invites the minister to be the first witness. There is now no way that the minister can support the proposal in the Council of Ministers. She votes with her Irish and other northern European colleagues; there is a blocking minority, and it is clear that the proposal cannot get through in its present state. It later reappears in a modest form that applies only to certain species of shellfish in the western Mediterranean.

How effective is the scrutiny process?

None of the institutions of the EU is accountable to any national parliament, so parliaments can exercise influence only through their own governments and ministers. No matter how strongly the shellfish proposal was criticised, the most the House of Commons could have done would have been to agree to a motion instructing the government to vote against in the Council of Ministers. The minister would have had to obey that instruction, but she could well have been outvoted in the Council.

The European scrutiny process is nevertheless valuable. It is comprehensive, and it catches a wide range of European proposals and other documents, on which ministers have to state their policy and provide evidence. It is open: EMs are public documents, and the committee's reports are published. And it also means that proposals are normally investigated and, if necessary, debated, before ministers vote on them in the Council – although last-minute drafting can still be a problem.

But the process depends crucially on the use that is made of it. It is a little like a burglar alarm. The scrutiny process can identify an EU proposal that might damage UK interests; and a burglar alarm can tell you that someone is attempting to get into your house through the kitchen window. But just as a bit more action is required to apprehend the burglar, so the scrutiny system depends on MPs (and anyone else affected by an EU proposal or policy) making effective use of the information.

What role for national parliaments?

The European Parliament sees itself as the democratic institution representing citizens across the European Union. It is reasonable to ask: in that case, what is there for national parliaments to do? The answer is that the European Parliament is in practice remote from the citizens it seeks to represent. It also exercises few of the key powers of a parliament: it does not sustain a government in office (it can dismiss the Commission, but it has no power over the Council of Ministers); it cannot impose taxes; and, although with the agreement of the Council it may make amendments, it cannot initiate legislation.

National parliamentarians are much closer to the citizens they represent. There are about 10,000 MPs in the national parliaments of member states, compared with 732 MEPs. Whereas a British MP represents an average of 94,400 people, a British MEP represents nearly 782,000 people. And although there is no cause for complacency about the 61 per cent turnout in the 2005 British general election, total EU turnout in European Parliament elections is lower and has fallen at every election, from 63 per cent at the first direct elections in 1979 to 61 per cent in 1984, 58.5 per cent in 1989, 56.8 per cent in 1994, below 50 per cent in 1999 (49.4 per cent) and again in 2004 (45.7 per cent) – despite voting being compulsory in several member states. In the UK – perhaps a country more Eurosceptic than some – turnout has never reached 40 per cent, but although in 1999 it was only 24 per cent, in 2004 it climbed to 38.5 per cent. This still put the UK at seventeenth out of twenty-five member states in terms of participation.

It is clear that, in most member states, voters see MPs, not MEPs, as their representatives; and in European elections they tend to vote on national issues, just as they would in a general election, and not on broader European policies. Nevertheless, the European Parliament has the important roles of considering legislation in detail (with the power to block it), and supervising the unelected Commission. The European Scrutiny Committee has said 'it is only necessary to imagine what the EU would be like without the Parliament; it would be a system totally dominated by bureaucrats and diplomats, loosely supervised by ministers flying periodically into Brussels'.

Even so, national parliaments seem certain to remain the key democratic element in the EU for at least the foreseeable future.

Closer cooperation between national parliaments

So how can national parliaments be more involved at the European level? It has been suggested that the European Parliament could have a second chamber composed of national MPs representing each member state parliament; but the idea has gathered little support, and it is difficult to see how national MPs could spare the time to make such a chamber much more than a symbol.

The Conference of European Affairs Committees (usually known by the French acronym COSAC), which every six months brings together representatives of the European committees in all the national parliaments of the member states and of the Constitutional Affairs Committee of the European Parliament, acts as a forum for exchanging ideas and best practice on European Scrutiny. Although COSAC has no formal powers, the protocol on the role of national parliaments in the European Union (part of the Amsterdam Treaty), recognises that it has a role to play with the right to transmit any submission to the Council, Commission or European Parliament.

The draft EU constitution seems unlikely to proceed in its present form, but it does attempt to address these issues. It states that national parliaments should ensure that EU proposals comply with the principles of subsidiarity (that is, whether action at European rather than national level is necessary) and proportionality (whether the action proposed meets the requirement, or whether it is more than necessary). On subsidiarity, any national parliament or any chamber of a national parliament of a member state would have to send a reasoned opinion to the Council, Commission or European Parliament stating why it considered that a proposal did not comply with the principle of subsidiarity. Where reasoned opinions on the same issue represented at least one-third of all the votes allocated to national parliaments (bicameral parliaments were to have one vote per chamber, unicameral parliaments two votes) the Commission would have to review its proposal and give a reasoned decision. With the draft EU constitution at present stalled, these proposals are more theoretical than practical.

Contacts also exist between policy and legislative committees of parliaments of member states that deal with similar subject areas. Arrangements for holding meetings of representatives of these committees are somewhat ad hoc, falling either to the initiative of the European Parliament or to the national parliament of the country holding the presidency, and many national parliaments are unhappy with current arrangements.

Perhaps most importantly, if national parliaments operate effective scrutiny systems, they can play an important part, not only in influencing their own governments but also in publicising the possible effects of European proposals. The European Scrutiny Committee has suggested that the agenda of the Council of Ministers should show whether a scrutiny reserve is still outstanding in any national parliament, and that, if the Council nevertheless proceeds, it should be required to state its reasons.

A closer relationship between MPs and MEPs?

How could MPs and MEPs be brought closer together, given that their roles are complementary? There is informal contact through party organisations; and most MPs will have a working relationship with the MEP whose constituency covers their 'patch' and the Commons European Scrutiny Committee has organised informal meetings. MEPs with dual mandates as MPs or peers used to provide something of a link between the institutions; but dual mandates have now been abolished.

Westminster is relatively unwelcoming to MEPs compared with, for example, the German parliament, which provides them with offices (although the pressure on space at Westminster is a powerful constraint). Nor do MEPs have any formal role in Westminster proceedings, unlike the Belgian parliament, where Belgian MEPs are full members of the European Committee in the House of Representatives.

Other suggestions have been made. The most recent, and one which seems likely to be implemented, was that of the Commons Modernisation Committee in March 2005 for a *Parliamentary European Committee* which would bring together MPs, peers and UK MEPs four times a year to debate EU issues of major importance. European Commissioners would be invited to attend the Committee to make statements and answer questions.

There may be a tendency to focus too much on the bilateral relationship between Westminster and the European Parliament. Just as important in many ways is the relationship between national parliaments throughout the EU, who have similar functions and many shared interests. Increased cooperation and understanding – whether through joint meetings of subject committees, the work of COSAC, the annual meetings of national parliament Speakers, or contacts between individual MPs – will be factors in maintaining and strengthening national parliaments as an essential democratic element in the European Union.

Other international relations

In this context, we should note the involvement of UK MPs and lords (and staff of both Houses) in a number of international assemblies. The *Parliamentary Assembly of the Council of Europe*, based in Strasbourg, was established in 1949 as the parliamentary organ of the Council of Europe, in some ways a forerunner of the European Community. The Council of Europe has had an important role in a range of social and cultural issues, but especially in human rights matters. It consists of 626 MPs representing forty-four countries (the British delegation has thirty-six members), and in recent years it has acted as a 'waiting room' for the new democracies of Eastern Europe that have become candidates for membership of the EU.

The *Assembly of Western European Union*, based in Paris, has ten member states, which are represented by the same delegations as in the Council of Europe Assembly, and eighteen associated countries. The WEU deals primarily with defence and security issues. The *NATO Parliamentary Assembly* brings together 214 parliamentarians from the nineteen NATO countries. It is based in Brussels but holds its sessions by turn in member countries. The *Parliamentary Assembly of the Organisation for Security and Co-operation in Europe (OSCE)*, based in Copenhagen, was set up in 1991. It consists of 317 delegates from the fifty-five OSCE participating states. The *British–Irish Inter-Parliamentary Body* brings together parliamentarians from Westminster and Dublin.

The UK branches of the *Inter-Parliamentary Union (IPU)* and the *Commonwealth Parliamentary Association (CPA)* are based at Westminster. The IPU represents parliaments worldwide, the CPA those within the Commonwealth. Both aim to increase international cooperation and understanding, and they play a considerable diplomatic role; for example, the first formal contacts between the United Kingdom and Argentina after the Falklands War between parliamentarians of the two countries under the auspices of the IPU, and the IPU-organised visit to the UK by Mikhail Gorbachev just before he became leader of the USSR proved hugely significant.

The Overseas Offices of the two Houses organise a large number of inward visits of officials and members of overseas parliaments, particularly Commonwealth parliaments, to Westminster. These contacts are greatly valued and reflect the wider world beyond the frontiers of the European Union, whose parliaments were in many cases modelled on Westminster principles.

The future of Parliament

Modernisation, reform and effectiveness

Many people would say, usually without thinking, that Parliament needs 'modernisation' or 'reform'. But these are words to be used with some care. To the person speaking, they really mean no more than 'change of which I approve'. After all, the 'Balfour reforms' of a century ago, which entrenched the government's control over the business and time of the House of Commons, were hardly a milestone in the democratic accountability of the executive. And in the present debate over the role of Parliament, 'modernisation' and 'reform' mean different things to different people.

It is much better to focus on the concept of 'effectiveness'. The traditional roles of Parliament include representing constituents, legislating, authorising taxation and spending, calling government to account, and acting as a forum for the testing of beliefs and opinions and a focus for national feeling. What do we expect Parliament to do for us, and how could it do those tasks more effectively?

Before we look in detail at some of the issues, it is worth establishing a sense of proportion. First of all, slagging off parliaments and parliamentarians is a national sport – all over the world as well as in the UK. When the Scottish Parliament was established, it was to be the epitome of a modern parliament: accessible, flexible, getting right what Westminster had got wrong. Yet only four years later, Sir David Steel, the parliament's first Presiding Officer, was writing ruefully:

> *Commentators on the Scottish Parliament spend a lot of time and energy questioning where the Scottish Parliament has 'got it wrong'. It is frustrating because we seldom read stories of the people who have benefited from the work of the Parliament, and there are many.*

It is also a strange irony that, even though most democratic rights have been purchased with blood, they often seem to be little valued by those who live in democracies. 'Oh, I don't vote', you hear people say, 'I don't know anything about politics, and I'm really not interested'. Yet the stuff of politics, and the business of Parliament, affects every aspect of our everyday lives: peace and war, the education of our children, the safety of our streets, the quality of the air we breathe, our civil liberties. This lack of interest may be a symptom of the disconnection between people and Parliament, but it is also the case that, however Parliament changes, there will always be a significant number of people who 'don't want to know'.

However, the fall in turnout at general elections, from nearly 78 per cent in 1992 to 61.5 per cent in 2005, suggests that Parliament is seen by the public as less important than it was. In 2005 disaffection was especially strong in the 18–24 age group, where only 37 per cent used their vote (and only 48 per cent of 25–34 year-olds voted). Not only the 'usual suspects' among pressure groups and commentators but also many MPs and others close to Parliament feel that something is wrong with the way it operates. These are things to be taken seriously; but there are no easy answers.

A reality check

Any proposal for changing the way Parliament – and particularly the House of Commons – works has to take into account the political and constitutional constraints. Here are eight practical factors:

◆ Some criticisms imply that Parliament should somehow simply stop the government doing things that are misguided or unpopular. As long as the UK has a constitutional system in which the government is *in* Parliament, *the executive is always going to get its way in the end, provided that it has a majority in the House of Commons and can persuade its back-benchers to support it issue by issue.* A separation of powers – a system in which the executive and legislature are entirely separate, as in the United States – could greatly increase the independent powers of Parliament, but it would require seismic constitutional change.

◆ Although many people are attracted by the more measured and less partisan approach of the House of Lords, *parliamentary politics is party politics*. Like it or not, free elections involve a clash of party policies and ideologies, and in any elected House – at Westminster or elsewhere – party discipline will always be a powerful factor.

◆ *Parliament is by its nature reactive.* It responds to events, to public opinion and constituency pressures, and to the proposals and actions of governments. There are relatively few genuinely parliamentary initiatives: at Westminster, the main ones are private members' bills (when these are indeed at the initiative of the individual MP and not government hand-out bills) and policy proposals made by select committees.

♦ *A wholly fresh start is virtually impossible.* The more starry-eyed reformers of Parliament might like to see a new Parliament on a green-field site somewhere in the centre of England, breaking the ties with London and shrugging off the burdens of history and tradition. But the executive arm of government would have to move as well, and it is difficult to see much enthusiasm for the establishment of a new administrative capital. The alternative might be a wholly new parliament building in London, but not at Westminster; but it is very difficult to imagine the huge expenditure and disruption being acceptable.

♦ *Parliament means different things to different people.* There are many who yearn for a measured, consensual approach to parliamentary politics. But there are also those who revel in the party battle, and see Parliament as an adversarial institution. As this book has shown, there is no reason why both cannot be accommodated; but one certainty is that there is no general agreement on *how* Parliament should change.

♦ *Parliament is not executive.* It approves principles (and in the case of legislation, detailed instructions) about what is to be done; but it is the government of the day that is responsible for the business and administration of the state and is answerable to Parliament and the electorate.

♦ *Parliament is an organism rather than an organisation.* It is made up of individual members, often unpredictable, who react to a range of influences but who also have their own views. This means that the law of unintended consequences is a powerful factor in parliamentary reform; it is easy to set out detailed procedural prescriptions but difficult to predict what effect they will have, or how they will be used.

♦ Perhaps most important, *Parliament – and especially the House of Commons – cannot change itself. It is the government of the day that has the power of initiative and the majority of votes*, and which controls the business. Parliament's interests and those of the government are often at odds; change may come about because of wider political pressure, but it has usually depended on there being something in it for the government as well as for Parliament.

We now look at the issues as they affect each House.

The House of Commons

The credit side

One morning not long ago, the BBC Radio 4 *Today* programme ran a 'Parliament dead' story, filled with gloom about the ineffectiveness of our democratic institutions. The piece that followed was about a select committee report on the government's planned public–private partnership for the London Underground. In a detailed, compelling report, the committee had done a remarkable demolition job on the government's proposals. Not only did the committee have a government majority, but the chairman was a government MP. The programme makers evidently saw no irony in the juxtaposition of the two items.

The fact is that the Westminster Parliament does a lot of things rather well – and some things better than many other parliaments. This is not an argument for complacency; but it is as well to remember that the more hysterical rumours of Parliament's death – too often fuelled by the media – are greatly exaggerated. Westminster is well regarded by people in the same business: other parliaments, as shown by the constant stream of visiting Speakers, members, committees and senior officials from overseas – from parliaments of all types, not only those in the Commonwealth that use the 'Westminster model'. So it is worth taking stock not only of the strengths of the House of Commons but also of some of the significant changes over the last four or five years.

Present strengths

The *close relationship with constituencies* means that Westminster MPs put a lot of effort into an ancient function of the House of Commons: representing constituents, and getting their voices heard by ministers who are often seen as remote and inaccessible. Success in solving constituents' problems depends on the tenacity of the MP and the strength of the case, but the 'satisfaction factor' of constituency cases was rated highly by MPs in a recent survey, and this aspect of MPs' work generally gets a good rating from the public.

Select committees are a key part of the work of the Commons. The system is flexible and comprehensive; it encourages independence of view amongst committee members; it produces well-researched and well-written reports; as well as exposing a wide range of government activity to scrutiny, it publishes a great deal of official information that would not otherwise be in the public domain; and, perhaps most important, it provides public access to the political process.

The complementary systems of European scrutiny in the Commons and the Lords are some of the best in any EU parliament (although their product is sadly underused).

Parliament attracts and retains high-quality staff; and its work is supported by committed and expert people who are highly regarded by their equivalents in parliaments worldwide. Other parliaments, when faced with a problem, often want to know 'how does Westminster tackle this?'

Parliamentary questions, used on a larger scale than in any other parliament, have their critics but are an important means of requiring governments to put information on the public record; and, in the hands of a determined MP, they can be remarkably effective. However, as we note on page 336, there is a risk that overuse may devalue them.

The House of Commons is *a natural focus of attention on historic occasions*. Following the terrorist attacks in the USA on 11 September 2001, upon the death of the Queen Mother, and in the bittersweet two days in July 2005 when the success of London's Olympic bid was followed by terrorist attacks in central London, the House was the forum for the expression of a national mood. In the build-up to war in Iraq, it also mirrored profound differences in the country at large.

We should not forget the more informal role that the House of Commons fulfils. It is *a place where opinions are exchanged and formed and laid open to the scrutiny of the media and the public*; where pressure groups and campaigners, as well as industries, the professions and a range of other players, put their case or seek a higher profile for their cause.

However, the Commons is seen as less effective in the key tasks of examining legislation and scrutinising public spending. We return to these below.

Recent change

There has been no shortage of drivers for change in the last nine years. In 1997, the incoming Labour government had a manifesto commitment to parliamentary reform; and the Modernisation Committee, which it established, together with the Liaison, Procedure, Public Administration, and Information Committees, the House of Commons Commission, the *Parliament First* group of MPs, the Hansard Society's Commission on Parliamentary Scrutiny chaired by former Leader of the House Tony Newton (Lord Newton of Braintree), the Commission to Strengthen Parliament, set up by William Hague when Leader of the Opposition and chaired by the distinguished academic Lord Norton of Louth, the Puttnam Commission on Parliament in the Public Eye and many other organisations and commentators, have become involved in the process.

There has been no shortage of changes either. Although none is in itself earth-shaking – and one or two have been controversial – as a whole they mark the most profound period of change for many decades.

The sitting hours have changed (and have partly been changed back again) (see page 147): the House now sits at 11.30 a.m. instead of 2.30 p.m. on Wednesdays and 10.30 a.m. on Thursdays, and the normal finishing time is 7.30 p.m. on Wednesdays, and 6.30 p.m. on Thursdays, instead of 10.30 p.m.

The traditional summer recess from late July to early October has twice been broken by *a two-week sitting period in the first half of September*. The aim of this was to prevent the government escaping scrutiny for so long a period. The additional sitting allowed time for more Question Times, the tabling and answering of more written questions, and more select committee activity; but also more time for government legislation. The September sittings proved extremely unpopular with most MPs.

A parliamentary calendar for a year ahead was first published in 2003, and appears now to be a fixture.

A 'parallel chamber' has been established in Westminster Hall (see page 296), which has provided additional opportunities for back-benchers to initiate debates and for select committee reports to be debated, and it has been the forum for 'cross-cutting' oral questions, in which ministers from several departments answer on a policy theme rather than on a single-department basis as in the Chamber (although few of these question periods have so far been held). (The adaptation of the parallel chamber idea from the Main Committee in the Australian House of Representatives is a reflection of the exchange of ideas and experience between parliaments; the Lords committee to scrutinise powers to be delegated to ministers in primary legislation also traces its origins to Australia.)

Oral questions to most ministers are now tabled only three sitting days before answer, rather than ten, and can be more topical as a result. *Written questions 'for a named day' are limited to five per MP per day* in an attempt to reduce the number of holding replies. *Questions may now be tabled electronically. Prime Minister's Questions now runs for half an hour on Wednesdays* rather than the pre-1997 quarter-hour on Tuesdays and Thursdays.

A new way of electing a Speaker has been established, differing from every other decision-making procedure in the House, with a secret ballot and the elimination of low-scoring candidates. *A more comprehensible Order Paper* has been introduced to assist MPs as well as those outside Parliament. In the Chamber, *the Speaker has been given the power to limit the length of speeches in over-subscribed debates. The rule against quoting in a supplementary at Question Time has been abolished. The comic method of raising a point of order during a vote*, in which an MP had to wear a hat in order to be recognised by the Chair, *has been scrapped. The motion 'that Strangers do now withdraw' has been replaced by the motion 'that the House sit in private'* (although this is purely cosmetic; the motion is used for exactly the same purposes – as a tactical waste of time, and by staging a division to test the numbers voting with the aim of getting the business postponed – as it was before). *The term 'Strangers'* – meaning anyone from outside the House – *has itself been abolished.*

'Deferred divisions' have been introduced for some categories of business, whereby, if after the normal finishing time a vote is forced, the vote takes place not on the spot but on the following Wednesday afternoon by MPs marking a ballot paper. This has contributed to earlier finishing times; and it is convenient for the government, which would otherwise have to keep more MPs until near the end of the sitting to make sure that the votes were not lost, but it has also attracted criticism precisely because it has made things easier for the government business managers, and because of the way in which it can separate debate and decision.

More methodical scrutiny by departmental select committees is now under-pinned by 'core tasks', and the committees produce annual reports on their work, which is drawn together by the Liaison Committee in an annual assessment of select committee effectiveness. *The Scrutiny Unit now supports select committees in scrutiny of financial papers and draft bills,* and the staffing of the Committee Office has been substantially increased to help committees to carry out the 'core tasks'. *A new format has greatly improved the presentation and user-friendliness of select committee reports.* Most *investigative committees can now operate more flexibly by being able to set up a sub-committee, and two or more committees and sub-committees of both Houses can work cooperatively through joint meetings.* However, the Modernisation Committee's proposal for a 'Committee of Nomination', which would have taken the selection of members of scrutiny committees out of the hands of the whips, was defeated.

On MPs' conduct issues, *the independence of the Parliamentary Commis-sioner for Standards has been entrenched, an additional inquiry mechanism established for the more difficult cases, and the Code of Conduct revised. An MP censured by the Standards and Privileges Committee may now have his or her pay docked* even if not suspended from the House.

On legislation, *more bills appear in draft for select committee scrutiny* (although the time available often limits the effectiveness of that scrutiny). *Better explanatory material is provided on bills* when they are formally introduced. *Programming is now routine for government bills* but has moved from its consensual origins to being a source of bitter disagreement between government and opposition, with almost every programming motion being the subject of a vote. The original expectation that more bills would be referred to special standing committees (see page 222), as recommended by the Modernisation Committee, has not been fulfilled.

A number of other recommendations on legislation made by the Modernisation Committee in the early days of the 1997 parliament have not been implemented: bills not previously published in draft to be considered by ad hoc first reading committees; limitation of speaking time in standing committee debates; debating the principle of a clause before considering amendments; reconvening a standing committee to consider non-controversial government amendments before report stage; considering Lords amendments in standing committee; and carrying out post-legislative scrutiny to see how Acts of Parliament have actually operated (although it is always open to any select committee to undertake this sort of scrutiny).

These changes have meant some more work for ministers and their departments, especially arising from the establishment of Westminster Hall and shorter periods of notice for oral questions. In the select committee world the changes have provided more opportunities and resources; the effectiveness of both will depend on what use committees make of them. Otherwise, although most of the changes would be seen by most people as improvements, they have not made much of a difference to the government–parliament relationship; in the Liaison Committee's phrase, they have not 'shifted the balance'. Indeed, some would claim that on legislation the routine programming of government bills has shifted the balance back the other way.

However, two events in the 2001 parliament are likely to work to the long-term benefit of Parliament. Despite later controversy about the reasons for going to war in Iraq, the fact remains that, unprecedentedly in modern times, the explicit approval of the House of Commons was sought for military action before troops were committed. If any future government engages in military action without seeking the view of the House of Commons, its mandate for doing so will be seen as doubtful. This may be one area of prerogative power that political circumstances have allowed the House to recapture. Second, the twice-yearly appearance of the Prime Minister before the Liaison Committee has been a symbolic as well as a substantive change. It is difficult to see any future Prime Minister being able to withdraw from the commitment, and the establishment of the principle may lead to more frequent sessions in the future.

What next?

We now look at areas where further changes are already under way, or where further reform might be more challenging.

Reconnecting Parliament and the public: voting

In a recent debate on turnouts in elections, one MP said:

> *We ask people to vote on a Thursday in one place and if they do not turn up at that place they do not get a vote. We ask them to vote on a slip of paper that seems to have been printed by the last remaining letterpress printer in the country. We then ask them to fill in their preference . . . using a carpenter's pencil attached to the wall by a piece of string. Finally, we ask them to do that in a horse box that has been set up in a school hall. That is probably one of the most bizarre activities that we ask people to do in their daily lives in expressing their opinions, preferences and thoughts.*

Getting more people to vote is clearly an important way of increasing interest in, and regard for, democratic institutions (although some would say that it puts the cart before the horse: get people interested in Parliament, and more of them will vote).

We assumed earlier in this chapter that low turnouts show a lack of interest and regard, but the picture is more complicated than that. Although many people prefer more consensual politics, sharper differences between the policies of the major parties may increase turnout, possibly on the principle of voting against candidates rather than for them. It may also be that when voters see the result of an election as a foregone conclusion (as many did in 2001 and 2005) they are more likely to stay at home.

The Electoral Commission set up under the Political Parties, Elections and Referendums Act 2000 has the duty of educating and informing the public about the importance of participation in the democratic process and of recommending ways in which electoral arrangements can be improved. Some changes have already been made: you do not need to have an address in order to vote; and under the 'rolling register' introduced in 2000 names can be added to the electoral register at any time during the year.

Postal voting

Before the 2005 election, postal voting was seen as an obvious answer to the problem of increasing turnout, not only because it is a convenient method for people to use but also because postal voting can be open for some time before polling day: voters do not have to get to a polling station between 7 a.m. and 10 p.m. on a particular day. And it seemed to work: for example, the all-postal pilot schemes tried out in the 2004 European Parliament elections raised turnout in the areas concerned from 20 per cent to 42 per cent.

However, the reputation of postal voting was seriously damaged in 2005 by a case heard by an Election Commissioner (a QC appointed for the purpose) that showed substantial fraud in elections for Birmingham City Council. The Commissioner declared the elections in two wards void; but his criticisms of ministers, and especially his remark that the system 'would disgrace a banana republic' undoubtedly tainted public perceptions of postal voting. Allegations of fraud in the 2005 general election – a week after polling day the police were investigating 25 cases, although no charges were eventually brought – cannot have helped.

The government sought to address these problems through the Electoral Administration Act 2006. There is general agreement that the key to secure postal voting is in accurate electoral registration information combined with appropriate security checks; but the reputation of postal voting may take time to recover.

Other ways of tackling the turnout problem

There have been experiments with *electronic voting* (although, like postal voting, this has security implications) and with *mobile polling stations* so that people can get to them more easily. Other proposals have involved: *voting on Sunday* (as in France) as this is the day of the week on which most people can make time to vote; *holding several types of elections on the same day* (as was done in 2004 for the European Parliament, local and Greater London Assembly elections); *making voting compulsory* (as it is in several EU and Commonwealth countries), although the Electoral Commission has said that it does not see this as the answer to the turnout problem; *reducing the voting age from 18 to 16* (as is the case for regional and municipal elections in Germany and Austria), but there is opposition to such a step, and in 2005 a ten-minute rule motion on the subject was defeated in the House of Commons.

It is often suggested that *funding political parties wholly from the public purse* might give voters greater ownership of the political process; but a recent survey by the Electoral Commission found that, although 70 per cent of those polled were worried that private donations to political parties allowed the 'peddling of influence', only 7 per cent actually supported wholly public funding. The issue made headlines with the 'loans for peerages' controversy in March 2006.

The cure for low turnouts most often suggested is a change to the electoral system itself, specifically *a move to one of the systems of proportional representation*. As we saw in Chapter 2, the fact that in 2005 the government was elected with the support of only one in five of the electorate provided new ammunition to the supporters of PR; but any early change seems unlikely.

Is this just a Westminster problem?

Emphatically no. In June 2004, for example, the average turnout across the EU for the European Parliament elections was only 45.5 per cent – which of course included the electorates of countries much more Europhile than the UK. Yet more striking was the turnout for the US Presidential Election in 2004. This was a straight head-to-head election of the nation's Chief Executive and Commander-in-Chief. The 2000 election had been nearly a dead heat. The war in Iraq was beginning to divide the country. There was intense voter registration effort by the two major parties. Yet the turnout, at 60.7 per cent, did not even get to the UK's 61.5 per cent for the 2005 general election.

What is one to conclude? That there is a cultural disengagement with politics, certainly. That this affects the young, who have not developed a habit of participating in elections, more than the old, who have – undoubtedly. (In the 2005 general election, only 37 per cent of 18 to 24-year-olds voted, but 75 per cent of those over 65 did so.) Clearly the level of turnout in the UK is a matter of concern. But the fact that this type of disengagement is seen widely in other countries with different parliamentary and electoral arrangements (despite the 81.2 per cent turnout in the April 2006 Italian elections) suggests that changes to our electoral systems might make only marginal improvements. And it suggests more clearly that changes to the UK Parliament – desirable though they may be in themselves if they make the institution more effective – will *by themselves* have little impact on public participation in politics.

Referendums

If participation in conventional voting cannot be increased, what about direct involvement in decision making through the use of referendums – an opportunity for all electors to vote on a specific proposition? Most democracies use referendums from time to time; in some systems (Switzerland

and California, for example) the result has the force of law; but elsewhere, as has so far happened in the United Kingdom, the result is advisory only (although a government may pledge itself to abide by that result).

Referendums have been used from time to time in the UK: in 1973 in Northern Ireland on the province's constitutional future; and in 1975 throughout the UK on the issue of continued membership of the EEC. They were used twice, in 1979 and 1997, on proposals for devolution to Scotland and Wales, more recently on proposals for elected mayors, and in 2005 on the setting up of a regional assembly in the north–east of England. In this case the government's proposal was heavily defeated, by 78 per cent to 22 per cent (on a 48 per cent turnout).

There are several disadvantages of referendums as a way of supplementing conventional democratic decision making in the UK. They can only be advisory; and they cannot be requisitioned by the people but are held at the government's initiative (and legislation is needed to authorise each referendum). The UK, without a written constitution, has no clear guidance about when referendums should be used; if, say, they should be used on constitutional issues, who decides what a constitutional issue is? For example, the government consistently refused the opposition's request for a referendum on the proposed new EU constitution, even though some other EU states held referendums as a matter of course.

If a referendum is held, what is a valid result? Should a minimum percentage of the electorate vote in favour, or should the requirement be an absolute majority, regardless of turnout? And what should be the question asked? (The Political Parties, Elections and Referendums Act 2000 provides that the government should consult the Electoral Commission on the 'intelligibility' of the question, but the final decision is still for ministers.) And however deftly the question may be phrased, what is to prevent the referendum becoming a vote of confidence on the government of the day? The decisive rejection of the draft EU constitution in French and Dutch referendums in 2005 probably had as much to do with national politics – at least in France – as with the constitution itself.

Historically, we have not had a habit of referendums in this country; but as interactive technology becomes more sophisticated and widespread, they (and some of these questions and problems) may become more important.

Reconnecting Parliament and the public: improving understanding

Many of the perceptions of Parliament and its work are provided by the media – indeed, many would say, that is part of the problem. But

Parliament does in fact make considerable efforts to explain its role and work.

The parliamentary website – www.parliament.uk – is a major resource for anyone who wants information about Parliament and parliamentary business. It carries the Order Paper, Question Book, *Hansard* (including the new 'rolling *Hansard*' that goes on the website throughout the day as the hard copy goes to the printer), bills before Parliament, select committee reports and evidence, early day motions, the Register of Members' Interests, factsheets and briefings on parliamentary and political subjects, and much more.

The website is not as easy to use and to navigate as it should be; it developed more as a tool for users who knew exactly what they were after rather than as a means of engaging people with Parliament more generally, and radical redesign is under way. Nevertheless, in financial year 2004/05 there were 29 million hits on the website, more than double the hits only two years before.

There is 'gavel-to-gavel' television coverage of proceedings in both Chambers and in Westminster Hall (about 70 hours a week), and extensive coverage of select committee hearings. All these proceedings are also webcast on www.parliamentlive.tv, with up to 18 live streams available, together with an on-demand archive.

Parliament's Central Tours Office hosted 114,000 people visiting Westminster in financial year 2004/05, and a new reception and visitor centre is under construction alongside Westminster Hall. The Parliamentary Education Unit provides support for teachers and students, including booklets and posters, visits programmes, videos and an education website at www.explore.parliament.uk. The Unit organises more than 10,000 teacher and student visits a year; and its visits programme, previously held only during the summer recess, runs all year round from 2006. A New Voter's Guide, for everyone in the country as they turn 18, will be published in 2006. The House of Commons Information Office answers questions from the public (some 60,000 a year, but falling as people make more use of what is on the website).

Both Houses use professional communications staff to publicise the work of Parliament, and especially of select committees, but there are practical limitations on far this can go. For example, if the government's case for something has been trounced in a major debate, or an opposition policy has been torn to shreds by a select committee, headlining these as examples of Parliament doing its job – as they are – is not going to play well with the government or the opposition in each case.

Reconnecting Parliament and the public: accessing the political process

If people are to feel involved in the business of Parliament, they must also feel that they can be a part of it, rather than voting for MPs every four years or so and then seeing the results on their television screens or in the newspapers.

Select committees provide one of the best ways of doing this. They draw on a wide range of evidence, not only from the 'great and the good' but also from people who know about a subject from a local or personal perspective. They can operate away from Westminster, seeing things first-hand and taking evidence. Increasing select committee consideration of draft bills provides new opportunities for people to be involved more directly in making the law. The Joint Committee on the Communications Bill ran a successful online consultation on the bill; but other select committees have found online consultation less rewarding. The process is complex and usually managed by external bodies such as the Hansard Society on the committee's behalf. It can also be expensive: in one recent case, a consultation with 160 responses cost £20,000 to run. The questions posed have to be simple and limited in number, whereas the success of select committees often lies in detail and subtlety. Many inquiries involve technical issues where the public at large are unlikely to have a view – and of course the responses are self-selecting. Online consultation has become one of the many tools at a committee's disposal, particularly where public opinion is at the heart of the subject matter of inquiry, but it is used more sparingly than had at first been thought by some. Public consultation is a key part of the regulatory reform procedure, and some of the suggestions for amendment of the law made by the Regulatory Reform Committee and its predecessor have had their origins in points put by members of the public.

In a sense, MPs' constituency work provides a link between Parliament and the public, but it has been suggested that this should be supplemented by a more formal way in which citizens can put their problems and concerns to the House of Commons. MPs can already present public petitions (see page 340) on behalf of their constituents, and this is a valued opportunity. However, although it may give a higher profile to an issue, and although the government usually publishes its observations on a petition (but is not required to do so), that is normally the end of the matter. Petitions are now referred to the relevant departmental committee, but none has yet been taken up. One option would be for a Select Committee on Public Petitions, which could hear the petitioners in person and could take up cases if it thought them justified.

Reconnecting Parliament and the public: the House's image

Concern is sometimes expressed about the image of Parliament as a factor in its public standing, in terms of both the sort of people who are MPs and some of its more old-fashioned or ceremonial aspects. As we saw in Chapter 2, the House of Commons is not a microcosm of the country as a whole. The average age of MPs is about 50; 20 per cent of them are women, as against more than 51 per cent in the general country as a whole; and 2 per cent are from ethnic minorities, compared with some 7 per cent in the general population. Many people believe that the House would be held in greater regard if all sectors of the population saw it as containing 'people like us' and that that would increase interest and participation. However, a greater democratisation of the House of Commons would not *of itself* increase its effectiveness, or the effectiveness of MPs as constituency representatives.

The prisoner of history?

If one is modernising something, cosmetic change always offers some quick hits; indeed, it is sometimes said that you know when the management consultants have been in because the canteen has been painted a different colour. As will have been clear from earlier chapters, there are often good reasons for some things in the House of Commons that appear strange to outside observers. But there are also many things that are the legacy of earlier centuries. Some, like the shape and size of the Chamber, probably do have a real influence on the way the House operates; it might be a very different place if the Chamber were a 646-seat hemicycle. Others are more picturesque; and although they have their critics, it is difficult to say that they really make much of a difference. How would the perception of the House change if the Clerks at the Table wore suits rather than their court dress and wigs, for example? Or if the Mace were not carried in procession into the Chamber every day? Many people rather like the dignified framework of the House's proceedings, perhaps seeing it as a counterweight to the rough and tumble of debate or Question Time. It is part of the House's image, but it makes little or no difference to the way that the House does its job. The danger is for people to focus on these superficialities and ignore the scope for real change that could help Parliament do a better job.

Information and communications technologies

ICT is intrinsic to the work of both Houses. The parliamentary network supports over 6,000 users, providing communications and information sources. Users can access the network remotely, for example from constituency offices; computer equipment for MPs has been installed in locations across the UK.

As well as providing communications and access to information, ICT is crucial to many of the functions of the two Houses. The 'camera-ready copy' that allows the rapid production of select committee reports, often overnight, is not produced by some specialist department but by a single person in each committee staff team. The Public Bill Offices of the two Houses use some of the world's most sophisticated text-handling software to produce lengthy bills, often incorporating hundreds of amendments, ready to print in a matter of hours. Select committees handle more than 98 per cent of their written evidence electronically, almost eliminating the need for typesetting, and tailor-made systems have revolutionised the production of *Hansard*. The House of Commons does not yet use ICT on the scale of its Canadian counterpart, which is probably the world leader in this field, but it is not far behind. One of the limitations is likely to be the preferences of MPs themselves; for example, one select committee has experimented with a paperless meeting, but there is little enthusiasm among other committees to move in this direction. And as we saw in Chapter 6 (page 174), there are arguments on both sides about the introduction of electronic voting.

However, many MPs see new technologies as offering more effective ways of communicating with their constituents, particularly in younger age groups through MPs' own websites, video-conferencing, online surgeries, better networking between Westminster and constituency offices, and the use of mobile devices to access information wherever the MP might be.

E-mail is increasingly used to communicate with constituents but, as we saw in Chapter 5 (page 114), it can bring its own problems: its speed leads many constituents to expect instant answers to what may be extremely complicated problems; and some very conscientious constituency MPs prefer not to use e-mail for this reason.

Although new technologies will inevitably play an increasing part in the relationship between Parliament and the citizen, there are two important caveats. First, if one creates expectations they need to be fulfilled. It is no good having an online consultation on a draft bill, for example, unless the process is moderated, and the results analysed and used. Websites need to be updated and e-mails responded to. All this needs effort and resources; otherwise the use of new technologies can actually risk a new form of disconnection with the public at large.

Second, although use of the Internet is constantly increasing, there is also what has become known as the 'digital divide'. Of the UK's population 60 per cent now have access to the Internet at home or at work, but for home access household income is an important factor: in the highest income group 78 per cent of households have access, whereas in the lowest income group the figure is only 36 per cent.

We have looked so far at the way in which the House is seen outside Westminster, and its relationship with those it represents. Let us now turn to the way in which it operates and some of the proposals that have been made for change.

The size of the House

As we saw in Chapter 2, the Commons is a comparatively large assembly. This has the advantage that each MP represents fewer people than he or she would in a smaller House. However, it also means that the competition for parliamentary time and opportunities is greater, and some commentators also see the size of the House as working in favour of the government of the day, diluting dissent and unfocusing opposition. The size of the government (in 2006 115 ministers in the two Houses, ninety-three of whom are in the Commons) also comes in for criticism; together with over fifty parliamentary private secretaries it represents a considerable exercise of patronage for the Prime Minister, and as 'the payroll vote' it is a rock-solid block of MPs voting the government line.

Most suggestions for reducing the size of the House focus around the 400 mark, often with the number of ministers being reduced further, to about fifty. However, although the Prime Minister could change the number of ministers in a morning, the lead time for any change in the size of the House is likely to be very long. It is certainly not an immediate prospect.

A related point is the 'West Lothian question': the ability of MPs from Scotland, Wales and Northern Ireland to vote at Westminster on matters that affect England but which in their own parts of the UK would be dealt with by the devolved administration and assemblies. This has always been an issue in devolution, but it has become more controversial; in the summer of 2003 many Scottish MPs voted for a total ban on fox-hunting and were also instrumental in saving the government's proposals for foundation hospitals from defeat. In Scotland, both subjects are the responsibility of the Scottish Parliament. It is sometimes suggested that the Speaker should certify bills so that they could be voted on only by those MPs in whose constituencies they would apply. Such a procedure is theoretically possible, but it would be complicated, to say the least.

The floor of the House

Here proposed changes have centred around more topical debates – perhaps chosen on the basis of the number of MPs who requested a debate on a particular subject. Another form of this proposal is that when an early day motion (see page 301) receives more than a certain number of signatures – perhaps half of the House's membership, or half of the membership less ministers and PPSs – time should be found to debate it; but this might simply lead to the canvassing of signatures on an industrial scale.

One rather surprising result of changes in recent years is that there is now no opportunity for an individual MP to put a proposition to the House for debate and decision, as used to be possible through the ballot for private members' motions. (The nearest equivalent is the ten-minute rule bill procedure (see page 229), although that allows only one speech against before a vote is taken.) It is very surprising that in the British House of Commons back-benchers do not have an opportunity that is available in most other parliaments in the world.

Parliamentary language

The language of Parliament is often cited as a factor that makes the institution less comprehensible and less attractive. There is a strong argument for all speeches to be made to the Chair, because this (as in meetings of all types) makes debate more orderly and avoids the possibly inflammatory 'you' when used of another MP. In turn this means that references to other MPs have to be in the third person.

The Commons has already dropped the terms 'learned' to describe a QC and 'gallant' for a former officer in the armed forces (although they are still occasionally used) and there is no particular need for an MP to be described as 'the honourable Member for such-and-such constituency'; 'Mr Smith' would do just as well.

This change might be welcomed by some; but it would be a superficial one. The language of parliamentary debate, on the other hand, is usually very plain and straightforward, and it is difficult to see what should be changed – or how. And when debate becomes complex, perhaps especially on legislation, that is usually because the matters themselves are complex.

A business committee

There has been increasing pressure for the establishment of a committee, on the same lines as the *bureau* in many continental parliaments, and similar committees in the devolved assemblies, to plan the business of the House. Its members would include representatives of all the parties in the House, and possibly the Speaker and his deputies. Some acknowledge that such a committee would have to meet in private; others believe that it could meet in public. A business committee is seen as a way of involving all parties in the House in the planning of business and of making the process more transparent. However, it is inevitable that the government of the day would see it as a serious threat to its control of the House's business.

Parliamentary questions

Some MPs would like to see oral questions with no notice to individual departments (as are most oral questions to the Prime Minister) in order to make Question Time more topical. The reduction in the period of notice required for oral questions has not produced quite the topicality that some hoped for, and so the proposal may resurface (although the Procedure Committee in 2002 did not support it).

The refusal of ministers to answer certain types of question, or the perceived unhelpfulness of replies, is seen by many MPs as frustrating. At the moment, the Public Administration Committee reports each session on ministerial accountability and refusals to answer. This process might bear more directly upon ministers – and their willingness to give full replies in every case – if there were some more immediate recourse, perhaps to a select committee that could in justified cases press (or, an even more daring reform, require) a minister to answer a particular question.

The Speaker's ability to grant an application for an urgent question, and summon a (perhaps reluctant) minister to come to the House at short notice to face MPs' questions, is an important part of calling the government to account. Some recent blueprints for reform have suggested that much greater use should be made of this power, and that the criteria for granting an urgent question should be relaxed.

The Royal Prerogative

As we saw in Chapter 4, many powers are exercised by ministers without reference to Parliament. These include entering into treaties, military action, public appointments and the organisation of government. Most proposals for making Parliament more effective include making the exercise of the prerogative subject to parliamentary approval, as canvassed by David Cameron, the new Leader of the Opposition, in 2006. Although some changes are occurring ad hoc, such as the remarkable precedent of parliamentary approval for British military intervention in Iraq, and select committees are starting to examine draft treaties and major public appointments, any change to make the role of Parliament decisive rather than advisory could happen only if the government of the day were to introduce legislation.

Select committees

Select committees already have a great deal of flexibility, and they exercise considerable independence. What use they make of it is very much up to them; determined and unanimous committees can achieve a great deal. The work of select committees has developed by leaps and bounds over the last ten years, but some see them as unduly constrained.

The back-up available to select committees has been an issue in the past, but the establishment of the Scrutiny Unit, the significant expansion of committee staff to deal with the core tasks (see page 372) and the flexibility of the specialist adviser system mean that committees are better resourced now than they have ever been. Even so, staff resources are fairly modest. There are two aspects to this: first, a successful and influential committee inquiry does not necessarily mean asking 5,000 questions; it may mean asking five questions *but getting answers*. Second, if select committees are going to maintain their political clout they must be member-driven, not staff-driven.

Modest resources do constrain committees in one way. They may be able to support several inquiries at the same time, but it is more difficult to keep a constantly roving eye across the committee's areas of responsibility to identify where the spotlight should turn next. In this respect, the Comptroller and Auditor General's constant monitoring of all government departments provides unique support for the Public Accounts Committee. Although some select committees have drawn upon the C&AG's reports, it is a little surprising that the PAC is supported by the work of 800 staff of the National Audit Office, while twenty-five or so other investigative committees are supported by 150 staff of the Committee Office. One way of rebalancing would be to put the resources of the NAO at the disposal of the select committee system as a whole, and for the PAC to return to its historical function of examining government accounts, rather than dealing with policy (which is in any event outside its terms of reference).

As we saw in Chapter 11, government replies to select committee reports are by convention given within two months of a report's publication. Although select committees should be well able to take action when a reply is late – such as calling a minister to give oral evidence – it would entrench the role of committees if the convention were to be made a formal requirement (perhaps with a slightly longer reply time), the breaching of which would have to be explained to the House by the responsible minister.

From time to time the powers of select committees become an issue, usually in the most high-profile and controversial inquiries. Select committees have the power to require the attendance of witnesses, but this may be difficult or counter-productive to enforce, and the power does not apply to ministers or civil servants. Although general undertakings to cooperate have been given by successive governments, select committees have often been dissatisfied with the results. Giving select committees a power of subpoena that could be directly enforced, and where non-compliance would carry an automatic penalty, is one possibility; but the legal difficulties, particularly from a human rights point of view, could be considerable.

The powers of select committees were thrown into sharp relief by Lord Hutton's inquiry into the death of the weapons expert Dr David Kelly, which reported in 2004. Largely unprompted, and even though the investigation was not a formal judicial inquiry with powers of subpoena, the government made available to Lord Hutton an extraordinary range of material, including internal papers, advice to ministers, e-mails between officials, and informal notes of meetings. Having set up the Hutton inquiry, it was in the government's interest to be as open as possible – not least to minimise the possibility of blame; but the material submitted was of a sort that any government would automatically have denied to a select committee undertaking a similar inquiry.

This should put select committees on their mettle. In October 2004 the government produced a revised version of the 'Osmotherly Rules' – the government's own guidance on what may or may not be given to a select committee (which is not a document that Parliament itself has agreed). The Commons Liaison Committee, consisting of all select committee chairmen, described the new edition as 'modest'. If select committees do not get from government what they need to do their job, they will be less effective and their reputation will suffer. As with so many aspects of Parliament, success in this will depend entirely on the determination, persistence – and independence – of MPs themselves.

One power that all committees have but that is almost never used (except in committees on private bills) is the ability to take evidence on oath. Under the Parliamentary Witnesses Oaths Act 1871, false evidence is then not something that has to be pursued through the cumbersome and largely ineffective mechanisms of privilege and contempt; the law's serious penalties for perjury come into play. In the small minority of cases where witnesses are thought to be misleading a committee, this might concentrate minds; and it might have a wider moral effect.

A number of other recommendations, mainly from the Liaison Committee and the Modernisation Committee, are still on the table. The proposal for a Committee of Nomination was defeated in the House in May 2002, but there is still some disquiet at the involvement of the whips in the appointment of those whose task it is to scrutinise government. The Liaison Committee's suggestion of a 'select committee half-hour' in prime time in the Chamber, to give immediate prominence to important select committee reports, was turned down by the government for reasons that the committee found profoundly unconvincing. The Liaison Committee also recommended that debates on select committee reports should take place on substantive motions to endorse recommendations, as a way of giving select committees a higher profile and connecting them more closely with the work of the House as a whole. This, too, was rejected by the government.

Two recent trends risk moving in the wrong direction: one is the increase in size of the major select committees from eleven members to fourteen. This has produced more unwieldy bodies that can lose focus – for example, in the questioning of witnesses – and committees will have to ensure that this does not make them less effective. The second has been the suggestion that committees might deliberate in public. A case can be made for this in very narrow circumstances – the five-yearly Select Committee on the Armed Forces Bill when it is actually considering and amending the bill, for example. But if select committees in general were to deliberate in public many of the strengths of the present system would be lost: the informality and directness of discussions that are crucial to creating political consensus; the ability to float radical ideas without looking over one's shoulder for the media or the whips; and the frankness with which committee staff are able to brief their members.

Joint committees

There has been an increase in the use of joint committees of the two Houses, most recently to examine a series of draft bills as well as human rights and the possibilities of Lords reform, and there may be scope for more cooperation. Detailed scrutiny needs considerable resources, which could be more efficiently provided on a joint basis. A suggestion made to the Royal Commission on the reform of the House of Lords was that joint committees might oversee areas of scrutiny, for example European business and delegated legislation (looking at merits, rather than the legal aspects already examined by the Joint Committee on Statutory Instruments). The 'product' of that scrutiny could then be used for investigations and recommendations by sub-committees that were specifically Commons or Lords, thus reflecting the different approaches of the two Houses.

Legislation

This is an area of the House's work that has come in for sustained criticism, and it has been made more contentious by the breakdown of consensus over the programming of bills. The huge quantity of delegated legislation made by ministers under powers given to them in Acts of Parliament is subject to relatively little scrutiny. The proposals in the Legislative and Regulatory Reform Bill, introduced in 2006, would have given sweeping order-making powers to ministers by which they could amend or repeal primary legislation. The Bill attracted immediate criticism on the grounds that it would enable a major increase in ministerial power at the expense of Parliament, and the government was forced to backtrack.

Finding better *ways* of examining legislation is in some ways a second-order question; the main problem is the sheer *volume*. It is a little like thinking of more efficient ways of mopping the floor when a better solution would be to turn the tap off. In July 2003 Robin Cook, the former Leader of the House, described the root cause of the problem, which is 'Whitehall's tendency to keep putting before us more legislation than we can properly scrutinise in any one session'.

Most would agree that the use of draft bills has allowed improved scrutiny and has contributed to better-quality legislation. However, the main complaint of committees that have examined draft bills is that they have had too little time to do a proper job.

In passing, it is worth observing that, although the House of Lords is usually seen as the chamber of detailed examination and revision, the House of Commons is perfectly capable of scrutinising legislation minutely – it just needs the time to do it.

It is possible to deploy an armoury of procedural solutions to the problems of legislative scrutiny: longer periods of notice for government amendments; prescribed intervals between different stages of bills; mandatory pre-legislative scrutiny except in certified cases of urgency; the use of Westminster Hall to increase the time available for debate on Committee of the whole House and report stages; sifting of delegated legislation for importance, combined with select committee investigation (the Procedure Committee's proposals for a sifting committee were turned down by the government, but such a committee has been established in the House of Lords); and so on.

However, the inability or unwillingness of governments of both main parties to legislate less will always be at the heart of the problem. A few years ago, an MP sought leave (only partly tongue in cheek) to bring in a ten-minute rule bill which would have required that, for every page of law put on to the statute book, a page should be deleted. Those who grapple with the scrutiny of legislation may feel that he had a point.

Private members' bill procedure is a fruitful source of proposals for change. As will have been clear from Chapter 6 (page 225), the tactics are complex and the likelihood of success very limited unless proposals are uncontentious and/or have government support. There are always back-bench MPs who have an enthusiasm for legislating that, if unchecked, could produce a volume of legislation rivalling that of the government. The frailty of private members' bills has always been a counterweight to that enthusiasm. However, there is some support for a system that would give a very few bills each session – perhaps five – a chance of success on the basis of being voted on (under some type of programming), rather than simply being talked out or obstructed by lengthy debate on preceding bills. One difficulty with such a change would be ensuring that it was used for genuinely back-bench initiatives rather than government hand-out bills – which would simply increase the government's legislative time.

Examining spending

Chapter 8 reviewed how Parliament, and especially the House of Commons, deals with spending and taxation, and the lack of detailed control over how the government spends taxpayers' money. Select committees' core tasks now require them to examine expenditure plans, and they are equipped to explore the detail in a way that would be impossible in a larger forum. But however strong their criticisms, the opportunity for committees to be any more than advisory is limited – in practice to six estimates day debates a year. And even then the committee may well be reluctant to use the 'nuclear option' of forcing a vote on the reduction of some individual estimate. However, the formal referral of estimates to select committees is often suggested. We consider this in a broader context below.

Reconnecting committees and the Chamber

The Chamber is the forum in which the House takes its decisions; committees are advisory and preparatory. In most cases – the main exception being when bills (as opposed to draft bills) are referred to committees – the result is *advice* rather than something with which the House has to *agree or disagree*.

One prescription for reform would allow the House to play to its acknowledged strength: select committees. Bills would invariably be referred to select committees after second reading, for scrutiny in the light of expert testimony and public involvement, and in a more flexible format than that provided by special standing committees.

The same approach could be used for the estimates, with the House being able to approve only on the basis of a report from the relevant select committee, which would be able to vary individual components up and down (if necessary, provided that the overall totals remained the same).

This radical approach would have a number of implications. Committees would be taking serious decisions that the government, if it disagreed, would have to ask the House to reverse. There would be more political pressure on select committees, and it might be difficult to maintain their generally consensual way of working. The process would demand more time and resources; but it would give power to back-benchers on both sides of the House in a way that would meet many of the current criticisms of the way the Commons operates.

This 'reconnecting committees and the Chamber approach' could be taken into a number of other areas: no statutory instrument could be debated until the Joint Committee on Statutory Instruments had reported upon it; the European Scrutiny Committee could have the power to specify a time within which debates on EU documents should be held and the power to require a debate in the Chamber on the most important proposals; debates in standing committees on delegated legislation could take place on a substantive motion; and the motion agreed to by the committee would have to be put to the House. A similar approach could be used for European standing committees, removing the government's right to substitute a motion of its own when a document was reported from standing committee. Debates on select committee reports could routinely take place on substantive motions.

Qualified majorities

The House has adopted a novel method of decision taking when electing its Speaker. Not all decisions need be taken by a simple majority. It is sometimes suggested that the rights of the opposition parties, and of back-benchers on both sides of the House, might be protected by requiring certain decisions, such as those suspending a normal rule of the House, to be taken by a qualified majority, perhaps two-thirds.

A zero-sum game

Qualified majorities and a mandatory role for select committees in matters of legislation and expenditure are the sorts of things that would cause business managers in governments of either main party to have apoplexy. Most procedural change takes place if there is some balance of advantage and disadvantage to the government of the day. What is noticeable in the studies of parliamentary effectiveness over the last few years is growing agreement that change really is a zero-sum game: that a greater role for Parliament means a net loss of the power of governments. Whether that happens is in the hands of MPs themselves, just as it is up to MPs how effectively they use the considerable parliamentary opportunities that already exist.

The House of Lords

The background

The changes that have taken place in the Commons in recent years, and the prospects for further change, have been evolutionary in character. The House of Lords too has seen evolutionary change, as we shall see. But because of a continuing debate about the composition and powers of the House – and indeed, as to whether the House should exist at all – the Lords has lived with the prospect of fundamental reform of a rather different order for much of the last hundred years. It is useful to see this in historical context.

We saw in Chapter 7 how the powers of the House of Lords over legislation were curtailed by the Parliament Act of 1911 and again in 1949 (page 244). Although reform of the composition of the House had been promised by the preamble to the 1911 Act, nothing was to happen for a very long time. Proposals for an indirectly elected House with a continuing hereditary element were developed by the Bryce Commission in 1918, but these proposals and variations of them found little favour at the time, not least because they would not have eliminated the Conservative Party's majority in the House.

1949

Serious discussion of reform did not resume until 1949, when, in the context of the passage of the second Parliament Bill, an all-party conference discussed powers and composition. No agreement was reached on any wider issue, and the 1949 Parliament Act was confined to reducing the period of operation of the so-called 'suspensory veto' from three sessions to two. But a statement of agreed principles on the future of the House was subsequently published. This statement suggested developments such as the admission of women to the House, some form of remuneration, development of a leave of absence scheme and the elimination of the then permanent majority of the Conservative Party – all of which, in time, were to come about. The most interesting idea of all was that in future the membership should be partly hereditary and partly for life. This latter concept was given effect by the Life Peerages Act in 1958, which included life peerages for women. In 1963, the Peerages Act allowed women hereditary peers to sit for the first time and any hereditary peer to disclaim his peerage for life on inheritance.

The Wilson proposals

In 1967, the Wilson government made a brave attempt to institute a two-tier House composed of 200 to 250 voting life peers, law lords and some bishops and a remainder of non-voting hereditary peers entitled to sit only for the remainder of their lives. Delaying powers over bills would be reduced to six months, and the government party would have a small majority over opposition parties. Although the proposals were approved in principle by the Lords, a curious alliance of Left and Right in the Commons opposed it, and progress in committee proved to be so slow that the bill was abandoned. The failure of this scheme had the effect of removing Lords reform from the agendas of the two main parties for a generation. The Conservative governments under Margaret Thatcher and John Major showed no interest in the question. Indeed, between 1977 and 1989 Labour Party policy was to abolish the House altogether.

The departure of the hereditary peers and a Royal Commission

Not until the election of Tony Blair's Labour government in 1997 did Lords reform reappear on the political agenda, with proposals to eliminate the hereditary members and set up a Royal Commission to consider long-term proposals. Thus the House of Lords Act of 1999 disqualified all hereditary peers from sitting, save for the ninety-two excepted by the Act (see page 38). And in January 2000 the Royal Commission chaired by Lord Wakeham produced its report *A House for the Future*. The Royal Commission confirmed most of the House's existing powers, including that of the suspensory veto under the Parliament Acts.

On composition, however, the Royal Commission made what were its only really radical recommendations. It suggested a chamber of about 550 members, a 'significant minority' of whom would be elected on a regional basis according to a list system of proportional representation, and the remainder appointed. Although the commission could not agree on the number to be elected – three alternative figures of sixty-five, eighty-seven and 195 were offered – the genie of election had been let out of the bottle and was to dominate the reform debate thereafter. Both elected and appointed members would serve fifteen-year terms. Existing life peers would become members for life in the new House. Finally, an Appointments Commission established on a statutory basis would vet nominations for membership of the new second chamber and make its own nominations, chiefly of independent members.

Appointment versus election

Although a House of Lords Appointments Commission with some of the functions recommended by the Royal Commission was established on a non-statutory basis in 2000, not until November 2001 did the government produce a White Paper responding to the Royal Commission's proposals. This proposed a largely nominated second chamber with 120 elected members, regionally based, and a guaranteed independent element. The representation of the political parties would reflect the votes cast in the preceding general election. The Appointments Commission would be a statutory body, but it would have no role in selecting the appointed party members.

The government's response was not well received in all quarters. In February 2002, the Commons Public Administration Committee recommended that 60 per cent of the Lords be elected, 20 per cent be nominated by the parties and 20 per cent be independent members. The Appointments Commission would appoint the non-elected members. Then a Commons early day motion called for any reformed House to be wholly or substantially elected and received the support of over 300 MPs. And the Conservative Party called for a smaller House of 300 predominantly elected members.

Against this increasingly confused background, the Lord Chancellor and Leader of the House of Commons finally announced the appointment of the long-delayed joint committee in order to forge the broadest possible parliamentary consensus on the way forward. The joint committee was to be asked as a first step 'to report on options for the composition and powers of the House of Lords once reform has been completed'. This was to be followed by free votes in both Houses and then a subsequent report to 'define in greater detail the proposed composition, role and powers of the reformed second chamber', taking account of the opinion expressed in the votes. It would also recommend the transitional strategy for transforming the existing House of Lords into its fully reformed state.

At the end of 2002, the joint committee duly published its first report setting out options for the composition of a reformed House against a background of what the committee saw as 'broad agreement on the role, functions and powers of a reformed second chamber', which would remain largely unchanged. On membership, seven options were put forward, ranging from fully appointed to fully nominated. The House would comprise about 600 members, each of whom would serve for twelve years. Nominations of appointed members would be scrutinised by a new, statutory, Appointments Commission.

The report was debated in both Houses in January 2003, and in February each House voted on each of the seven options. The outcome was confusing. The Lords voted overwhelmingly in favour of the fully appointed option and rejected the others. The Commons on the other hand rejected all options, although the 80 per cent elected, 20 per cent appointed option was lost by only three votes. In view of this, the joint committee made a second report in May 2003 identifying the consensus that had been achieved – chiefly on powers – and outlining the further work that needed to be done on questions such as the future of the remaining hereditary peers, the appointments system, the size of the House and the conditions of tenure of the members. The report spelled out the five qualities required in the membership of a House that can perform the functions currently assigned to it – legitimacy, representativeness, no domination by one party, independence, and expertise – and, in effect, invited the government to indicate what view it now took of the future of Lords reform.

The government's response, published in July 2003, accepted the joint committee's assessment that a consensus had now been reached over the role, functions and powers of the House. It also accepted the qualities required in the membership. But, in the absence of a consensus as to what the membership should be, the government's interest in further reform would be confined to making the House work as effectively as possible in the medium term.

Thus in September 2003, the government published its consultation paper 'Constitutional reform: next steps for the House of Lords', in which it announced its intention to introduce a bill 'when Parliamentary time allows' to remove all remaining hereditary peers from the House and to establish a statutory Appointments Commission. The government proposed that the commission would be accountable to Parliament and would determine the number and timing of appointments, select independent members of the House and oversee party nominations. The commission would be obliged to ensure that the balance of new nominations between the parties reflected the distribution of the vote at the previous general election. Twenty per cent of new appointments would be non-party, and the target membership of the House would probably not exceed 600.

In some ways it is difficult to see what else the government could have done in the light of the decisions of the two Houses. But, on the other hand, those who hoped for more radical change will no doubt have agreed with Robin Cook, former Leader of the House of Commons, who recorded in his diary as this policy was being formulated: 'Modernisation is to be limited to moving from the fifteenth century principle of heredity to the eighteenth century principle of patronage'.

It had been expected that a bill to give effect to changes on these lines would be introduced in March 2004 but instead the government announced that it would not, after all, legislate in that Parliament.

Backbenchers have their say

As in the past, when government schemes for Lords reform lose momentum, back-bench members kept the issues alive. In the Lords, a group of seven Labour back-benchers chaired by Lord Hunt of Kings Heath held a series of meetings in 2004 to consider reform of powers and procedures rather than composition. Its report, published in July of that year, made a number of recommendations, the chief of which was that a new Parliament Act should be passed which, while retaining the current two session suspensory veto or something like it, would introduce a sixty-day time limit for Lords consideration of bills; provide that Lords bills would be subject to the Parliament Acts; redefine time limits for delay so as to facilitate carry-over of bills; and provide for a formal reconciliation machinery to resolve disagreements between the Houses. The group's other chief recommendation was to recast the current stages on bills into three stages – deliberation, decision and revision. While the decision and revision stages broadly equate to the current report and third reading, the deliberation stage would take place off the floor and would combine elements of the current second reading debate (but with participation of officials) with the current grand committee style of committee stage for the detailed consideration and disposal of non-contentious amendments. A debate on these proposals was held in the House of Lords in January 2005 and they were badly received by the opposition parties.

Not long afterwards a cross-party group of distinguished members of the House of Commons (chaired by Paul Tyler, then Liberal Democrat shadow Leader of the House and including Kenneth Clarke and Sir George Young (Conservative), and the late Robin Cook and Tony Wright (Labour)) published an initiative entitled 'Breaking the Deadlock'. Their proposals were for a 70 per cent elected upper house, with sixteen bishops and archbishops, and the remainder appointed by a statutory Appointments Commission. The total membership would be 385 and each member would serve the equivalent of three House of Commons terms (i.e. in practice twelve to fourteen years). Existing members of the House would leave in three stages – one-third at each of three elections. They would be free to stand for election. The system of election would be single transferable vote using European Parliament 'constituencies'. A draft bill to give effect to these changes was appended to the report. These proposals are consistent with the findings of the Royal Commission but the relatively high proportion of elected members may deter some from supporting the package.

The 2005 Labour Manifesto and beyond

The Labour party manifesto for the 2005 general election called for a reformed upper chamber that is 'more representative without challenging the primacy of the House of Commons'. It called for the establishment of a joint committee once again, this time to focus more on codifying the conventions of the House, new forms of scrutiny, time limits on bills and so forth – to validate, in other words, some of the findings of Lord Hunt of Kings Heath's working group. The remaining hereditary members would be removed and a free vote offered on composition. Following informal consultations between the parties initiated by Lord Falconer of Thoroton, a joint committee was finally established in May 2006 to consider the practicality of codifying the Salisbury convention; conventions on delegated legislation; the assumptions about "reasonable time" for passage of bills; and practices surrounding disagreements on bills ('ping-pong'). Curiously the remit does not include any review of the provisions of the Parliament Acts relating to the so-called 'suspensory veto' of one year.

Any recommendation which materially affects the powers of the Lords is unlikely to find favour in the House, though codification of the ways in which these powers are actually currently applied may well have more chance of adoption. The Government for its part will wish to see some shift in the way that the House exercises its powers in return for a vote in both Houses and a further bill on composition which – were it to remove the remaining hereditary element and provide for the election of a proportion of the House – would give the House a democratic legitimacy it has hitherto lacked.

Meanwhile the loans and cash for peerages scandal surrounding the working peers list finally published in April 2006 has strengthened calls for reform of composition. Will 2006 be the year when these issues are finally resolved?

Would-be reformers of the House of Lords have always faced two virtually irresolvable problems: first, how to reconcile reform of membership with the heightened sense of legitimacy vis-à-vis the House of Commons that would inevitably result; and, second, how to reconcile a heightened sense of legitimacy with the exercise of a range of powers that, while retaining the practical utility of the upper House, nevertheless reflects the ultimate supremacy of the House of Commons. Until answers can be found to these questions that are acceptable both across the political spectrum and within the current administration, the prospect of success will remain elusive.

The Lord Chancellor and the Lords of Appeal in Ordinary

The office of Lord Chancellor dismembered

On 12 June 2003, Lord Irvine of Lairg resigned as Lord Chancellor and Lord Falconer of Thoroton was appointed in his place. But at the same time the announcement was made that steps would be taken to separate the functions of the Lord Chancellor. The new Lord Chancellor would cease to sit judicially; an independent Judicial Appointments Commission set up on a statutory basis would recommend candidates for appointment as judges; and the House of Lords would be invited to consider an alternative method for appointing its own Speaker. The appellate functions of the House of Lords would be transferred to a Supreme Court. The Lord Chancellor's Department was renamed the Department of Constitutional Affairs and acquired overall responsibility for the Scotland and Wales Offices. Lord Falconer became Secretary of State of the Department. In the longer term, the post of Lord Chancellor would be abolished.

Although the announcement of these changes surprised many, the role of the Lord Chancellor as Speaker of a chamber of Parliament, government minister, judge and head of the judiciary had come to be questioned by some lawyers and constitutionalists. While there is no evidence to suggest that holders of the office in recent times were unable successfully to separate their various functions and exercise them impartially, the office appeared to offend the doctrine of separation of powers. After all, the Lord Chancellor embodied in his person parliamentary, executive and judicial office. (Indeed, he illustrated only too well how the concept of separation of powers has always existed only imperfectly in the United Kingdom!)

A bill, the Constitutional Reform Bill, was introduced in 2004 to give effect to main changes – abolishing the office of Lord Chancellor, making the Lord Chief Justice head of the judiciary, providing for the establishment of a Supreme Court and setting up a Judicial Appointments Commission. The eventual Act received Royal Assent just before dissolution in 2005, after the bill had most unusually been committed to a select committee in the Lords and carried over into the following session for completion of Lords stages and consideration by the Commons. All the main provisions of the original bill were enacted except that, following a committee stage defeat in the Lords, the government agreed to retain the office of Lord Chancellor. However the duties of the post will be much reduced and there will be no obligation for the occupant to be a lawyer or a member of the House of Lords. Meanwhile, Lord Falconer has continued to fulfil all aspects of the job, although he has not sat judicially.

The changes to the office of Lord Chancellor will have a profound effect on the speakership of the House of Lords and the creation of a Supreme Court (unlikely before 2009) will end a centuries old appellate function and exclude serving justices from membership of the House. We consider these effects next.

The Speaker

On 12 July 2005 the House agreed that it should elect its own presiding officer and it reconvened a select committee on the speakership which had previously met and considered the issue in 2003. This committee, chaired by Lord Lloyd of Berwick, a retired law lord, had already recommended in 2003 that the House should elect a Speaker by ballot, using the alternative vote system currently in use for by-elections for the excepted hereditary members. The successor committee reported on 19 December 2005. It reaffirmed the mode of election. While the earlier committee had suggested that the Speaker might have a new role as 'guardian of the Companion to Standing Orders', the later committee took a more cautious line, reflecting the mood of the House. The House would continue to keep its own order, though the Speaker might intervene to offer procedural advice. In addition the Lord Speaker would take over adjudication of Private Notice Question and the *sub judice* rule from the Leader of the House, and the power of recall of the House and certain statutory functions – such as appointment of Lords members of the Ecclesiastical Committee – from the Lord Chancellor. The Speaker would be expected to preside over proceedings for up to three hours each day and would be assisted by a reduced panel of twelve deputies. The Speaker would assume chairmanship of the House Committee but otherwise the office of Lord Chairman would remain intact. The Speaker would, of course, undertake representative functions at home and abroad, meet and greet, and so forth. The election of a Speaker of the House of Lords, on 28 June 2006, represents a momentous change. Ironically, it requires no legislation but merely the replacement of Standing Order 18, dating from 1660, which provided that the Lord Chancellor should be Speaker of the House of Lords. And while initially the post will, in human resources jargon, be somewhat lightly loaded, it would be surprising if it did not develop over the years to come. The Committee also recommended that the Speaker be called 'Lord Speaker' which, though an old style of address commonly used within the House, may not find favour with some MPs. The House agreed these proposals in April 2006.

The Supreme Court

This book does not concern itself with the role of the House of Lords as a court of final appeal, although we saw in Chapter 2 how, under the Appellate Jurisdiction Act 1876, the Lords of Appeal in Ordinary are given life peerages to hear appeals; they and retired Lords of Appeal currently number twenty-eight.

It is intended that the proposed Supreme Court will assume the current appellate functions of the House of Lords as the final court of appeal in the United Kingdom, save in Scottish criminal cases. It will also acquire from the Judicial Committee of the Privy Council functions in respect of contested devolution issues. The appellate function of the House has for centuries been distinct from the parliamentary function. So vesting it in a Supreme Court, subject to appropriate legislative and administrative arrangements being put in place, will not impinge on the other work of the House at all. Indeed, parliamentary accommodation and staff will become available for other uses.

The chief effect will be the potential loss of eminent lawyers – the law lords appointed under the 1876 Act – as members of the House. At the moment, it is possible for the serving and retired Lords of Appeal to take part in proceedings of the House and to serve on its committees. Some contribute to debates on bills, especially those that relate to the administration of justice or the criminal law, and even move and vote on amendments. Others play an active part in committees – chairing the Joint Committee on Consolidation Bills, the Ecclesiastical Committee, Sub-Committee E of the European Union Committee and the Privileges Committee, for example. They provide a valuable in-house resource of legal and forensic expertise.

Under the provisions of the Constitutional Reform Act the Justices of the Supreme Court (as the Lords of Appeal in Ordinary will become) will no longer be eligible to sit in the Lords and new Justices will not be given peerages. Indeed they will be disqualified from membership until they retire as judges. While the House will still include practising lawyers amongst its members it will no longer have the advantage of the advice of some of the highest legal brains in the land – not before they finally retire, at any rate.

Although the establishment of the Judicial Appointments Commission and the modifications in the office of Lord Chancellor (and hence the speakership of the House) took place in the early part of 2006, the Supreme Court is unlikely to be established until October 2009. Indeed, the Supreme Court cannot be set up until the intended new premises at the old Middlesex Guildhall on Parliament Square have been prepared.

Modernisation of practice and procedure in the Lords

The House of Lords has undergone its own programme of change in working practices and procedures in recent years. Unlike the Commons, the

Lords has no continuing Modernisation Committee, although the former Leader of the House's Working Group on the Working Practices of the House in 2001–02, and somewhat earlier the Select Committee on the Committee Work of the House in 1992 (the Jellicoe Committee) and the Group on Sittings of the House in 1995 (the Rippon Group) performed very similar functions. In addition, the Procedure Committee continually develops the way in which things are done. For many years, in the absence of proposals for reform of the House, it was by means such as these that the House developed – indeed reformed – itself. Developments continue in a number of areas, and while they have been recounted elsewhere in this book it is useful to pull them together here to illustrate the capacity of the House to renew itself.

Committee work

The expansion of the work of select committees since the establishment of the European Union (then Communities) Committee in 1974 was one of the most visible signs of renewal. The process continues, although, as we saw in Chapter 11, the Liaison Committee now arbitrates on competing claims for resources. Thus since 1997 the Economic Affairs and Constitution Committees have been established as sessional committees and the Human Rights Committee as a joint committee. Following recommendations of the Group on Working Practices in 2002, the Finance Bill Sub-Committee of the Economic Affairs Committee was established in 2003, and a Select Committee on the Merits of Statutory Instruments was set up as a sessional committee at the beginning of the 2003–04 session. Further demands for the establishment of committees on an ad hoc or sessional basis are continually being made.

Like the Commons, Lords committees seek to engage the public in their inquiries to the extent that it is practicable. Online consultation has been used twice since the experience of the Joint Committee on the Draft Communications Bill. But for the reasons set out at page 202, most committees appear to find the process of limited value.

Grand committees

As we saw in Chapter 7, following a recommendation of the Rippon Group in 1995, some bills have been committed to unselected 'grand committees', which any lord may attend. The Group on Working Practices recommended in 2002 that more use be made of this procedure. The number of bills referred is determined by the usual channels but is now much higher than when the procedure was introduced.

In 2003, on the initiative of the then Leader of the House, the House agreed that the grand committee procedure could be used to debate some Northern Ireland Orders. The intention was to improve scrutiny of what was, effectively, primary legislation during a period of suspension of the Northern Ireland Assembly. The Orders then return to the floor of the House for approval.

Then in 2004, two years on from the original Leader's Group on Working Practices, a new group under the chairmanship of Baroness Amos met to review those recommendations that had been made on a trial basis. The Group confirmed the grand committee's procedures and activities. It further recommended that other delegated legislation might also be considered in that forum and that debates on some select committee reports and unstarred questions could also be held. The Procedure Committee agreed and as a result, since the beginning of the 2004–05 session, the grand committee has all the makings of a parallel Chamber, capable of transacting the committee stages of bills, debates (though no final approval) on Northern Ireland Orders and other affirmative instruments, debates on select committee reports and unstarred questions.

Sitting hours

Following recommendations of the Group on Working Practices, the House agreed to make changes to its hours of sitting with effect from the 2002–03 session. A convention has been established that the House will normally rise at 10.00 p.m. on Mondays to Wednesdays. On Thursdays the House now sits at 11.00 a.m. and business ends at 7 p.m. In addition, the House agreed to sit for two weeks in September in line with the Commons, having risen in mid-July. None of these developments at first proved an unqualified success. The 10.00 p.m. cut-off, combined with the relatively late start to business in the afternoons after questions and statements, has reduced the ability of the government to get its business through. The arrangement of Thursday business originally with a lunchtime adjournment followed by Question Time was not liked and has been further refined, particularly as debates on motions now take place on Thursdays rather than Wednesdays. There are many who question the value of sitting in September. Neither House sat in September 2005.

Other developments, such as increased pre-legislative scrutiny of bills (see page 201), carry-over of such bills if they are subsequently introduced late in a session, as recommended by the Group on Working Practices, and more Lords participation in Commons standing committees on EU matters (see page 404), may also come about in coming years. Taken alone, none of these changes amounts to a 'reform' in the traditional sense of the word, but taken collectively, incremental changes such as these have a tremendous effect both on what the House does and on the way in which it does it.

Conclusion

Parliament is an *organism* as much – or more – than it is an *organisation*. And it has all the classic attributes of an organism: reactive, unpredictable, sometimes illogical. But at the start of the twenty-first century it has much to offer its citizens – and could still play as important a part in the life of the nation as at any time in its history.

'Modernisation', a word with no precise meaning, is not to be confused with 'effectiveness'. The changes made in both Houses over the last few years prompt some thoughts about the way ahead.

Parliamentary reform has become a zero-sum game. The process of modernisation is one of diminishing marginal returns: there were some obvious things to do early on, but after a while the only alternatives are either to fiddle with details or to make real changes that shift the balance in favour of Parliament and away from the government of the day. Given that the power of initiative lies in the hands of the government, this suggests the need either for unprecedented altruism on the part of the government of the day, or for the powers of Parliament to matter so much to its members that they force change, even against the political interests of the parties to which they belong.

In turn this suggests that a more rigorous view of any proposed change is required. Will it make Parliament more effective in discharging its key functions – authorising and controlling spending, getting value for money, holding the government to account, representing constituents effectively? Or does it simply make the lives of MPs or ministers easier?

A key element in this is the Civil Service. Things that make a government's life easier also make life more comfortable for its officials. There has never been any enthusiasm in Whitehall for additional parliamentary powers, or for reforms that make life less predictable, and this is an additional challenge for advocates of change.

An important factor in the future health and effectiveness of Parliament is somehow tackling the urge to legislate. Under the heading 'Ministers must avoid becoming prisoners of the Whitehall machine' a leader in *The*

Times in May 2005 observed 'all governments come to believe that every social ill demands a legislative response from Parliament'; and, as the late Robin Cook said from his perspective as a former Leader of the House, the main problem is 'Whitehall's tendency to keep putting before us more legislation than we can properly scrutinise in any one session'. Poorly scrutinised law, passed too quickly, does nothing for the reputation of Parliament, nor for the law itself.

Whether or not these things matter enough to members of both Houses, they do not yet matter enough to the public and the media. When the House of Commons made permanent the system of programming of bills, a bitterly contentious issue that went directly to the power of the executive to get its way over legislation, every national newspaper the next day covered instead, in more or less jokey terms, the abolition of the term 'Strangers', which had been dealt with at the same sitting.

Some parliamentary changes in the last five years have produced unintended consequences. The changes in sitting hours were intended to make the House of Commons more family-friendly, with a working day closer to that of most of the population. But the Commons has ended up with a weekly timetable on which only two of the five days are the same, which makes it more, not less difficult for the media and others outside Parliament to engage with what is happening. And at the same time earlier sittings in both Houses have reduced the opportunities for constituents to tour Parliament. To take another example, would-be reformers often criticise the complexity of parliamentary procedures. Yet the programming of bills has required the addition of twelve pages of intricate standing orders.

There can be no doubt that the general public are not enthusiastic about parliamentary politics. In the run-up to the 2005 election, the BBC's *Question Time* programme featured a debate between the three party leaders. It attracted an audience of 4.1 million; but *Footballers' Wives*, broadcast at the same time on a rival channel, beat it easily with 5.8 million viewers. The turnout in the subsequent general election only just beat the record low of 2001; but this apparent disaffection is not unique to the UK.

Reputational issues are a factor. In September 2004 the Committee on Standards in Public Life published the findings of its extensive survey of attitudes to public standards. Of those polled 11 per cent rated standards in public life as low or very low; but only 27 per cent trusted MPs generally to tell the truth, as opposed to 67 per cent who did not (incidentally, almost exactly the same score as for TV journalists). But when respondents were asked whether they trusted their local MP to tell the truth, the 'yes' score went up to 47 per cent – no doubt the human tendency to stereotype people but at the same time making exceptions for those we know.

Our adversarial political culture may be partly to blame. Sir Peter Ustinov, when asked why he never went into politics, said 'because I couldn't bear to be right all the time'; which perhaps underlines the need for Parliament's traditional, but sometimes forgotten, role as a place in which debate and evidence change minds.

All that said, the United Kingdom Parliament at the start of the twenty-first century has real strengths and even greater potential, which this book has attempted to portray. Parliament is also more active and vibrant than it has been for decades. Fifty years ago there was no broadcasting or tele-vising of proceedings, little constituency work, and no attempt to reach out to the public. The relatively few select committees were much weaker, had minimal back-up and did not challenge policy. And only 2.5 per cent of votes in the Commons showed any dissent at all. By contrast, in 2004–05 the percentage was 39 per cent, and in that session the government was also defeated thirty-seven times in the House of Lords.

The last few years have seen something of a 'Parliament dead' industry, in which facile criticisms of the institution have obscured what really needs to be changed to make it more effective (combined with using the con-siderable *existing* opportunities to greater advantage). The attitude of some parliamentarians towards making Parliament do a better job was recently described as 'Here am I, send my neighbour'. There is no doubt that achiev-ing a more powerful Parliament will not be easy, and will have a political price; but in the end it is parliamentarians alone who can make it happen.

Glossary of parliamentary terms

In each definition, words in *italics* are further explained elsewhere in the glossary.

accounting Officer the individual (usually the *Permanent Secretary* of a government department or the chief executive of an executive agency) who is personally responsible for the regularity and propriety of expenditure voted under a particular estimate.

Act paper paper laid before Parliament because an Act of Parliament requires it.

additional costs allowance an allowance to cover an MP's costs of staying away from home while at Westminster.

Address a formal communication from either House to the sovereign. The debate on the Queen's Speech takes place on a motion of thanks for the speech (often called the 'Humble Address').

adjournment the end of a *sitting*. An 'adjournment debate' takes place on a motion 'That this House do now adjourn'. It may be either the half-hour adjournment debate at the end of each sitting in the Commons (where MPs may 'raise a subject on the Adjournment'), or a more significant debate as part of the main business of the day. For the government, the advantage of an adjournment debate (sometimes called in the media a 'technical motion') is that any vote at the end is not on a substantive issue but only on whether the House should adjourn or not. An adjournment (for example 'the summer adjournment') is also a more formal name for a *recess*.

Administration Estimate in the Commons, pays for the staff of the House and the services provided by the House departments.

advisory cost limit the estimated cost of answering a parliamentary question (at present £600) above which a minister may decline to answer the question.

affirmation a secular promise of allegiance to the Crown made by MPs or peers who do not wish to take a religious oath.

affirmative instrument a piece of *delegated legislation* that the parent Act requires Parliament to approve explicitly before it can come into effect ('the affirmative procedure').

allocation of time order see *guillotine*.

all-party groups of greater or lesser formality, these bring together MPs and peers from all parties to discuss matters of common interest. They are established by MPs and peers themselves rather than being creations of either House. The total varies: in 2006 there were some 320 groups. 'Associate parliamentary groups' (about 40) also include people who are not members of one or other House. 'Country groups' (about 120) bring together MPs and peers interested in the affairs of particular countries.

ambit of an estimate the formal description of the services to be financed from that *estimate*.

amendment proposal to change the text of a bill, motion or draft select committee report.

amendment of the law motion moved by the Chancellor of the Exchequer after his *Budget* statement: 'that it is expedient to amend the law with respect to the National Debt and to make further provision in respect of public finance'. It is the vehicle for the broad Budget debate that follows.

amendment in lieu amendment proposed by one House to the other as an alternative to one that has been rejected by the former.

annually managed expenditure (AME) a category of government expenditure that is less predictable or controllable than that under *departmental expenditure limits*; for example, social security and Common Agricultural Policy payments.

annulment the act of making a *Statutory Instrument* of no effect. See also *prayer*.

Appellate Committee the committee of law lords that hears appeals in the House of Lords.

back-bencher an MP or peer who is neither a minister nor (in opposition) a spokesperson for his or her party.

back of the Chair bill see *presentation bill*.

backsheet the last page of a bill, which repeats the *long* and *short title* of the bill, gives the bill number and the session, and lists the MP introducing the bill ('the member in charge') and his or her supporters.

ballot bills in the Commons, the twenty *private members' bills* introduced following the ballot on the second Thursday of each session.

bill draft *primary legislation*.

bill of aids and supplies old name for a bill granting *Supply* and *Ways and Means*.

Black Rod ('the Gentleman Usher of the Black Rod') an officer of the Lords responsible for accommodation, services, security and ceremonial.

blocking minority the number of votes required to block a proposal in the Council of Ministers of the European Union under *qualified majority voting* (*QMV*). The voting strengths of the member states are: France, Germany, Italy, the United Kingdom, 29 each; Poland, Spain, 27 each; the Netherlands, 13; Belgium, the Czech Republic, Greece, Hungary, Portugal, 12 each; Austria, Sweden, 10 each; Denmark, Ireland, Lithuania, Slovakia, Finland, 7 each; Cyprus, Estonia, Latvia, Luxembourg, Slovenia, 4 each; Malta 3. The total of all the votes is 321. For the approval of a proposal by QMV, 72.3 per cent of votes (or 232) have to be cast in favour. So a blocking minority is 321 less 231, or 90 votes. In addition, a member state may ask for confirmation that the votes cast represent at least 62 per cent of the population of the EU. If this is not the case, then the proposal is defeated. Voting in the UK Parliament is somewhat simpler.

Boundary Commissions the four bodies that keep under review the size, boundaries and numbers of parliamentary *constituencies*, especially to take account of population changes.

Budget oral statement by the Chancellor of the Exchequer, usually in March, which reviews the nation's finances and makes taxation proposals.

Business Questions (strictly, 'the Business Question') in the Commons, a type of *urgent question* asked of the *Leader of the House* every Thursday, in response to which he announces the business for the next fortnight and answers questions.

by-election an election in a single *constituency* when a seat becomes vacant because the MP dies or is otherwise no longer eligible to sit.

casting vote the vote cast by the Chair to decide the issue when the numbers voting are equal. How the vote is cast is usually dictated by precedent, except in select committees.

CCLA Commons consideration of *Lords amendments*.

Chairman of Committees (or 'Lord Chairman') the principal Deputy Speaker of the House of Lords and Chairman of the House Committee, which oversees Lords administration. He organises the panel of deputy speakers and deputy chairmen and assigns them their duties, and he has special responsibility for *private bills*. He also chairs the Liaison Committee and the Procedure Committee.

Chairman of Ways and Means the principal Deputy Speaker of the Commons, with special responsibilities for Committees of the whole House, *private bills* and *Westminster Hall*. In the House, he is assisted by First and Second Deputy Chairmen of Ways and Means, who act as Deputy Speakers. He chairs the Speaker's Panel of Chairmen, which provides chairmen for *standing committees*.

Chiltern Hundreds the posts of steward or bailiff of Her Majesty's three Chiltern Hundreds of Stoke, Desborough and Burnham, or of the manor of Northstead, are symbolic 'offices of profit' used to allow an MP to resign his or her seat. If an MP is appointed to one, he or she is disqualified as holding an 'office of profit under the Crown' (an MP cannot simply resign).

clause the basic unit of a *bill*, divided into subsections, then paragraphs, then sub-paragraphs. When a bill becomes an Act, 'clauses' become 'sections' but the names of the other subdivisions stay the same.

Clerk of the House the principal officer of the Commons. Chief executive of the House Service and corporate officer as well as the House's principal adviser on the practice, law and privilege of the House.

Clerk of the Parliaments the principal officer of the Lords, with functions similar to those of the Clerk of the House of Commons, but who is also Registrar of the Court when the House acts in its judicial capacity.

closure in the Commons, a device for curtailing debate, or for securing a decision on a matter that would otherwise be *talked out*. An MP moves a *motion* 'That the Question be now put', which (if allowed by the Chair) is put to a decision immediately, without debate. If a division is forced upon it, not fewer than 100 MPs must vote in the majority for the closure, otherwise the motion is lost. If it is agreed to, the Question originally proposed from the Chair must be put immediately.

collective responsibility the doctrine under which all members of the government – that is, ministers – support the policies of the government and take responsibility for government action, even if there are elements with which they privately disagree. Open disagreement is normally followed by resignation.

Command Paper paper presented to Parliament by the government, formally 'by Command of Her Majesty'.

commencement the coming into effect of legislation. For Acts of Parliament, this is usually done by an order made by the responsible minister. If there is no commencement provision, the Act comes into force from midnight at the beginning of the day on which *Royal Assent* was given.

Committee of the whole House used for the committee stage of bills in the House itself rather than in a *standing committee*. In the Commons, Committee of the whole House is presided over by the *Chairman of Ways and Means* rather than the *Speaker*, and the *Mace* (normally on top of the *Table*) is placed on brackets below the Table to show that the House is in committee. Any MP may take part in proceedings, just as in the House itself.

Commons amendment an amendment made by the Commons to a bill passed by the Lords.

Comptroller and Auditor General a statutorily independent officer of the Commons who heads the National Audit Office (NAO); who approves the release of money from the Consolidated Fund; who audits some 600 accounts of government departments and a range of public bodies; and who carries out 'value for money' (VFM) inquiries into the economy, efficiency and effectiveness of public spending. He has a close relationship with the Public Accounts Committee, which considers his reports.

consideration see *report stage*.

Consolidated Fund the government's account at the Bank of England.

Consolidated Fund (Appropriation) Bill the detailed legislative authority for *Supply*. It sets out the *ambit* of each estimate and the amount to be paid ('appropriated') in respect of each, any receipts to be set against expenditure, and the numbers of personnel authorised for the armed services.

Consolidated Fund Bill a bill giving legislative authority to the Commons *resolutions* approving the *estimates*.

consolidation bill one that seeks to set out the law in a particular subject area in a clearer and more up-to-date form without changing its substance.

constituency the area of the country 'returning', or being represented by, each MP.

constituency Friday a non-sitting Friday in a sitting week.

COSAC (known by the French acronym) the Conference of European Affairs Committees, which every six months brings together representatives of the European Affairs Committees in all the national parliaments of the member states of the EU, and of the Constitutional Affairs Committee of the European Parliament.

Cranborne money financial assistance to opposition parties in the Lords, named after the then Leader of the House, Viscount Cranborne. The Commons equivalent is *Short money*.

cross-benches benches in either House facing the Chair rather than on one side or the other of the Chamber. In the Lords, cross-benchers are those peers without party allegiance.

crossing the floor changing party allegiance (even if the MP's new party in fact sits on the same side of the House).

decision any decision of the EU Council of Ministers is binding upon those to whom it is addressed.

deferred division in the Commons, when on certain types of business an attempt is made to force a vote after the *moment of interruption*, that vote is held in one of the division lobbies between 12.30 p.m. and 2.00 p.m. on the next sitting Wednesday.

delegated legislation sometimes called 'subordinate legislation' or 'secondary legislation' (or 'Statutory Instruments', which most but not all are): legislation made by a minister, or occasionally by a public body, under powers conferred by an Act of Parliament. Different types of delegated legislation are called variously orders, rules, regulations, schemes or codes, depending on what the 'parent Act' calls them.

departmental annual reports published between March and May each year, these report on a government department's activities, spending and achievements, especially performance against objectives.

departmental expenditure limit (DEL) total planned expenditure for a government department, but excluding *annually managed expenditure*.

deposit sum of £500 forfeited if a candidate receives less than 5 per cent of the votes cast at a parliamentary election.

de-referral in the Commons, a motion to take business (typically, debate on a Statutory Instrument or European Union document) on the floor of the House rather than in the committee to which is has been automatically referred.

despatch boxes boxes at the *Table* of either House, from which *front-benchers* speak.

dilatory motion a delaying motion, for the adjournment of the debate, committee or House; or to adjourn further consideration of a bill.

directive European legislation binding on member states in terms of the result to be achieved by a certain date.

dissolution the ending of a parliament by royal proclamation, followed by a *general election*.

division a vote 'to divide the House' (or committee) to force a vote. In the Commons the votes are 'Aye' or 'No'; in the Lords 'Content' or 'Not Content'.

draft bill a bill, not yet formally introduced into either House, that is made available for pre-legislative scrutiny by a select or joint committee.

dummy bill a sheet of paper, with the *short* and *long titles* and list of supporters, presented at the *Table* by a back-bench MP introducing a *private member's bill*.

early day motion (EDM) motions set down for 'an early day' and so – apart from *prayers*, which first appear in this form – almost certain not to be debated. EDMs are mainly used to make political points and to test opinion.

elector someone who has a vote in a parliamentary election.

electoral quota the total number of electors divided by the number of constituencies.

estimate a request from the government to the Commons for the resources required for each main area of public expenditure.

estimates days in the Commons, three days in the course of a session when the *estimates* are approved; select committee reports selected by the Liaison

Committee, and linked to particular estimates, provide the subjects for debate on those days.

excess Votes these seek retrospective authorisation when a government department's spending in a financial year has exceeded what Parliament has authorised, or has been incurred for a purpose that was not authorised.

exempted in the Commons, business that may be taken after the *moment of interruption*, either because it falls into an exempted category, or because it is covered by an order (at the initiative of the government) that specifically exempts it.

explanatory memorandum the government's evidence on each EU document, which is subject to the European scrutiny system of each House.

Explanatory Notes a document accompanying a government bill that sets out the bill's intention and background, explains the clauses in lay person's language and gives an assessment of the bill's effects on public service manpower and costs, and on private sector business.

Father of the House in the Commons, the MP with the longest continuous service.

first past the post the voting system in which the candidate with the most votes – a relative majority – wins regardless of how many other candidates there are or how close they come to the winning number of votes.

first reading the formal first stage of a bill's passage through Parliament, taken without debate when the bill is introduced. The bill is then ordered to be printed.

floor of the House the Chamber of either House. A matter debated 'on the floor' is discussed in a plenary sitting rather than in a separate committee.

front-bencher a minister or *shadow minister*.

the gallery collective term for the journalists primarily concerned with reporting proceedings rather than the interpretation of parliamentary and political events, which is more the province of the *lobby*.

general election following a dissolution of Parliament, an election for every seat in the new House of Commons.

giving way allowing another member to intervene briefly in a speech to make a point or to ask a question.

grand committee in the Lords, for considering the committee stage of bills off the floor of the House. In the Commons, the Scottish, Welsh and

Northern Ireland Grand Committees may be used for statements from ministers, oral questions, the consideration of bills and *delegated legislation*, and *adjournment debates*.

green card available in the Central Lobby of the Palace of Westminster and filled in by a constituent seeking a meeting with his or her MP.

Green Paper document for consultation on possible policy options.

grouping the grouping of related *amendments* for debate.

guillotine in the Commons; also known as an 'allocation of time order': at any stage in the passage of a bill, an order that imposes time limits on the remainder of its progress.

hand-out bill a bill that the government wishes to see enacted and that is drafted by *parliamentary counsel*, offered to a back-bencher to take forward as a *private member's bill*, usually with the continuing support and briefing of the government department concerned.

Hansard see *Official Report*.

hemicycle a semicircular debating chamber, as in the French Assemblée nationale, or the European Parliament.

hereditary peer a member of the House of Lords by virtue of inheriting a title (usually, a son inheriting from a father, although some hereditary peerages can pass to a daughter); 92 hereditary peers have seats as a result of the House of Lords Act 1999 (which removed the right of other hereditary peers to sit in the Lords).

House of Lords Appointments Commission a non-statutory commission that makes recommendations to the Queen for non-political peers and vets for propriety all nominations for peerages, including those from the political parties.

hung parliament after a *general election*, when no one party has a majority in the House of Commons.

hybrid bill a bill that combines the characteristics of a public bill (changing the general law) and a private bill (making provision with local or personal effect).

incidental expenses provision an MP's allowance principally to cover the costs of constituency offices.

introduction the formal start of a bill's passage through Parliament. The bill is formally given a first reading at the same time and ordered to be printed. Also used of the formal introduction of a new MP or peer.

joint committee a *select committee* with a membership drawn from both Houses.

Journal the legal record of the proceedings of both Houses (of decisions and events rather than words spoken).

knives the deadlines within a *programme order*. When a knife falls, only specified decisions may be taken, and it may not be possible to debate or decide on certain clauses or amendments.

LCCA Lords consideration of *Commons amendments*.

Leader of the House in the Commons, a cabinet minister dealing with House affairs and the organisation of business, who also chairs the Modernisation Committee. The Leader of the House of Lords has a similar role but plays an additional part in guiding the course of business during a sitting.

life peer a member of the House of Lords for life, having been appointed under the Appellate Jurisdiction Act 1876 (law lords) or the Life Peerages Act 1958 (other peers).

lobby (1) a room, as in division lobbies, the Central Lobby, Members' Lobby or Peers' Lobby; (2) to come to Westminster to put a case, either to an individual MP or as part of a demonstration ('mass lobbies'); (3) the group of parliamentary journalists with special access to the Palace of Westminster, reporting parliamentary and political news and opinion.

lobby terms information given to journalists on the basis that it may be disclosed but not attributed.

lobby standi the position of someone directly affected by the provisions of a *private bill*, who therefore has the right to petition against it.

long title the passage at the start of a bill that begins 'a Bill to . . .' and then lists its purposes. The content of the bill must be covered by the long title.

Lord Chancellor presiding officer of the House of Lords (until replaced by a Lord Speaker), Secretary of State for Constitutional Affairs and a member of the Cabinet.

Lords amendment amendment made by the Lords to a bill passed by the Commons.

LP the Cabinet Committee on the Legislative Programme, chaired by the *Leader of the House of Commons*. Other members include the *Leader of the House of Lords* and the Chief Whips in both Houses.

Mace a silver gilt ornamental mace symbolises the authority of each House. It is carried in procession before a sitting and remains on the *Table* (in the Commons, under the *Table* when the House is in *Committee of the whole House*) while the House is sitting.

main estimates the principal request from the government to the Commons for the resources required to run the state in the following financial year. There is one for each government department (and for other bodies such as the Office of Rail Regulation and the NHS Pension Scheme). Usually published in late March or early April.

main Question if an *amendment* to a *motion* has been moved, the original motion is known as the main Question.

manifesto statement of policies and intentions on which a political party fights a *general election*.

measure legislation of the Church of England, agreed by the General Synod, then considered by the Ecclesiastical Committee (a statutory committee consisting of members of both Houses) and then presented to both Houses for approval.

Members Estimate in the Commons, pays for members' pay and allowances.

message formal communication between one House and the other.

minister of state the second rank of ministers (below secretaries of state).

Ministry of Defence Votes A published in February, these seek the annual authorisation by the Commons of the maximum numbers of personnel in the armed services.

the Minute daily working papers of the House of Lords.

moment of interruption the time at which the main business of the Commons day normally ends (10.00 p.m. on Mondays and Tuesdays, 7.00 p.m. on Wednesdays, 6.00 p.m. on Thursdays and 2.30 p.m. on Fridays).

money bill a bill whose only purpose is to authorise expenditure or taxation.

money resolution a motion (when approved, a resolution) to authorise government expenditure in relation to a bill.

motion a proposal 'moved' by a member. When approved, it becomes a *resolution* or an *order*.

named-day questions in the Commons, written questions for answer on a stated day, with a minimum notice period of three sitting days (but including non-sitting Fridays). An individual MP may ask no more than five such questions per day.

naming (of an MP) a power used by the Chair in the Commons, usually for more serious offences, usually including disregard for the authority of the Chair. Following naming, a motion to suspend the MP concerned (to bar him or her from the precincts and stop payment of salary for a stated period) is moved by the senior minister present and invariably agreed to.

National Audit Office see *Comptroller and Auditor-General*.

negative instrument a piece of *delegated legislation* that under the parent Act may be made and come into effect unless one or other House decides otherwise ('the negative procedure').

new clause a substantial *amendment* to a bill, usually introducing a separate subject or issue rather than seeking to amend the provisions already in the bill (but to be in order a new clause must be within the *scope* of the bill).

1922 Committee (sometimes called 'the 22') body consisting of all Conservative MPs but especially important as a reflection of back-bench opinion.

nod to secure agreement to something 'on the nod' is without debate or a vote.

official Opposition the largest opposition party, sometimes known as 'Her Majesty's Opposition'.

Official Report the verbatim report of debates in both Houses, Westminster Hall, standing committees and grand committees. Also contains written answers to questions. Known as *Hansard*.

Ombudsman see *Parliamentary Commissioner for Administration*.

opposition days in the Commons, twenty days in the course of a session on which the subject of the main debate is chosen by the opposition parties.

order a decision of either House or of a committee on a matter within the power of the body making the order for example, 'That a select committee be appointed to . . .'. See also *resolution*.

Order in Council a type of *delegated legislation*, made in the name of the sovereign rather than that of a minister.

orders of reference *orders* made by either House when setting up a select committee. They set out the committee's task and define its powers.

ordinary written questions in the Commons, written questions that are put down for answer two sitting days after they are received and that by convention the government answers within a week.

Outlawries Bill an antique bill 'for the more effectual preventing of clandestine outlawries' given a formal first reading in the Commons as a symbol of their right to deal with their own business before proceeding to debate the *Queen's Speech* after the *State Opening* of Parliament. The Lords equivalent is the Select Vestries Bill.

packaging the grouping of Lords amendments together for debate and decision in the Commons. Even though a particular proposition may have been defeated, its appearance as part of a *package* in which *amendments in lieu* are offered may avoid 'double insistence': that is, when neither House will give way and the bill in question will be lost.

pairing an arrangement between two MPs on opposite sides of the House not to vote in a particular division, so that their absences cancel each other out.

a parliament the main division of parliamentary time: the period between one *general election* and the next.

parliamentary agent a specialist lawyer who represents the *promoter* of a private bill.

Parliamentary Commissioner for Administration (Ombudsman) an independent officer, reporting to Parliament, who investigates maladministration by government departments and other public bodies which has caused injustice that has not been put right. She also holds the posts of Health Service Commissioner for England and for Wales (in the latter role she reports to the National Assembly for Wales). She has a close relationship with the Public Administration Select Committee in the Commons, which considers her reports.

Parliamentary Commissioner for Standards an independent officer of the Commons who maintains the Register of Members' Interests and other registers of interests; advises MPs and the Committee on Standards and Privileges on interests and standards issues; monitors the operation of the Code of Conduct; and investigates complaints about MPs' conduct.

parliamentary counsel a small group of government lawyers who are expert in legislative drafting and who draft all government bills, including '*hand-out*' bills. *Delegated legislation* is usually drafted not by parliamentary counsel but by the lawyers in the government department concerned.

parliamentary private secretary (PPS) an unpaid MP aide to a secretary of state or a minister of state.

parliamentary secretary *or* **parliamentary under-secretary of state** the third rank of ministers, below *secretaries of state* and *ministers of state*.

Patronage Secretary formal title for the government Chief Whip in the Commons.

payroll vote government ministers and *parliamentary private secretaries* – the most reliable supporters of the government in any votes.

Permanent Secretary (in some departments, more formally 'Permanent Under-Secretary of State') the senior civil servant in a government department. Usually also the *Accounting Officer*.

personal statement a statement (in the Commons, made by permission of the Speaker), usually of apology, or explaining the reasons for a ministerial resignation.

petition either a *public petition* or, in the case of a *private bill*, a case made against it by someone who would be directly affected by its provisions.

ping-pong the to and fro of bills and amendments between the two Houses towards the end of a session.

point of order an appeal to the Chair for guidance or a ruling on a matter of order or procedure, but also a means (through 'bogus points of order') of furthering political argument.

polling day the day on which votes are cast in a *general election* or *by-election*.

PLP Parliamentary Labour Party, consisting of all Labour MPs and peers. Especially important as a reflection of back-bench opinion.

PMQs Prime Minister's Questions (in the Commons, for half an hour every sitting Wednesday).

PPC prospective parliamentary candidate: someone selected by a party organisation to contest the next election.

PPR a *select committee's* power to send for 'persons, papers and records'.

PPS see *parliamentary private secretary*.

prayer a motion seeking the *annulment* of a *Statutory Instrument*.

praying time the period (usually of forty days, excluding time when both Houses are adjourned for more than four days) during which a motion for the *annulment* of a *Statutory Instrument* must be taken.

pre-legislative scrutiny see *draft bill*.

prerogative sometimes 'the Royal Prerogative': power of ministers to act in the Queen's name without the approval of Parliament.

presentation bill a bill presented at the *Table*, notice having been given on the Order Paper.

previous Question an old-fashioned *dilatory motion* in the form 'That the Question be not now put'. If it is agreed to, the House moves to the next business; if it is not agreed to, then the matter that was interrupted must be decided immediately, as with a *closure*.

primary legislation Acts of Parliament.

Prince of Wales's Consent signification by the Prince of Wales that Parliament may proceed to consider legislation that would affect his interests.

private bill a bill – a draft Act – that, if passed, will have only local or personal, rather than general, effect.

private business proceedings on *private bills* and related matters. In the Commons, taken immediately after prayers (the religious prayers at the start of the sitting); if opposed, time for debate is found by the *Chairman of Ways and Means*.

private member's bill a public bill introduced by a 'private member' (not a minister). Not to be confused with *a private bill*. In the Lords, 'private peer's bill'.

private notice question in the Lords, a question of urgent importance asked orally of the government. In the Commons, the term has been replaced by *urgent question*.

privilege parliamentary privilege (a better name would be 'public interest immunity') gives the two Houses, their committees and members, the protection from outside interference or legal action necessary to perform their roles. The two main elements are freedom of speech and the right of both Houses to regulate their own affairs. Also (as 'financial privilege') used to describe the pre-eminence of the Commons in financial matters.

privilege amendment a polite fiction to preserve the pre-eminence of the Commons in financial matters; a subsection in a bill starting in the Lords that involves an increase in expenditure or taxation says 'Nothing in this Act shall impose any charge on the people or on public funds'. The subsection is removed when the bill is in committee in the Commons.

Privy Counsellor a member of the Privy Council, consisting of senior politicians past and present, senior judges, some Commonwealth statesmen and certain others of distinction. Members of the Privy Council are styled 'right honourable'.

proclamation a royal proclamation by the sovereign dissolves Parliament and sets a day for the new parliament to meet after the ensuing *general election*.

programming in the Commons, the imposition of a timetable on the passage of a bill immediately after *second reading*. Originally designed to provide an allocation of time more in proportion to the importance or contentiousness of various parts of a bill – a compromise between informal agreement and a *guillotine* – but now the source of profound disagreement between government and opposition.

programming committee in the Commons, when a programme order applies to proceedings in *Committee of the whole House*, *report stage* or *third reading*, a programming committee (chaired by the *Chairman of Ways and Means* and consisting of up to eight other MPs) may propose how the available time should be allocated; but such committees are in practice not used, unlike a **programming sub-committee** (chaired by the chairman of the *standing committee*, with seven members of the committee), which deals with proceedings in a standing committee.

programme order a timetable for a bill once agreed to by the House.

promoter the body or individual outside Parliament sponsoring a *private bill*.

proposing the Question when the Chair states the proposition on which the House or committee must decide.

prorogation the formal end of a parliamentary *session*, which brings to an end almost all parliamentary business.

public bill a bill – a draft Act – that, if passed, will have general effect in some or all of the constituent parts of the UK.

public business generally, proceedings on the main business of the day (in the Commons following Question Time and statements).

public petition an application by one or more people outside Parliament to one House or the other (usually the Commons) for some particular action or relief.

qualified majority voting (QMV) a weighted system of voting in the EU Council of Ministers in which larger countries have more votes. See *blocking minority*.

Queen's Consent signification by the sovereign that Parliament may proceed to consider legislation that would affect her interests.

Queen's Speech sometimes called 'the Gracious Speech'; written by the government and delivered by the Queen at the *State Opening* of Parliament, it recalls the events of the previous year (such as state visits) and outlines the government's plans for the new session, especially its legislative programme.

Question (as well as the conventional meaning) a matter for decision.

Question rota in the Commons, the order in which ministers answer oral questions.

quorum the number of members required to be present to transact business. In the Lords the quorum is 3; but on a division on a bill or on *delegated legislation* at least 30 peers must vote to constitute a quorum.

    In the Commons there is no quorum except on a division, when at least 40 MPs must be present (35 voting, the 4 tellers and the occupant of the Chair). The quorum of a *standing committee* is one-third of the membership, counting the chairman (but the chairman does not count towards whether a quorum is present); in *select committees* it is 3 or a quarter of the membership, counting the chairman (who also counts towards the quorum). Fractions are rounded up. In *Westminster Hall* the quorum is 3.

reasoned amendment one tabled for the *second* or *third reading* of a bill that sets out why the bill should not proceed (or proceed in its current form).

reasons given by one House to the other for rejecting *amendments* to a bill.

recall the return of Parliament during a recess. In the Commons, it is authorised by the *Speaker* on the request of the government. In the Lords, the power is exercised by the *Lord Chancellor*.

recess a longer time of adjournment than over a weekend, usually at Christmas, for a week in February, at Easter, the late spring bank holiday, and from late July to early October (if there is not a two-week September sitting). Strictly speaking, the word applies to the period of *prorogation* but is rarely used in this sense.

regulation (1) in the UK, a type of *delegated legislation*; (2) in European legislation, regulations have the force of law throughout the EU without member states having to take any action.

regulatory reform order an order under the Regulatory Reform Act 2001 made by a minister to lift burdens on anyone carrying on any activity. An order may be made only after public consultation on a proposal, which is then scrutinised by committees of both Houses. The committees also scrutinise the draft order that is brought forward as a result. A regulatory reform order is an unusual type of *delegated legislation* in that it may amend *primary legislation*.

remedial order an order made by a minister that amends *primary legislation* when that has been found incompatible with the Human Rights Act 1998. Draft remedial orders are scrutinised by the Joint Committee on Human Rights and are then approved by both Houses. Urgent procedure orders may be made without advance scrutiny but must be confirmed by the approval of both Houses within 120 days.

repeal to make the whole or part of an Act of Parliament have no further effect.

report stage consideration of a bill in the form in which it left committee, and an opportunity for any member to propose amendments, not just those who were on the committee.

reserved matter one not devolved to Scotland, Wales or Northern Ireland.

resolution a decision of either House, or of a committee, that expresses an opinion (for example, 'That this House has no confidence in Her Majesty's Government'). See also *order*.

resource accounting records the economic cost of the provision of services and the consumption of assets (including depreciation, the cost of using capital assets, and future liabilities such as those for compensation for early retirement). **Resource accounts** must be laid before Parliament by 31 January following the financial year to which they relate (although this is now being speeded up).

revised estimates change the *ambit of an estimate* if it appears that funds already authorised may have to be spent on something outside the present ambit.

Royal Assent the sovereign's agreement to a bill passed by both Houses.

ruling a decision by the *Speaker* of the Commons or any other occupant of the Chair (or chairman of a *standing committee*) on a matter of order or procedure.

Salisbury convention (dating from 1945 and named after the fifth Marquess of Salisbury) that the Lords should not reject at second reading any government legislation that has been passed by the Commons and that carries out a *manifesto* commitment.

schedule schedules appear after the *clauses* of a bill and fill in detail.

scope the ambit of a bill; to be in order, *amendments* must not go beyond the purposes of the bill as summarised in the *long title*.

scrutiny reserve resolutions constrain ministers from giving agreement in the EU Council of Ministers to a proposal that has not cleared the European scrutiny systems in both Houses.

second reading approval in principle of a bill. A second reading debate is a discussion of the principle rather than the details of individual *clauses*.

second reading committee in the Commons, a (temporary) committee to which an uncontroversial bill may be referred for a *second reading* debate. There is then no debate when the bill is reported to the House for its second reading.

secretary of state one of the top rank of ministers; senior minister in a government department; always a member of the Cabinet.

section the basic unit within an Act of Parliament, divided into subsections, then paragraphs, then sub-paragraphs.

select committee a committee of members of either House charged with investigating a matter and reporting (ad hoc select committees), or of monitoring a government department (Commons departmental select committees) or a subject area, or a category of legislative or other proposals) and reporting from time to time. Select committees also advise on the administration of both Houses. Select committees that are not ad hoc are normally permanent institutions, with their members nominated for the length of a Parliament.

selection the decision by the *Speaker*, the *Chairman of Ways and Means* or the chairman of a *standing committee* as to which *amendments* (or, in some cases, *motions*) shall be debated or voted upon.

Senior Salaries Review Body an independent body that, amongst other things, makes recommendations on parliamentary pay and allowances.

Serjeant at Arms the officer of the Commons responsible for works, housekeeping, ICT, ceremonial and security.

session the main subdivision of time during a parliament: the period from the *State Opening* to *prorogation* (usually from early November to late October in the following year).

sessional orders any order of either House that has effect only for the rest of that session of Parliament; but particularly used of the traditional orders passed by the Commons on the day of the *State Opening* at the start of a *session*, providing for good order and access to the House, the protection of witnesses, and the now unknown circumstance of an MP elected for two seats deciding which one to represent.

Sewel motion a means whereby the Scottish Parliament demonstrates its agreement to Westminster legislating on a devolved matter.

shadow Cabinet those opposition front-benchers who 'shadow' members of the Cabinet, presided over by the Leader of the Opposition.

shadow minister an MP who is the spokesperson of an opposition party on a particular subject, mirroring the responsibilities of the 'real' minister in the government.

Short money financial support for opposition parties in the Commons, named after Edward Short, the Leader of the House when it was introduced. The Lords equivalent is *Cranborne money*.

short title the title by which a bill is known during its passage through Parliament; for example, 'Criminal Justice Bill'. See also *long title*.

sitting a meeting of either House, usually in a single day, at the end of which the House adjourns. Also a meeting of a committee.

Speaker the presiding officer of the Commons and chairman of the House of Commons Commission, which oversees House administration.

special public bill committee in the Lords, a committee that may take written and oral evidence on a bill within twenty-eight days of the committee's appointment, thereafter proceeding as a public bill committee.

special report a report from a *select committee* that is not a substantive report on an inquiry but is used as a vehicle for publishing government replies or informing the House of some difficulty the committee has encountered.

special standing committee in the Commons, a hybrid of the deliberating/evidence-taking method of a *select committee* and the debating method of a *standing committee*, to which bills may be sent for their committee stage.

spillover the period (usually in October) preceding prorogation.

staffing allowance an allowance for each MP to meet the cost of up to three staff.

standing committee in the Commons, a committee to which most bills are referred for their committee stage. Standing committees are laid out like the Chamber of the House, are chaired by an impartial chairman and cease to exist when they have finished considering a bill. A number of standing committees may be in existence at the same time.

standing orders the rules made by both Houses for the regulation of their proceedings. Standing orders remain in force until they are amended or repealed. 'Temporary standing orders' are typically made for the length of a *session* or *parliament*.

starred questions in the Lords, four oral questions on Mondays and Thursdays (five on Tuesdays and Wednesdays) taken at the start of business. In the Commons, the term is not used, but a star on the Order Paper against a question indicates that it is for oral answer.

State Opening the ceremonial start to a session of Parliament. The main event is the *Queen's Speech*.

statute an Act of Parliament. 'Statute law' and 'the statute book' are collective terms for all Acts in force.

statute law repeal bill a bill that removes parts of the law that have become redundant.

Statutory Instrument see *delegated legislation*.

strangers the old-fashioned and rather unfriendly description of visitors to Parliament. Now being superseded by 'visitors'.

sub judice rule the rule against referring to a current or impending court case (more precisely, when someone has been charged in a criminal case, or, in a civil action, when a case has been set down for trial), to avoid influencing the outcome. The rule may be relaxed at the Speaker's discretion, and it need not prevent the consideration of legislation.

subordinate legislation see *delegated legislation*.

subsidiarity in the European context, the principle that a decision should be taken at national level unless the aim could be achieved only by action at EU level.

substantive motion a motion expressing an opinion or taking a decision; not an *adjournment* motion (even though that involves the narrow decision of whether the House or a committee shall adjourn).

sunset clause a provision in legislation that makes it time-limited (and which may also provide for renewal by Parliament after a prescribed period).

supplementary estimates seek additional resources.

supplementary question a follow-up oral question.

Supply the granting of money to the Crown for the running of the country.

surgery the time when an MP makes himself or herself available in the constituency for meetings with constituents, usually to discuss their problems.

suspend informally interrupt the sitting of a House or committee. For suspension of an MP, see *naming*.

table to deposit formally before the House or committee, as 'to table an *amendment*' (or *motio*n, question or paper). 'The Table' in both Houses is the table between the front benches, and also a collective term for the Clerks at the Table.

talking out in the Commons, debating a *motion* or a proceedings on a bill up to the *moment of interruption*, when the business is lost or postponed.

tax law re-write bills bills that tidy and clarify existing tax law. Similar to *consolidation bills* but with greater latitude as to the scope of amendment.

tellers two members from each side who count the votes at a *division*.

ten-minute rule bill in the Commons (on Tuesdays and Wednesdays), a bill introduced by leave of the House (with a vote if one is forced) following a speech of not more than ten minutes from the sponsor of the proposal. An opponent may speak for not more than ten minutes in opposition.

test roll a bound parchment book signed by MPs when they take the oath or make *affirmation* after an election (also in the Lords).

third reading the final stage of the passage of a bill through one House of Parliament; a final review of the contents of the bill, with debate limited to what is actually in the bill rather than, as at *second reading*, what might be included. Substantive *amendments* are allowed at this stage in the Lords but not in the Commons.

unopposed return   a motion for an unopposed return seeks the laying of a report or other paper before Parliament, thus giving it the protection of parliamentary *privilege*.

unstarred questions   in the Lords, questions that give rise to short debates of an hour and a half at the end of the day's business. In the Commons, a question that has been unstarred has been converted from one for oral answer to one for written answer.

urgent debate   in the Commons, an application is made to the Speaker under S.O. No. 24 to debate 'a specific and important matter that should have urgent consideration'. Such debates are rare.

urgent procedure order   see *remedial order*.

urgent question   (formerly known as a private notice question (PNQ)) in the Commons, an oral question to a minister on an urgent matter of public importance, granted by the Speaker.

usual channels   the informal and private contacts between the *whips* and business managers on the two sides of each House.

virement   moving funds between the subheads of an *estimate* with Treasury approval but without further parliamentary authority.

the Vote bundle   the daily working papers of the Commons.

Votes and Proceedings   the legal record of the proceedings of the Commons: decisions taken, papers laid and so on. Later becomes the *Journal*.

Votes on Account   come before the Commons each November and cover some 45 per cent of the estimated expenditure of each government department over the coming year; they are to tide the government over until the *main estimates* are approved in July. They must be agreed by the House by 6 February.

Ways and Means resolution   a *motion* (when approved, a *resolution*) to authorise the raising of a tax or imposition of a charge in relation to a bill. 'Ways and Means' is an old name for taxation.

West Lothian question   named after Tam Dalyell MP, then member for that constituency: why should Scottish MPs at Westminster be able to speak, question and vote on matters affecting the rest of the UK when in Scotland those matters are devolved to the Scottish Parliament and the Scottish Executive?

Westminster Hall as well as the Great Hall on the west side of the Palace, the parallel debating chamber 'the House sitting in Westminster Hall', which takes place in the Grand Committee Room off the northern end of Westminster Hall. Used mainly for non-controversial debates on subjects put forward by back-benchers as well as by the government; for debates on select committee reports; and 'cross-cutting' oral question times (on subjects that span the responsibilities of several departments).

whips members responsible for parliamentary party organisation and discipline. 'The Whip' is circulated weekly by the whips of each party to their own members; it lists the business for the following week, together with the party's expectations as to when its MPs will vote.

White Paper a published statement of government policy (see also *Green Paper*).

wrecking amendment one designed to frustrate the purpose of a bill already approved at *second reading*, or of a *clause* already approved in committee.

written ministerial statements in the Commons, statements by ministers that appear in the next day's *Official Report*, before answers to oral questions. A minister's intention to make a written statement is signalled in the Order Paper at the end of the day's business.

Yeoman Usher Black Rod's deputy.

Sources of information
about Parliament

Books

This is not a bibliography but a highly selective list of publications that may be of further help to readers of this book.

Companion to the Standing Orders and Guide to the Proceedings of the House of Lords, The Stationery Office, 2005.
The chief work of reference on House of Lords practice and procedure. The *Companion* describes every aspect of the House's practice and procedure as established by the standing orders, ancient practice, and decisions of the Procedure Committee and the House itself. It complements *Erskine May* (see below), which for some areas provides more detail and gives precedents.

Dod's Parliamentary Companion, Vacher Dod Publishing, 2006.
The annually published reference work with biographies of MPs and peers, detailed results of the last general election, and a great deal of contact and other information on political parties, government departments, public bodies, the devolved institutions and the European Parliament. It also has a useful website directory.

Erskine May's Treatise on the Law, Privileges, Proceedings and Usage of Parliament, twenty-third edition, edited by Sir William McKay, LexisNexis Butterworths, 2004.
Usually known simply as 'Erskine May', it is technical and comprehensive rather than highly readable, but it is the pre-eminently authoritative textbook on Parliament and the one most used by practitioners.

Griffith and Ryle on Parliament: Functions, Practice and Procedures, second edition, by Robert Blackburn and Andrew Kennon with Sir Michael Wheeler-Booth, Sweet & Maxwell, 2003.

A detailed survey of the workings of both Houses, with a huge amount of statistical information and examples of every type of event. As well as providing shrewd analysis, it also usefully sets the present operation of Parliament in the context of the institution's development over the last half-century.

Handbook of House of Commons Procedure, fifth edition, by Paul Evans, and *Handbook of House of Lords Procedure*, by Mary Robertson, Vacher Dod Publishing, 2004.

Two excellent practical guides to procedure, logically laid out and well cross-referenced. They are written in straightforward language and will be especially useful for those involved at first hand with proceedings in the two Houses.

House of Commons Weekly Information Bulletin, The Stationery Office.

Published when the House is sitting, it provides a digest of current and forthcoming business, state of play on bills and some types of delegated legislation, forthcoming public meeting of select committees in both Houses, and forthcoming inquiries. It also lists recently published select committee and National Audit Office reports, and the titles of recently tabled early day motions. It has a useful summary of the current state of the parties in the Commons, together with a record of all by-elections in the current parliament. It is also available on-line from 4.00 p.m. each Friday at www.parliament.uk

The British Constitution in the Twentieth Century, edited by Vernon Bogdanor, Oxford University Press for the British Academy 2003.

A definitive account of the development of all major British constitutional institutions in the twentieth century, with separate chapters on the House of Commons and the House of Lords. A valuable work of reference for those interested in the recent historical development of Parliament.

The Standing Orders of the House of Commons: Public Business, The Stationery Office, 2005 (also available on the parliamentary website).

The Standing Orders of the House of Lords relating to Public Business, The Stationery Office, 2005 (also available on the parliamentary website).

Parliament websites

The principal site is www.parliament.uk. This site, at present undergoing major redesign, provides a huge amount of parliamentary information and text. Content includes:

- what's on: current and future business in both Houses and forthcoming meetings of committees;

- the text of Commons *Hansard* from session 1988–89 onwards and Lords *Hansard* from session 1994–95; and the *Hansard* of all standing committee debates of bills and other matters from session 1997–98 onwards. The *Hansard* for the previous day in the two Chambers is put up on the website at 8.00 a.m. the following day and a rolling *Hansard* appears at intervals on the same day;

- the text of all bills, both public and private, that are before Parliament, and their current status;

- standing orders of both Houses, for both public and private business;

- via the Stationery Office site, the text of Acts of Parliament (public Acts from 1988 onwards and private Acts from 1991);

- for the House of Lords in its judicial role, practice notes, Appellate Committee reports, judgements and cases to be heard;

- lists of: MPs by constituency, county, gender and party; peers; ministers and PPSs; opposition spokespeople; all-party groups and country groups; together with the state of the parties and by-election results;

- the Locata system, which will tell you who your MP is from your post-code (www.locata.co.uk/commons/);

- registers of interests;

- for select committees in both Houses, and joint committees: committee home pages with membership, terms of reference and contact details; press notices; text of reports, all oral and much written evidence (from session 1997–98 onwards); a guide for witnesses; weekly bulletins of forthcoming meetings;

- explanatory notes and factsheets on many aspects of the work of Parliament;

- Commons Library research papers on matters of current interest, together with research notes and longer papers produced by the Parliamentary Office of Science and Technology;

- useful links;

- current job opportunities in Parliament.

www.parliamentlive.tv gives access to webcast proceedings of both Houses, Westminster Hall, and select committees taking evidence in public, together with a searchable archive.

www.explore.parliament.uk is the website of the Parliamentary Education Unit, which provides an education service on behalf of both Houses; provides resources and support for students and teachers; works closely with bodies such as the Hansard Society for Parliamentary Government and the Citizenship Foundation; and advises and supports MPs and peers in their work with young people. The unit produces 'Parliament explained' booklets, available on the website. The website gives details of other material, including wallcharts and videos.

www.commonsleader.gov.uk is the website of the Leader of the House of Commons. It carries information about future business, and the government's views on issues such as improving engagement, electoral policy and young people and politics.

The Parliament website also has a useful link page at www.parliament.uk/useful/related_links.cfm, which gives websites of central government departments, international organisations, the monarchy and so on.

www.lordswhips.org.uk (the website of the Lords Government Whips Office) gives details of forthcoming business in the Lords, speakers' lists, groupings of amendments, ministerial responsibilities, and so on.

Other websites

Websites useful for Parliament and politics include:

www.electoralcommission.org.uk The Electoral Commission was set up under the Political Parties, Elections and Referendums Act 2000 to provide advice on all aspects of the electoral process. This website gives details of the Commission's work, and the texts of a series of useful reports.

www.theyworkforyou.com and www.publicwhip.org.uk are the sites of pressure groups seeking to show constituents MPs' voting records, attitudes to issues, rebelliousness, speed of response to constituents' letters and activity levels. But beware of crude rankings of numbers of questions tabled, speeches made and so on. Activity is not achievement, and some of the statistics are flawed. For example, www.theyworkforyou.com, counts a one-word intervention in a debate as a speech!

www.w4mp.org is a site designed for all those working for an MP, but its material is of general interest too. It has ninety downloadable guides on subjects ranging from the rules about using Commons stationery to handling the media. It also carries advertisements for jobs as MPs' assistants and researchers.

The Hansard Society at www.hansardsociety.org.uk describes its mission as 'promoting democracy – strengthening Parliament'. It seeks to explain Parliament and increase involvement in parliamentary politics, and researches and publishes on a wide range of issues, as well as organising a range of lectures, seminars and other events.

The Constitution Unit, based in the Department of Political Science at University College London (www.ucl.ac.uk/constitution-unit) is an authoritative academic group that publishes briefings on topical constitutional and political issues, and organises seminars and other events.

www.psr.keele.ac.uk (Keele University) provides extensive web resources relating to politics, Parliament and government.

The respected Centre for Legislative Studies at Hull University (www.hull.ac.uk/cls/) provides a great deal of useful information and links, ranging much more widely than legislation.

www.revolts.co.uk is the website of Philip Cowley, an academic who has made the subject of political revolts and parliamentary voting patterns his own. Essential for anyone researching this subject.

www.politicos.co.uk is the website of an excellent online bookshop with a wide range of political books and other material.

There are hundreds of online media sites that provide coverage of Parliament and politics, but the BBC site (via www.bbc.co.uk then to 'news') is especially good, with constantly updated reports, more reflective pieces, video clips, etc.

Television

In addition to normal news coverage, and live broadcasts of Prime Minister's Questions and some other occasions on various channels, BBC Parliament provides a dedicated channel, with real-time coverage of the Commons and 'time-shifted' coverage of the Lords and select committees.

Visiting Parliament

To see proceedings

Both Houses have public galleries, and it is often possible, especially later in the day, to get a seat just by turning up. However, this is difficult on particularly newsworthy occasions (and, in the Commons, for Question Time, and especially Prime Minister's Questions). Then a public queue forms at St Stephen's Entrance (see map on page 20); but it may not be possible to get in until ticket-holders (see below) have left.

To get a ticket for the Gallery of the House of Commons, UK residents should write to their MP (if you don't know who your MP is, put your postcode into www.locata.co.uk/commons/, which is also accessible through the parliamentary website). Members have only a small allocation of tickets, so it is a good idea to write well in advance. Overseas visitors should write to their Embassy or High Commission.

It is also possible to attend public sittings of standing committees (see page 211), select committees in both Houses (see Chapter 11), and debates in the 'parallel Chamber' in Westminster Hall (see page 296). You should go to the Central Lobby and seek directions from the reception desk there. It is not possible to reserve seats, and high-profile select committee hearings may be crowded. But if you can get in, some select committee hearings can offer the best theatre in London!

To tour Parliament
People who are resident in the UK should contact their local MP (if necessary, find out who it is using www.locata.co.uk/commons/) or a peer they know. At times when both Houses are sitting, tours are available on Mondays, Tuesdays, Wednesdays and Fridays (on Fridays, all day if the Commons are not sitting, late afternoon if they are). There is no access to the Commons Chamber after 9.30 a.m. on Wednesdays. Tours are normally conducted in English, but other languages are also available.

During recesses, UK residents should continue to arrange tours through their MP, or through a peer they know. But during the summer recess, the Palace also arranges pre-booked tours at a charge; this is particularly aimed at overseas visitors (who cannot normally arrange a tour on sitting days) but anyone may book tickets. Details are available through www.parliament.uk/directories/hcio/tours.cfm. The Central Tours Office, which organises all tours, may be contacted on 020 7219 3003 or e-mail CTO@parliament.uk.

Schools visits
Schools and other educational institutions based in this country may contact their MP to arrange a tour. However, throughout the year the Parliamentary Education Unit offers a range of educational visits for students in Years 3 to 10. Visits for older students (KS4) take place in the autumn; this

programme is advertised in the *Times Educational Supplement* in March each year. The best thing is to consult the Parliamentary Education Unit well in advance, at:

Parliamentary Education Unit,
Norman Shaw Building (North),
London SW1A 2TT
Telephone 020 7219 2105
e-mail edunit@parliament.uk
Fax: 020 7219 0818

Other useful contact details

Palace of Westminster switchboard: 020 7219 3000.
House of Commons Information Office: House of Commons, London
   SW1A 2TT, telephone 020 7219 4272, fax 020 7219 5839,
   hcinfo@parliament.uk
House of Lords Information Office: House of Lords, London SW1A 0PW
   telephone 020 7219 3107, hlinfo@parliament.uk
House of Lords Record Office: London SW1A 0PW, telephone
   020 7219 3074, fax 020 7219 2570, hlro@parliament.uk
House of Commons Committee Office: general enquiry lines:
   020 7219 3267/4300; recorded message service about
   forthcoming meetings: 020 7219 2033
House of Lords Committee Office: general enquiries 020 7219 5791/3150
Parliamentary Bookshop: 12 Bridge Street, Parliament Square, London
   SW1A 2JX; enquiries and telephone orders 020 7219 3890; fax
   orders 020 7219 3866
The Stationery Office: (mail, telephone and fax orders) PO Box 29,
   Norwich NR3 1GN; general enquiries 0870 600 5522; orders
   through the parliamentary hotline *Lo-call* 0845 7 023474; fax orders
   0870 600 5533, bookorders@tso.co.uk

Devolved parliament and assemblies

Northern Ireland Assembly: Parliament Buildings, Stormont, Belfast
   BT4 3XX, telephone 028 90 521333, fax 028 90 521961; website
   www.niassembly.gov.uk
Scottish Parliament: Edinburgh EH99 1SP, telephone 0131 348 5000;
   website www.scottish.parliament.uk
National Assembly for Wales: Cardiff Bay, Cardiff CF99 1NA, telephone
   029 20 898 200; website www.wales.gov.uk

The European Union

European Commission: 1049 Brussels, Belgium, telephone
00 322 299 1111; website www.europa.eu.int. The
Commission's Office in the UK: Jean Monnet House,
8 Storey's Gate, London SW1P 3AT, telephone 020 7973 1992
European Parliament: rue Wiertz, 1047 Brussels, Belgium, telephone
00 322 284 2111; website www.europarl.eu.int. The European
Parliament's Office in the UK: 2 Queen Anne's Gate, London SW1H
9AA, telephone 020 7227 4300; website www.europarl.org.uk

Political parties

Conservative Party: 25 Victoria Street, London SW1H 0DL, telephone
020 7222 9000; website www.conservatives.com
Democratic Unionist Party: 91 Dundela Avenue, Belfast BT4 3BU,
telephone 028 90 471155; website www.dup.org.uk
Labour Party: 16 Old Queen Street, London SW1H 9HP, telephone
08705 900200; website: www.labour.org.uk
Liberal Democrats: 4 Cowley Street, London SW1P 3NB, telephone
020 7222 7999; website www.libdems.org.uk
Plaid Cymru: 18 Park Grove, Cardiff CF10 3BN, telephone
029 20 646000; website www.plaidcymru.org.uk
Scottish National Party: 107 McDonald Road, Edinburgh EH7 4NW,
telephone 0131 525 8900; website www.snp.org.uk
Sinn Féin: 44 Parnell Square, Dublin 1, telephone 00 3531 872 6932;
website www.sinnfein.ie
Social Democratic and Labour Party: 121 Ormeau Road, Belfast BT7 1SH,
telephone 028 90 247700; website www.sdlp.ie
Ulster Unionist Party: 429 Holywood Road, Belfast BT4 2LN, telephone
028 90 765500; website www.uup.org.uk

Index

Abbott (Speaker) 128, 177
Aberdeen, Lord 356
accountability principle 96–7
accounting officer 277, 446
Act paper 171, 446
ad hoc committees 355–6
additional costs allowance 65, 446
Address 71, 139, 150, 446
addressing the house 302
adjournment 140, 142, 144–6, 446
adjournment debate 159, 165–6
adjournment motion 294–6
Administration Committee 355
Administration estimate (Commons) 58,
    76–7, 446
Administration Estimate Audit Committee
    77
advisory cost limit 316, 447
affirmation 137, 154, 447
affirmative instrument 254, 255, 257, 447
allocation of time order 198, 447
all-party groups 447
All-Party Whip 120
ambit of an estimate 276, 447
amendment 213, 215–17, 288, 447
amendment in lieu 243, 447
amendment of the law motion 271, 447
Amos, Baroness 442
Amsterdam, Treaty of (1997) 387
Anderson, Donald 360
annual calendar 145–6
annually managed expenditure (AME) 275,
    447
annulment 256–7, 447
Appeal judges 7
Appellate Committee 16, 447
Appellate Jurisdiction Act (1876) 35–6,
    439
Assembly of Western European Union 405
assent procedure (EU) 393

Association of Professional Political
    Consultants 124
Astor, Countess 32
Audit Committee (Commons) 61

back of the Chair bill 225, 448
back-bench debates (Lords) 307–8
back-bencher 10, 95, 157, 448
    and Lords reform 435–6
back-benchers' motions 294
backsheet 208, 448
balance sheet 282
Balfour, Prime Minister A.J. 96, 278
ballot bills 228–9, 448
Beckett, Margaret 349
'behind the chair' 100
Belfast (Good Friday) Agreement 91
Bell, Martin 23
Benn, Hilary 331
Benn, Tony 100, 232
Benton, Joe 29
bill of aids and supplies 266, 448
bills 170, 190, 448
    government 192–208
        anatomy of 204–8
        origins 192–3
        from proposal to 193–6
        stages 203, 208–34
Black Rod, Gentleman Usher of 75, 138,
    448
Blair, Prime Minister Tony 28, 29, 106, 111,
    317, 330, 433
blocking minority 448
blocking motion 250
Blunkett, David 128
Board of Management (Commons) 57–8, 61
Boothroyd, Betty (Speaker) 46, 47, 53, 54,
    201
Boundary Commission 22–3, 53–4, 448
breaking the sitting 159

British-Irish Inter-Parliamentary Body 405
Brittan, Leon 97
broadcasting parliament 179–81
Broadcasting Unit 62
Brooke, Peter 47
Brown, Gordon 270
Budget 141, 448
  annual pattern 268–9
  information 273
  unified 273–4
Budget cycle 267, 270–4
Budget day 270
Burke, Edmund 113
business committee (Commons) 424
Business Questions 154, 448
by-election 154–5, 449
  expenses 27
  when held 25
Byers, Stephen 97, 184

cabinet, daily routine of 162–3
Cabinet Office Code of Practice 194
Cameron, David 80, 111, 331, 391, 425
Campaign Group (Labour Party) 110
Campbell, Sir Menzies 112
cash flow statement 282
'cash for questions' affair 125
casting vote 52–3, 449
CCLA (Commons consideration of Lords
    amendments) 142, 449
Central Tours Office 418
ceremonial speeches 155–6
Chairman of Committees 360–1, 449
  and committees' reports 165
  elected 139
  on private legislation 251
  roles of 72–3, 75
Chairman of Ways and Means 55–6, 250,
    270, 298, 449
Chalfont, Lord 380
Chamberlain, Prime Minister Neville 295
Chancellor of the Exchequer 270–1
Chief whip 46, 100, 106
Chiltern Hundreds 25, 449
Church of England 264
Churchill, Sir Winston S. 15, 295
Clarke, Kenneth 111, 436
clause 204, 208, 449
Clerk of Legislation 195
clerk of the committee 361–2
Clerk of the House 55, 57–8, 62, 449
Clerk of the Parliaments 74–5, 449
Clwyd, Ann 108

closure 51, 158, 198, 449–50
Code of Practice on Access to Government
    Information 314
co-decision procedure (EU) 393
collective responsibility 95, 450
Command Paper 79, 170, 450
commencement 157, 450
Committee on the Inter-Governmental
    Conference on the Future of Europe
    300
Committee of Permanent Representatives
    (COREPER) 390
Committee of Public Accounts (PAC) 284,
    346, 425–6
Committee of the Regions (EU) 392
Committee of Selection 228, 354–5
Committee on Standards and Privileges 52,
    129, 133, 355, 412
Committee of Supply 55
Committee of the whole House 55, 210,
    215, 450
  types of bills debated 221–2
Committee Office (Commons) 62
Committee on Standards in Public Life 121,
    125–6, 129, 133, 444
committee stage of a bill 141, 210–23
Commons amendment 142, 450
Commons consideration of Lords
    amendments (CCLA) 142, 449
Commons Disqualification Act (1975) 23
Commonwealth Parliamentary Association
    (CPA) 120, 405
complaint of privilege 52, 183–4
Comptroller and Auditor General 128, 171,
    273, 282, 283, 425, 450
Conference of European Affairs Committees
    (COSAC) 403, 451
Conservative Party
  candidate selection 24
  on dissent 107
  financial support for 68
  organisation in parliament 109
  parliamentary research unit 66
  party leadership 111
consideration 223, 450
consolidation bill 193, 210, 248, 451
Consolidated Fund 276, 277, 278
Consolidated Fund and Appropriation Bill
    210, 244–5, 266, 279, 450–1
constituency 22–3, 112–20, 419, 451
  constituent's problems 114–16
  constituent's views 117
  dealing with 114–16, 119–20

constituency (*continued*)
  MP's relationship with 112–14
  MPs representing 118–19
  profile of 117–18
constituency Friday 114, 141, 451
Constitution Committee (Lords) 378
Constitutional Affairs, Department of 438
Constitutional Reform Act (2005) 71, 438,
      440
contempts 184
  punishment for 184–5
Cook, Robin 435, 444
  as Leader of the House 345, 349, 375
  and Modernisation Committee 147, 428
  resignation of 95, 155
  and whips 101
cooperation procedure (EU) 393
COREPER (Committee of Permanent
      Representatives) 390
Cornerstone Group 110
COSAC (Conference of European Affairs
      Committees) 403, 451
Council of Europe 404–5
Council of Ministers 390, 392–3
Court of Auditors 392
CPA (Commonwealth Parliamentary
      Association) 120, 405
Cranborne, Lord 38, 76
Cranborne money 76, 132, 451
cross-benches 7, 451
cross-cutting committees (Commons)
      348–51
cross-cutting committees (Lords) 378
crossing the floor 13, 107, 423, 451
Crossman, Richard 147, 220

Dalyell, Tam 87, 335
Davis, David 111
debate
  language of 303–4
  in Lords 306–10
    conventions of 308–9
  purpose of 304–5
  on Queen's Speech 139–40
  rules and conventions 301–3
  uses of 305–6
  in Westminster Hall 296–8
decision 392, 451
deferred division 175, 412, 451
delegated legislation 165, 191, 252–64, 437
  definitions 252–3
  parliamentary control 255
  see also Statutory Instrument

Delegated Powers and Regulatory Reform
      Committee (Lords) 254, 261, 352
Democratic Unionist Party 68, 110
Denham, John 289
Department of the Official Report *see*
      Hansard
departmental annual reports 275, 280–2,
      451
departmental expenditure limit (DEL) 275,
      452
deposit 24, 252
Deputy Chief Whip 99, 360
Deputy Speakers 55–6
de-referral 257, 452
despatch boxes 163, 309, 452
devolution 85–91
dilatory motion 291, 452
directive 389, 392, 452
dissent 103–7
  crossing the floor 107
  dynamics of 105–6
  punishment for 106–7
dissolution 25, 452
division 13–14, 171–3, 452
draft bill 195, 196, 201–2, 372, 413, 452
draft order 261–2
drafting on the hoof 197, 201
Dugdale, Sir Thomas 96
dummy bill 208, 452
Duncan Smith, Iain 111
Dunwoody, Gwyneth 360

early day motion 144, 300–1, 452
Economic Affairs Committee (Lords) 378,
      382
Economic and Fiscal Strategy Report 273
Economic and Social Committee (EU) 392
elections *see* by-election; general election
elective dictatorship, parliament as 94
elector 26, 452
Electoral Administration Act (2006) 415
Electoral Commission 54, 414–15
electoral quota 22–3, 452
electronic voting 173–4, 415, 421
emergency adjournment debates 296
engagements question 329–30
England, electoral quota 22
Enhanced Legislative Competence Orders 90
Ennis, Jeff 331
Environmental Audit Committee 348
Erskine May 48, 57, 80, 311
estimate 274, 452
Estimates Committee 346

estimates cycle 267, 274–80
  annual pattern 268–9
estimates days 94, 141, 142, 277–8, 452–3
ethnic minorities in parliament 32–3
European Central Bank 392
European Commission 391
European Communities Act (1972) 80, 84,
    85, 190, 388, 389–90
European Convention on Human Rights 81,
    82–3
European Council 390
European Court of Justice 389, 392
European Parliament 391–2
  and national parliaments 401–2
  cooperation between 402–3
European Scrutiny Committee (Commons)
    349, 396–7, 400–1, 403
  effectiveness of 401
European Standing Committee (Commons)
    397–8
European Union 84–5
  closer union 386–8
  Council of Ministers 390
  debates on 388–9
  explanatory memorandum 395–6
  law making and sovereignty 389–90
  legislation
    influence on 393–5
    procedure 392–3
    types of 392
  membership 386
  Westminster scrutiny of 395
    debates on 397–8
    in House of Commons 396–7
    scrutiny reserve 400–1
European Union, Treaty of (Maastricht
    Treaty, 1992) 387, 388
European Union Committee (Lords), 378,
    383, 398–400
excess votes 141, 279–80, 453
exclusive cognisance of each House 182–3
exempted business 453
Expenditure Committee 346
explanatory memorandum 395–6, 453
Explanatory Notes 208, 453

Falconer of Thoroton, Lord 437
'fast-track' procedure 210
Father of the House 47, 453
Finance Bill 271–3
Finances and Services Committee
    (Commons) 355
financial bills 192

financial privilege of Commons 266
Financial Statement and Budget Report
    (FSBR) 273
final disagreement 244
first past the post 27, 29, 453
first reading 141, 157, 208–9, 453
Flight, Howard 25
floating voter 29
floor of the House 13, 453
forecast operating cost statement 277
Forth, Eric 200
founding resolutions 271
Fox, Liam 111
Freedom of Information Act 314–15
freedom of speech 181–2
front-bencher 10, 453
FSBR (Financial Statement and Budget
    Report) 273
Future Business 298, 335

gallery, the 176–8, 453
Galloway, George 24, 107
'Gang of Four' 107
general election 453
  expenses 27
  timetable for 26
  turnouts to 34, 414–16
  voting patterns, 2005 28
  when held 25
  who votes 25–6
Gilbert, John 377
giving way 303, 453
government adjournment motion 294–5
government bill 192–208
  anatomy of 204–8
  origins 192–3
  from proposal to 193–6
  stages 203, 208–34
government motions (Lords) 308
Government of Ireland Act (1920) 90
Government of Wales Act (1998) 85–6
Government Resources and Accounts Act
    (2000) 274–5
government substantive motions 293–4
Graham, Sir Alastair 121, 126
grand committee 235, 320, 441–2, 453
Gray, James 122–3
Green Budget 274
green card 7, 454
Green Paper 171, 194, 454
Griffiths, Jane 24–5
grouping 215–16, 217, 454
guillotine 198–200, 454

Hague, William 289, 411
Hailsham, Viscount 23
half-hour adjournment motion 295–6
hand-out bill 226, 230, 454
Hansard 10, 63, 74, 169–70, 454
    in Lords 171
Hansard Society's Commission on
        Parliamentary Scrutiny 410
Haselhurst, Sir Alan 56, 289
Hawkins, Nick 25
Heal, Sylvia 56
Heald, Oliver 200
Heath, Prime Minister Edward 41, 47
hemicycle 15, 454
Henry VIII clause 254, 260
hereditary peers 37–8, 454
    departure of 433
Heseltine, Michael 111
High Court judges 7
Hogg, Douglas 23
House Administration (Commons) 59–61
House Committee (Lords) 73, 75
House of Commons
    age of members 31
    attendance in 163–4
    chamber of 7, 10–11, 13, 430
    cost of 77–8
    departments 61–4
    development of 3
    disagreement with Lords 242–7
    government's control of 93–7
        accountability 96–7
        patronage and collective responsibility
            94–5
        practical matters 95–6
        time 93–4
    and Lords, relationships between 130–1
    modernisation of 409–31
        joint committees 428
        legislative process 428–9
        parliamentary questions 424
        qualified majorities 431
        recent changes 410–14
        select committees 425–7, 430
        spending 429–30
        strengths 409–10
    occupation and education of members
        31
    paying for 76–7
    pressures on 16–17
    questions in *see* Questions
    scrutiny of European Union 396–7
    services shared with Lords 64

sitting day 148–60, 444
    after Question time 153–7
    to end of Question time 150–3
    exempted business 159
    late sittings 159–60
    moment of interruption 158
    public business 157–8
    start of 149–50
sitting week 146–8
size of 21–2, 422–3
time in 160–1
voting in 171–5
House of Commons (Administration) Act
    (1978) 60
House of Commons Commission 58, 60,
    410
House of Lords
    accommodation for 18–19
    administration of 75
    attendance 38–9
    bills, stages of 234–42
        differences from Commons 234–7
    chamber of 5–7, 8
    as chamber of experts 309–10
    and Commons, relationship between
        130–1
    composition 39
    cost of 78
    debatable motions in 306
    debates in 306–10
    development of 3
    disagreement with Commons 242–7
    European Union Committee in 398–400
    expenses paid 76
    government, position of in 131
    independence of 135, 241–2
    influences on 130–5
    legislation, impact on 237–40
    limitations on powers 244–6
    lobby groups in 135
    membership 35–8
    modernisation of 431–7
        appointment *versus* election 433–5
        backbenchers' say on 435–6
        committee work 441
        future of 436–7
        Grand committees 441–2
        hereditary peers, departure of 433
        Lord Chancellor 437–8
        of practice and procedure 440–3
        sitting hours 442
        Speaker 439
        Wilson proposals 432–3

House of Lords (*continued*)
  paying for 77
  personal interests 132–3
  political parties in 132
  proceedings on Statutory Instruments
    258
  registration of interests 133–4
  running of 69–76
  services shared with Commons 64
  sittings and use of time 164–8
  voting in 176
  working papers 171–2
House of Lords Acts (1998, 1999) 38, 39,
    237, 247, 433
House of Lords Appointments Commission
    37, 433–4, 435, 454
House of Lords Business 171
House Service (Commons) 57, 58–9
housekeeping bills 193
Howard, Michael 111
Howe, Sir Geoffrey 155
Hughes, Simon 112
Huhne, Chris 112
Human Rights Act (1998) 82–4, 183, 262–3
Humble Address 139–40
hung parliament 41–2, 454
Hungerford, Sir Thomas (Speaker) 44
Hunt of Kings Heath, Lord 435, 436
Hunting Act (2005) 81
Hutton, Lord 153, 426
hybrid bill 143, 191, 252, 454
Hylton-Foster (Speaker) 46

Identity Cards Bill 240, 242
incidental expenses provision 65, 454
Independent Commission on the Voting
    System 29–30
Information Committee 410
instruction 166
Intelligence and Security Committee 356–7
interdependent amendments 216
Inter-Parliamentary Union (IPU) 120, 405
interventions 303
introduction 208, 454
Irvine of Lairg, Lord 71, 437

Jakobovits, Lord 35
Jenkins, Roy 107
Joint Committee on Consolidation &c., Bills
    352
Joint Committee on Human Rights 352
Joint Committee on Parliamentary Privilege
    183, 384

Joint Committee on Statutory Instruments
    352–3
joint committees 384–5, 428
Jopling, Michael 147, 199
journal 62, 455
Journal Office (Commons) 62
Judicial Appointments Commission 438, 440
junior minister *see* under-secretary of state

Kelly, Dr David 153, 359, 426
Kennedy, Charles 30, 332
Khan, Sadiq 331–2
Kilfoyle, Peter 289
King (Speaker) 47
knives 201, 455

Labour Party
  candidate selection 24
  dissent in 104–5
  organisation in Commons 107–8
  party leadership 111
  political groups in 110
  regional groups 108
Lamont, Norman 155
late sittings 159–60
Law, Peter 23–4
LCCA (Lords consideration of Commons
    amendments) 142, 455
lead amendment 217
Leader of the House 46, 56–7, 455
Leader of the House of Lords 73–4, 132
Leader of the Opposition 67, 68, 140
  at Prime Minister's questions 330
Legal Services Office (Commons) 62
Legg, Sir Thomas 153
legislation
  examining, modernisation of 428–9
  pressure of 196–7
  types of 190–1
  see also bill
Legislative and Regulatory Reform Bill 240,
    262
Legislative Programme (LP) (Cabinet
    Committee) 57, 194–5, 197, 456
legislative supremacy of parliament 79–82
Lester of Herne Hill, Lord 83
Liaison Committee 73, 202, 277, 410, 426
  on select committees 278, 374, 376, 377,
    427
  work of 349–50, 412
Liberal Democratic Party
  candidate selection 24
  and electoral reform 30

Liberal Democratic Party (*continued*)
  financial support for 68
  in parliament 109–10
  party leadership 111–12
Library (Commons) 63
Life Peerages Act (1958) 36–7
life peers 455
  under Appellate jurisdiction Act (1876)
    35–6
  under Life Peerages Act (1958) 36–7
Lloyd of Berwick, Lord 71, 439
Lloyd George, Prime Minister David
    266
lobby 7, 10, 121–4, 177–8, 455
lobby terms 177, 455
locus standi 249, 455
long title 204, 455
Lord, Sir Michael 56
Lord Chancellor 69–71, 455
  reform of 437–8
  reform of post 71–2
Lord Speaker 7, 69–70, 72–3
Lords amendment 142, 455
Lords bills 229–30
Lords consideration of Commons
    amendments (LCCA) 142, 455
Lords of Appeal in Ordinary 439
Lords Select Committee on Delegated
    Powers and Regulatory Reform 236,
    259–60
lost questions 321
LP (Legislative Programme) (Cabinet
    Committee) 57, 194–5, 197, 456

Mace 10, 62, 456
Main, Anne 331
main estimates 276–7, 456
main Question 288, 293, 456
Major, Prime Minister John 103, 126, 330,
    388–9
manifesto 192, 456
manuscript amendment 288
Markievicz, Countess 32
marshalled list 215
Martin, Michael (Speaker) 45, 46, 47,
    48, 49, 54, 56
Mates, Michael 106
Mawer, Sir Philip 129
Mayer, Sir Christopher 350
measure 191, 264, 456
Members' Lobby 7, 10, 14
members of European Parliament 402
  and MPs 404

members of parliament 23–5
  age of 31
  allowances 65–6
  attendance in chamber 163–4
  daily routine 161–4
    of ministers 162–3
  interests of 126–30
    declaration of 127–8
    lobbying 128
    registration of 126–7
    voting 128
  job description 92–3
  letters
    from constituents 342–3
    to ministers 342–3
  and MEPs 404
  and parliamentary standards 124–5
  pay 64–5
  personal influences 112
  staff 66–7
Members Estimate 58, 77, 456
Members Estimate Committee 77
Members Estimate Audit Committee 77
Merits of Statutory Instruments Committee
    259
message 224, 243, 456
ministerial accountability 96
minister of state 94, 456
Ministerial Code 128
ministers
  daily routine of 162–3
  letters to 342–3
Ministry of Defence Votes A 276, 456
Minute, the 171, 456
mobile polling stations 415
Modernisation Committee 160, 175, 353–4,
    410
  on programming 199–201
  sitting hours, changes 147–8, 149, 411
  on standing committees 223
  and Westminster Hall 297
  see also House of Commons; House of
    Lords
moment of interruption 158, 295, 456
money bill 245, 266–7, 456
money resolution 210, 228, 456
Moore, Jo 96–7
Morrison (Speaker) 46
motion for a new writ 150, 153
motions 287–96, 457
  adjournment 294–6
  back-benchers 294
  disposing of 290–1

motions (*continued*)
  in Lords 306
  on opposition days 292–3
  superseding 291
  withdrawal of 290
Murphy, Paul 356

named-day question 333–4, 411, 457
naming (of an MP) 49, 457
National Assembly for Wales 87–90
National Audit Office 77, 283, 426, 457
NATO Parliamentary Assembly 405
negative instrument 254, 255, 256–7,
    457
Neill of Bladen, Lord 126
net cash requirement 277
new clause 220, 457
Newton of Braintree, Lord 410
Nice, Treaty of (2001) 387
Nick's Diner (Conservative Party) 110
1922 Committee (Conservative Party) 109,
    457
the 92 (Conservative Party) 110
No Turning Back 110
nod 13, 157, 209, 457
Nolan, Lord 126, 133
non-exempted business 158
Northern Ireland
  devolution of 85, 90–1, 263–4
  electoral quota 22
  proportional representation in 30
  questions on 313
Northern Ireland Acts (1974, 1998) 85, 91,
    263
Northern Ireland grand committee 299–300,
    320
Northern Ireland Orders 235
Northern Ireland select committee 348
Norton of Louth, Lord 411
notices of motions 158

O'Brien, Stephen 331
offices of profit 25
official Opposition 95, 307, 457
Official Report see Hansard
Ombudsman 117, 351, 457
Onslow, Arthur (Speaker) 45
operating cost statement 277, 282
Operations Directorate (Serjeant at Arms
    Department) 63
opposition days 94, 142, 457
  motions on 292–3
opposition debates (Lords) 307–8

opposition parties 13
  financing 67–9
oral questions 316–17, 337, 411, 424
  tabling 320–2
order 191, 253, 288, 457
Order in Council 191, 253, 457
Order of Business (Commons) 151–2,
    158
Order Paper 48, 168–9, 412
  in Lords 166, 167, 171
orders of reference 357–8, 458
orders of the day 158
ordinary written questions 333, 458
OSCE (Parliamentary Assembly of the
    Organisation for Security and
    Co-operation) 405
Osmotherly Rules 426
Outlawries Bill 139, 458
Overseas Office (Commons) 62
Owen, David 107

PAC *see* Committee of Public Accounts
packaging 244, 458
pairing 101, 458
parent Act 191, 253
parliament
  beginning of 137–8
  and courts 183
  effectiveness of 406–7
  as elective dictatorship 94
  ethnic minorities in 32–3
  fire (1934) 4
  as King's palace 2
  modernisation of
    access to 419–20
    constraints on 407–8
    image of House 420
    information and communication
      technologies 421–2
    and tradition 420–1
    understanding of, improving 417–18
    voting 414–16
  reputation of 33
  secondary legislation, control of 258–60
  televising of 179–81, 418
  women in 31–2
  see also House of Commons; House of
    Lords
a parliament 136, 458
Parliament Acts (1911, 1949) 81, 136,
    245–6, 266, 432
Parliament First group 410
parliamentary agent 249, 458

Parliamentary Assembly of the Council of
   Europe 404
Parliamentary Assembly of the Organisation
   for Security and Co-operation in
   Europe (OSCE) 405
parliamentary calendar 136–66, 372
Parliamentary Commissioner for
   Administration (Ombudsman) 117,
   351, 457
Parliamentary Commissioner for Standards
   126, 129, 412, 458
Parliamentary Committee of the Labour
   Party 108
Parliamentary Constituencies (Scotland)
   Order (2005) 87
Parliamentary Corporate Bodies Act (1992)
   74
parliamentary counsel 195, 196, 458–9
Parliamentary Education Unit 418
parliamentary estate 19, 20
Parliamentary Estates Directorate 63, 75
Parliamentary European Committee 404
Parliamentary Information and
   Communications Technology Service
   (PICTS) 64, 75
Parliamentary Labour Party (PLP) 106,
   107–8, 459
parliamentary language 423–4
Parliamentary Office of Science and
   Technology (Commons) 62
parliamentary papers 168–71
   vote bundle 168–9
parliamentary private secretary (PPS) 93, 95,
   459
Parliamentary Recording Unit 180
parliamentary secretary or parliamentary
   under-secretary of state 322, 459
Parliamentary Secretary to the Treasury
   (Chief Whip) 99
parliamentary sleaze 125, 129
parliamentary vocabulary 13–14
parliamentary website 418
Parliamentary Works Services Directorate
   (Lords) 75
Parliamentary Works Services Directorate
   (Serjeant at Arms Department) 63
Patronage Secretary 99, 459
payroll vote 95, 141, 241
personal statement 155–6, 459
persons, papers and records (PPR) 358, 459
Peter de Montfort (Speaker) 44
petition 340–1, 419–20, 459
ping pong 142, 225, 242–4, 385, 437, 459

Plaid Cymru 110
   financial support for 68
PLP (Parliamentary Labour Party) 106,
   107–8, 459
point of order 156, 459
political parties
   all-party groups 120–1
   in Lords 132
   in parliament 98–112
      whips 98–107
   party leadership 110–12
   public funding of 415–16
   state funding for 69
   see also individual parties
Political Parties, Elections and Referendums
   Act (2000) 68, 414, 417
polling day 26, 41, 459
Portcullis House 17–18
postal voting 415
PPC (prospective parliamentary candidate)
   24, 459
PPR (persons, papers and records) 358, 459
PPS (parliamentary private secretary) 93, 95,
   459
practice (ancient usage) 185
prayer 256, 459
praying time 257, 260, 460
pre-Budget report 274
pre-legislative scrutiny 201–2, 442–3, 460
prerogative 79, 460
presentation bill 157, 208, 225, 229–30, 460
previous question 291, 460
primary legislation 83, 190, 460
Prime Minister's Questions (PMQs) 50, 317,
   329–32, 411, 459
   select committee on 350
Prince of Wales's Consent 196, 460
private bill 94, 190–1, 460
private business 153, 249–51, 460
private members' bills 94, 191, 225–34, 429,
   460
   success and failure 230–2
   tactics and procedure 227–9
   see also ballot bills
private notice question 51, 165, 332, 460
   in Lords 340
privilege 156, 181–5, 315, 460
   complaints of 52, 183–4
privilege amendment 267, 461
Privy Counsellor 302, 461
probing amendment 215
procedure 185–8
   complications of 186–8

Procedure Committee (Commons) 354,
    410
  on election of Speakers 47, 53
  on the guillotine 199
  on money bills 271, 285
  on oral questions 320
  on questions 335, 337
  on scrutiny 260
  on select committees 346, 361
  on supplementary questions 328
Procedure Committee (Lords) 165, 441
proceedings, freedom of speech in 182
proclamation 25, 143, 461
programme motion 210
programming 199–201, 461
programming committee 213, 461
promoter 249, 461
proportional representation 30, 416
proposing the Question 172, 217, 288,
    461
prorogation 140, 143–4, 461
prospective parliamentary candidate (PPC)
    24, 459
Public Administration Select Committee
    (PASC) 315–16, 350–1, 410, 424,
    433
public bill 157, 190–1, 461
  Lords on 165–6
Public Bill Office 227, 421
public business 157–8, 461
public petition 159, 462
public service agreements (PSAs) 275, 280,
    373
public spending 275
Puttnam, Lord 239

qualified majorities (Commons) 431
qualified voting majority (QVM) 387,
    462
Queen, H.M. 40–3
  political neutrality of 40–1
  prime minister, choosing 41–2
  as statesman 42–3
Queen's Consent 196, 462
Queen's Speech 139
  debate on 139–40
Question rota 318–19, 462
Question Time 10, 94, 142, 153
  pattern of 317–19
  preparation for 328–9
  questions answered at end of 333
  in sitting day 150–3, 322–7
  Speaker's influence on 50

Questions 462
  in Commons 311–37, 410
    answers to 313–14
    changes to 424
    costs of 316
    definition 311–12
    effectiveness of 335–6
    increase in 336–7
    and Public Administration Committee
      315–16
    rules for 312–13
  engagements question 329–30
  in Lords 338–40
    for oral answers 338–9
    for written answers 339–40
  see also Prime Minister's Questions
quorum 291–2, 462
QMV (qualified majority voting) 387, 462

reasoned amendment 290, 462
reasons 267, 462
recall 53, 146, 462
  in Lords 70
recess 144–5, 411, 462–3
recess debates 296
referendums 416–17
Referendums (Scotland and Wales) Bill
    (1997) 85
Refreshment Department (Commons) 64
Regional Affairs Committee 299–300
regulation 191, 392, 463
Regulatory Reform Act (2001) 261
Regulatory Reform Committee 352
regulatory reform order 191, 260–2, 463
remedial order 83, 191, 262–3, 463
repeal 195, 463
report stage 141, 220, 223–4, 463
reporting cycle 267, 280–4
  annual pattern 268–9
Representation of the People Act (1983) 26
reserved matter 86, 463
resignation speeches 155–6
resolution 208, 288, 306, 463
resource accounting 274–5, 282, 463
resource outturn 282
responsibility 96
revised estimates 278, 463
Richard, Lord 89, 90
robing room 5–7, 138
Rodgers, William 107
Rome, Treaty of 386–7
routine programming of bills 160
Royal Assent 40, 234, 247, 464

Royal Commission on Reform of the House
    of Lords 258, 259
royal gallery 5–7
Royal Prerogative 40, 43, 425, 460
royal summons 2
rules 191
ruling 186, 464

Salisbury convention 131, 246–7, 385, 437,
    464
schedule 204, 464
scope 215, 464
Scotland
    devolution of 85
    electoral quota 23
    legislative powers 86
    proportional representation in 30
    questions on 313
Scotland Act (1998) 85–6, 190
Scott, Sir Richard 153
Scottish grand committee 299–300, 320
Scottish National Party 110
    financial support for 68
Scottish select committee 348
scrutiny reserve resolutions 400–1, 464
scrutiny unit 362, 372, 412, 425
second reading 141, 209–10, 464
second reading committee 209, 464
secondary legislation 191, 252
    parliamentary control of 258–60
secretary of state 94, 322, 464
section 204, 464
select committee 201, 210, 222, 409–10,
    419, 464
    in Commons 344–63
        achievements of 374–7
        activities of 371–4
        ad hoc committees 355–6
        chairmen 360–1
        compulsion 358–9
        cross-cutting committees 348–51
        dealing with 370–1
        Intelligence and Security Committee
            356–7
        internal committees 353–5
        legislative committees 351–3
        list of 347
        membership of 359–60
        modernisation of 425–7, 430
        orders of reference and powers 357–8
        scrutiny 346–7, 412
        staffing 361–2
        work of 362–3

development of 345–6
inquiry procedure 363–70
    consensus in 369–70
    government reply 368–9
    report of 366, 368
    start 363–4
    taking evidence 364–6
    travel 366
joint committees 384–5
in Lords 378–84, 441
    committees 378–80
    outcomes 381–4
    process 380–1
reports in Lords 306–7
Select Committee on Administration and
    Works (Lords) 73, 74
Select Committee on House of Lords Offices
    75
Select Committee on Members' Interests
    125
Select Committee on Statutory Instrument
    353
Select Committee on the Crash of Chinook
    Helicopter ZD576 (Lords) 380
Select Committee on the Modernisation of
    the House 57
Select Vestries Bill 139
selection 215–16, 290, 464
selection list 217
Selwyn-Lloyd (Speaker) 46
Senior Salaries Review Body see SSRB
Serjeant at Arms 62–3, 148, 465
session 138–44, 465
    pattern of 140–3
sessional orders 139, 465
Sewel motion 86, 465
shadow Cabinet 108, 465
shadow minister 10, 163, 293, 322,
    465
Short, Clare 156
Short, Edward 67
Short money 67–8, 465
short title 204, 465
Single European Act (1987) 387
Sinn Fein 110
sitting 13, 465
    hours 147–8, 149, 411, 442, 444
    pattern of 144–5
Skinner, Dennis 303
Smith, Chris 289
Smoking Room 14
Social Democratic Party 107
South Staffordshire constituency 26–7

Speaker 44–55, 465
  collecting the voices 172
  election of 46–8, 137, 411–12
  formal communication by 150
  independence of 45–6
  in Lords 439
  office of 44–5
  precedent and change 54–5
  roles of 48–54
    on Boundary Commissions 53–4
    calling members to speak 49–50
    casting vote 52–3
    powers of 50–2
    recalling the house 53
    as voice of the house 54
  and sitting day 148, 149
special public bill committee 235, 465
special report 368, 465
special standing committee 210, 222–3, 466
Spicer, Sir Michael 109
spillover 140, 142, 466
SSRB (Senior Salaries Review Body) 92, 466
  MPs' pay and allowances 64–5, 76, 77
St John-Stevas, Norman 346
staffing allowance 65, 466
standing committee 141, 211–20, 466
  chairmanship 212–13
  on delegated legislation 257
  on Finance Bill 272
  going through a bill 217–20
  meetings 213
  membership 212
  scrutiny 220
standing orders 98, 144, 185, 466
starred questions 165, 466
State Opening 138–9, 466
statement by ministers 153–4
statute 190, 466
statute law repeal bill 210, 466
Statutory Instrument 83, 191, 235, 253, 466
  Lords proceedings on 258, 259–60
  procedure 256
  purpose 253–5
Steel, Sir David 406
strangers 291, 466
Straw, Jack 56
sub judice rule 48, 183, 300, 303, 312, 466
subject committees of Labour Party 108
subordinate legislation 253, 466
subsidiarity 396, 467

substantive motion 158, 287–90, 467
  by government 293–4
Sunset clause 467
superseding a motion 291
supplementary estimates 141, 278–9, 467
supplementary question 48, 322, 467
  in Lords 339
  rules for 327
  tactics of 322, 327
Supply 266, 467
supreme court, House of Lords as 36, 439–40
surgery 114, 145, 467
suspend 139, 467
swearing in 137, 155

table 13, 311, 467
Table Office (Commons) 62
talking out 158, 228, 290, 467
tax law re-write bills 210, 467
Tax Law Rewrite Committee 353
taxation
  annual cycle 267–9
  constitutional principles of 265–7
Taylor, Ann 353
Taylor, Richard 23
Tea Room 14
tellers 172–3, 467
ten-minute rule bill 157, 225, 229–30, 467
Terrorism Bill (2005–6) 204–7, 240
test roll 137, 155, 467
Thatcher, Prime Minister Margaret 335–6
  and poll tax 106
  resignation of 41, 111, 155
  on transfer of questions 330
third reading 224–5, 467–8
Thomas (Speaker) 46, 50
three-line whip 101
Thurso, Viscount 23
top-up members 30
totally managed expenditure 275
Treasurer of HM Household (Deputy Chief Whip) 99
Treasury Committee 273
Trevor, Sir John (Speaker) 124–5, 302
Tyler, Paul 123, 436

UK Independence Party 28
under-secretary of state 322, 459
unopposed return 153, 468
unstarred questions 165, 235, 306, 468
urgent debate 155, 468
urgent procedure order 83, 468

urgent question 51–2, 54, 153, 332–3, 468
Ustinov, Sir Peter 445
usual channels 95, 100–1, 468
  on Queen's speech 140
  and select committee chairmen 360

Vaizey, Edward 331
virement 259, 277, 468
Vote bundle, the 168, 215, 468
Vote Office (Commons) 62
Votes and Proceedings 169, 208, 468
Votes on Account 141, 275–6, 277, 468

Wakeham, Lord 433
Wales
  devolution of 85
  electoral quota 22
  National Assembly 87–90
  proportional representation in 30
  questions on 313
Walpole, Prime Minister Sir Robert 270
wasted votes 28
ways and means 265
Ways and Means resolution 210, 468
Weatherill (Speaker) 46, 47
Weekly Bulletin (Lords) 171
Weleminsy, Judy 184
Welsh grand committee 299–300, 320
Welsh select committee 348
West Lothian question 87, 468–9
Westminster, Palace of 1

Westminster Hall 4, 13, 411, 415
  debates in 296–8
  oral questions in 320
Whip, The 101
whips 46, 98–107, 469
  dissent 103–7
  party discipline 101–3
  rebellion 103
  usual channels 100–1
  see also Chief Whip
White Paper 171, 194, 469
Wicks, Sir Nigel 126
Williams, Shirley 107
Williams, Stephen 29
Williams of Mostyn, Lord 74, 166
Wilson, Prime Minister Harold 41
Wilson proposals on House of Lords reform
  432–3
winding-up speeches 100
withdrawal of motion 290
women in parliament 31–2
Woolsack 5, 7
wrecking amendment 215, 469
Wright, Tony 436
Writs of Assistance 7
written answers (Lords) 339–40
written ministerial statements 334–5, 469
written questions 333–4, 337, 411

Yeoman Usher 469
Young, Sir George 436